MOOD DISORDERS
A HANDBOOK OF SCIENCE AND PRACTICE

Edited by

Mick Power
*University of Edinburgh
and Royal Edinburgh Hospital*

John Wiley & Sons, Ltd

Other Wiley Editorial Offices

John Wiley & Sons Inc., 111 River Street, Hoboken, NJ 07030, USA

Jossey-Bass, 989 Market Street, San Francisco, CA 94103-1741, USA

Wiley-VCH Verlag GmbH, Boschstr. 12, D-69469 Weinheim, Germany

John Wiley & Sons Australia Ltd, 33 Park Road, Milton, Queensland 4064, Australia

John Wiley & Sons (Asia) Pte Ltd, 2 Clementi Loop #02-01, Jin Xing Distripark, Singapore 129809

John Wiley & Sons Canada Ltd, 22 Worcester Road, Etobicoke, Ontario, Canada M9W 1L1

Wiley also publishes its books in a variety of electronic formats. Some content that appears in print may not
be available in electronic books.

Library of Congress Cataloging-in-Publication Data

Mood disorders : a handbook of science and practice / edited by Mick Power.
        p.   cm.
    Includes bibliographical references and index.
    ISBN 0-470-84390-X (Cloth : alk. paper)
        1. Affective disorders—Physiological aspects.   2. Affective disorders—Treatment.   3. Affective
disorders—Chemotherapy.   I. Power, Michael J.
RC537 .M6627   2004
616.85'27—dc21   2003012946

British Library Cataloguing in Publication Data

A catalogue record for this book is available from the British Library

ISBN 0-470-84390-X

Typeset in 10/12pt Times and Helvetica by TechBooks Electronic Services, New Delhi, India
Printed and bound in Great Britain by Antony Rowe Ltd, Chippenham, Wiltshire
This book is printed on acid-free paper responsibly manufactured from sustainable forestry
in which at least two trees are planted for each one used for paper production.

P

MOOD DISORDERS
A HANDBOOK OF SCIENCE AND PRACTICE

TO SILKE

For I have sworn thee fair, and thought thee bright,
Who art as black as hell, as dark as night.
(Shakespeare, Sonnet 147)

CONTENTS

Part III: GENERAL ISSUES   **305**

ABOUT THE EDITOR

Mick Power is Professor of Clinical Psychology and Director of the Clinical Psychology Training Programme at the University of Edinburgh. He is a practising clinical psychologist in the Royal Edinburgh Hospital. In the past he has been a Senior Lecturer at the University of London and has worked as a clinical psychologist at Guy's Hospital, and at the Bethlem and Maudsley Hospitals. He has worked for the Medical Research Council and has acted for many years as a Research Adviser to the World Health Organization. He is a founding editor of the journal *Clinical Psychology and Psychotherapy.*

LIST OF CONTRIBUTORS

Paul Bebbington, *Department of Psychiatry and Behavioural Sciences, Archway Campus, Highgate Hill, London N19 5LW, UK*

Annika Berge, *Division of Psychiatry, Royal Edinburgh Hospital, Edinburgh EH10 5HF, UK*

Peter J. Bieling, *Department of Psychology, St Joseph's Hospital, 50 Charlton Avenue East, Hamilton, Ontario, L8N 4A6, Canada*

Douglas Blackwood, *Division of Psychiatry, Royal Edinburgh Hospital, Edinburgh EH10 5HF, UK*

Jonathan Cavanagh, *Department of Psychological Medicine, Gartnavel Royal Hospital, 1055 Great Western Road, Glasgow G12 0XH, UK*

Anthony J. Cleare, *Division of Psychological Medicine, Institute of Psychiatry, De Crespigny Park, London SE5 8AF, UK*

Klaus P. Ebmeier, *Division of Psychiatry, Royal Edinburgh Hospital, Edinburgh EH10 5HF, UK*

Ellen Frank, *Department of Psychiatry, University of Pittsburgh School of Medicine, Pittsburgh, PA 15213, USA*

Paul Gilbert, *Mental Health Research Unit, Kingsway Hospital, Derby DE22 3LZ, UK*

Ian H. Gotlib, *Department of Psychology, Building 420 Jordan Hall, Stanford University, Stanford, CA 94305-2130, USA*

Richard Harrington, *Department of Child and Adolescent Psychiatry, Royal Manchester Children's Hospital, Pendlebury, Manchester M27 1HA, UK*

Kay Redfield Jamison, *Department of Psychiatry, Johns Hopkins School of Medicine, 720 Rutland Avenue, Baltimore, MD 21205, USA*

Sidney H. Kennedy, *University Health Network, 200 Elizabeth Street, Eaton North, 8th Floor, Room 222, Toronto M5G 2C4, Canada*

David J. Kupfer, *Department of Psychiatry, University of Pittsburgh School of Medicine, Pittsburgh, PA 15213, USA*

Ken Laidlaw, *Section of Clinical and Health Psychology, University of Edinburgh, Royal Edinburgh Hospital, Edinburgh EH10 5HF, UK*

Dominic Lam, *Department of Psychology, Institute of Psychiatry, De Crespigny Park, London SE5 8AF, UK*

Andrew K. MacLeod, *Department of Psychology, Royal Holloway, Egham, Surrey TW20 0EX, UK*

John C. Markowitz, *Department of Psychiatry, Weill Medical College of Cornell University, 525 East 68th Street, Room 1322, New York, NY 10021, USA*

Walter Muir, *Division of Psychiatry, Royal Edinburgh Hospital, Edinburgh EH10 5HF, UK*

Anne Palmer, *Mood Disorders Service, Kingfisher House, Wensum Meadows, Hellesdon Hoop, Norwich NR6 5BN, UK*

Sagar V. Parikh, *Department of Psychiatry, Toronto Western Hospital, 399 Bathurst Street, Toronto M5T 2S8, Canada*

Dave Peck, *Department of Clinical Psychology, Craig Dunain Hospital, Inverness IV3 6PJ, UK*

Mick Power, *Section of Clinical and Health Psychology, University of Edinburgh, Royal Edinburgh Hospital, Edinburgh EH10 5HF, UK*

Jonathan Rottenberg, *Department of Psychology, Building 420 Jordan Hall, Stanford University, Stanford , CA 94305-2130, USA*

Matthias Schwannauer, *Section of Clinical and Health Psychology, University of Edinburgh, Royal Edinburgh Hospital, Edinburgh EH10 5HF, UK*

Jan Scott, *Institute of Psychiatry, King's College London, De Crespigny Park, London SE5 8AF, UK*

Zindel V. Segal, *Clarke Institute of Psychiatry, 250 College Street, Toronto M5T 1R8, Canada*

David Semple, *Division of Psychiatry, Royal Edinburgh Hospital, Edinburgh EH10 5HF, UK*

Premal Shah, *Division of Psychiatry, Royal Edinburgh Hospital, Edinburgh EH10 5HF, UK*

Heather N. Spielvogle, *Department of Psychiatry, University of Pittsburgh School of Medicine, Pittsburgh, PA 15213, USA*

Douglas Steele, *Division of Psychiatry, Royal Edinburgh Hospital, Edinburgh EH10 5HF, UK*

Holly A. Swartz, *Department of Psychiatry, University of Pittsburgh School of Medicine, Pittsburgh, PA 15213, USA*

Kim Wright, *Department of Psychology, Institute of Psychiatry, De Crespigny Park, London SE5 8AF, UK*

FOREWORD

Moods are so essential to our navigating the world that when they go awry it is only a matter of time until distress and disaster hit. Moods allow us to gauge people and circumstance, alert us to danger or opportunity, and provide us with the means to convey our emotional and physical state to others. If we act rashly when we ought to be prudent or hang back when we could move forward to advantage, difficulties accrue. Problems compound if, in addition to disruptions in mood, energy, sleep, and thinking also are affected. Disorders of mood which result from this combined disturbance are common, painful, and too often lethal. Fortunately, they are usually treatable.

Scientists and clinicians have learned a remarkable amount about depression and manic-depression, or bipolar disorder, during the past decade. These advances in our understanding of diagnosis, pathophysiology, epidemiology, comorbidity, and treatment are lucidly presented in this excellent handbook. There is a strong emphasis upon a complex approach to mood disorders, with the authors providing important coverage of both psychological and biological perspectives on the causes and treatment of depression and mania. The thorny issues of diagnostic categories, the ever-expanding spectrum of pathological into normal affective states, and the unsettled relation of major depression to bipolar disorder, are well addressed, as are the topics of evolutionary psychology, suicide, and pharmacological and psychotherapeutic treatments.

There remain many important questions: ethical and clinical considerations which will arise after the first genes for mood disorders are located; the intriguing psychological issues raised by mania—its relation to violence and creativity, its addictive qualities, and its place in the field of positive emotions; cross-species comparisons which will be possible as a result of mapping the human and other mammalian genomes; and the increased understanding of normal moods which will follow from research into more pathological ones. Neuroscientists, clinicians, psychologists, and molecular biologists make a powerful alliance. This handbook gives an outstanding overview of their accomplishments to date and a sense of the excitement to come.

Kay Redfield Jamison, Ph.D.
Professor of Psychiatry
The Johns Hopkins School of Medicine

Part I

UNIPOLAR DEPRESSION

THE CLASSIFICATION AND EPIDEMIOLOGY OF UNIPOLAR DEPRESSION

Paul Bebbington

INTRODUCTION

In this chapter, I will deal with the difficult problem of classifying a disorder that looks more like the expression of a continuum than a useful category. The way affective symptoms are distributed in the general population calls into serious question the utility of a medical classification, and certainly makes procedures of case definition and case finding very difficult. Nevertheless, researchers do rely on these procedures to establish the epidemiology of the disorder, and in the second part of the chapter I will pull together recent findings on the prevalence and distribution of unipolar depression.

CLASSIFICATION AND UNIPOLAR DEPRESSION

The idea of unipolar depression is primarily a medical one; that is, it involves a particular way of looking at psychological disturbance. This centres on the notion of a *syndrome* that is distinct from other psychiatric syndromes. Some of these can be relatively easily distinguished—for example, paranoid schizophrenia—while others are acknowledged to be related. The disorders that most resemble unipolar depression are other affective disorders, that is, conditions that are characterized centrally by mood disturbance. They cover a number of anxiety disorders, other depressive conditions, and bipolar mood disorder.

Bipolar disorder is identified by the presence of two sorts of episode in which the associated mood is either depressed or predominantly elated. It is distinct from unipolar disorder in a variety of ways (such as inheritance, course, and outcome), and the distinction is therefore almost certainly a useful one. However, depressive episodes in bipolar disorder cannot be distinguished symptomatically from those of unipolar depression. As perhaps half of all cases of bipolar disorder commence with a depressive episode, this means that unipolar depression is a tentative category—the disorder will be reclassified as bipolar in 5% of cases (Ramana & Bebbington, 1995).

Mood Disorders: A Handbook of Science and Practice. Edited by M. Power.
© 2004 John Wiley & Sons, Ltd. ISBN 0-470-84390-X.

Psychiatric disorders are classified in the hope that the classification can provide mutually exclusive categories to which cases can be allocated unambiguously (case identification). Categories of this type are the basis of the medical discipline of *epidemiology*, which is the study of the distribution of diseases (that is, medical classes) in the population. This has been a very powerful method for identifying candidate causal factors, and is thus of great interest to psychiatrists as well as to clinicians from other specialities.

Syndromes are the starting point of aetiological theories, and of other sorts of theory as well—theories of course and outcome, of treatment, and of pathology (Wing, 1978). There is no doubt that the medical approach to malfunction has been a very effective one, generating new knowledge quickly and efficiently by testing out theories of this type (Bebbington, 1998).

SYMPTOMS AND SYNDROMES

The first stage in the establishment of syndromes is the conceptualization of individual symptoms. Symptoms in psychiatry are formulations of aspects of human experience that are held to indicate abnormality. Examples include abnormally depressed mood, impaired concentration, loss of sexual interest, and persistent wakefulness early in the morning. They sometime conflate what is abnormal for the individual and what is abnormal for the population, but they can generally be defined in terms that are reliable. Signs (which are unreliable and rarely discriminating in psychiatry, and thus tend to be discounted somewhat) are the observable concomitants of such experiences, such as observed depressed mood, or behaviour that could be interpreted as a response to hallucinations. Different symptoms (and signs) often coexist in people who are psychologically disturbed, and this encourages the idea that they go together to form recognizable syndromes. The formulation of syndromes is the first stage in the disease approach to medical phenomena, as syndromes can be subjected to investigations that test the various types of theories described above.

While syndromes are essentially lists of qualifying symptoms and signs, individuals may be classed as having a syndrome while exhibiting only some of the constituent symptoms. Moreover, within a syndrome, there may be theoretical and empirical reasons for regarding some symptoms as having special significance. Other symptoms may be relatively non-specific, occurring in several syndromes, but, even so, if they cluster in numbers with other symptoms, they may achieve a joint significance. This inequality between symptoms is seen in the syndrome of unipolar depression: depressed mood and anhedonia are usually taken as central, while other symptoms (such as fatigue or insomnia) have little significance on their own. This reflects serious problems with the raw material of human experience: it does not lend itself to the establishment of the desired mutually exclusive and jointly exhaustive categories.

In an ideal world, all the symptoms making up a syndrome would be discriminating, but this is far from true, and decisions about whether a given subject's symptom pattern can be classed as lying within a syndrome usually show an element of arbitrariness. The result is that two individuals may both be taken to suffer from unipolar depression despite exhibiting considerable symptomatic differences.

This is tied in with the idea of symptom severity: disorders may be regarded as severe either from the sheer number of symptoms, or because several symptoms are present in severe degree. In practice, disorders with large numbers of symptoms also tend to have a greater severity of individual symptoms.

COMPETING CLASSIFICATIONS

The indistinctness of psychiatric syndromes and of the rules for deciding whether individual disorders meet symptomatic criteria has major implications for attempts to operationalize psychiatric classifications. There are currently two systems that have wide acceptance, the *Diagnostic and Statistical Manual* (DSM) of the American Psychiatric Association (APA) and the World Health Organization (WHO)'s *International Classification of Disease* (ICD). In the early days, revision of classificatory schemata relied almost wholly on clinical reflection. However, since the classifications are set up primarily for scientific purposes, they should properly be modified in the light of empirical research that permits definitive statements about their utility. The standardized and operationalized classifications that are now in existence offer an opportunity for using research in this way.

Unfortunately, much of the pressure for change has continued to originate from clinical and political demands. Revisions have sometimes had the appearance of tinkering in order to capture some imagined essence of the disorders included (Birley, 1990). What looks like fine-tuning can nevertheless make considerable differences to whether individual cases meet criteria or not, and thus disproportionately affects the putative frequency of disorders. We should jettison classifications only on grounds of inadequate scientific utility and as seldom as possible, since too rapid revision defeats the objective of comparison. Like all such classifications, DSM and ICD are created by committees. The natural tendency to horse-trading between experts selected precisely because they are powerful and opinion-ated leads to an over-elaborate structure, an excess of allowable classes and subclasses, and complicated defining criteria. Thus, in DSM-IV-R (APA, 1994), there are potentially 14 categories to which depressed mood can be allocated, and in ICD-10 (WHO, 1992) there are 22. Greater utility would probably accrue from limiting the primary categories to three (bipolar disorder, unipolar depressive psychosis, and unipolar non-psychotic depression), and epidemiological research often uses these categories in any case. In Table 1.1, I have provided a comparison of the definitions of depressive disorder under DSM-IV (APA, 1994) and ICD-10 (WHO, 1992), slightly simplified. Over the years, there has been considerable convergence between the systems. However, the differences remain important. The cate-gories are too close together for empirical studies to establish their relative validity, but far enough apart to cause discrepancies in identification. Relatively severe cases are likely to be classified as depressive disorder under both systems. However, milder disorders may be cases under one system, and not the other. This becomes important in epidemiological studies of depressive disorder in the general population because such studies usually report their results under one system or the other, and the degree of comparability is hard to quan-tify. Thus, the use of different classificatory systems is one barrier to comparison between studies: there are others.

It is of interest to see the effect of applying algorithms for the diagnostic categories defined by different systems to a common set of symptom data. The Schedules for Clinical Assessment in Neuropsychiatry (SCAN) (WHO, 1992) allows diagnosis under both DSM and ICD. In Table 1.2, I have illustrated the effect of applying ICD-10 and DSM-IV criteria to the data from the Derry Survey (McConnell et al., 2002) on the identification of cases of depressive episode (ICD) and depressive disorder (DSM). Of the 18 participants diag-nosed as having a depressive condition by one classification, two-thirds were diagnosed by both. Five cases of depressive episode were not diagnosed as DSM depressive disorder, whereas only one case of depressive disorder was not diagnosed as ICD depressive episode. In contrast, DSM recognized many more cases of anxiety disorder. Fifteen of the cases

Table 1.1   Criteria for depressive episode

DSM-III-R/DSM-IV	ICD-10
Symptoms present nearly every day in same 2-week period	**Episode must have lasted at least 2 weeks with symptoms nearly every day**
Change from normal functioning	**Change from normal functioning**
Key symptoms ($n = 2$) Depressed mood Anhedonia	**Key symptoms ($n = 3$)** Depressed mood Anhedonia Fatigue/loss of energy
Ancillary symptoms ($n = 7$) Fatigue/loss of energy Weight/appetite loss/gain Insomnia/hypersomnia Observed agitation/retardation Low self-esteem/guilt Impaired thinking/concentration Suicidal thoughts	**Ancillary symptoms ($n = 7$)** Weight and appetite change Sleep disturbance Subjective or objective Agitation/retardation Low self-esteem/confidence Self reproach/guilt Impaired thinking/concentration Suicidal thoughts
Criteria: one key, five symptoms in total **Plus** Significant distress **Or** Social impairment	**Criteria:** Mild episode: two key, four symptoms in total Moderate: two key, six symptoms in total Severe: three key, eight symptoms in total
Exclusions Not mixed episode Not substance related Not organic Not bereavement Not psychotic	**Exclusions** No history (ever) of manic symptoms Not substance related Not organic

Table 1.2   DSM-III-R and ICD-10 classification based on the same symptom data. The Derry Survey (McConnell et al., 2002)

	No depressive diagnosis	Depressive disorder DSM
No depressive diagnosis	289 (94%)	1 (0.3%)
Depressive episode ICD-10	5 (1.6%)	12 (3.9%)
Kappa =	**0.79**	
	No anxiety diagnosis	Anxiety disorder DSM
No anxiety diagnosis	269 (87%)	15 (4.9%)
Anxiety disorder ICD	2 (0.7%)	21 (6.8%)
Kappa =	**0.68**	

defined by DSM were not classed as anxiety disorders by ICD, while only two classified by ICD were not so classed by DSM. Thus, the ICD criteria appear to be less stringent for depressive episode, while the reverse is true of anxiety. The results suggest that the difference between the two systems arises because of differing thresholds rather than because of wide differences in the symptom contents of the classes.

THE LIMITS OF CLASSIFICATION

As classification aspires to 'carve nature at the joints', the empirical relationships between psychiatric symptoms create special difficulties of their own. In particular, symptoms are related non-reflexively: thus, some symptoms are common and others are rare, and, in general, they are hierarchically related, rather than being associated in a random manner. Rare symptoms often predict the presence of common symptoms, but common symptoms do not predict rare symptoms. Deeply (that is, 'pathologically') depressed mood is commonly associated with more prevalent symptoms, such as tension or worry, while, in most instances, tension and worry are *not* associated with depressed mood (Sturt, 1981). Likewise, depressive delusions are almost invariably associated with depressed mood, whereas most people with depressed mood do not have delusions of any kind. The consequence is that the presence of the rarer, more 'powerful' symptoms indicates a case with many other symptoms as well, and therefore a case that is more symptomatically severe. It is because of this set of empirical relationships between symptoms that psychiatric syndromes are themselves largely arranged hierarchically. Thus, schizophrenia is very often accompanied by affective symptoms, although these are not officially part of the syndrome. Likewise, psychotic depression is not distinguished from non-psychotic depression by having a completely different set of symptoms, but by having extra, discriminating, symptoms, such as depressive delusions and hallucinations.

LEAKY CLASSES AND COMORBIDITY

The operational criteria set up to identify and distinguish so-called common mental disorders cut across the natural hierarchies existing between symptoms. The consequence is that many people who have one of these disorders also meet the criteria for one or more of the others. This *comorbidity* has generated much interest, and was even responsible for the name of one of the major US epidemiological surveys (the National Comorbidity Survey) (Kessler et al., 1994). Researchers, then, divide into two camps: those who think the comorbidity represents important relationships between well-validated disorders; and those who think it arises as an artefact of a classificatory system that is conceptually flawed and fails adequately to capture the nature of affective disturbance.

Thus, Kessler (2000) has defended the status of generalized anxiety disorder (GAD) as an independent condition, despite its high comorbidity, arguing that it does, for example, precede major depression, and also outlasts it. However, this would be expected if GAD represented a low threshold disorder that could transmute into a higher threshold disorder with the addition of a few symptoms. GAD and depression certainly share a common genetic diathesis (Mineka et al., 1998). The superimposition of major depression on a long-lasting minor depressive disturbance (dysthymia) has been called double depression (Keller et al., 1997). The comorbidity of anxiety and depression may arise because anxiety states can transform into depressive disorders with the addition of relatively few symptoms (Parker et al., 1997). Depression/anxiety is equally apparent in adolescents (Seligman & Ollendick, 1998), as is the link between dysthymia and major depression (Birmaher et al., 1996). The idea that there are several distinguishable affective disorders is, to some extent, self-perpetuating, as it prevents clinicians from seeking out the full range of symptoms that are reflected in comorbidity. I imagine that it will turn out to be much more useful to see these comorbidities as an indication of common underlying processes leading to, but not necessarily reaching, a common destination.

DEPRESSION AND THE THRESHOLD PROBLEM

Another important empirical aspect of affective disorders is the distribution of symptoms in the general population. Many people have a few symptoms, while few people have many. This means that decisions have to be made about the threshold below which no disorder should be identified. People who have few symptoms may still be above this threshold if some of their symptoms are particularly discriminating, but, in general, the threshold is defined by the number of symptoms. There is always a tendency in medicine to move the threshold down, particularly as a sizeable proportion of the people with mental symptoms who are seen by primary-care physicians fall below the thresholds of DSM-IV or ICD-10. However, others in the medical profession have serious reservations about what they regard as medical imperialism, the medicalization of normal human experience (Double, 2002).

In response to the threshold problem, there has been a burgeoning literature recently relating to subthreshold, subclinical, minor, and brief recurrent affective disorder (Schotte & Cooper, 1999). The tendency to extend the threshold downwards is apparent in the establishment of the category of *dysthymia*, referred to above, a depressive condition characterized only by its mildness (that is, a *lack* of symptoms) and its chronicity. The category has, nevertheless, become a study it its own right: it has clear links with major depression, presumably because it is relatively easy for someone who already has some depressive symptoms to acquire some more and meet criteria for the more severe disorder. It is also associated with psychosocial distress, both recent and distant. Some authors have gone so far as to suggest that it reflects abnormalities of neuroendocrine and neurotransmitter function (Griffiths et al., 2000).

The imposition of a threshold on an apparent continuum lacks some of its arbitrariness if it is possible to demonstrate a naturally occurring 'step-change' in the distribution. Thus, while the distribution of IQ is largely continuous, there is a clear excess of subjects at the bottom of the continuum who are characterized by a distinct and identifiable pathology (Penrose, 1963). Many have argued that no such distinction exists in affective symptoms (Goldberg, 2000; Tyrer, 1985). While it might be possible to create a threshold that represented a step-change in social disability (Hurry et al., 1983), the evidence does, overall, suggest that affective symptoms are distributed more like blood pressure than IQ. Melzer and his colleagues (2002) have recently used symptom data from the British National Survey of Psychiatric Morbidity to test the smoothness of the distribution. A single exponential curve provided the best fit for the whole population, but there were floor effects that produced deviations at symptom counts of 0–3. Truncation of the data to take account of this provided an excellent fit (Figure 1.1). This was not affected by selecting for analysis subgroups characterized by especially high or low prevalence.

It can be concluded from this discussion that the epidemiological literature on depressive disorder is likely to be a mess. We have disorders that are identified as classes imposed on what is empirically a continuum. This is made worse by the fact that the classificatory schemes are changed at regular intervals. Moreover, two major schemes exist side-by-side. Added to this is the issue of how the symptoms of common mental disorders can be elicited,

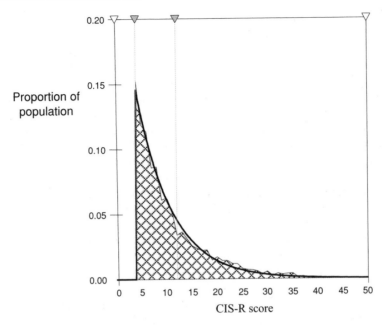

Figure 1.1 Proportion of population by truncated range of CIS-R scores, and fitted exponential curve. Reproduced from Melzer, D. et al. (2002). Common mental disorder symptom counts in populations: Are there distinct case groups above epidemiological cut-offs? *Psychological Medicine, 32*, 1195–1201. Reproduced by permission of Cambridge University Press

identified, and used, in order to decide whether, together, they can be said to constitute a case.

CASE IDENTIFICATION IN RESEARCH

Case identification is the basis of epidemiology. The process of diagnosis involves allocating symptom patterns to a diagnostic class according to given rules. In recent years, these rules have been set out explicitly in the diagnostic criteria for research (DCRs) attached to specific classifications, such as DSM-III-R, DSM-IV, and ICD-10, so precisely that it is possible to incorporate them into computer algorithms such as CATEGO (Wing et al., 1990) and OPCRIT (McGuffin et al., 1991).

Once the presence of symptoms has been established, the information can be entered into one of these computer programs in order to provide a diagnostic classification. Human idiosyncrasy can be reduced to an absolute minimum in this process. However, researchers must still decide how carefully the underlying symptoms should be identified. The choices include unstructured clinical assessment, responses to questionnaires, and semi-structured research interviews.

The first option, unstructured clinical judgement, introduces variability into the process of case allocation, since researchers are relying merely on their devotion to a common educational tradition. This situation is even worse when the judgements of others (for example, the treating physician) are used, as with the diagnostic information recorded in case registers or in national statistics.

In order to be practicable, questionnaires should seek simple responses to unelaborated questions. However, symptoms are traditionally recognized through an assessment of mental experiences that demand quite elaborate enquiry (Brugha et al., 1999). They are usually established by a process of clinical cross-examination. This process is rather complicated since it requires the questioner to frame further questions in a flexible way in the light of the answers given by the subject. While it might be possible to encapsulate this procedure in a standard questionnaire by using a branching algorithm, it would be exhaustive and exhausting—it might require paths comprising over a dozen questions just to establish the presence of pathologically depressed mood. In these circumstances, there are clearly practical limits to the process of standardization, and it is probably better to rely on the short cuts available from using the skills of trained clinicians. Since diagnosis is built around symptoms defined and elicited in this manner, redefinition in terms of answers to much more limited questions would involve changing the concept of diagnosis itself. No one has seriously suggested that the way psychiatric symptoms are conceptualized should be changed; therefore, if a questionnaire is used, phenomena may be recorded as present when subsequent clinical enquiry might reveal otherwise, and vice versa. Nevertheless, structured questionnaires do allow lay interviewers to be used, with considerable cost savings. The Diagnostic Interview Schedule (DIS) (Robins et al., 1981) and the Composite International Diagnostic Interview (CIDI) (Robins et al., 1988) are fully structured questionnaires that have been widely used, and have good reliability.

Semi-structured research interviews are costly in clinical time, and the way in which symptoms are established makes it impossible to standardize the procedure entirely (Robins, 1995). Because of the reliance on clinical judgement and the effect this has on the choice of follow-up questions, some variability will remain. This is the price paid for greater validity, that is, the closer approximation to the clinical consensus about the nature of given symptoms. The Schedules for Clinical Assessment in Neuropsychiatry (SCAN) (Wing et al., 1990) are based on a semi-structured interview, and are increasingly used in epidemiological research studies (e.g., Ayuso-Mateos et al., 2001; Bebbington et al., 1997; McConnell et al., 2002; Meltzer et al., 1995). SCAN has good interrater reliability despite its semi-structured format.

QUESTIONNAIRES AND INTERVIEWS

If, as I have argued, there are doubts in principle about the validity of structured questionnaires, it is worth knowing how their performance compares with semi-standardized interviews. One head-to-head comparison has been made between SCAN and CIDI (Brugha et al., 2001). This permits two separate questions:

(1) Does the questionnaire provide a similar frequency of disorder to that established by the semi-structured interview?
(2) To what extent are the same cases identified by the two instruments?

Differences in frequencies would, at the very least, indicate some systematic biases separating the instruments. However, even if, for example, CIDI recognized more cases than SCAN, it could still be the case that CIDI picked up most or all of the cases identified by SCAN. This would imply that the constraints of a rigid questionnaire tended to lower the threshold of case identification, as might be the case if the rigidity and the paucity of elaborative questions led to over-recognition of specific symptoms. If, however, in addition to over-recognition of cases, there were little overlap between the cases found by the two systems, this would indicate a more general failure of rigid questioning to establish symptoms properly.

Brugha and his colleagues (2001) conducted a two-phase study of the general population of Leicestershire, UK. In the second phase, 172 subjects selected for an increased probability of exhibiting cases of psychiatric disorder were interviewed with both CIDI and SCAN, in random order. The coefficients of concordance for the various ICD-10 diagnoses varied between poor and fair. The authors calculated that using CIDI would give prevalences about 50% greater than those obtained from SCAN. The index of agreement for any depressive episode was poor (0.14). As expected, the discrepancies arose particularly from cases around the threshold for recognition.

BOTTOM-UP AND TOP-DOWN CASE IDENTIFICATION

The other way in which instruments differ is whether they are diagnosis-driven or symptom-driven. Instruments that are diagnosis-driven do not require to elicit the same set of symptoms in each case in order to establish the appropriate diagnostic category. All they have to do is to confirm that the required diagnostic criteria are met. DIS and CIDI are examples of such instruments. The advantage is that they can cut corners by not having to check out all symptoms once a diagnosis has been made: this is often the way clinicians work in their ordinary practice.

Symptom-driven instruments are exhaustive in their coverage of symptoms, and only then do they use the symptomatic information to check whether diagnostic criteria have been met (for example, SCAN and CIS-R). This has two advantages. The first is that, in theory, it should be possible to use the symptom information to serve a new algorithm if the diagnostic criteria were changed. This might be extremely arduous in practice, although attempts of this sort have been made (e.g., Murphy, 1994). The other advantage is of particular relevance to the study of the common affective disorders. Establishing whether or not a set range of symptoms is present allows an overall symptoms count to be made, and this is useful when it is appropriate to study the distributions of symptoms in the general population, as in the study by Melzer and his colleagues (2002) mentioned above.

THE FREQUENCY OF DEPRESSIVE DISORDER

Frequency can be measured in a variety of ways: incidence; point, period, and lifetime prevalence; and morbid risk. Table 1.3 defines commonly used rates in epidemiology. General population surveys usually report period or lifetime prevalence rates, while investigations of clinical series often use first contact or admission as a proxy for incidence. In this chapter, I shall rely largely on studies of prevalence.

While community psychiatric surveys date back nearly a century, it is only in the past 25 years that they have used standardized methods of assessment that allow the comparison of research from different locations. I have reviewed studies based on the superseded

Table 1.3 Epidemiological rates

Incidence rate: the number of new cases in a given period as a proportion of a population at risk

Point prevalence rate: the number of cases identified at a point in time as a proportion of a total population

Period prevalence rate: the number of cases identified as in existence during a specified period as a proportion of a total population

Lifetime prevalence rate: a variant of period prevalence where the period for case identification comprises the entire lifetime of each subject at the point of ascertainment

---

PSE-ID-CATEGO system (Wing et al., 1978) elsewhere (Bebbington, 1998). Those using the Diagnostic Interview Schedule (DIS) (Robins et al., 1985) developed for the US Epidemiological Catchment Area (ECA) surveys have been summarized by Weissman et al. (1996). Table 1.4 provides 1-year and lifetime prevalence rates according to this system from around the world.

Although Weissman and her colleagues (1996) argue that variation between locations is not great, the annual prevalences rates, in fact, range from 0.8% to 5.8%, and the lifetime prevalence from 1.5% to 16.4%.

The range of prevalences given in Table 1.4 is difficult to explain, as it does not correspond to the obvious cultural differences between the locations of the surveys. So, for instance, there are high rates in Europe compared with the USA, but the studies from Canada and New Zealand are also high. High rates in Beirut are perhaps understandable. The difficulties in the overall interpretation of these results suggest differences in the application of the interview.

Since these surveys, data have been published from a number of large-scale investigations based on national probability samples. These include the US National Comorbidity Survey (Kessler et al., 1993, 1994); two British National Surveys of Psychiatry Morbidity (Jenkins et al., 1997; Singleton et al., 2001), the Australian National Survey of Mental Health and Well-Being (Henderson et al., 2000), and the Finnish National Survey (Lindeman et al., 2000). They each involved interviews with several thousand subjects (see Table 1.5). All but the British surveys used variants of CIDI (the Composite International Diagnostic Interview)

Table 1.4 Annual and lifetime prevalence of major depressive episode from studies using DIS

Site	N	Annual	Lifetime
United States (ECA) (Robins & Regier, 1991)	18 571	3.0	5.2
Edmonton, Alberta (Bland et al., 1988)	3258	5.2	9.6
Puerto Rico (Canino et al., 1987)	1513	3.0	4.3
Paris (Lepine et al., 1989)	1746	4.5	16.4
West Germany[1] (Wittchen et al., 1992)	481	5.0	9.2
Florence (Faravelli et al., 1990)	1000	–	12.4
Beirut (Karam, 1992)	528	–	19.0
Taiwan (Hwu et al., 1989)	11 004	0.8	1.5
Korea (Lee et al., 1990)	5100	2.3	2.9
Christchurch, New Zealand (Oakley-Browne et al., 1989)	1498	5.8	11.6

[1] Aged 26–64.
Data from Weissman et al. (1996). References in table are to base papers from original studies.

Table 1.5   Prevalence rates for depressive disorders: recent large-scale surveys

Survey	N	Prevalence	Notes
National Comorbidity Survey (Kessler et al., 1993)	8098		Age 15–54; 1-year prevalence University of Michigan version of CIDI DSM-IV major depressive disorder
Australian National Survey (Henderson et al., 2000)	10 600	5.1%	1-year prevalence ICD-10 depressive episode Automated presentation of CIDI
Finnish National Survey (Lindeman et al., 2000)	5993	9.3%	1-year prevalence Automated presentation of short form of UM—CIDI
First British National Survey (Jenkins et al., 1997)	10 108	2.3%	1-week prevalence—CIS-R ICD-10 depressive disorder
Second British National Survey (Singleton et al., 2001)	8580	2.6%	1-week prevalence—CIS-R ICD-10 depressive disorder

(Robins et al., 1988). The British Surveys also used lay interviewers, but was based on the revised version of the Clinical Interview Schedule (CIS-R) (Lewis et al., 1992), an interview that provides ICD-10 diagnoses (WHO, 1992). It can be seen from Table 1.5 that despite the similar procedure of the CIDI and the DIS, the prevalences in the ECA studies, which used the latter, are closer to those in the British National Survey of Psychiatric Morbidity than to the CIDI-based surveys. The rate of affective disorders with CIDI in Ethiopia was low, and it is not clear whether this represents a methodological problem or a real difference (Kebede & Alem, 1999).

Some community psychiatric studies using SCAN have now been published (WHO, 1992). Two are British and are located in Camberwell (inner south London) and Derry (Londonderry), Northern Ireland, respectively (Bebbington et al., 1997; McConnell et al., 2002). The 1-year prevalence rates of ICD-10 depressive episode were 6% and 7%, respectively. The rate in Derry would be expected to be higher than in towns of comparable size, given its considerable poverty and legacy of sectarian violence. The multinational ODIN project also used SCAN, but the results so far published are difficult to interpret, as the authors provide prevalences for depressive disorder of all types, whether identified according to ICD-10 or DSM-IV (Ayuso-Mateos et al., 2001). Not surprisingly, in view of this confused decision, the prevalences are among some of the highest quoted, and cannot be compared with any other studies.

What, then, can be concluded from this exercise in counting? First, if we are going to establish a category of depressive disorder, we should be consistent. There is no real way of choosing between ICD-10 and DSM-IV criteria, although they differ somewhat in the cases they identify, but one or other system should be adhered to, as they are the most commonly used. The criteria for depressive disorder (DSM-IV) are more restrictive than those of ICD-10 major depressive episode, and, in principle, should result in lower prevalences. However, epidemiological studies presenting DSM-IV major depressive disorder (MDD) often use CIDI, and this probably results in quoted prevalences around 50% above what they would be if a semi-structured clinical interview were used. The short form of the CIDI, as used in the Finnish study (Lindeman et al., 2000), may result in particularly high prevalences (Patten, 1997; 2000).

The consequence of these two countervailing influences is that we cannot use the epidemiological surveys to make very sensible statements about whether the different locations in which they were carried out are characterized by true differences in prevalence. For that, we have to rely on studies that cover more than one area, in a way that permits inferences about consistent influences; for instance, the relatively low rates of depression in rural areas (Paykel et al., 2000).

My best guess is that annual prevalence rates of ICD depressive episode may be around 4%, and that of DSM depressive disorder around 5%. Prevalence related to shorter periods (1-week, 1-month) will be around one-half to two-thirds these rates.

Nevertheless, one can use these essentially questionable procedures to come to certain limited but interesting conclusions concerning the factors that influence prevalence.

DEPRESSION AND SEX

One of the most consistent findings in the whole of psychiatric epidemiology is that women are more likely to suffer from depression than men. Thus, in the summary of the DIS studies (Weissman et al., 1996), the sex ratio for the lifetime prevalence of depression ranged from 1.6 to 3.0. The two British national surveys gave a sex ratio for 1-week prevalence on the low side, at 1.5 and 1.2, respectively. The Finnish national study gave a value of 1.5 (Lindeman et al., 2000). There have been numerous reviews (Bebbington, 1996; Maier et al., 1999; Merikangas, 2000; Piccinelli & Wilkinson, 2000). The very large, six-nation European study DEPRES (Depressive Research in European Society) (Angst et al., 2002) establishes the sex difference at the level both of MDD (F:M = 1.7) and of the various depressive symptoms. Very few studies have shown ratios close to unity, and they have usually been in restricted populations.

This consistency of the sex ratio is not matched by any clarity of explanation. Before considering the possible causes, we must consider the influence of age on depression.

DEPRESSION AND AGE

There are clear general statements that can be made about the relationship between age and depression. First, the propensity for depression is rare before adolescence (Birmaher et al., 1996). Secondly, the prevalence of depression declines in late middle age or early old age (e.g., Figure 1.2). Thirdly, the female to male sex ratio for depression is not constant over the lifespan, being around unity in childhood, rising during adulthood, and declining once again in elderly groups (Jorm, 1987).

The relationship between sex differences and age is of interest, as it may be linked to explanations for the former. The onset of the difference in adolescence may be related to the emergence of adult hormonal status. However, adolescence is both a biological and a social transformation. Some authors have argued that the social process of 'gender intensification' may be responsible for additional stresses on girls. Others adhere to the idea that hormonal changes increase female vulnerability. Until recently, the burden of evidence favoured the social hypothesis, as the sex ratio appeared to be related to chronological age

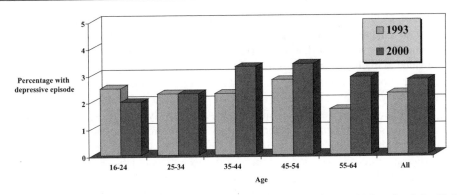

Figure 1.2   Prevalence of depressive episode by age in 1993 and 2000 for all adults. Data taken from Meltzer et al. (1995) and Singleton et al. (2001)

rather than to hormonal development (Bebbington, 1996). However, two very good, recent epidemiological studies (Angold et al., 1999; Patton et al., 1996) are both in favour of a relationship with menarche rather than social transition.

The issue nevertheless remains unresolved, as does the age at which the sex ratio once again tends towards unity. One possibility is that the rate of depression in women declines (thus reducing the sex ratio) after the menopause. This would be interesting, in view of the idea that in women the hormonal status of the child-rearing years is particularly associated with vulnerability to depression. Because the menopause coincides with a number of social transitions, and is in any case an event of psychological significance, it is necessary to try to control for confounding by social variables that serve to mark these transitions. Using data from the first British National Survey, Bebbington and his colleagues (1998) found that the decline in prevalence rates of depression after age 55 could not be accounted for by obvious social factors, such as the end of involvement in childcare or changes in marital or employment status. This would be consistent with a possible hormonal influence. However, in the second national survey, the decline in female depression occurred to a greater degree after age 65. Such a shift is easier to explain in (unspecified) social terms.

OTHER SOCIODEMOGRAPHIC VARIABLES THAT INFLUENCE RATES OF DEPRESSION

The age effects confirm the embarrassing situation that we have no clear explanation of the sex difference: we cannot say for sure what weight should be accorded to biological, social, and psychological explanations (Bebbington, 1996, 1998).

Nevertheless, social factors may well be of considerable importance because the sex ratio is not universally maintained across all sociodemographic categories. It is, for instance, much more marked in married than in never-married groups (Bebbington et al., 1981; Lindeman et al., 2000; Weissman & Klerman, 1977). Young married women looking after small children appear to be particularly at risk, at least in some societies (Brown & Harris, 1978; Ensel, 1982). Unsupported mothers appear to be even more at risk (Targosz et al., 2003). However, marital status has different associations with affective disorder in different cultures. Married women are at low risk of disorder in Mediterranean countries (Mavreas et al., 1986; Vazquez-Barquero et al., 1987), in rural New Zealand (Romans-Clarkson et al., 1988), and among British Orthodox Jews (Lowenthal et al., 1995). These societies all accord a high value to the home-making role.

This variation in the impact of marital status on the sex ratio of depression might be taken as merely epiphenomenal, a sort of froth on the central fact that women are inherently vulnerable to depression for biological reasons. Alternatively, it might suggest not only that social variables are important in determining the sex ratio for depression, but also that the association with relatively simple sociodemographic factors is itself affected by more subtle sociocultural influences. The pervasiveness of the sex ratio could then be seen as a reflection of the all-pervading hydra of social disadvantage experienced by women worldwide.

In most Western societies, women are even now less likely to be employed than men. Employment generally has beneficial effects on psychological health: it brings interest, income, fulfilment, social contacts, and status, and provides structure and a sense of control (Jahoda, 1982; Krause & Geyer-Pestello, 1985). The availability of these benefits is likely to differ both among women, and between men and women. The advantages of employment are weaker in married women (Roberts & O'Keefe, 1981; Roberts et al., 1982; Warr & Parry, 1982), more so if they have children (McGee et al., 1983; Parry, 1986), most so when the children are of pre-school age (Haw, 1995). Full-time employment is particularly demanding (Cleary & Mechanic, 1983; Elliott & Huppert, 1991). The most likely explanation for these findings is role conflict and overload. Thus, part of the excess of depressive disorders in women may be related both to their reduced involvement in employment and to the particular strains they are exposed to if they do work.

BIOLOGICAL EXPLANATIONS FOR THE SEX RATIO IN DEPRESSION

My interpretation of the evidence for a specific biological vulnerability to depression in women may be politically driven, since the choice between social and biological theories can be represented at the choice between seeing women either as universally disadvantaged, or as inherently vulnerable with all the associated implications of inferiority.

Direct evidence linking hormone status to depressive disorder has some face validity: oestradiol and progesterone seem to modulate the neurotransmitter and neuroendocrine systems, including those involving monamines, and there are transitions in women's lives characterized by hormonal shifts that may also be associated with mood disturbance (child-birth and the menopause).

The evidence in this area is extremely complicated (Bebbington, 1996). Moreover, there is a more plausible neuroendocrine hypothesis for depression involving glucocorticoids. This offers an explanation for a range of other neurohumoral phenomena, and a mechanism whereby extrinsic stress may result in the features of depressive disorder (Checkley, 1998; Dinan, 1994). It links overactivation of the hypothalamico-pituitary-adrenal (HPA) axis and the associated hypercortisolism with the changes in the central monaminergic pathways thought to underlie depression and the actions of antidepressants. These changes will probably turn out to be the major hormonal concomitants of depressive disorder. Unfortunately for our purpose, they cannot explain the sex difference: specifically, the function of the HPA axis in general does not differ by sex in the required manner (Allen & Pitts, 1984; Ansseau et al., 1987; Hunt et al., 1989; Maes et al., 1989).

The failure to find a convincing sex-related biological mechanism for depression that would account for the sex difference has its parallel in genetic studies. It is extremely unlikely that biological differences between women would be unaffected by intrafamilial (specifically, genetic) factors. The most plausible model is one based on multiple threshold liability. This assumes that the familial liability to a disorder is continuously distributed, comprising both genetic factors and familial-environmental effects. Depression in women can be conceived as a broad form of disorder with a lower threshold than the narrow male form, thus accounting for the higher prevalence rate in women. Under this model, the relatives of male probands will be more frequently affected, because in them the loading of familial factors will be greater (Carter, 1969). In practice, the relatives of male depressives are not at higher risk than the relatives of female depressives (Kupfer et al., 1989; Merikangas et al., 1985). Kendler and Prescott (1999) and Sullivan and colleagues (2002) were led to conclude that the heritability of the liability to depression was similar in men and women, even though the specific genetic factors might not overlap completely. Thus, it seems that the sex ratio must be explained in terms of extra-familial influences. This still allows for genetic effects in the transmission of depression, we merely assert that they do not cause the sex difference.

LIFE STRESS AND DEPRESSION

Life event research has been a major topic in the aetiology of depression for more than 30 years. The idea is intuitively appealing, and this is exactly why there is a conceptual problem with this type of research. Humans try to make sense of their experience by identifying patterns of apparent cause and effect, and this applies to the relationship between social circumstances, feelings, and behaviour. People understand that individuals are often distressed when upsetting things happen. Sociologists and social psychiatrists developed the concept of significant life events from the upset that can be caused by rapid adverse changes in circumstances, while psychiatrists' conceptualization of affective disorders derives from the features that characterize distress. Distress is recognized from emotional and cognitive responses that, in severe or persistent forms, strongly resemble the symptoms of depressive disorder.

At a technological level, 'life events' differ from ordinary experience, and depressive disorder differs from ordinary distress only in degree. So what is the status of the assertion 'life events cause depression'? It could be regarded as definitional: things defined as being likely to distress people often do cause distress. At the very best, it is a hypothesis with low information value. Popper (1959) particularly admired theories (such as relativity) that were of inherently low a priori probability: the change in knowledge if they were corroborated, was thus great. However, our theory about life events has high a priori probability: everybody already believes it, not just the scientists, and thus corroboration does not add much to our knowledge. Given this preamble, it is not surprising that studies in both clinical and general populations, whether methodologically sophisticated or not, display remarkable consistency in finding that life events are associated with the onset of depressive disorder.

While this finding is not very interesting in itself, it does lead to more interesting questions. Thus, although there is an overall association, some people put up with considerable stress without becoming depressed. What is the nature of this resilience? People may vary in the way they handle events (coping), or particular individuals may have been exposed to events that happen not to be very threatening to them. Vulnerability itself may be the consequence of exposure to prior experiences that caused particular psychological predispositions. Alternatively, relevant temperamental variation may be under genetic control. Finally, genetic inheritance may influence the frequency with which individuals experience life events, even those that do not appear to be under their control.

THE CHILDHOOD ANTECEDENTS OF LATER DEPRESSION

There are clear associations between certain childhood experiences, circumstances, and characteristics, and later depression. This is despite the rarity of childhood depressive disorder. What links there are must therefore usually be indirect—the causal connection appears to operate over a gap of years. This suggests some enduring change that mediates the later propensity to depression. Such changes might include psychological, temperamental, and biological predispositions, and an increased sensitivity to adult stress is a plausible mechanism. For example, the tendency of women to become depressed in response to domestic violence in adulthood is increased if they had also experienced abuse in childhood (Roberts et al., 1998).

The identification of childhood antecedents is an essentially epidemiological task, particularly when it involves longitudinal cohorts with follow-up over many years. Later depression is associated with childhood neuroticism, childhood symptoms of depression and anxiety, and reduced cognitive abilities. It has been suggested that these antecedents render individuals more sensitive to later life events (van Os et al., 1997; van Os & Jones, 1999).

A variety of childhood traumas are associated with later depressive episodes (De Marco, 2000). Childhood abuse, whether physical, emotional, or sexual, is associated with later psychopathology (Bifulco et al., 1991; Fergusson et al., 1996; Mullen et al., 1996). This seems particularly likely to be mediated through low self-esteem and later difficulties in forming relationships (Romans et al., 1995, 1996). In these New Zealand studies, only the most severe forms of abuse were unequivocally related to adult affective disorder. Abuse usually occurs in the context of other problems, and it may be this matrix that leads to adult disorder (Finkelhor et al., 1990; Higgins & McCabe, 1994; Rind & Tromovitch, 1997). Abuse is associated with many types of adult psychopathology, indicating a less than specific relationship with depression.

Childhood sexual abuse is associated with adult-onset depression in both men and women, but abuse is much more frequent in girls (Weiss et al., 1999). It may be mediated by its effects on psychological disparities, but also by dysregulating the HPA axis. Moreover, in females, the HPA axis may be inherently vulnerable to dysregulation by early stress (Weiss et al., 1999).

The link between child sexual abuse and adult depression is all too plausible. There has been some debate, however, whether parenting style in itself is sufficient to account for much of the variance in adult depression. One school of thought is that children have a built-in plasticity in the face of quite considerable disparities in levels of care. However, it is becoming increasingly clear that parenting style does have considerable impact. Much of this work has resulted from the development of simple methods of assessment. The Parental Bonding Instrument (PBI) (Parker, 1990; Parker et al., 1979) is a self-report inventory designed to measure perceived parental care. It divides parenting style into the aspects of *care* and *overprotection*, and these seem stable over time. Optimal parenting comprises high care and low overprotection (Parker, 1990). While lack of care is consistently related to adult depression, the association of overprotection is less consistent (Parker et al., 1995).

Clearly, the PBI is a self-report measure, and might merely represent a querulous response set in people whose mood is depressed, but in fact, there is little evidence of this (Parker, 1981). Parker (1981) assessed the validity of the PBI by showing correspondence between sibling ratings of the subject's parenting with the subject's own. It is of interest that perceived parental care of twins correlates better for monozygotic than dizygotic twins (Kendler, 1996). Finally, it is possible that a third variable (neuroticism, for instance) might lead to a spurious relationship between reports of parenting and depression, by itself, being responsible for the propensity towards both. It is also possible that neuroticism might mediate between the experience of poor parenting and depression (Kendler et al., 1993). However, Duggan and his colleagues (1998) found that poor parenting and neuroticism had effects on later depression that were independent of each other.

Of course, it is possible that suboptimal parenting style may be linked to child sexual abuse. Hill and his colleagues (2001) demonstrated that low care was associated with sexual abuse, not only by relatives, but also by non-relatives. However, low care and child sex abuse were independently related to depression. However, this led Hill and his colleagues (2001) to suggest that the links between childhood sexual abuse and poor parenting with adult depression are mediated through different pathways.

THE EPIDEMIOLOGY OF TREATMENT FOR DEPRESSION

There are various ways in which the delivery of treatment for depression can be assessed (Bebbington et al., 1996). One is to assume that identified depressive disorders need treatment of one sort or another, and to establish how often they actually received it. This is technically a measure of *utilization*. Another approach is to establish directly whether treatment was actually needed before quantifying how often it was delivered. Need can be defined either by experts, or by the individual in question (when it is called want, demand, or subjective need). Investigations of general population samples are the obvious source of such information. The obvious questions are as follows. Did this person have a need for professional treatment? Did he or she seek psychiatric help at either primary or secondary care level? Was he or she then prescribed treatment? Did he or she take the treatment prescribed? Studies of any kind are rare, but give a clear picture of under-treatment.

The Australian National Survey of Mental Health and Well-Being (Andrews *et al.*, 2001) reports data on service utilization. Thus, two-thirds of all subjects had no contact with services in the previous year, while 29% had seen GPs and 7.5% psychiatrists (Henderson et al., 2000). However, the survey gives data only from the combined category of major depressive disorder and dysthymia—the use of a broad category like theirs would reduce the likelihood of service contact.

Table 1.6 lists two direct studies of expert-defined need that provide data for depression. While the proportion of the population requiring treatment for depression was similar in Camberwell and Derry, it does appear that people were more likely to receive treatment in

Table 1.6 Need and utilization of treatment for depressive disorders

Study	Location	N stage2/stage 1	One-year treatment needs for depression	Proportion of needs met
Bebbington et al., 1997	Camberwell, London	408 (760)	6.0%	20%
McConnell et al., 2002	Derry, N. Ireland	307 (923)	7.1%	48%

Study	Location	N	Contact with primary care services	Proportion treated	Antidepressant treatment	Other drugs	Counselling
Bebbington et al., 2000	First British National Survey	10 108	48%	28%	16%	9%	15%
Singleton et al., 2001	Second British National Survey	8580	62%	44%	34%	12%	17%

the latter: Derry appears to have inner-city levels of depression, but small-town levels of primary-care services.

The other results listed in Table 1.6 are of particular interest—the two British National Surveys used the same methods, but the data were gathered seven years apart (1993 and 2000). There are significant improvements in the treatment of cases of depressive disorder at primary-care level: more people saw their GP with their mental health problem, and more received appropriate treatment, indicated by the noteworthy rise in antidepressant drug prescription.

Large surveys of this type offer rather crude indications of treatment levels, but the general finding of under-treatment is so marked that it clearly represents a serious public health problem, requiring education both of primary-care physicians and of the public at large.

THE GENETIC EPIDEMIOLOGY OF MAJOR DEPRESSION

The study of genetic epidemiology is of interest because it seeks to attribute a relative weight to the effects of genes, the shared and non-shared environment, and gene–environment interactions. Sullivan and colleagues (2002) have recently reviewed the literature on the genetic epidemiology of major depression, using specific inclusion criteria. On the basis of the five family studies that met their criteria, they concluded that the odds ratio of being affected with major depression in the first-degree relatives of probands compared with those of unaffected comparison subjects was around 2.8.

Twin studies are capable of providing estimates for the relative strength of genetic effects and the effects of the shared and non-shared environments. Sullivan and colleagues (2002) reviewed five studies covering 21 000 individuals that met their criteria. Although the studies showed appreciable variation in the heritability of major depression, all reported significant heritability estimates, while the estimates for *shared* environmental effects were non-significant in all the studies. There were no consistent sex differences in the results.

Despite problems in aggregating data of this type from different studies, it did prove possible. The best-fitting model included only genetic and individual-specific environmental factors, with the former contributing about 37% of variance. Heritability may be particularly increased in depression with an early onset, and is almost certainly so in recurrent depression. It should be noted that, as calculated, heritability estimates would cover gene–environment interactions as well as purely genetic effects.

CONCLUSIONS

In this chapter, I have considered the practical difficulties facing the epidemiological study of depression. Epidemiology is a medical approach that relies initially on the conceptualization of impaired functions as disorders, followed by a requirement to identify these disorders in a reliable way. Depression as conceived shades both into normal experience and into other affective disorders. Distinguishing it in a way at once useful and consistent is thus difficult, as I have argued in some detail. In particular, the comparability of studies is jeopardized by differences between classifications and instruments and in the way these are applied. The consequence is that no two research teams are likely to identify the same sets of respondents as cases; indeed, in practice, the overlap is small, and there may be systematic over- or under-identification, resulting in different prevalence rates. I now think these obstacles to precise case identification are probably insuperable. Nevertheless, the arguments remain strong for doing the best we can. Two things alleviate this rather miserable conclusion. Because most cases identified in general populations are around the threshold that distinguishes them from non-cases, different studies are likely to end up with case groups that have similar characteristics. Robust associations—for example, the association of depression with life events or with poverty—will therefore survive the inadequacies of our instrumentation.

The second way around these inadequacies is to supplement the medical case approach with studies that look at the correlates of total symptom score. In this way, important findings can be triangulated, as they are in the study of blood pressure.

REFERENCES

Allen, R.E. & Pitts, F.N. (1984). Dexamethasone suppression in depressed elderly outpatients. *Journal of Clinical Psychiatry, 45*, 397–398.

American Psychiatric Association (APA) (1994). *Diagnostic and Statistical Manual of Mental Disorders*, 4th edn, revised. Washington, DC: American Psychiatric Association.

Andrews, G., Issakidis, C. & Carter, G. (2001). Shortfall in mental health service utilisation. *British Journal of Psychiatry, 179*, 417–425.

Angold, A., Costello, E.J., Erkanli, A. & Worthman, C.M. (1999). Pubertal changes in hormone levels and depression in girls. *Psychological Medicine, 29*, 1043–1053.

Angst, J., Gamma, A., Gastpar, M., Lépine, J.P., Mendlewicz, J. & Tylee, A. (2002). Gender differences in depression: Epidemiological findings from the European Depression I and II Studies. *European Archives of Psychiatry and Clinical Neuroscience, 252*, 201–209.

Ansseau, M., Depauw, Y., Charles, G., et al. (1987). Age and gender effects on the diagnostic power of the DST. *Journal of Affective Disorders, 12*, 185–191.

Ayuso-Mateos, J.L., Vazquez-Barquero, J.L., Dowrick, C., et al. & the ODIN GROUP (2001). Depressive disorders in Europe: Prevalence figures from the ODIN study. *British Journal of Psychiatry, 179*, 308–316.

Bebbington, P., Hurry, J., Tennant, C., Sturt, E. & Wing, J.K. (1981). The epidemiology of mental disorders in Camberwell. *Psychological Medicine, 11*, 561–580.

Bebbington, P., Meltzer, H., Brugha, T., et al. (2000). Unequal access and unmet need: neurotic disorders and the use of primary care services. *Psychological Medicine, 30*, 1359–1368.

Bebbington, P.E. (1996). The origins of sex differences in depressive disorder: Bridging the gap. *International Review of Psychiatry, 8*, 295–332.

Bebbington, P.E. (1998). The assessment and epidemiology of affective disorder. In: S. Checkley (Ed.), *The Management of Depression* (pp. 1–26). Oxford: Blackwell Science.

Bebbington, P.E., Dunn, G., Jenkins, R., et al. (1998). The influence of age and sex on the prevalence of depressive conditions: Report from the National Survey of Psychiatric Morbidity. *Psychological Medicine, 28*, 9–19.

Bebbington, P.E., Marsden, L. & Brewin, C.R. (1997). The need for psychiatric treatment in the general population: The Camberwell Needs for Care survey. *Psychological Medicine, 27*, 821–834.

Bebbington, P.E., Marsden, L., Brewin, C.R. & Lesage, A. (1996). Measuring the need for psychiatric treatment in the general population: the Community Version of the MRC Needs for Care Assessment. *Psychological Medicine, 26*, 229–236.

Bifulco, A., Brown, G.W. & Adler, A. (1991). Early sexual abuse and clinical depression in adult life. *British Journal of Psychiatry, 159*, 115–122.

Birley, J.L.T. (1990). DSM-III: From left to right or from right to left? *British Journal of Psychiatry, 157*, 116–118.

Birmaher, B., Ryan, N.D., Williamson, D.E., et al. (1996). Childhood and adolescent depression: A review of the past 10 years. I. *Journal of the American Academy of Child and Adolescent Psychiatry, 35*, 1427–1439.

Bland, R.C., Newman, S.C. & Orn, H. (1988). Epidemiology of psychiatric disorders in Edmonton. *Acta Psychiatrica Scandinavica, 77, Suppl. 338.*

Brown, G.W. & Harris, T. (1978). *Social Origins of Depression*. London: Tavistock.

Brugha, T.S., Bebbington, P.E. & Jenkins, R. (1999). A difference that matters: Comparisons of structured and semi-structured psychiatric diagnostic interviews in the general population. *Psychological Medicine, 5*, 1013–1020.

Brugha, T., Jenkins, R., Taub, N., Meltzer, H. & Bebbington, P. (2001). A general population comparison of the Composite International Diagnostic Interview (CIDI) and the Schedules for Clinical Assessment in Neuropsychiatry (SCAN). *Psychological Medicine, 31*, 1001–1013.

Canino, G.J., Bird, H.R., Shrout, P.E., et al. (1987). The prevalence of specific psychiatric disorders in Puerto Rico. *Archives of General Psychiatry, 44*, 727–735.

Carter, C.D. (1969). Genetics of common disorders. *British Medical Bulletin, 25*, 52–57.

Checkley, S. (1998). Neuroendocrine changes in depression. *International Review of Psychiatry*, 584–590.

Cleary, P.D. & Mechanic, D. (1983). Sex differences in psychological distress among married people. *Journal of Health and Social Behaviour, 6*, 64–78.

De Marco, R.R. (2000). The epidemiology of major depression: Implications of occurrence, recurrence, and stress in a Canadian community sample. *Canadian Journal of Psychiatry, 45*, 67–74.

Dinan, T.G. (1994). Glucocorticoids and the genesis of depressive illness. A psychobiological model. *British Journal of Psychiatry, 164*, 365–371.

Double, D. (2002). The limits of psychiatry. *British Medical Journal, 324*, 900–904.

Duggan, C., Sham, P., Minne, C., Lee, A. & Murray, R. (1998). Quality of parenting and vulnerability to depression: Results from a family study. *Psychological Medicine, 28*, 185–191.

Elliott, J. & Huppert, F.A. (1991). In sickness and in health: Associations between physical and mental well-being, employment and parental status in a British nation-wide sample of married women. *Psychological Medicine, 21*, 515–524.

Ensel, W.M. (1982). The role of age in the relationship of gender and marital status to depression. *Journal of Nervous and Mental Disease, 170*, 536–543.

Faravelli, C., Degl'Innocenti, B.G., Aiazzi, L., Incerpi, G. & Pallanti, S. (1990). Epidemiology of mood disorders: A community survey in Florence. *Journal of Affective Disorders, 20*, 135–141.

Fergusson, D.M., Horwood, J. & Lynskey, M.T. (1996). Childhood sexual abuse and psychiatric disorder in young adulthood. II. Psychiatric outcomes of childhood sexual abuse. *Journal of the American Academy of Child and Adolescent Psychiatry, 34*, 1365–1374.

Finkelhor, D., Hotaling, G., Lewis, I.A. & Smith, C. (1990). Sexual abuse in a national survey of adult men and women: Prevalence, characteristics and risk factors. *Child Abuse and Neglect, 14*, 19–28.

Goldberg, D. (2000). Plato versus Aristotle: Categorical and dimensional models for common mental disorders. *Comprehensive Psychiatry, 41*, 8–13.

Griffiths, J., Ravindran, A.V., Merali, Z. & Anisman, H. (2000). Dysthymia: A review of pharmacological and behavioural factors. *Molecular Psychiatry, 5*, 242–261.

Haw, C.E. (1995). The family life cycle: A forgotten variable in the study of women's employment and wellbeing.*Psychological Medicine, 25*, 727–738.

Henderson, S., Andrews, G. & Hall, W. (2000). Australia's mental health: An overview of the general population survey. *Australian and New Zealand Journal of Psychiatry, 34*, 197–205.

Higgins, D.J. & McCabe, M.P. (1994). The relationship of child sexual abuse and family violence to adult adjustment: Toward an integrated risk-sequelae model. *Journal of Sex Research, 31*, 255–266.

Hill, J., Pickles, A., Burnside, E., et al. (2001). Child sexual abuse, poor parental care and adult depression: Evidence for different mechanisms. *British Journal of Psychiatry, 179*, 104–109.

Hunt, G.E., Johnson, G.F. & Caterson, I.D. (1989). The effect of age on cortisol and plasma dexamethasone concentrations in depressed patients and controls. *Journal of Affective Disorders, 17*, 21–32.

Hurry, J., Sturt, E., Bebbington, P.E. & Tennant, C. (1983). Sociodemographic associations with social disablement in a community sample. *Social Psychiatry, 18*, 113–122.

Hwu, H.-G., Yeh, E.-K. & Chang, L.Y. (1989). Prevalence of psychiatric disorders in Taiwan defined by the Chinese Diagnostic Interview Schedule. *Acta Psychiatrica Scandinavica, 79*, 136–147.

Jahoda, M. (1982). *Employment and Unemployment.* Cambridge: Cambridge University Press.

Jenkins, R., Bebbington, P.E., Brugha, T., et al. (1997). The National Psychiatric Morbidity Surveys of Great Britain—strategy and methods. *Psychological Medicine, 27*, 765–774.

Jorm, A.F. (1987). Sex and age differences in depression: A quantitative synthesis of published research. *Australian and New Zealand Journal of Psychiatry, 21*, 46–53.

Karam, E. (1992). Depression et guerres du Liban: Méthodologie d'une recherche. *Annals of Psychological Education.* Beirut, Lebanon: Université, St Joseph: 99–106.

Kebede, D. & Alem, A. (1999). Major mental disorders in Addis Ababa, Ethiopia. II. Affective disorders. *Acta Psychiatrica Scandinavica*, Suppl. *397*, 18–23.

Keller, M.B., Hirschfeld, R.M. & Hanks, D. (1997). Double depression: A distinctive subtype of unipolar depression. *Journal of Affective Disorders, 45*, 65–73.

Kendler, K.S. (1996). Parenting: A genetic-epidemiologic perspective. American *Journal of Psychiatry, 153*, 11–20.

Kendler, K.S. & Prescott, C.A. (1999). A population-based twin study of lifetime major depression in men and women. *Archives of General Psychiatry, 56*, 39–44.

Kendler, K.S., Kessler, R.C., Neale, M.C. Heath, A.C. & Eaves, L.J. (1993). The prediction of major depression in women: Toward an integrated etiologic model. *American Journal of Psychiatry, 150*, 1139–1148.

Kessler, R.C. (2000). The epidemiology of pure and comorbid generalized anxiety disorder: A review and evaluation of recent research. *Acta Psychiatrica Scandinavica*, Suppl. *406*, 7–13.

Kessler, R.C., McGonagle, K.A., Nelson, C.B., Hughes, M., Swartz, M. & Blazer, D.G. (1994). Sex and depression in the National Comorbidity Survey. II. Cohort effects. *Journal of Affective Disorders, 30*, 15–26.

Kessler, R.C., McGonagle, K.A., Swartz, M., Blazer, D.G. & Nelson, C.B. (1993). Sex and depression in the National Comorbidity Survey. I. Lifetime prevalence, chronicity and recurrence. *Journal of Affective Disorders, 29*, 85–96.

Krause, N. & Geyer-Pestello, H.F. (1985). Depressive symptoms among women employed outside the home. *American Journal of Community Psychology, 13*, 49–67.

Kupfer, D.J., Frank, E., Carpenter, L.L. & Neiswanger, K. (1989). Family history in recurrent depression. *Journal of Affective Disorders, 17*, 113–119.

Lee, C.K., Kwak, Y.S., Yamamoto, J., et al. (1990). Psychiatric epidemiology in Korea. I. Gender and age differences in Seoul. *Journal of Nervous and Mental Disorder, 178*, 247–252.

Lepine, J.P., Pariente, P., Boulenger, J.P., et al. (1989). Anxiety disorders in a French general psychiatric outpatient sample. Comparison between DSM-III and DSM-IIIR criteria. *Social Psychiatry and Psychiatric Epidemiology, 24*, 301–308.

Lewis, G., Pelosi, A., Araya, R.C. & Dunn, G. (1992). Measuring psychiatric disorder in the community: A standardized assessment for use by lay interviewers. *Psychological Medicine, 22*, 465–486.

Lindeman, S., Hamalainen, J., Isometsa, E., et al. (2000). The 12-month prevalence and risk factors for major depressive episode in Finland: Representative sample of 5993 adults. *Acta Psychiatrica Scandinavica, 102*, 178–184.

Lowenthal, K., Goldblatt, V., Gorton, T., et al. (1995). Gender and depression in Anglo-Jewry. *Psychological Medicine, 25*, 1051–1064.

Maes, M., DeRuyter, M. & Suy, E. (1989). Use of the dexamethasone suppression test in an inpatient setting: A replication and new findings. *Psychoneuroendocrinology, 14*, 584–590.

Maier, W., Gansicke, M., Gater, R., Rezaki, M., Tiemens, B. & Urzua, R.F. (1999). Gender differences in the prevalence of depression: A survey in primary care. *Journal of Affective Disorders, 53*, 241–252.

Mavreas, V.G., Beis, A., Mouyias, A., Rigoni, F. & Lyketsos, G.C. (1986). Prevalence of psychiatric disorder in Athens: A community study. *Social Psychiatry, 21*, 172–181.

McConnell, P., McClelland, R., Gillespie, K., Bebbington, P. & Houghton, S. (2002). Prevalence of psychiatric disorder and the need for psychiatric care in Northern Ireland. Population study in the District of Derry. *British Journal of Psychiatry, 181*, 214–219.

McGee, R., Williams, S., Kashani, J. & Silva, P. (1983). Prevalence of self reported depressive symptoms and associated factors in mothers in Dunedin. *British Journal of Psychiatry, 143,* 473–479.

McGuffin, P., Farmer, A. & Harvey, I. (1991). A polydiagnostic application criterion in studies of psychotic illness. Development and reliability of the OPCRIT system [news]. *Archives of General Psychiatry, 48,* 764–770.

Meltzer, H., Gill, B., Petticrew, M. & Hinds, K. (1995). *The Prevalence of Psychiatric Morbidity Among Adults Living in Private Households. OPCS Survey of Psychiatric Morbidity in Great Britain.* Report 1. London: HMSO.

Melzer, D., Tom, B.D.M., Brugha, T.S., Fryers, T. & Meltzer, H. (2002). Common mental disorder symptom counts in populations: Are there distinct case groups above epidemiological cut-offs? *Psychological Medicine, 32,* 1195–1201.

Merikangas, K.R. (2000). Epidemiology of mood disorders in women. In: M. Steiner, K. Yonkers & E. Eriksson (Eds), *Mood Disorders in Women* (pp. 1–14). London: Martin Dunitz.

Merikangas, K.R., Weissman, M.M. & Pauls, D.L. (1985). Genetic factors in the sex ratio of major depression. *Psychological Medicine, 15,* 63–69.

Mineka, S., Watson, D. & Clark, L.A. (1998). Comorbidity of anxiety and unipolar mood disorders. *Annual Review of Psychology, 49,* 377–412.

Mullen, P.E., Martin, J.L., Anderson, J.C., Romans, S.E. & Herbison, G.P. (1996). The long-term impact of the physical, emotional, and sexual abuse of children: A community study. *Child Abuse and Neglect, 20,* 7–21.

Murphy, J.M. (1994). The Stirling County study: Then and now. *International Review of Psychiatry, 6,* 329–348.

Oakley-Browne, M.A., Joyce, P.R., Wells, J.E., Bushnell, J.A. & Hornblow, A.R. (1989). Christchurch Psychiatric Epidemiology Study. I. Six-month and other period prevalences of specific psychiatric disorders. *Australian and New Zealand Journal of Psychiatry, 23,* 327–340.

Parker, G. (1981). Parental reports of depressives: An investigation of several explanations. *Journal of Affective Disorders, 3,* 131–140.

Parker, G. (1990). Parental rearing style: Examining for links with personality vulnerability factors for depression. *Social Psychiatry and Psychiatric Epidemiology, 28,* 97–100.

Parker, G., Hadzi-Pavlovic, D., Greenwald, S. & Weisssman, M. (1995). Low parental care as a risk factor to lifetime depression in a community sample. *Journal of Affective Disorders, 33,* 173–180.

Parker, G., Roussos, J., Hadzi-Pavlovic, D., Mitchell, P., Wilhelm, K. & Austin, M.P. (1997). The development of a refined measure of dysfunctional parenting and assessment of its relevance in patients with affective disorders. *Psychological Medicine, 27,* 1193–1203.

Parker, G., Wilhelm, K. & Asghari, A. (1979). Early onset depression: The relevance of anxiety. *Social Psychiatry and Psychiatric Epidemiology, 32,* 30–37.

Parry, G. (1986). Paid employment, life events, social support and mental health in working class mothers. *Journal of Health and Social Behaviour, 27,* 193–208.

Patten, S.B. (1997). Performance of the Composite International Diagnostic Interview Short Form for major depression in community and clinical samples. *Chronic Diseases in Canada, 18,* 109–112.

Patten, S.B. (2000). Major depression prevalence in Calgary. *Canadian Journal of Psychiatry, 45,* 923–926.

Patton, G.C., Hibbert, M.E., Carlin, J., et al. (1996). Menarche and the onset of depression and anxiety in Victoria, Australia. *Journal of Epidemiology and Community Health,* 50, 661–666.

Paykel, E.S., Abbott, R., Jenkins, R., Brugha, T.S. & Meltzer, H. (2000). Urban-rural mental health differences in Great Britain: Findings from the National Morbidity Survey. *Psychological Medicine, 30,* 269–280.

Penrose, L.S. (1963). *The Biology of Mental Defect.* London: Sidgwick & Jackson.

Piccinelli, M. & Wilkinson, G. (2000). Gender differences in depression. Critical review. *British Journal of Psychiatry, 177,* 486–492.

Popper, K.R. (1959). *The Logic of Scientific Discovery.* London: Hutchinson.

Ramana, R. & Bebbington, P.E. (1995). Social influences on bipolar affective disorder. *Social Psychiatry and Psychiatric Epidemiology, 30,* 152–160.

Rind, B. & Tromovitch, P. (1997). A meta-analytic review of findings from national samples on psychological correlates of child sexual abuse. *Journal of Sex Research, 34*, 237–255.

Roberts, C.R., Roberts, R.E. & Stevenson, J.M. (1982). Women, work, social support and psychiatric morbidity. *Social Psychiatry, 17*, 167–173.

Roberts, G.L., Lawrence, J.M., Williams, G.M. & Raphael, B. (1998). The impact of domestic violence on women's mental health. *Australian and New Zealand Journal of Public Health, 22*, 796–801.

Roberts, R.E. & O'Keefe, S.J. (1981). Sex differences in depression re-examined. *Journal of Health and Social Behaviour, 22*, 394–400.

Robins, L.N. (1995). How to choose among the riches: Selecting a diagnostic instrument. In: M.T. Tsuang, M. Tohen & G.E.P. Zahner (Eds), *Textbook in Psychiatric Epidemiology* (pp. 243–252). New York: Wiley-Liss.

Robins, L.N. & Regier, D.A. (1991). *Psychiatric Disorders in America: The Epidemiological Catchment Area Study*. New York: Free Press.

Robins, L.N., Helzer, J.E., Croughan, J. & Ratcliff, K.S. (1981). National Institute of Mental Health Diagnostic Interview Schedule: Its history, characteristics and validity. *Archives of General Psychiatry, 38*, 381–389.

Robins, L.N., Helzer, J.E., Orvaschel, H., et al. (1985). The Diagnostic Interview Schedule. In W.W. Eaton & L.G. Kessler (Eds), *Epidemiologic Field Methods in Psychiatry: The NIMH Epidemiologic Catchment Area Program* (pp. 143–170). Orlando, FL: Academic Press.

Robins, L.N., Wing, J.K., Wittchen, H.U., et al. (1988). The Composite International Diagnostic Interview. *Archives of General Psychiatry, 45*, 1069–1077.

Romans, S., Martin, J. & Mullen, P. (1996). Women's self-esteem: A community study of women who report and do not report childhood sexual abuse. *British Journal of Psychiatry, 169*, 696–704.

Romans, S.E., Martin, J.L., Anderson, J.C., O'Shea, M.L. & Mullen, P.E. (1995). Factors that mediate between child sexual abuse and adult psychological outcome. *Psychological Medicine, 25*, 127–142.

Romans-Clarkson, S.E., Walton, V.A., Herbison, G.P. & Mullen, P.E. (1988). Marriage, motherhood and psychiatric morbidity in New Zealand. *Psychological Medicine, 18*, 983–990.

Schotte, K. & Cooper, B. (1999). Subthreshold affective disorders: A useful concept in psychiatric epidemiology? *Epidemiologia e Psichiatria Sociale, 8*, 255–261.

Seligman, L.D. & Ollendick, T.H. (1998). Comorbidity of anxiety and depression in children and adolescents: An integrative review. *Clinical Child and Family Psychology Review, 1*, 125–144.

Singleton, N., Bumpstead, R., O'Brien, M., Lee, A. & Meltzer, H. (2001). *The prevalence of psychiatric Morbidity Among Adults Living in Private Households, 2000*. London: HMSO.

Sturt, E. (1981). Hierarchical patterns in the incidence of psychiatric symptoms. *Psychological Medicine, 11*, 783–794.

Sullivan, P.F., Neale, M.C. & Kendler, K.S. (2002). Genetic epidemiology of major depression: Review and meta-analysis. *American Journal of Psychiatry, 157*, 1552–1562.

Targosz, S., Bebbington, P., Lewis, G., et al. (2003). Lone mothers, social exclusion and depression. *Psychological Medicine, 33*, 715–722.

Tyrer, P. (1985). Neurosis divisible? *Lancet, i*, 685–688.

Van Os, J. & Jones, P.B. (1999). Early risk factors and adult person environment relationships in affective disorder. *Psychological Medicine, 29*, 1055–1067.

Van Os, J., Jones, P., Lewis, G., Wadsworth, M. & Murray, M. (1997). Developmental precursors of affective illness in a general population birth cohort. *Archives of General Psychiatry, 54*, 625–631.

Vazquez-Barquero, J-L., Diez-Manrique, J.F., Pena, C., et al. (1987). A community mental health survey in Cantabria: a general description of morbidity. *Psychological Medicine, 17*, 227–242.

Warr, P. & Parry, G. (1982). Paid employment and women's psychological well-being. *Psychological Bulletin, 91*, 498–516.

Weiss, E.L., Longhurst, J.G. & Mazure, C.M. (1999). Childhood sexual abuse as a risk factor for depression in women: Psychosocial and neurobiological correlates. *American Journal of Psychiatry, 156*, 816–828.

Weissman, M.M. & Klerman, G.L. (1977). Sex differences and the epidemiology of depression. *Archives of General Psychiatry, 3*, 98–112.

Weissman, M.M., Bland, R.D., Canino, G.J., et al. (1996). Cross natural epidemiology of major depression and bipolar disorder. *Journal of the American Medical Association, 276*, 292–299.

Wing, J.K. (1978). *Reasoning About Madness*. London: Oxford University Press.

Wing, J., Wing, J.K., Babor, T., Brugha, T., Burke, J. & Cooper, J.E. (1990). SCAN: Schedules for Clinical Assessment in Neuropsychiatry. *Archives of General Psychiatry, 47*, 589–593.

Wing, J.K., Mann, S.A., Leff, J.P. & Nixon, J.N. (1978). The concept of a case in psychiatric population surveys. *Psychological Medicine, 8*, 203–219.

Wittchen, H.U., Esau, C.A., von Zerssen, D., Kreig, J.C. & Zaudig, M. (1992). Lifetime and six-month prevalence of mental disorders: The Munich follow-up study. *European Archives of Psychiatry and Clinical Neuroscience, 241*, 247–258.

World Health Organization (1992). *Tenth Revision of the International Classification of Diseases*. Geneva: WHO.

2

BIOLOGICAL MODELS OF UNIPOLAR DEPRESSION

Anthony J. Cleare

INTRODUCTION

In this chapter, the focus will be on reviewing what is currently known about biological dysfunction in depression, and attempting to develop coherent models of the relevance of these changes. The parallels and interactions of the biology of depression with other features will be referred to throughout.

GENETIC MODELS OF DEPRESSION

Research findings

It has been clear for decades that there is a significant genetic predisposition to depression. Evidence of a genetic component of unipolar depression comes from the usual sources for genetic studies. Family studies show increased familial risk—the earlier the age of onset, the higher the familial risk—and twin and adoption studies confirm a clear genetic component, though less for community-sampled or 'neurotic' depression, suggesting a lesser biological component (Hirschfield & Weissman, 2002). What is less clear is how this genetic risk translates into the expression of depressive illness. No evidence exists for true Mendelian inheritance. The few studies finding linkage have not been replicated.

Conceptual models

There are a number of theories as to what mediates the genetic risk. Suggestions include:

- other biological changes (such as genetic polymorphisms)
- the response to stress

Mood Disorders: A Handbook of Science and Practice. Edited by M. Power.
© 2004 John Wiley & Sons, Ltd. ISBN 0-470-84390-X.

- the tendency to have life events
- other factors and/or behaviours within the syndrome.

Several attempts have been made to look for polymorphic variation in gene alleles that might be linked to depression (Cravchik & Goldman, 2000). Thus, affective disorder has been associated with polymorphisms of serotonin (5-HT) receptor subtypes, of tryptophan hydroxylase (the enzyme controlling 5-HT synthesis), and of the 5-HT transporter. Some allele pairs have a functional significance, such as a differential rate of reuptake of serotonin. They could therefore provide a link between the genetics of depression and the 5-HT hypothesis of depression (see below).

There is little evidence to suggest that a higher personal genetic loading leaves an individual needing less environmental stress to become depressed. Instead, it is the tendency to become depressed in response to life events that is inherited (Hirschfield & Weissman, 2002). Moreover, recent family and twin studies show a clear genetic component of life events themselves (Kendler & Karkowski Shuman, 1997). Thus, both the tendency to suffer adversity and to respond to it by becoming depressed have genetic components.

One interesting question relates to the observation that depression tends to be recurrent, and that there is a tendency for each recurrence to be less dependent on precipitating stress, a process likened to kindling (see below). Kendler and colleagues investigated the genetic contribution to this phenomenon in their large twin-pair sample; they found that genetic risk tended to place people in a 'pre-kindled' state rather than speeding up the process of kindling (Kendler et al., 2001).

Future genetic research may also integrate elements of post-transcriptional changes and modifications, the so-called proteomics—much of the *expression* of genetic risk appears to be dependent on what happens during this post-transcriptional period.

ENDOCRINE MODELS OF DEPRESSION

Hypothalamo-pituitary-adrenal (HPA) axis

RESEARCH FINDINGS

The HPA axis mediates the response of the body to stress; as such, it has been a natural focus of biological research into a disorder with a close link to stress. A schematic representation of the HPA axis is shown in Figure 2.1. The HPA axis has been extensively studied in depression; about 50% of depressed patients show a picture of hypercortisolaemia. However, this varies with the symptomatic picture: rates are higher in those with features of DSM-IV melancholic depression, strong somatic symptoms, or psychosis (Schatzberg et al., 2002).

Assessing the HPA axis can be problematic. Cortisol is a pulsatile hormone, has a strong diurnal rhythm, and is released in stressful circumstances, such as blood sampling. For this reason, more detailed methods of endocrinological assessment are needed. A widely used method in depression has been the dexamethasone-suppression test (DST). Dexamethasone is a synthetic glucocorticoid which suppresses hypothalamic corticotrophin-releasing hormone (CRH) and pituitary adrenocorticotrophic hormone (ACTH) via glucocorticoid receptors (Figure 2.1). In a proportion of depressed individuals, such suppression fails to occur, averaging around 60–70% in melancholic depression and 30–40% in 'neurotic' depression. The test is not specific to depression, as non-suppression can be seen in other

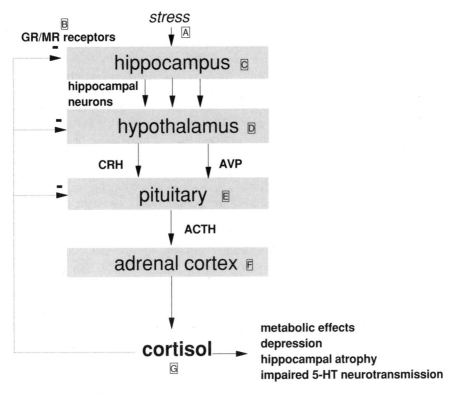

Figure 2.1 Schematic representation of the control of the hypothalamo-pituitary-adrenal (HPA) axis. CRH: corticotrophin-releasing hormone; ACTH: corticotrophin; AVP: argenine vasopressin; MR: mineralocorticoid receptors; GR: glucocorticoid receptors. Abnormalities in this axis in depression are shown in Table 2.1.

conditions. A further refinement of this test is the combined dexamethasone-CRH test. Dexamethasone pre-administration usually attenuates the cortisol response to CRH; in depression, this effect is less pronounced due to downregulated glucocorticoid receptors. This test has proved more able to distinguish depressed subjects from normals that the simple DST (Heuser et al., 1994). Table 2.1 outlines the specific findings of the various tests applied to components of the HPA axis.

Table 2.1 HPA axis abnormalities in depression relating to Figure 2.1

A	Increased incidence of life events and chronic stress
B	Impaired hippocampal fast (rate-sensitive) feedback
C	Hippocampal atrophy
D	Raised CRH levels in the cerebrospinal fluid; impaired negative feedback by dexamethasone
E	Impaired pituitary ACTH response to CRH administration; this may represent downregulated CRH receptors or negative feedback from high cortisol levels. Pituitary hypertrophy
F	Hypertrophied adrenal cortices
G	Hypercortisolism

CONCEPTUAL MODELS

Thus, in a substantial proportion of depressed patients, there is oversecretion of cortisol and reduced negative feedback at the hypothalamus and pituitary. Can cortisol hypersecretion be considered a plausible biological mechanism for depression? First, since cortisol is the main stress hormone, it is easy to see how it might mediate between life events and biological changes in depression. Evidence that raised cortisol levels may be driving depression rather than vice versa comes from studies showing that lowering cortisol levels, as for example, by administering cortisol synthesis inhibitor drugs such as metyrapone or ketoconazole, can alleviate depression (Murphy, 1997). However, raised cortisol secretion in endogenous Cushing's disease is associated with depression in 50–85% of cases. Furthermore, abnormally high cortisol levels have been shown to be associated with other biological changes, such as inhibitory effects on neuronal 5-HT neurotransmission; given the links between 5-HT neurotransmission and mood changes, this is a feasible mechanism by which 5-HT neurotransmission could become dysregulated. There are also suggestions that prolonged periods of high cortisol can lead to hippocampal atrophy—indeed, in Cushing's disease, the decreased hippocampus size can be correlated with plasma cortisol levels and cognitive impairment. Recent studies also suggest hippocampal atrophy in depression (Sheline & Minyun, 2002).

However, the role of the HPA may also be seen in other ways. Adverse circumstances in childhood, such as losing parents or suffering abuse, are well known to predispose an individual to depression. Recent work suggests that the HPA axis may provide some further understanding of the mechanism of this link. Experiencing childhood abuse leads to a long-term alteration of the stress response (Heim et al., 2000). Thus, it is also possible to see the HPA axis changes as a biological link between early life stresses and an increased vulnerability to stress and depression.

Others have noted that changes elsewhere in the HPA axis may mediate symptoms. For example, CRH may also act as a neurotransmitter, and it produces symptoms of agitation, insomnia, and reduced feeding in animals. The amount of CRH expressed in cells, and the co-occurrence of CRH with its synergistic ACTH releaser, vasopressin, is increased in depressed suicide victims. CRH levels in the cerebrospinal fluid (CSF) are increased. Furthermore, CRH receptors are found in the cortex, and show a reduced density in suicide victims, consistent with high levels of CRH release. Thus, increased CRH in depression could contribute to some symptoms (Nemeroff, 1996).

The importance of the HPA axis changes in depression go beyond the apparent ability to provide a neat mediator between stressful events and symptoms, and also concerns prognostic indicators. There are suggestions that DST non-suppression is associated with a poorer response to placebo (though not a superior response to medication) and a poorer response to cognitive therapy (Thase et al., 1996). More strikingly, if clinical response to treatment is associated with continued non-suppression, there is a fourfold increase in the risk of short-term relapse or suicide attempt. Recently, the long-term risk of suicide was also found to be more closely linked to DST non-suppression than any other factor, more so even than past suicide attempts (Coryell & Sehlesser, 2001).

In summary, there is no doubt that HPA axis dysfunction is present in a large proportion of depressed patients, particularly those with more melancholic symptom patterns. The HPA axis provides a plausible biological mechanism for some of the most replicated causal theories of depression. Thus, the links between depressive symptoms and stressful life

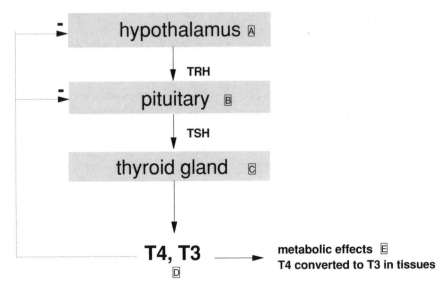

Figure 2.2   Schematic representation of the control of the hypothalamo-pituitary-thyroid (HPT) axis. TRH: thyrotrophin-releasing hormone; TSH: thyroid-stimulating hormone; T4: thyroxine; T3: tri-iodothyronine. Abnormalities in this axis in depression are shown in Table 2.2.

events, chronic social adversity, or traumatic or abusive childhoods could all be explained by the mediating role of the HPA axis.

Hypothalamo-pituitary-thyroid (HPT) axis

Clinical disorders of thyroid function are known to cause alteration in mood. Classically, patients with hypothyroidism frequently report features similar to depression and, while usually more closely linked to feelings of anxiety, depressive reactions are also sometimes seen in hyperthyroid patients.

In depression, several abnormalities in thyroid function have been described. Figure 2.2 shows the axis, and Table 2.2 lists the abnormalities described. While not entirely consistent, the blunted thyroid-stimulating hormone (TSH) response to thyrotrophin-stimulating hormone (TRH) could be due to hypersecretion of TRH that causes downregulation of pituitary TRH receptors.

Table 2.2   Thyroid axis abnormalities in depression relating to Figure 2.2

A	Increased TRH in cerebrospinal fluid
B	Reduced TSH response to TRH administration (30%)
C	Antithyroid antibodies (9–20%)
D	Subclinical hypothyroidism
E	Treatment response to T3 or T4 augmentation strategies

Given the suggestions of subclinical hypothyroidism in depression, albeit in a minority, it is natural to ask about the effects of thyroid hormone treatment. A recent review found six randomised, controlled trials, and concluded that thyroid hormone may potentiate both the speed and the efficacy of antidepressant medication (Altshuler et al., 2001). Furthermore, there is also evidence that patients resistant to other treatments may respond to such treatment, although there have been no studies linking pre-treatment, subclinical hypothyroidism to this response. There is also some evidence that low tri-iodothyronine (T3) levels are prospectively associated with a higher rate of relapse in the long term (Joffe & Marriott, 2000), and that antithyroid antibodies predict post-partum depression (Harris et al., 1992).

DHEA

There has been much recent interest in the role of DHEA, in both healthy ageing and depression. Although this role is not entirely clear, what has emerged is that, in many ways, DHEA has an anticortisol effect. It has been argued, therefore, that increased 'net' effects of cortisol may occur if there is low DHEA, and that high levels of cortisol may not be biologically damaging if they are accompanied by high DHEA levels. Thus, many have started to measure the cortisol/DHEA ratio as an index more likely to be relevant to the causation of depression. Work to date suggests that this ratio may be higher in patients with depression (Young et al., 2002). Moreover, in a large cross-sectional study, DHEA and DHEA-S were found to be inversely correlated with depression scores (Barrett-Connor et al., 1999). Finally, some studies do suggest that DHEA treatment may be an effective antidepressant, presumably acting by reducing the biological effects of cortisol (Wolkowitz et al., 1999). However, this work remains in its early stages.

NEUROCHEMICAL MODELS OF DEPRESSION

Brain neurochemistry was one of the first suspects in the search for the biological basis of depression. The original monoamine hypothesis of depression derived from the findings that monoamine depletion by the drug reserpine caused depression, while antidepressants inhibited monoamine reuptake. Subsequent reports that there were reduced monoamine breakdown products in the CSF led to the theory that there is a deficiency of noradrenaline, dopamine, 5-HT, or all three at monoaminergic synapses. From this original hypothesis, several proposed biological models of depression are worth discussing.

Serotonin hypothesis of depression

Classically, several pieces of evidence are cited to support the serotonin theory (see Maes & Meltzer, 1995, for review). First, there is evidence of a reduced availability of the 5-HT precursor tryptophan. Studies suggest reduced plasma levels of tryptophan and also enhanced non-CNS pathways for tryptophan catabolism, such as the kynurenine pathway in the liver.

Second, there is evidence of changes in the normal physiology of serotonin metabolism. For example, there is reduced uptake of 5-HT into the platelets (a model of the neuronal 5-HT transporter system).

Third, there are several ways of demonstrating 5-HT receptor changes in depression. Early work relied on the use of brains from post-mortem studies of depressed suicides. Several studies reported increased $5\text{-}HT_2$ receptors, a factor that was felt to be secondary to low 5-HT content, and reduced $5\text{-}HT_{1A}$ hippocampal and amygdala binding. A further approach was to use neuropharmacological challenge tests. These tests are used to determine the integrity of neurotransmitter systems. Standardised serotonergic drug challenges are given, and a physiological response is measured, such as hormone release or temperature change. The magnitude of the response is taken as an index of the activity of the system challenged. Many, although by no means all, of these studies have reported impairments in depression. One example is of a blunted prolactin response to fenfluramine, a 5-HT-releasing drug.

Fourth, the technique of tryptophan depletion (TD) suggests that there may be a causal relationship between 5-HT changes and depression. The TD paradigm involves administration of a mixture of amino acids without tryptophan. This leads to a large and rapid fall in plasma tryptophan, reduced brain tryptophan entry, and reduced 5-HT synthesis. TD in depressed subjects has not revealed consistent results, perhaps because the system is maximally dysregulated. However, TD depletion temporarily induces depressive symptoms in vulnerable groups such as remitted depressed patients, those with a family history of depression, and females (Reilly et al., 1997). This research provides powerful evidence that serotonergic function is causally related to mood states rather than merely showing a cross-sectional association. This technique may also have a predictive value, in that depressed patients in remission who show a mood-reducing effect of TD have higher rates of true relapse in the following 12 months (Moreno et al., 2000). This suggests that certain individuals may have a biological vulnerability to the short-term depressogenic effects of reduced brain 5-HT availability, a vulnerability which places them at increased risk of future major depression, possibly as a response to other biological or environmental causes of reduced 5-HT availability.

One anomaly is the observation that the mood-lowering effect of tryptophan depletion does not occur to a significant degree in remitted depressed patients receiving continuation treatment with desipramine, a noradrenergic-specific tricyclic (Delgado et al., 1999). They do, however, experience the effect if noradrenaline synthesis is inhibited; however, this procedure does not affect patients taking SSRIs (Delgado et al., 1999).

More recently, neuroimaging techniques have increased our knowledge about 5-HT changes in depression; these will be described later in the chapter.

One argument against the significance of serotonergic changes in depression comes from observations that several enduring character traits may be closely related to 5-HT function. Thus, while early studies of CSF concentrations of the 5-HT breakdown product 5-HIAA reported reduced levels in depression, more recent studies suggest that low CSF levels of 5-HIAA and other indices of reduced serotonergic function are linked more specifically to suicide, impulsivity, aggression, or other personality variables (Cleare & Bond, 1997; Mann, 1995). Thus, 5-HT changes in depression may reflect these factors.

A further issue is whether or not the serotonergic changes are state or trait related. Many of the neuroendocrine challenge tests, such as fenfluramine, normalise with treatment of the depression (Maes & Meltzer, 1995). However, the reduced $5\text{-}HT_{1A}$ receptor binding seen with positron emission tomography (PET) does not normalise after treatment with SSRI medication (Sargent et al., 2000). This suggests that some of the observed changes in depression may indeed be trait markers, and could therefore be linked to vulnerability or personality rather than the depressive state.

Noradrenergic theories

There is evidence of noradrenergic dysfunction in depression. Many antidepressants are potent inhibitors of the reuptake of noradrenaline, with little effect on serotonin reuptake. Neuroendocrine challenge studies have found evidence of reduced noradrenergic function. For example, there is a reduced GH response to the α_2-agonists clonidine and desipramine, suggesting impaired α_2-receptor function. This abnormality remains blunted when patients are off medication and non-depressed, suggesting that it could be a trait marker. Post-mortem and platelet studies also provide some support for changes in α and β adrenergic receptors. Several studies have shown that low urinary levels of the noradrenaline metabolite MHPG predict a favourable response to tricyclics (Schatzberg et al., 2002).

A novel, though highly invasive, method has recently been described that provides further evidence of reduced catecholamine availability in the brain in depression (Lambert et al., 2000). Patients with treatment-resistant depression underwent catheterisation in the brachial artery for arterial blood and in the internal jugular vein for venous blood draining from the brain. The main findings were that there was a reduced concentration gradient in depression for noradrenaline and its metabolites and for the dopamine metabolite, homovanillic acid; this suggests reduced amounts of these neurotransmitters stemming from the brain.

Dopaminergic theories

There is some evidence of a reduced GH response to apomorphine, a dopamine receptor agonist, in depression, but results are inconsistent with this challenge (Schatzberg et al., 2002). Interest in the dopaminergic system has been rekindled by the introduction of bupropion, an antidepressant that works primarily on dopamine reuptake.

Cholinergic theories

Studies have shown an enhanced GH response to the anticholinesterase drug pyridostigmine, a measure of acetylcholine receptor function. Further evidence comes from the observation of reduced rapid eye movement (REM) latency and increased REM sleep in depression, effects that may represent increased cholinergic activity. Furthermore, depressed patients show supersensitivity to the REM sleep effects of cholinergics. Janowsky proposed the cholinergic-adrenergic balance theory of depression, hypothesising that increased cholinergic function and reduced noradrenergic function were both important in generating symptoms in depression (Janowsky & Overstreet, 1995).

GABA-ergic theories

There is a reduced GH response to baclofen, a GABA-B receptor agonist, suggesting reduced GABA receptor activity in depression (O'Flynn & Dinan, 1993). Plasma GABA may also be low (Schatzberg et al., 2002).

Interactions of monoamines

There is now increasing evidence that drugs that affect one neurotransmitter system can also affect another through downstream effects. If one looks simply at serotonin, there are innumerable examples. Thus, serotonergic heteroceptors are found on neurons primarily involved in the release of other neurotransmitters; there is evidence that 5-HT_{1D} receptors may act in an inhibitory manner in this way. Noradrenergic receptors may be present on serotonergic nerve cell bodies and terminals: α_1-receptors on serotonergic cell bodies act to increase cell firing and 5-HT release, while α_2-receptors are present on serotonergic nerve terminals and inhibit 5-HT release. Projections of serotonergic neurons to other areas of the brain are known to inhibit dopaminergic function in the cortex and elsewhere. The serotonin transporter protein is thought to interact with the ability of α_2-receptors to inhibit 5-HT cell firing. Finally, noradrenaline reuptake inhibition is potentiated in the presence of simultaneous 5-HT reuptake inhibition.

It is likely that a number of neurotransmitter alterations are present in depression. Clinically, it is of relevance that drugs that act on both serotonin and noradrenaline, such as amitriptyline (Barbui & Hotopf, 2001) and venlafaxine (Smith et al., 2002), may have slightly enhanced efficacy in the treatment of depression.

NEUROIMAGING MODELS OF DEPRESSION

Recent rapid advances in neuroimaging methodology have heralded attempts to relate the phenomenological abnormalities seen in depression to changes in brain structure and function (Fu et al., 2003). Neuroimaging can broadly be broken up into structural and functional techniques.

Structural

There is increasing evidence that depression may be associated with structural brain pathology. Magnetic resonance imaging (MRI) has revealed decreased volume in cortical regions, particularly the frontal cortex, but also in subcortical structures, such as the hippocampus, amygdala, caudate, and putamen (see Sheline & Minyun, 2002, for review). These findings are supported by post-mortem studies. Furthermore, some of these neuroanatomical changes may relate to some of the cognitive features of depression; thus, hippocampal volume loss has been associated with changes in functions such as memory performance.

It has been known for some time that elderly depressives have features of cerebral atrophy (sulcal widening and ventricular enlargement) midway between that in depression and dementia. Patients with pseudo-dementia have more abnormalities than those without. More recently, a model of 'vascular depression' occurring later in life has emerged, suggesting that some individuals with depression in old age have underlying cerebrovascular disease affecting areas of the brain important in the control of mood. While perhaps more obvious in the case of post-stroke depression, microvascular disease seems also to be associated with depression. For example, MRI scans and measures of depression were taken in 1077 non-demented, elderly adults (Cees de Groot et al., 2000). Virtually all subjects had white-matter lesions; the 5% of patients without them had lower depression scores than the rest. When adjusted for other relevant variables, those with more severe white-matter lesions were up to five times more likely to have depressive symptoms than those with only mild white-matter lesions. Of those with a depressive disorder, those with an on-set after age 60 had more severe white-matter lesions than those with an onset before age 60.

The implications of such vascular contributions to depression include the question of whether it can be prevented by early monitoring and intervention with respect to the cardiovascular risk factors thought to underlie white-matter lesions. Clinically, depression associated with vascular disease appears to be more resistant to treatment.

Functional imaging

Functional neuroimaging assesses neural function in different brain regions by measuring metabolism (such as glucose utilisation) or blood flow, both of which are thought to be closely coupled to neural activation. Most studies of resting activity have described hypo-frontality, particularly in the dorsolateral prefrontal and anterior cingulate cortices, and several groups have also described decreased activity in the basal ganglia (see Fu et al., 2003, for review). However, criticisms of these studies include the difficulty in standardising what the brain is actually doing in the resting state (Sheline & Minyun, 2002).

This has led to the use of functional neuroimaging while subjects undertake neuropsychological tasks; as well as standardising what the brain is doing, this allows particular areas of the brain, or particular psychological functions, relevant to depression to be probed. In depression, this approach has uncovered impaired activation in, among other areas, the left anterior cingulate, right prefrontal cortex, and left caudate (Fu et al., 2003). Induction of low mood in normals can induce similar changes to depressed subjects. More recently, Elliott and colleagues used a cognitive task with emotional valence (happy, neutral, or sad). They found that depressed subjects demonstrated an attenuated response to neutral or happy objects, but an enhanced one to sad objects, again focused in anterior cingulate and prefrontal cortical regions (Elliott et al., 2002). Thus, there may be a definable neural substrate underlying the perceptual cognitive bias in depression.

It should also be noted that many of these changes are not specific to depression, and indeed can be seen in other psychiatric states. It has been suggested that changes in brain regions are more likely to be related to specific psychological dysfunctions rather than diagnoses. Thus, specific patterns of changes have been ascribed to the presence of, for example, psychomotor retardation or depressive pseudo-dementia (Fu et al., 2003).

A number of studies have investigated the response to treatment in depression. Many show that pretreatment abnormalities reverse with treatment. The most consistent finding has been in the subgenual prefrontal cortex: activity is *increased* activation during an acute depressive state, and this *decreases* following effective antidepressant treatment (Fu et al., 2003; Mayberg et al., 2000).

Finally, rather than simply looking at one part of the brain in isolation, it may be most important to look at the various networks of the brain and how they are interlinked. These functional connections may be disrupted in the depressed state. Thus, one study revealed a complex picture of cortical and subcortical changes associated with treatment response to fluoxetine, with increases in the dorsal prefrontal cortex but decreases in the hippocampus (Mayberg et al., 2000). The study of changes in brain connectivity by path analysis and other statistical methods may yield more understanding of the clearly complex pathways in brain neurocircuitry.

Neurochemical imaging

Neuroimaging has also helped in the further investigation of the neurochemical deficits in depression. PET and SPET imaging can use radiolabelled ligands to measure receptor binding (a product of receptor density and receptor sensitivity) for specific neurochemical targets in the different brain regions.

The status of brain 5-HT$_2$ receptors in depression and the effect of antidepressant treatment remain unclear, and vary depending on the method used to assess them: studies have found receptor binding to be increased, normal or decreased. While the largest study to date using PET found a marked global reduction in receptor binding (22–27% in various regions), there remains difficulty in reconciling the accumulating finding of reduced binding with the fact that effective antidepressant treatments lead to further downregulation of 5-HT$_2$ receptors (Sheline & Minyun, 2002).

Using a recently introduced radioligand, Sargent and colleagues (Sargent et al., 2000) found a generalised reduction in 5HT$_{1A}$ receptor binding throughout the cortex. However, this was not altered by treatment with an SSRI. The authors note that receptor numbers may not represent receptor function, but they hypothesise a trait reduction in 5HT$_{1A}$ receptors that is unaffected by treatment. Reduced 5-HT$_{1A}$ binding has been replicated elsewhere (Fu et al., 2003).

One of the pieces of evidence making up the serotonin hypothesis of depression is the impaired endocrine response to challenge with serotonergic drugs such as fenfluramine (see above). This same approach has now been transferred to neuroimaging: challenge with the serotonin releaser fenfluramine leads to marked changes in neural activity. These serotonergically mediated changes were found to be markedly attenuated in depression, suggesting impaired central 5-HT neurotransmission. However, a study using the more specific *d*-isomer of fenfluramine could not replicate this finding (Fu et al., 2003).

As described earlier, a proportion of subjects show a depressive relapse after tryptophan depletion. When undertaken in the PET scanner, this depressive relapse was correlated with reduced activity in the orbito-frontal cortex, anterior cingulate, left caudate nucleus, and superior parietal cortex, like those seen in unmedicated depressed subjects (Smith et al., 1999). Furthermore, while a verbal fluency task was performed, there was a significant attenuation of usual task-induced activation in the anterior cingulate. These results help link changes in serotonin function with changes in activity in specific brain areas during depressive relapse. Furthermore, they also provide a possible neurobiological link between 5-HT changes and the cognitive effects of depression.

Finally, support for dysfunction in other neurochemical systems is also emerging. For example, the use of the challenge drug clonidine reveals evidence of noradrenergic dysfunction in depression, postulated to arise from functionally impaired pre-synaptic alpha2-adrenoceptors as well as regionally supersensitive post-synaptic cortical alpha2-adrenoceptors (Fu et al., 2001).

CELLULAR MODELS OF DEPRESSION

Kindling model

Neurons which are repeatedly subjected to convulsions or electrical stimuli show a process of *kindling*, whereby the fit threshold is gradually lowered, and the cells eventually fire autonomously. Post has suggested that this phenomenon might underlie the tendency for some patients with affective disorder to suffer increasingly severe or refractory episodes of depression, or to require fewer provoking life events, with passing time. Strong support was provided by a study from Virginia (Kendler et al., 2000), which followed up over 2000 community-based female twin pairs over 9 years, measuring depression and life-event severity in this period. They found a clear tendency for each episode of depression to be followed by an increased subsequent risk of a further episode of depression. There was also a general tendency for each successive episode of depression to be less strongly related to preceding life stress. The mechanisms underlying this effect remain unclear, although suggestions are now being made that relate to the effects of gene expression, neural growth factors, and gene transcription changes; further work on these intriguing possibilities is needed.

Intracellular signalling models

There is evidence that antidepressants are able to modify intracellular signalling, as for example, by enhancing the cyclic AMP pathway activation occurring after serotonergic receptor stimulation. It has been hypothesised that G proteins, important signal transducers in the phosphoinositol system, are overactive in depression; they are also potentially important in the mechanism of action of lithium. Several growth factors and neurotrophins are altered in depression, and may be important in neuronal changes seen in depression. Antidepressants also have effects on the expression of these factors. A new cellular model of depression is evolving in which there are felt to be impairments in signalling pathways that regulate neuroplasticity and cell survival (Manji et al., 2001).

Other models of depression have been developed from observations in animals of the effects of certain cytokines on behaviour, and of the effects of some of these cytokines in humans (Kronfol & Remick, 2000).

IS SOME DEPRESSION MORE BIOLOGICAL THAN OTHER FORMS?

The concept of core depression

While most agree that depression is a heterogeneous condition, there have been innumerable attempts to subdivide depression according to symptom patterns. Relevant to this chapter, most studies of depression have identified a group of patients characterised by certain symptoms: early morning waking, weight loss, poor appetite, anhedonia, and agitation. This symptom grouping has been variously labelled as *endogenous*, *nuclear*, and *melancholic* depression. Early conceptualisations of this category noted that they were said to show a preferential response to physical treatments, and to show more dysfunction of biological correlates of depression, such as the DST. Few good studies have made direct comparisons between melancholic depression and other types, preventing firm conclusions from being drawn. However, many of the studies referred to in this chapter have tended to select patients with more melancholic features, and how applicable the findings are to the more common but less severe cases remains unknown.

Psychotic depression

The clinical importance of separating out psychotic depression relates to the preferential response of this group to antidepressant–antipsychotic combinations or electroconvulsive treatment (ECT). In terms of neurobiology, some authors have argued that psychotic depression represents a separate and distinct category, based on clinical, genetic, treatment response and biological features. There is some evidence that there may be biological differences between psychotic depression and non-psychotic depression in terms of a more disturbed HPA axis (see above), increased dopamine turnover (that is, higher HVA levels in the CSF), and different patterns of disturbance of serotonin pathways (Wheeler Vega et al., 2000). Overall, however, a separation on the basis of neurobiology remains premature.

Atypical depression

Atypical depression has been used in the past to mean a number of different conditions, including non-endogenous depression, depression secondary to another condition, depression associated with anxiety or panic, and depression with reversed biological features. However, as the concept has evolved, atypicality has been more tightly defined, and the disorder is now included in DSM-IV.

VALIDITY OF ATYPICAL DEPRESSION AS A SUBTYPE

Atypical depression does appear to be a valid concept. Sullivan and colleagues (Sullivan et al., 1998) used data from the large US National Comorbidity Survey, and identified six syndromes, two of which correspond to mild atypical depression and severe atypical depression, respectively. A study of 1000 female twin pairs also found an atypical depression syndrome; furthermore, individuals tended to have the same syndrome on each recurrence, and the concordance of syndrome type was greater in monozygotic than in dizygotic pairs (Kendler et al., 1996).

NEUROBIOLOGY OF ATYPICAL DEPRESSION

In view of the relatively recent addition of atypical depression to the psychiatric nosology, few data exist on the similarities and differences between typical and atypical depression. One of the most frequently observed differences relates to the HPA axis. While hypercortisolaemia is characteristic of melancholic major depression (see above), several studies have now suggested that atypical depression is associated with hypocortisolaemia. Gold and colleagues have suggested that, while typical major depression can be characterised by an excessive activation of both the physiological stress systems, the locus ceruleus-noradrenergic

Table 2.3   Organic causes of a depressive syndrome

Endocrine:	disorders of cortisol, thyroxine or parathormone production; hypopituitarism; hypoglycaemia
Infections:	glandular fever, syphilis, AIDS, encephalitis
Neurological:	stroke, Parkinson's disease, multiple sclerosis, brain tumours (classically meningioma), trauma, cerebral lupus
Carcinoma:	common non-metastatic manifestation, especially pancreatic carcinoma, which may otherwise remain occult, and lung carcinoma
Nutritional:	deficiencies of folate, nicotinamide (pellagra), and vitamins B_{12}, B_1 (thiamine), and B_6
Other:	cerebral ischaemia, myocardial infarction

system, and the HPA axis, the opposite changes are present in atypical depression (Gold et al., 1995). Some support for this is provided by studies showing that the control of noradrenergic function is relatively preserved in atypical compared to typical depression (Asnis et al., 1995). Gold and colleagues suggest that it is diminished central CRH activity that is specifically related to the symptoms of hypoarousal of the syndrome (Gold et al., 1995). Evidence that it is low CRH rather than low cortisol that is related to the atypicality syndrome comes from one detailed study of Cushing's syndrome, in which cortisol is high and CRH low, where atypical depression was the predominant depressive syndrome (Dorn et al., 1995). Studies of serotonergic function are lacking, though one study suggested that platelet serotonin function is unaltered in atypical depression (Owens & Nemeroff, 1994).

Post-partum and seasonal depression

Post-partum depression and seasonal depression represent other specifiers used in the DSM-IV classification. There are some suggestions of particular biological therapeutic modalities for seasonal depression (light therapy) and post-partum depression (oestradiol). However, there are few indications that post-partum depression or seasonal depression represent biologically distinct subtypes.

Depression as a result of organic illness

There are a number of systemic diseases in which depression may be a presenting feature or a common accompaniment (over and above the 'normal' rate of depression). These are shown in Table 2.3. Drugs that may cause or exacerbate depression are shown in Table 2.4.

INTEGRATING THE NEUROBIOLOGY OF DEPRESSION

We can attempt to integrate the neurobiological findings in depression to the 'whole' in several ways. These include integrating neurobiological with other levels of understanding or research modalities, linking neurobiology to treatment, and attempting to relate the neurobiological changes to each other.

Table 2.4   Drugs associated with depressive syndromes

Cardiovascular:	methyl-dopa, reserpine, beta-blockers, clonidine, diuretics, digoxin
Endocrine:	steroids, combined oral contraceptive (high dose)
Neurological:	L-Dopa, bromocriptine
Others:	pentazocine, indomethacin, chloroquine, mefloquine
On withdrawal:	psychostimulants (e.g., amphetamines, cocaine), benzodiazepines
Alcohol:	cause and consequence

This chapter has already given some examples of how the biological models of depression can be tied in with other characteristics of depression from other disciplines such as epidemiology. The predisposition to suffer depression entailed by childhood experiences can be paralleled by the presence of 'endocrine scars'. Acute and chronic stress from the environment can be shown to have profound neurobiological correlates. High cortisol levels are associated with cognitive dysfunction (Van London et al., 1998). Recent neuroimaging studies reveal a brain that is overresponsive to unhappy stimuli and underresponsive to happy ones (Elliott et al., 2002). It is easy to see how such a brain dysfunction can be linked to the perceptual biases in depression, and also to cognitive theories of depression in which such cognitive distortions are felt to be a primary disturbance in depression.

Neurobiology may have relevance to the choice of different treatments available. For example, certain neurobiological disruption, such as a disrupted HPA axis or shortened REM latency, may be associated with a preferential response to physical rather than psychological treatments (Thase et al., 1993; 1996). Exciting enquiries are now being made into whether neuroimaging can inform the response to therapy. In what promises to be the beginning of a series of studies, two papers report changes in brain function occurring during treatment of depression with either psychological therapy or drug therapy. Brody et al. (2001) took 24 subjects with unipolar major depression and obtained resting PET scans of glucose metabolism at baseline and after 12 weeks of treatment with either interpersonal therapy or paroxetine. With treatment, both groups showed a similar tendency for baseline abnormalities to normalise, although the paroxetine-treated subjects had a greater decrease in depression scores. This differential response and the lack of randomisation at baseline mean that there may be explanations other than the different treatments for these changes. A second paper measured brain blood flow, using SPET, in 28 patients with major depression (Martin et al., 2001). In this case, subjects were randomised—receiving venlafaxine or interpersonal therapy—with scans being repeated at 6 weeks. Once again, the antidepressant group had a larger fall in depression scores. On this occasion, the two treatments produced a differential change, with the venlafaxine-treated group showing posterior temporal and right basal ganglia activation, whereas the IPT group had limbic, right posterior cingulate, and right basal ganglia activation. Thus, both treatments caused basal ganglia activation, whereas only interpersonal therapy showed limbic blood-flow increase. Problems with this trial include the short duration of treatment, probably before the main effects of psychological therapy would have been detectable.

Certain treatments have a more fundamental basis in neurobiology than others. One of the more controversial treatments in psychiatry is psychosurgery. This is now only very rarely used as a last resort, in cases of severe, intractable depression under strict controls.

Stereotactic techniques are used for more specific ablation, and a variety of operations have been developed to focus on limbic areas and their cortical connections. Clinically, approximately one-third of patients are reported to gain marked benefit, though the side effects can include frontal lobe syndromes and epilepsy. There has been recent interest in deep-brain stimulation in neurology and psychiatry: implanted electrodes can induce functional lesions, but have the advantage over psychosurgery of being reversible if not successful. The advances in the understanding of the neural basis of depression outlined in this chapter may allow an informed refinement of these techniques for those unfortunate cases of severe and resistant depression.

Finally, it is worth reminding ourselves that separate biological systems do not act independently. Neurochemical systems modulate the activity of each other, endocrine systems act on neurochemical systems, neurochemical activation leads to intracellular activation, and so on. Understanding the different changes in parallel and on several levels is rarely undertaken, and this remains a huge obstacle at present to a full understanding of the neurobiology of mood disorders.

REFERENCES

Altshuler, L.L., Bauer, M., Frye, M.A., et al. (2001). Does thyroid supplementation accelerate tricyclic antidepressant response? A review and meta-analysis of the literature. *Am J Psychiatry, 158,* 1617–1622.

Asnis, G.M., McGinn, L.K. & Sanderson, W.C. (1995). Atypical depression: Clinical aspects and noradrenergic function. *Am J Psychiatry, 152,* 31–36.

Barbui, C. & Hotopf, M. (2001). Amitriptyline v. the rest: Still the leading antidepressant after 40 years of randomised controlled trials. *Br J Psychiatry, 178,* 129–144.

Barrett-Connor, E., von Muhlen, D., Laughlin, G.A. & Kripke, A. (1999). Endogenous levels of dehydroepiandrosterone sulfate, but not other sex hormones, are associated with depressed mood in older women: The Rancho Bernardo Study. *J Am Geriatr Soc, 47,* 685–691.

Brody, A.L., Saxena, S., Stoessel, P., et al. (2001). Regional brain metabolic changes in patients with major depression treated with either paroxetine or interpersonal therapy: Preliminary findings. *Arch Gen Psychiatry, 58,* 631–640.

Cees de Groot, J.C., de Leeuw, F.-E., Oudkerk, M., Hofman, A., Jolles, J. & Breteler, M.M.B. (2000). Cerebral white matter lesions and depressive symptoms in elderly adults. *Arch Gen Psychiatry, 57,* 1071–1076.

Cleare, A.J. & Bond, A.J. (1997). Does central serotonergic function correlate inversely with aggression? A study using d-fenfluramine in healthy subjects. *Psychiatry Res, 69,* 89–95.

Coryell, W. & Sehlesser, M. (2001). The dexamethasone suppression test in suicide prediction. *Am J Psychiatry, 158,* 748–753.

Cravchik, A. & Goldman, D. (2000). Genetic diversity among human dopamine and serotonin receptors and transporters. *Arch Gen Psychiatry, 57,* 1105–1114.

Delgado, P.L., Miller, H.L., Salomon, R.M., et al. (1999). Tryptophan depletion challenge in depressed patients treated with desipramine or fluoxetine: Implications for the role of serotonin in the mechanism of antidepressant action. *Biol Psychiatry, 46,* 212–220.

Dorn, L.D., Burgess, E.S., Dubbert, B., et al. (1995). Psychopathology in patients with endogenous Cushing's syndrome: 'Atypical' or melancholic features. *Clin Endocrinol, 43,* 433–442.

Elliott, R., Rubinsztein, J.S., Sahakian, B.J., & Dolan, R.J. (2002). The neural basis of mood-congruent processing biases in depression. *Arch Gen Psychiatry, 59,* 597–604.

Fu, C.H., Reed, L.J., Meyerm, J.H., et al. (2001). Noradrenergic dysfunction in the prefrontal cortex in depression: An [15O] H2O PET study of the neuromodulatory effects of clonidine. *Biol Psychiatry, 49,* 317–325.

Fu, C.H.Y., Walsh, N.D. & Drevets, W.C. (2003). Neuroimaging studies of mood disorders. In: C.H.Y. Fu, T. Russell, C. Senior, D.R. Weinberger & R.M. Murray (Eds), *neuroimaging in psychiatry.* Martin Dunitz.

Gold, P.W., Licinio, J., Wong, M.L. & Chrousos, G.P. (1995). Corticotropin releasing hormone in the pathophysiology of melancholic and atypical depression and in the mechanism of action of antidepressant drugs. *Ann N Y Acad Sci, 771*, 716–729.

Harris, B., Othman, S., Davies, J.A., et al. (1992). Association between postpartum thyroid dysfunction and thyroid antibodies and depression. *BMJ, 305*, 152–156.

Heim, C., Newport, D.J., Heit, S., et al. (2000). Pituitary-adrenal and autonomic responses to stress in women after sexual and physical abuse in childhood. *JAMA, 284*, 592–597.

Heuser, I., Yassouridis, A. & Holsboer, F. (1994). The combined dexamethasone/CRH test: A refined laboratory test for psychiatric disorders. *J Psychiatr Res, 28*, 341–356.

Hirschfeld, R.M.A. & Weissman, M.M. (2002). Risk factors for major depression and bipolar disorder. In: K.L. Davis, D. Charney, J.T. Coyle & C. Nemeroff (Eds), *Neuropsychopharmacology. The Fifth Generation of Progress* (pp. 1017–1026). Philadelphia: Lipincott Williams & Wilkins.

Janowsky, D.S. & Overstreet, D.H. (1995). The role of acetylcholine mechanisms in mood disorders. In: D.J. Kupfer & F.E. Bloom (Eds), *Psychopharmacology: The Fourth Generation of Progress* (pp. 945–956). New York: Raven Press.

Joffe, R. & Marriott, M. (2000). Thyroid hormone levels in recurrence of major depression. *Am J Psychiatry, 157*, 1689–1691.

Kendler, K.S., Eaves, L.J., Walters, E.E., Neale, M.C., Heath, A.C. & Kessler, R.C. (1996). The identification and validation of distinct depressive syndromes in a population-based sample of female twins. *Arch Gen Psychiatry, 53*, 391–399.

Kendler, K.S. & Karkowski Shuman, L. (1997). Stressful life events and genetic liability to major depression: Genetic control of exposure to the environment? *Psychol Med, 27*, 539–547.

Kendler, K.S., Thornton, L.M. & Gardner, C.O. (2000). Stressful life events and previous episodes in the etiology of major depression in women: An evaluation of the 'kindling' hypothesis. *Am J Psychiatry, 157*, 1243–1251.

Kendler, K.S., Thornton, L.M. & Gardner, C.O. (2001). Genetic risk, number of previous depressive episodes, and stressful life events in predicting onset of major depression. *Am J Psychiatry, 158*, 582–586.

Kronfol, Z. & Remick, D.G. (2000). Cytokines and the brain: Implications for clinical psychiatry. *Am J Psychiatry, 157*, 683–694.

Lambert, G., Johansson, M., Ågren, H. & Friberg, P. (2000). Reduced brain norepinephrine and dopamine release in treatment-refractory depressive illness: Evidence in support of the cate-cholamine hypothesis of mood disorders. *Arch Gen Psychiatry, 57*, 787–793.

Maes, M. & Meltzer, H. (1995). The serotonin hypothesis of major depression. In: F.E. Bloom & D.J. Kupfer (Eds), *Psychopharmacology. Fourth Generation of Progress* (pp. 933–944). New York: Raven Press.

Manji, H.K., Drevets, W.C. & Charney, D.S. (2001). The cellular neurobiology of depression. *Nat Med, 7*, 541–547.

Mann, J.J. (1995). Violence and aggression. In: F.E. Bloom & D.J. Kupfer (Eds), *Psychopharmacology: The Fourth Generation of Progress* (pp. 1919–1928). New York: Raven Press.

Martin, S.D., Martin, E., Rai, S.S., Richardson, M.A. & Royall, R. (2001). Brain blood flow changes in depressed patients treated with interpersonal psychotherapy or venlafaxine hydrochloride: Preliminary findings. *Arch Gen Psychiatry, 58*, 641–648.

Mayberg, H.S., Brannan, S.K. & Tekell, J.L., et al. (2000). Regional metabolic effects of fluoxetine in major depression: Serial changes and relationship to clinical response. *Biol Psychiatry, 48*, 830–843.

Moreno, F.A., Heninger, G.R., McGahueya, C.A. & Delgado, P.L. (2000). Tryptophan depletion and risk of depression relapse: A prospective study of tryptophan depletion as a potential predictor of depressive episodes. *Biol Psychiatry, 48*, 327–329.

Murphy, B.E. (1997). Antiglucocorticoid therapies in major depression: A review. *Psychoneuroendocrinology, 22*, S125–132.

Nemeroff, C. (1996). The corticotropin-releasing factor (CRF) hypothesis of depression: New findings and new directions. *Mol Psychiatry, 1*, 336–342.

O'Flynn, K. & Dinan, T.G. (1993). Baclofen-induced growth hormone release in major depression: Relationship to dexamethasone suppression test result. *Am J Psychiatry, 150*, 1728–1730.

Owens, M.J. & Nemeroff, C.B. (1994). Role of serotonin in the pathophysiology of depression: Focus on the serotonin transporter. *Clin Chem, 40*, 288–295.

Reilly, J.G., McTavish, S.F.B. & Young, A.H. (1997). Rapid depletion of plasma tryptophan: A review of studies and experimental methodology. *J Psychopharmacol, 11*, 381–392.

Sargent, P.A., Kjaer, K.H., Bench, C.J., et al. (2000). Brain serotonin 1A receptor binding measured by positron emission tomography with [11C]WAY-100635: Effects of depression and antidepressant treatment. *Arch Gen Psychiatry, 57*, 174–180.

Schatzberg, A.F., Garlow, S.J. & Nemeroff, C.B. (2002). Molecular and cellular mechanisms in depression. In: K.L. Davis, D. Charney, J.T. Coyle & C. Nemeroff (Eds), *Neuropsychopharmacology. The Fifth Generation of Progress* (pp. 1039–1050). Philadelphia: Lipincott Williams & Wilkins.

Sheline, Y.I. & Minyun, M.A. (2002). Structural and functional imaging of affective disorders. In: K.L. Davis, D. Charney, J.T. Coyle & C. Nemeroff (Eds), *Neuropsychopharmacology. The Fifth Generation of Progress* (pp. 1065–1080). Philadelphia: Lipincott Williams & Wilkins.

Smith, D., Dempster, C., Glanville, J., Freemantle, N. & Anderson, I. (2002). Efficacy and tolerability of venlafaxine compared with selective serotonin reuptake inhibitors and other antidepressants: A meta-analysis. *Br J Psychiatry, 180*, 396–404.

Smith, K.A., Morris, J.S., Friston, K.J., Cowen, P.J. & Dolan, R.J. (1999). Brain mechanisms associated with depressive relapse and associated cognitive impairment following acute tryptophan depletion. *Br J Psychiatry, 174*, 525–529.

Sullivan, P.F., Kessler, R.C. & Kendler, K.S. (1998). Latent class analysis of lifetime depressive symptoms in the national comorbidity survey. *Am J Psychiatry, 155*, 1398–1406.

Thase, M.E., Dube, S., Bowler, K., et al. (1996). Hypothalamic-pituitary-adrenocortical activity and response to cognitive behavior therapy in unmedicated, hospitalized depressed patients. *Am J Psychiatry, 153*, 886–891.

Thase, M.E., Simons, A.D. & Reynolds, C.F.D. (1993). Psychobiological correlates of poor response to cognitive behavior therapy: Potential indications for antidepressant pharmacotherapy. *Psychopharmacol Bull, 29*, 293–301.

Van London, L., Goekoop, J.G., Zwinderman, A.H., Lanswer, J.B.K., Wiegent, V.M. & De Wied, D. (1998). Neuropsychological performance and plasma cortisol arginine vasopressin and oxytocin in patients with major depression. *Psychol Med, 28*, 275–284.

Wheeler Vega, J., Mortimer, A. & Tyson, P.J. (2000). Somatic treatment of psychotic depression: Review and recommendations for practice. *J Clin Psychopharmacol, 20*, 504–519.

Wolkowitz, O.M., Reus, V.I., Keebler, A., et al. (1999). Double-blind treatment of major depression with dehydroepiandrosterone. *Am J Psychiatry, 156*, 646–649.

Young, A.H., Gallagher, P. & Porter, R.J. (2002). Elevation of the cortisol-dehydroepiandrosterone ratio in drug-free depressed patients. *Am J Psychiatry, 159*, 1237–1239.

3

COGNITIVE MODELS AND ISSUES
IN DEPRESSION

Peter J. Bieling and Zindel V. Segal

OVERVIEW

Among the various psychological theories of depression, cognitive models continue to
be informed by empirical tests of both the theoretical framework and clinical outcomes
associated with this approach (Clark et al., 1999). Several scholarly reviews (Clark et al.,
1999; Coyne & Gotlib, 1983; Haaga et al., 1991; Kwon & Oei, 1994; Teasdale, 1983) suggest
consistent support for important aspects of the model, and there is general agreement that
cognitive therapy is an effective treatment for depression, with an efficacy that equals that
of antidepressant pharmacotherapy (Clark et al., 1999; DeRubeis & Crits-Cristoph, 1998;
Dobson, 1989; Robinson et al., 1990). Our aim in this chapter is to describe the current
cognitive model of depression and the evidence that supports this theoretical framework.
We will focus on a number of important research questions within the cognitive model, as
well as point to patterns of evidence identified in previous reviews (e.g., Clark et al., 1999;
Haaga et al., 1991). Beyond examining the evidence, we will also point out areas where
evidence is weak or contradictory. Thus, our aim is to capture the current state of the field,
but also to suggest important future directions and unresolved issues.

THE COGNITIVE MODEL

At its most general, the cognitive model of depression suggests that there is a strong connection between people's construal of events, their behaviour, and their emotional state.
The model postulates that incoming information from the environment is processed via
meaning-making structures that result in particular interpretations for each individual, and
that in depression such cognitive structures are negatively oriented in their processing and
tone, generating negative emotions and problematic behaviours (Beck, 1967). The cognitive
model sees the processing of information as a primary, though not necessarily causal, factor
in depression.

Mood Disorders: A Handbook of Science and Practice. Edited by M. Power.
© 2004 John Wiley & Sons, Ltd. ISBN 0-470-84390-X.

The cognitive model has its roots in two of the dominant currents of contemporary psychological thought, behaviourism and cognitivism. The developer of the cognitive model, A.T. Beck, was influenced considerably by behaviourism and learning theory, which suggested that psychopathology could be learned and did not necessarily result from repressed psychosexual conflicts, the prevailing view into the 1960s (Clark et al., 1999). At the same time, theorists and researchers began to turn their attention away from straightforward associationist connections between a stimulus and a response, to information processing that connected the external environment and behaviour through meaning construction. Beck's critical clinical observation was that patients who are depressed construe many of their circumstances as negative, and that while this ran counter to the objective reality of the situation, it was the negative processing that kept problematic emotions and behaviours in place (Beck, 1967). Consistent with learning theory, he postulated that this negative information processing was the result of early learning, and he began to pursue the idea that this kind of information processing was intimately connected with the signs and symptoms of depression. Since the 1960s, the cognitive model has evolved (Beck, 1967; Beck et al., 1979; Clark et al., 1999) and has been elaborated by others (e.g., Teasdale & Barnard, 1993).

Cognitive theory posits that the processing of information is crucial for the survival of any organism. Because the number of external stimuli in the environment is practically infinite, an organism needs to be able to filter out irrelevant inputs while selecting only the most relevant information for further attention. In psychopathology, these filters, or schemas, are thought to be rigid, absolute, and automatic as a result of early learning. The content of schemas is thought to differ across various disorders including depression, anxiety, and personality disorders. For example, in depression, schemas are thought to centre on unlovability and inadequacy (J. Beck, 1995); during an episode of depression, negative schemas are believed to dominate the meanings that patients assign to events, while between episodes these schemas are less pronounced.

Schemas do not operate in a vacuum; quite the opposite, these systems of beliefs are brought to bear on everyday life events encountered by the person. The major avenue through which these schemas are thought to operate is by the production of automatic thoughts; that is, specific, observable cognitions that occur in response to a situation and whose theme is often consistent with the schema's content. Such automatic thoughts play a central role in negative emotions and behavioural decisions (Clark et al., 1999).

EVIDENCE FOR THE COGNITIVE MODEL

The predictions of the cognitive model have been investigated in a variety of research areas including information processing, assessment of emotions and change in emotions, coping behaviours, treatment process and outcome, and developmental psychopathology. Researchers have tended to focus on a set of very specific predictions the model makes and to develop a paradigm to test those ideas. Conclusions about the cognitive model's integrity, therefore, rely on examination and review of numerous studies of specific predictions, which can be assembled into similar themes in order to draw inferences about the overall value of the model.

Other reviewers have used several organizing principles to assemble their review of the literature. For instance, the first comprehensive review of the area by Haaga and colleagues (1991) specified nine specific hypotheses that could be derived from the cognitive model. Similarly, Clark et al. (1999) derived nine hypotheses from the cognitive model, although these nine hypotheses differed considerably from the nine hypotheses created by Haaga and colleagues. The approach of listing very narrow hypotheses has the benefit of being straightforward, especially when the task at hand is the review of studies numbering in the hundreds. Our approach was to use many of these hypotheses as a point of departure, but we also use another level of organization that is partly derived from the cognitive conceptualization of clinical disorders (see J.S. Beck, 1995). Our purpose in using this different approach is to offer a somewhat simpler but still meaningful heuristic to help the reader organize the large amount of information and number of studies. The questions we pose concern core predictions of the model of psychopathology and are relatively less focused on treatment issues, such as the efficacy of cognitive therapy or mechanisms of action. The following questions will guide our examination of the evidence for cognitive models:

(1) What is the evidence regarding the existence of negative distortions in the thoughts of depressed individuals?
(2) Are these cognitive distortions related to environmental stimuli, and do these distortions have an impact on emotion and behaviour?
(3) What is the evidence that there are different levels of cognition, and that the presence of the different types of cognitions is important to the experience of depression?
(4) What is the evidence that early life experiences influence the development of negative cognitive structures?

For each question, we will review the weight of evidence and describe seminal studies in that area. We will also describe any issues that remain unresolved within each of those areas.

What is the evidence regarding the existence of negative distortions in the thoughts of depressed individuals?

The cognitive model of depression takes as its starting point the notion that it is the depressed person's moment-to-moment negative misinterpretation of an event, rather than the event itself, that leads to emotional distress (Beck et al., 1979; Clark et al., 1999). What is the empirical status of the assertion that depressed people are more likely to have negative thoughts? As reviewers have done previously, we frame the questions about negative cognitions in terms of central tenets. To examine the issue of cognitive distortions, we focus on the following two specific hypotheses:

(1) Negativity—depression is characterized by the presence of self-referent negative thinking,
(2) Specificity—depression has a distinct cognitive profile in terms of both content and process.

With regard to the first hypothesis, the large majority of studies and reviews support this notion of negativity. Since A.T. Beck's original research comparing the level of negative cognitions expressed by depressed patients during interviews to that of non-depressed psychiatric patients (Beck, 1967), the large majority of studies have supported this hypothesis. Later studies focused on objective "checklists" of depressotypic thoughts such as the Cognitions Checklist (Beck et al., 1987) or the Automatic Thoughts Questionnaire (Hollon & Kendall, 1980), in which participants use Likert scales to assess the frequency of negative thoughts. These studies suggest that cognitions can be reliably measured and are associated with depression. That is, a higher frequency of negative thoughts characterizes depressed individuals when compared to a variety of control groups, including non-depressed normals and non-depressed patients (e.g., Dobson & Shaw, 1986; Hollon et al., 1986; Ingram et al., 1987; Whisman et al., 1993).

Related to negativity is the notion of specificity, which holds that psychological disorders can be distinguished from one another by distinct cognitive profiles. In other words, when contrasted with other disorders, depression is predicted to be more associated with thoughts concerning loss or deprivation (Clark et al., 1999). This hypothesis has been tested by group comparisons (contrasting those who have a diagnosis of depression with other diagnostic categories on self-report measures of a variety of cognitions) and by examining correlations between continuous measures of psychiatric symptoms and different kinds of cognition. Most studies in this area have suggested specificity of depression and negative cognition when compared to individuals with generalized anxiety, social phobia, or test anxiety (Beck et al., 1992; Clark et al., 1990; Sanz & Avia, 1994; Steer et al., 1994). Specificity has also been examined with information-processing paradigms, such as having participants recall previously endorsed self-referent adjectives. Here, too, depressed individuals appear to recall more negative content adjectives than anxious individuals (Greenberg & Beck, 1989; Ingram et al., 1987). Similarly, correlational studies examining the pattern of relations between symptom measures and measures of cognition suggest that depression is specifically associated with negative thoughts, even when controlling for the presence of anxiety or threat cognitions (e.g., Alford et al., 1995; Jolly & Dykman, 1994). These studies generally converge on the conclusion that, indeed, depressed states are typically associated with negative thoughts that do not characterize normal emotional states or anxiety. In fact, depressed states are typically associated with thoughts of loss, failure, and pessimism (Clark et al., 1999; Greenberg & Beck, 1989; Haaga et al., 1991; Sanz & Avia, 1994; Steer et al., 1994).

Finally, early formulations of the cognitive model argued for exclusivity of negative thinking; that is, depression should be characterized by an absence of positive thoughts. However researchers have found that depressed people do report some positive cognitions and positive self-views, a finding which challenges the notion of the exclusivity of negative thoughts (Derry & Kuiper, 1981; Segal & Muran, 1993). However, later writing on the cognitive model of depression emphasizes not an absolute lack of positive cognition, but rather a preponderance of negative thoughts (Clark et al., 1999). Indeed, the research literature does support the notion that depressed individuals have a relatively higher ratio of negative to positive thoughts, with a general consensus that in depression negative thoughts outnumber positive thoughts approximately 2 to 1 (Schwartz, 1986; 1997). Taken together, evidence for the negativity and specificity hypotheses lends good support to the notion that depressive thinking is characterized by numerous negative biases.

Are these cognitive distortions related to environmental stimuli, and do these distortions have an impact on emotion and behaviour?

This question is equally important because the cognitive model specifies that negative thoughts will not occur randomly, but in response to specific events that are misinterpreted by the individual. Moreover, this misinterpretation is said to fuel a cycle of negative emotions, and influence the behaviour of the depressed individual. Phrased in more technical terms, these ideas have been termed selective processing and primacy. The selective-processing hypothesis states that depression is characterized by a processing bias for negative self-referent information from the environment. The primacy hypothesis posits that negative cognition influences both behaviour and emotion (Clark et al., 1999; Haaga et al., 1991).

It is important to note that the cognitive theory of depression does not suggest that depressed persons are always biased in their information processing (Segal, 1988). Rather such biases are most likely to emerge in situations that are personally relevant, and that offer a degree of ambiguity (Beck, 1967; Clark et al., 1999). Unlike the research on negativity and specificity, which often involves simple self-report, evaluation of the selective-processing hypothesis involves more laboratory-based studies. Participants in such studies are placed in a variety of specifically constructed situations, ranging from imagined scenarios in which an outcome is predicted, to performing a task and receiving feedback from others. Indeed, these studies do suggest that depressed individuals find negative and positive interpretations of ambiguous stimuli equally acceptable, whereas non-depressed individuals prefer positive interpretations (Crowson & Cromwell, 1995, Moretti et al., 1996). Depressed individuals are more likely to perceive their own performance of an experimental task as less positive and more negative (e.g., Dykman et al., 1989; Weary & Williams, 1990), though some studies have suggested that depressed individuals see their performance as less positive only (DeMonbreun & Craighead, 1977). Similarly, depressed individuals judge their social performances to be more negative than do non-depressed individuals (Dow & Craighead, 1987; Gotlib & Meltzer, 1987). Depressed individuals selectively recall more negative self-referent adjectives in memory-based tasks, although in some studies depressed individuals recall fewer positive adjectives and not necessarily more negative adjectives (e.g., Kuiper & Derry, 1982). Moreover, the responses of depressed individuals to standardized, open-ended vignettes of typical achievement and interpersonal experiences often contain negative distortions (Krantz & Hammen, 1979; Krantz & Liu, 1987; Watkins & Rush, 1983), especially when the vignette is itself negative (Krantz & Gallagher-Thompson, 1990). This is true whether the comparison group comprises non-distressed controls or mixed psychiatric controls (Haaga et al., 1991). Similarly, an examination of the thought records of depressed patients in treatment has revealed cognitive errors in response to situations that patients had recorded themselves (Blackburn & Eunson, 1989). Moreover, whether responses are gathered in the context of a laboratory or in the clinic, the types of cognitive errors made by depressed individuals appear to be similar. Arbitrary inference (for example, attributing a cause in the absence of evidence), magnification (such as making a small mistake and seeing this out of all proportion), overgeneralization (as in taking a single case and seeing that as a general, negative rule), and personalization (such as attributing a negative outcome to the self) are the most common cognitive errors reported in these studies (Clark et al., 1999). Such studies certainly support the notion of selective, negative processing of information in depression.

However, there are also several issues in the area of selective processing that have been controversial. In some studies of information processing, depressed individuals have actually been found to be more accurate than those of non-depressed individuals. This effect has been termed "depressive realism" or the "sadder but wiser" phenomenon (Abramson & Alloy, 1981). Obviously, if the perceptions of depressed people are sometimes more accurate than those of non-depressed people, the notion of selective processing and the cognitive model itself are open to challenge. However, closer examination of the experimental findings has suggested that there are specific conditions under which depressed individuals are more accurate, and that the depressive realism notion does not hold uniformly (Clark et al., 1999). Specifically, it seems that depressed people may be more accurate when asked to judge the probability of abstract outcomes, but not when judging personally relevant, everyday situations, which are much more central in the experience of depression (Clark et al., 1999; Haaga & Beck, 1995). Another issue, and one that remains unresolved despite its prominence in the cognitive model, is the empirical status of the cognitive distortions. Depending on which source reference is used, the cognitive model sets out variable numbers and types of cognitive distortions. It has been relatively straightforward to demonstrate that depressed individuals have biases that are negative in tone. It has been more difficult to construct a comprehensive empirical taxonomy of the kinds of distortions depressed individuals make.

The next hypothesis to be explored in this section, that of primacy, predicts that there is a link between negative distortions and the individual's emotions and behaviour. One programme of research has illustrated that ruminative, self-focused negative thoughts are systematically related to enduring negative mood, particularly among depressed women (Nolen-Hoeksema, 1991; Nolen-Hoeksema et al., 1993). Other studies attempt to reduce negative thought content to examine the impact of such cognitive change on affect (Persons & Burns, 1985; Teasdale & Fennell, 1982). Overall, both types of studies demonstrate a reciprocal link between negative moods and negative thoughts. There is also evidence that negative cognition is associated with both peripheral physiological changes and changes in cortical activity. Negative cognition has been linked to increased heart rate (Schwartz et al., 1981) and respiration rate (Schuele & Wiesenfeld, 1983), as well as to cerebral blood flow through the limbic, paralimbic, and brainstem structures in positron emission tomography (PET) studies (George et al., 1995). The difficulty with such physiological studies is teasing apart the nature of relationships between cognition and emotion. The design of these studies has typically been correlational rather than experimental, and the degrees of association are sometimes modest. For better establishment of causality, some studies induce a negative mood and then examine the impact of the mood on cognitive networks, and these studies also support the primacy hypothesis (Ingram et al., 1998).

Unfortunately, less research is available on the connection between depressive thinking, mood, and overt behaviour. Nonetheless, numerous authors have argued that depression is associated with actions that precipitate stress in the long term (Hammen, 1991; Monroe & Peterman, 1988; Monroe & Simons, 1991; Rutter, 1986). Indeed, in one study, depressed women were found to generate more interpersonal stress in a 1-year period, particularly in an interpersonal context (Hammen, 1991). In that study, depressed women had more life stressors that could be seen as random, but the behavioural choices of the women also contributed to the creation of more difficult circumstances. There is also recent evidence from a very large population-based twin registry that supports the notion that self-generated stress contributes to the onset of depression (Kendler et al., 1999; 2000). What is not well understood is whether the correlation between depression and problematic, potentially stress-generating behaviours is cognitively mediated. That is, do the distortions of depressed individuals lead them to select behavioural strategies that are not optimal, and do these strategies lead eventually to increased stressors or other self-defeating behaviours? These ideas could be tested within presently available experimental paradigms and would be further evidence in positing cognition as a central feature in the experience of depression.

What is the evidence that there are different levels of cognition, and that the presence of the different types of cognitions is important to the experience of depression?

The cognitive model makes clear that negative cognition exists at different levels or layers. Some of these layers or levels are accessible to the person and can be spontaneously described, but other levels are under less effortful control and cannot be reported by the individual directly, without training. At the most observable level, negative thinking, we have seen that there is good evidence that depressed individuals are likely to have more negative thoughts. Is there also evidence that there are other levels of cognition, and that these have a negative tone in depression? Moreover, are these other levels of cognition important in initiating or maintaining depression? These questions, though they seem simple, are complex and pose several dilemmas for researchers. First, how does one ascertain the existence of cognitive processes that cannot be described by the individual or observed directly? Second, if evidence for more implicit cognition exists, how might explanations drawing on these constructs demonstrate their incremental utility compared to accounts based on negative thoughts alone?

As in other areas of the model, one of the critical questions is whether one can measure the phenomenon of interest reliably and validly. These more implicit types of cognition are termed either "beliefs" or "schemas", and there have been attempts to measure them through self-report. The earliest and most established measure of these more deeply held beliefs is the Dysfunctional Attitudes Scale (DAS) (Weissman & Beck, 1978). The DAS has three forms, a 100-item version, and two more commonly used, 40-item versions (forms A and B). The DAS and its different forms have been found to display adequate psychometric properties (Beck et al., 1991; Oliver & Baumgart, 1985), and many of the DAS items are explicitly written as "if . . . then" statements to distinguish them from measures of automatic thoughts. The latter have strongly self-relevant negative content, while beliefs are expressed mainly as rules or conditional assumptions.

Clearly, implicit beliefs need to be sufficiently differentiated from automatic negative thoughts in order to be useful concepts or to have explanatory power that goes beyond negative thoughts. The conditional nature of beliefs and their content (such as "if . . . then" rules) is one factor that differentiates them. However, beliefs also need to meet additional criteria if they are to be useful in cognitive models. First, beliefs should be correlated moderately but significantly with negative thoughts; a correlation that is too high would suggest redundancy of concepts, whereas no correlation would suggest that beliefs and thoughts are independent of one another. Second, one may hypothesize that beliefs would be more stable than negative thoughts since the former are less tied to specific mood states or situations. Finally, the presence of these maladaptive beliefs should increase vulnerability to onset or relapse of depression. These hypotheses have received positive support from research to date (Clark et al., 1999). For example, the DAS has been found to correlate moderately but significantly with negative thoughts and depressive symptoms in many studies (Clark et al., 1999). Second, there is evidence that markers of these beliefs are evident even between episodes of depression (Gemar et al., 2001; Ingram et al., 1998). Finally, a large body of research supports the notion that these kinds of beliefs, especially when coupled with stressors, lead to the emergence of depressive symptoms (Hammen et al., 1985; 1995; Segal et al., 1992).

Another interesting issue in the literature on beliefs is the question of the content of these beliefs. Research has shown that the underlying factor structure of the DAS is determined by which version is at issue, and that the two forms (A and B) appear to have different factor structures. Form A factors are needed for approval, perfectionism, and avoidance of risk. Form B factors are need for success, need to impress others, need for approval, and need to control feelings (Oliver & Baumgart, 1985). The most comprehensive analysis of the DAS items, using the entire 100-item pool as a starting point, suggests that nine types of conditional assumptions are reliably measured by the DAS (Beck et al., 1991). The nine types of conditional assumptions are vulnerability, need for approval, success-perfectionism, need to please others, imperatives, need to impress, avoidance of appearing weak, control over emotions, and disapproval-dependence. Two studies have also addressed the issue of DAS and coping, that is, the connection between beliefs and behaviour. One study found no relationship between DAS scores and perceived social support (Kuiper et al., 1987). However, in a study of depressed inpatients, elevated DAS scores were associated with perceiving one's support as inadequate and having lower social adjustment (Norman et al., 1988). This research represents a promising line of inquiry, but it is too early to draw any conclusions about the link between conditional beliefs and coping strategies.

According to the cognitive model, beliefs contain meaning (or content), but are also processing constructs (Clark et al., 1999; Williams et al., 1997). There are numerous inherent difficulties in measuring the products of "implicit cognitive processing". Indeed, a self-report measure in which the respondent essentially endorses the content of an item cannot, in and of itself, support the notion of belief-based information-processing (Gotlib & McCabe, 1992; Segal & Swallow, 1994). To study the information-processing functions of beliefs, researchers have used a variety of experimental paradigms, including sentence completion, trait adjective ratings, and autobiographical memory recall. These studies suggest that depression increases accessibility to negative self-referent schema content (Clark et al., 1999). Studies in this area share an underlying conceptual and methodological framework. Researchers compare individuals at risk of depression (for example, patients who were formerly depressed, but are currently remitted or recovered) with never depressed or non-depressed psychiatric control groups. The two groups are exposed to an experimental stimulus, usually a "mood prime" designed to activate temporary negative emotions and thereby a negative set of beliefs. Comparison of the beliefs of groups before and after mood priming can demonstrate the presence of activated negative beliefs. Using this paradigm, numerous studies have demonstrated that, as a result of mood priming, remitted depressed individuals are likely to have more negative content in their thoughts and more negative recall and encoding of information than controls, and problems with focusing their attention (Ingram et al., 1998). Thus, the induced negative mood may be seen to be an analogue of negative environmental events, and the activation in cognitive structures to be a vulnerability, or risk factor for depression. More recently, one study has found a link between degree of activation of negative beliefs and vulnerability to depressive relapse, suggesting an important link between latent negative beliefs and the onset of full depression (Segal et al., 1999). These lines of research support the idea that deep cognition is a powerful explanatory construct in depression and that deep cognitive processes are distinct from negative automatic thoughts.

An elaboration of this approach to "deep" cognitive structures in depression has been provided by the interacting cognitive subsystems (ICS) approach of Teasdale and Barnard (1993). This approach suggests that depression does not increase activation of negative core beliefs, but rather results in the application of a different set of mental models. Furthermore, these mental models encode more globally negative views of self and views that are more closely allied with notions of lack of social approval and lack of success. This model, while relatively more recent, does have some empirical support (e.g., Teasdale et al., 1995). For example, Teasdale and colleagues were able to show that depressed patients completed sentence stems with positive words when doing so changed the overall meaning of the belief to be dysfunctional. For example, in the sentence, "Always seeking the approval of other people is the road to————", the depressed individuals were more likely to use the word "success", whereas non-depressed individuals were more likely to use a word such as "unhappiness". This finding suggests that depressed individuals do not process information in a monolithic or simplistic negative manner, but apply a template of beliefs that set them up to experience negative consequences (Teasdale et al., 1995).

On the whole, the investigation of beliefs has proven to be one of the most important challenges for researchers investigating the cognitive model. Thus far, the literature is sharply divided into information-processing paradigms and self-report content categories. Each has its limitations. Investigations that focus on content tell us little about the operation of these beliefs. Likewise, studies examining the processing associated with these beliefs tell us little about the content of the beliefs that have been activated. Future approaches may be helpful if they can combine these two approaches. First, for example, can situation-specific "mood prime" paradigms demonstrate the activation of specific types of beliefs? Second, do these specific beliefs then influence the subsequent processing of information? This research will require considerable rigour, and probably awaits the creation of new experimental paradigms that can test such complex questions.

What is the evidence that early life experiences influence the development of negative cognitive structures?

We have now reviewed the evidence that supports the idea that specific cognitive processes are associated with depression. We have seen that these processes operate on both the overt level and at deeper levels that can be detected indirectly but reliably. A logical question is, where do these beliefs and thoughts come from? The cognitive model suggests that a "child learns to construe reality through his or her early experiences with the environment, especially with significant others. Sometimes, these early experiences lead children to accept attitudes and beliefs that will later prove maladaptive" (Beck & Young, 1985, p. 207). Based on this assumption, the cognitive-mediation hypothesis states that cognitive processes and maladaptive beliefs mediate between developmental risk factors and subsequent onset of depression (Ingram et al., 1998). We next address the scientific basis of the cognitive-mediation hypothesis.

Certainly, the children of depressed parents are at increased risk of psychiatric problems, particularly major depression in adolescence and adulthood (Cohn et al., 1986; Field, 1984; Tronick & Gianino, 1986). Furthermore, depressed adults do tend to report having been parented in problematic ways in childhood (e.g., Brewin et al., 1992; Koestner et al., 1991; Zemore & Rinholm, 1989). However, these findings could be due to a number of factors. What is more important to demonstrate, from the perspective of the cognitive model, is that early experiences influence the formation of cognitive systems that make an individual vulnerable to depression. Unfortunately, this mediation hypothesis has not been studied sufficiently to draw a conclusion. In one study using an undergraduate sample, very limited support was found for a mediating relationship of cognitive variables between reports of maladaptive parenting and subsequent depression (Whisman & McGarvey, 1995). Moreover, among depressed patients, a history of developmental adversity, most notably sexual abuse, is associated with more dysfunctional cognitive styles (Rose et al., 1994). In another study using a young adolescent sample, self-worth was found to mediate between reports of maternal parenting and depressive symptoms (Garber & Robinson, 1997; Garber et al., 1997). To date, only limited innovative work is beginning to address cognitive mechanisms directly. This work tentatively suggests that maladaptive beliefs about the self and others may emerge early in the development of at-risk children (e.g., Bartholomew & Horowitz, 1991; Coyne & Whiffen, 1995; Taylor & Ingram, 1999).

In summary, the research suggests guarded evidence for the cognitive-mediation hypothesis in several circumscribed areas. Childhood loss coupled with inadequate post-bereavement care, poor parenting (particularly lack of care, rejection or criticism, and over-controlling disciplinary practices), insecure attachments, and childhood sexual abuse appear to set the stage for subsequent depression. However, the available evidence suggests that these factors are neither necessary nor sufficient causal factors, but are risk factors for subsequent problems that predate depression.

CONCLUSION

The cognitive model, originally proposed over 30 years ago, has continued to be refined and modified on the basis of empirical feedback and conceptual challenges (Clark et al., 1999). This approach has responded to numerous challenges through the development of more refined research strategies and paradigms that have addressed many of its critics' concerns. In the future, the model is also likely to benefit from the convergence of cognitive psychology, clinical psychology, and psychiatric neurosciences informed by imaging technologies. Many of the paradigms developed to test the cognitive model of depression could be adapted to a neuroimaging context. This could further specify the anatomical mechanisms that underlie cognitive and emotional processes related to depression. In sum, the model offers significant explanatory power and theoretical coherence to support the continued reliance on cognitive interventions as a front-line psychological treatment for unipolar depression.

REFERENCES

Abramson, L.Y. & Alloy, L.B. (1981). Depression, nondepression, and cognitive illusions: A reply to Schwartz. *Journal of Experimental Psychology: General, 110*, 436–447.

Alford, B.A., Lester, J.M., Patel, R.J., Buchanan, J.P. & Giunta, L.C. (1995). Hopelessness predicts future depressive symptoms: A prospective analysis of cognitive vulnerability and cognitive content specificity. *Journal of Clinical Psychology, 51*, 331–339.

Bartholomew, K. & Horowitz, L.M. (1991). Attachment styles among young adults: A test of a four category model. *Journal of Personality and Social Psychology, 61*, 226–244.

Beck A.T. (1967). *Depression: Causes and Treatment*. Philadelphia: University of Pennsylvania Press.

Beck, A.T. & Young, J.E. (1985). Cognitive therapy of depression. In D. Barlow (Ed.), *Clinical Handbook of Psychological Disorders: A Step-By-Step Treatment Manual* (pp. 206–244). New York: Guilford.

Beck A.T., Brown, G., Steer, R.A., Eidelson, J.I. & Riskind, J.H. (1987). Differentiating anxiety and depression: A test of the cognitive content-specificity hypothesis. *Journal of Abnormal Psychology, 96*, 179–183.

Beck, A.T., Brown, G., Steer, A.N. & Weissman, A.N. (1991). Factor analysis of the Dysfunctional Attitude Scale in a clinical population. *Psychological Assessment, 3*, 478–483.

Beck, A.T., Rush, A.J., Shaw, B.F. & Emery, G. (1979). Cognitive therapy of depression. New York: Guilford.

Beck, A.T., Steer, R.A. & Epstein, N. (1992). Self-concept dimensions of clinically depressed and anxious outpatients. *Journal of Clinical Psychology, 48*, 423–432.

Beck, J.S. (1995). *Cognitive Therapy: Basics and Beyond.* New York: Guilford.

Blackburn, I.M. & Eunson, K.M. (1989). A content analysis of thoughts and emotions elicited from depressed patients during cognitive therapy. *British Journal of Medical Psychology, 62*, 23–33.

Brewin, C.R., Firth-Cozens, J., Furnham, A. & McManus, C. (1992). Self-criticism in adulthood and recalled childhood experience. *Journal of Abnormal Psychology, 101*, 561–566.

Clark, D.A. & Beck, A.T. with Alford, B.A. (1999). *Scientific Foundations of Cognitive Theory and Therapy of Depression.* Chichester: Wiley.

Clark, D.A., Beck, A.T. & Stewart, B. (1990). Cognitive specificity and positive-negative affectivity: Complementary or contradictory views on anxiety and depression? *Journal of Abnormal Psychology, 99*, 148–155.

Cohn, J.F., Matias, R., Tronick, E.Z., Connell, D. & Lyons-Ruth, K. (1986). Face to face interactions of depressed mothers and their infants. In E.Z. Tronick & T. Field (Eds), *Maternal Depression and Infant Disturbance* (pp. 31–45). New Directions for Child Development, No. 34. San Francisco, CA: Jossey-Bass.

Coyne, J.C. & Gotlib, I.H. (1983). The role of cognition in depression: A critical appraisal. *Psychological Bulletin, 94*, 472–505.

Coyne, J.C. & Whiffen, V.E. (1995). Issues in personality as diathesis for depression: The case of sociotropy-dependency and autonomy-self-criticism. *Psychological Bulletin, 118*, 358–378.

Crowson, J.J. & Cromwell, R.L. (1995). Depressed and normal individuals differ both in selection and in perceived tonal quality of positive-negative messages. *Journal of Abnormal Psychology, 104*, 305–311.

DeMonbreun, B.G. & Craighead, W.E. (1977). Distortion of perception and recall of positive and neutral feedback in depression. *Cognitive Therapy and Research, 1*, 311–329.

Derry, P.A. & Kuiper, N.A. (1981). Schematic processing and self reference in clinical depression. *Journal of Abnormal Psychology, 90*, 286–297.

DeRubeis, R.J. & Crits-Christoph, P. (1998). Empirically supported individual and group psychological treatments for adult mental disorders. *Journal of Consulting and Clinical Psychology, 66*, 37–52.

Dobson, K.S. (1989). A meta-analysis of the efficacy of cognitive therapy for depression. *Journal of Consulting and Clinical Psychology, 57*, 414–419.

Dobson, K.S. & Shaw, B.F. (1986). Cognitive assessment with major depressive disorders. *Cognitive Therapy and Research, 10*, 13–29.

Dow, M.G. & Craighead, W.E. (1987). Social inadequacy and depression: Overt behavior and self-evaluation processes. *Journal of Social and Clinical Psychology, 5*, 99–113.

Dykman, B.M., Abramson, L.Y., Alloy, L.B. & Hartlage, S. (1989). Processing of ambiguous and unambiguous feedback by depressed and nondepressed college students: Schematic biases and their implications for depressive realism. *Journal of Personality and Social Psychology, 56*, 431–445.

Field, T.M. (1984). Early interactions between infants and their post-partum mothers. *Infants Behavior and Development, 7*, 527–532.

Garber, J. & Robinson, N.S. (1997). Cognitive vulnerability in children at risk for depression. *Cognition and Emotion, 11*, 619–635.

Garber, J., Robinson, N.S. & Valentiner, D. (1997). The relation between parenting and adolescent depression: Self-worth as a mediator. *Journal of Adolescent Research, 12*, 12–33.

Gemar, M., Segal, Z., Sagrati, S. & Kennedy, S. (2001). Mood-induced changes on the Implicit Association Test in recovered depressed patients. *Journal of Abnormal Psychology, 110*, 282–289.

George, M.S., Ketter, T.A., Parekh, P.I., Horwitz, B., Herscovitch, P. & Post, R.M. (1995). Brain activity during transient sadness and happiness in healthy women. *American Journal of Psychiatry, 152*, 341–351.

Gotlib, I.H. & McCabe, S.B. (1992). An information processing approach to the study of cognitive functioning in depression. In E.F. Walker, B.A. Cornblatt, & R.H. Dworkin (Eds), *Progress in Experimental Personality and Psychopathology Research* (vol. 15, pp. 131–161). New York: Springer.

Gotlib, I.H. & Meltzer, S.J. (1987). Depression and the perception of social skills in dyadic interaction. *Cognitive Therapy and Research, 11*, 41–54.

Greenberg, M.S. & Beck, A.T. (1989). Depression versus anxiety: A test of the content-specificity hypothesis. *Journal of Abnormal Psychology, 98*, 9–13.

Haaga, D.A.F. & Beck, A.T. (1995). Perspectives on depressive realism: Implications for cognitive therapy of depression. *Behaviour Research and Therapy, 19*, 121–142.

Haaga, D.A.F., Dyck, M.J. & Ernst, D. (1991). Empirical status of cognitive theory of depression. *Psychological Bulletin, 110*, 215–236.

Hammen, C. (1991). Generation of stress in the course of unipolar depression. *Journal of Abnormal Psychology, 100*, 555–561.

Hammen, C.L., Burge, D., Daley, S.E., Davila, J., Paley, B. & Rudolph, K.D. (1995). Interpersonal attachment cognitions and prediction of symptomatic responses to interpersonal stress. *Journal of Abnormal Psychology, 104*, 436–443.

Hammen, C., Marks, T., Mayol, A. & deMayo, R. (1985). Depressive self-schemas, life stress, and vulnerability to depression. *Journal of Abnormal Psychology, 94*, 308–319.

Hollon, S.D. & Kendall, P.C. (1980). Cognitive self-statements in depression: Development of an automatic thoughts questionnaire. *Cognitive Therapy and Research, 4*, 383–395.

Hollon, S.D., Kendall, P.C. & Lumry, A. (1986). Specificity of depressotypic cognitions in clinical depression. *Journal of Abnormal Psychology, 95*, 52–59.

Ingram, R.E., Kendall, P.C., Smith, T.W., Donnell, C. & Ronan, K. (1987). Cognitive specificity in emotional disorders. *Journal of Personality and Social Psychology, 53*, 734–742.

Ingram, R.E., Miranda, J. & Segal, Z.V. (1998). *Cognitive Vulnerability to Depression.* New York: Guilford.

Jolly, J.B. & Dykman, R.A. (1994). Using self-report data to differentiate anxious and depressive symptoms in adolescents: Cognitive content specificity and global distress? *Cognitive Therapy and Research, 18*, 25–37.

Kendler K.S., Karkowski, L.M., & Prescott, C.A. (1999). Causal relationship between stressful life events and the onset of major depression. *American Journal of Psychiatry, 156*, 837–841.

Kendler, K.S., Thornton, L.M. & Gardner, C.O. (2000). Stressful life events and previous episodes in the etiology of major depression in women: An evaluation of the kindling hypothesis. *American Journal of Psychiatry, 157*, 1243–1251.

Koestner, R., Zuroff, D.C. & Powers, T.A. (1991). Family origins of adolescent self-criticism and its continuity into adulthood. *Journal of Abnormal Psychology, 100*, 191–197.

Krantz, S.E. & Gallagher-Thompson, D. (1990). Depression and information valence influence depressive cognition. *Cognitive Therapy and Research, 14*, 95–108.

Krantz, S.E. & Hammen, C. (1979). Assessment of cognitive bias in depression. *Journal of Abnormal Psychology, 88*, 611–619.

Krantz, S.E. & Liu, C. (1987). The effect of mood and information valence on depressive cognition. *Cognitive Therapy and Research, 11*, 185–196.

Kuiper, N.A. & Derry, P.A. (1982). Depressed and nondepressed content self-reference in mild depressives. *Journal of Personality, 50*, 67–80.

Kuiper, N.A., Olinger, L.J. & Swallow, S.R. (1987). Dysfunctional attitudes, mild depression, views of self, self-consciousness, and social perceptions. *Motivation and Emotion, 11*, 379–401.

Kwon, S. & Oei, T.P.S. (1994). The roles of two levels of cognitions in the development, maintenance, and treatment of depression. *Clinical Psychology Review, 14*, 331–358.

Monroe, S.M. & Peterman, A.M. (1988). Life stress and psychopathology. In L. Cohen (Ed.), *Research on Stressful Life Events: Theoretical and Methodological Issues* (pp. 31–63). Newbury Park, CA: Sage.

Monroe, S.M. & Simons, A.D. (1991). Diathesis-stress in the context of life stress research: Implications for the depressive disorders. *Psychological Bulletin, 111*, 406–425.

Moretti, M.M., Segal, Z.V., McCann, C.D., Shaw, B.F., Miller, D.T. & Vella, D. (1996). Self-referent versus other-referent information processing in dysphoric, clinically depressed, and remitted depressed subjects. *Personality and Social Psychology Bulletin, 22*, 68–80.

Nolen-Hoeksema, S. (1991). Responses to depression and their effects on the duration of depressive episodes. *Journal of Abnormal Psychology, 100*, 569–582.

Nolen-Hoeksema, S., Morrow, J. & Fredrickson, B.L. (1993). Response styles and the duration of episodes of depression. *Journal of Abnormal Psychology, 102*, 20–28.

Norman, W.H., Miller, I.W. & Dow, M.G. (1988). Characteristics of depressed patients with elevated levels of dysfunctional cognitions. *Cognitive Therapy and Research, 12*, 39–52.

Oliver, J.M. & Baumgart, E.P. (1985). The Dysfunctional Attitude Scale: Psychometric properties and relation to depression in an unselected adult population. *Cognitive Therapy and Research, 9*, 161–167.

Persons, J.B. & Burns, D.D. (1985). Mechanisms of action of cognitive therapy: The relative contributions of technical and interpersonal interventions. *Cognitive Therapy and Research, 9*, 539–551.

Robinson, L.A., Berman, J.S. & Neimeyer, R.A. (1990). Psychotherapy for the treatment of depression: A comprehensive review of controlled outcome research. *Psychological Bulletin, 108*, 1–20.

Rose, D.T., Abramson, L.Y., Hodulik, C.J., Halberstadt, L. & Leff, G. (1994). Heterogeneity of cognitive style among depressed inpatients. *Journal of Abnormal Psychology, 103*, 419–429.

Rutter, M. (1986). Meyerian psychobiology, personality development, and the role of life experiences. *American Journal of Psychiatry, 143*, 1077–1087.

Sanz, J. & Avia, M.D. (1994). Cognitive specificity in social anxiety and depression: Self-statements, self-focused attention, and dysfunctional attitudes. *Journal of Social and Cognitive Psychology, 13*, 105–137.

Schuele, J.G. & Wiesenfeld, A.R. (1983). Autonomic response to self-critical thought. *Cognitive Therapy and Research, 7*, 189–194.

Schwartz, G.E., Weinberger, D.A. & Singer, J.A. (1981). Cardiovascular differentiation of happiness, sadness, anger and fear following imagery and exercise. *Psychosomatic Medicine, 43*, 343–364.

Schwartz, R.M. (1986). The internal dialogue: On the asymmetry between positive and negative coping thoughts. *Cognitive Therapy and Research, 10*, 591–605.

Schwartz, R.M. (1997). Consider the simple screw: Cognitive science, quality improvements, and psychotherapy. *Journal of Consulting and Clinical Psychology, 65*, 970–983.

Segal, Z.V. (1988). Appraisal of the self-schema construct in cognitive models of depression. *Psychological Bulletin, 103*, 147–162.

Segal, Z.V., Gemar, M. & Williams, S. (1999). Differential cognitive response to a mood challenge following successful cognitive therapy or pharmacotherapy for unipolar depression. *Journal of Abnormal Psychology, 108*, 3–10.

Segal, Z.V. & Muran, J.C. (1993). A cognitive perspective on self-representation in depression. In Z.V. Segal & S.J. Blatt (Eds), *The Self in Emotional Distress: Cognitive and Psychodynamic Perspectives* (pp. 131–170). New York: Guilford.

Segal, Z.V., Shaw, B., Vella, D. & Katz, R. (1992). Cognitive and life stress predictors of relapse in remitted unipolar depressed patients: Test of the congruency hypothesis. *Journal of Abnormal Psychology, 101*, 26–36.

Segal, Z.V. & Swallow, S.R. (1994). Cognitive assessment of unipolar depression: Measuring products, processes, and structures. *Behaviour Research and Therapy, 32*, 147–158.

Steer, R.A., Beck, A.T., Clark, D.A. & Beck, J.S. (1994). Psychometric properties of the Cognition Checklist with psychiatric outpatients and university students. *Psychological Assessment, 6*, 67–70.

Taylor, L. & Ingram, R.E. (1999). Cognitive reactivity and depressotypic information processing in children of depressed mothers. *Journal of Abnormal Psychology, 108*, 202–210.

Teasdale, J.D. (1983). Negative thinking in depression: Cause, effect or reciprocal relationship? *Advances in Behaviour Research and Therapy, 5*, 3–25.

Teasdale, J.D. & Barnard, P.J. (1993). *Affect, Cognition, and Change: Remodeling Depressive Thought*. Hove: Erlbaum.

Teasdale, J.D. & Fennell, M.J.V. (1982). Immediate effects on depression of cognitive therapy interventions. *Cognitive Therapy and Research, 6*, 343–352.

Teasdale, J.D., Taylor, M.J., Cooper, Z., Hayhurst, H. & Paykel, E.S. (1995). Depressive thinking: Shifts in construct accessibility or in schematic mental models? *Journal of Abnormal Psychology, 104*, 500–507.

Tronick, E.Z. & Gianino, A. (1986). The transmission of maternal disturbance to the infant. In E.Z. Tronick & T. Field (Eds), *Maternal Depression and Infant Disturbance* (pp. 5–12). New Directions for Child Development, No. 34. San Francisco, CA: Jossey-Bass.

Watkins, J.T. & Rush, A.J. (1983). Cognitive response test. *Cognitive Therapy and Research, 7*, 425–436.

Weary, G. & Williams, J.P. (1990). Depressive self-presentation: Beyond self-handicapping. *Journal of Personality and Social Psychology, 58*, 892–898.

Weissman, A.N. & Beck, A.T. (1978). Development and validation of the Dysfunctional Attitudes Scale: A preliminary investigation. Paper presented at the meeting of the Association for the Advancement of Behavior Therapy, Chicago.

Whisman, M.A., Diaz, M.L. & Luboski, J.A. (1993). Cognitive specificity of major depression and generalized anxiety disorder. Paper presented at the annual meeting of the Association for Advancement of Behavior Therapy, Atlanta, GA.

Whisman, M.A. & McGarvey, A.L. (1995). Attachment, depressotypic cognitions, and dysphoria. *Cognitive Therapy and Research, 19*, 633–650.

Williams, J.M.G., Watts, F.N., MacLeod, C. & Matthews, A. (1997). *Cognitive Psychology and the Emotional Disorders* (2nd edn). Chichester: Wiley.

Zemore, R. & Rinholm, J. (1989). Vulnerability to depression as a function of parental rejection and control. *Canadian Journal of Behavioural Science, 21*, 364–376.

4

SOCIOEMOTIONAL FUNCTIONING IN DEPRESSION

Jonathan Rottenberg and Ian H. Gotlib

Major depressive disorder (MDD) is a psychiatric syndrome characterized by impaired functioning in multiple domains, including biology, behavior, emotion, and cognition. Investigators working within each of these domains face an ever-expanding corpus of theory, methodology, and empirical findings. Perhaps in part due to these burgeoning literatures, different groups of researchers have typically focused on only one of these domains of functioning. While understandable, the consequence of this situation is that there is a lack of integrative theory and research in which the range of dysfunctions that are associated with depression are synthesized to form a meaningful overall pattern (Gotlib & Hammen, 1992, 2002).

For several reasons, the social and emotional dysfunctions observed in depression appear to be particularly good candidates with which to begin to develop such an integrative approach. It is clear, for example, that depressed individuals exhibit striking deficits in both of these domains. And perhaps more important, the social and emotional deficits in MDD *appear* to be interwoven. It is not difficult to imagine, for instance, that a depressed woman's inability to experience pleasure (emotion deficit) might lead her to withdraw from pleasant activities involving others (social deficit). Indeed, a growing body of research conducted with "normal" samples reinforces the formulation that there are strong bidirectional linkages between the social and the emotional domains (e.g., Fridja, 1986; Fridlund, 1992). Emotions are critical in coordinating the trajectory of social interactions (Ekman, 1992). In turn, social interactions set the conditions under which the majority of all emotional episodes occur (Scherer et al., 1986). These insights concerning the linkage of social and emotional phenomena have only recently been applied to the understanding of psychopathology (e.g., Keltner & Kring, 1998). We believe that this is an opportune time, therefore, for researchers and theorists in the field of depression to consider the interconnections between the social dysfunctions (e.g., Barnett & Gotlib, 1988) and the emotional dysfunctions (e.g., Rottenberg et al., 2002) that are typically observed in individuals who are experiencing this debilitating disorder.

Mood Disorders: A Handbook of Science and Practice. Edited by M. Power.
© 2004 John Wiley & Sons, Ltd. ISBN 0-470-84390-X.

Certainly, the formulation of a socioemotional linkage in MDD is not entirely novel. Several well-validated interventions for depression, such as interpersonal therapy (IPT) (Klerman et al., 1984), social skills training (Becker et al., 1987), and marital and family therapy (Beach & Jones, 2002), make strong assumptions about the existence of tight connections between the state of depressed persons' interpersonal functioning and their emotional state. In fact, a central claim of these interventions is that improving depressed patients' social functioning will alleviate their depressive symptoms (including the emotional symptoms). Despite the demonstrated efficacy of these therapies, the mechanisms through which socially based therapies effect changes in emotional functioning remain largely unknown.

The purpose of this chapter is to present an overview and integration of the literatures on social and emotional functioning in depression. Using the general concept of socioemotional linkage as a framework, we begin this chapter by discussing normative aspects of the relation between social and emotional functioning. Our overarching goal in using the concept of socioemotional linkage is to go beyond a simple "snapshot" description of how depressed individuals function in social settings and offer a more dynamic explanation of *why* depressed persons engage in dysfunctional social behaviors. In this context, examining the emotional functioning of depressed individuals can provide important insights concerning their social behaviors. After reviewing the literatures concerning the social and emotional functioning of depressed persons, we attempt to integrate these literatures by considering the contributions both of broad motivational systems and of specific emotion deficits to the problematic social functioning of depressed individuals. We conclude this chapter with recommendations for future research designed to examine the roles of social and emotional functioning, over time and across clinical state, as possible risk factors for MDD.

SOCIOEMOTIONAL LINKAGE IN NORMATIVE FUNCTIONING

For all people, social and emotional functioning are undoubtedly connected in a multitude of ways. In examining these associations, we will focus on two levels of analysis or examination—macro and micro—that differ both in their breadth and in their timescale. Whereas the macro level of analysis involves an examination of the nature of the relation between broad motivational systems and overall patterns of social activity, the micro level of analysis considers the role of emotional responses in shaping the course of ongoing social interaction. We now consider each of these levels of analysis in turn.

Macro-level linkages

Attachment behavior offers one illustration of a macro-level association between social and emotional functioning. At its core, attachment theory describes how emotional states such as love and anxiety concerning separation can motivate interactive behaviors aimed at forming and maintaining social bonds (e.g., Bowlby, 1969, 1973). More specifically, attachment theory posits that proximity to available and responsive caretakers during development is critical in enabling children to manage anxiety and distress successfully, a process that will be reflected in a secure attachment style and adequate coping to deal with anxiety and distress later in life. Conversely, early disturbance of this comfort- and security-seeking attachment system is posited to lead to maladaptive social behavior later in life in the face of significant stressors (Bowlby, 1973). Three attachment styles, each with accompanying socioemotional behaviors, have been described: secure attachment is associated with trust, relationship satisfaction, and constructive approaches to conflict; avoidant attachment is related to low levels of intimacy, commitment, and care; and anxious/ambivalent attachment is linked with dependency, relationship conflict, and low relationship satisfaction (e.g., Collins & Read, 1990). As we will discuss later in this chapter, there is considerable evidence indicating that this socioemotional node is disturbed in depressed individuals.

Neurobiological models of motivation and personality provide a second macro-level link between social and emotional functioning. A number of researchers, most notably Gray (1982), have used animal models to identify two distinct motivational systems: an approach-related, positive-incentive system (the behavioral activation system [BAS]), and a withdrawal-related, threat-sensitive system (the behavioral inhibition system [BIS]). These two motivational systems have been found to be useful in conceptualizing human emotional functioning. Indeed, several other theorists have postulated similar functionally indepen- dent systems involved in behavioral regulation (e.g., Higgins, 1997; Watson et al., 1999). Importantly, researchers and theorists have now begun to relate BIS/BAS system activity to social functioning. For example, BAS levels have been related conceptually to levels of extraversion and positive affect (Gable et al., 2000; Jorm et al., 1999), two aspects of personality that themselves have been linked to sociability (Clark & Watson, 1988). Simi- larly, levels of behavioral inhibition have been linked conceptually to difficulties in social functioning through neuroticism, negative affectivity, and shyness (Asendorpf, 1989). Em- pirical work is lagging behind these conceptual formulations of the relation of the BAS and BIS systems to social behavior, representing an important direction for future research in this area. Nevertheless, as we discuss later in this chapter, several investigators have already begun to examine how abnormalities in the BIS and BAS systems might be implicated in a number of different forms of psychopathology (e.g., Fowles, 1988; Kring & Bachorowski, 1999) and, more specifically, in depressive illness (e.g., Beevers & Meyer, 2002; Depue & Iacono, 1989; Kasch et al., 2002).

Micro-level linkage

Much of human emotion unfolds in social contexts. Indeed, the close association of social and emotional functioning in the context of ongoing interpersonal transactions has been noted by several investigators (Campos et al., 1989; Ekman, 1992; Lazarus, 1991). In par- ticular, a number of specific interconnections of social and emotional functioning have been identified (see Keltner & Haidt, 1999, for a review). In very systematic ways, for example, emotional experience relates to specific types of social relationships. The experience of em- barrassment and shame relates to perceptions of low social status vis-à-vis others (Gilbert & Trower, 1990); the experience of anger arises from the perception of wrongful actions by others (Lazarus, 1991); and the experience of joy arises from unfettered social play (Boulton & Smith, 1992).

Ever since Darwin's (1872) work on emotional expression, scientists have recognized the critical role of emotional behavior in signaling conspecifics. One type of behavioral signaling performs an *informative* function. That is, facial and vocal displays of emotion communicate information in a fairly reliable fashion to receivers about the senders' emotion and their social intentions (e.g., Ekman, 1993, Fridlund, 1992; Scherer, 1986). For example, senders' displays of embarrassment communicate appeasement and a future intent to submit to the receivers' desires (Keltner & Buswell, 1997). Emotions also clearly have an *evocative* function in social interactions. That is, emotional behaviors have the capacity to elicit responses from others that are relevant to the emotional situation or event. For example, smiling evokes affiliative tendencies (Keltner & Bonanno, 1997); displays of anger motivate fear responses in others (Oehman, 1986); and, perhaps most relevant to this chapter, displays of sadness and distress typically elicit sympathy, helping, and increased proximity to the individual (Averill, 1968). In sum, it is clear that social and emotional functioning work together to form a dense network, and that disturbances in various parts of this network might contribute to the problematic interpersonal functioning that is characteristic of depression.

SOCIAL FUNCTIONING IN DEPRESSION

Depressed individuals are characterized by a wide range of social deficits (see Barnett & Gotlib, 1988; Segrin, 2000, for reviews). It is noteworthy that there is no single cohesive theory to account for the origins of these social difficulties. Instead, relatively isolated bodies of empirical research (for example, studies examining the associations between depression and stressful life events, social networks, marital functioning, etc.) have implicated different aspects of interpersonal functioning as being important in understanding the etiology and maintenance of depression, as well as relapse of this disorder. Given recent reviews of the social functioning of depressed persons (e.g., Hirschfield et al., 2000; Segrin, 2000), we will not attempt to present an exhaustive review of this research in this chapter. Rather, we will organize our discussion of the social functioning of depressed persons by describing two main types of social deficit in MDD: those that involve problems with the *quantity* of social interactions, and those that involve the *quality* of social interactions.

Quantity of social interactions in MDD

One major characteristic of the interpersonal functioning of individuals while they are experiencing an episode of depression is a reduced overall level of social activity. Not only do depressed persons report having fewer people in their social networks than do nondepressed individuals, but they also have less frequent contact with people in their social networks (e.g., Youngren & Lewinsohn, 1980). In addition, compared with nondepressed controls, depressed persons report having fewer social intimates (Gotlib & Lee, 1989) and fewer friends (Brim et al., 1982), and experiencing fewer contacts outside their immediate families (Henderson et al., 1981). Importantly, these findings of reduced levels of social interaction in depression are obtained in studies using both self-report and interview methodologies; moreover, they are corroborated by other informants, such as family members (e.g., Billings et al., 1983; Brim et al., 1982).

It is important to note that this pattern of reduced levels of social activity appears to be a relatively stable characteristic of individuals who are vulnerable to depressive episodes. For example, investigators who have tested depressed individuals both during and after depressive episodes have found that although there was some recovery in the number of social contacts reported by depressed individuals 1 year following their depressive episode, they continued to report restricted social networks even when they were no longer symptomatic (Billings & Moos 1985a, 1985b; Gotlib & Lee, 1989). Moreover, there is strong evidence that depression is associated with such stable characteristics as low assertiveness, social withdrawal, avoidance, and shyness—all traits that have been found to be associated with reduced social activity (Alfano et al., 1994; Anderson & Harvey, 1988). In fact, both the lack of assertiveness (Ball et al., 1994) and the presence of social withdrawal (Boivin et al., 1995) have been found to predict future depression, a pattern of results that suggests that reduced social activity may serve as a risk factor for depression. Although promising, it is clear that more research using prospective designs needs to be conducted before we are able to understand fully the causal nature of the relation between reduced social activity and episodes of depression.

In this context, there are several reasons why depression may be associated with reduced social activity. One possibility is that because depressed persons do not find social activities pleasurable or reinforcing (e.g., Lewinsohn, 1974), they actively curtail or avoid social activity. Another, albeit not mutually exclusive, possibility is that the impetus for reduced social activity comes from the interaction partners of depressed persons. Indeed, it has been postulated that because partners find interacting with a depressed person to be aversive, they ultimately seek to limit further contact with him or her (Coyne, 1976; Gotlib & Robinson, 1982). Regardless of the explanation, it is clear that when depressed persons interact with strangers, friends, or family members, the interactants are often dissatisfied. Therefore, it is clear that it is not simply the quantity, but also the *quality* of social interactions that is reduced during episodes of depression.

Quality of social interactions in MDD

Depressed persons report lower quality in a wide variety of social relationships relative to nondepressed persons. These differences appear to be pervasive and are observed when depressed individuals report on their relationships with their parents (Gotlib et al., 1988), their spouses (Whisman, 2001), their friends (Gotlib & Lee, 1989), or their children (Goodman et al., 1994). Moreover, evidence indicates that these differences are veridical, and not the simple result of a negative reporting bias in depression (Gotlib et al., 1988; Gotlib & Lee, 1989).

Not surprisingly, therefore, a significant body of literature has examined impairments in the quality of social interactions in depression. For example, early behavioral formulations of depression viewed depression as resulting from a lack of environmental reinforcement (e.g., Lewinsohn, 1974). According to this perspective, depressed persons lack the skills that are critical in eliciting reinforcement from others in social situations. Subsequent studies have demonstrated that, in both dyadic and group interactions with strangers, depressed individuals do indeed exhibit a number of behaviors that are indicative of social-skill deficits. For example, when engaging in conversation, depressed individuals have been found to smile less frequently than do nondepressed individuals (Gotlib, 1982; Gotlib & Robinson, 1982). Compared with nondepressed controls, depressed persons tend to make less eye contact with those with whom they are interacting (Gotlib, 1982); they speak more slowly and more monotonously (Gotlib & Robinson, 1982; Libet & Lewinsohn, 1973; Youngren & Lewinsohn, 1980), and with less volume and voice modulation; and they have longer pauses in their speech patterns, and take longer to respond when someone else addresses them (e.g., Talavera et al., 1994; Teasdale et al., 1980; Youngren & Lewinsohn, 1980). Depressed individuals also take longer to respond to others in a conversation and offer responses that are inappropriately timed (Gotlib & Robinson, 1982; Jacobson & Anderson, 1982; Libet & Lewinsohn, 1973). They are also more self-centered in the interactions and tend to direct the conversations to negative content, often communicating themes of self-devaluation and helplessness (Biglan et al., 1985; Hokanson et al., 1980). Understandably, as a result of these behaviors, many individuals will express a desire to withdraw from interactions with depressed partners (Segrin, 2000).

While these effects are clearly observable in interactions of depressed individuals with strangers, it is apparent that depression affects meaningful social relationships to a greater extent than it does more superficial relationships. For example, Segrin and Flora (1998) found that depressed individuals were more likely to disclose negative topics when talking with a friend than when talking with a stranger. Perhaps the most dramatic effects, however, are found in the marital relationships of depressed persons. Beach and Jones (2002) present considerable data indicating that the marital interactions of depressed persons are characterized by high levels of anger, conflict, and negative affect. Depressed spouses have been found to derogate themselves and their partners, and both spouses escalate their negative affect and behaviors over the course of the interactions. Interestingly, expressions of sad affect in the depressed spouse appear to have the effect of suppressing anger and aggression in the partner, suggesting that depression may play a functional albeit maladaptive role in the marriage (e.g., Hops et al., 1987). With respect to their children, depressed individuals report that they find it difficult to be warm and consistent parents, that they do not derive satisfaction from their children, and that they feel inadequate in their parenting role (Goodman et al., 1994). Consistent with these self-reports, in interactions with their children depressed mothers display sad and irritable affect (e.g., Cohn et al., 1990), and are either unresponsive or intrusive (see Gotlib & Goodman, 1999, for a more detailed review of this literature). Interestingly, depressed individuals report experiencing their own relationships with their parents as children as being relatively low in quality, and characterize their parents as being cold and overprotective (Gotlib et al., 1988). These findings suggest that later problems in relating to significant others may be a consequence of earlier attachment difficulties.

In sum, there is evidence that depressed persons have difficulties in their relationships with both intimates and nonintimates, and are generally less engaged in social activity. Undoubtedly, these patterns of problematic interpersonal functioning are complex and stem from a number of sources. However, a number of recent findings increasingly point to the possibility that disturbances in emotion processing can explain several aspects of dysfunctional social behavior in this disorder. To clarify the role that emotion plays in depressed persons' social dysfunction, we now briefly review the emerging literature on emotional functioning in depression.

EMOTIONAL FUNCTIONING IN DEPRESSION

Emotions are usually conceptualized as multisystem responses that involve changes in linguistic, behavioral, and/or physiological functioning (e.g., Lang, 1978). When an organism is confronted by relevant stimuli and challenges in the environment (such as a charging bear), its emotion systems generate responses that prepare it for adaptive action (Ekman,

1992; Tooby & Cosmides, 1990). Two of the major challenges faced by organisms are obtaining the resources necessary for survival and reproduction (such as food or sex), and avoiding situations or experiences that might threaten these goals (such as physical damage or loss of status). Consequently, a number of theorists have posited the existence of two primary motivational systems that are responsible for different forms of emotional activation: an appetitive system, associated with positive feeling states and prototypically expressed by behavioral approach, and a defensive system, associated with negative feeling states and prototypically expressed by behavioral escape or avoidance (Gray, 1982; Lang, 1995).

How does depression affect the generation of emotional states? From depressed patients' prototypical reports of emotion, it appears that MDD involves disturbances in both appetitive (positive) and defensive (negative) motivational systems. That is, depressed individuals typically report experiencing low levels of positive feeling states such as joy or amusement, and high levels of negative feeling states such as sadness, anxiety, and shame (Clark et al., 1994). Given this pattern of reporting, it is reasonable to hypothesize that depression should serve to decrease responsiveness to positive incentives and increase responsiveness to negative incentives. Interestingly, empirical research examining emotional reactivity in MDD provides only partial support for this hypothesis, suggesting instead that depression serves to diminish emotional reactivity to *both* positive and negative stimuli.

Appetitive motivation in MDD

A number of theorists have hypothesized that appetitive motivation is deficient in depression (Clark et al., 1994; Depue & Iacono, 1989; Fowles, 1988). Evidence for this idea is robust. A common set of clinical features of depression, for example, involves impairment in appetitive motivation: depressed individuals frequently exhibit anhedonia, psychomotor retardation, fatigue, anorexia, and apathy. These features are all easily interpretable in terms of a reduced responsivity to appetitive stimuli and/or a reduced drive to engage with positive or rewarding features of the external environment in MDD. Not surprisingly, and also consistent with this interpretation, depressed individuals have been found to report lower levels of appetitive motivation than do nondepressed controls (Kasch et al., 2002).

Perhaps the strongest evidence of appetitive deficits comes from laboratory studies in which positive emotional stimuli are presented to depressed individuals. For example, compared with nondepressed controls, depressed individuals have been found to exhibit less positive emotion-expressive behavior in response to pleasant film and pleasant drink stimuli (Berenbaum & Oltmanns, 1992), and pleasant slides (Sloan et al., 2001), and to be less behaviorally responsive to reward contingencies (Henriques & Davidson, 2000). Depressed individuals have also been shown to be characterized by attenuated reports of positive emotion in response both to slides depicting pleasant scenes (Allen et al., 1999; Sloan et al., 1997, 2001) and to an amusing film clip (Rottenberg et al., 2002). Finally, and perhaps most germane to our focus on social functioning, in our laboratory we have found that smiling human faces evoke less neural reactivity (as measured by functional magnetic resonance imaging [fMRI]) in depressed individuals than in nondepressed controls (Gotlib et al., 2001). Indeed, based in part on this accumulating evidence, clinical theorists and researchers have argued that deficits in appetitive motivation are a characteristic emotional "signature" of depression that distinguishes this disorder from other forms of psychopathology (e.g., Clark et al., 1994; Henriques & Davidson, 1991).

Defensive motivation in MDD

Certainly, no overall characterization of emotional responding in MDD is complete without a consideration of how depressed individuals respond to negative emotional stimuli. From early psychoanalytic formulations of depression to contemporary cognitive conceptualizations of this disorder, theorists have postulated that depressed individuals are characterized by a magnified response to negative stimuli. For example, cognitive theories of depression conceptualize this disorder in terms of biases in information processing, in which attention to, and/or memory for, negative stimuli or environmental events are potentiated (e.g., Beck, 1967, 1976; Beck et al., 1979). Indeed, given the pervasiveness of negative thinking and negative affect in this disorder, the hypothesis that depression enhances reactivity to negative stimuli is a reasonable one.

Surprisingly, however, there is little empirical evidence to support the view that depression enhances reactivity to negative stimuli. Not only have several investigators obtained null results (e.g., Sloan et al., 2001), but also a growing number of experimental studies have actually reported findings in the opposite direction, indicating that depressed persons exhibit *diminished* reactivity to negative stimuli. For instance, in early studies comparing depressed individuals and nondepressed controls, depressed participants have been found to report experiencing less pain in response to heat (Hall & Stride, 1954; Hemphill et al., 1952), pressure (Merskey, 1965), and electric shock (Davis et al., 1979; von Knorring & Espvall, 1974; but also see Lewinsohn et al., 1973). This pattern of findings has been replicated in more recent studies using pressure and cold stimuli (Lautenbacher et al., 1999), and heat stimuli (Dworkin et al., 1995; Lautenbaucher et al., 1994; but see also Adler & Gattaz, 1993). In fact, in our laboratory, this pattern of blunted, rather than enhanced, responding has even been observed in tearful crying, an emotional response that one would reasonably expect to be enhanced by depression. Crying is ordinarily associated with the report and display of sadness and with physiological arousal (Gross et al., 1994). Given the clear elevations among depressed people in reports and displays of sadness, combined with clinical reports of crying as a characteristic of depression, we hypothesized that individuals diagnosed with MDD would be more likely than would nondepressed controls to cry in response to a sad film. Contrary to this prediction, we found, first, that depressed individuals were no more likely to cry than were nondepressed controls, and, second, that crying-related increases in the report and display of sadness and in heart rate and electrodermal responding were *smaller* among depressed than among nondepressed individuals (Rottenberg et al., 2002).

Response stereotypy: A reformulation of emotional deficits in MDD

Considered collectively, these findings indicate, contrary to what might be assumed, that diminished emotional reactivity in depression is not restricted to positively valenced stimuli. Rather, it appears that depressed persons exhibit a more general insensitivity to environmental stimuli. Although there is not yet a fully developed theoretical framework to account for this stereotyped and inflexible pattern of emotional reactivity (Davidson et al., 2000), it is nevertheless consistent with conceptualizations that emphasize depressed persons' pervasive withdrawal from environmental events (Nesse, 2000). Indeed, considerable evidence indicates that depressed persons exhibit a reduced sensitivity to changing emotional contexts. For example, compared with nondepressed controls, depressed persons have been found to show less affective modulation of startle (Allen et al., 1999), less electromyographic modulation during affective imagery (Gehricke & Shapiro, 2000; Greden et al., 1986), less facial reactivity in response to expressive facial stimuli (Wexler et al., 1993), less valence-related modulation of event-related brain potentials (Deldin et al., 2001), less differential neural responding to emotion face stimuli (Gotlib et al., 2001), and a lack of autonomic responding to a variety of stimuli (Dawson et al., 1977).

The results of naturalistic studies also indicate that depressed individuals exhibit emotional stereotypy, showing little modulation of their facial affect (e.g., Andreasen, 1979; Kulhara & Chadda, 1987) or vocal characteristics (e.g., Hargreaves et al., 1965). These findings are especially important because they indicate that depressed individuals exhibit stereotyped emotional responses in social situations. Indeed, as we will discuss in the following section, we believe that the capacity to shift affect appropriately is crucial if one is to interact effectively with others. In this context, therefore, the lack of affective modulation among depressed individuals is likely to have important implications for their social functioning.

TOWARD AN INTEGRATION: SOCIOEMOTIONAL LINKAGE IN DEPRESSION

A growing body of work aimed at understanding normative functioning has demonstrated close interconnections between the social and emotional domains. Investigators examining depression (and other forms of psychopathology) have only recently begun to take advantage of these insights. Despite the fact that depressed individuals exhibit characteristic impairments in both the social and emotional domains, our overall picture of depressive deficits remains fragmented and in need of a unifying theory. In this section, we will outline a conceptual basis for integrating social and emotional impairments in MDD by identifying two areas of socioemotional linkage that differ in their breadth and timescale of operation.

Macro-level linkages

We have considered evidence indicating that individuals who are vulnerable to depression exhibit lower overall levels of social activity (e.g., Gotlib & Lee, 1989). In light of this evidence, one question that remains unanswered is *why* levels of social activity are persistently low in vulnerable individuals. Although several factors are almost certainly involved, our account here will focus on macro-level socioemotional links between typical levels of social activity and the appetitive and defensive motivational systems. These two motivational systems, as we have reviewed, influence a person's characteristic affective reactions to stimuli in the environment (including social stimuli). Consistent with this premise, temperament research indicates that a person's characteristic affective style (Davidson, 1998) develops from an early age, is stable, and has a significant biological basis (e.g., Kagan, 1998). The long-range stability exhibited by the appetitive and defensive motivational systems raises the possibility that the motivational systems of depression-vulnerable individuals "set" social activity at abnormally low levels.

The appetitive system has a role in facilitating social relations. Supporting this notion, individuals who typically experience high levels of positive affect also report higher levels of social activity (Clark & Watson, 1988). In contrast, low levels of positive affect (such as that reported during depressive episodes) are associated with a reduced drive to socialize with others (e.g., Blanchard et al., 2001). If weakness in the appetitive system generates the low prevailing levels of social activity seen in individuals who are vulnerable to experiencing depression, appetitive system abnormalities should be observable during well periods independently of depressive symptomatology. To date, however, empirical findings bearing on this point are mixed. Although self-reports of social anhedonia have been found to track depression symptom levels (Blanchard et al., 2001), other indicators of appetitive deficits, such as low levels of self-reported reward responsiveness (Kasch et al., 2002) and hypoactivation of the left frontal lobes (e.g., Henriques & Davidson, 1990), occur independently of current depression symptom levels. These latter findings underscore the possibility that the smaller and less active social networks characteristic of depression-vulnerable individuals originate from low tonic activation of the appetitive system. This formulation, we think, is inherently plausible. For example, depression-vulnerable individuals might not seek out novel social contacts because they do not anticipate receiving pleasure from such contacts. Clearly, further examination of the relation between social activity and appetitive deficits in depression will be an important avenue for future work

There is reason to believe that the defensive motivation system also exerts an ongoing influence on social activity levels. In contrast to the appetitive system, which facilitates socializing, activation of the defensive system dampens social exploration. Previous work in other areas suggests that behaviorally inhibited children (that is, children who are fearful when confronted with novel persons or stimuli) are less likely to seek out new friendships and are considered shy by their peers (Kagan, 1998). Importantly, both adults and children who are vulnerable to depression have been found to have high scores on measures of defensive motivation (that is, behavioral inhibition) (Kasch et al., 2002; Rosenbaum et al., 2000). These findings are also consistent with the possibility that the high tonic activation of the defense system sets social activity levels at low prevailing levels. Indeed, consistent with the idea that individuals who are vulnerable to depression are highly tuned to social threats, depression-vulnerable individuals appear to be differentially sensitive to the effects of peer rejection (Boivin et al., 1995) and to criticism by intimates (Hooley & Gotlib, 2000). And, as we will discuss in the following section, currently depressed persons' social behavior appears to be shaped more by the harm-avoidance function of the defense system than by the pleasure-seeking function of the appetitive system.

Micro-level linkages

A variety of evidence indicates that depressed individuals experience low quality in their interactions with others. Again, a consideration of emotion processes might help explain *why* it is that depressed individuals exhibit this pattern of social dysfunction. An emerging view of emotional functioning in depression suggests that the primary problem in depressed individuals is that they exhibit emotional stereotypy, or a loss in the capacity to generate emotional responses that are appropriate to changing environmental contexts. Stereotypy of emotional behaviors has a number of implications for social functioning. We now consider the effects of emotional stereotypy on the interaction partners of depressed individuals, highlighting the role of micro-level socioemotional linkages between social and emotional behavior as it unfolds in specific interactions over relatively brief periods of time.

Because emotions provide such valuable social information, disturbances in emotional responsiveness are likely to disrupt relationships in important ways. As we have reviewed, a growing body of evidence indicates that depressed individuals exhibit stereotyped emotional behaviors that are insensitive to changing environmental contexts. This emotional stereotypy often leads to inappropriate social behavior. Consistent with the chronic over-activation of their defense system, depressed individuals' social behaviors often communicate self-derogation, helplessness, and problem disclosure. Importantly, because these emotional behaviors are often emitted without respect for the immediate audience or social context, they are naturally judged as often being inappropriately self-disclosing (Jacobson & Anderson, 1982). Indeed, when they are motivated to socialize, depressed individuals often communicate to others that they are overwhelmed by their problems, seek reassurance, and attempt to draw others in to solve their problems—requests that may or may not be granted (Joiner, 2002). Interestingly, in some contexts, this set of depressed behaviors can be successful in reducing threat and eliciting support. For instance, Biglan et al. (1985) and Hops et al. (1987) have shown that depressive behavior can serve to reduce the likelihood of aversive responses from family members. In this respect, depressive behavior appears to be similar to displays of distress in nondepressed individuals, which have the capacity to elicit signs of distress, concern, and overt attempts at helping in others (e.g., Batson & Shaw, 1991; Zahn-Waxler et al., 1992).

Although the stereotypy of emotional behavior in depression might temporarily recruit social support, it is likely to carry with it extremely high costs for the quality of the social interaction. For example, it is clear that stereotyped emotional behavior violates a number of assumptions about how typical interactions should proceed (e.g., Davis, 1982; Segrin & Abramson, 1994). Theorists have observed, for instance, that most communicative behaviors carry an implicit demand for an appropriately elaborate and relevant response (e.g., Davis, 1982). People whose behavior is rigid and unchanging over the course of one or several interactions would naturally frustrate their partners' desire for dynamic feedback both about their own performance and about the state of their relationship. Emotional stereotypy also is likely to be aversive to others because it violates basic expectations about emotion-expressive reciprocity. Indeed, considerable research indicates that, while interacting, people mirror one another when they are emotionally expressive. This pattern of behavior has been observed with respect to both embarrassment (Miller, 1987) and laughter (Provine, 1992). In short, we believe that emotional stereotypy erodes the quality of social interactions. Clearly, this is an important deficit to understand as we begin to integrate social and emotional functioning in depressive disorders. Further study of this deficit has the potential to illuminate several different elements of depressive social behavior, including the paradoxical finding that behaviors that are emitted by depressed people have the capacity to elicit both care and rejection from their interaction partners (Coyne, 1976).

CONCLUDING REMARKS

In this chapter, we have developed and illustrated the idea of socioemotional linkage, an idea with wide application to normal and pathological states. In depression research, this idea holds particular promise as a basis for integrating the disparate literatures on social and emotional functioning, and synthesizing the pattern of deficits that are observed in this disorder. To bring this integration forward to a full fruition will require investigators to deal with several unresolved issues.

Perhaps the most pressing of these issues concerns how socioemotional linkages evolve over time and across changes in clinical state. One problem in commenting on this question at the present time is that in the overwhelming majority of studies of emotional functioning in depression, individuals have been assessed only when they are acutely ill. Without inclusion of groups of participants who have a history of MDD but who do not have current symptoms of the disorder, or without following participants after recovery from depression, it remains possible that deficits in emotion processing (that is, reduced reactivity and/or emotional stereotypy) are simply products, or symptoms, of the depressed state. Determining whether or not these emotion deficits are more stable characteristics of depression-vulnerable individuals that are present independently of depressive symptomatology will be critical for clarifying their role in social dysfunction and for determining their etiological role in precipitating depressive episodes.

Another issue related to the causal status of emotion deficits involves an examination of their interactions with other factors in contributing to a vulnerability to depression. It is unlikely that a chronic deficit in emotional functioning (such as low tonic activation of the appetitive system) would operate as *sufficient* or *proximal* cause of depressive episodes, given that individuals who possess the risk factor are generally not in an episode of depression. Far more likely, then, is the possibility that emotional deficits interact with other factors such as stress or social support to lead to depression. For example, it is plausible that trait-like weakness in appetitive motivation leads to weakness or deterioration in social support networks that, in turn, renders a person more vulnerable to effects of stress. Therefore, studies that examine multiple factors in predicting future episodes of depression, as well as investigations that tease apart the relative predictive power of the appetitive/defense motivational systems, will be useful in moving this field forward.

Finally, it is critical that research designed to understand and improve interventions for depression (and other forms of psychopathology) consider the treatment implications of the idea of socioemotional linkage. Because social and emotional functioning form a dense network of interconnections, it is almost certainly the case that modifying emotion in a client affects his or her social functioning, and vice versa. Indeed, interventions might be more effective if therapists were cognizant of these socioemotional linkages, and of their connections to depressive symptomatology. To this end, research examining the efficacy of psychological treatments for depression would profit from a systematic investigation of different nodes in this socioemotional network, with the goal of determining which of these nodes offers the most efficient and most effective point of intervention, both to facilitate recovery from depression and to prevent relapse of this disorder.

REFERENCES

Adler, G. & Gattaz, W.F. (1993). Pain perception threshold in major depression. *Biological Psychiatry, 34*, 687–689.

Alfano, M.S., Joiner, Jr., T.E., Perry, M. & Metalsky, G.I. (1994). Attributional style: A mediator of the shyness-depression relationship? *Journal of Research in Personality, 28*, 287–300.

Allen, N.B., Trinder, J. & Brennen, C. (1999). Affective startle modulation in clinical depression: Preliminary findings. *Biological Psychiatry, 46*, 542–550.

Anderson, C.A. & Harvey, R.J. (1988). Discriminating between problems in living: An examination of measures of depression, loneliness, shyness, and social anxiety. *Journal of Social and Clinical Psychology, 6*, 482–491.

Andreasen, N.C. (1979). Affective flattening and the criteria for schizophrenia. *American Journal of Psychiatry, 136*, 944–947.

Asendorpf, J.B. (1989). Shyness as a final common pathway for two different kinds of inhibition. *Journal of Personality and Social Psychology, 57*, 481–492.

Averill, J.R. (1968). Grief: Its nature and significance. *Psychological Bulletin, 70*, 721–748.

Ball, S.G., Otto, M.W., Pollack, M.H. & Rosenbaum, J.F. (1994). Predicting prospective episodes of depression in patients with panic disorder: A longitudinal study. *Journal of Consulting and Clinical Psychology, 62*, 359–365.

Barnett, P.A. & Gotlib, I.H. (1988). Psychosocial functioning and depression: Distinguishing among antecedents, concomitants, and consequences. *Psychological Bulletin, 104*, 97–126.

Batson, C.D. & Shaw, L.L. (1991). Evidence for altruism: Toward a pluralism of prosocial motives. *Psychological Inquiry, 2*, 107–122.

Beach, S.R.H. & Jones, D.J. (2002). Marital and family therapy for depression in adults. In I.H. Gotlib & C.L. Hammen (Eds), *Handbook of Depression* (pp. 422–440). New York: Guilford.

Beck, A.T. (1967). *Depression: Clinical, Experimental, and Theoretical Aspects*. New York: Harper and Row.

Beck, A.T. (1976). *Cognitive Therapy and the Emotional Disorders*. Madison, CT: International Universities Press.

Beck, A.T., Rush, A.J., Shaw, B.F. & Emery, G. (1979). *Cognitive Therapy of Depression*. New York: Guilford.

Becker, R.E., Heimberg, R.G. & Bellack, A.S. (1987). *Social Skills Treatment for Depression*. New York: Pergamon Press.

Beevers, C.G. & Meyer, B. (2002). Lack of positive experiences and positive expectancies mediate the relationship between BAS responsiveness and depression. *Cognition and Emotion, 16*, 549–564.

Berenbaum, H. & Oltmanns, T.F. (1992). Emotional experience and expression in schizophrenia and depression. *Journal of Abnormal Psychology, 101*, 37–44.

Biglan, A., Hops, H., Sherman, L., Friedman, L.S., Arthur, J. & Osteen, V. (1985). Problem-solving interactions of depressed women and their husbands. *Behavior Therapy, 16*, 431–451.

Billings, A.G. & Moos, R.H. (1985a). Life stressors and social resources affect posttreatment outcomes among depressed patients. *Journal of Abnormal Psychology, 94*, 140–153.

Billings, A.G. & Moos, R.H. (1985b). Psychosocial processes of remission in unipolar depression: Comparing depressed patients with matched community controls. *Journal of Consulting and Clinical Psychology, 53*, 314–325.

Billings, A.G., Cronkite, R.C. & Moos, R.H. (1983). Social-environmental factors in unipolar depression: Comparisons of depressed patients and nondepressed controls. *Journal of Abnormal Psychology, 92*, 119–133.

Blanchard, J.L., Horan, W.P. & Brown, S.A. (2001). Diagnostic differences in social anhedonia: A longitudinal study of schizophrenia and major depressive disorder. *Journal of Abnormal Psychology, 110*, 363–371.

Boivin, M., Hymel, S. & Burkowski, W.M. (1995). The roles of social withdrawal, peer rejection, and victimization by peers in predicting loneliness and depressed mood in childhood. *Development and Psychopathology, 7*, 765–785.

Boulton, M.J. & Smith, P.K. (1992). The social nature of play fighting and play chasing: Mechanisms and strategies underlying cooperation and compromise. In J.H. Barkow, L. Cosmides & J. Tooby (Eds), *The Adapted Mind: Evolutionary Psychology and the Generation of Culture* (pp. 429–444). New York: Oxford University Press.

Bowlby, J. (1969). *Attachment and loss. Vol. 1: Attachment*. New York: Basic Books.

Bowlby, J. (1973). *Attachment and Loss. Vol. 1. Attachment*. New York: Basic Books.

Brim, J.A., Witcoff, C. & Wetzel, R.D. (1982). Social network characteristics of hospitalized depressed patients. *Psychological Reports, 50*, 423–433.

Campos, J.J., Campos, R.G. & Barrett, K.C. (1989). Emergent themes in the study of emotional development and emotion regulation. *Developmental Psychology, 25*, 394–402.

Clark, L.A. & Watson, D. (1988). Mood and the mundane: Relations between daily life events and self-reported mood. *Journal of Personality and Social Psychology, 54*, 296–308.

Clark, L.A., Watson, D. & Mineka, S. (1994). Temperament, personality, and the mood and anxiety disorders. *Special Issue: Personality and Psychopathology. Journal of Abnormal Psychology, 103*, 103–116.

Cohn, J.F., Campbell, S.B., Matias, R. & Hopkins, J. (1990). Face-to-face interactions of postpartum depressed and nondepressed mother–infant pairs at 2 months. *Developmental Psychology, 26*, 15–23.

Collins, N.L. & Read, S.J. (1990). Adult attachment, working models, and relationship quality in dating couples. *Journal of Personality and Social Psychology, 58*, 644–663.

Coyne, J.C. (1976). Toward an interactional description of depression. *Psychiatry, 39*, 28–40.

Darwin, C. (1872). *The Expression of Emotions in Man and Animals*. New York: Philosophical Library.

Davidson, R.J. (1998). Affective style and affective disorders: Perspectives from affective neuroscience. *Cognition and Emotion, 12*, 307–330.

Davidson, R.J., Jackson, D.C. & Kalin, N.H (2000). Emotion, plasticity, context, and regulation: Perspectives from affective neuroscience. *Psychological Bulletin, 126*, 890–909.

Davis, D. (1982). Determinants of responsiveness in dyadic interaction. In W. Ickes & E.S. Knowles (Eds), *Personality, Roles, and Social Behavior* (pp. 85–139). New York: Springer-Verlag.

Davis, G.C., Buchsbaum, M.D. & Bunney, W.E. (1979). Analgesia to painful stimuli in affective illness. *American Journal of Psychiatry, 136*, 1148–1151.

Dawson, M.E., Schell, A.M. & Catania, J.J. (1977). Autonomic correlates of depression and clinical improvement following electroconvulsive shock therapy. *Psychophysiology, 14*, 569–578.

Deldin, P.J., Keller, J., Gergen, J.A. & Miller, G.A. (2001). Cognitive bias and emotion in neuropsychological models of depression. *Cognition and Emotion, 15*, 787–802.

Depue, R.A. & Iacono, W.G. (1989). Neurobehavioral aspects of affective disorders. *Annual Review of Psychology, 40*, 457–492.

Dworkin, R.H., Clark, W.C. & Lipsitz, J.D. (1995). Pain responsivity in major depression and bipolar disorder. *Psychiatry Research, 56*, 173–181.

Ekman, P. (1992). An argument for basic emotions. *Cognition and Emotion, 6*, 169–200.

Ekman, P. (1993). Facial expression and emotion. *American Psychologist, 48*, 384–392.

Fowles, D.C. (1988). Psychophysiology and psychopathology: A motivational approach. *Psychophysiology, 25*, 373–391.

Fridja, N. (1986). *The Emotions*. Cambridge: Cambridge University Press.

Fridlund, A.J. (1992). The behavioral ecology and sociality of human faces. In M.S. Clark (Ed.), *Emotion* (pp. 190–221). Newbury Park, CA: Sage.

Gable S.L., Reis H.T. & Elliot A.J. (2000). Behavioral activation and inhibition in everyday life. *Journal of Personality and Social Psychology, 78*, 1135–1149.

Gehricke, J.G. & Shapiro, D. (2000). Reduced facial expression and social context in major depression: Discrepancies between facial muscle activity and self-reported emotion. *Psychiatry Research, 95*, 157–167.

Gilbert, P. & Trower, P. (1990). The evolution and manifestation of social anxiety. In W.R. Crozier (Ed.), *Shyness and Embarrassment* (pp. 144–177). New York: Cambridge University Press.

Goodman, S.H., Adamson, L.B., Riniti, J. & Cole, S. (1994). Mothers' expressed attitudes: Associations with maternal depression and children's self-esteem and psychopathology. *Journal of the American Academy of Child and Adolescent Psychiatry, 33*, 1265–1274.

Gotlib, I.H. (1982). Self-reinforcement and depression in interpersonal interaction: The role of performance level. *Journal of Abnormal Psychology, 91*, 3–13.

Gotlib, I.H. & Goodman, S.H. (1999). Children of parents with depression. In W.K. Silverman & T.H. Ollendick (Eds), *Developmental Issues in the Clinical Treatment of Children* (pp. 415–432). Boston, MA: Allyn & Bacon.

Gotlib, I.H. & Hammen, C.L. (1992). *Psychological Aspects of Depression: Toward a Cognitive-Interpersonal Integration*. New York: Wiley.

Gotlib, I.H. & Hammen, C.L. (Eds) (2002). *Handbook of Depression*. New York: Guilford.

Gotlib, I.H. & Lee, C.M. (1989). The social functioning of depressed patients: A longitudinal assessment. *Journal of Social and Clinical Psychology, 8*, 223–237.

Gotlib, I.H. & Robinson, L.A. (1982). Responses to depressed individuals: Discrepancies between self-report and observer-rated behavior. *Journal of Abnormal Psychology, 91*, 231–240.

Gotlib, I.H., Mount, J.H., Cordy, N.I. & Whiffen, V.E. (1988). Depressed mood and perceptions of early parenting: A longitudinal investigation. *British Journal of Psychiatry, 152*, 24–27.

Gotlib, I.H., Sivers, H., Canli, T., Kasch, K.L. & Gabrieli, J.D.E. (November, 2001). Neural activation in depression in response to emotional stimuli. In I.H. Gotlib (Chair), New Directions in the Neurobiology of Affective Disorders. Symposium presented at the Annual Meeting of the Society for Research in Psychopathology, Madison, Wisconsin.

Gray, J.A. (1982). *The Neuropsychology of Anxiety: An Enquiry into the Functions of the Septo-Hippocampal System.* Oxford: Oxford University Press.

Greden, J.F., Genero, N., Price, H.L., Feinberg, M. & Levine, S. (1986). Facial electromyography in depression. *Archives of General Psychiatry, 43*, 269–274.

Gross, J.J., Frederickson, B.L. & Levenson, R.W. (1994). The psychophysiology of crying. *Psychophysiology, 31*, 460–468.

Hall, K.R. & Stride, E. (1954). The varying response to pain in psychiatric disorders. A study of abnormal psychology. *British Journal of Medical Psychology, 27*, 48–60.

Hargreaves, W., Starkweather, J. & Blacker, K. (1965). Voice quality in depression. *Journal of Abnormal Psychology, 70*, 218–229.

Hemphill, R.E., Hall, K.R.L. & Crookes, T.G. (1952). A preliminary report on fatigue and pain tolerance in depressive and psychoneurotic patients. *Journal of Mental Science, 98*, 433–440.

Henderson, A.S., Byrne, D.G. & Duncan-Jones, P. (1981). *Neurosis and the Social Environment.* Sydney: Academic Press.

Henriques, J.B. & Davidson, R.J. (1990). Regional brain electrical asymmetries discriminate between previously depressed and healthy control subjects. *Journal of Abnormal Psychology, 99*, 22–31.

Henriques, J.B. & Davidson, R.J. (1991). Left frontal hypoactivation in depression. *Journal of Abnormal Psychology, 100*, 535–545.

Henriques, J.B. & Davidson R.J. (2000). Decreased responsiveness to reward in depression. *Cognition and Emotion, 14*, 711–724.

Higgins, E.T. (1997). Beyond pleasure and pain. *American Psychologist, 52*, 1280–1300.

Hirschfeld, R.M.A., Montgomery, S.A., Keller, M.B., et al. (2000). Social functioning in depression: A review. *Journal of Clinical Psychiatry, 61*, 268–275.

Hokanson, J.E., Sacco, W.P., Blumberg, S.R. & Landrum, G.C. (1980). Interpersonal behavior in depressive individuals in a mixed-motive game. *Journal of Abnormal Psychology, 89*, 320–332.

Hooley, J.M. & Gotlib, I.H. (2000). A diathesis-stress conceptualization of expressed emotion and clinical outcome. *Journal of Applied and Preventive Psychology, 9*, 135–151.

Hops, H., Biglan, A., Sherman, L., Arthur, J., Friedman, L. & Osteen, V. (1987). Home observations of family interactions of depressed women. *Journal of Consulting and Clinical Psychology, 55*, 341–346.

Jacobson, N.S. & Anderson, E.A. (1982). Interpersonal skill and depression in college students: An analysis of the timing of self-disclosures. *Behavior Therapy, 13*, 271–282.

Joiner, T.E. (2002). Depression in its interpersonal context. In I.H. Gotlib & C.L. Hammen (Eds), *Handbook of Depression* (pp. 295–313). New York: Guilford.

Jorm, A.F., Christensen, H., Henderson, A.S., Jacomb, P.A., Korten, E. & Rodgers, B. (1999). Using the BIS/BAS scales to measure behavioural inhibition and behavioural activation: Factor structure, validity and norms in a large community sample. *Personality and Individual Differences, 26*, 49–58.

Kagan, J. (1998). *Galen's Prophecy: Temperament in Human Nature.* Boulder, CO: Westview Press.

Kasch, K.L., Rottenberg, J., Arnow, B.A. & Gotlib, I.H. (2002). Behavioral activation and inhibition systems and the severity and course of depression. *Journal of Abnormal Psychology.*

Keltner, D. & Bonnano, G.A. (1997). A study of laughter and dissociation: Distinct correlates of laughter and smiling during bereavement. *Journal of Personality and Social Psychology, 73*, 687–702.

Keltner, D. & Buswell, B.N. (1997). Embarrassment: Its distinct form and appeasement functions. *Psychological Bulletin, 122*, 250–270.

Keltner, D. & Haidt, J. (1999). Social functions of emotions at four levels of analysis. *Cognition and Emotion Special Issue: Functional Accounts of Emotion, 13*, 505–521.

Keltner, D. & Kring, A.M. (1998). Emotion, social function, and psychopathology. *Review of General Psychology, 2*, 320–342.

Klerman, G.L., Weissman, M.M., Rounsaville, B.J. & Chevron, E.S. (1984). *Interpersonal Therapy for Depression*. New York: Basic Books.

Kring, A.M. & Bachorowski, J. (1999). Emotions and psychopathology. Special Issue: Functional Accounts of Emotion. *Cognition and Emotion, 13*, 575–599.

Kulhara, P. & Chadda, R.A. (1987). A study of negative symptoms in schizophrenia and depression. *Comprehensive Psychiatry, 28*, 229–235.

Lang, P.J. (1978). Anxiety: Toward a psychophysiological definition. In H.S. Akiskal & W.L. Webb (Eds), *Psychiatric Diagnosis: Exploration of Biological Criteria* (pp. 265–389). New York: Spectrum.

Lang, P.J. (1995). The emotion probe: Studies of motivation and attention. *American Psychologist, 50*, 372–385.

Lautenbacher, S., Roscher, S., Strian, D., Fassbender, K. & Krumrey, K., & Krieg, J.C. (1994). Pain perception in depression: Relationships to symptomatology and naloxone-sensitive mechanisms. *Psychosomatic Medicine, 56*, 345–352.

Lautenbacher, S., Spernal, J., Schreiber, W. & Krieg, J. (1999). Relationship between clinical pain complaints and pain sensitivity in patients with depression and panic disorder. *Psychosomatic Medicine, 61*, 822–827.

Lazarus, R.S. (1991). *Emotion and Adaptation*. New York: Oxford University Press.

Lewinsohn, P.M. (1974). A behavioral approach to depression. In R.J. Friedman & M.M. Katz (Eds), *The Psychology of Depression: Contemporary Theory and Research* (pp. 157–178). Washington, DC: Winston-Wiley.

Lewinsohn, P.M., Lobitz, W.C. & Wilson, S. (1973). "Sensitivity" of depressed individuals to aversive stimuli. *Journal of Abnormal Psychology, 81*, 259–263.

Libet, J.M. & Lewinsohn, P.M. (1973). Concept of social skill with special reference to the behavior of depressed persons. *Journal of Consulting and Clinical Psychology, 40*, 304–312.

Merskey, H. (1965). The effect of chronic pain upon the response to noxious stimuli by psychiatric patients. *Journal of Psychosomatic Research, 8*, 405–419.

Miller, R.S. (1987). Empathic embarrassment: Situational and personal determinants of reactions to the embarrassment of another. *Special Issue: Integrating Personality and Social Psychology. Journal of Personality and Social Psychology, 53*, 1061–1069.

Nesse, R.M. (2000). Is depression an adaptation? *Archives of General Psychiatry, 57*, 14–20.

Oehman, A. (1986). Face the beast and fear the face: Animal and social fears as prototypes for evolutionary analyses of emotion. *Psychophysiology, 23*, 123–145.

Provine, R.R. (1992). Contagious laughter: Laughter is a sufficient stimulus for laughs and smiles. *Bulletin of the Psychonomic Society, 30*, 1–4.

Rosenbaum, J., Biederman, J., Hirshfeld-Becker, D.R., et al. (2000). A controlled study of behavioral inhibition in children of parents with panic disorder and depression. *American Journal of Psychiatry, 157*, 2002–2010.

Rottenberg, J., Kasch, K.L., Gross, J.J. & Gotlib, I.H. (2002). Sadness and amusement reactivity differentially predict concurrent and prospective functioning in major depressive disorder. *Emotion, 2*, 135–146.

Rottenberg, J., Gross, J.J., Wilhelm, F.H., Najmi, S. & Gotlib, I.H. (2002). Crying threshold and intensity in major depressive disorder. *Journal of Abnormal Psychology, 111*, 302–312.

Scherer, K.R. (1986). Vocal affect expression: A review and a model for future research. *Psychological Bulletin, 99*, 143–165.

Scherer, K.R., Wallbott, H.G. & Summerfield, A.B. (Eds) (1986). *Experiencing Emotion: A Cross-Cultural Study*. New York: Cambridge University Press.

Segrin, C. (2000). Social skills deficits associated with depression. *Clinical Psychology Review, 20*, 379–403.

Segrin, C. & Abramson, L.Y. (1994). Negative reactions to depressive behaviors: A communication theories analysis. *Journal of Abnormal Psychology, 103*, 655–668.

Segrin, C. & Flora, J. (1998). Depression and verbal behavior in conversations with friends and strangers. *Journal of Language and Social Psychology, 17*, 492–503.

Sloan, D.M., Strauss, M.E., Quirk, S.W. & Sajatovic, M. (1997). Subjective and expressive emotional responses in depression. *Journal of Affective Disorders, 46*, 135–141.

Sloan, D.M., Strauss, M.E. & Wisner, K.L. (2001). Diminished response to pleasant stimuli by depressed women. *Journal of Abnormal Psychology, 110*, 488–493.

Talavera, J.A., Saz-Ruiz, J. & Garcia-Toro, M. (1994). Quantitative measurement of depression through speech analysis. *European Psychiatry, 9*, 185–193.

Teasdale, J.D., Fogarty, S.J. & Williams, J.M. (1980). Speech rate as a measure of short-term variation in depression. *British Journal of Social and Clinical Psychology, 19*, 271–278.

Tooby, J. & Cosmides, L. (1990). The past explains the present: Emotional adaptations and the structure of ancestral environments. *Ethology and Sociobiology, 11*, 375–424.

Von Knorring, L. & Espvall, M. (1974). Experimentally induced pain in patients with depressive disorders. *Acta Psychiatrica Scandinavica*, Suppl. *255*, 121–134.

Watson, D., Wiese, D., Vaidya, J. & Tellegen, A. (1999). The two general activation systems of affect: Structural findings, evolutionary considerations, and psychobiological evidence. *Journal of Personality and Social Psychology, 76*, 820–838.

Wexler, B.E., Levenson, L., Warrenburg, S. & Price, L.H. (1993). Decreased perceptual sensitive to emotion-evoking stimuli in depression. *Psychiatry Research, 51*, 127–138.

Whisman, M.A. (2001). The association between depression and marital dissatisfaction. In S.R.H. Beach (Ed.), *Marital and Family Processes in Depression: A Scientific Foundation for Clinical Practice*. Washington, DC: American Psychological Association.

Youngren, M.A. & Lewinsohn, P.M. (1980). The functional relationship between depression and problematic behavior. *Journal of Abnormal Psychology, 89*, 333–341.

Zahn-Waxler, C., Radke-Yarrow, M., Wagner, E. & Chapman, M. (1992). Development of concern for others. *Developmental Psychology, 28*, 126–136.

5

DEVELOPMENTAL PERSPECTIVES ON DEPRESSION IN YOUNG PEOPLE*

Richard Harrington

INTRODUCTION: WHAT IS A DEVELOPMENTAL PERSPECTIVE?

During the past two decades, developmental psychopathology, which is the study of the origins and course of individual patterns of behavioural maladaptation, has emerged as a new science. It brings together and integrates a variety of disciplines, including epidemiology, genetics, psychiatry, psychology, the neurosciences, and sociology. There are many features of developmental psychopathology that could make it important, but the defining features can be reduced to three key issues (Rutter & Sroufe, 2000). The first central concept, which is at the core of much developmental research, is an emphasis on understanding the processes of development, of investigating the emergence of patterns of adaptation and maladaptation over time. Developmental analyses tend therefore to be progressive, with one step leading to another. It is recognized that the mechanisms involved in causation may involve dynamic processes over time, with several routes to the same outcome. It is also recognized that development comprises not only continuities over time, but also discontinuities. It is important to understand, for example, why depressive phenomena seem to be less prevalent at some developmental stages than others.

The second key concept is a focus on the understanding of causal processes. It is now widely understood that most mental disorders are not due to single linear causes. Individual risk factors are seldom that powerful. More often, psychopathology arises from the complex interplay of multiple risk and protective factors, some genetic and others environmental. A third key concern has been a focus on the links between normality and pathology. Much causal research in psychiatry has been based on the idea that diagnostic categories represent some kind of reality or "truth" distinct from normal behaviour. By contrast, many developmental psychopathological concepts are dimensional, with the need to take account of variations along dimensions.

---

* This chapter contains extracts previously published in Harrington, R. & Dubicka, B. (2001). Natural history of mood disorders in children and adolescents. Chapter 13 in I.M. Goodyer (Ed.) *The Depressed Child and Adolescent* (2nd edn), Cambridge University Press. Reproduced with permission.

Mood Disorders: A Handbook of Science and Practice. Edited by M. Power.
© 2004 John Wiley & Sons, Ltd. ISBN 0-470-84390-X.

The present chapter presents a developmental perspective on depression, with a particular focus on depression among children and adolescents. The chapter is divided into six parts. The first describes briefly the clinical features and assessment of depressive conditions among the young, the second reviews continuities of these disorders over time, and the third reviews the processes involved in continuity. The fourth section looks at the issue of discontinuity, and the factors that might protect young people from further problems. The fifth reviews the links between depression as a disorder and depressive symptoms. The chapter concludes with a review of some of the implications for treatment and prevention.

DIAGNOSIS OF DEPRESSION IN YOUNG PEOPLE

Concepts of depression

The concept of a depressive syndrome that is distinct from the broad class of other child and adolescent emotional disorders has a relatively short history. Until the 1970s, it was believed that depressive disorders resembling adult depression were uncommon among the young. Children were thought incapable of experiencing depression. Depression in older adolescents was often seen as a normal feature of development, so-called adolescent turmoil. However, in the 1970s and early 1980s, several investigators began to diagnose depression in young people by adult criteria (Pearce, 1978; Puig-Antich, 1982; Weinberg et al., 1973). These studies showed that conditions resembling adult depression could occur from middle childhood upwards. Indeed, recent epidemiological studies have reported that as many as one in 10 adolescent girls suffer from depressive disorders (Angold et al., 1999; Olsson & von Knorring, 1999).

Since these estimates come from the application of operational criteria in the *Diagnostic and Statistical Manual of Mental Disorders* (American Psychiatric Association, 1987; 1994), which states that the core symptoms of depression in young people are the same as adults, it might be thought that any remaining doubts about the validity of the concept had been dispelled. However, there are still uncertainties.

Issues in the diagnosis of depression among the young

Defining the boundaries between extremes of normal behaviour and psychopathology is a dilemma that pervades all of psychiatry. It is especially problematic to establish the limits of depressive disorder in young people because of the cognitive and physical changes that take place during this time. Adolescents tend to feel things particularly deeply, and marked mood swings are common during the teens (Rutter et al., 1976). It can be difficult to distinguish these intense emotional reactions from depressive disorders. By contrast, young children do not find it easy to describe how they are feeling and often confuse emotions such as anger and sadness (Kovacs, 1986). They have particular difficulty in describing certain of the key cognitive symptoms of depression, such as hopelessness and self-denigration. Indeed, there are developmental changes in many of the cognitive abilities that may underlie these depressive cognitions. Thus, for instance, during middle childhood (age 7–9 years), the self is conceived in outward, physical terms. If asked to describe themselves, children of this age will tend to frame their descriptions in terms of external characteristics, or what they do. It is only by adolescence that young people regularly describe themselves in terms of psychological characteristics.

A further issue arises from the fact that all epidemiological studies conducted up to now have found that depressive disorder very commonly occurs in conjunction with other psychiatric problems. Indeed, one of the best discriminators in community studies between children with any form of psychiatric disorder and children with no psychiatric disorder is the symptom of depression (Rutter et al., 1970). Moreover, some of the symptoms that are part of the depressive constellation may arise as a symptom of other disorders. Thus, restlessness is seen in agitated depression, hypomania, and hyperkinetic syndrome. As a general rule, the double diagnosis should be made only when symptoms that are not simply part of another disorder clearly indicate the separate presence of a depressive disorder.

CONTINUITIES AND DISCONTINUITIES IN DEPRESSION

Continuities in the short term

Many studies of clinical samples have reported that young people with a depressive disorder have a high risk of recurrence or persistence (Asarnow et al., 1988; Emslie et al., 1997b; Goodyer et al., 1991; 1997b; Kovacs et al., 1984a; McCauley et al., 1993). For example, Kovacs and colleagues (Kovacs et al., 1984a) undertook a systematic follow-up of child patients with a major depressive disorder, a dysthymic disorder, an adjustment disorder with depressed mood, and some other psychiatric disorder. The development of subsequent episodes of depression was virtually confined to children with major depressive disorders and dysthymic disorders. Thus, within the first year at risk, 26% of children who had recovered from major depression had had another episode; by 2 years this figure had risen to 40%; and by 5 years the effected cohort ran a 72% risk of another episode! On long-term follow-up, major depression and dysthymia were associated with similar rates of most outcomes (Kovacs et al., 1994).

Surveys of community samples have generally also found that depressive disorders among young people tend to be recurrent (Fleming et al., 1993; Garrison et al., 1997; Lewinsohn et al., 1993; 1994a; McGee et al., 1992; McGee & Williams, 1988). For instance, Lewinsohn et al. (1993; 1994a) found that the 1-year relapse rate for unipolar depression (18.4%) was much higher than the relapse rate found in most other disorders. Interestingly, among adolescents in that study who experienced two episodes of depression, there was low concordance across episodes in the symptoms of depression (Roberts et al., 1995). Only one community study has failed to find significant continuity for depressive disorder (Cohen et al., 1993a; 1993b).

Similarly, investigators of the short-term stability of questionnaire ratings of depressive *symptoms* in community samples of young people have also found significant correlations over time (Charman, 1994; Edelsohn et al., 1992; Garrison et al., 1990; Larsson et al., 1991; Stanger et al., 1992).

Continuities in the long term

It seems, then, that both depressive symptoms and depressive disorder show significant continuity over time. Do these continuities extend into adulthood? The available data suggest that they do. Harrington et al. (1990) followed up 63 depressed children and adolescents on average 18 years after their initial contact. The depressed group had a substantially greater risk of depression after the age of 17 years than a control group who had been matched on a large number of variables, including non-depressive symptoms and measures of social impairment. This increased risk was maintained well into adulthood and was associated with significantly increased rates of attending psychiatric services and of using medication, as compared to the controls. Depressed children were no more likely than the control children to suffer non-depressive disorders in adulthood, suggesting that the risk of adult depression was specific and unrelated to comorbidity with other psychiatric problems. Rao et al. (1995) also found high rates of recurrence of major depression in a clinical sample of depressed adolescents who were followed up 7 years later. Weissman and colleagues reported similar findings (Weissman et al., 1999).

Continuity from childhood into adult life has also been found in community surveys, such as the Dunedin Multidisciplinary Health and Development Study (DMHDS). In the DMHDS, mental health data were gathered at ages 11, 13, 15, 18, and 21 years. Follow-back longitudinal analyses found that subjects with a mood disorder at age 21 years were much more likely to have a history of previous mood disorder than of non-depressive disorders earlier in life (Newman et al., 1996). Similarly, prospective longitudinal analyses from the Oregon Adolescent Depression Project (Lewinsohn et al., 1999) found significant continuity from late adolescence (age 17 years) into early adult life (age 24 years). Thus, major depression in young adulthood was significantly more common in subjects who had had major depression in late adolescence than subjects who had had non-affective mental disorders or no psychiatric disorder (average annual rate 9.0%, 5.6%, and 3.7%, respectively). About 45% of adolescents with a history of major depression developed a new episode of depression between the ages of 19 and 24. In the New York longitudinal study (Cohen et al., 1993a; 1993b), anxiety or depression in adolescence predicted anxiety or depression in early adult life (Pine et al., 1998). Most adult anxiety or depression was preceded by earlier anxiety or depression. The British birth cohort follow-up of individuals born in 1946 found that evidence of affective disturbance at ages 13 and 15 years was a strong predictor of major affective disorder in middle life (Os et al., 1997).

Subsequent social impairment

There are a number of reasons for thinking that early-onset depression might not only predict further depression, but also could be associated with effects on social and cognitive functioning. Thus, depression in young people is frequently accompanied by social withdrawal and irritability, and so depressed youngsters may find it more difficult to establish and maintain social relationships. In addition, symptoms such as loss of concentration and psychomotor retardation may interfere with the process of learning. This, in turn, might lead to low self-esteem and so on to further academic failure. Kovacs and Goldston (1991) pointed out that young people suffering from major depression are impaired for a significant proportion of the lifespan, and they are handicapped at a time when learning takes place rapidly. Perhaps, then, they will eventually show cognitive as well as social delays.

Several studies have examined the social outcomes of depressed young people. In one of the first systematic studies, Puig-Antich and his colleagues (Puig-Antich et al., 1985a; 1985b) found that impairment of peer relationships persisted for several months after recovery from depression. In the longer term, Kandel and Davies (1986) reported that self-ratings of dysphoria in adolescence were associated with heavy cigarette smoking, greater involvement in delinquent activities, and impairment of intimate relationships as young adults. Garber et al. (1988) found that depressed adolescent inpatients reported more marital and relationship problems when they were followed-up 8 years after discharge than non-depressed psychiatric control subjects.

These findings have important theoretical as well as clinical implications since they suggest that the social isolation and lack of a supporting relationship that have been found in cross-sectional studies of adult depression (Brown & Harris, 1978) may reflect social selection as much as social causation. However, none of these studies excluded the effects that childhood conduct problems, which are commonly associated with adolescent depression, could have on these outcomes. Harrington et al. (1991) found that juvenile depression seemed to have little direct impact on social functioning in adulthood, whereas comorbid conduct disorder was a strong predictor of subsequent social maladjustment. Similar findings were reported by Renouf and colleagues (Renouf et al., 1997) in an intensive longitudinal study of depressed children and non-depressed psychiatric controls. Social dysfunction associated with comorbid depression and conduct disorder seemed to be mainly related to the effects of conduct disorder. Bardone et al. (1998) found that adolescent conduct disorder predicted more smoking, sexually transmitted diseases, and early pregnancy in adult life. Adolescent depression only predicted tobacco dependence and more medical problems. The implication is that it is important to differentiate the course of depressive disorder from the course of other, comorbid disorders.

PROCESSES INVOLVED IN CONTINUITY

Direct persistence of the initial depression

The review thus far suggests that depression in young people is associated with a variety of adverse outcomes, particularly further episodes of depression and suicidal behaviour. What processes could underpin these strong continuities over time? The first point is that the strength and specificity of the continuities clearly support the idea that in some cases there may be *direct* persistence of the initial depression. At first sight, the finding that most cases of major depression among the young remit within a year (see below) would seem to suggest that direct persistence is uncommon. However, a detailed, 12-year prospective study of adults who had presented with major depression found that while only 15% had major depressive disorder (MDD)-level symptoms during the follow-up, 43% had subthreshold depression (Judd et al., 1998). The same may apply to depression in young people; major depression and dysthymia often overlap and one can lead to the other (Kovacs et al., 1994). The symptomatic course of depression seems to be malleable, and symptoms of major depression, dysthymia, and minor depression alternate over time in the same patients.

Scarring or sensitization

Another potential mechanism of continuity is that individuals are changed in one way or another by their first episode, so that they become more likely to have subsequent ones.

This notion, sometimes referred to as *"scarring"* or *"sensitization"*, has attracted a good deal of attention from investigators of the neurobiological (Post, 1992) and psychological (Rohde et al., 1990) processes that may be involved in the relapsing and remitting course of depression in adults. Post and colleagues (Post, 1992), for instance, have suggested that the first depressive episode may sensitize people to further episodes. They hypothesized that such sensitization may help to explain three characteristics of depression in adults: the tendency to recur, the decreasing length of interval between episodes, and the greater role of psychosocial stress at the first episode. The idea is that the first episode of depression, which can often be linked to a psychosocial stressor, is associated with long-lasting changes in biology and responsivity to stressors. There may be biochemical and microstructural changes in the central nervous system that put the individual at risk of further episodes (Post et al., 1996).

The idea of scarring may also be relevant to depression in young people. Lewinsohn and colleagues (Lewinsohn et al., 1994b) found in cross-sectional comparisons that formerly depressed individuals shared many psychosocial characteristics with depressed individuals. A subsequent prospective study by the same research group identified 45 adolescents who experienced and recovered from a first episode of depression between two assessment points (Rohde et al., 1994). Psychosocial scars (characteristics evident after but not before the episode) included stressful life events, excessive emotional reliance on others, and subsyndromal depressive symptoms. This level of scarring was more severe than that found in previous research by the same team with depressed adults.

Cognitive vulnerability

Scarring should be distinguished from the related concept of vulnerability, in which the predisposition to depression precedes the first episode.

Two types of cognitive problem are thought to make young people vulnerable to depression: (a) general cognitive deficits, such as reading retardation or low intelligence, and (b) cognitive distortions, such as a negative attributional style, that are believed to be specific to depression.

There may be early neurodevelopmental precursors of affective illness in both childhood and adult life. In a retrospective study of hospital records, Sigurdsson et al. (1999) found that adolescents with severe affective disorders (bipolar, manic, or psychotic depression) were significantly more likely to have experienced delayed language, social, or motor development. Associations between childhood developmental problems (such as low cognitive ability) and affective disorder were studied prospectively in the British 1956 national birth cohort study (Os et al., 1997). Affective disorder was assessed at interview when subjects were aged 36 and 43 years. Teacher questionnaires at ages 13 and 15 years also identified subjects with evidence of affective disturbance. Early cognitive ability independently predicted both adolescent affective disturbance and affective disorder in adult life. So, continuity could be due to an underlying neurodevelopmental problem that increases the liability to depression in both childhood and adult life.

Biological vulnerability

The search for evidence of biological indices has up to now been focused on the kinds of markers that have been studied in depressed adults, such as abnormalities of cortisol physiology (Casat & Powell, 1988), melatonin (Shafii et al., 1996), thyroid-hormone levels (Dorn et al., 1996; Kutcher et al., 1991), sleep (Emslie et al., 1987), and brain imaging (Steingard et al., 1996). Several studies have shown that, in comparison with non-depressed patients, depressed young people are less likely to show suppression of cortisol secretion when the exogenous corticosteroid dexamethasone is administered (Casat & Powell, 1988) and more likely to have sleep abnormalities (Appelboom-Fondu et al., 1988; Cashman et al., 1986; Emslie et al., 1987; Kutcher et al., 1992; Lahmeyer et al., 1983; Riemann & Schmidt, 1993).

There has been very little longitudinal research on most of these measures. There is, however, some evidence that cortisol levels predict subsequent depression. Goodyer and colleagues (Goodyer et al., 1998) found that higher cortisol/DHEA levels at night predicted both the persistence of major depression and subsequent disappointing life events. They hypothesized that adrenal steroids might be involved in abnormal cognitive or emotional processes associated with the continuation of disturbed interpersonal behaviour. Susman et al. (1997) reported that adolescents who showed increased cortisol levels in a challenging situation had higher levels of depressive symptoms a year later than adolescents whose cortisol did not change or decreased.

Family-genetic vulnerability

The offspring of depressed parents are at greatly increased risk of depression, especially in childhood and early adult life (Wickramaratne & Weissman, 1998). Many other forms of psychopathology are increased among these children (Wickramaratne & Weissman, 1998), and they are also at increased risk of medical problems (Kramer et al., 1998). Several prospective longitudinal studies have suggested that these increased risks extend for many years (Beardslee et al., 1993; Hammen, 1991; Weissman et al., 1997). For example, Weissman and her colleagues (Weissman et al., 1997) evaluated the effects of parental depression on offspring over a 10-year period. High rates of depression, panic disorder, and alcoholism were found among the children.

There is evidence that affective disorders in adults have a genetic component. Genetic influences seem strongest for bipolar disorders (McGuffin & Katz, 1986), but unipolar major depressions also show significant heritability (Kendler et al., 1993), as do seasonal affective disorders (Madden et al., 1996). There have thus far been no large systematic twin or adoption studies of depressive disorder in young people. There is, however, evidence from twin studies of modest genetic influences on depressive symptoms in late childhood and adolescence (Eaves et al., 1997; Thapar & McGuffin, 1994), though this has not been replicated in adoption studies (Eley et al., 1998). Twin studies also suggest that some of the stability in depressive symptoms arises from genetic factors (O'Connor et al., 1998).

Family environment

It is likely, however, that family environment also plays an important role in continuities. Some kinds of family adversity, such as marital discord, can be highly persistent (Richman et al., 1982; Rutter & Quinton, 1984), and there is growing evidence of the relevance of these factors to continuities of depressive disorders in young people. For example, Hammen and colleagues found a close temporal relationship between episodes of depression in children and episodes of depression in the mother (Hammen et al., 1991). Fergusson et al. (1995) reported that maternal depression was only associated with depressive symptoms in adolescent offspring insofar as maternal depression was associated with social disadvantage or family adversity. Depression in parents is associated with many problems that could lead to depression in offspring, including impaired child management practices, insecure attachment, poor marital functioning, and hostility towards the child (Cummings & Davies, 1994). Indeed, Asarnow and colleagues reported (Asarnow et al., 1993) that relapse of depression after discharge from a psychiatric inpatient sample was virtually confined to children who returned to a home environment characterized by high expressed emotion and hostility. Goodyer et al. (1997c) found that family dysfunction and lack of a confiding relationship with the mother predicted persistent psychiatric disorder in a sample with major depression.

Other environments

Other kinds of adverse experience may also contribute to the persistence of depression. For example, events such as physical assault or sexual abuse are strongly associated with subsequent depressive symptoms, even when the association of both with previous symptoms and family relationship problems is controlled statistically (Boney-McCoy & Finkelhor, 1996). A history of childhood physical or sexual abuse may be associated with a particular pattern of reversed neurovegetative depressive symptoms, such as increased appetite and hypersomnia (Levitan et al., 1998). Poor peer relationships are also associated with persistence of depression (Goodyer et al., 1997c).

Role of comorbidity with nondepressive psychopathology

Several studies have reported that comorbidity with non-depressive disorders predicts a worse outcome for juvenile depressive disorder (Goodyer et al., 1997a; Kovacs et al., 1997; Sandford et al., 1995). For instance, Kovacs et al. (1997) found that comorbid externalizing disorder predicted a much more protracted recovery from dysthymic disorder. Goodyer et al. (1997a) reported that comorbid obsessive-compulsive disorder was associated with persistence of major depression at 36 weeks' follow-up.

Combinations of risk factors

It seems, then, that the risk of further episodes of depression is predicted by many factors. It is likely that it is the combination of several of these risk factors that poses the greatest risk. Thus, for instance, Beardslee et al. (1996) examined risk factors for affective disorder within a random sample of 139 adolescents. Single risk factors such as parental major depression, parental non-affective diagnosis, or a previous child psychiatric diagnosis increased the risk of subsequent affective disorder from 7% to 18%. However, when all three risk factors were present, the risk jumped to 50%!

It is not clear whether the factors that lead to continuity simply add up, or whether there is some kind of interaction such that some risk factors operate only in the presence of others. There is some evidence of such interactions in adult depression. For instance, studies of major depression in women suggest that genetic influences may alter the sensitivity of individuals to the depression-inducing effect of adverse life events (Kendler et al., 1995). In other cases, it seems as if people act in ways that increase their likelihood of adversity, a pattern which in turn increases their risk of depression. One of the best-known examples of this phenomenon comes from the research of Brown et al. (1986) with inner-city young women. They found that women who had experienced lack of care during childhood (such as abuse) were more likely to become pregnant while young. In turn, early pregnancy increased the risk of other forms of adversity, such as marrying an abusive partner. These later forms of adversity were strongly associated with depression.

Similar kinds of processes may occur in juvenile depression. Daley and colleagues (Daley et al., 1998) conducted a community study of personality functioning in older adolescents, who were then followed up for 2 years. They found that certain personality disorder features seemed to generate chronic interpersonal stress, which increased vulnerability to depression. Goodyer and Altham (1991) reported that the families of depressed girls seemed to become "life event prone" as a result of parental psychopathology. In their study, it seemed that young people became depressed when depressed parents were no longer able to protect them from adversity.

DISCONTINUITY AND RECOVERY

Developmental discontinuities

The findings thus far suggest that juvenile depressive disorders show significant continuities over time. Nevertheless, the available data also suggest that many depressed young people will *not* go on to have another episode, and so it is important to consider the reasons for *discontinuity*. There is a surprising lack of knowledge on this issue, but some limited evidence is available.

The first point to make is that there may be developmental differences in the continuity of depressive disorders. Interest in the possibility of such differences has been increased by the finding of marked age differences in the prevalence of affective phenomena such as depression, suicide, and attempted suicide (Harrington et al., 1996). Thus, for example, it seems that depressive disorders show an increase in frequency during early adolescence (Angold et al., 1998). The reasons for these age trends are still unclear, but there is some evidence that they are accompanied by developmental differences in *continuity*. Thus, in our child-to-adult follow-up of depressed young people, continuity to major depression in adulthood was significantly stronger in pubescent/postpubertal depressed probands than in prepubertal depressed subjects (Harrington et al., 1990). All five cases of bipolar disorder in adulthood occurred in the postpubertal group. Similarly, Kovacs et al. (1989) reported that among patients who had recovered from their index episode of major depression, older children would go into a new episode faster than younger ones. Other studies, too, have found that older age predicts greater persistence of depression (Goodyer et al., 1997b; Sandford et al., 1995).

What do these differences mean? Clearly, the association with age, puberty, or both suggests that maturational factors could play an important part. For example, perhaps the relative cognitive immaturity of younger children protects them from the development of cognitive "scars" arising from an episode of depression. Or, it may be that the massive changes in sex-hormone production that occur around the time of puberty are involved. However, it would be unwise to dismiss the effects of environment altogether. After all, puberty is associated not only with maturational changes but also with marked changes in social/family environment (Buchanan et al., 1992). Indeed, there is evidence that children who develop depression are more likely to be those from families in which there is much discord and expressed emotion than depressed adolescents (Harrington et al., 1997). It could be that for depression to occur at a developmentally inappropriate period (that is, early childhood), stressors need to be particularly severe.

Recovery from an episode of depression

It is important to distinguish between long-term continuities/discontinuities in the course of depressive disorders and the prognosis for the index attack. Indeed, the available data suggest that the majority of children with major depression will recover within 2 years. For example, Kovacs et al. (1984b) reported that the cumulative probability of recovery from major depression by 1 year after onset was 74% and by 2 years, 92%. The median time to recovery was about 28 weeks. This study included many subjects who had previous emotional-behavioural problems and some form of treatment, and might therefore have been biased towards the most severe cases. However, very similar results were reported by Keller et al. (1988) in a retrospective study of recovery from first episode of major depression in young people who had mostly not received treatment (Keller et al., 1991), and by Warner et al. (1992) in a study of the children of depressed parents. In a community survey, Garrison et al. (1997) found that only one-fifth of those with major depression at baseline continued to have it at 1 year. The probability of recovery for adolescent inpatients with major depression also appears to be about 90% by 2 years (Strober, 1992), though those with long-standing depression seem to recover less quickly than those whose presentation was acute (Shain et al., 1991).

How do young people recover from an episode of depression? The paucity of systematic studies among the young makes it impossible to draw firm conclusions about this issue. Indeed, even the adult literature is sparse and has for the most part been concerned with recovery in the context of treatment trials rather than with the process itself. It has provided, however, a number of pointers about the mechanisms that could be involved in young people. It may be, for instance, that environmental circumstances change. For example, perhaps there is a reduction in adversity. Alternatively, it could be that some kind of positive event needs to occur before depression will abate (Brown et al., 1992; Needles & Abramson, 1990).

There are also a number of biological explanations for the periodicity of affective disorders. It could be, for instance, that the physiological systems involved in recurrent affective conditions oscillate "endogenously". The recovery phase occurs because homeostatic mechanisms come into force in order to correct underlying biochemical imbalances. Or, it might be that there is some kind of external photic or temperature-related seasonal cue that leads to cycling. Recovery occurs when the external biological cue has ceased.

Treatment may also influence recovery from depression. There is quite a lot of evidence that some psychological therapies, particularly cognitive-behavioural therapies, are effective in mild or moderately severe depression in this age group (Harrington et al., 1998b). Pharmacological treatments, too, may be effective (Emslie et al., 1997a).

DEPRESSION AS A CATEGORY AND A DIMENSION

As described in the introduction, a third key concern of a developmental approach has been a focus on the links between normality and pathology.

Depression can be conceptualized both as a dimension and as a category (see Chapter 1). Epidemiological studies suggest that juvenile depression is a continuum that is associated with problems at most levels of severity. Even minor forms of depression are associated with social impairment (Pickles et al., 2001). Indeed, it seems that there is no "good" level of depression; it is better for an adolescent to have no symptoms of depression at all than to be averagely depressed (Harrington & Clark, 1998). Thus, in the Oregon Adolescent Depression Project, the level of psychosocial impairment increased as a direct function of the number of depressive symptoms (Lewinsohn et al., 1998). Moreover, in line with studies of adults (Angst et al., 1997), much of the morbidity associated with depression occurred in the "milder" but more numerous cases of minor depression. Mild forms of adolescent depression are a risk factor for depression in early adulthood (Pine et al., 1999). The implication is that, from the public health perspective of lowering the total burden of morbidity associated with depression, it might be better to regard depression as a continuum.

In clinical practice, however, depression is viewed not only as a dimension but also as a category. This is partly because many clinical decisions are dichotomous. For example, if a patient has a depressive disorder, a course of treatment is initiated; if not, the patient is reassured that all is well. Clinicians do not generally prescribe a little bit of antidepressant for a little bit of depression. To clinicians, then, depression usually means a diagnosis, something that a patient either does or does not have.

CLINICAL IMPLICATIONS

Implications for initial management

The time course of major depression in young people is highly regular across studies (see above). Once triggered, 50% of all episodes last around 7 months and 80% last 1 year. Only 10% or less last 2 years or longer. It is important, therefore, that clinicians enquire carefully about the duration of depressive symptoms. Patients who present shortly after the onset of symptoms have a good chance of recovering within the next few months. In such cases, a sensible initial approach might consist of a relatively brief intervention, especially as there is evidence that the response rate to inactive interventions or placebo is around 30–40% (Harrington et al., 1998a; Hazell et al., 1995). By contrast, those who present for treatment after, say, 6 months may be less likely to recover spontaneously within the next 4 weeks. In such cases, there is a stronger case for initiating an intensive form of treatment straight away.

Need for continuation and maintenance treatments

There has been widespread agreement on the finding that juvenile affective disorders tend to be recurrent. This finding is important because it has been taught for many years that while behavioural difficulties such as conduct disorders show strong continuity over time, "emotional" problems among the young tend to be short-lived. The studies described here suggest that this view is mistaken, at least so far as clinical cases of depressive disorders are concerned. They are associated with considerable impairment of psychosocial functioning, and in severe cases vulnerability extends into adult life.

It is apparent, then, that both assessment and treatment need to be viewed as extending over a prolonged period of time. Young people with severe depressive disorders are likely to have another episode, and so it is important that we develop effective prophylactic treatments. But for how long should these treatments continue? Research with depressed adults distinguishes between the need for continuation treatments and maintenance treatments. The idea behind continuation treatments is that although treatment may suppress the acute symptoms of depression, studies of the natural history suggest that the underlying illness process is continuing. Thus, for example, untreated major depression in adolescents often lasts for many months (see above). Treatment therefore needs to continue until the hypothesized underlying episode has finished. There have been no randomized trials of continuation treatments for juvenile depressive disorders. However, data from a non-randomized trial with depressed adolescents suggest that continuing psychological treatment for 6 months after remission is feasible and may be effective in preventing relapse (Kroll et al., 1996). Moreover, there is good evidence from randomized trials with depressed adults that continuation psychological and pharmacological treatments are effective (Kupfer, 1992). Most investigators therefore recommend that the treatment given during the acute episode of adolescent depression should be continued after remission, until the patient has been free of depression for around 6 months.

Maintenance treatments have a different objective, which is to prevent the development of a new episode of depression. Research with adult patients suggests that both pharmacotherapy and psychotherapy may reduce the risk of relapse if maintained for several years after the index depressive episode (Frank et al., 1990; Kupfer et al., 1992). Clearly, such treatments will be very time-consuming and expensive. At present, they cannot be contemplated for more than a small minority of depressed young people. Clinical experience suggests that indications for maintenance treatment include a history of highly recurrent depressive disorder, severely handicapping episodes of depression, and chronic major depression.

The form of maintenance treatment may vary from case to case. Since early-onset depressive disorders seem to have a significant self-perpetuating quality, there is clearly a need to help individuals to develop coping strategies that will enable them to deal with the illness in the long term. However, there is also evidence that relapses are linked to changes in environmental circumstances, especially family disturbances such as parenting difficulties and mental illness (see above). Accordingly, clinicians treating young people with depressive disorders need to assess the extent to which these factors are relevant. It may be possible to intervene therapeutically to improve patterns of family relationships. Parents who are depressed or suffering from some other form of mental disorder also need to be helped. In other words, there needs to be a concern with the family as a whole, and not just with the patient as an individual.

In patients with milder cases who are relatively well between episodes, it is important that we teach the child and his parents early recognition of the signs of a relapse, and encourage them to return to us when the first symptoms appear. Alternatively, it may be useful to see the young person from time to time for "check-ups", rather like going to the dentist.

Need for vigorous treatment of the first episode

The finding that the first episode of depression can lead to "scarring" is important because it suggests that much greater attention should be paid to the recognition and treatment of the first episode of depression. Since late adolescence is a common period for the onset of adult depressive disorders (Smith & Weissman, 1992), the implication is that child and adolescent psychiatry could have an important part to play in the prevention of depression in adulthood. Indeed, there are plenty of developmental examples of the ways in which early disorders that are not managed appropriately can lead to permanent changes in both the biology of individuals and their psychosocial functioning (Wolkind & Rutter, 1985).

Implications for preventive policies

The evidence on the course of early-onset depressive disorders also has implications for preventive policies. For example, it may be that intensive work with at-risk groups, such as the children of depressed parents, will reduce the risk of depression in the children. Unfortunately, so far, data are lacking on the extent to which primary preventive interventions are, in fact, protective, so it may be better to concentrate on the early recognition and intensive treatment of the first episode of depression (Harrington & Clark, 1998). There is some evidence that in adults the earlier the intervention, the shorter the episode (Kupfer et al., 1989). It remains to be seen whether the same will be found in juvenile depression.

Finally, it should be noted that much of the impairment associated with depression occurs below the threshold for MDD (Harrington & Clark, 1998; Pickles et al., 2001). Therefore, future preventive programmes may need to focus as much on symptoms as on disorders.

ACKNOWLEDGEMENTS

The author's research on affective disorders is currently supported by the Health Technology Assessment and the PPP Foundation. The views expressed in this article do not necessarily reflect those of either organization. Portions of this chapter are based on a chapter by the author in *Depression in Childhood and Adolescence*, edited by I.M. Goodyer, and the author is grateful for permission to reproduce them here.

REFERENCES

American Psychiatric Association (1987). *Diagnostic and Statistical Manual of Mental Disorders—DSM-III-R (3rd edn—revised)*. Washington, DC: American Psychiatric Association.

American Psychiatric Association (1994). *Diagnostic and Statistical Manual of Mental Disorders—DSM-IV (4th edn)*. Washington, DC: American Psychiatric Association.

Angold, A., Costello, E.J., Erkanli, A. & Worthman, C.M. (1999). Pubertal changes in hormone levels and depression in girls. *Psychological Medicine, 29*, 1043–1053.

Angold, A., Costello, E.J. & Worthman, C.M. (1998). Puberty and depression: The roles of age, pubertal status and pubertal timing. *Psychological Medicine, 28*, 51–61.

Angst, J., Merikangas, K.R. & Preisig, M. (1997). Subthreshold syndromes of depression and anxiety in the community. *Journal of Clinical Psychiatry, 58* (Suppl. 8), 6–10.

Appelboom-Fondu, J., Kerkhofs, M. & Mendlewicz, J. (1988). Depression in adolescents and young adults—polysomnographic and neuroendocrine aspects. *Journal of Affective Disorders, 14*, 35–40.

Asarnow, J.R., Goldstein, M.J., Carlson, G.A., Perdue, S., Bates, S. & Keller, J. (1988). Childhood-onset depressive disorders. A follow-up study of rates of rehospitalization and out-of-home placement among child psychiatric inpatients. *Journal of Affective Disorders, 15*, 245–253.

Asarnow, J.R., Goldstein, M.J., Tompson, M. & Guthrie, D. (1993). One-year outcomes of depressive disorders in child psychiatric inpatients: Evaluation of the prognostic power of a brief measure of expressed emotion. *Journal of Child Psychology and Psychiatry, 34*, 129–137.

Bardone, A.M., Moffitt, T.E., Caspi, A., Dickson, N., Stanton, W.R. & Silva, P.A. (1998). Adult physical health outcomes of adolescent girls with conduct disorder, depression, and anxiety. *Journal of the American Academy of Child and Adolescent Psychiatry, 37*, 594–601.

Beardslee, W.R., Keller, M.B., Lavori, P.W., Staley, J. & Sacks, N. (1993). The impact of parental affective disorder on depression in offspring: A longitudinal follow-up in a nonreferred sample. *Journal of the American Academy of Child and Adolescent Psychiatry, 32*, 723–730.

Beardslee, W.R., Keller, M.B., Seifer, R., et al. (1996). Prediction of adolescent affective disorder: Effects of prior parental affective disorders and child psychopathology. *Journal of the American Academy of Child and Adolescent Psychiatry, 35*, 279–288.

Boney-McCoy, S. & Finkelhor, D. (1996). Is youth victimization related to trauma symptoms and depression after controlling for prior symptoms and family relationships? A longitudinal, prospective study. *Journal of Consulting and Clinical Psychology, 64*, 1406–1416.

Brown, G.W. & Harris, T. (1978). *Social Origins of Depression*. London: Tavistock.

Brown, G.W., Harris, T.O. & Bifulco, A. (1986). Long-term effects of early loss of parent. In M. Rutter, C.E. Izard & P.B. Read (Eds), *Depression in Young People: Developmental and Clinical Perspectives* (pp. 251–296). New York: Guilford.

Brown, G.W., Lemyre, L. & Bifulco, A. (1992). Social factors and recovery from anxiety and depressive disorders. A test of specificity. *British Journal of Psychiatry, 161*, 44–54.

Buchanan, C.M., Eccles, J.S. & Becker, J.B. (1992). Are adolescents the victims of raging hormones? Evidence for activational effects of hormones on moods and behavior at adolescence. *Psychological Bulletin, 111*, 62–107.

Casat, C.D. & Powell, K. (1988). The dexamethasone suppression test in children and adolescents with major depressive disorder: A review. *Journal of Clinical Psychiatry, 49*, 390–393.

Cashman, M.A., Coble, P., McCann, B.S., Taska, L., Reynolds, C.F. & Jupfer, D.J. (1986). Sleep markers for major depressive disorder in adolescent patients. *Sleep Research, 15*, 91.

Charman, T. (1994). The stability of depressed mood in young adolescents: A school-based survey. *Journal of Affective Disorders, 30*, 109–116.

Cohen, P., Cohen, J. & Brook, J. (1993a). An epidemiological study of disorders in late childhood and adolescence. II. Persistence of disorders. *Journal of Child Psychology and Psychiatry, 34*, 869–877.

Cohen, P., Cohen, J., Kasen, S., et al. (1993b). An epidemiological study of disorders in late childhood and adolescence. I. Age- and gender-specific prevalence. *Journal of Child Psychology and Psychiatry, 34*, 851–867.

Cummings, E.M. & Davies, P.T. (1994). Maternal depression and child development. *Journal of Child Psychology and Psychiatry, 35*, 73–112.

Daley, S.E., Hammen, C., Davila, J. & Burge, D. (1998). Axis II symptomatology, depression, and life stress during the transition from adolescence to adulthood. *Journal of Consulting and Clinical Psychology, 66*, 595–603.

Dorn, L.D., Burgess, E.S., Dichek, H.L., Putnam, F.W., Chrousos, G.P. & Gold, P.W. (1996). Thyroid hormone concentrations in depressed and nondepressed adolescent: Group differences and behavioral relations. *Journal of the American Academy of Child and Adolescent Psychiatry, 35*, 299–306.

Eaves, L.J., Silberg, J.L., Meyer, J.M., et al. (1997). Genetics and developmental psychopathology. II. The main effects of genes and environment on behavioral problems in the Virginia twin study of adolescent behavioral development. *Journal of Child Psychology and Psychiatry, 38*, 965–980.

Edelsohn, G., Ialongo, N., Werthamer-Larsson, L., Crockett, L. & Kellam, S. (1992). Self-reported depressive symptoms in first-grade children: Developmentally transient phenomena? *Journal of the American Academy of Child and Adolescent Psychiatry, 31*, 282–290.

Eley, T.C., Deater-Deckard, K., Fombonne, E., Fulker, D.W. & Plomin, R. (1998). An adoption study of depressive symptoms in middle childhood. *Journal of Child Psychology and Psychiatry, 39*, 337–345.

Emslie, G.J., Roffwarg, H.P., Rush, A.J., Weinberg, W.A. & Parkin-Feigenbaum, L. (1987). Sleep EEG findings in depressed children and adolescents. *American Journal of Psychiatry, 144*, 668–670.

Emslie, G., Rush, A., Weinberg, W., et al. (1997a). A double-blind, randomized placebo-controlled trial of fluoxetine in depressed children and adolescents. *Archives of General Psychiatry, 54*, 1031–1037.

Emslie, G.J., Rush, J.A., Weinberg, W.A., Gullion, C.M., Rintelmann, J. & Hughes, C.W. (1997b). Recurrence of major depressive disorder in hospitalized children and adolescents. *Journal of the American Academy of Child and Adolescent Psychiatry, 36*, 785–792.

Fergusson, D.M., Horwood, L.J. & Lynskey, M.T. (1995). Maternal depressive symptoms and depressive symptoms in adolescents. *Journal of Child Psychology and Psychiatry, 36*, 1161–1178.

Fleming, J.E., Boyle, M.H. & Offord, D.R. (1993). The outcome of adolescent depression in the Ontario Child Health Study. *Journal of the American Academy of Child and Adolescent Psychiatry, 32*, 28–33.

Frank, E., Kupfer, D.J., Perel, J.M., et al. (1990). Three-year outcomes for maintenance therapies in recurrent depression. *Archives of General Psychiatry, 47*, 1093–1099.

Garber, J., Kriss, M.R., Koch, M., Lindholm, L. (1988). Recurrent depression in adolescents: A follow-up study. *Journal of the American Academy of Child and Adolescent Psychiatry, 27*, 49–54.

Garrison, C.Z., Jackson, K.L., Marsteller, F., McKeown, R. & Addy, C. (1990). A longitudinal study of depressive symptomatology in young adolescents. *Journal of the American Academy of Child and Adolescent Psychiatry, 29*, 581–585.

Garrison, C.Z., Waller, J.L., Cuffe, S.P., McKeown, R.E., Addy, C.L. & Jackson, K.L. (1997). Incidence of major depressive disorder and dysthymia in young adolescents. *Journal of the American Academy of Child and Adolescent Psychiatry, 36*, 458–465.

Goodyer, I.M. & Altham, P.M.E. (1991). Lifetime exit events and recent social and family adversities in anxious and depressed school-age children and adolescents. I. *Journal of Affective Disorders, 21*, 219–228.

Goodyer, I.M., Germany, E., Gowrusankur, J. & Altham, P. (1991). Social influences on the course of anxious and depressive disorders in school-age children. *British Journal of Psychiatry, 158*, 676–684.

Goodyer, I.M., Herbert, J. & Altham, P.M. (1998). Adrenal steroid secretion and major depression in 8- to 16-year-olds. III. Influence of cortisol/DHEA ratio at presentation on subsequent rates of disappointing life events and persistent major depression. *Psychological Medicine, 28*, 265–273.

Goodyer, I.M., Herbert, J., Secher, S.M. & Pearson, J. (1997a). Short-term outcome of major depression. I. Comorbidity and severity at presentation as predictors of persistent disorder. *Journal of the American Academy of Child and Adolescent Psychiatry, 36*, 179–187.

Goodyer, I.M., Herbert, J., Tamplin, A., Secher, S.M. & Pearson, J. (1997b). Short-term outcome of major depression. II. Life events, family dysfunction, and friendship difficulties as predictors of persistent disorder. *Journal of the American Academy of Child and Adolescent Psychiatry, 36*, 474–480.

Goodyer, I.M., Herbert, J., Tamplin, A., Secher, S.M. & Pearson, J. (1997c). Short-term outcome of major depression. II. Life events, family dysfunction, and friendship difficulties as predictors of persistent disorder. *Journal of the American Academy of Child and Adolescent Psychiatry, 36*, 474–480.

Hammen, C. (1991). *Depression Runs in Families. The Social Context of Risk and Resilience in Children of Depressed Mothers*. New York: Springer-Verlag.

Hammen, C., Burge, D. & Adrian, C. (1991). Timing of mother and child depression in a longitudinal study of children at risk. *Journal of Consulting and Clinical Psychology, 59*, 341–345.

Harrington, R., Rutter, M. & Fombonne, E. (1996). Developmental pathways in depression: Multiple meanings, antecedents and endpoints. *Development and Psychopathology, 8*, 601–616.

Harrington, R., Whittaker, J., Shoebridge, P. & Campbell, F. (1998a). Systematic review of efficacy of cognitive behaviour therapies in child and adolescent depressive disorder. *British Medical Journal, 316*, 1559–1563.

Harrington, R.C. & Clark, A. (1998). Prevention and early intervention for depression in adolescence and early adult life. *European Archives of Psychiatry and Clinical Neuroscience, 248*, 32–45.

Harrington, R.C., Fudge, H., Rutter, M., Pickles, A. & Hill, J. (1990). Adult outcomes of childhood and adolescent depression. I. Psychiatric status. *Archives of General Psychiatry, 47*, 465–473.

Harrington, R.C., Fudge, H., Rutter, M., Pickles, A. & Hill, J. (1991). Adult outcomes of childhood and adolescent depression. II. Risk for antisocial disorders. *Journal of the American Academy of Child and Adolescent Psychiatry, 30*, 434–439.

Harrington, R.C., Rutter, M., Weissman, M., et al. (1997). Psychiatric disorders in the relatives of depressed probands. I. Comparison of prepubertal, adolescent and early adult onset forms. *Journal of Affective Disorders, 42*, 9–22.

Harrington, R.C., Whittaker, J. & Shoebridge, P. (1998b). Psychological treatment of depression in children and adolescents: A review of treatment research. *British Journal of Psychiatry, 173*, 291–298.

Hazell, P., O'Connell, D., Heathcote, D., Robertson, J. & Henry, D. (1995). Efficacy of tricyclic drugs in treating child and adolescent depression: A meta-analysis. *British Medical Journal, 310*, 897–901.

Judd, L.L., Akiskal, H.S. & Maser, J.L., et al. (1998). A prospective 12-year study of subsyndromal and syndromal depressive symptoms in unipolar major depressive disorders. *Archives of General Psychiatry, 55*, 694–700.

Kandel, D.B. & Davies, M. (1986). Adult sequelae of adolescent depressive symptoms. *Archives of General Psychiatry, 43*, 255–262.

Keller, M.B., Beardslee, W., Lavori, P.W., Wunder, J., Drs D.L. & Samuelson, H. (1988). Course of major depression in non-referred adolescents: A retrospective study. *Journal of Affective Disorders, 15*, 235–243.

Keller, M.B., Lavori, P.W., Beardslee, W.R., Wunder, J. & Ryan, N. (1991). Depression in children and adolescents; new data on "undertreatment" and a literature review on the efficacy of available treatments. *Journal of Affective Disorders, 21*, 163–171.

Kendler, K.S., Kessler, R.C., Walters, E.E., et al. (1995). Stressful life events, genetic liability, and onset of an episode of major depression in women. *American Journal of Psychiatry, 152*, 833–842.

Kendler, K.S., Neale, M.C., Kessler, R.C., Heath, A.C. & Eaves, L.J. (1993). A longitudinal twin study of 1–year prevalence of major depression in women. *Archives of General Psychiatry, 50*, 843–852.

Kovacs, M. (1986). A developmental perspective on methods and measures in the assessment of depressive disorders: The clinical interview. In M. Rutter, C.E. Izard & R.B. Read (Eds), *Depression in Young People: Developmental and Clinical Perspectives* (pp. 435–465). New York: Guilford.

Kovacs, M., Akiskal, H.S., Gatsonis, C. & Parrone, P.L. (1994). Childhood-onset dysthymic disorder. Clinical features and prospective naturalistic outcome. *Archives of General Psychiatry, 51*, 365–374.

Kovacs, M., Feinberg, T.L., Crouse-Novak, M., Paulauskas, S.L., Pollock, M. & Finkelstein, R. (1984a). Depressive disorders in childhood. II. A longitudinal study of the risk for a subsequent major depression. *Archives of General Psychiatry, 41*, 643–649.

Kovacs, M., Feinberg, T.L., Crouse-Novak, M.A., Paulauskas, S.L. & Finkelstein, R. (1984b). Depressive disorders in childhood. I. A longitudinal prospective study of characteristics and recovery. *Archives of General Psychiatry, 41*, 229–237.

Kovacs, M., Gatsonis, C., Paulauskas, S. & Richards, C. (1989). Depressive disorders in childhood. IV. A longitudinal study of comorbidity with and risk for anxiety disorders. *Archives of General Psychiatry, 46*, 776–782.

Kovacs, M. & Goldston, D. (1991). Cognitive and social cognitive development of depressed children and adolescents. *Journal of the American Academy of Child and Adolescent Psychiatry, 30*, 388–392.

Kovacs, M., Obrosky, S., Gatsonis, C. & Richards, C. (1997). First-episode major depressive and dysthymic disorder in childhood: Clinical and sociodemographic factors in recovery. *Journal of the American Academy of Child and Adolescent Psychiatry, 36*, 777–784.

Kramer, R.A., Warner, V., Olfson, M., Ebanks, C.M., Chaput, F. & Weissman, M.M. (1998). General medical problems among the offspring of depressed parents: A 10-year follow-up. *Journal of the American Academy of Child and Adolescent Psychiatry, 37*, 602–611.

Kroll, L., Harrington, R.C., Gowers, S., Frazer, J. & Jayson, D. (1996). Continuation of cognitive-behavioural treatment in adolescent patients who have remitted from major depression. Feasibility and comparison with historical controls. *Journal of the American Academy of Child and Adolescent Psychiatry, 35*, 1156–1161.

Kupfer, D. (1992). Maintenance treatment in recurrent depression: Current and future directions. *British Journal of Psychiatry, 161*, 309–316.

Kupfer, D., Frank, E. & Perel, J.M. (1989). The advantage of early treatment intervention in recurrent depression. *Archives of General Psychiatry, 46*, 771–775.

Kupfer, D.J., Frank, E. & Perel, J.M., et al. (1992). Five-year outcome for maintenance therapies in recurrent depression. *Archives of General Psychiatry, 49*, 769–773.

Kutcher, S., Malkin, D., Silverberg, J., et al. (1991). Nocturnal cortisol, thyroid stimulating hormone, and growth hormone secretory profiles in depressed adolescents. *Journal of the American Academy of Child and Adolescent Psychiatry, 30*, 407–414.

Kutcher, S., Williamson, P., Marton, P. & Szalai, J. (1992). REM latency in endogenously depressed adolescents. *British Journal of Psychiatry, 161*, 399–402.

Lahmeyer, H.W., Poznanski, E.O. & Bellur, S.N. (1983). EEG sleep in depressed adolescents. *American Journal of Psychiatry, 140*, 1150–1153.

Larsson, B., Melin, L., Breitholtz, E. & Andersson, G. (1991). Short-term stability of depressive symptoms and suicide attempts in Swedish adolescents. *Acta Psychiatrica Scandinavica, 83*, 385–390.

Levitan, R.D., Parikh, S.V., Lesage, A.D., et al. (1998). Major depression in individuals with a history of childhood physical or sexual abuse: Relationship to neurovegetative features, mania, and gender. *American Journal of Psychiatry, 155*, 1746–1752.

Lewinsohn, P.M., Clarke, G.N., Seeley, J.R. & Rohde, P. (1994a). Major depression in community adolescents: Age at onset, episode duration, and time to recurrence. *Journal of the American Academy of Child and Adolescent Psychiatry, 33*, 809–818.

Lewinsohn, P.M., Hops, H., Roberts, R.E., Seeley, J.R. & Andrews, J.A. (1993). Adolescent psychopathology. I. Prevalence and incidence of depression and other DSM-III-R disorders in high school students. *Journal of Abnormal Psychology, 33*, 133–144.

Lewinsohn, P.M., Roberts, R.E., Seeley, J.R., Rohde, P., Gotlib, I.H. & Hops, H. (1994b). Adolescent psychopathology. II. Psychosocial risk factors for depression. *Journal of Abnormal Psychology, 103*, 302–315.

Lewinsohn, P.M., Rohde, P., Klein, D.N. & Seeley, J.R. (1999). Natural course of adolescent major depressive disorder. I. Continuity into young adulthood. *Journal of the American Academy of Child and Adolescent Psychiatry, 38*, 56–63.

Lewinsohn, P.M., Rohde, P. & Seeley, J.R. (1998). Major depressive disorder in older adolescents: Prevalence, risk factors, and clinical implications. *Clinical Psychology Review, 18*, 765–794.

Madden, P.A.F., Heath, A.C., Rosenthal, N.E. & Martin, N.G. (1996). Seasonal changes in mood and behavior. *Archives of General Psychiatry, 53*, 47–55.

McCauley, E., Myers, K., Mitchell, J., Calderon, R., Schloredt, K. & Treder, R. (1993). Depression in young people: Initial presentation and clinical course. *Journal of the American Academy of Child and Adolescent Psychiatry, 32*, 714–722.

McGee, R. & Williams, S. (1988). A longitudinal study of depression in nine-year-old children. *Journal of the American Academy of Child and Adolescent Psychiatry, 27*, 342–348.

McGee, R., Feehan, M., Williams, S. & Anderson, J. (1992). DSM-III disorders from age 11 to age 15 years. *Journal of the American Academy of Child and Adolescent Psychiatry, 31*, 50–59.

McGuffin, P. & Katz, R. (1986). Nature, nurture and affective disorder. In J.F.W. Deakin (Ed.), *The Biology of Depression* (pp. 26–52). London: Royal College of Psychiatrists.

Needles, D.J. & Abramson, L.Y. (1990). Positive life events, attributional style, and hopefulness: Testing a model of recovery from depression. *Journal of Abnormal Psychology, 99*, 156–165.

Newman, D.L., Moffitt, T.E., Caspi, A., Magdol, L., Silva, P.A. & Stanton, W.R. (1996). Psychiatric disorder in a birth cohort of young adults: Prevalence, comorbidity, clinical significance, and new case incidence from ages 11 to 21. *Journal of Consulting and Clinical Psychology, 64*, 552–562.

O'Connor, T.G., Neiderhiser, J.M., Reiss, D., Hetherington, E.M. & Plomin, R. (1998). Genetic contributions to continuity, change, and co-occurrence of antisocial and depressive symptoms in adolescence. *Journal of Child Psychology and Psychiatry, 39*, 323–336.

Olsson, G.I. & von Knorring, A.L. (1999). Adolescent depression: Prevalence in Swedish high-school students. *Acta Psychiatrica Scandinavica, 99*, 324–331.

Os, Jv., Jones, P., Lewis, G., Wadsworth, M. & Murray, R. (1997). Developmental precursors of affective illness in a general population birth cohort. *Archives of General Psychiatry, 54*, 625–631.

Pearce, J.B. (1978). The recognition of depressive disorder in children. *Journal of the Royal Society of Medicine, 71*, 494–500.

Pickles, A., Rowe, R., Simonoff, E., Foley, D., Rutter, M. & Silberg, J. (2001). Child psychiatric symptoms and psychosocial impairment: Relationship and prognostic significance. *British Journal of Psychiatry, 179*, 230–235.

Pine, D.S., Cohen, E., Cohen, P. & Brook, J. (1999). Adolescent depressive symptoms as predictors of adult depression: Moodiness or mood disorder? *American Journal of Psychiatry, 156*, 133–135.

Pine, D.S., Cohen, P., Gurley, D., Brook, J. & Ma, Y. (1998). The risk for early-adulthood anxiety and depressive disorders in adolescents with anxiety and depressive disorders. *Archives of General Psychiatry, 55*, 56–64.

Post, R.M. (1992). Transduction of psychosocial stress into the neurobiology of recurrent affective disorder. *American Journal of Psychiatry, 149*, 999–1010.

Post, R.M., Weiss, S.R.B., Leverich, G.S., George, M.S., Frye, M. & Ketter, T.A. (1996). Developmental psychobiology of cyclic affective illness: Implications for early therapeutic intervention. *Development and Psychopathology, 8*, 273–305.

Puig-Antich, J. (1982). Major depression and conduct disorder in prepuberty. *Journal of the American Academy of Child and Adolescent Psychiatry, 21*, 118–128.

Puig-Antich, J., Lukens, E., Davies, M., Goetz, D., Brennan-Quattrock, J. & Todak, G. (1985a). Psychosocial functioning in prepubertal major depressive disorders. I. Interpersonal relationships during the depressive episode. *Archives of General Psychiatry, 42*, 500–507.

Puig-Antich, J., Lukens, E., Davies, M., Goetz, D., Brennan-Quattrock, J. & Todak, G. (1985b). Psychosocial functioning in prepubertal major depressive disorders. II. Interpersonal relationships after sustained recovery from affective episode. *Archives of General Psychiatry, 42*, 511–517.

Rao, U., Ryan, N.D., Birmaher, B., et al. (1995). Unipolar depression in adolescence: Clinical outcome in adulthood. *Journal of the American Academy of Child and Adolescent Psychiatry, 34*, 566–578.

Renouf, A.G., Kovacs, M., Mukerji, P. (1997). Relationship of depressive, conduct, and comorbid disorders and social functioning in childhood. *Journal of the American Academy of Child and Adolescent Psychiatry, 36*, 998–1004.

Richman, N., Stevenson, J. & Graham, P. (1982). *Pre-school to School: A Behavioural Study.* London: Academic Press.

Riemann, D. & Schmidt, M.H. (1993). REM sleep distribution in adolescents with major depression and schizophrenia. *Sleep Research, 22*, 554.

Roberts, R.E., Lewinsohn, P.M. & Seeley, J.R. (1995). Symptoms of DSM-III-R major depression in adolescence: Evidence from an epidemiological survey. *Journal of the American Academy of Child and Adolescent Psychiatry, 34*, 1608–1617.

Rohde, P., Lewinsohn, P.M. & Seeley, J.R. (1990). Are people changed by the experience of having an episode of depression? A further test of the scar hypothesis. *Journal of Abnormal Psychology, 99*, 264–271.

Rohde, P., Lewinsohn, P.M. & Seeley, J.R. (1994). Are adolescents changed by an episode of major depression? *Journal of the American Academy of Child and Adolescent Psychiatry, 33*, 1289–1298.

Rutter, M. & Quinton, D. (1984). Parental psychiatric disorder: Effects on children. *Psychological Medicine, 14*, 853–880.

Rutter, M. & Sroufe, L.A. (2000). Developmental psychopathology: Concepts and challenges. *Development and Psychopathology, 12*, 265–296.

Rutter, M., Graham, P., Chadwick, O.F. & Yule, W. (1976). Adolescent turmoil: Fact or fiction? *Journal of Child Psychology and Psychiatry, 17*, 35–56.

Rutter, M., Tizard, J. & Whitmore, K. (1970). *Education, Health and Behaviour.* London: Longmans.

Sandford, M., Szatmari, P., Spinner, M., et al. (1995). Predicting the one-year course of adolescent major depression. *Journal of the American Academy of Child and Adolescent Psychiatry, 34*, 1618–1628.

Shafii, M., MacMillan, D.R., Key, M.P., Derrick, A.M., Kaufman, N. & Nahinsky, I.D. (1996). Nocturnal serum melatonin profile in major depression in children and adolescents. *Archives of General Psychiatry, 53*, 1009–1013.

Shain, B.N., King, C.A., Naylor, M. & Alessi, N. (1991). Chronic depression and hospital course in adolescents. *Journal of the American Academy of Child and Adolescent Psychiatry, 30*, 428–433.

Sigurdsson, G., Fombonne, E., Sayal, K. & Checkley, S. (1999). Neurodevelopmental antecedents of early-onset bipolar affective disorder. *British Journal of Psychiatry, 174*, 121–127.

Smith, A.L. & Weissman, M.M. (1992). Epidemiology. In E.S. Paykel (Ed.), *Handbook of Affective Disorders* (2nd edn., pp. 111–129). Edinburgh: Churchill Livingstone.

Stanger, C., McConaughy, S.H. & Achenbach, T.M. (1992). Three-year course of behavioral/emotional problems in a national sample of 4- to 16-year-olds. II. Predictors of syndromes. *Journal of the American Academy of Child and Adolescent Psychiatry, 31*, 941–950.

Steingard, R.J., Renshaw, P.F., Yurgelun-Todd, D., et al. (1996). Structural abnormalities in brain magnetic resonance images of depressed children. *Journal of the American Academy of Child and Adolescent Psychiatry, 35*, 307–311.

Strober, M. (1992). Bipolar disorders: Natural history, genetic studies, and follow-up. In M. Shafii & S.L. Shafii (Eds), *Clinical Guide to Depression in Children and Adolescents* (pp. 251–268). Washington, DC: American Psychiatric Press.

Susman, E., Dorn, L.D., Inoff-Germain, G., Nottelmann, E.D. & Chrousos, G.P. (1997). Cortisol reactivity, distress behavior, and behavioral and psychological problems in young adolescents: A longitudinal perspective. *Journal of Research on Adolescence, 7*, 81–105.

Thapar, A. & McGuffin, P. (1994). A twin study of depressive symptoms in childhood. *British Journal of Psychiatry, 165*, 259–265.

Warner, V., Weissman, M.M., Fendrich, M., Wickramaratne, P. & Moreau, D. (1992). The course of major depression in the offspring of depressed parents. Incidence, recurrence, and recovery. *Archives of General Psychiatry, 49*, 795–801.

Weinberg, W.A., Rutman, J., Sullivan, L., Penick, E.C. & Dietz, S.G. (1973). Depression in children referred to an educational diagnostic centre: Diagnosis and treatment. *Journal of Paediatrics, 83*, 1065–1072.

Weissman, M.M., Warner, V., Wickramaratne, P., Moreau, D. & Olfson, M. (1997). Offspring of depressed parents. 10 years later. *Archives of General Psychiatry, 54*, 932–940.

Weissman, M.M., Wolk, S., Goldstein, R.B., et al. (1999). Depressed adolescents grown up. *Journal of the American Medical Association, 281*, 1707–1713.

Wickramaratne, P.J. & Weissman, M.M. (1998). Onset of psychopathology in offspring by developmental phase and parental depression. *Journal of the American Academy of Child and Adolescent Psychiatry, 37*, 933–942.

Wolkind, S. & Rutter, M. (1985). Separation, loss and family relationships. In M. Rutter & L. Hersov (Eds), *Child and Adolescent Psychiatry: Modern Approaches* (pp. 34–57). Oxford: Blackwell.

6

DEPRESSION: A BIOPSYCHOSOCIAL, INTEGRATIVE, AND EVOLUTIONARY APPROACH

Paul Gilbert

Our moods and feelings are the basis for our quality of life; one can be happy in less than ideal circumstances and depressed in relatively benign ones. Many years ago, a suicidal, depressed man I was working with told of the terror of killing himself, going to heaven, but still being depressed (no escape). When we explored the idea of depression in heaven, we became aware that the 'if not recovered — why not' reasons reveal much about our cultural views of depression. In fact, for many centuries, different cultures have had a myriad of explanations for suffering (including depression) and its cure. Beliefs about causes include bad luck, life events and losses, poor childhood, consequences of past misdeeds (bad karma), the anger of God (sinner), a test of spirit, attachment and cravings, soul loss, social oppression, black bile, and, more recently, hormones and genes (Radden, 2000; Shweder et al., 1997). Depending on the meanings given to depression, different people have tried different things: changing one's luck, a variety of psychotherapies, working off bad karma, passing the spiritual tests, earning the love or forgiveness of God, communing with dead ancestors, seeking release from oppression, light therapy, exercise, various diets, bodily cleansings, herbs, pills, potions, and alcohol. A recent American community-based study found that, of those with 'self-diagnosed' depression and anxiety, 53.6% with severe depression and 56.7% with anxiety reported using complementary medicine and alternative therapies to treat their conditions (Kessler et al., 2001).

Although depression has been recognised as a common disorder for over 2000 years, with many sharp and insightful descriptions (Radden, 2000), unlike some more recently discovered illnesses and infections, consensus about its cause and treatment is tenuous. There remains doubt about its physiology and whether (or which type of) depression can be construed as a defect/error, a normal reaction to abnormal circumstances, or the extreme of a normally distributed variation in defensive strategies. Nonetheless, modern Western views, while perhaps less prosaic than many of the cultural variations, are still multifactorial. For some peoples and social groups, life is so harsh that depression may be a common

Mood Disorders: A Handbook of Science and Practice. Edited by M. Power.
© 2004 John Wiley & Sons, Ltd. ISBN 0-470-84390-X.

experience of life. For others, thinking styles, early schema, and coping behaviours can drive depression even for people whose environments are not so bad. For yet others, there are genetic sensitivities to some types of depression. And for all those who are depressed, modulation of the affect systems that have evolved over millions of years is key to the puzzle of depression. The biopsychosocial approach focuses on the *interactions* between processes, and, as Akiskal and McKinney (1975) pointed out many years ago, depression is a final common pathway of many different processes. To be depressed in heaven (if it exists of course), you would have to retain an evolved mind, built like other primate minds that could construe and feel in certain ways.

DEPRESSION

Depression can be classified in various ways and can take many forms, including bipolar or manic depression (Akiskal & Pinto, 1999; Goodwin & Jamison, 1990), major depression (Beckham et al., 1995), and dysthymia (Griffiths et al., 2000). The symptoms of major depression include loss of pleasure (anhedonia) (Clark, 2000; Willner, 1993); loss of motivation/interest (Klinger, 1975; 1993; Watson & Clark, 1988); negative thinking about the self, world and future (Beck et al., 1979); increased negative emotions (such as anxiety and anger) (van Praag, 1998); problems in cognitive functions such as memory, attention, and concentration (Gotlib et al., 2000; Watts, 1993); dysfunctional changes in sleep and restorative processes (Moldofsky & Dickstein, 1999); and a host of biological changes in various neurotransmitter and hormonal systems (McGuade & Young, 2000; Thase & Howland, 1995), and various brain areas such as the frontal cortex (Davidson, 2000). Major depression, although highly heterogeneous, is a common disorder with a point prevalence of around 5% (Kaelber et al., 1995), and a 12-month prevalence twice this — 7.7% for men and 12.9% for women (Kessler et al., 1994)—although both point and yearly prevalence can be much higher in some disadvantaged and traumatised communities (Bebbington et al., 1989). One in 4–5 women and one in 7–10 men will have an episode at some time in their lives (Bebbington, 1998). At least 50% of people with major depression will have more than one episode, with early-onset depression (on or before 20 years) being particularly vulnerable to relapse (Giles et al., 1989). Indeed, major depression is often a relapsing condition, and in about 20% of cases it can become chronic (McCullough, 2000; Scott, 1988). The World Heath Organisation has pointed out that depression constitutes one of the most common mental health problems; is a major personal, social, and economic burden; and is increasing (Murray & Lopez, 1996; Fombonne, 1994, 1999).

Types, categories, dimensions, and discontinuities

Despite the undoubted usefulness of syndromic approaches to mental disorders, from which the above is derived, there is concern with them. This is partly because they tend to see symptom clusters as disorders and distinct categories that can overlap with other disorders, and vary in levels of severity, but are distinct nonetheless (Gilbert, 1992). It is clear, however, that depression is a highly heterogeneous disorder with a variety of proposed subtypes, such as neurotic-psychotic, bipolar-unipolar, endogenous-reactive, primary-secondary, early onset versus late onset, angry versus anxious, agitated-retarded, serotonion versus noradrenalin based, and various mixed states (Gilbert, 1984, 1992), with a new category of atypical depression also being suggested (Posternak & Zimmerman, 2002). In fact, depression is more often than not comorbid with other (especially anxiety) disorders (Brown et al., 2001). To complicate the picture further, Akiskal and Pinto (1999) suggest that a substantial minority of depressions are related to a spectrum of bipolar disorders, some of which may be destabilised on traditional antidepressants. Coyne (1994) raised major concerns about dimensional approaches (for example, mild, moderate, and severe), and, assuming that results from studying mildly depressed or dysphoric people (for example, some students) can be extrapolated to more severe depression, as there may be quite different process involved.

Coyne's view has been challenged (e.g., Vredenburg et al., 1993), but this debate on types of depression and spectrums of disorder, and variations in physiological, psychological, and social processes, raises a key issue about the models we use to investigate processes. We can consider the question of discontinuities in severity of depression (that is, some people have more severe depressions than others) and whether discontinuities necessarily suggest different processes (such as causes and vulnerability factors) and/or different relationships (interactions) between processes. For example, catastrophe theory (Zeeman, 1977), later to evolve into chaos theory, points out that processes that are themselves dimensional and linear can produce discontinuous effects according to the state of the system. Many systems are like this in fact; for example, the straw that breaks the camel's back, the wave breaking on the beach, or the animal that is fighting and then suddenly, as fear gets the better of it, turns tail and runs away. And in anxiety disorders we talk of 'panic attacks' as a sudden onset of a major change in the system. These, then, are points of sudden shifts and discontinuities. Hence, in 1984, I argued that taking a dimensional approach to depression is *not to assume linearity* (that is, a bit more of this causes a bit more of that). I used what is called the 'cusp catastrophe' (Zeeman, 1977) to explore this (Gilbert, 1984, pp. 199–215). Hence, although there are different types of depression with different severities, there may still be *similarities in the processes and types of stressor that trigger them*. However, due to system organisation factors (such as genes or early trauma), small variations in one dimension (for example, a rejection that makes one feel unloved) can produce catastrophic effects in another part of the system (such as stress hormones). This then causes the system to spiral down or dramatically shift to a new equilibrium (catastrophe shift) way below what (say) someone else might experience. We often call these pre-depression factors 'vulnerability factors', but another way to think of them is as 'system setters'; they set a system up in a certain way and can produce catastrophic effects in some contexts. We will return to this concept as we proceed through the chapter. More recently, Meehl (1995) has offered a fascinating and important discussion of these difficulties in classification (for example, categorical versus dimensional) and calls for new mathematical models for their study.

Positive affect (PA) and negative affect (NA)

Costello (1993) has drawn attention to both the heterogeneity problem in depression, and the reliability of current classifications, and recommends a more focused approach on specific symptoms. Hence, rather than focus on syndromes, another approach has been to focus on affect systems and in particular positive affect (PA) and negative affect (NA) (Davidson, 2000; Watson et al., 1995a;b), which are orthogonal (that is, one can feel both excited and frightened) (Clark, 2000). This approach makes sense of comorbidity data, for while depression is primarily a disorder of (low) PA, or anhedonia, it can be associated with a variety of NAs (such as anxiety, sadness, and anger) and coping efforts (such as alcohol use).

There are, however, slightly different conceptualisations of anhedonia. One focuses on anhedonia as a broad category, encompassing general apathy with a marked lack of motivation to engage in almost all activities (Klinger, 1993) and diminished interest or pleasure in activities, reflecting a generalised lack of PA (Watson & Clark, 1988; Watson et al., 1995a;b). This definition views depression as the result of reductions in a range of PAs such as joy, energy, enthusiasm, alertness, self-confidence, and interest. Others (e.g., Willner, 1993) have suggested that anhedonic patients can remain 'interested' in hedonic experiences (they would like to engage in certain activities), but anticipate that they will be unable to enjoy them if they do engage in them. Loss of interest or lack of motivation may *develop* from repeated experiences of wanting but failing to feel pleasure or reward from various activities (Snaith et al., 1995).

Davidson (2000) offers another angle on PA systems by suggesting that there are different regulators for the anticipation of rewards that motivate engagement and effort, compared to the enjoyment of rewards if one's efforts are successful. This distinction may be important for a number or reasons. First, cognitive therapists (Beck et al., 1979) advocate the use of pleasure and mastery recording to help patients plan activities and to discover that they may enjoy them (and achieve) more than they thought they would. Clearly, if patients continued to enjoy them less than they predicted, this may be a less helpful intervention. If this is a successful approach, it suggests that it is the *anticipation* of rewards and enjoyment that is compromised in depression (that is, Willner's [1993] view). Second, if this is the affect system that is compromised, it suggests that one of the functions of anhedonia in depression may be to inhibit engagement with the environment. As we shall see, this may have important implications for an evolutionary model to be presented shortly.

There have been a few studies that have explored the regulators of PA and NA separately. Clark's (2000) review indicates that NA is associated with threats and irritations, whereas PA seems particularly associated with social engagement and activity. Interestingly, MacDonald (1988) argued that PA systems have undergone extensive evolutionary modification in the last few millions years. The 'drive' for this has been the role of social relationships (especially affiliative ones) in our evolution, making us into the highly social and interactive species we are. PA capacity and control have evolved along with the complexity of, and multiple functions of, social relationships. Interestingly, there have been suggestions in the literature that some people may suffer from *social* anhedonia as a trait (that is, they have less interest in, and enjoyment of, social relationships). Such a trait may be related to vulnerabilities to schizophrenia (e.g., Blanchard et al., 2000). However, anhedonia in depression is often a change in state and is not specific to social interactions (Snaith et al., 1995). This again suggests that in the context of depressive disorders anhedonia serves to inhibit general engagement in activities and functions as a variable strategy.

Whereas NA provides an individual with information about dangers and threats, and the type of emotion (anxiety and anger) indicates the defensive response (such as fight–flight), PAs are part of a safeness (Gilbert, 1993), behavioural approach (Davidson, 2000; Gray, 1987) and/or resource-seeking system (Panksepp, 1998) that controls levels of engagement in the environment and energy expenditure. Affect and energy expenditure are also separable systems, however, as when there is high PA but low activity (relaxing on a warm beach on holiday), the result of goals having been meet. In agitated depressions, there is low PA with high-energy expenditure. Many depressions are marked by high fatigue and loss of energy, which some patients feel preceded their anhedonia and other depression symptoms clinically, although there is little research in this area.

BIOPSYCHOSOCIAL APPROACHES

Systems change as a function of both the forces acting upon them and their own internal dynamics. The same is true for a switch from a non-depressed to a depressed state (Gilbert, 1984). There is now increasing recognition that depression is typically related to a host of interacting processes in the domains of physiological processes (genes and stress hormones), psychological processes (negative beliefs, rumination, and social withdrawal), and social factors (life events and social support) that interact over time (Akiskal & McKinney, 1975). This is depicted in Figure 6.1.

Note the ongoing, dynamic, and reciprocal nature of these interactions. Thus, one's early life (for example, love or abuse) interacting with genetically given temperament will affect physiological processes, social behaviour, and the schema of relationships. Thoughts and

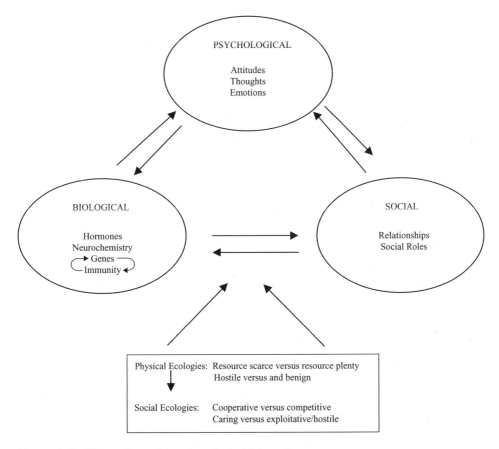

Figure 6.1   Biopsychosocial and ecological interactions

beliefs about relationships (such as fear of abandonment) can reflect and affect physiological process and social behaviour. Manifest social behaviour (for example, clingy attachment or quickness to take offence) can mean that relationships are stormy and break up easily, affecting physiology (such as stress hormones), relational schema, and social behaviour. These biopsychosocial relations are themselves contextualised in different types of physical and social ecologies. Not only are interactions key to understanding the emergence of states such as depression, but also there can be discontinuities in each domain. For example, there may be genetic or early sensitisation effects that increase the instability of key neuronal affect modulators. Or consider how Beck (1967, p. 277) described the vulnerability of negative latent schema that can persist 'like an explosive charge ready to be detonated by an appropriate set of conditions'; *explosions* are hardly smooth transitions. And, of course, in the social domain, life events can be sudden (such as the death of a loved one, the break-up of a relationship, or serious illness or injury). Understanding interacting processes that produce discontinuities and state shifts are, then, often the rule rather than the exception.

Early forerunners of the biopsychosocial approach can be found in Meyers' psychobiology approach (Rutter, 1986), behavioural medicine, and psychosomatic medicine (Kiesler, 1999). The biopsychosocial approach is critical of narrow-focused or single-process approaches and is critical of 'the dualisms' (mind versus body; nature versus nature)—which Eisenberg (2000) aptly termed 'brainless and mindless science'—that still plague our theorising. One thing is clear, however; that although many clinicians of all types pay lip service to a biopsychosocial approach, few actually adopt it in their clinical practice or research. The main reasons are that clinicians do not understand it and rarely study interactions of processes, and so radical shifts in research, training, and practice are needed (Kiesler, 1999).

Given the high incidence and prevalence rates of depression, it is not surprising that there have been a vast number of theories about the vulnerability, onset, and maintenance factors (Gilbert, 1992). As will be noted below, these focus variously on genetic vulnerabilities, acquired vulnerabilities (for example, via aversive early life experiences), and/or current social contexts. Despite our long recognition that the study of ongoing, reciprocal, dynamic processes of individual–environment interactions is central to understanding states such as depression (Akiskal & McKinney, 1975), many theories of psychopathology, let alone depression, rarely address issues of complex biopsychosocial interactions (Eisenberg, 2000). Many have lamented the way social and biological theories often operate in isolation from each other (Cacioppo et al., 2000), and studies are often on groups, thus losing in the variance the individual nature of interactions. It is, however, true that many theorists of major depression endorse some form of a stress-diathesis model, which suggests that stressors affect underlying vulnerabilities (e.g., Akiskal & McKinney, 1973; Hankin & Abramson, 2001).

The importance of multicomponent interactions

The biopsychosocial approach, then, focuses on interactions, and so we need to conceptualise what kinds of interactions are salient, and to recognise the importance of feedback and feed-forward processes. We can depict possible domains of interaction relevant to depression with a simple flow diagram derived from numerous studies on various elements of depression. This is given in Figure 6.2 and depicts early vulnerability factors, current

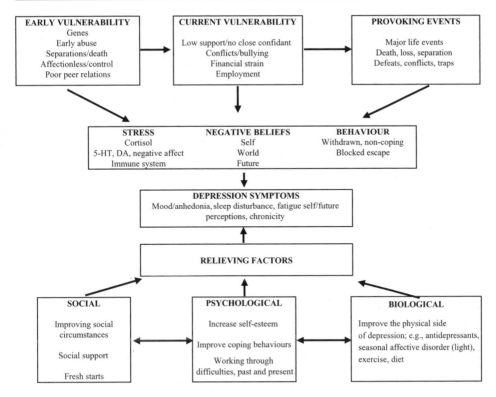

Figure 6.2   Biopsychosocial interactions in depression

vulnerability, and provoking agents or triggers. Each of these alone or in combination affects physiological states, appraisal processes (for example, of self, world, and future), and coping behaviours, and gives rise to the symptoms of depression.

Note that there are arrows across and between processes. For example, early vulnerability factors (such as abuse) can affect how people engage their social lives (for example, have difficulty in developing supportive, stable, and intimate relationships), making them more currently vulnerable (for example, poor social support) and susceptible to stressors (such as early pregnancy) (see Andrews, 1998). As Hankin and Abramson (2001) note, some events can be independent (such as collapse of the stock market and financial or job loss), but others are dependent (for example, some personality dispositions reduce the probability of developing close supportive relationships and increase the probability of relationship break-up and conflict). Thus, early vulnerability, current vulnerability, and provoking agents can interact.

Physiological changes themselves, as may stem from a major life stress (such as loss of one's job), can interact, as, for example, the discovered interactions between the endocrine and immune systems, each of which can affect neurotransmitter systems and mood (Anisman & Merali, 1999). Physiological processes also affect cognitive processes. For example, increasing levels of cortisol (a stress hormone) tend to focus attention on threats and negative events; animals with high cortisol are more sensitive and attentive to possible threats than low-cortisol animals (Rosen & Schulkin, 1998; Toates, 1995), and, as we will note below, people from abusive backgrounds have high levels of cortisol. In a major review, Taylor et al. (2000) explored how differences in gender evolution and sex hormones can differently affect stress and depression in the genders. They called for greater gender-sensitive research.

Recovery

We also know something of the relieving factors for depression, and these, too, can be delineated in biopsychosocial domains. Antidepressants or exercise may change physiological systems (such as serotonin [5-HT] transmission) such that people sleep better and are less exhausted, and boost PA, leading to increased confidence to make changes in their lives. Changing how one thinks about oneself (via psychological interventions) may produce various physiological changes that aid mood. Physiological treatments have major psychosocial effects, and psychological treatments affect physiological processes (e.g., Gabbard, 2000; Thase et al., 1996). Brown et al. (1987) have shown that depression can often remit in the face of fresh-start (positive) life events.

At its best, the biopsychosocial approach is *holistic*. However, it also recognises the importance of individual differences. These differences can show up in how stressors trigger defensive responses, the intensity of the response(s), and the speed and form of recovery from them (Davidson, 2000). Hence, how your systems interact may be different from mine. Therefore, our needs and responses to treatment will be different, and this includes responses to biological and psychological treatments. Regarding alcohol, it is clear that some people drink to relax and have fun, but others become aggressive. Some like to feel tipsy while others hate it. Some can take it or leave it, while others become addicted. For most trials of treatment, effectiveness is based on averages and applies to the average patient, but there is no such thing as 'the average patient'. We are all individuals in so many unique ways, from our genes to our histories, to the context of our lives. So we should not be surprised to find that some like antidepressants and find them life-savers, while others feel detached, suffer awful side effects, and hate them; some may be worse off with an antidepressant because of the nature of the mood disorder (Akiskal & Pinto, 1999). Some people take to cognitive therapy like ducks to water and do well (Blackburn & Moorhead, 2000), but others do not. For biopsychosocial clinicians, these individual differences guide therapy, and it becomes the role of clinician and patient to work out which is the best treatment or combination of treatments for that individual. Such a procedure requires detailed understanding of family and personal history (Akiskal & Pinto, 1999). Theories guide our understanding, and frameworks and evidence guide our interventions, but, ultimately, therapy is a process that must respect the individual. It has been the failure of clinicians to address the problems of individual differences in treatment, and their inclination to see depression only as 'a disease' that has caused many of the problems in the use of antidepressants (Healy, 2001). Similarly, psychologists need to be sensitive to genetic, physiological, and social factors in some depressions. So, clearly, we cannot outline all the many and salient pathways of interaction here, and, in any case, there are likely to be unique individual variations for people. Integrationist approaches are best orientated to the complexity of interactions for research and intervention.

In what follows, we will explore some of the interactions that seem pertinent to depression. Space requires some selection of focus of these, and if any seem to be played down, or ignored, it should not be taken to imply their unimportance but, more probably, the limitations of the author.

DEPRESSION AND STRESS

We can make a start at integration by focusing on that well-known but tricky concept, stress. The simple reason for this is that there is little doubt now that major depression is a state of *chronic* stress as measured by subjective reports, life events (Morriss & Morriss, 2000), physiological indicators of autonomic nervous system hyperarousal (Toates, 1995), and overactivity of the hypothalamic-pituitary-adrenal (HPA) system, which results in high cortisol levels, called hypercortisolaemia (Levitan et al., 2000; McGuade & Young, 2000; Nemeroff, 1998; Raadsheer et al., 1994). Importantly, hypercortisolaemia has many detrimental effects on the immune system (Maes, 1995), and various internal organs and brain areas (Sapolsky, 1996, 2000), and by feedback interactions it downgrades 5-HT, an important neurotransmitter in mood regulation (McGuade & Young, 2000). There is good evidence that even in the less severe depression of dysthymia there are significant physiological disturbances of functioning (as in the HPA system, immune systems, and neurotransmitters) (Griffiths et al., 2000). Although there are a variety of regulators of the HPA system (Nemeroff, 1996) that may operate differently in different types of depression (Posener et al., 2000), so important is the HPA system in depression that new therapeutic efforts are being targeted at hypercortisolaemia (McGuade & Young, 2000).

In a large epidemiological study, Kessler and Magee (1993) found that childhood adversities are related to both onset and recurrent episodes of depression. In a follow-up of 121 student women, Hammen et al. (2000) found that women with a history of childhood adversity needed less stress to trigger depression than those without childhood adversity. Andrews (1998) has shown that chronic depression in women is linked to childhood sexual abuse. Hence, aversive early relationships can skew development towards anxiety, depression, suspiciousness, shame sensitivity, non-affiliation (poor help-seeking), aggressiveness, and social wariness or avoidance. It is possible that part of the difficulty for people abused or neglected as children is that, via a process of repeated activation of stress and the defensive behaviours (such as protest-despair or submissive inhibition to an aggressive parent), there is a sensitisation and kindling of the key neurocircuitry of these defensive strategies, similar to that for fear (Rosen & Schulkin, 1998). Additionally, other strategies, e.g. for more relaxed and secure social behaviour, are understimulated or underdeveloped (Perry et al., 1995). In effect, the person approaches his/her environment needing to spot harms quickly, go on the defensive, and minimise harms (Gilbert, 1995). Genetic effects can make some individuals especially sensitive to these social contexts (Suomi, 1997).

Thus, the physiological states of depression are real enough (just as they are for heart disease and other diseases), but this does not mean they 'cause depression' on their own, for they could be consequences of other factors (such as high-stress environments). Rather, we should constantly think about interactions and that depression emerges or takes the patterns it does from interactions of processes (Gilbert, 2001a). In a way, this is like cake making—where, although we can try to identify the ingredients of a cake, it is difficult to separate out the ingredients once it is cooked—and it is the cooking that makes the cake. However, there are some ingredients that seem important.

WHAT TYPE OF STRESS AND WHAT TYPE OF DEFENCE? SOME EVOLVED REGULATORS

Although we can be stressed by many different life events and loss of control, from an evolutionary point of view we need to identify stressors that can be chronic and that down-regulate PA. Depression (low PA) makes us withdraw effort from things that are unlikely to work out—this is called disengagement (Klinger, 1975)—or where to continue to engage in activities increases the risk of harm (Nesse, 2000). However, there are at least two meaningful evolutionary contexts where downregulation of PA may have been adaptive: *attachment loss* and *entrapped defeat*. This is not a new idea but has been suggested by many researchers (e.g., Beck, 1987; Sloman, 2000a). There are two central concepts to understanding how these work. First, in earlier evolutionary times, in certain contexts, *the signals an animal emits may themselves be threats*. This is because the animal may behave in a way that draws unwanted attention to itself (as from a predator or hostile conspecifics). Hence, an adaptive defensive response would be to stop the animal from behaving (emitting signals) in certain ways and thus reduce the risk of harm. The second point is that many defensive responses are designed for rapid action, and to be accessed quickly and produce discontinuities in behaviour; for example, when an animal needs to stop feeding and run from a predator, or to shift from one defence to another—for example, from fight to flight (Gilbert, 1984). Hence, a shutting down of 'signal emission' and a rapid shift in behaviour may be part of an evolved design for both attachment loss and defeats—a theme we will explore below.

The idea that some defensive responses are designed to stop an animal from engaging with its environment (Gilbert, 1989) and from seeking resources fits with the idea that the primary PA system that will be downregulated for this behaviour is the anticipatory PA system (Davidson, 2000). Moreover, studies of nonverbal behaviour in depression by Schelde (1998a;b) suggest that depression is marked by a reduction in signals for social engagements (as in eye gaze, facial expression, and speech), a feature which changes with recovery. Ellgring (1989), however, notes that there are sizeable individual differences in the non-verbal behaviour of depressed people, and much depends on what other affects are part of the clinical picture (for example, some patients are more anxious, and others more angry).

Abandonment-separation

When separated from their mother, juveniles show a protest-despair reaction (Bowlby, 1969, 1973, 1980; Suomi, 1997). Protest is designed to engage in urgent searching and *signal/communicate* distress to elicit help and/or reunion; that is, the signal is designed to search for, and affect (call to) others/mother (Panksepp, 1998). However, for most mammals, a distressed-calling/searching, young individual on its own is in danger of attracting predators, being harmed by conspecifics, getting lost, and/or becoming exhausted. Better in such contexts to sit tight and wait for the parent to return. Despair (which seems to be rooted in downregulation of PA, among other things) (Panksepp, 1998) is thus designed to stop signalling and moving, and disengage approach or resource-seeking behaviour when not to do so might be dangerous. Despair is a form of behavioural and PA deactivation when protest does not work. In animals, despair is associated with heightened activity in the HPA system, and antidepressants can moderate it (Panksepp, 1998). The shifts from calm/secure, to awareness of mother's absence and anxious protest, to despair (shutting down PA) can be quick, and the *intensity* of the response in each phase can be in influenced by multiple factors (such as genes, age, and history of reunions). Moreover, the speed of return to a state of calm or safeness on reunion can be quick or slow.

There is evidence that these primitive strategies/mechanisms (behavioural and affect regulators) are still powerful templates for coping with separations, with evidence for genetic differences in susceptibility to the intensity of protest-despair responses (Suomi, 1997). Moreover, both animal and human studies show that depressed states are often triggered by social losses (Bowlby, 1980; Brown & Harris, 1978), and the physiology of protest-despair has many overlapping features with depression (Panksepp, 1998; Reite & Field, 1985). In line with others at the time, Gilbert (1984) suggested that although animals and humans can switch from protest to despair, some depressions may represent agitated searches and 'protest'. These people are likely to feel more sad and tearful, and to seek reassurance. Once despair (or defeat) is firmly activated, the experience is more one of retardation and feeling inwardly dead. Such folk are likely to say they wish they could feel sad or cry—to feel anything other than their *flattened affect*. Indeed, many clinicians have noted that while some patients are flat and need 'boosting up', others need calming down. However, while these two states (called A states and R states) (Gilbert, 1984) probably reflect different defensive strategies, and may have different regulators, they can also overlap and compete for expression; hence, there can be mixed states.

Involuntary subordination

Conspecifics can threaten and harm each other. Hence, animals need to be wary of those who can inflict harm and coordinate their behaviour accordingly (not acting above their station). Animals that do not follow these social rules are at risk of injury and death (Higley et al., 1996). Hence, subordination can also be a situation where it is important for an animal to have an internal, inhibitory, regulating process that limits acquisition and 'seeking' behaviour (Gilbert, 1984). Sapolsky (1989) notes that subordinate baboons are vulnerable to stress-induced hypercortisolism, in part from the harassment and threat signals issued by more dominant animals, and because they have less control over adversities. Sapolsky (1994) also found that blood pressure in subordinate baboons remained higher for much longer after a conflict than it did in dominant animals. In both monkey (Spalosky, 1989, 1994) and human studies (Wilkinson, 1996), subordinate individuals can be at increased risk of a variety of disorders. Interestingly, social signals themselves may have direct regulatory effects on these strategies. Raleigh et al. (1984) found that threat displays of a dominant are capable of suppressing the 5-HT of subordinates, while subordinate signals (such as retreating, fear grin, and crouch) have powerful (enhancing) effects on the 5-HT of the dominant (Gilbert & McGuire, 1998). Indeed, there is increasing research in monkeys showing that threats from dominants have powerful effects on stress hormones and many neurotransmitter systems, including dopamine (Gilbert, 2001b). Dopamine is a potent regulator of reward sensitivity and PA (Willner, 1985). There is also some evidence that drugs that affect dopamine and 5-HT systems have different effects according to whether the animal they are given to is dominant or subordinate (Gilbert, 2001b).

A different piece of evidence that social ranks are important for understanding depression comes from the medical sociologist Richard Wilkinson (1996). He has explored differences in rates of certain types of disorder, including depression, between countries and groups. He argues that there are higher rates of depression in societies with large disparities in social wealth, social power, and social comparisons (and where people may have to compete vigorously for their jobs and some are at risk of being placed in harassed, subordinate positions).

Evidence that some kind of internal regulator or mental mechanism(s) for subordination is operative in depression is offered by findings that depression is associated with seeing oneself as inferior, subordinate, or subordinated; with increased inclination to behave submissively, and to withdraw from conflicts with more powerful others (Allan & Gilbert, 1997); and with failed efforts to be assertive (Arrindell et al., 1990). Vulnerability to depression has long been linked with low self-esteem (e.g., Brown & Harris, 1978), but self-esteem is itself rooted in social rank (social comparison) judgements (Price, 2000). Whether self-esteem is trait-like or state-like, low self-esteem seems to operate like a subordinate defensive strategy in that it is associated with damage-limitation strategies (trying to stop bad things from happening) rather than a PA-enhancement strategy (Baumeister et al., 1989). In line with the idea that damage-limitation (subordinate) strategies are important in some depressions, Forrest and Hokanson (1975) found that, in a conflict situation, depressed people showed more autonomic arousal reduction if they could give a submissive and self-punitive response (rather than an assertive response), whereas, for non-depressed people, an assertive response had more effect. Arrindell et al. (1990) have shown that the degree of distress and NA in assertiveness is central to poor assertiveness and is associated with depression. Interestingly, there is some evidence that non-depressed people have positive biases (or a warm glow) in their information processing about the self. Based on the idea that subordinates are less 'free' to take social risks and could not afford positive biases, Gilbert et al. (1996) hypothesised that it was perceptions of social rank rather than mood that would be associated with positive biases. In a study of students, we found that, as predicted, measures of social comparison (feeling inferior to others) and submissive behaviour were better predictors of confidence estimates than a measure of depression. One can lose the 'warm glow' in contexts where one feels inferior to others. All these different studies, then, point to the role of subordinate, damage-limitation strategies in depression.

However, for humans, low rank is not always a position of anxiety or threat sensitivity, especially if one sees the higher ranks as benevolent and helpful. Moreover, submissiveness is made up of a complex set of behaviours, not all of which may be associated with stress or depression (Gilbert, 2000a). Hence, we can make a distinction between *voluntary* and *involuntary* submission (Gilbert, 1992, 2000a). Voluntary submissiveness would be behaviours such as willingly following the requests and demands of a leader or significant other (and from which one benefits), whereas involuntary submission is having to do things one does not wish to, when not to do so will result in conflicts and losses (for example, having to comply to a bullying other, or someone one is dependent on). As Sloman (2000a) makes clear, in the involuntary submissive situation there is submissiveness but *with continual arousal of fight and flight*. In this context, although submissive behaviour may reduce the chances of injury, it is ineffective in its function to reduce stress arousal because the person is still trapped in the aversive situation and may be still orienttaed to resist, fight, or escape. And, of course, in situations where the dominant is shaming, undermining, or abusive, the stress will be the greater. Thus, involuntary submissive behaviour may protect from threats to a degree but not do much to lift one's PA.

Defeats

Although low-ranking animals are commonly stressed, they are not necessarily depressed. Moreover, socially anxious people and low self-esteem people can feel inferior and behave submissively but may not be depressed (Gilbert, 2001b). Indeed, Brown and Harris (1978) suggest that low self-esteem is a vulnerability factor that can fuel depression in the face of provoking agents. There are, in fact, two other ingredients that may need to be present for depression: defeat and entrapment. Price (1972, Price & Sloman, 1987) first argued that depression might be an evolved response to social defeats where either there is a loss in social standing (rank) and/or an animal is being harassed from above and cannot escape to somewhere else or try something else. He argued that under such conditions the best response may be a form of demobilisation which stops the animal from engaging in behaviour that elicits further attacks, and signals to potential attackers that 'one is defeated and out of action'. Price originally called this kind of demobilisation a yielding subroutine of a subordinate strategy set, where the downregulation of PA forces the animal to yield and stay out of action for a while (Price et al., 1994). However, we have subsequently called it an involuntary defeat strategy (see Sloman & Gilbert, 2000). One reason for this is that socially anxious and low self-esteem people may use some subordinate strategies, and they may yield (be non-assertive) in many contexts, but it is the involuntary defeat strategy that may underpin some depressions.

Social defeats in animals have major physiological effects and can produce quite rapid and profound effects; that is, they set the system in a new state. Levitan et al. (2000) have reviewed data on the biology of submissive and defeat states, finding that defeated and/or harassed subordinates are chronically stressed, with increased HPA activation (Ray & Sapolsky, 1992; Sapolsky, 1989). Laboratory studies on rodents show that defeat experiences reliably result in physiological and behavioural consequences, including a decrease in offensive aggression, an increase in defensive responses, decreases in subsequent exploratory behaviour, increases in freezing, weight loss, reduction of appetitive behaviours, and disruption of escape learning (Gilbert, 2000a). Social defeats are also associated with retardation (Sloman et al., 2003). Importantly, however, within populations, there are individual differences in strategies (perhaps gene or early history related) for coping with down-rank agonism, rejection, and social defeats. For example, Von Holst (1986) studied tree shrews and found that defeated losers adopted one of two different strategies. Some continued with activities but in a timid and cautious way. They showed an elevated stress response and elevated tyrosine hydroxylase activity. However, other defeated animals became seriously demobilised, with greatly elevated cortisol responses and reductions in tyrosine hydroxylase. They died within 14 days of the confrontation. Even separating victor and loser by a wire mesh did not save these animals.

Mental defeat

It is, of course, a huge step to jump from animal studies of social harassment and defeat to those of human depression, and for all such attempts the devil is in the detail. Nonetheless, guided by animal work, Steven Allan and I decided to test whether perceptions of defeat were related to depression (Gilbert & Allan, 1998). We designed a defeat, self-report scale that asked about feelings of 'having lost important battles in one's life', 'fallen in social standing', and 'feeling defeated by life'. Note that, for humans, a sense of defeat can come from many sources; for example, one may feel one's life goals are defeated by a health problem or financial loss, but the key sense of defeat is of being knocked down, squashed, worse off than other people, and unable to recover (Gilbert, 1992, 2000a). Our defeat scale was highly correlated with depression (Gilbert & Allan, 1998; Gilbert et al., 2002).

We did not make the distinction between feeling defeated and mental defeat. However, important research in the field of post-traumatic disorders after torture has found that severity of symptoms and duration are related to experiences of mental defeat. Ehlers et al. (2000) point out that many victims of torture may feel defeated and sign false confessions, but they may not feel *inwardly or personally defeated* in the sense that they have lost autonomy. Mental defeat, however, is defined as 'the perceived loss of all autonomy, a state of giving up in one's mind all efforts to retain one's identity as a human being with a will of one's own' (p. 45). Mental defeat, in this context, was also associated with total subordination, such as feeling merely an object to the other; and with loss of self-identity, as if prepared to do whatever the other asked, and not caring whether one lived or died. Those who experienced mental defeat had more chronic post-traumatic stress disorder (PTSD) symptoms and higher depression. In the social-rank model, mental defeat would be related to feeling personally inferior in some way. Indeed, Ehlers et al. (2000) indicated that refusing to feel personally inferior to one's torturers (or perhaps others in the same situation) might help to avoid mental defeat.

Gilbert (1992, pp. 209–217) noted that similar themes (of feeling controlled by others and not caring whether one lives or dies) are common in some depressions. Clearly, for humans who make symbolic representations of the self and develop identities, the mechanisms of defeat will operate in and through these competencies (see below). Scott's (1990) anthropological studies indicate that, even though groups can be beaten down (for example, slaves in North America), their ability to hold on to their own identities and values affect their adjustment and resistance. Clearly, more research is needed on the differences between feeling defeated, loss of status and control, and mental defeat related to an internal sense of inferiority and a loss of self-identity. Interestingly, severely depressed people may feel that the illness itself robs them of their identity and makes them into a 'no-thing', and may feel mental defeat as part of the experience of being depressed. Such experiences raise questions of what evolved mechanisms may underpin defeat states and can be triggered by various routes.

Defeats and helplessness

Although there is good evidence that loss of control and beliefs about control are powerfully implicated in depression (Peterson et al., 1993), the point about social defeat and social harassment is that this is not just about losing control—though, of course, in one sense (loss of) control is key to a defeat and/or a harassed position. Rather, it is the knock-on effects of a defeat that are crucial, especially the way a defeat forces a change in social standing, comparison of oneself with others, and social behaviour (Gilbert, 2000a). It should be noted that in animal studies of learned helplessness (LH) (such as that induced by inescapable shock), helpless states tend to remit quite quickly, within 48–72 hours or so, and this has been a serious criticism of this model of depression (see Irwin, 2000). Recognising this, Weiss et al. (2000), rather than explore whether different types of stressor produce different effects, chose to try to breed a strain of rats that would show a longer-lasting response to inescapable shock. They failed, although they did find a strain that showed early life hyperactivity, and when young showed a more prolonged LH response.

Not only is prolonged exposure to shock a totally unnatural type of stress, but it is also a stress that requires no change in social communication, social cognition, or social activity. However, not only has social agonism been a common stressor for many animals for millions of years, because competition for resources can be acute, but also there is a range of evolved behaviours for coping with it; for example, submissive behaviour and defeat-demobilisation. Moreover, in response to a defeat (or ongoing harassment if an animal tries to mount a challenge), animals must change their social behaviour and downgrade exploration and acquisitive, confident social engagement behaviours—those very behaviours associated with PA. Furthermore, unlike shock-stress, social defeats and attacks can have long-term effects. Meerlo et al. (1996) found that a single episode of social defeat in rats could have measurable effects on biological rhythms, and eating and social behaviour in an open field up to 7 days later. Indeed, animals can die shortly after social defeats—and not from their injuries (MacLean, 1990; Von Holst, 1986). What emerges from the literature, then, is that defeats can produce rapid shifts (discontinuities) in functioning and be long lasting.

Gilbert et al. (2002), using a structural equation model, found that feeling defeated had specific effects on PA. Rooke and Birchwood (1998) found that loss of status, sense of defeat, and entrapment were also powerfully related to depression in people suffering from schizophrenia. In an interesting test of the defeat/entrapment model, Willner and Goldstein (2001) studied 76 stressed mothers and found that entrapment and defeat mediated the link between depression and stress. It is when stress is associated with a sense of personal defeat and entrapment that stress is associated with depression. In another test of the defeat and social-rank theory, Brenninkmeyer et al. (2001) explored symptoms of burnout (which has overlapping features with depression such as fatigue). Burnout interacted with feelings of inferiority to affect significantly levels of depression. Such findings need replication of course, and the direction of causality remains unclear.

From their studies of torture victims, Ehlers et al. (2000) have also argued that mental defeat is different from loss of control (helplessness). Clearly, to be subjected to torture is to lose control, but some people can still retain a sense of their identity. It is those who feel mentally defeated that suffer the higher depression and chronic PTSD symptoms, even after controlling for severity of the torture.

Defeats and hopelessness

Although hopelessness (a derivative of LH theory) has been put forward as a model for depression (Abramson et al., 1989), it should be noted that hopelessness is a relatively high-level cognition that, presumably, most animals could not have—yet animals clearly can (in some sense) show behavioural and physiological patterns of depression. We cannot test for hopelessness in animals, nor is it easy to study physiological mediators as we can for social losses, harassments of subordinates, entrapments, and defeats. In a way, hopelessness (which is undoubtedly a powerful factor in human depression) is an *outcome* of defeats and entrapments; it is a measure of predictions of long-term or continuing defeat and powerlessness; one is caught in a place, circumstances, or state of mind that one cannot get away from. This may be why it is correlated with entrapment (Gilbert & Allan,

1998) and is associated with suicide (Williams, 1997). Hopelessness also says little about social behaviour—except indirectly. The social-defeat and social-ranking model (Gilbert, 1992, 2000a; Price 1972; Sloman & Gilbert, 2000), however, suggests that defeats and subordination are intimately linked at the level of evolved mechanisms that regulate social behaviour, NA, and PA. Moreover, these regulators can produce rapid shifts in functioning. In the Gilbert & Allan (1998) study, we found not only that this measure was highly correlated with depression and hopelessness, but also that hopelessness was no longer significantly correlated with depression once defeat is controlled for. However, when we controlled for hopelessness, defeat was still highly correlated with depression.

Defeats and provoking agents

If humans carry within them a potential defeat strategy (no different from saying we have anger-attack strategies or anxious-flight strategies coded in the limbic system), it seems to operate by downgrading PA, and explorative and social engagement (Gilbert et al., 2002). Clearly, in humans, the elicitors and modulators of an involuntary defeat strategy are much more complex than they are in animals. Nonetheless, the typical elicitors of depression have the essence of 'defeat' about them. For example, Brown et al. (1987) and Brown et al. (1988) found that it is only life events that have long-term negative consequences that are related to depression. Such events include loss of resources and setbacks that force people to lower their standard of living (e.g., Ganzini et al., 1990); direct attacks on self-esteem that are shaming and humiliating, such as criticism and general putting-down in salient relationships (e.g., Belsher & Costello, 1988; Brown et al., 1995; Hooley & Teasdale, 1989); loss of (control over) core roles which are important for a person's sense of self and offer a sense of status, value, or prestige (e.g., Champion & Power, 1995; Gilbert, 1992; Rooke & Birchwood, 1998); and indirect attacks such as being ignored, marginalised, and lacking support and/or a confidant, indicating low access to social resources (Brown & Harris, 1978).

Blocked and ineffective defensive-coping behaviour

Van Praag (1998) suggested that certain types of depression can arise from dysregulation of the anxiety and aggression systems, and, undoubtedly, anger and anxiety are often part of depressed states. In recent years, I have been interested in the idea that, when people are in aversive situations (for example, losing control over situations, or, subject to shaming or non-supportive environments), not only are these stressful but also there is an automatic triggering of basic evolved defensive behaviours (Gilbert 2000a). There is a range of such behaviours, including fight, flight, submission, and help-seeking (Gilbert, 2000a, 2001c). Dixon (1998; personal communication, 1993) pointed out that if one arouses *but then blocks the execution of a defensive response* (such as flight and escape) in animals (such as rodents), one often sees passivity and immobility. Gilbert (1992) noted that LH studies in animals often involve arousing but blocking the innate defence of active escape behaviour. Moreover, many of the serious life difficulties associated with chronic stress (Morriss & Morriss, 2000) and depression, as found by Brown and Harris (1978; Brown et al., 1987), could be seen as *entrapments*; that is, people are highly motivated to get away from their current situation (aroused flight motivation) but feel unable to. Brown et al. (1995) explored this possibility and found that loss events associated with a sense of humiliation (feeling subordinated) and feeling trapped (unable to get away from the situation) were more predictive of depression than major loss events alone. Viewing a psychotic illness as a serious life event, Birchwood et al. (1993) found that those who felt unable to control the illness, and where flight motivated to their illness (wanted to get away from it), were more vulnerable to depression than those who engaged with and managed their illness. Gilbert and Allan (1998) developed an entrapment questionnaire and found that feelings of wanting to get away (high flight motivation) but being trapped were highly associated with depression, defeat, and hopelessness. Using focus groups of depressed people, Gilbert and Gilbert (2003) found that feeling trapped by both life events *and the depression itself* was a common experience of depression. Indeed, I am struck by how often the theme of entrapment comes up in depression—including its archetypal imagery—being stuck in a dark hole and unable to escape or get out. Rowe (1983) has long argued that depression is experienced as 'a prison', powerfully capturing the notion of entrapment. Of course, torture, as discussed above, is clearly one of entrapment. It has also been commonly observed that when some depressed people make plans to kill themselves (escape), their affect can improve, sometimes quite substantially. Here, at least, escape seems the primary affect regulator because after death there is not much hope of achieving anything (see Baumeister, 1990, for a discussion of these issues).

It can be useful for clinicians to explore and work with these themes (Gilbert, 2000b; Swallow, 2000), not least because people can feel trapped and resentful for a host of reasons, and entrapment can be associated with suicide (Williams, 1997). Moreover, Leahy (2000) has suggested that people can remain stuck or trapped in unhelpful situations or relationships because they feel they have invested too much in them to let go ('sunk costs'). This is not to suggest that, say, fight or flight would be adaptive if acted on. While sometimes aiding flight (as in leaving an abusive spouse) can be therapeutic, at other times turning off flight motivation may involve helping people to 'take on' their problems (engage rather than avoid or take flight), change their thinking, and cope in different ways. Moreover, learning how to be assertive might limit brooding resentment and rage. There might be many ways to lower fight/flight activation, but lowering it could do much to take pressure off the stress systems (Gilbert, 2000b).

In fact, if one considers the idea that depression is associated with an array of aroused defensive behaviours, such as fight, flight, help-seeking, and submission, one finds evidence that all these tend to be blocked, ineffective, or poorly regulated in depressed people. As reviewed elsewhere (Gilbert, 2001a), depressed people can be anxious and avoidant; can have raised irritation and anger levels; can be fearful of their anger, although they can have anger attacks (Brody et al., 1999); and may be ashamed and avoidant help seekers (Cramer, 1999), or their help seeking may turn people away (Segrin & Abramson, 1994). Suffice it to say that it looks as if the limbic system is in a high state of stress arousal, firing off defensive impulses to fight or escape, but because these are blocked or ineffective (or, if acted on, make things worse), the system stays in a state of chronic stress with all the disruptive feedback such states produce.

Summary

In brief, then, we have explored the types of evolved strategy (for dealing with separation, social defeats/involuntary low rank, and entrapments) that are designed to reduce resource seeking, confident exploration, and engagement in the environment. From an evolutionary point of view, activating these defences may be designed to be rapid (produce shifts in state), and switching from one defensive strategy to another (for example, from protest to despair) may also represent a switching point. This is not to say that some depressions are not the result of cumulative stress or that depression cannot emerge slowly. Nor is it to say that innate factors are the main controllers of the rapidity or intensity of switching into these states. Indeed, for some people, rapid shifting of states may be learned as a result of kindling (repeated activation of), conditioning, and sensitivity in key neurocircuitry (Sloman et al., 2003). Cognitive therapists use the idea of latent (explosive) schema activation (Beck, 1967). So the question of how human systems shift from one pattern to another is complex and multifactorial, but the question of 'what states' underpin depression can be illuminated by exploration of natural defences (such as protest-despair and entrapped defeat). Within this general frame, however, it has been stressed that for the severity of protest-despair, and demobilisation to defeats and mental defeats, there are major individual differences, found in both humans and animals, the source of which requires more research.

Even though today there are few major predators that threaten human infants, or the types of defeats humans encounter can be different from those of our primate ancestors, the templates of protest-despair and defeat-submission are still clearly available in our neuroarchitecture (Panksepp, 1998). Moreover, children and adults can be subject to a good deal of bullying, harassment, and rejection by parents, siblings, peers, or bosses, which has clear links to depression (Schuster, 1996). As I shall discuss in the last part of this chapter, even for those people who currently are not externally bullied, rejected, or harassed, there can be an ongoing internal harassment in the form of *self-criticism and self-blame*.

I should also say that the idea that depressed states are rooted in primitive evolved defensive strategies is not to undervalue models that stress the importance of control over one's life goals (e.g., Peterson et al., 1993)—defeats and entrapments can be inflicted in many ways (Gilbert, 1992). I am simply saying that to understand the changes in social cognition (such as the sense of self-as-inferior), social behaviour (such as submissiveness), and, often, intense changes of state in depression, we can suggest the activation of earlier evolved strategies that regulate NA and PA, and which are recruited to cope with a variety of stressors. So, for me, feeling abandoned and emotionally cut off from others, defeated and/or harassed with no way out; feeling trapped in a painful state of mind, inferior and/or subordinated in some way; and experiencing increases in poorly controlled defensive emotions, such as anger and anxiety, all these are ingredients in my 'depression cake'. These are the repeating themes in the clinic. But when we try to zero in on these themes, we must remember we are looking at a 'cooked cake'. In what follows, we will explore how the various interacting processes outlined, in this evolutionary biopsychosocial approach, can be mapped onto protest-despair and defeat-involuntary subordination mediators of low PA. A further discussion of the interaction between attachment and social rank can be found in Sloman et al. (2003).

VULNERABILITY

As noted, dimensional processes can produce discontinuities; that is, sudden changes or shifts. One person responds to a love rejection with mild dysphoria, but in another person the rejection triggers a serious depression. Much depends on the state of 'the system' before a stressor is encountered. Although cognitive therapists are fond of concepts such as latent schema, these are only part of the story. *System setters* that are going to influence how a stressor affects a system can operate in multiple domains. System setters are, of course, vulnerability factors.

Having identified some evolved regulators of PA and NA (such as separation-abandonment, defeats, and entrapments) that show clear evolutionary continuities between animals and humans, we can now explore a range of vulnerability factors (or system setters) and consider how these relate to sensitivity to protest-despair and entrapped-defeat defences. We will also explore the way our evolved capacity for self-schema can interact with these evolved strategic defences.

Genes

Vulnerability to bipolar disorders is highly heritable, and, in some types, mood systems are highly unstable (Akiskal & Pinto, 1999; Wilson, 1998). For some unipolar major depressions, there is a genetic vulnerability (McGuffin et al., 1991). It also seems likely that there may be a variety of genotypes for different types of depression. However, consider that cystic fibrosis is an inherited disease, but only if one inherits two copies (one from the father and one from the mother) of the genes. One copy increases lung mucus, but this can be highly protective against some lung diseases. Thus, a gene or genes for a disorder or degree of severity may manifest themselves only when associated with other genes, and in different combinations can give a positive advantage or a milder vulnerability. Or consider sickle-cell anaemia; its gene also protects against malaria (Wilson, 1998). Hence, it remains unclear whether the genes associated with depression also confer benefits, and, if so, which genes in what combinations, and in what contexts do they create serious problems.

The study of the ongoing, reciprocal, dynamic processes of individual–environment interactions suggests that the genotypic possibilities of functions can have unpredictable phenotypic outcomes. For example, there are variations in genetic sensitivity to depressed states possibly related to the 5-HT transporter gene that influences the metabolism of 5-HT. However, cross-fostering research in primates (that is, placing genetically at-risk infants with highly responsive mothers) suggests that such an apparent genetic sensitivity is only manifested in certain contexts. Indeed, animals with this genotype can do exceptionally well in certain developmental (such as high-care) contexts but badly in others (such as low-care) (Suomi, 1997; personal communication, September, 2000). So it is unclear whether genes affect the degree of shift (intensity of a response) to a stressor, and/or make one sensitive to learning in particular social contexts. If the latter, this could mean one's nervous system is more plastic and open to social shaping for good or bad. This seems to be the implication of Suomi's findings. Genes themselves can also be turned on and off by the environment. We cannot explore this here, but for a fascinating and highly readable account of the way the environment—including internal physiological processes such as cortisol—can have gene-controlling effects, see Ridley (2000).

Considering the two (possible) evolved regulators of mood states—attachment loss and social-rank defeat—there is good evidence that for attachment loss there are genetic differences in the intensity and duration of response to separation (Suomi, 1997). It is probable (although there is no good evidence) that the same is true for social rank and defeat. In bipolar spectrum disorders, hypomania is associated with a heightened sense of being up-rank and with sexuality, feeling important and confident, and having energy. Such a profile has been associated with high rank, and recent acquisition of high rank, in many animals (Gardner, 1982). Frenetic activity, including sexual behaviour, may be adaptive, in that one's position may not last for long—so one should make hay while it does (Wilson, 1998). In so far as the mechanisms for this profile may be a form of generalised disinhibition, this can spread through human cognitive systems, giving rise to poorly controlled thinking processes and preoccupation with high-rank (status) activity—being a world leader or the chosen one, or solving the riddles of the meaning of life. Depression is typically associated with the opposite—loss of confidence, feeling inferior and a failure, loss of energy, and social withdrawal. Just as there may be genetic variation in populations in the intensity and ease of triggering protest-despair, so there may be genetic influences underpinning the intensity and ease of triggering in the winner go-for-it strategies and in the loser defeat and failure (stop going for it) strategies (Wilson, 1998). It is unclear whether these are related to the same genetic sensitivities.

The evolution of self-schema

At this point, some readers might say, 'Yes, but even if we can understand animal depression in terms of primitive defences against abandonment, defeats, and harassments, we cannot apply these models to humans because we are a thinking, conceptualising species with complex cultures and meaning-making systems. Moreover, human depression is about self-awareness and self-conscious feelings such as shame and guilt.' To take this view is to misunderstand the evolved functions of self-conscious feelings. In fact, the capacity to develop self-conscious self-schema has arisen for evolutionary reasons. They are designed to serve certain functions—one of which is to regulate social behaviour in the competition for resources (Gilbert & McGuire, 1998).

Emotions such as rage/anger, fear/anxiety, sadness/despair, and joy/happiness (and their behavioural output systems, such as fight, flight, and approach) are often considered primary or basic emotions (Panksepp, 1998) and are the main components of our NA and PA systems (Clark, 2000). We share these emotions with many other animals. They can be elicited by simple threats and losses, and we know something of their evolutionary history (Nesse, 1998) and neurophysiology (Panksepp, 1998). Emotions such as shame, embarrassment, pride, and guilt are sometimes referred to as secondary, higher-order, or self-conscious emotions (Lewis, 1992; Tangney & Fischer, 1995). These emotions are indeed less shared (if at all) with animals, and are relatively new on the evolutionary stage, and we know much less about their neurophysiology (but see Schore, 2001). Self-conscious emotions may develop later than primary emotions and are dependent on various *competencies* (Zahn-Waxler, 2000). These competencies begin to unfold from around 2 years of age and include the ability to recognise the self as an object for others, theory of mind (ability to make judgements about what others are thinking), awareness of the ability for approval and disapproval, and ability for role taking and understanding social rules, and symbolic representations. However, although fairly new in evolution, these self-conscious competencies *blend* with primary emotions to give rise to self-conscious emotions of shame, pride, and guilt. Thus, a threat to the self as a social agent (such as shame) can recruit negative primary emotions (such as anxiety, anger, and disgust) and reduce positive emotions in various ways. Self-conscious emotions are key to the development of the self as a social agent and come to regulate social behaviour, and one's defences if abandoned, bullied, or defeated (Gilbert, 1998a).

Animals respond to signals in their environment and coordinate their behaviour via social-detection and output systems. They have little capacity for self-reflection, in part because they do not compete for symbolic indicators of status and investment from others and cannot work out detailed plans of how to present the self to others for good effect. Although chimpanzees can be cautious of a dominant animal and seek sexual opportunities, we have yet to find chimpanzees who wake in the morning wondering what to wear to impress a job interviewer or what to buy to impress a girlfriend on St Valentine's Day. Self-conscious awareness, however, is highly focused on how one exists in the eyes of others (the kind of emotions and feelings we think others have about us). It is built, in part at least, for self-presentation manipulations and reputation building (Leary, 1995). Such abilities and competencies allow us to build models of ourselves in relation to others, but the purpose of doing this is to compete for resources and achieve the same types of biosocial goals that other animals seek (such as good-quality alliances, sexual partners, and social success and acceptance).

Although many psychological researchers in depression believe that the two most salient schema underpinning depressions are related to schema for attachment loss (sense of unlovableness and abandonment sensitivity) and social defeat (feeling a loser or inferior) (e.g., Beck, 1987), such schema may reflect unconscious, evolved strategies. In fact, many human schemas probably have their origins in social signal-detection systems that enabled the decoding of social signals and coordinating of responses (to enact social roles) (Gilbert, 2000c). For example, even primitive reptiles adopt submissive postures in contexts of a dominant attack, or engage in courting displays to a potential mate. They do not need to 'know' they are doing this, let alone have any self-awareness of what they are doing or why. The human evolution of self-awareness and sense of self has given us opportunities to engage in social roles in a far more sophisticated way, but many basic *role patterns* are of old design (Gilbert, 1989; Gilbert & McGuire, 1998).

Early life experiences and interpersonal relationships

Even though there may be genetic and inherited variations in strategies for what to do if cut off from care, or if one is a winner or loser, many strategies are open to modification through learning and social contexts (Schore, 1994; Suomi, 1997). As noted above, there is increasing evidence that early life may sensitise stress, mood, and social behavioural systems. Humans have evolved into a highly socially intelligent species, with competencies for self-conscious emotions and self-schema, but one that requires a long and important period of parental dependency to develop. This dependency turns out to be a two-edged sword that carries great potential benefits but also potentially high costs (Gilbert & Miles, 2000). This is because early relationships play a powerful role in the maturation of the stress system and the cortical areas that modulate limbic-emotion systems (Hofer, 1994; Meaney et al., 1996; Schore, 1994, 2001). For example, physical affection, in the form of touch, holding, and cuddling, reduces HPA activity to stress (Field, 1998). Positive social experiences link positive affect with close relationships (Schore, 1994). Negative experiences (such as parental unresponsiveness, coldness, and abuse) activate defensive systems and are associated with various stress responses (Perry et al., 1995). People abused as children exhibit increased HPA activation and poorer recovery from stress than non-abused people (Heim et al., 2000), a fact which has been related to depression vulnerability

(Hart et al., 1996). Abusive experiences affect the maturation of the frontal orbital cortex, which is an important brain area for the regulation of affect (Davidson, 2000; Schore, 2001).

The physiological effects of social relationships

Leaving aside for a moment the fact that, for humans, social signals (like other stimuli) are subject to various forms of complex processing that give meaning to them, social signals can be physiological regulators in their own right, and this regulation starts from birth. For example, the presence of a mother and the way she interacts with her infant have major impacts on the infant's physiological states (Hofer, 1994) and brain maturation (Schore, 1994, 2001). There is increasing evidence that depression in new mothers affects the interactional styles between infant and mother, such as holding, comforting, and looking at the infant, and these can have serious impacts on infant development (Murray & Cooper, 1997). Moreover, unresolved abuse issues or neglect in a mother can have a major impact on her interactional style with her own child (Liotti, 2000; Sloman et al., 2003).

Miller & Fishkin (1997) review the evidence on how close adult–adult bonds evolved with physiologically regulating impacts on the mood, stress, sex hormones, and immune systems of participants (see Cacioppo et al., 2000; Zeifman & Hazan, 1997). There is good evidence that living in supportive and caring relationships has many physiological benefits for the stress and immune systems (Cacioppo et al., 2000; Uchino et al., 1996). Roy et al. (1998) found that social support moderates physiological stress responses to life events. Attachment, and affectionate and supportive relationships, then, are powerful physiological regulators influencing stress hormones, PA and NA, and other processes in interactional patterns between participants. Social relationships are not just sources of rewards and punishments, and sources for schema development; they are also sources of physiological regulation (McGuire & Troisi, 1998a).

Affecting the minds and emotions of others and the development of experiences of self

Let us take a closer look at the social relationship regulators of PA and NA and how these are related to the development of self-schema. Evolutionary theorists point out that much of our social behaviour is designed to affect the minds of others and particularly their feelings towards us. Gilbert (1989, 1997, 2001b; Gilbert & McGuire, 1998) suggested that internal models of self-worth are (in part) built up from experiences of successfully stimulating positive emotions in the minds of others. This process begins early in life, perhaps even from the first facial communications between infant and parent. For example, a mother's smile can induce a smile in the infant. Not only does the mother's smile activate PA in the infant, but also the infant's response involves the activation of various neural pathways of affect and psychomotor movement to produce the smile (Schore, 1994, 2001). In effect, the parent is stimulating and coordinating the maturation of various neuropathways and, in so doing, is sensitising certain types of PA- and NA-linked behavioural strategies in the child.

There is little doubt we have evolved to be highly sensitive and to respond with PA to the affection and approval of parents and peers (MacDonald, 1988). We do not (in the first instance) learn to respond to such signals with PA but are biologically set up to do so, and these early automatic responses become the sources for later self-schema (Greenberg & Pascual, 1997). But note that how a child is able to create PA and NA in a parent will feed back into internalised PA and NA about the self. Imagine Jane, a 3-year-old, drawing a picture, and then proudly holding it up for Mum's approval and admiration. Mum responds by kneeling down and saying, 'Wow—that's wonderful. What a clever girl.' Now, in this encounter, Jane not only experiences her mother as proud of her (she has generated PA in her mother), but also has emotions *in herself about herself*—she feels good about herself. PAs become associated with confident display and self-expression (in this case, a drawing). The triggering of PA in the self from having *stimulated the positive emotions in others* can then build into positive schema of the self: 'I am someone others like; therefore, I am likable.'

Suppose, however, Mum responds with, 'Oh no, not another of those drawings. They're all over the house, making a mess.' Clearly, Jane has failed to generate positive emotions in her mother but has instead inspired NA and is then unlikely to have good feelings about herself. Her head may drop, and she moves away, possibly in a state of disappointment and shame (Gilbert, 1998a). If such experiences are frequently repeated, internal models of the self will be linked to a history of failures in eliciting positive feelings in others (and/or generating negative feelings) and shame in the self. Such emotional experiences will then regulate the development of self-other schema and the organisation of PA and NA in the self, expectations of being able to elicit positive (valuing) attention from others, and risks of rejection and criticism (put-downs).

To offer another example, if a child experiences physical abuse and fear in interactions with her father, the typical way she *automatically* behaves around him may be with anxiety and submission-avoidance. From these patterns of activation, she may develop conditioned defensive responses to 'men in authority'. Thus, when dealing with 'men in authority', her stress-defence system is primed with biases in information processing (sensitivity to any threat signal from certain men) and a readiness to behave defensively with anxiety, submission inhibition, or avoidance. At this point, no high-level cognitive schema are necessary, and associative learning, based on repeated threat → evolved defensive behaviour activation (such as fearful submission), is sufficient to explain the behaviour (Gilbert, 1992). However, as she becomes able to observe and make sense of her own reactions (fear of men in authority and poor assertive behaviour) and the (social/cultural) implications of being abused, she may develop (reinforce) notions of herself as (say) submissive and weak or bad. Her schema developed from experiences of being threatened and frightened, as she had to take (evolved) defensive actions (submit) even before she could articulate a sense of a self as 'weak or bad'. In other words, we can develop a schema of being weak, lovable, etc., by how we have in the past (and recently) automatically felt and behaved in certain situations.

In this example, it is not that people develop a schema of 'self as weak' and *then* behave submissively, but, rather, they first behave submissively (automatic triggering of a fear-submissive responses) and then gradually articulate these automatic reactions into self-schema. This is to ask, what does it mean to be a person who feels and acts like this or has had these experiences of abuse? These meaning systems can be superimposed on more basic strategies. So, for both PA and NA, schema generated in interpersonal contexts (failure to elicit PA in others and/or having to respond from an early age to threats, criticism, and abuse) can be as much explanations of why we behave as we do, as causes.

In terms of schema development, as noted above, subordinate positions are not necessarily anxious positions if one sees more powerful or dominant others as helpful and benevolent.

Indeed, for such individuals, one might accentuate approach behaviours. Therefore, what various forms of abuse can do is to develop schema of more powerful-dominant others (and one's parent is always more powerful in the first instance) as hostile, exploitative, or unhelpful. As Liotti (2000) discusses, there may be intense ambivalence that produces approach avoidance conflicts with parental figures. These experiences, then, are 'system setters' that set up our psychobiological systems with the potential for making discontinuous jumps into defensive strategies.

Competing to be valued and loved (and losing)

As we emphasised, human relationships provide an array of valuable resources to individuals in the form of protection, care, support, and opportunities for reproduction (Buss, 1999; Gilbert, 1989). They are also physiologically powerful, including effects on the immune system (Cacioppo et al., 2000). It is worth remembering that viruses (and other pathogens) have played a large role in human evolution; the mortality rate was often high in early hominids. The influenza epidemic of 1918, at the end of the First World War, killed more people than died in that war. If access to affectionate, supportive relationships aids the immune system, survival from illness, and disability, and offers advantages of cooperative activity and sharing, then abilities to secure these relationships will be key drivers in evolution. Hence, we would expect humans to be highly attuned and responsive to them (Cacioppo et al., 2000), to be affected by their presence or loss, and to compete for them.

Barkow (1989) suggests that human competition has evolved from aggressive conflict into competing for 'prestige' and being seen as attractive and useful to others, and such competition is clearly linked to PA. Similarly, Gilbert (1984, 1989, 1997) suggested that not only do people compete to be seen as attractive/desirable but they also develop internal working models of their relative attractiveness/desirability to others (laid down in the first instance via relationships with siblings, peers, and parents), and from this derive confidence to engage in competing for social resources. Not only do signals of being valued and cared for raise PA but also raised PA is generally attractive to others. Those who feel relatively inferior and place themselves (or are placed) in unwanted, subordinate positions are likely to experience or perceive reduced control over valued social resources and more defeats in trying to obtain them. Keep in mind, though, that such perceptions are always impersonally linked. Feeling inferior to others who are seen as accepting, benevolent, and helpful will be quite different from seeing oneself as inferior to those who are hostile or rejecting, or to whom one has to 'prove one's worth' to be accepted. In fact, Gara et al. (1993) found that depressed people have negative views of themselves *and others.*

In fact, control over social resources is often exercised in social contexts in which others are seeking the same resources. Thus, as Tooby and Cosmides (1996) suggest, in successfully engaging in many forms of social relationship, such as eliciting parental investment, sibling rivalry, developing supportive peer relationships, and attracting desirable mates, there is an underlying competition. This is because investing in relationships is not cost free, and participants in roles will exercise some choice over whom they form a relationship with (whom they will invest their time and energy in, value, and support). Generally, people want to form relationships with and invest in people who are in some way useful to their own interests. Knowing this, people track their place in 'the competition' by *social comparisons* and *opinion tracking* (how much others value and support them in comparison with how much others criticise, reject, or ignore them) in whatever domain is important to them, be it physical beauty, intelligence, or popularity (Gilbert, 1997; Gilbert et al., 1995). However, as noted above, by the time children enter the world of peers, ready to compete for resources and find their place in a group, they will already have a history of being able (or not) to create PA in others. This history (in combination with genes and temperament) will have partly 'set the system' to move forward with relative confidence to seek affiliative relationships, or to be highly attuned to social rank, power issues, and threats.

Given that we have to compete in social arenas to 'prove our worth' (stimulate positive feelings in others) in order to engage them in helpful roles, Santor and Walker (1999) found that having qualities that one thinks others will value is especially related to self-esteem. Leary et al. (1995) suggested that self-esteem is a form of internal tracking of one's attractiveness to others and sense of belonging. In other words, it is what one thinks others will value about the self that is often key to self-esteem and confidence. It is the *competitive element* which tells us much about why depressed people are often so focused on rank evaluations of self-worth and self-esteem (Price, 2000), typically think about themselves in social comparative terms, and see themselves as inferior to non-depressed others (Buunk & Brenninkmeyer, 2000). Herein lies a link to the subordination and defeat strategies we discussed earlier.

The self-conscious emotion of shame is the human archetypal experience of put-down and rejection—of involuntary subordination (Gilbert, 1998a, 2000d). People who have a deep sense of shame feel unattractive to others; feel unworthy (do not deserve) or feel unable to win love, affection, or respect; and think they will lose in competitions for friends, sexual partners, affection, and help from others. They are also very sensitive to the signals they emit and the things they reveal about themselves. There is good evidence that shame is linked to negative social comparison, beliefs that others see the self as inferior, negative self-evaluation, submissive behaviour, and depression (Gilbert, 2000c; Tangney et al., 1992). If shame and needing to compete for social recognition are salient in depression, one would expect to find these themes in the recall of parenting in patients. Indeed, Gilbert and Gerlsma (1999) found that recall of being shamed as a child and being a less favoured child (that is, seeing oneself as inferior to one's siblings) was highly associated with psychopathology, even after controlling for warmth. Shame was also linked to hostility. There is little research here, but, clinically, it is not uncommon to find depressed people who feel their families were highly competitive (rank orientated) for attention and care, and/or feel they have lived in the shadow of a sibling, or were regarded as the 'black sheep' of the family. The common theme is that they see life as a competition and that they have lost in the competitions for place and recognition in the family (and later in wider social groups).

Hence, it is not only that depressed people have negative thoughts about the self and their futures (as, of course, they do) but also that the sense of self is associated with *low* PA, shame, and, at times, high NA (such as self-dislike or even self-hatred). Moreover, they often believe that 'it is because of their personal deficits' that they will be defeated (or are defeated) in their efforts to compete for and raise their social standing or attractiveness. For example, Kay had a major weight problem and had been bullied at school. She had tried many diets but had made one big effort with a new diet she had found on the Internet. When that, too, failed, she slipped into a serious, suicidal depression. She felt both trapped in, and defeated by, her body, ugly, and of very low rank in regard to her attractiveness. I suspect that any therapy that is helpful for depression, be it by challenging negative thoughts or via drugs, must change the affective orientation to the self. I will return to this shortly with a discussion of compassionate mind work. I suspect that many people need a certain amount of positive signals to keep the PA system toned up (stimulated), although, as in all these processes, there are likely to be individual variations.

RELATING STYLES

In the model I am suggesting, social contexts and relating styles (mediated by self–other schema) that make it difficult to elicit or maintain a flow of positive affiliative relationships, or achieve evolutionarily meaningful biosocial goals (McGuire & Troisi, 1998b), as well as disruptions of relationships that recruit perceptions of inferiority and low rank, are likely to be vulnerability factors for depression (Sloman et al., 2003). Brown et al. (1995) found that social losses associated with humiliation (perceptions of reduced social rank) were more depressogenic than loss events alone. In a study of grief-triggered depression, Horowitz et al. (1980) found that some people had negative latent self-schema (associated with feelings of worthlessness and inferiority), which their spouse had helped to keep latent. When the spouse died, these negative self-schema become reactivated (self as inferior and helpless), complicating grief and increasing the risk of depression. Some limited research on monkeys has also shown that low rankers show a more intense and prolonged response to separation and attachment disruption than high rankers (e.g., Rasmussen & Reite, 1982).

Attachment theorists have illuminated some key interpersonal styles that increase vulnerability to depression. Collins and Feeney (2000) summarise these:

> Adult attachment researchers typically define four prototypic attachment styles derived from two underlying dimensions; *anxiety* and *avoidance*.... The anxiety dimension refers to one's sense of self worth and acceptance (vs. rejection) by others and the avoidance dimension refers to the degree to which one approaches (vs. avoids) intimacy and interdependence with others. Secure adults are low in both attachment-related anxiety and avoidance; they are comfortable with intimacy, willing to rely on others for support, and confident that they are valued by others. *Preoccupied* (anxious-ambivalent) adults are high in anxiety and low in avoidance; they have an exaggerated desire for closeness and dependence, coupled with a heightened concern with being rejected. *Dismissing avoidant* individuals are low in attachment-related anxiety but high in avoidance; they view close relationships as relatively unimportant and they value independence and self-reliance. Finally, *fearful avoidant* adults are high in both attachment anxiety and avoidance; although they desire close relationships and the approval of others, they avoid intimacy because they fear being rejected. (p. 1054)

In a number of studies, Mario Mikulincer, a prominent researcher on attachment relations, has found that securely attached people see others as relatively benevolent and can regulate stress by appropriate support seeking and self-management, while anxiously attached people show typical 'protest' behaviour to stress and become clingy and controlling. Avoidant attached people do not seek help for stress, do not have views of others as benevolent, use repression as a coping mechanism, and are overly self-reliant (see Mikulincer et al., 2000). Sloman et al. (2003) also note that secure attachments make it easier to deal with defeats and regulate affect and cognition in the context of defeat.

A related concept has been that of rejection sensitivity. Rejection-sensitive children and adults expect rejection when asking for help and respond with more NA (anger and anxiety) to rejection (Downey et al., 1998a,b). In an ongoing study of depressed people in our department, we have found that rejection sensitivity is significantly correlated with depression, seeing the self as inferior to others, and submissive behaviour. Based on Bowlby's (1969, 1973) idea of attachment as a safe base, Gilbert (1989, 1993) noted that securely attached children feel relatively safe in interpersonal contexts, feel lovable (as well as loved), and thus have confidence to build helpful and PA-boosting relationships, whereas the insecurely attached do not. Sloman (2000b) has outlined how rejection sensitivity can develop from attachment difficulties and be manifested in inferiority sensitivities. In a series of studies, Allan (2000) found that insecure attachment was highly correlated with rank perceptions (for example, seeing the self as inferior and thinking that others look down on the self), with some evidence that social rank and perceptions of defeat may mediate the link between attachment insecurity and depression.

If low or threatened social rank conveys vulnerability to depression, one would expect that social anxiety would be a vulnerability factor. Although not all socially anxious people are depressed, of course, social anxiety is comorbid with other disorders, including depression, schizophrenia, eating disorders, and substance misuse and often precedes these disorders (Schneier et al., 1992). Again, one reason for such comorbidity, and why social anxiety may often precede a mood disorder (Alpert et al., 1997), is that social anxiety can reduce the ability to develop supportive/affiliative relationships (Gilbert, 1992). Spence et al. (1999) found that socially phobic children have more negative cognitions, expect more negative outcomes from interactions, express anxiety, are more submissive, and thus have less positive interactions with peers and are more likely to be rejected. Socially anxious adults see their anxious behaviours and symptoms as unattractive to others (Creed & Funder, 1998); indeed, social phobics, in first encounters, are liked less and seen as less sympathetic or desirable as friends than low socially anxious people (Alden & Wallace, 1995). They are then disadvantaged in eliciting PA in, and positive responses from, others (Gilbert, 2001b).

Other researchers have focused on generalised raised anxieties in social relationships, often referred to as 'interpersonal sensitivity'. Davidson et al. (1989) explored a measure of interpersonal sensitivity in depression and suggested that:

> Interpersonal sensitivity (IPS) is a construct that refers to an individual's hypersensitivity to perceived self-deficiencies in relation to others. It embraces sensitivity to rejection and criticism on the part of others; it also embodies a sense of personal inadequacy, inferiority, and poor morale. Such individuals are quick to take offense, are unduly sensitive to ridicule, feel uncomfortable in the presence of others, and show a negative set of expectations in their dealings with others. A close relationship with social phobia is suggested. (p. 357)

Their study showed that high scorers, compared to low(er) scorers had an earlier age of onset, more chronicity, and more severe depression; were more retarded; had higher guilt and suicidality; and were more paranoid. Again the themes of low rank are strongly implicated.

Social rank again

A potential limitation of this type of research is that it does not clearly delineate the exact nature of the threat and the defensive response. Protest-despair was designed to cope with attachment loss and unavailability, but the defeat-submissive defences are to cope with the threat posed by potentially hostile or rejecting others (Gilbert, 2000a). Hence, as noted by Gilbert and Gerslma (1999), while attachment relationships in families have been well studied, competitive styles (such as competing to win affection and sibling rivalries) and rank-orientated ways of relating have been less well researched (see Dunn, 1992).

For the activation and use of rank-related defensive responses, there are two very important domains that can lead to vulnerability. The first is where child–parent relationships are abusive and/or are marked by high expressed emotion (over-involvement, intrusiveness, and criticism) (Wearden et al., 2000). The second domain is sibling and peer bullying. It is now well known that sexual abuse is a major risk factor for later depression, especially chronic depression in women (Andrews, 1998). In a recent major review and study on child maltreatment in the UK for the National Society for the Prevention of Cruelty to Children (NSPCC), Cawson et al. (2000) found that there are numerous ways in which children can be threatened: humiliation/ and degradation, withdrawal of love, harming something dear to a child, showing marked dislike of a child, and terrorizing. In their large community study, they found that 33% of men and 34% of women acknowledged some experiences of being terrorized by their parents (Table 37).

Peer and sibling bullying is also a risk factor for depression (Schuster, 1996; Smith & Myron-Wilson 1998). As reviewed by Smith and Myron-Wilson (1998), bullies, bully/victims (who oscillate between subordinate and aggressive dominant behaviours), and victims show disturbances in early attachment relationships, and bullies often learn their behaviour in families high in conflict (parents or siblings act as hostile dominants) with harsh and inconsistent discipline (that is, non-safe environments). Victims, however, may come from families that are over-enmeshed. In a different paradigm, Vinokur and van Ryn (1993) found that social undermining (defined as social hindrance, negative social support, and social conflict) had a stronger, though more volatile, impact on mental health than social support over two time periods.

Both parental maltreatment or abuse and peer or sibling bullying can be seen as forms of harassment that inflict defeats/controls on the child. Moreover, they seriously interfere with efforts to stimulate PA in others—to be liked and accepted. In both cases, the commonly activated defences may be fight, flight-withdrawal, or submissive inhibition. However, these may be unhelpful in developing positive relationships—the things humans compete for and can stimulate PA.

Gender differences

Considerations of gender touch on something we cannot explore here in detail but should mention. If one experiences early childhood as one of rejection or bullying by parents and/or peers, what is it that determines whether defensive strategies will take the low-rank, anxious, and submissive route (where there is as least the hope of developing affiliative and caring relations), as opposed to aggressive strategies (becoming a self-reliant bully or exploiter)? These are sometimes linked to internalising and externalising disorders. There are many possibilities here, but one that may throw light on sex differences in depression is that, because females carry their young in their womb and care for them subsequently, they can less afford to fight because of risk of injury to themselves and their young. Taylor et al. (2000) discuss this theme in depth and conclude that women are more orientated to 'tend and befriend' as stress-controlling strategies, making them more susceptible to loss of affiliative relationships. Men (from abusive backgrounds) may have more to gain (as a reproductive strategy) by switching to aggressive strategies and forming loose bonds, with little commitment.

Women, then, may be more orientated to submissive defences (or, at least, less orientated to fight) and more competitive in domains of 'love and support seeking' than men. Interacting with these dispositions are the cultural rules that shape the identities of men and women (for example, men should be tough and fearless and women submissive and agreeable). Cohen (2001) offers a fascinating discussion of these themes. Gender differences in depression, then, require explanations that take account of differences in male and female reproductive strategies, hormonal-affect regulators, basic defensive strategies (submissive versus aggressive), cultural depictions of status and desirability (such as thin and beautiful versus tough and hard driving), peer styles of bullying, and cultural contexts that frustrate people's ability to achieve their goals (see McGuire & Troisi, 1998b, for a discussion of these issues).

EVOLUTION, DEFENSIVE PROCESSING, AND THE SELF

There is little doubt that depression involves biases and distortions in attention, memory, and information processing (Gotlib et al., 2000). One has to ask whether these can be adaptive. To answer this, we should distinguish between adaptations and 'exaptations'. Exaptations are adaptations that are recruited for new uses for which they were not originally designed, or triggered by contexts which were not present in the ancestral environment (Buss, 1999). They can be helpful; we did not evolve our finger dexterity or memory systems to perform piano concertos, but systems already evolved can be used and developed for these extraordinary feats. However, some exaptations can be unhelpful liabilities.

There is good evidence that many 'normal' information-processing routines have built-in biases, including biases to think more positively of one's own group and kin than outgroups and non-kin, self-serving biases, and sexual-attraction biases (Tobena et al., 1999). As noted elsewhere (Gilbert, 1998b), cognitive distortions can also be linked to a basic *defensive* heuristics and biases in information processing; for example, *better safe than sorry*. Thus, if an animal hears a sound in the bushes, it may be better for it to assume a predator and run away than stay to gather the evidence. Overestimating danger may lead to the expenditure of effort by running away when one did not need to, but underestimating a danger could be fatal. Algorithms for information processing under stress are thus often based on quick, safety-first heuristics rather than logic or rationality.

For a harassed subordinate, the defeated, or an unprotected juvenile, downregulation of PA that puts powerful breaks on exploration and resource-seeking behaviour could be adaptive. These same processes may be involved in reducing access to memories of positive events or being able to anticipate positive outcomes of efforts to improve one's position. However, these mechanisms evolved long before humans evolved competencies of self-awareness and self-reflection ('I am a failure'), and capacities to ruminate on oneself and, via self-criticism, to 'harass oneself'. These higher-level possibilities for metarepresentations can both reflect and feed back onto evolved strategies that regulate affect. Such processes can create highly maladaptive feedback loops of spiralling depression and state shifts. This touches on the important new area of research into metacognition (thinking and reflecting on one's thoughts and feelings) (Wells, 2000). It is highly unlikely that metacognitive abilities evolved to worsen depression (more likely, they evolved because they gave advantages in competing for social attractiveness via working out advantageous self-presentation) (Gilbert, 1997). Nonetheless, because evolved functions can be used in ways for which they were not designed, metacognitive abilities may work to reduce thresholds for, intensify, and maintain depression by setting up maladaptive feedback cycles. Some of the therapeutic manoeuvres used when working with metacognitions (Wells, 2000) may work if they help to decouple evolved mechanisms (as for defeat or subordination) from higher self-defining competencies; for example, 'I may feel like a failure because this is the program my primate limbic system is running, but this does not mean I am a failure.' Note that in evolutionary cognitive therapy we might sometimes use notions of underlying evolved algorithms as explanations for why people feel as they do, and to underline the importance of exploring one's thinking in a more detached way.

Another aspect to this has been noted by Teasdale (1988), who suggested that as people face setbacks or become depressed, some are able to self-sooth and limit the slide, while, for others, memories of past defeats and harm, self-attacking, and more extreme types of negative thinking come to the fore. Indeed, it is not just metacognition that sets up painful spirals, but, as Reynolds and Brewin (1999) have found, depressed people can suffer from painful intrusive negative memories, especially those of loss, rejection, failure, and/or being bullied; in a way, perhaps, they are being 'reinfected' with these negative signals.

Internal harassment

One of the criticisms of the social-rank model of depression is that people can occupy a low rank in society but have positive (personal) self-esteem and not be depressed, while those in high social positions (such as top models, pop stars, or actors) can still experience feelings of low self-esteem and depression. This also suggests that having access to resources (such as wealth or social position) does not always protect from depression. This is one of the reasons I am dubious about depression being only an issue of control over goals (Peterson et al., 1993) or a monitor of good and bad circumstances, as suggested by Nesse (2000)— although, of course, poverty and negative life events are certainly major risk factors (Morriss & Morriss, 2000; Wilkinson, 1996). Social-rank theory offers a different explanation for the depressed pop star. First, successful people can be competitive and perfectionist, sometimes as efforts to make up for earlier failures to win love and affection (insecure attachments). In fact, some forms of perfectionism are related to underlying feelings of inferiority (Wyatt & Gilbert, 1998) and probably a sense of defeat if standards cannot be met. Cognitive therapists (Beck et al., 1979) suggest that a small defeat or setback can, via a process of overgeneralisation, spread to more global self-perceptions such that people believe that anything they try to do will end in defeat or not be good enough. Second, many successful people I have worked with can feel *internally harassed,* put down, and defeated by their own negative and self-attacking thoughts. Their self-attacking is both a drive to achieve and a liability. Third, people often feel trapped by their own self-attacking thoughts and would like to escape from them (Gilbert & Allan, 1998; Gilbert et al., 2001). Fourth, self-attacking affects the ability to form affiliative relationships. Zuroff et al. (1999) found that those high on dependency needs are submissive and inhibit hostility to others. Self-critics, however, behave in hostile and resentfully submissive ways, are relatively poor at validating others, and have problems in developing affiliative relationships. Zuroff et al. (1994) found that the degree of self-criticism in childhood is a predictor of later adjustment.

One can often trace the origins of these ways of treating the self back to abusive or neglectful experiences, or trying to please a parent, and analysts have long talked about internalised relationships coming to control one's view of oneself (see Baldwin & Fergusson,

2001, for research and discussion of this). But whatever their sources, there is an ongoing set of signals that people are giving themselves that are *basically put-downs and attacks.* Cognitive therapists, of course, call these 'negative automatic thoughts' and link them to self-other schema. But the point is that negative automatic thoughts do not operate in a physiological vacuum; some forms of them depict internal (social-like) relationships, and may activate more primitive strategic defences (Gilbert, 2000c).

Internal stimuli, one's thoughts and images, can act like external ones. For example, generating sexual imagery (even when alone) can lead to sexual arousal, and focusing on the enjoyment of a holiday can lead to excitement (with the relevant physiological elements). Similarly, one's own self-attacking thoughts can be sources of stress. The negative self-cognitions ('I'm no good, a complete loser, a failure; no one could love me') so typical of depression (Beck et al., 1979), can, for example, also stimulate desires to submit to (to appease or agree) and/or escape from these put-downs (Gilbert & Allan, 1998; Gilbert et al., 2001). Greenberg et al. (1990) suggested that depression is more likely when individuals cannot defend themselves against their own attacks and feel beaten down and defeated by them. In a fascinating study of these ideas, Whelton (2000) measured students' levels of self-criticism with the Depressive Experiences Questionnaire. He then asked the students to sit in one chair and spend 5 minutes imagining themselves sitting in the other chair, and to criticise themselves. They were then invited to switch chairs and respond to the self-criticism. Those high in self-criticism often submitted to (agreed with) their own self-criticisms, exhibited shame postures (slumbered with head down) and sad faces, and felt weak and unable to counteract their own self-criticisms—in other words, submissive and defeat-like profiles were activated by their own attacks. In an ongoing study in our department, we are finding that students high in a self-report measure of self-attacking find it relatively easy to imagine and visualise a self-critical part of themselves, but less easy to imagine and visualise a self-supporting part. For those low in self-attacking, the reverse is the case. It is difficult not to get the impression that what is going on inside a self-critical person is a kind of war—a war of shaming and dominating parts and submitting and defeated parts (that is, internal high expressed emotion (HEE) and bullying harassment). Internal mechanisms for enacting social roles (dominating and subordinating) are playing off (interacting) with each other (Gilbert, 2000c). As one recent patient said, 'I don't need others to put me down, I do it so well myself!'

Gilbert et al. (2001) used this idea to explore negative self-cognitions (self-attacking) in depression and malevolent voices in schizophrenia. They found that for both depressed people and those with schizophrenia, depression was associated with how powerful and dominating they felt their thoughts or voices to be. Moreover, be it a hostile voice or a self-attacking thought, depression was associated with desires to escape but feeling trapped with it. People can want to escape from their own thoughts and feelings, especially when these are subordinating, hostile, and painful (Baumeister, 1990).

Self-blame and subordination

Self-blame can be part of internal harassment, especially if people focus and ruminate on how (they believe) they may have caused bad things to happen. The origins of self-blame are many; for example, it may be guilt or shame based (Gilbert, 1997). People may blame themselves for not being able to live up to others' expectations, or parents may blame themselves for how their children turn out. Cognitive therapists (Beck et al., 1979) often see depression-linked self-blame as a cognitive distortion or error. However, as noted above, in some contexts, it is important that animals and humans control the signals they emit, and these controls are exerted via unconscious strategies. Hence, some forms of self-blame may be linked to subordinate strategies and the control of aggression. As noted above, subordinates often cannot risk being aggressive up rank. We can think about it from the point of view of a child who needs to win love and protection from a parent. An angry, accusing child who blames the parents for their bad behaviour towards the child (such as scolding or hitting) might court more trouble, and, as noted above, a subordinate defence (such as a shame profile of head down and non-aggression) might be more automatic and useful (see Keltner & Harker, 1998). Indeed, Bowlby (1980) argued that children can use *defensive exclusion* in such contexts. This requires screening out the bad behaviour of the other (which could activate aggressive retaliation) and hence helps to control the child's aggression. Moreover, such defensive exclusion blocks from awareness the more serious and threatening possibility that one's parent is dangerous and bad. Self-blame also carries the hope, at least, that one can find out how to conduct oneself so as to reduce harm. If one focuses on what is bad in the parents (but cannot control them because they are more powerful), one is less orientated to focus on one's own ability to avoid punishment. Allen and Gilbert (2000) explored this as form of inner deception.

If self-blame is, at times, part of a subordination strategy, we would expect to see it emerge when people are under serious threat from powerful others. There is good evidence that this is so. For example, many studies on child sexual abuse find that, although it is quite illogical, many children (and later) adults blame themselves. Ligezinska et al. (1996) found that self-blame and guilt in children for extrafamilial abuse was associated with higher fear and depression. Kimberly (1990) found that adults who blamed themselves as children for abuse had higher depression and lower self-esteem. Andrews and Brewin (1990) found that women living with abusive men often blamed themselves for the violence, but changed their attributional style when they moved away; that is, when it was safe to do so. So sometimes it may be safer to blame oneself because this will inhibit one's anger when its outward expression could be dangerous—that is, the dominant other will simply retaliate powerfully and escalate. In many religious texts, people blame themselves for what they perceive as God's persecution of them (Jung 1952/1992). Gilbert (1992) suggested that these may be examples of defensive cognitive strategies, but humans can experience them, not as the defensive strategies they are (I blame myself because it is safer), but as a reflection of reality (I really am to blame). In other words, they are themselves deceived (Allen & Gilbert, 2000). Self-blame then turns out to be an extremely complex form of human processing that can have many different functions (such as defensive) (see Driscoll, 1988), and may be as much a part of a defensive strategy (such as, subordination) as a cause; therefore, to treat it only as a schema-driven cognitive distortion may be overly simplistic.

COMPASSIONATE MIND

If I may return to the 'depression in heaven' idea and the cultural beliefs about the reasons that life can be so harsh, I must admit I share the Buddhist view here (Dalai Lama, 2001). And over the years I have, like many others, come to the view that compassion is a powerful antidote to depression (e.g., Rubin, 1975). Compassion is an important perceived element in therapists; that is, they are seen as empathic, as trying to understand, share in the pain of depression, and find a way out (they offer a flow of positive acceptance signals)—and certainly not as shaming or degrading. However, there can also be compassion for the 'suffering of the self', from the self. The theory behind this view is derived from what is known about the physiological effects of supportive as opposed to hostile signals (Gilbert, 2000c). If people give themselves negative signals and put themselves down a lot, they can get depressed, just as if someone else were abusing and bullying them. The brain (limbic system) responds to bullying signals it cannot defend against with stress reactions and ultimately demobilisation (Whelton, 2000). And if a person feels defeated and unlovable, this will lower PA. However, we know that if people receive positive signals in the form of being valued, supported, and cared for (and the affect of these signals is crucial), this is good for their physiology (Cacioppo et al., 2000). Hence, it can be suggested that developing self-supporting signals (or the care-giving mentality; Gilbert, 1989) for the self can be physiologically regulating. The details of the therapy approach can be found elsewhere (Gilbert, 2000c), but a flavour of it can be given briefly.

In compassionate mind work, we are trying to raise PA for the self and develop new internalised (caring), self-to-self relationships. To do this, people might first learn to identify things they feel depressed about, such as failing in a relationship for which they blame themselves. As in basic cognitive therapy, a person might test certain ideas (evidence for and against) about blame or 'being unlovable' and so forth. Hence, one may have a chain of negative thoughts and a set of alternatives. However, it can be important to help people to be empathic to their own distress (for example, it is sad that I have this difficulty) and give space to grieving, if this is appropriate. Some people bypass their sadness and grief. They do not know how to process it, are frightened of it, or may focus on anger and have thoughts such as: 'I am stupid or weak to let this upset me; I should be stronger', or 'It's my own fault anyway, so I deserve it.' They use a basic dominating, bullying style even when distressed. If they treated other people this way (kicking them when they are down), they would be seen as somewhat psychopathic.

So we try to point this out; it is not just the unreasonableness of some of the attacks but the anger and contempt that is salient (Greenberg et al., 1990). To counter this, we focus on the feelings of warmth and compassion, perhaps using imagery of a compassionate person and how such a person might look or sound as a helper. Once this affect is elicited (to some degree), they go over their 'alternative coping thoughts' in their mind, trying to generate as much compassion and warmth as possible. The therapist may say, 'Let's go though these alternative thoughts again, but as you read them through try to imagine hearing them in your mind, as if a compassionate part of you were speaking them.' Or the therapist might say, 'Can you imagine the voice of someone who is very understanding of the distress you feel, and who is speaking warmly and compassionately to you to encourage and support you.' The idea here is to get a warm *emotional tone* in the alternative thoughts. This can be practised a number of times in the therapy. The idea is directly to undermine *the affect* of the self-attacking, to get into the 'limbic' processes. In a way, it is like trying to generate an alternative incompatible affect, not unlike teaching people relaxation as a counter-affect to anxiety. Warmth can be a counter to hostility and contempt, and it touches many other aspects of ongoing work, such as forgiveness (Gilbert, 2000c;e).

To date, there is no clear evidence that this approach gives any additional advantage over evidence-based challenges and behavioural change. However, since we developed this approach with self-critical depressed people, a number of them have suggested that this was a key aspect for them in beginning to believe in their alternative thoughts and generate internal feelings of being supported. One patient said that when she felt bad she sometimes did not challenge her thinking at first, but recognised her distress (rather than focus on 'self as bad'), used her imagery, took a moment to try to focus on feelings of warmth, *and then* gradually was able to challenge her thinking. Helping people become compassionate to their own distress and mistakes, cope with grief processes if necessary, learn how to challenge negative automatic thoughts with warm affect in the challenge (rather than detached logic), and develop compassionate imagery is an ingredient *added* to a basic cognitive approach. However, helping people develop inner warmth can be difficult. For example, it can put people in touch with enormous grief that for a variety of reasons can seem overwhelming.

In the last 10 years, there has been a quiet revolution in ideas of how to work with depressed people's thinking; one form is called *mindfulness* (e.g., Teasdale, 1999). We lack the space to explore this here, except to say that this approach focuses on the importance of detached observation of one's own thinking, acceptance, non-judgement, non-striving, and letting go. Some of these practices are derived from Buddhist approaches to mind regulation and philosophy (for example, the Buddha's Four Noble Truths, teaching that a root of our suffering lies in our attachment to and cravings for things that are impermanent). Moreover, Buddhism has had a strong focus on metacognition (although Buddhists do not call it that) (Dalai Lama, 2001). Hence, these approaches may also be ideal for learning how to work with one's evolved archetypal mind that can push and pull in all directions. Personally, I am also interested in Buddhist approaches to compassionate healing imagery (Mullen, 2001)—an affective element not prominent in mindfulness as yet. Compassionate mind work is linked to an evolution-physiology theory about the role of external and internal supportive caring signals, and is part of a larger theory of mental processes called 'mentality theory' (Gilbert, 1992, 2000c).

CONCLUSION

We started this chapter by wondering whether one could be depressed in heaven. It turns out that the 'if not—why not' reasons illuminate many common assumptions about depression, and based on these assumptions/beliefs, many people over the ages have tried many different things. Our modern Western assumptions fall (fairly) neatly into biopsychosocial ones of social contexts, early life sensitisation, internal psychology, and physiology (Akiskal & McKinney, 1975). However, the biopsychosocial approach is not just a set of different assumptions and models thrown together. As argued elsewhere (Gilbert, 1995), we need to understand *interactions* and why some interactions cause the effects they do. My own biopsychosocial approach has always had strong evolutionary flavourings because I think that many of the elicitors of depressed states have a lot to do with how our brains and needs have been shaped over millions of years.

We noted that the onset of depression can be gradual, or there may be marked and intense shifts in states. For these, we need models that can account for system discontinuities in function when a system can switch between states (as in catastrophe theory). We also suggested that it is shifts in PA that might be the key to depression. We then went in search of evolved regulators that might produce shifts of states (especially loss of PA), and we suggested that protest-despair and entrapped defeat might be good candidates. For there, we explored the evolution of human needs for care and to be seen as attractive and able to secure important and evolutionarily meaningful biosocial goals (for example, close alliances, access to sexual opportunities, and freedom from oppression)—social relationships are powerful biological regulators. We noted how people compete for them and how early life prepares us to enter the competition. We also noted that control theory, attachment theory, and social-rank theory are not competitive models—but the devil is in the detail of how such biopsychosocial processes interact—on this, far more research is needed. Finally, contrary to what some people think about social-rank theory, while its therapeutic implications can be about helping people escape adversity or become more assertive and independent, it is also about helping people become more inwardly compassionate and give up excessive competitiveness and internal self-attacking (called internal bullying and harassment), in order to develop a compassionate rationality (Gilbert, 2000b;c;e).

I agree with Nesse (2000) that it is not possible to say whether serious depression itself (or what type) is an adaptation, is at times adaptive, or is simply an unfortunate side effect of the evolution of other mechanisms, such as competencies for self-reflection and rumination. I guess that if we had not evolved the capacity to plan, fantasise about our futures, reflect on ourselves, and ruminate for good or ill, some of the sources of our depression and the maintenance of it would not be there. But though these are powerfully involved in human depression, the state itself speaks to something deeper, darker, and older in us. It is about physiological systems that evolved long ago, primitive defensive responses that become compromised; about feeling defeated, trapped, and excluded. It is about old-time regulators of PA and NA. It is old brain stuff in new minds. Our new minds will take us to the moon and create great concertos, but they can also give conscious feeling to the most primitive of affect regulators.

To lose the ability to feel PA does literally turn the lights off, and creates the blackest of despair. While evolution may well have made it possible to downregulate PA systems for defensive reasons, to become conscious of this is the stuff of nightmares. For many, then, heaven is associated with love, union, and belonging; with PA; with bliss even. Hell is its absence. No wonder, when people enter depressed states, some would rather give up all consciousness of a self (kill themselves) than be conscious of a life without PA and where NA runs amuck. The terror of no escape is a terror indeed that perhaps compassion can help bridge.

REFERENCES

Abramson, L.Y., Metalsky, G.I. & Alloy, L.B. (1989). Hopelessness depression: A theory based subtype of depression. *Psychological Bulletin, 96*, 358–372.

Akiskal, H.S. & McKinney, W.T. (1973). Depressive disorders: Toward a unified hypothesis. *Science, 182*, 20–29.

Akiskal, H.S. & McKinney, W.T. (1975). Overview of recent research in depression: Integration of ten conceptual models into a comprehensive frame. *Archives of General Psychiatry, 32*, 285–305.

Akiskal, H.S & Pinto, O. (1999). The evolving bipolar spectrum: Prototypes I, II, III, and IV. In H.S Akiskal (Ed.), *Bipolarity: Beyond Classic Mania. Psychiatric Clinics of North America, 22*, 517–534.

Alden, L.E. & Wallace, S.T. (1995). Social phobia and social appraisal in successful and unsuccessful social interaction. *Behaviour Research and Therapy, 33*, 497–505.

Allan, S. (2000). Social Rank and Attachment in Relationship to Depression. PhD thesis, University of Derby.

Allan, S. & Gilbert, P. (1997). Submissive behaviour and psychopathology. *British Journal of Clinical Psychology, 36*, 467–488.

Allen, N.B. & Gilbert, P. (2000). Social intelligence, self deception, and vulnerability to psychopathology: A challenge for the cognitive therapies? In P. Gilbert & K.G. Bailey (Eds), *Genes on the Couch: Explorations in Evolutionary Psychotherapy* (pp. 151–175). Hove: Psychology Press.

Alpert, J.E., Uebelacker, L.A., McLean, N.E., et al. (1997). Social phobia, avoidant personality disorder and atypical depression: Co-occurrence and clinical implications. *Psychological Medicine, 27*, 627–633.

Andrews, B. (1998). Shame and childhood abuse. In P. Gilbert & B. Andrews (Eds), *Shame: Interpersonal Behavior, Psychopathology and Culture* (pp. 176–190). New York: Oxford University Press.

Andrews, B. & Brewin, C.R. (1990). Attributions of blame for marital violence: A study of antecedents and consequences. *Journal of Family and Marriage, 52*, 757–767.

Anisman, H. & Merali, Z. (1999). Anhedonic and anxiogenic effects of cytokine exposure. *Advances in Experimental Medical Biology, 461*, 199–233.

Arrindell, W.A., Sanderman, R., Hageman, W.J.J.M., et al. (1990). Correlates of assertiveness in normal and clinical samples: A multidimensional approach. *Advances in Behaviour Theory and Research, 12*, 153–282.

Baldwin, M.W. & Fergusson, P. (2001). Relational schemas: The activation of interpersonal knowledge structures in social anxiety. In W.R. Crozier & L.E. Alden (Eds), *International Handbook of Social Anxiety: Concepts, Research and Interventions to the Self and Shyness* (pp. 235–257). Chichester: Wiley.

Barkow, J.H. (1989). *Darwin, Sex and Status: Biological Approaches to Mind and Culture.* Toronto: University of Toronto Press.

Baumeister, R.F. (1990). Suicide as escape from self. *Psychological Review, 97*, 90–133.

Baumeister, R.F., Tice, D.M. & Hutton, D.G. (1989). Self-presentational motivation of differences in self-esteem. *Journal of Personality, 57*, 547–579.

Bebbington, P. (1998). Editorial: Sex and depression. *Psychological Medicine, 28*, 1–8.

Bebbington, P., Katz, R., McGuffin, P., Sturt, E. & Wing, J.K. (1989). The risk of minor depression before age 65: Results from a community survey. Psychological Medicine, *19*, 393–400.

Beck, A.T. (1967). *Depression: Clinical, Experimental and Theoretical Aspects.* New York: Harper & Row.

Beck, A.T. (1987). Cognitive models of depression. *Journal of Cognitive Psychotherapy: An International Quarterly, 1*, 5–38.

Beck, A.T., Rush, A.J., Shaw, B.F. & Emery, G. (1979*). Cognitive Therapy of Depression.* New York: Wiley.

Beckham, E.E., Leber, W.R. & Youll, L.K. (1995). The diagnostic classification of depression. In E.E. Beckham & W.R. Leber (Eds), *Handbook of Depression*, (2nd edn) (pp. 36–60). New York: Guilford.

Belsher, G. & Costello, C.G. (1988). Relapse after recovery from unipolar depression: A critical review. *Psychological Bulletin, 104*, 84–86.

Birchwood, M., Mason, R., MacMillan, F. & Healy, J. (1993). Depression, demoralization and control over psychotic illness: A comparison of depressed and non-depressed patients with chronic psychosis. *Psychological Medicine, 23*, 387–395.

Blackburn, I.M. & Moorhead, S. (2000). Update in cognitive therapy for depression. *Journal of Cognitive Psychotherapy: An international Quarterly, 14*, 305–336.

Blanchard, J.J., Gangestad, S.W., Brown, S.A. & Horan, W.P. (2000). Hedonic capacity and schizotypy revisited: A taxometric analysis of social anhedonia. *Journal of Abnormal Psychology, 109*, 87–95.

Bowlby, J. (1969). *Attachment: Attachment and Loss*, vol. 1. London: Hogarth Press.

Bowlby, J. (1973). *Separation, Anxiety and Anger. Attachment and Loss*, vol. 2. London: Hogarth Press.

Bowlby, J. (1980). *Loss: Sadness and Depression. Attachment and Loss*, vol. 3. London: Hogarth Press.

Brenninkmeyer, V., Yperen, N.W. & Buunk, B.P. (2001). Burnout and depression are not identical twins: Is decline of superiority a distinguishing feature? *Personality and Individual Differences, 30*, 873–880.

Brody, C.L., Haag, D.A.F., Kirk, L. & Solomon, A. (1999). Experiences of anger in people who have recovered from depression and never-depressed people. *Journal of Nervous and Mental Disease, 187*, 400–405.

Brown, G.W., Adler, W.Z. & Bifulco, A. (1988). Life events, difficulties and recovery from chronic depression. *British Journal of Psychiatry, 152*, 487–498.

Brown, G.W. & Harris, T.O. (1978). *The Social Origins of Depression*. London: Tavistock.

Brown, G.W., Bifulco, A. & Harris, T.O. (1987). Life events, vulnerability and onset of depression: Some refinements. *British Journal of Psychiatry, 150*, 30–42.

Brown, G.W., Harris, T.O. & Hepworth, C. (1995). Loss, humiliation and entrapment among women developing depression: A patient and non-patient comparison. *Psychological Medicine, 25*, 7–21.

Brown, T., Campbell, L.A., Lehman, C.L., Grisham, J.R. & Mancill, R.B. (2001). Current and lifetime comorbidity of the DSM-IV anxiety and mood disorders in a large clinical sample. *Journal of Abnormal Psychology, 110*, 585–599.

Buss, D.M. (1999). *Evolutionary Psychology: The New Science of Mind*. Boston, MA: Allyn and Bacon.

Buunk, B.P. & Brenninkmeyer, V. (2000). Social comparison among depressed individuals: Evidence for the evolutionary perspective on involuntary subordinate strategies? In L. Sloman & P. Gilbert (Eds), *Subordination and Defeat: An Evolutionary Approach to Mood Disorders and their Treatment* (pp. 147–164). Mahwah, NJ: Erlbaum.

Cacioppo, J.T., Berston, G.G., Sheridan, J.F. & McClintock, M.K. (2000). Multilevel integrative analysis of human behavior: Social neuroscience and the complementing nature of social and biological approaches. *Psychological Bulletin, 126*, 829–843.

Cawson, P., Wattam, C., Brooker, S. & Kelly, G (2000). Child maltreatment in the United Kingdom: A study of the prevalence of child abuse and neglect: London NSPCC (for further information: e-mail *infounit@nspcc.org.uk*).

Champion, L.A. & Power, M.J. (1995). Social and cognitive approaches to depression. *British Journal of Clinical Psychology, 34*, 485–503.

Clark, L.A. (2000). Mood, personality and personality disorder. In R.J. Davidson (Ed.), *Anxiety, Depression and Emotion* (pp. 171–200). New York: Oxford University Press.

Cohen, D. (2001). Cultural variation: Considerations and implications. *Psychological Bulletin, 127*, 451–471.

Collins, N.L. & Feeney, B.C. (2000). A safe haven: An attachment theory perspective on support seeking and care giving in intimate relationships. *Journal of Personality and Social Psychology, 78*, 1053–1073.

Costello, C.G. (1993). The advantages of the symptom approach to depression. In C.G. Costello (Ed.), *Symptoms of Depression* (pp. 1–21). New York: Wiley.

Coyne, J.C. (1994). Self-reported distress: Analog or ersatz depression? *Psychological Bulletin, 116*, 29–45.

Cramer, K.M. (1999). Psychological antecedents to help-seeking behavior: A reanalysis using path modelling structures. *Journal of Counselling Psychology, 46*, 381–387.

Creed, A.T. & Funder, D.C. (1998). Social anxiety: From the inside and outside. *Personality and Individual Differences, 25*, 19–33.

Dalai Lama (2001). *An Open Heart: Practising Compassion in Everyday Life* (edited by N. Vreeland). London: Hodder & Stoughton.

Davidson, R.J. (2000). Affective style, mood, and anxiety disorders: An affective neuroscience approach. In R.J. Davidson (Ed.), *Anxiety, Depression and Emotion* (pp. 88–108). New York: Oxford University Press.

Davidson, J., Zisook, S., Giller, E. & Helms, M. (1989). Symptoms of interpersonal sensitivity in depression. *Comprehensive Psychiatry, 30*, 357–368.

Dixon, A.K. (1998). Ethological strategies for defence in animals and humans: Their role in some psychiatric disorders. *British Journal of Medical Psychology, 71*, 417–445.

Downey, G., Freitas, A.L., Michaels, M. & Khouri, H. (1998a). The self-fulfilling prophecy in close relationships: Rejection sensitivity and rejection by romantic partners. *Journal of Personality and Social Psychology, 75*, 545–560.

Downey, G., Lebolt, A., Rincon, C. & Freitas, L.A. (1998b). Rejection sensitivity and children's interpersonal difficulties. *Child Development, 69*, 1074–1091.

Driscoll, R. (1988). Self-condemnation: A conceptual framework for assessment and treatment. *Psychotherapy, 26*, 104–111.

Dunn, J. (1992). Sisters and brothers: Current issues in developmental research. In F. Boers & J. Dunn (Eds), *Children's Sibling Relationships: Developmental and Clinical Issues* (pp. 1–17). Hillsdale, NJ: Erlbaum.

Ehlers, A., Maercker, A. & Boos, S. (2000). Posttraumatic stress disorder following imprisonment: Role of mental defeat, alienation, and perceived permanent change. *Journal of Abnormal Psychology, 109*, 45–55.

Eisenberg, L. (2000). Is psychiatry more mindful or brainier than it was a decade ago? *British Journal of Psychiatry, 176*, 1–5.

Ellgring, H. (1989). *Nonverbal Communication in Depression*. Cambridge: Cambridge University Press.

Field, T.M. (1998). Touch therapy effects on development. *International Journal of Behavioral Development, 22*, 779–797.

Fombonne, E. (1994). Increased rates of depression: Update of epidemiological findings and analytical problems. *Acta Psychiatrica Scandinavica, 90*, 145–156.

Fombonne, E. (1999). Time trends in affective disorders. In P. Cohen, C. Slomkowski & L. Robins (Eds), *Historical and Geographical Influences on Psychopathology* (pp. 115–140). Mahwah, NJ: Erlbaum.

Forrest, M.S. & Hokanson, J.E. (1975). Depression and autonomic arousal reduction accompanying self-punitive behavior. *Journal of Abnormal Psychology, 84*, 346–357.

Gabbard, G.O. (2000). A neurobiologically informed perspective on psychotherapy. *British Journal of Psychiatry, 177*, 117–122.

Ganzini, L., McFarland, B.H. & Cutler, D. (1990). Prevalence of mental disorder after a catastrophic financial loss. *Journal of Nervous and Mental Disease, 178*, 680–685.

Gara, M.A., Woolfolk, R.L., Cohen, B.D., Goldston, R.B., Allen, L.A. & Novalany, J. (1993). Perception of self and other in major depression. *Journal of Abnormal Psychology, 193*, 93–100.

Gardner, R. (1982). Mechanisms of manic-depressive disorder: An evolutionary model. *Archives of General Psychiatry, 39*, 1436–1441.

Gilbert, P. (1984). *Depression: From Psychology to Brain State*. London: Erlbaum.

Gilbert, P. (1989). *Human Nature and Suffering*. Hove: Erlbaum.

Gilbert, P. (1992). *Depression: The Evolution of Powerlessness*. Hove: Erlbaum.

Gilbert, P. (1993). Defense and safety: Their function in social behaviour and psychopathology. *British Journal of Clinical Psychology, 32*, 131–154.

Gilbert, P. (1995). Biopsychosocial approaches and evolutionary theory as aids to integration in clinical psychology and psychotherapy. *Clinical Psychology and Psychotherapy, 2*, 135–156.

Gilbert, P. (1997). The evolution of social attractiveness and its role in shame, humiliation, guilt and therapy. *British Journal of Medical Psychology, 70*, 113–147.

Gilbert, P. (1998a). What is shame? Some core issues and controversies. In P. Gilbert & B. Andrews (Eds), *Shame: Interpersonal Behavior, Psychopathology and Culture* (pp. 3–38). New York: Oxford University Press.

Gilbert, P. (1998b). The evolved basis and adaptive functions of cognitive distortions. *British Journal of Medical Psychology, 71*, 447–463.

Gilbert, P. (2000a). Varieties of submissive behavior as forms of social defense: Their evolution and role in depression. In L. Sloman & P. Gilbert (Eds), *Subordination and Defeat: An Evolutionary Approach to Mood Disorders and their Treatment* (pp. 3–45). Mahwah, NJ: Erlbaum.

Gilbert, P. (2000b). *Counselling for Depression. 2nd edn*. London: Sage.

Gilbert, P. (2000c). Social mentalities: Internal 'social' conflicts and the role of inner warmth and compassion in cognitive therapy. In P. Gilbert & K.G. Bailey (Eds), *Genes on the Couch: Explorations in Evolutionary Psychotherapy* (pp. 118–150). Hove: Brenner-Routledge.

Gilbert, P. (2000d). The relationship of shame, social anxiety and depression: The role of the evaluation of social rank. *Clinical Psychology and Psychotherapy, 7*, 174–189.

Gilbert, P. (2000e). *Overcoming Depression: A Self-Guide Using Cognitive Behavioural Techniques* (rev. edn). London: Robinson-Constable (New York: Oxford University Press).

Gilbert, P. (2001a). Depression and stress: A biopsychosocial exploration of evolved functions and mechanisms. *Stress: International Journal of the Biology of Stress, 4*, 121–135.

Gilbert, P. (2001b). Evolution and social anxiety: The role of social competition and social hierarchies. In F. Schnieder (Ed.), *Social Anxiety: Psychiatric Clinics of North America, 24*, 723–751.

Gilbert, P. (2001c). Evolutionary approaches to psychopathology: The role of natural defences. *Australian and New Zealand Journal of Psychiatry, 35*, 17–27.

Gilbert, P. & Allan, S. (1998). The role of defeat and entrapment (arrested flight) in depression: An exploration of an evolutionary view. *Psychological Medicine, 28*, 584–597.

Gilbert, P. & Gerlsma, C. (1999). Recall of favouritism in relation to psychopathology. *British Journal of Clinical Psychology, 38*, 357–373.

Gilbert, P. & Gilbert, J. (2003). Entrapment and arrested anger in depression: An exploration using focus groups. *Psychology and Psychotherapy: Theory Research and Practice, 76*, 173–188.

Gilbert, P. & McGuire, M. (1998). Shame, social roles and status: The psychobiological continuum from monkey to human. In P. Gilbert & B. Andrews (Eds), *Shame: Interpersonal Behavior, Psychopathology and Culture* (pp. 99–125). New York: Oxford University Press.

Gilbert, P. & Miles, J.N.V. (2000). Evolution, genes, development and psychopathology. *Clinical Psychology and Psychotherapy, 7*, 246–255.

Gilbert, P., Allan, S., Ball, L. & Bradshaw, Z. (1996). Overconfidence and personal evaluations of social rank. *British Journal of Medical Psychology, 69*, 59–68.

Gilbert, P., Allan, S., Brough, S., Melley, S. & Miles, J.N.V. (2002). Anhedonia and positive affect: Relationship to social rank, defeat and entrapment. *Journal of Affective Disorders, 71*, 141–151.

Gilbert, P., Birchwood, M., Gilbert, J., et al. (2001). An exploration of evolved mental mechanisms for dominant and subordinate behaviour in relation to auditory hallucinations in schizophrenia and critical thoughts in depression. *Psychological Medicine, 31*, 1117–1127.

Gilbert, P., Price, J.S. & Allan, S. (1995). Social comparison, social attractiveness and evolution: How might they be related? *New Ideas in Psychology, 13*, 149–165.

Giles, D., Jarrett, R., Biggs, M., Guzick, D. & Rush, J. (1989). Clinical predictors of reoccurrence in depression. *American Journal of Psychiatry, 146*, 764–767.

Goodwin, D. & Jamison, K.R. (1990). *Manic Depressive Illness*. Oxford: Oxford University Press.

Gotlib, I.H., Gilboa, E. & Sommerfeld, B.K. (2000). Cognitive functioning in depression. In, R.J. Davidson (Ed.), *Anxiety, Depression and Emotion* (pp. 133–165). New York: Oxford University Press.

Gray, J.A. (1987). *The Psychology of Fear and Stress* 2nd edn. Cambridge: Cambridge University Press.

Greenberg, L.S., Elliott, R.K. & Foerster, F.S. (1990). Experiential processes in the psychotherapeutic treatment of depression. In C.D. McCann & N.S. Endler (Eds), *Depression: New Directions in Theory, Research and Practice* (pp. 157–185). Toronto: Wall & Emerson.

Greenberg, L.S. & Pascual, J. (1997). Emotion in the creation of personal meaning. In M. Power & C. Brewin (Eds), *The Transformation of Meaning: Reconciling Theory and Therapy in Cognitive, Behaviour and Related Therapies* (pp. 157–173). Chichester: Wiley.

Griffiths, J., Ravindran, A.V., Merali, Z. & Anisman, H. (2000). Dysthymia: A review of pharmacological and behavioral factors. *Molecular Psychiatry, 5*, 242–261.

Hammen, C., Henry, R. & Daley, S.E. (2000). Depression and sensitization to stressors among young women as a function of childhood adversity. *Journal of Clinical and Consulting Psychology, 68*, 782–787.

Hankin, B.L. & Abramson, L.Y. (2001). Development of gender differences in depression: An elaborated cognitive vulnerability-transactional stress theory. *Psychological Bulletin, 127*, 773–796.

Hart, J., Gunnar, M. & Cicchetti, D. (1996). Altered neuroendocrine activity in maltreated children related to symptoms of depression. *Development and Psychopathology, 8*, 201–214.

Healy, D. (2001). The dilemmas posed by new fashionable treatments. *Advances in Psychiatric Treatment, 7*, 322–327.

Heim, C., Newport, J., Heit, S., et al. (2000). Pituitary-adrenal and autonomic responses to stress in women after sexual and physical abuse in childhood. *Journal of American Medical Association, 284*, 592–597.

Higley, J.D., Mehlman, P.T., Higley, S., et al. (1996). Excessive mortality in young free-ranging male nonhuman primates with low cerebrospinal fluid 5-hydroxyindoleacetic acid concentrations. *Archives of General Psychiatry, 53*, 537–543.

Hofer, M.A. (1994). Early relationships as regulators of infant physiology and behavior. *Acta Paediatrica Supplement, 397*, 9–18.

Hooley, J.M. & Teasdale, J.D. (1989). Predictors of relapse in unipolar depressives: Expressed emotion, marital distress and perceived criticism. *Journal of Abnormal Psychology, 98*, 229–235.

Horowitz, M.J., Wilner, N., Marmar, C. & Krupnick, J. (1980). Pathological grief and the activation of latent self-images. *American Journal of Psychiatry, 137*, 1157–1162.

Irwin, W. (2000). Depression in rodents and humans: Commentary on Jay Weiss. In R.J. Davidson (Ed.), *Anxiety, Depression and Emotion* (pp. 36–49). New York: Oxford University Press.

Jung, C.G. (1952/1992). *Answer to Job.* London: Routledge.

Kaelber, C.T., Moul, D.E. & Farmer, M.E. (1995). Epidemiology of depression. In E.E. Beckham & W.R. Leber (Eds), *Handbook of Depression (2nd edn)* (pp. 3–35). New York: Guilford.

Keltner, D. & Harker, L.A. (1998). The forms and functions of the nonverbal signal of shame. In P. Gilbert & B. Andrews (Eds), *Shame: Interpersonal Behavior, Psychopathology and Culture* (pp. 78–98). New York: Oxford University Press.

Kessler, R.C. & Magee, W. (1993). Childhood adversities and adult depression: Basic patterns of association in a U.S. national survey. *Psychological Medicine, 23*, 679–690.

Kessler, R.C., McGonagle, K.A., Zhao, S., et al. (1994). Lifetime and 12–month prevalence of DSM-111R psychiatric disorders in the United States: Results from the National Comorbidity Survey. *Archives of General Psychiatry, 51*, 8–19.

Kessler, R.C., Soukup, J., Davis, R.B., et al. (2001). The use of complementary and alternative therapies to treat anxiety and depression in the United States. *American Journal of Psychiatry, 158*, 289–294.

Kiesler, D.J. (1999). *Beyond the Disease Model of Mental Disorders.* New York: Praeger.

Kimberly, H. (1990). Blame and adjustment among women sexually abused as children. *Women and Therapy, 9*, 89–110.

Klinger, E. (1975). Consequences and commitment to aid disengagement from incentives. *Psychological Review, 82*, 1–24.

Klinger, E. (1993). Loss of interest. In C.G. Costello (Ed.), *Symptoms of Depression* (pp. 43–62). New York: Wiley.

Leahy, R.L. (2000). Sunk costs and resistance to change. *Journal of Cognitive Psychotherapy: An International Quarterly, 14*, 355–371.

Leary, M.R. (1995). *Self-Presentation: Impression Management and Interpersonal Behavior.* Madison, WI: Brown & Benchmark's.

Leary, M.R., Tambor, E.S., Terdal, S.K. & Downs, D.L. (1995). Self-esteem as an interpersonal monitor: The sociometer hypothesis. *Journal of Personality and Social Psychology, 68*, 519–530.

Levitan, R., Hasey, G. & Sloman, L. (2000). Major depression and the involuntary defeat strategy; biological correlates. In L. Sloman & P. Gilbert (Eds), *Subordination and Defeat: An Evolutionary Approach to Mood Disorders and Their Therapy* (pp. 95–114). Mahwah, NJ: Erlbaum.

Lewis, M. (1992). *Shame: The Exposed Self.* New York: Free Press.

Ligezinska, M., Firestone, P., Manion, I.G., McIntyre, J., Ensom, R. & Wells, G. (1996). Children's emotional and behavioral reactions following the disclosure of extrafamilial sexual abuse: Initial effects. *Child Abuse and Neglect, 20*, 111–125.

Liotti, G. (2000). Disorganised attachment, models of borderline states and evolutionary psychotherapy. In P. Gilbert & B. Bailey (Eds), *Genes on the Couch: Explorations in Evolutionary Psychotherapy* (pp. 232–256). Hove: Brunner-Routledge.

MacDonald, K.B. (1988). *Social and Personality Development: An Evolutionary Synthesis.* New York: Plenum Press.

MacLean, P.D. (1990). *The Triune Brain in Evolution.* New York: Plenum Press.

Maes, M. (1995). Evidence for an immune response in major depression: A review and hypothesis. *Progress in NeuroPsychopharmacology and Biological Psychiatry, 19*, 11–38.

McCullough, J.P. Jr. (2000). *Treatment for Chronic Depression: Cognitive Behavioral Analysis System of Psychotherapy*. New York: Guilford.

McGuade, R. & Young, A.H. (2000). Future therapeutic targets in mood disorders: The glucorticoid receptor. *British Journal of Psychiatry, 177*, 390–395.

McGuffin, P., Katz, R. & Rutherford, J. (1991). Nature, nurture and depression: A twin study. *Psychological Medicine, 21*, 329–335.

McGuire, M.T. & Troisi, A. (1998a). *Darwinian Psychiatry*. New York: Oxford University Press.

McGuire, M.T. & Troisi, A. (1998b). Prevalence differences in depression among males and females: Are there evolutionary explanations? *British Journal of Medical Psychology, 71*, 479–492.

Meaney, M.J., Diorio, J., Francis, D., et al. (1996). Early environmental regulation of forebrain glucocorticoid receptor gene expression: Implications for adrenocortical responses to stress. *Developmental Neuroscience, 18*, 49–72.

Meehl, P.E. (1995). Bootstrap taxometrics: Solving the classification problem in psychopathology. *American Psychologist, 50*, 266–275.

Meerlo, P., de Boer, S.F., Koolhaas, J.M., Daan, S. & van den Hoofdakker, R.H. (1996). Changes in daily rhythms of body temperature and activity after a single social defeat in rats. *Physiology and Behaviour, 59*, 735–739.

Mikulincer, M., Birnbaum, G., Woddis, D. & Nachmias, O. (2000). Stress and accessibility of proximity-related thoughts: Exploring intraindividual components of attachment theory. *Journal of Personality and Social Psychology, 78*, 509–523.

Miller, L.C. & Fishkin, S.A. (1997). On the dynamics of human bonding and reproductive success: Seeking windows on the adapted-for-human-environment interface. In J. Simpson & D.T. Kendrick (Eds), *Evolutionary Social Psychology* (pp. 197–235). Mahwah, NJ: Erlbaum.

Moldofsky, H. & Dickstein, J.B. (1999). Sleep and cytokine-immune functions in medical, psychiatric and primary sleep disorders. *Sleep Medicine Reviews, 34*, 325–337.

Morriss, R.K. & Morriss, E.E. (2000). Contextual evaluation of social adversity in the management of depressive disorder. *Advances in Psychiatric Treatment, 6*, 423–431.

Mullen, K. (2001). Pleasing to behold: Healing and the visualized body. *Mental Health Religion and Culture, 4*, 119–132.

Murray, L. & Cooper, P.J. (1997). *Postpartum Depression and Child Development*. New York: Guilford.

Murray, C.J.L. & Lopez, A.D. (1996). *The Global Burden of Disease: A Comprehensive Assessment of Mortality and Disability from Diseases. Injuries and Risk Factors in 1990 and Projected to 2020*. Cambridge MA: Harvard University Press.

Nemeroff, C.B. (1996). The corticotropin-releasing factor (CRF) hypothesis of depression: New findings and new directions. *Molecular Psychiatry, 1*, 336–342.

Nemeroff, C.B. (1998). The neurobiology of depression. *Scientific American*, June, 28–35.

Nesse, R. (1998). Emotional disorders in evolutionary perspective. *British Journal of Medical Psychology, 71*, 397–416.

Nesse, R. (2000). Is depression an adaptation? *Archives of General Psychiatry, 57*, 14–20.

Panksepp, J. (1998). *Affective Neuroscience*. New York: Oxford University Press.

Perry, B.D., Pollard, R.A., Blakley, T.L., Baker, W.L. & Vigilante, D. (1995). Childhood trauma, the neurobiology of adaptation and 'use-dependent' development of the brain: How 'states' become 'traits'. *Infant Mental Health Journal, 16*, 271–291.

Peterson, C., Maier, S.F. & Seligman, M.E.P. (1993). *Learned Helplessness: A Theory for the Age of Personal Control*. New York: Oxford University Press.

Posener, J.A., deBattista, C., Willimans, G.H., Chmura, H., Kalehzan, M. & Scatzberg, A.F. (2000). 24-hour monitoring of cortisol and corticotropin secretion in psychotic and nonpsychotic major depression. *Archives of General Psychiatry, 57*, 755–760.

Posternak, M.A. & Zimmerman, M. (2002). Partial validation of the atypical features subtype of major depressive disorders. *Archives of General Psychiatry, 59*, 70–76.

Price, J.S. (1972). Genetic and phylogenetic aspects of mood variations. *International Journal of Mental Health, 1*, 124–144.

Price, J.S. (2000). Subordination, self-esteem and depression. In L. Sloman & P. Gilbert (Eds), *Subordination and Defeat: An Evolutionary Approach to Mood Disorders and Their Therapy* (pp. 165–177). Mahwah, NJ: Erlbaum.

Price, J.S. & Sloman, L. (1987). Depression as yielding behaviour: An animal model based on Schjelderup-Ebb's pecking order. *Ethology and Sociobiology, 8* (Suppl.), 85–98.

Price, J., Sloman, L., Gardner, R., Gilbert, P. & Rohde, P. (1994). The social competition hypothesis of depression. *British Journal of Psychiatry, 164*, 309–315.

Raadsheer, F.C., Hoogendijk, W.J.G., Stam, F.C., Tilders, F.J.H. & Swaab, D.F. (1994). Increased numbers of corticotropin-releasing hormone expressing neurones in the hypothalamic paraventricular nucleus of depressed patients. *Clinical Neuroendocrinology, 60*, 436–444.

Radden, J. (2000). *The Nature of Melancholy: From Aristotle to Kristeva.* New York: Oxford University Press.

Raleigh, M.J., McGuire, M.T., Brammer, G.L. & Yuwiler, A. (1984). Social and environmental influences on blood serotonin concentrations in monkeys. *Archives of General Psychiatry, 41*, 405–410.

Rasmussen, K.L.R. & Reite, M. (1982). Loss-induced depression in an adult macaque monkey. *American Journal of Psychiatry, 139*, 679–681.

Ray, J.C. & Sapolsky, R.M. (1992). Styles of social behavior and their endocrine correlates among high-ranking wild baboons. *American Journal of Primatology, 28*, 231–250.

Reite, M. & Field, T. (1985). *The Psychobiology of Attachment and Separation.* New York: Academic Press.

Reynolds, M. & Brewin, C.R. (1999). Intrusive memories in depression and posttraumatic stress disorder. *Behavior Research and Therapy, 37*, 201–215.

Ridley, M. (2000). *Genome: The Autobiography of a Species.* London: Fourth Estate.

Rooke, O. & Birchwood, M. (1998). Loss, humiliation and entrapment as appraisals of schizophrenic illness: A prospective study of depressed and non-depressed patients. *British Journal of Clinical Psychology, 37*, 259–268.

Rosen, J.B. & Schulkin, J. (1998). From normal fear to pathological anxiety. *Psychological Bulletin, 105*, 325–350.

Rowe, D. (1983). *Depression and the Way Out of Your Prison.* London: Routledge.

Roy, M.P., Steptoe, A. & Kirschbaum, C. (1998). Life events and social support as moderators of individual differences in cardiovascular and cortisol reactivity. *Journal of Personality and Social Psychology, 5*, 1273–1281.

Rubin, T.I. (1975). *Compassion and Self-Hatred: An Alternative to Despair.* New York: Touchstone.

Rutter, M. (1986). Meyerian psychobiology, personality development and the role of life experiences. *American Journal of Psychiatry, 143*, 1077–1087.

Santor, D. & Walker, J. (1999). Garnering the interests of others: Mediating the effects among physical attractiveness, self-worth and dominance. *British Journal of Social Psychology, 38*, 461–477.

Sapolsky, R.M. (1989). Hypercortisolism among socially subordinate wild baboons originates at the CNS level. *Archives of General Psychiatry, 46*, 1047–1051.

Sapolsky, R.M. (1994). Individual differences and the stress response. *Seminars in the Neurosciences, 6*, 261–269.

Sapolsky, R.M. (1996). Why stress is bad for your brain. *Science, 273*, 749–750.

Sapolsky, R.M. (2000). Glucocorticoids and hippocampus atrophy in neuropsychiatric disorders. *Archives of General Psychiatry, 57*, 925–935.

Schelde, J.T. (1998a). Major depression: Behavioral markers of depression and recovery. *Journal of Mental and Nervous Disease, 186*, 133–140.

Schelde, J.T. (1998b). Major depression: Behavioral parameters of depression and recovery. *Journal of Mental and Nervous Disease, 186*, 141–149.

Schneier, F.R., Johnson, J., Hornig, C.D., Liebowitz, M.R. & Weissman, M.M. (1992). Social phobia: Comorbidity and morbidity in an epidemiologic sample. *Archives of General Psychiatry, 49*, 282–288.

Schore, A.N. (1994). *Affect Regulation and the Origin of the Self: The Neurobiology of Emotional Development.* Hillsdale, NJ: Erlbaum.

Schore, A.N. (2001). The effects of early relational trauma on right brain development, affect regulation, and infant mental health. *Infant Mental Health Journal, 22*, 201–269.

Schuster, B. (1996). Rejection, exclusion, and harassment at work and in schools. *European Psychologist, 1*, 293–317.

Scott, J. (1988). Chronic depression. *British Journal of Psychiatry, 153*, 287–297.

Scott, J.C. (1990). *Domination and the Arts of Resistance*. New Haven, CT: Yale University Press.

Segrin, C. & Abramson, L.Y. (1994). Negative reactions to depressive behaviours: A communication theories analysis. *Journal of Abnormal Psychology, 103*, 655–668.

Shweder, R.A., Much, N.C., Mahapatra, M. & Park, L. (1997). The 'big three' of morality (autonomy, community and divinity) and the 'big three' explanations of suffering. In A.M. Brandt & P. Rozin (Eds), *Morality and Health* (pp. 119–169). New York: Routledge.

Sloman, L. (2000a). How involuntary defeat is related to depression. In L. Sloman & P. Gilbert (Eds), *Subordination and Defeat: An Evolutionary Approach to Mood Disorders and Their Therapy* (pp. 47–66). Mahwah, NJ: Erlbaum.

Sloman, L. (2000b). The syndrome of rejection sensitivity. In P. Gilbert & B. Bailey (Eds), *Genes on the Couch: Explorations in Evolutionary Psychotherapy* (pp. 257–275). Hove: Brunner-Routledge.

Sloman, L. & Gilbert, P. (Eds) (2000). *Subordination and Defeat: An Evolutionary Approach to Mood Disorders and Their Therapy*. Mahwah, NJ: Erlbaum.

Sloman, L., Gilbert, P. & Hasey, G. (2003). The role and interaction of attachment and social rank in depression. *Journal of Affective Disorders*.

Smith, P.K. & Myron-Wilson, R. (1998). Parenting and school bullying. *Clinical Child Psychology and Psychiatry, 3*, 405–417.

Snaith, R.P., Hamilton, M., Morley, S., Humayan, A., Hargreaves, D. & Trigwell, P. (1995). A scale for the assessment of hedonic tone. The Snaith Hamilton Pleasure Scale. *British Journal of Psychiatry, 167*, 99–103.

Spence, S.H., Donovan, C. & Brechman-Toussaint, M. (1999). Social skills, social outcomes, and cognitive features of childhood social phobia. *Journal of Abnormal Psychology, 108*, 211–221.

Suomi, S.J. (1997). Early determinants of behavior: Evidence from primate studies. *British Medical Bulletin, 53*, 170–184.

Swallow, S.R. (2000). A cognitive behavioural perspective on the involuntary defeat strategy. In L. Sloman & P. Gilbert (Eds), *Subordination and Defeat: An Evolutionary Approach to Mood Disorders and Their Therapy* (pp. 181–198). Mahwah, NJ: Erlbaum.

Tangney, J.P. & Fischer, K.W. (Eds) (1995). *Self-Conscious Emotions: The Psychology of Shame, Guilt, Embarrassment and Pride*. New York: Guilford.

Tangney, J.P., Wagner, P. & Gramzow, R. (1992). Proneness to shame, proneness to guilt, and psychopathology. *Journal of Abnormal Psychology, 101*, 469–478.

Taylor, S.E., Klein, L.B., Lewis, B.P., Gruenwald, T.L., Gurung R.A.R. & Updegaff, J.A. (2000). Biobehavioral responses to stress in females: Tend and befriend, not fight and flight. *Psychological Review, 107*, 411–429.

Teasdale, J.D. (1988). Cognitive vulnerability to persistent depression. *Cognition and Emotion, 2*, 247–274.

Teasdale, J.D. (1999). Emotional processing: Three modes of mind and the prevention of relapse in depression. *Behaviour Research and Therapy, 37*, 29–52.

Thase, M.E. & Howland, R.H. (1995). Biological processes in depression: An update and integration. In E.E. Beckham & W.R. Leber (Eds), *Handbook of Depression, 2nd edn* (pp. 213–279). New York: Guilford.

Thase, M.E., Dub, J.S., Bowler, K., et al. (1996). Hypothalamic-pituitary-adrenocortical activity and response to cognitive behavior therapy in unmedicated, hospitalised depressed patients. *American Journal of Psychiatry, 144*, 1253–1262.

Toates, F. (1995). *Stress: Conceptual and Biological Aspects*. Chichester: Wiley.

Tobena, A., Marks, I. & Dar, R. (1999). Advantages of bias and prejudice: An exploration of their neurocognitive templates. *Neuroscience and Behavioral Reviews, 23*, 1047–1058.

Tooby, J. & Cosmides, L. (1996). Friendship formation and the bankers paradox: Other pathways to the evolution of adaptations for altruism. *Proceedings of the British Academy, 88*, 119–143.

Uchino, B.N., Cacioppo, J.T. & Kiecolt-Glaser, J.K. (1996). The relationship between social support and physiological processes: A review with emphasis on underlying mechanisms and implications for health. *Psychological Bulletin, 119*, 488–531.

van Praag, H.M. (1998). Anxiety and increased aggression as pacemakers of depression. *Acta Psychiatrica Scandinavica, 98* (Suppl. 393), 81–88.

Vinokur, A.D. & van Ryn, M. (1993). Social undermining: Their independent effects on the mental health of unemployed persons. *Journal of Personality and Social Psychology, 65*, 350–359.

Von Holst, D. (1986). Vegetative and somatic components of tree shrews' behaviour. *Journal of the Autonomic Nervous System* (Suppl.), 657–670.

Vredenburg, K., Flett, G.L. & Krames, L. (1993). Analogue versus clinical depression: a critical reappraisal. *Psychological Bulletin, 113*, 327–344.

Watson, D. & Clark, L.A. (1988). Positive and negative affectivity and their relation to anxiety and depressive disorders. *Journal of Abnormal Psychology, 97*, 346–353.

Watson, D., Clark, L.A., Weber, K., et al. (1995a). Testing a tripartite model. I. Evaluating the convergent and discriminate validity of anxiety and depression symptom scales. *Journal of Abnormal Psychology, 104*, 3–14.

Watson, D., Clark, L.A., Weber, K., Assenheimer, J., Strauss, M.E. & McCormick, R.A. (1995b). Testing a tripartite model. II. Exploring the symptom structure of anxiety and depression in student, adult and patient samples. *Journal of Abnormal Psychology, 104*, 15–25.

Watts, F. (1993). Problems with memory and concentration. In C.G. Costello (Ed.), *Symptoms of Depression* (pp. 113–140). New York: Wiley.

Wearden, A.J., Tarrier, N., Barrowclough, C., Zastowny, T.R. & Rahil, A.A. (2000). A review of expressed emotion research in health care. *Clinical Psychology Review, 5*, 633–666.

Weiss, J.M., Demetrikopoulos, M.K., McCurdy, P.M., West, C.H.K. & Bonsall, R.W. (2000). Depression seen through an animal model: An expanded hypothesis of pathophysiology and improved models. In R.J. Davidson (Ed.), *Anxiety, Depression and Emotion* (pp. 3–35). New York: Oxford University Press.

Wells, A. (2000). *Emotional Disorders and Metacognition: Innovative Cognitive Therapy.* Chichester: Wiley.

Whelton, W.J. (2000). Emotion in Self-Criticism. Unpublished PhD thesis: University of York: Montreal, Canada.

Wilkinson, R.G. (1996). *Unhealthy Societies: The Affiliations of Inequality.* London: Routledge.

Williams, M. (1997). *Cry of Pain.* London: Penguin Books.

Willner, P. (1985). *Depression: A Psychobiological Synthesis.* Chichester: Wiley.

Willner, P. (1993). Anhedonia. In C.G. Costello (Ed.), *Symptoms of Depression* (pp. 63–84). New York: Wiley.

Willner, P. & Goldstein, R.C. (2001). Mediation of depression by perceptions of defeat and entrapment in high-stress mothers. *British Journal of Medical Psychology, 74*, 473–485.

Wilson, D.R. (1998). Evolutionary epidemiology and manic depression. *British Journal of Medical Psychology, 71*, 375–395.

Wyatt, R. & Gilbert, P. (1998). Perfectionism and social rank. *Personality and Individual Differences, 24*, 71–79.

Zahn-Waxler, C. (2000). The development of empathy, guilt and internalization of distress: Implications for gender differences in internalizing and externalizing problems. In R.J. Davidson (Ed.), *Anxiety, Depression and Emotion* (pp. 222–265). New York: Oxford University Press.

Zeeman, E.C. (1977). *Catastrophe Theory: Selected Papers 1972–1977.* Reading: Addison Wesley.

Zeifman, D. & Hazan, C. (1997). Attachment: The bond in pair-bonds. In J. Simpson & D.T. Kendrick (Eds), *Evolutionary Social Psychology* (pp. 237–263). Mahwah, NJ: Erlbaum.

Zuroff, D.C., Koestner, R. & Powers, T.A. (1994). Self-criticism at age 12: A longitudinal study of adjustment. *Cognitive Therapy and Research, 18*, 367–385.

Zuroff, D.C., Moskowitz, D.S. & Cote, S. (1999). Dependency, self-criticism, interpersonal behaviour and affect: Evolutionary perspectives. *British Journal of Clinical Psychology, 38*, 231–250.

7

BIOLOGICAL TREATMENTS OF MOOD DISORDERS

Klaus P. Ebmeier, Annika Berge, David Semple, Premal Shah,
and Douglas Steele

PHARMACOLOGICAL TREATMENTS

The pharmacological treatment of unipolar disorder

Mood disorders, particularly depression, are among the more psychologically plausible of mental health problems. For this reason, the general public assumes that psychotherapeutic approaches are the naturally effective treatment for these conditions. Even after a targeted public campaign (Defeat Depression, Royal Colleges of General Practitioners and Psychiatrists), this belief persists together with the conviction that antidepressants are addictive (Paykel et al., 1998). In contrast to this public belief, the evidence for the efficacy and safety of pharmacotherapy far outstrips that of any psychological treatment. Antidepressants are traditionally divided by chemical and historical criteria into first-generation tricyclic antidepressants, such as amitriptyline, nortriptyline, imipramine and desipramine, trimipramine and clomipramine; second-generation tricyclics, such as doxepine and dothiepin; serotonin reuptake inhibitors (SRIs), such as citalopram, fluvoxamine, paroxetine and sertraline; noradrenalin (norepinephrine) reuptake inhibitors, such as reboxetine and maprotiline; and miscellaneous drugs, such as venlafaxine, mianserin, mirtazepine, trazodone, reboxetine and buproprion (see Table 7.1). In addition, there are reversible and irreversible monoamine-oxidase inhibitors, such as moclobemide, and phenelzine and tranylcypromine, respectively. Augmentation strategies (Hawley et al., 2000) and poorly empirically supported therapies, such as polypharmacy, which are nevertheless commonly used. (Frye et al., 2000; Stimpson et al., 2002), have to be left to more specific pharmacological texts. While controlled studies clearly indicate the specific antidepressant effects of many antidepressants, there is also more indirect secular evidence of a general decline in suicide: 'The risk of suicide in follow-up studies of affective disorder has decreased compared to that reported in previous reviews. The availability of ECT [electroconvulsive treatment] and

Mood Disorders: A Handbook of Science and Practice. Edited by M. Power.
© 2004 John Wiley & Sons, Ltd. ISBN 0-470-84390-X.

Table 7.1 Commonly used antidepressants

Class of antidepressant	Monoamine affected	Mode of action	Other notes
Tricyclic antidepressants (TCAs)	Noradrenalin (NA) and serotonin (5-HT)	Reuptake inhibition	• Individual TCAs vary in the proportion of NA and 5-HT reuptake • Larger number of side effects • May be more effective in severe depression
SRIs	Mainly 5-HT, but can have NA and Dopamine (DA) effects as well	Reuptake inhibition	• Now used as first-line treatment • More selective action than TCAs • Generally fewer side effects than TCAs, and better tolerated
5-HT *and* NA-RIs (Venlafaxine)	5-HT and NA, at higher doses possibly DA	Reuptake inhibition	• At lower doses, mainly 5-HT action • At moderate doses, NA action • Pronounced withdrawal effects
NA-RIs	NA	Reuptake inhibition	• Increased risk of seizures
NA and DA reuptake inhibitor	NA and DA	Reuptake inhibition	• Only licensed in USA
Monoamine oxidase inhibitors	NA and 5-HT and DA	Prevents synaptic breakdown of NA and 5-HT	• Tranycypromine is activating • Tyramine-low diet required
5-HT$_2$ antagonists plus reuptake inhibitors (Trazodone)	5-HT and NA	Blocks post-synaptic 5-HT$_2$ receptors, less powerful re-uptake inhibition	• Acts both pre- and post-synaptically • Belief that both components are important for therapeutic effect
Mianserin, Mirtazepin	NA and 5-HT	Blocks pre-synaptic α_2-receptors	• Pre-synaptic α_2-receptors usually inhibit release of NA and 5-HT • Blocking these receptors stops the inhibition
Lithium	5-HT and others		• Possibly influences post-synaptic second messenger systems once receptor is activated

antidepressants may have contributed to this decrease, but prescription of these treatments cannot be assumed for all patients'. (O'Leary et al., 2001).

Pharmacological treatments of depression continue to be based on the *monoamine hypothesis of depression*. In its original form, this stated that 'depression is associated with a central depletion of noradrenaline' (Bunney & Davis, 1965; Schildkraut, 1965). It has since been elaborated to encompass reductions in the other monoamines (serotonin and dopamine) and to postulate alterations in monoamine receptor sensitivities in order to explain the delay of the treatment response (Charney et al., 1990). It developed from the observation that antihypertensive agents, such as reserpine, which deplete neurons of noradrenalin, could trigger depressive symptoms. Because of limited access to the human brain in vivo, the confirmation of this hypothesis has proven difficult. Investigators have used peripheral biological markers, such as serotonin metabolite concentrations in urine and cerebrospinal fluid (CSF) as indices of central monoamine function, sometimes with contradictory results. The introduction of functional neuroimaging techniques for the in vivo examination of receptor systems promises more direct hypothesis testing (Ebmeier & Kronhaus, 2002).

TRICYCLIC ANTIDEPRESSANTS (TCAs)

Since Kuhn first described the use of imipramine in treating depression (Kuhn, 1958), convincing evidence has accumulated to support the effectiveness of TCAs in the acute treatment of depression of moderate to severe severity, in improving both response and recovery. Overall, randomised, controlled trials of acute treatment find that 50–60% of patients respond to antidepressants compared with 25–30% on placebo (Schulberg et al., 1999). This means that only three to four patients need to be treated with an antidepressant in order for one more patient to respond than on placebo. Tricyclic antidepressants, particularly amitriptyline, thus remain the reference standard for antidepressant therapy (Barbui & Hotopf, 2001). They generally generate more severe side effects, including sedation and, in particular, anticholinergic symptoms, such as dry mouth, blurred vision, constipation and urinary retention. This is associated with reduced acceptability for patients compared with some of the newer drugs (Anderson, 2001; Barbui et al., 2000). There is a hotly disputed conflict between the lower doses used in general practice (100 mg and less of a tricyclic) and the expert opinion that doses above 100 mg are required for optimum response (Furukawa et al., 2002). Tricyclics are now used mainly as second-line treatment after newer drugs have proved ineffective, not least because their cardiac effects render them more dangerous in overdose.

SEROTONIN REUPTAKE INHIBITORS (SRIs)

The attempt to isolate the effective principle of tricyclics and the following effort of diversification and market penetration have, over the past couple of decades, resulted in a whole generation of SRIs. These drugs are generally better tolerated than tricyclics, but have a side-effect profile of their own, including headache, nausea, akathisia and a characteristic withdrawal syndrome that is not, however, associated with behavioural dependence (Haddad, 2001). Certain authors have considered psychomotor restlessness (akathisia) as a side effect of SRIs, along with emergent suicidal thoughts and behaviour, but the evidence accumulated so far is limited and unconvincing (Hansen, 2001). However, adding benzodiazepines to these drugs can increase adherence and effectiveness (Furukawa et al., 2000). It has long been known that in the course of treatment with any antidepressants there is a vulnerable period when psychomotor retardation and indecision improve at a time when suicidal and depressive symptoms still persist. All practitioners should be aware of this risk and discuss it with staff, relatives and patients as part of the overall management plan, although, as yet, it is not clear which educational or informational interventions are best to achieve adherence and optimise efficacy. (Pampallona et al., 2002). In summary, and comparing SRIs with each other and with other antidepressants, there appears to be 'a slower onset of therapeutic action of fluoxetine over other [S]SRIs; a different side effect profile of [S]SRIs to TCAs with superior general tolerability of [S]SRIs over TCAs; poorer tolerability of fluvoxamine than other [S]SRIs in a within group comparison; [and] no increased the risk of suicidal acts or ideation in fluoxetine compared with TCAs (or placebo) in low-risk patients' (Anderson, 2001).

OTHER ANTIDEPRESSANTS

Other antidepressants share certain behaviours in animal models of depression with the older drugs (which is usually how they have entered clinical trials), but possess a diversity of potential mechanisms of action (Table 7.1). At normal doses, venlafaxine behaves like an SRI, but at higher doses also has noradrenalin reuptake-inhibiting properties. It may be more effective than SRIs, but probably not TCAs. (Anderson, 2001; Smith et al., 2002). Other antidepressants (see above) may have certain advantages in terms of side effects or may be used by the specialist in the course of a systematic trial-and-error procedure to find an effective treatment in treatment-resistant patients. Finally, although the presence of a major depressive episode is a good predictor of treatment response, antidepressants have been used effectively in anxiety disorders and in patients with dysthymia (Lima & Moncrieff, 2000).

L-Tryptophan (Table 7.2) is an essential amino acid and the precursor of serotonin (5-HT), tryptophan-hydroxylation being the rate-limiting step in 5-HT production. Thus, it has been suggested as an adjunct treatment for depression, to be added to a conventional antidepressant. The rationale is that, with reuptake inhibition, more 5-HT is available for degradation, eventually leading to a central 5-HT deficit state. Some evidence supports this view. In those recovered from depression, the exclusion of tryptophan from the diet and administration of a tryptophan-depleting drink can lead to a rapid resurgence of depressive symptoms (Delgado et al., 1999).

Most pharmacological attention has focused on 5-HT and noradrenalin-augmenting strategies. However, there are a number of lines of evidence to suggest that dopamine function is altered in depression, and that patients may benefit from dopaminergic intervention. In Parkinson's disease, which is associated with dopamine deficiency, up to 40% of patients develop depression (Cummings, 1992). Both parkinsonian and the associated depressive symptoms can be treated with pramipexole, a drug which directly stimulates the dopamine D_2 receptors. Interestingly, pramipexole appears to exhibit antidepressant properties also in non-parkinsonian patients (Corrigan et al., 2000). Reduced dopaminergic turnover has been found in depressed patients (Jimerson, 1987), and many antidepressant treatments, including ECT, buproprion and amphetamines, have a direct or indirect effect on dopamine (Diehl & Gershon, 1992). More direct evidence comes from in vivo receptor imaging in depression. Investigators (Ebert et al., 1994; Shah et al., 1997) have found evidence of reduced dopamine D_2 receptor occupancy in depressed patients, a feature which was associated with motor slowing.

For many years, it has been recognised that depressive episodes often succeed psychologically or physically stressful events. A large body of evidence suggests that the regulation of 'stress hormones', particularly of cortisol, is abnormal in depression. This has given rise to the glucocorticoid-cascade hypothesis of depression (Sapolsky et al., 1986). In severe depression, cortisol levels are often raised (Carroll et al., 1976). Monoamine systems and cortisol are interdependent, and, at least in animal models, raised cortisol can have neurodegenerative effects (Sapolsky et al., 1986). An increasing number of studies indicate

Table 7.2   Other agents with possible use in depression

Drug	Possible action	Notes
L-Tryptophan	Increases production of 5-HT	1. L-tryptophan is a basic amino acid found in food 2. Only L-tryptophan can be converted to 5-HT 3. Usually used as an add-on treatment
Amphetamines Methylphenidate	Pre-synaptic dopamine release	1. Addiction potential
Pramipexole	Dopamine D_2 receptor agonist	1. One randomised control trial of its effectiveness in depression 2. Useful for depression in Parkinson's disease
Oestrogens	Downregulate 5-HT_2 receptors	1. May be a useful adjunct treatment in post-menopausal women lacking oestrogens
Thyroxine	Unclear; possible sensitisation of NA receptors	1. Usually used as an adjunct treatment 2. Based on the observation that hypothyroidism can mimic clinical depression 3. 20% of depressed patients have evidence of biochemical thyroid abnormalities
Antiglucocorticoid drugs	Inhibits the action or production of cortisol	1. Systematic review indicates positive evidence for antidepressant effect 2. May influence the reciprocal cortisol-monoamine systems
Folic acid	May aid neuronal regeneration	1. Recent studies suggest that it may be useful in women with depression 2. Action remains unclear

structural brain changes in depressed patients (Drevets et al., 1998; Shah et al., 2001; Sheline et al., 1996). If this were the case, drugs which control the production or effect of cortisol could have antidepressant effects. A recent review has suggested that antiglucocorticoid drugs have some form of antidepressant effect in about 67–77% of patients, roughly equivalent to the size of response seen with conventional antidepressants (Wolkowitz & Reus, 1999). The best response was observed in depressed, hypercortisolaemic patients, suggesting a causal role for HPA dysfunction in some patients. Preliminary pathological evidence has emerged of neuronal cell loss in the brains of previously depressed patients, in areas innervated by monoamine systems (Rajkowska et al., 1999). The recent finding that many antidepressant treatments, including TCAs, SSRIs, ECT and lithium, promote the production of brain-derived nerve growth factor (BDNF), which may help neuronal regeneration (Vogel, 2000), has made some investigators speculate that some of the therapeutic effects of antidepressants are due to neuroregeneration (Miguel-Hidalgo & Rajkowska, 2002). This may also explain the recent finding of an antidepressant effect of folic acid (Coppen & Bailey, 2000), a substance critical for the growth of healthy neuronal tissue.

ST JOHN'S WORT

St John's wort (*Hypericum perforatum*), has been used for its therapeutic effects for centuries. Lately, the plant extracts have been increasingly popular as a herbal antidepressant.
In many European countries, St John's wort is available on prescription, while in others it
is sold as a dietary supplement. In Germany, in fact, St John's wort is the leading treatment
for anxiety, and depressive and sleep disorders, and the herb is outselling the standard antidepressant fluoxetine (Prozac) by a factor of four to one (Di Carlo et al., 2001). An increasing number of people self-medicate with various extracts of this plant, so there is an urgent
need for information about their exact mechanism of action and about possible side effects
and drug interactions. *Hypericum* extracts available commercially contain a large number
of constituents, and it is unknown which is responsible for the antidepressant properties
of the herb. Some of the most researched compounds are the napthodiathrones, including
hypericin and pseudo-hypericin, and the phloroglucinols, such as hyperforin, tannins and
flavinoids. The concentrations of constituents vary among the different extracts due to different plant types, growing conditions, preparations and processing procedures, making it
difficult to establish active mechanisms of *Hypericum* extracts. In the following, we aim to
outline the available evidence for an antidepressant action of *H. perforatum*.

In 1996, Linde *et al.* published a systematic review and meta-analysis of the evidence
of 23 placebo-controlled clinical trials of St John's wort in the *British Medical Journal*
(Linde et al., 1996). Its objective was to establish whether extracts of St John's wort are
more effective than placebo in treating depressive disorders, whether the herb is as effective
as standard antidepressants, and whether it has fewer side effects. *H. perforatum* extracts
were significantly superior to placebo: 55% of the active treatment group responded to the
treatment, compared with only 22% in the placebo group. When *Hypericum* extracts were
compared with standard antidepressants, both treatments showed similar effectiveness, 64%
responding to *Hypericum* compared with 58% receiving standard antidepressant treatment.
Hypericum extracts appeared to be better tolerated than treatment with antidepressants;
fewer patients in the *Hypericum* group dropped out due to side effects. Since then, in randomised, double-blind and controlled trials of depression, *Hypericum* extracts have been
found to be as effective as and better tolerated than imipramine (Woelk, 2000) and amitriptyline (Wheatley, 1997). Philipp and colleagues (Philipp et al., 1999) randomised over 250
patients to either 1050 mg *Hypericum* extract (0.2–0.3% hypericin and pseudo-hypericin
and 2–3% hyperforin according to HPLC), 100 mg of imipramine or placebo. *Hypericum*
and imipramine were equally effective, but were better than placebo at 4, 6 and 8 weeks of
the trial. The imipramine dose was clearly suboptimal, and *Hypericum* was prescribed at
a higher than usual dose; nevertheless, both treatments were effective. In contrast, a large
multicentre study (Hypericum Depression Trial Study Group 2002) could not find a significant difference in efficacy between placebo and St John's wort. Figures 7.1a and 1b illustrate
the effect of *Hypericum* compared with placebo and comparator drugs, respectively. From
the variability of the placebo-controlled results (Q-'non-combinability' for risk difference =
123.5, df = 14, P < 0.0001), it appears that study outcomes are significantly diverse due
to design, drug composition or patient selection, so that results cannot be pooled.

One of the possible impediments to optimising the efficacy of *Hypericum* studies is that
the active principle has not yet been identified (Chatterjee et al., 1998, 2001; Müller et al.,
1997, 1998; Singer et al., 1999). Although this may go against the principles of some of

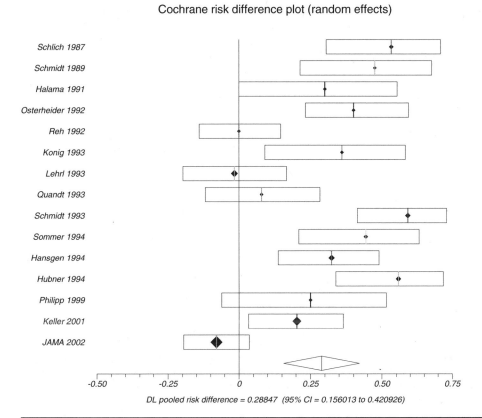

Figure 7.1a   Comparison of St John's wort with placebo—proportion of patients improved after St John's wort minus those improved after placebo (risk difference). Data previous to 1997 cited from (Linde et al., 1996). Computation and graphics were done with StatsDirect, Version 1.9.15, May 2002

its proponents, only detailed analysis of its components' antidepressant actions will make *Hypericum* a reliably effective and acceptable antidepressant.

The pharmacological treatment of bipolar disorder

LONG-TERM PROPHYLAXIS

The primary aim of long-term treatment is the prevention of recurrent episodes (either mania or depression) (see also Chapter 11). According to current guidelines, any patient who has had at least two episodes in 5 years is likely to benefit from prophylactic treatment (American Psychiatric Association, 1994). Despite problems with tolerability, lithium still remains the 'gold standard' against which other treatments are measured. The effectiveness of long-term treatment with lithium to prevent recurrences in bipolar disorder is supported

Cochrane risk difference plot (random effects)

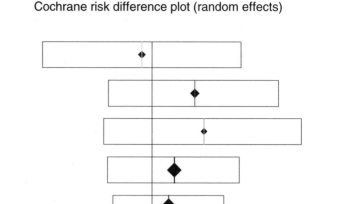
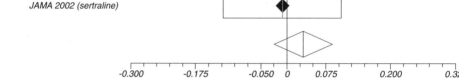

DL pooled risk difference = 0.031472 (95% CI = -0.024581 to 0.087525)

Figure 7.1b Comparison of St John's wort with comparator drug—proportion of patients improved after St John's wort minus those improved after comparator (risk difference). Data previous to 1997 cited from (Linde et al., 1996). Computation and graphics were done with StatsDirect, Version 1.9.15, May 2002

by at least nine controlled, double-blind studies (Baldessarini et al., 1996; Burgess et al., 2001; Price & Heninger, 1994; Tondo et al., 2001). To date, lithium remains the first-line choice for maintenance treatment in patients with a 'classical' course of illness (Maj, 2000).

Some subtypes of what has become known as the 'bipolar spectrum' may not respond as well to lithium. These include patients with 'mixed mania', that is, depression during mania. (Swann et al., 1997), and 'rapid cycling' (Dunner & Fieve, 1974). Emerging evidence would seem to suggest a role for anticonvulsants in these patients. For example, carbamazepine, compared with lithium or placebo, is effective in the long-term treatment of bipolar disorder, with an overall response rate of 63% in 14 controlled or partially controlled studies. (Dunn et al., 1998). Although it does not have worldwide approval as yet, carbamazepine does seem to be more effective in the treatment of bipolar spectrum than classical bipolar disorder. (Berky et al., 1998; Greil et al., 1998). Similarly, sodium valproate has demonstrated efficacy in rapid-cycling bipolar disorder (Calabrese et al., 1993), and controlled studies on the prophylactic benefits of valproate are beginning to emerge. (Bowden et al., 2000).

There have been promising reports on the efficacy of the newer anticonvulsants, such as lamotrigine, gabapentin and topiramate (De León, 2001) (Calabrese et al., 2002). Until evidence from controlled studies is available, it remains prudent to reserve these drugs for refractory cases.

Alternative treatment strategies, or potential augmentative agents, include a number of other compounds which may have some clinical utility, but for which the evidence remains weak. These include calcium channel antagonists such as verapamil, nifedipine and nimodipine (Dubovsky, 1993); thyroid hormones. (Bauer et al., 1998; Baumgartner et al., 1994); the antipsychotic clozapine. (Hummel et al., 2002); and some of the 'novel' antipsychotics, including risperidone and olanzapine (Yatham, 2002). With long-term treatment, it is essential that patients are well informed about the risks and implications of stopping medication. Substantial evidence exists that abrupt discontinuation of lithium is associated with an increased risk of relapse (Baldessarini et al., 1999). The risk, particularly of mania, may be minimised by gradually reducing the lithium dose (Faedda et al., 1993). Although comparable studies are not available for the anticonvulsants, a similarly cautious approach would seem advisable.

MANAGEMENT OF ACUTE MANIA

Early research supported the use of lithium in the treatment of acute mania. More recently, the *superiority* of lithium to other treatments, such as valproate, has been questioned (Bowden et al., 1994). Nonetheless, the efficacy of lithium is without doubt. In an early review of 10 uncontrolled trials of 413 patients with bipolar disorder, 81% displayed reduced manic symptoms during acute lithium treatment (Goodwin & Ebert, 1973). The overall response rate to lithium in four placebo-controlled studies of 116 patients with acute mania was 78% (Goodwin et al., 1969; Maggs, 1963; Schou et al., 1954; Stokes et al., 1971). These studies also demonstrated that up to 2 weeks of treatment with lithium may be necessary to reach maximal effectiveness for manic patients. Due to this delayed effect, particularly in instances of severe mania or psychotic symptoms, with associated acute behavioural disturbance, additional use of an antipsychotic or a benzodiazepine is usually required. Antipsychotics, such as haloperidol and chlorpromazine, have been shown to be useful in the rapid control of severely agitated or psychotic patients with bipolar disorder (Gelenberg & Hopkins, 1996). Despite their widespread use, the high frequency of extrapyramidal side effects has led to caution, particularly in the long term, due to the risk of tardive dyskinesia. There is also evidence that antipsychotic medication, far from helping patients with depressive episodes, may in fact worsen symptoms (Kane, 1999). For these reasons, the use of 'novel' antipsychotics has been advocated, and positive evidence is accumulating to support the treating of acute mania with risperidone, olanzapine or clozapine (Yatham, 2002).

Another approach to reduce the need for antipsychotics is the adjunctive use of benzodiazepines. Clonazepam and lorazepam are the most widely studied compounds, either alone or in combination with lithium. The interpretation of many of these studies is confounded by small sample sizes, short durations of treatment, use of antipsychotics and difficulties in distinguishing possible antimanic effects from nonspecific sedative effects (Bradwejn et al., 1990; Edwards et al., 1991). However, taken together, these studies suggest that benzodiazepines are effective, in place of or in conjunction with a neuroleptic, to sedate the acutely agitated manic patient while waiting for the effects of other primary mood-stabilizing agents to become evident. The fact that lorazepam is well absorbed after intramuscular injection (unlike other benzodiazepines) has made it particularly useful for some very agitated patients (Chouinard et al., 1993).

Carbamazepine has been widely used in the treatment of acute mania where its sedative effects may be advantageous (Post et al., 1998). The results of 19 controlled trials, since 1978, support the efficacy of carbamazepine, or its derivative oxcarbazepine, in the treatment of acute mania, either alone or in combination with lithium or antipsychotics (McElroy & Keck, 2000).

Valproate has also been shown to be effective in the treatment of acute mania. A review of 16 uncontrolled studies (McElroy et al., 1992) reported an overall response rate of 63% in 663 patients. The only placebo-controlled parallel-group study of valproate versus lithium for acute mania published to date (Bowden et al., 1994) showed a significant improvement in 49% of patients receiving lithium, 48% of those receiving valproate and 25% of those receiving placebo. Valproate is well tolerated and has very few drug interactions, making it more suitable for combined treatment regimens (Freeman & Stolle, 1998).

Of the newer anticonvulsants, a review of the recent literature suggests that there is no current evidence to recommend the use of gabapentin in bipolar disorder (mania or hypomania). The strongest evidence is for lamotrigine, but in depressive episodes, not mania or hypomania. Topiramate has shown some promise in both depressed and manic bipolar patients, with the added benefit of promoting weight loss (Calabrese et al., 2002; De León, 2001). Overall, however, the evidence is still very limited.

It is worthwhile mentioning that electroconvulsive therapy (ECT) has been shown to be one of the best treatment options in acute mania (Mukherjee et al., 1994). Current practice, influenced as it is by political as well as clinical issues, reserves ECT for clinical situations where pharmacological treatments may not be possible, such as pregnancy or severe cardiac disease, or when the patient's illness is refractory to drug treatments (American Psychiatric Association, 1994).

MANAGEMENT OF DEPRESSIVE EPISODES

The pharmacological treatment of depressive episodes in bipolar disorder represents a particular challenge. Although almost all of the antidepressants used in the treatment of unipolar depression are effective in the treatment of bipolar depression, the response rates are lower, and there is the risk of precipitating a manic episode or inducing or accelerating rapid cycling (Compton & Nemeroff, 2000; Sachs et al., 2000). The first steps in managing depression in a bipolar patient should involve the initiation of a 'mood stabiliser', if patients are 'drug-free'. If patients are taking prophylaxis, this must be optimised, serum levels checked, and any associated problems, such as hypothyroidism, excluded or treated. If depressive symptoms persist, a decision needs to be taken whether to add an antidepressant or an additional mood stabiliser (Sachs et al., 2000).

Although evidence is scarce, recent studies have suggested that the selective serotonin reuptake inhibitors (SSRIs) may be better tolerated, work more quickly, and have a lower associated risk of inducing mania or rapid cycling than the tricyclic antidepressants (Bauer et al., 1999; Nemeroff et al., 2000). Similarly, although controlled clinical trials comparing standard clinical treatments for depression in patients with bipolar disorder are lacking, it is a widely accepted clinical practice to add a second mood stabilizer to the treatment regimens of patients with bipolar disorder. A recent study compared the addition of an antidepressant with that of a second mood stabilizer in depressed patients who were receiving lithium carbonate or valproate. Both groups showed significant improvement in depressive symptoms during the 6-week trial, the antidepressant group tolerating the combination better (Young et al., 2000).

As mentioned previously, monotherapy with lamotrigine appears to have utility, particularly in the treatment of refractory bipolar depression, but further confirmation of this is awaited (Calabrese et al., 1999). Other suggested strategies include the use of adjunctive thyroxin (Bauer et al., 1998) and the novel use of inositol (Chengappa et al., 2000). Again, the use of ECT, in severe depression, or where urgent treatment is necessary, should not be overlooked (American Psychiatric Association, 1994).

SUICIDE PREVENTION

Since patients with bipolar disorder represent a group at high risk of suicide, it is reasonable to ask whether the above treatment strategies reduce the occurrence of suicidal acts. Retrospective and prospective studies do suggest that long-term lithium therapy reduces the risk of suicide, and may even reduce the known associated risk of cardiovascular disease (Schou, 2000; Tondo et al., 1997). At present, there are still few data available on the antisuicidal effects of the anticonvulsants in bipolar disorder (Goodwin, 1999). Prospective studies looking at the issue of outcome in bipolar disorder suggest that lithium may be significantly superior to carbamazepine in this regard (Greil et al., 1997).

PHYSICAL TREATMENTS

Electroconvulsive treatment (ECT)

ECT is one of the more controversial treatments in psychiatry. It has been vilified as barbaric and irrational, because of its (past) practice and potential side effects (Fink, 2001; Glass, 2001). However, some authors have argued that most of these are just symptoms and signs of the underlying (depressive) illness (Brodaty et al., 2001). There is good evidence that the majority of patients in experimental as well as routine clinical settings improve during a course of ECT (www.sean.org.uk/home.htm). It appears to be superior in action to placebo, that is, general anaesthesia without ECT, but for obvious reasons only limited data are available (Anonymous, 1984; Brandon et al., 1985; Buchan et al., 1992; Johnstone et al., 1980; Stuart, 1985).

Nevertheless, the frequency of the use of ECT appears to be declining in countries where its use had continued unabated since the end of the last world war (Glen & Scott, 1999). In particular, there seems to be considerable variation in its use, even between clinicians working in the same setting (Glen & Scott, 1999). This is, however, not an argument against the efficacy or rationality of prescribing ECT, as it merely confirms the influence other, non-evidence-related factors have on medical decisions. In fact, there has been a renaissance of ECT research in the USA, which appears to be associated with an upward trend in ECT prescriptions. (Sackeim et al., 2000). One of the drawbacks of ECT is its time-limited action, which tends to dissipate after a couple of weeks and requires follow-up medication. (Sackeim et al., 2001). Another is the occasionally occurring retrograde amnesia, which tends to resolve completely or, more rarely, with some residual impairment (Lisanby et al., 2000; Weiner, 2000). It would be difficult to understand why patients submit to such a worrying procedure, without the appreciation that depression is one of the most distressing and painful medical conditions. It is particularly insidious, as it undermines the ability of the sufferer to cope with functional impairment, with mental and physical pain, and with the self-destructive impulses and thoughts that accompany depression. ECT is also occasionally used for treatment-resistant psychosis and mania, where it appears to be effective in 50–60% of cases (www.sean.org.uk/home.htm). Finally, ECT has been successfully employed to resolve neurological crises, such as extreme parkinsonian symptoms (on–off phenomena) (Andersen et al., 1987) and drug-induced states, such as neuroleptic malignant syndrome (Trollor & Sachdev, 1999).

Other electromagnetic stimulation: magnetoconvulsive treatment (MCT)

The potential hazard of seizure induction during repetitive transcranial magnetic stimulation (rTMS) has recently been turned into a potential strength, by using a varying magnetic field to induce seizures during magnetoconvulsive therapy (MCT) (Lisanby et al., 2001). Without the vagaries of poor and variable electric conductivity that allows only a small proportion of the current applied during ECT to pass through the brain, MCT can focus and dose the brain stimulation more accurately and reliably, with the potential benefit of limiting stimulation to the brain structures essential for treatment response, and reducing side effects, such as memory impairment.

Other electromagnetic stimulation: transcranial magnetic stimulation (TMS)

In spite of the absence of major corporate sponsors, a fair amount of therapeutic research has been conducted into the possible antidepressant effects of repetitive transcranial magnetic stimulation (rTMS). A number of good recent reviews describe the studies in detail. (Burt et al., 2002; George et al., 1999; Holtzheimer et al., 2002; Pridmore et al., 2001). However, compared with the evidence necessary for the licensing of antidepressant drugs, the number and quality of trials, as well as the number of subjects included in those trials, are limited. The stimulation parameters employed in different studies are rather diverse, suggesting the familiar 'apples and oranges' problem. For example, George et al. (1997) treated 12 outpatients in a blind, crossover study, using 20 Hz over the left dorsolateral prefrontal cortex and sham treatment. The simple rationale for this approach was that neuroimaging studies had shown reduced metabolism in this brain area, and stimulation at higher frequencies was expected to increase cortical activity under the coil.

Based on a rather similar hypothesis, Klein et al. (1999) treated 71 depressed patients with the slow stimulation frequency of 1 Hz over the right dorsolateral prefrontal cortex. Their assumption was that TMS at 1 Hz would reduce cortical activity in the right prefrontal cortex and bring the relative imbalance between left and right hemisphere deactivation back into equilibrium. It is clearly problematic to lump these two studies together to compute an average effect size, although they are based on similar theoretical premises. Spontaneous remission and placebo response rates in depressive illness vary considerably (20–60%), so

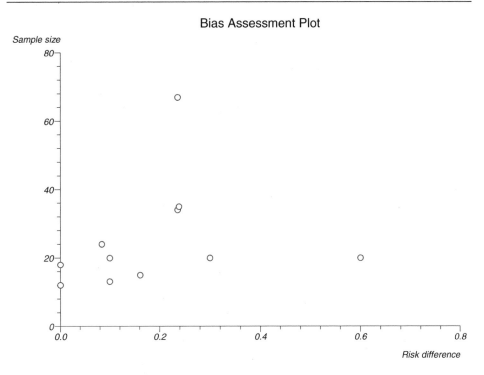

Figure 7.2   Funnel plot of effect size (risk difference, *x*-axis) plotted against number of patients in study (*y*-axis); sham-controlled trials of TMS. Kendall's test of bias on standardised effect versus variance (Begg and Mazumdar): −0.27, P = 0.22 (NS). Computation and graphics were done with StatsDirect, Version 1.9.15, May 2002

that even sizeable improvement rates in open TMS studies of depression may not indicate superiority to placebo.

A serious problem in evaluating TMS is the absence of a true placebo condition. Previous strategies include angling the stimulation coil away from the head surface. However, there is some evidence that subjects can distinguish between flat and angled coil positions by the strength of superficial nerve and muscle stimulation. Some authors have further cast doubt on the assumption that with an angled coil no activation of cortical tissue occurs, arguing that therapeutic effects may be expected from this supposed placebo treatment (George et al., 1999).

With these caveats, it is of interest to look at the effect sizes of some published studies. We recently computed the effect sizes of 11 randomised sham-controlled studies with 102 actively treated patients, using StatsDirect (Version 1.9.15; 5 May 2002; www.statsdirect.com) and a modification of the data provided by Holtzheimer (Holtzheimer et al., 2002). Studies with smaller numbers clearly show a larger variability (Figure 7.2) and Q ('non-combinability' for risk difference) is 18.3 (df = 10, P = 0.0501), just missing statistical significance. This suggests that, as predicted above, some variability exists between studies. The (random-effects) pooled risk difference is 16%, with an approximate 95% confidence interval of 7–26% (DerSimonian-Laird-x^2 = 11.9, df = 1, P = 0.0006; Figure 7.3).

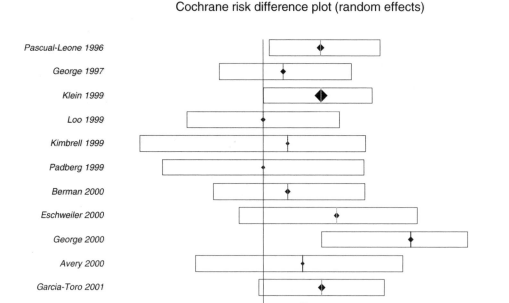

Figure 7.3   Meta-analysis of randomised, sham controlled trials of TMS, comparing proportion of patients improved after TMS with those improved after sham intervention (risk difference). Computation and graphics were done with StatsDirect, Version 1.9.15, May 2002

In summary, these are interesting preliminary results, suggesting that TMS may have antidepressant effects. However, there is no convincing evidence so far that a particular stimulation mode, be it frequency or placement over the head, is superior to others. This casts doubt on any hypotheses about the action of TMS and suggests that non-specific effects may be important.

Other electromagnetic stimulation: vagus nerve stimulation (VNS)

Most recently, vagus stimulation by implanted pacemaker, a treatment method previously used for the control of epileptic seizures, has been applied to the treatment of depression (George et al., 2000). Thirty treatment-resistant, but non-psychotic, depressed patients received an implant of a pacemaker stimulating the left cervical vagus nerve by bipolar electrodes, attached below the cardiac branch. Stimulation was mostly with 0.5-ms pulse-width, at 20–30 Hz, with 30-s stimulation periods alternating with 5-min breaks. This open protocol was sustained over 10 weeks, with a response rate of 40% at the end point. Patients had failed to respond to at least two robust treatment attempts, and had an average duration of illness episode of 10 years (0.3–49.5 years). The most common stimulation-related adverse event was voice alteration (usually hoarseness) in 40%, and there was pain, coughing and dysphagia (10% each). Longer-term follow-up appeared to support the efficacy of VNS (Marangell et al., 2002). Considering the severity of illness, this is an encouraging result that warrants further controlled studies.

Other electromagnetic stimulation: light therapy (see also Doris et al., 1999)

A simple and therefore attractive and widely researched idea is that there is an inverse relationship between short duration of the local daylight period and the incidence of depression (Young et al., 1997). This correlation has not always been replicated, and possible confounds, such as seasonal unemployment, have to be considered (Murray & Hay, 1997). There is some evidence for the effectiveness of light therapy in seasonal affective disorder. (Lee et al., 1997). However, the usual irradiation at 10 000 lx is not always without side effects. About half the patients suffer from headaches and visual problems early in treatment (Kogan & Guilford, 1998). There have also been reports of emerging suicidal tendencies during light therapy (Praschak et al., 1997), so that this treatment should not be given without psychiatric supervision. Proof that seasonal depression is in any way different from major depressive illness is still lacking. Its symptoms are consistent with (atypical) depression, with hypersomnia, hyperphagia, and tiredness. As in other types of depressive illness, symptoms respond to standard antidepressants, such as fluoxetine (Ruhrmann et al., 1998).

Neurosurgery for mental disorder (NMD)

Neurosurgery for mental disorder (NMD) is rarely undertaken; between 1984 and 1994, a total of only 20 operations per year in the UK (CRAG Working Group, 1996) were done. Even fewer operations per year are done now. Therefore, for practical purposes, this form of treatment has effectively ceased, although it was common up until 40 years ago.

The only contemporary indications for such treatment are severe mood disorder or obsessive compulsive disorder (OCD), when the patient wants the operation, when all other reasonable treatments have repeatedly failed, and the patient remains ill but competent to provide informed consent (CRAG Working Group, 1996). For example, under Section 97 of the Mental Health (Scotland) Act, independent certification by the Mental Welfare Commission of a patient's ability to consent and the appropriateness of treatment is required.

Modern NMD operations comprise subcaudate tractotomy, anterior cingulotomy, limbic leucotomy and anterior capsulotomy (CRAG Working Group, 1996). Operations such as amygdalotomy and hypothalamotomy are no longer practised (CRAG Working Group, 1996).

EARLY HISTORY OF NMD

NMD was originally developed because of a need to treat intractable psychotic disorders at a time when there were no effective treatments (Malhi & Bartlett, 2000). Fulton and Jacobsen, while investigating primate frontal lobe function, discovered that bilateral removal of the orbitofrontal cortex subdued the animals, making them appear less anxious (Fulton &

Jacobsen, 1935). Soon afterwards, Lima operated on humans (Fenton, 1999), and Freeman and Watts (Freeman et al., 1978) began 'psychosurgery' in the USA, devising the standard prefrontal leucotomy. Subsequently, 40 000 patients in the USA and 12 000 patients in the UK were operated on until the mid-1950s (Malhi & Bartlett, 2000).

At this point, the number of such operations declined because of the development of the first effective drug treatments and reports of a 'post-lobotomy syndrome' (Malhi & Bartlett, 2000). The operations to date had employed relatively crude 'freehand' methods, reflecting neurosurgical practice at the time.

RECENT HISTORY OF NMD

It became apparent that the existing operations lesioned very variable brain regions and that there was considerable variability in clinical outcome. An early consensus arose that patients with mood disorders and OCD appeared to benefit most (Knight, 1964), regardless of operation type.

In such patients, it was claimed that lesions confined to the white-matter tracts deep to the orbitomedial prefrontal cortex had minimal effect on intellect and personality while benefit with regard to illness recovery was maintained (Knight, 1964). A stereotactic operative procedure designed to make reproducible lesions in this brain area was then devised (Knight, 1964). Subsequent post-mortem studies of lesion location confirmed this reproducibility (Newcombe, 1975).

The new procedure was termed 'stereotactic subcaudate tractotomy' (SST) and became by far the most common modern NMD used in the UK over the next 40 years (CRAG Working Group, 1996). In other countries, two other stereotactic operations were developed: cingulotomy and anterior capsulotomy (CRAG Working Group, 1996). The combination of what was essentially SST and cingulotomy was termed 'limbic leucotomy' (Richardson, 1973).

STEREOTACTIC SUBCAUDATE TRACTOTOMY (SST)

For the first few decades following the introduction of SST, large patient follow-up studies indicated a significant improvement in 40–60% of otherwise treatment-refractory patients (Bridges et al., 1994; Goktepe et al., 1975). No operative mortality was reported, and there appeared to be minimal effects on personality, with an epilepsy rate of a few per cent. A substantial reduction in completed suicide rate in comparison to untreated depressive illness was noted. These outcome studies have been strongly criticised because of a number of limitations (Cawley & Tarish, 1994). Constructive recommendations for future study have been made (CRAG Working Group, 1996).

CINGULOTOMY AND ANTERIOR CAPSULOTOMY

Lack of space prevents much comment on these other procedures. However, discussion of operative technique and clinical outcome is available (Ballantyne et al., 1987; Meyerson & Mindus, 1988; Richardson, 1973). It should be noted that the location of the cingulotomy lesion was deliberately variable (Richardson, 1973) though not necessarily for a good reason.

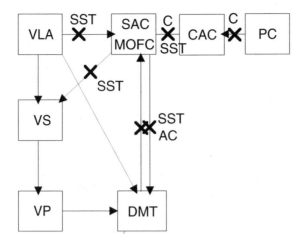

X White-matter tract damage

Figure 7.4 Limbic cortical basal ganglia re-entrant loop with superimposed lesion locations. PC: posterior cingulate; SAC: subgenual anterior cingulate; MOFC: medial orbitofrontal cortex; CAC: caudal anterior cingulate; VLA: ventrolateral nucleus of the amygdala; VS: ventral striatum; VP: ventral pallidum; DMT: dorsomedial thalamic nucleus; SST: stereotactic subcaudate tractotomy; C: cingulotomy; AC: anterior capsulotomy. Limbic loop circuitry based on Alexander et al., 1990; Price, 1999. Lesion locations derived from Ballantyne et al., 1987; Knight, 1964; Meyerson & Mindus, 1988; Richardson, 1973. Cingulotomy lesion location is very variable and often deep to caudal anterior cingulate

Moreover, conventional anterior capsulotomy does not attempt to avoid damage to fibres passing to the dorsolateral cortex (Meyerson & Mindus, 1988), a fact which might account for reports of significant postoperative apathy and weight gain (Meyerson & Mindus, 1988) with this procedure.

NMD LESION LOCATIONS

Anatomically, the prefrontal cortex is now recognised as being organised into five parallel cortical basal-ganglia re-entrant loops (Alexander et al., 1990), providing the substrate for motor (skeletomotor and oculomotor), cognitive (dorsolateral) and emotional (orbitofrontal and anterior cingulate) function. The orbitofrontal and anterior cingulate loop is also known as the 'limbic' loop, and considerable evidence links this brain region with emotion and mood (Alexander et al., 1990).

Figure 7.4 shows the limbic loop with lesion locations for the various NMD procedures superimposed. Clearly, these operations would be expected to cause marked disruption of function in this particular loop. It has been argued that these loops comprise functional units (Alexander et al., 1990), and lesions anywhere within such a unit may cause similar clinical syndromes (Megga & Cummings, 1994). This might begin to explain why apparently different NMD procedures have similar reported effects, though, clearly, this does not suggest a mechanism of action.

NATIONAL AND INTERNATIONAL AVAILABILITY OF NMD

NMD has always been a controversial treatment and lack of space prevents detailed discussion of evidence for its efficacy and safety versus adverse outcome, or the limitations of that knowledge. The CRAG Working Group for Mental Illness investigated this issue for the NMD procedures of interest here, and their report constitutes the largest and most recent enquiry into NMD in the UK (CRAG Working Group, 1996). They concluded that 'Subject to existing and recommended additional safeguards and procedures, neurosurgery for mental disorder should continue to be available in Scotland, but only as a treatment for intractable obsessive compulsive disorder and affective disorders (e.g. major depressive illness).' Dundee is currently the only centre in the UK practising NMD. Most other countries still allow NMD, though with variable safeguards on its use (Malhi & Bridges, 1997).

REFERENCES

Alexander, G.E., Crutcher, M.D. & DeLong, M.R. (1990). Basal ganglia-thalamocortical circuits: Parallel substrates for motor, oculomotor, "prefrontal" and "limbic" functions. In H.B.M. Uylings et al. (Eds), *Progress in Brain Research*. New York: Elsevier.

American Psychiatric Association (1994). Practice guideline for the treatment of patients with bipolar disorder. *American Journal of Psychiatry, 151* (Suppl.), 1–36.

Andersen, K., Balldin, J., Gottfries, C.G., et al. (1987). A double-blind evaluation of electroconvulsive therapy in Parkinson's disease with "on-off" phenomena. *Acta Neurologica Scandinavica, 76,* 191–199.

Anderson, I.M. (2001). Meta-analytical studies on new antidepressants. *British Medical Bulletin, 57,* 161–178.

Anonymous (1984). The Northwick Park ECT trial. Predictors of response to real and simulated ECT. Clinical Research Centre, Division of Psychiatry. *British Journal of Psychiatry, 144,* 227–237.

Baldessarini, R.J., Tondo, L., Faedda, G.L., Suppes, T.R., Floris, G. & Rudas, N. (1996). Effects of the rate of discontinuing lithium maintenance treatment in bipolar disorders. *Journal of Clinical Psychiatry, 57,* 441–448.

Baldessarini, R.J., Tondo, L. & Viguera, A.C. (1999). Discontinuing lithium maintenance treatment in bipolar disorders: Risks and implications. *Bipolar Disorders, 1,* 17–24.

Ballantyne, H.T., Bouckoms, A.J., Thomas, E.K. & Giriunas, I.E. (1987). Treatment of psychiatric illness by stereotactic cingulotomy. *Biological Psychiatry, 22,* 807–819.

Barbui, C. & Hotopf, M. (2001). Amitriptyline v. the rest: Still the leading antidepressant after 40 years of randomised controlled trials. *British Journal of Psychiatry, 178,* 129–144.

Barbui, C., Hotopf, M., Freemantle, N., et al. (2000). Selective serotonin reuptake inhibitors versus tricyclic and heterocyclic antidepressants: Comparison of drug adherence. *Cochrane Database Systematic Review*, no. 4, p. CD002791.

Bauer, M., Hellweg, R., Gräf, K.J. & Baumgartner, A. (1998). Treatment of refractory depression with high-dose thyroxine. *Neuropsychopharmacology, 18,* 444–455.

Bauer, M., Zaninelli, R., Müller-Oerlinghausen, B. & Meister, W. (1999). Paroxetine and amitriptyline augmentation of lithium in the treatment of major depression: A double-blind study. *Journal of Clinical Psychopharmacology, 19,* 164–177.

Baumgartner, A., Bauer, M. & Hellweg, R. (1994). Treatment of intractable non-rapid cycling bipolar disorder with high-dose thyroxine: An open clinical trial. *Neuropsychopharmacology, 10,* 183–189.

Berky, M., Wolf, C. & Kovacs, G. (1998). Carbamazepine versus lithium in bipolar affective disorder. *European Archives of Psychiatry and Clinical Neuroscience, 248,* S119.

Bowden, C.L., Brugger, A.M., Swann, A.C., Calabrese, J.R., Janicak, P.G. & Petty, F. (1994). Efficacy of valproate and lithium in the treatment of acute mania. *American Journal of Psychiatry, 149,* 108–111.

Bowden, C.L., Calabrese, J.R., McElroy, S.L., Gyulai, L., Wassef, A. & Petty, F. (2000). A randomised, placebo-controlled trial of divalproex and lithium in the treatment of outpatients with bipolar I disorder. *Archives of General Psychiatry, 57,* 481–489.

Bradwejn, J., Shriqui, C., Koszycki, D. & Meterissian, G. (1990). Double-blind comparison of the effects of clonazepam and lorazepam in acute mania. *Journal of Clinical Psychopharmacology, 10,* 403–408.

Brandon, S., Cowley, P., McDonald, C., Neville, P., Palmer, R. & Wellstood, E. (1985). Leicester ECT trial: Results in schizophrenia, *British Journal of Psychiatry, 146,* 177–183.

Bridges, P.K., Bartlett, J.R., Hale, A.S., Poynton, A.M., Malizia, A.L. & Hodgkiss, A.D. (1994). Psychosurgery: Stereotactic subcaudate tractotomy. An indispensable treatment. *British Journal of Psychiatry, 165,* 599–611.

Brodaty, H., Berle, D., Hickie, I. & Mason, C. (2001). "Side effects" of ECT are mainly depressive phenomena and are independent of age. *Journal of Affective Disorders, 66,* 237–245.

Buchan, H., Johnstone, E., McPherson, K., Palmer, R.L., Crow, T.J. & Brandon, S. (1992). Who benefits from electroconvulsive therapy? Combined results of the Leicester and Northwick Park trials. *British Journal of Psychiatry, 160,* 355–359.

Bunney, W.E. Jr. & Davis, J.M. (1965). Norepinephrine in depressive reactions: A review. *Archives of General Psychiatry, 13,* 483–494.

Burgess, S., Geddes, J., Hawton, K., Townsend, E., Jamison, K. & Goodwin, G. (2001). Lithium for maintenance treatment of mood disorders. *Cochrane Database Systematic Review, 3,* CD003013.

Burt, T., Lisanby, S.H. & Sackeim, H.A. (2002). Neuropsychiatric applications of transcranial magnetic stimulation: A meta-analysis. *International Journal of Neuropsychopharmacology, 5,* 73–103.

Calabrese, J.R., Bowden, C.L., Sachs, G.S., Ascher, J.A., Monaghan, E. & Rudd, G.D. (1999). A double-blind placebo-controlled study of lamotrigine monotherapy in outpatients with bipolar I depression. *Journal of Clinical Psychiatry, 60,* 79–88.

Calabrese, J.R., Rapport, D.J., Kimmel, S.E., Reece, B. & Woyshville, M. (1993). Rapid cycling bipolar disorder and its treatment with valproate. *Canadian Journal of Psychiatry—Revue Canadienne de Psychiatrie, 38,* 57–61.

Calabrese, J.R., Shelton, M.D., Rapport, D.J. & Kimmel, S.E. (2002). Bipolar disorders and the effectiveness of novel anticonvulsants. *Journal of Clinical Psychiatry, 63,* (Suppl. 3), 5–9.

Carroll, B.J., Curtis, G.C. & Mendels, J. (1976). Neuroendocrine regulation in depression. II. Discrimination of depressed from non-depressed patients. *Archives of General Psychiatry, 138,* 1218–1221.

Cawley, R. & Tarish, M. (1994). Peer review of "Psychosurgery: Stereotactic subcaudate tractotomy. An indispensable treatment". *British Journal of Psychiatry, 165,* 612–613.

Charney, D.S., Southwick, S.M., Delgado, P.L. & Krystal, J.H. (1990). Current status of receptor sensitivity hypothesis of antidepressant action: Implications for the treatment of severe depression. In J.D. Amsterdam (Ed.), *Pharmacotherapy of Depression,* pp. 13–34. Basel: Marcel Dekker.

Chatterjee, S., Biber, A. & Weibezahn, C. (2001). Stimulation of glutamate, aspartate and gamma-aminobutyric acid release from synaptosomes by hyperforin. *Pharmacopsychiatry, 34S,* S11–S19.

Chatterjee, S., Nöldner, M., Koch, E. & Erdelmeier, C. (1998). Antidepressant activity of *Hypericum perforatum* and hyperforin: The neglected possibility. *Pharmacopsychiatry, 31S,* S7–S15.

Chengappa, K.N.R., Levine, J. & Gershon, S. (2000). Inositol as an add-on treatment for bipolar depression. *Bipolar Disorders, 2,* 47–55.

Chouinard, G., Annable, L., Turnier, L., Holobow, N. & Szkrumelak, N. (1993). A double-blind randomized clinical trial of rapid tranquillization with I.M. clonazepam and I.M. haloperidol in agitated psychotic patients with manic symptoms. *Canadian Journal of Psychiatry—Revue Canadienne de Psychiatrie, 38* (Suppl. 4), S114–S121.

Compton, M.T. & Nemeroff, C.B. (2000). The treatment of bipolar depression. *Journal of Clinical Psychiatry, 61* (Suppl.) 57–67.

Coppen, A. & Bailey, J. (2000). Enhancement of the antidepressant action of fluoxetine by folic acid: A randomised, placebo controlled trial. *Journal of Affective Disorders, 60*, 121–130.

Corrigan, M.H., Denahan, A.Q., Wright, C.E., Ragual, R.J. & Evans, D.L. (2000). Comparison of pramipexole, fluoxetine, and placebo in patients with major depression. *Depression and Anxiety, 11*, 58–65.

CRAG Working Group (1996). *Neurosurgery for Mental Disorder*. Scotland: HMSO (J2318 7/96).

Cummings, J.L. (1992). Depression and Parkinson's disease: A review. *American Journal of Psychiatry, 4*, 443–454.

De León, O.A. (2001). Antiepileptic drugs for the acute and maintenance treatment of bipolar disorder. *Harvard Review of Psychiatry, 9*, 209–222.

Delgado, P.L., Miller, H.L. & Salomon, R.M. (1999). Tryptophan–depletion challenge in depressed patients treated with desipramine or fluoxetine: Implications for the role of serotonin in the mechanism of antidepressant action. *Biological Psychiatry, 46*, 212–220.

Di Carlo, G., Borelli, F., Ernst, E. & Izzo, A. (2001). St John's wort: Prozac from the plant kingdom. *Trends in Pharmacological Sciences, 22*, 292–297.

Diehl, D.J. & Gershon, S. (1992). The role of dopamine in mood disorders. *Comprehensive Psychiatry, 33*, 115–120.

Doris, A., Ebmeier, K. & Shajahan, P. (1999). Depressive Illness. *Lancet, 354*, 1369–1375.

Drevets, W.C., Ongur, D. & Price, J.L. (1998). Neuroimaging abnormalities in the subgenual prefrontal cortex: Implications for the pathophysiology of familial mood disorders. *Molecular Psychiatry, 3*, 220–221.

Dubovsky, S.L. (1993). Calcium channel antagonists in manic-depressive illness. *Neuropsychobiology, 27*, 184–192.

Dunn, R.T., Frye, M.S., Kimbrell, T.A., Denicoff, K.D., Leverich, G.S. & Post, R.M. (1998). The efficacy and use of the anticonvulsants in mood disorders. *Clinical Neuropharmacology, 21*, 215–235.

Dunner, D.L. & Fieve, R.R. (1974). Clinical factors in lithium carbonate prophylaxis failure. *Archives of General Psychiatry, 30*, 229–233.

Ebert, D., Feistel, H., Kaschka, W., Barocka, A. & Pirner, A. (1994). Single photon emission computerized tomography assessment of cerebral dopamine D2 receptor blockade in depression before and after sleep deprivation—preliminary results. *Biological Psychiatry, 35*, 880–885.

Ebmeier, K.P. & Kronhaus, D. (2002). Brain imaging in mood disorders. In H.D'Haenen et al. (Eds), *Textbook of Biological Psychiatry*, pp. 815–828. New York: Wiley.

Edwards, R., Stephenson, U. & Flewett, T. (1991). Clonazepam in acute mania: A double-blind trial. *Australian and New Zealand Journal of Psychiatry, 25*, 238–242.

Faedda, G.L., Tondo, L., Baldessarini, R.J., Suppes, T. & Tohen, M. (1993). Outcome after rapid vs. gradual discontinuation of lithium treatment in bipolar disorders. *Archives of General Psychiatry, 50*, 448–455.

Fenton, G.W. (1999). Neurosurgery for mental disorder: Past and present. *Advances in Psychiatric Treatment, 5*, 261–270.

Fink, M. (2001). Convulsive therapy: A review of the first 55 years. *Journal of Affective Disorders, 63*, 1–15.

Freeman, C.P.L., Basson, J. & Crighton, A. (1978). A double-blind controlled trial of ECT and simulated ECT in depressive illness. *Lancet, i*, 738–740.

Freeman, M.P. & Stolle, A.L. (1998). Mood stabilizer combinations: A review of the safety and efficacy. *American Journal of Psychiatry, 155*, 12–21.

Frye, M.A., Ketter, T.A., Leverich, G.S., et al. (2000). The increasing use of polypharmacotherapy for refractory mood disorders: 22 years of study. *Journal of Clinical Psychiatry, 61*, 9–15.

Fulton, J.E. & Jacobsen, C.F. (1935). The functions of the frontal lobes. A comparative study in monkey, chimpanzee and man. II. *International Neurological Congress*, pp. 70–71.

Furukawa, T., Streiner, D.L. & Young, L.T. (2000). Antidepressant plus benzodiazepine for major depression. *Cochrane Database Systematic Review*, 4, p. CD001026.

Furukawa, T.A., McGuire, H. & Barbui, C. (2002). Meta-analysis of effects and side effects of low dosage tricyclic antidepressants in depression: Systematic review. *British Medical Journal, 325*, 991–995.

Gelenberg, A.J. & Hopkins, H.S. (1996). Antipsychotics in bipolar disorder. *Journal of Clinical Psychiatry, 57* (Suppl.), 49–52.

George, M.S., Lisanby, S.H. & Sackeim, H.A. (1999). Transcranial magnetic stimulation: Applications in neuropsychiatry. *Archives of General Psychiatry, 56*, 300–311.

George, M.S., Sackeim, H.A., Rush, A.J., et al. (2000). Vagus nerve stimulation: A new tool for brain research and therapy. *Biological Psychiatry, 47*, 287–295.

George, M.S., Wassermann, E.M., Kimbrell, T.A., et al. (1997). Mood improvement following daily left prefrontal repetitive transcranial magnetic stimulation in patients with depression: A placebo-controlled crossover trial. *American Journal of Psychiatry, 154*, 1752–1756.

Glass, R.M. (2001). Electroconvulsive therapy—time to bring it out of the shadows. *Journal of the American Medical Association, 285*, 1346–1348.

Glen, T. & Scott, A.I.F. (1999). Rates of electroconvulsive therapy use in Edinburgh (1992–1997). *Journal of Affective Disorders, 54*, 81–85.

Goktepe, E.O., Young, L.B. & Bridges, P.K. (1975). A further review of the results of stereotactic subcaudate tractotomy. *British Journal of Psychiatry, 126*, 270–280.

Goodwin, F.K. (1999). Anticonvulsant therapy and suicide risk in affective disorders. *Journal of Clinical Psychiatry, 60*, (Suppl. 2), 89–93.

Goodwin, F.K. & Ebert, M. (1973). Lithium in mania: Clinical trials and controlled studies. In S. Gershon & B. Shopsin (Eds), *Lithium: Its Role in Psychiatric Research and Treatment.* New York: Plenum Press.

Goodwin, F.K., Murphy, D.L. & Bunney, W.F. Jr. (1969). Lithium carbonate treatment in depression and mania: A longitudinal double-blind study. *Archives of General Psychiatry, 21*, 486–496.

Greil, W., Kleindienst, N., Erazo, N. & Müller-Oerlinghausen, B. (1998). Differential response to lithium and carbamazepine in the prophylaxis of bipolar disorder. *Journal of Clinical Psychopharmacology, 18*, 455–460.

Greil, W., Ludwig-Mayerhofer, W. & Erazo, N. (1997). Lithium versus carbamazepine in the maintenance treatment of bipolar disorders: A randomised study. *Journal of Affective Disorders, 43*, 151–161.

Haddad, P.M. (2001). Antidepressant discontinuation syndromes. *Drug Safety, 24*, 183–197.

Hansen, L. (2001). A critical review of akathisia, and its possible association with suicidal behaviour. *Human Psychopharmacology, 16*, 495–505.

Hawley, C.J., Loughlin, P.J., Quick, S.J., et al. (2000). Efficacy, safety and tolerability of combined administration of lithium and selective serotonin reuptake inhibitors: A review of the current evidence. Hertfordshire Neuroscience Research Group. *Int Clin Psychopharmacol, 15*, 197–206.

Holtzheimer, P.E., Russo, J. & Avery, D.H. (2002). A meta-analysis of repetitive transcranial magnetic stimulation in the treatment of depression. *Psychopharmacology Bulletin, 35*, 149–169.

Hummel, B., Dittmann, S., Forsthoff, A., Matzner, N., Amann, B. & Grunze, H. (2002). Clozapine as add-on medication in the maintenance treatment of bipolar and schizoaffective disorders. A case series. *Neuropsychobiology, 45*, (Suppl. 1), 37–42.

Hypericum Depression Trial Study Group (2002). Effect of *Hypericum perforatum* (St John's wort) in major depressive disorder. *Journal of the American Medical Association, 287*, pp. 1807–1814.

Jimerson, D.C. (1987). Role of dopamine mechanisms in the affective disorders. In H.Y. Meltzer (Ed), *Psychopharmacology. The Third Generation of Progress* (pp. 505–511). New York: Raven Press.

Johnstone, E.C., Deakin, J.F., Lawler, P., et al. (1980). The Northwick Park electroconvulsive therapy trial. *Lancet, 2*, 8208–8209, 1317–1320.

Kane, J.M. (1999). Tardive dyskinesia in affective disorders. *Journal of Clinical Psychiatry, 60*, (Suppl. 5), 43–47.

Klein, E., Kreinin, I., Chistyakov, A., et al. (1999). Therapeutic efficacy of right prefrontal slow repetitive transcranial magnetic stimulation in major depression: A double-blind controlled study. *Archives of General Psychiatry, 56*, 315–320.

Knight, G. (1964). The orbital cortex as an objective in the surgical treatment of mental illness. *British Journal of Surgery, 51*, 114–124.

Kogan, A.O. & Guilford, P.M. (1998). Side effects of short-term 10,000-lux light therapy. *American Journal of Psychiatry, 155*, 293–294.

Kuhn, R. (1958). The treatment of depressive states with G22355 (imipramine hydrochloride). *American Journal of Psychiatry, 115*, 459–464.

Lee, T.M., Chan, C.C., Paterson, J.G., Janzen, H.L. & Blashko, C.A. (1997). Spectral properties of phototherapy for seasonal affective disorder: A meta-analysis. *Acta Psychiatrica Scandinavica, 96,* 117–121.

Lima, M.S. & Moncrieff, J. (2000). A comparison of drugs versus placebo for the treatment of dysthymia. *Cochrane Database Systematic Review, 2,* p. CD001130.

Linde, K., Ramirez, G., Mulrow, C.D., Pauls, A., Weidenhammer, W. & Melchart, D. (1996). St John's wort for depression—an overview and meta-analysis of randomised clinical trials. *British Medical Journal, 313,* no. 7052, 253–258.

Lisanby, S.H., Maddox, J.H., Prudic, J., Devanand, D.P. & Sackeim, H.A. (2000). The effects of electroconvulsive therapy on memory of autobiographical and public events. *Archives of General Psychiatry, 57,* 581–590.

Lisanby, S.H., Schlaepfer, T.E., Fisch, H.U. & Sackeim, H.A. (2001). Magnetic seizure therapy of major depression. *Archives of General Psychiatry, 58,* 303–305.

Maggs, R. (1963). Treatment of manic illness with lithium carbonate. *British Journal of Psychiatry, 109,* 56–65.

Maj, M. (2000). The impact of lithium prophylaxis on the course of bipolar disorder: A review of the research evidence. *Bipolar Disorders, 2,* 93–101.

Malhi, G.S. & Bartlett, J.R. (2000). Depression: A role for neurosurgery? *British Journal of Neurosurgery, 14,* 5, 415–423.

Malhi, G.S. & Bridges, P.K. (1997). Neurosurgery for mental disorders (NMD). A clinical worldwide perspective: Past, present and future. *International Journal of Psychiatry in Clinical Practice, 1,* 119–129.

Marangell, L., Rush, J., George, M.S., et al. (2002). Vagus nerve stimulation (VNS) for major depressive episodes: One year outcomes. *Biological Psychiatry, 51,* 280–287.

McElroy, S.L. & Keck, P.E., Jr. (2000). Pharmacological agents for the treatment of acute bipolar mania. *Biological Psychiatry, 48,* 539–557.

McElroy, S.L., Keck, P.E. Jr., Pope, H.G. & Hudson, J.I. (1992). Valproate in the treatment of bipolar disorder: Literature review and clinical guidelines. *Journal of Clinical Psychopharmacology, 12,* (Suppl. 1), S42–S52.

Megga, M.S. & Cummings, J.L. (1994). Frontal-subcortical circuits and neuropsychiatric disorders. *Journal of Neuropsychiatry and Clinical Neurosciences, 6,* 358–370.

Meyerson, B.A. & Mindus, P. (1988). The role of the anterior internal capsulotomy in psychiatric surgery. In L.D. Lunsford (Ed.), *Modern Stereotactic Neurosurgery,* (pp. 353–363). Lancaster: Martinus Nijhoff.

Miguel-Hidalgo, J.J. & Rajkowska, G. (2002). Morphological brain changes in depression: Can antidepressants reverse them? *Central Nervous System Drugs, 16,* 372.

Mukherjee, S., Sackheim, H.A. & Schnurr, D.B. (1994). Electroconvulsive treatment of acute manic episodes: A review. *American Journal of Psychiatry, 151,* 169–176.

Müller, W., Rolli, M., Schäfer, C. & Hafner, U. (1997). Effects of *Hypericum* extract (LI 160) in biochemical model of antidepressant activity. *Pharmacopsychiatry, 30S,* S102–S107.

Müller, W., Singer, A., Wonnermann, M., Hafner, U., Rolli, M. & Schäfer, C. (1998). Hyperforin represents the neurotransmitter reuptake inhibiting constituent of *Hypericum* extract. *Pharmacopsychiatry, 31S,* S16–S21.

Murray, G.W. & Hay, D.A. (1997). Seasonal affective disorder in Australia: Is photoperiod critical? *Australian and New Zealand Journal of Psychiatry, 31,* 279–284.

Nemeroff, C.B., Evans, D.L. & Gyulai, L. (2000). Double-blind, placebo-controlled comparison of imipramine and paroxetine in the treatment of bipolar depression. *American Journal of Psychiatry, 158,* 906–912.

Newcombe, R. (1975). The lesion in stereotactic subcaudate tractotomy. *British Journal of Psychiatry, 126,* 478–481.

O'Leary, D., Paykel, E., Todd, C. & Vardulaki, K. (2001). Suicide in primary affective disorders revisited: A systematic review by treatment era. *Journal of Clinical Psychiatry, 62,* 804–811.

Pampallona, S., Bollini, P., Tibaldi, G., Kupelnick, B. & Munizza, C. (2002). Patient adherence in the treatment of depression. *British Journal of Psychiatry, 180,* 104–109.

Paykel, E.S., Hart, D. & Priest, R.G. (1998). Changes in public attitudes to depression during the Defeat Depression Campaign. *British Journal of Psychiatry, 173,* 519–522.

Philipp, M., Kohnen, R. & Hiller, K.O. (1999). *Hypericum* extract versus imipramine or placebo in patients with moderate depression: Randomised multicentre study of treatment for eight weeks. *British Medical Journal, 319,* (7224) 1534–1538.

Post, R.M., Frye, M., Deniciff, K., Leverich, G.S., Kimbrell, T.A. & Dunn, R.T. (1998). Beyond lithium in the treatment of bipolar illness. *Neuropsychopharmacology, 19,* 206–219.

Praschak, R., Neumeister, A., Hesselmann, B., Willeit, M., Barnas, C. & Kasper, S. (1997). Suicidal tendencies as a complication of light therapy for seasonal affective disorder: A report of three cases. *Journal of Clinical Psychiatry, 58,* 389–392.

Price, J.L. (1999). Prefrontal cortical networks related to visceral function and mood. *Annals of the New York Academy of Sciences, 877,* 383–396.

Price, L.H. & Heninger, G.R. (1994). Lithium in the treatment of mood disorders. *New England Journal of Medicine, 331,* 591–598.

Pridmore, S., Khan, U.A., Reid, P. & George, M.S. (2001). Transcranial magnetic stimulation in depression: An overview. *German Journal of Psychiatry, 4,* 43–50.

Rajkowska, G., Miguel-Hidalgo, J.J., Wei, J., et al. (1999). Morphometric evidence for neuronal and glial prefontal cell pathology in major depression. *Biological Psychiatry, 45,* 1085–1098.

Richardson, A. (1973). Stereotactic limbic leucotomy: Surgical technique. *Postgraduate Medical Journal, 49,* 860–864.

Ruhrmann, S., Kasper, S., Hawellek, B., et al. (1998). Effects of fluoxetine versus bright light in the treatment of seasonal affective disorder. *Psychological Medicine, 28,* 923–933.

Sachs, G.S., Koslow, C.L. & Ghaemi, S.N. (2000). The treatment of bipolar depression. *Bipolar Disorders, 2,* 256–260.

Sackeim, H.A., Haskett, R.F., Mulsant, B.H., et al. (2001). Continuation pharmacotherapy in the prevention of relapse following electroconvulsive therapy—a randomized controlled trial. *Journal of the American Medical Association, 285,* 1299–1307.

Sackeim, H.A., Prudic, J., Devanand, D.P., et al. (2000). A prospective, randomized, double-blind comparison of bilateral and right unilateral electroconvulsive therapy at different stimulus intensities. *Archives of General Psychiatry, 57,* 425–434.

Sapolsky, R.M., Krey, L.C. & McEwen, B. (1986). The neuroendocrinology of stress and ageing: The glucocorticoid cascade hypothesis. *Endocrine Reviews, 7,* 284–301.

Schildkraut, J.J. (1965). The catecholamine hypothesis of affective disorders: A review of supporting evidence. *Americal Journal of Psychiatry, 122,* 509–522.

Schou, M. (2000). Suicidal behaviour and prophylactic lithium treatment of major mood disorders: A review of reviews. *Suicide and Life-Threatening Behavior, 30,* 289–293.

Schou, M., Juel-Nielson, J., Strömgren, E. & Voldby, H. (1954). The treatment of manic psychoses by administration of lithium salts. *Journal of Neurology, Neurosurgery, and Psychiatry, 17,* 250–260.

Schulberg, H.C., Katon, W.J., Simon, G.E. & Rush, A.J. (1999). Best clinical practice: Guidelines for managing major depression in primary medical care. *Journal of Clinical Psychiatry, 60,* 19–26.

Shah, P.J., Glabus, M.F., Goodwin, G.M. & Ebmeier, K.P. (2001). Chronic, treatment resistant depression—MRI changes and clinical correlates. *British Journal of Psychiatry.*

Shah, P.J., Ogilvie, A., Goodwin, G.M. & Ebmeier, K.P. (1997). Clinical and psychometric correlates of dopamine D2 binding in depression. *Psychological Medicine, 27,* 1247–1256.

Sheline, Y.I., Wang, P.W., Gado, M.H., Csernansky, J.G. & Vannier, M.W. (1996). Hippocampal atrophy in recurrent major depression. *Proceedings of the National Academy of Sciences of the United States of America, 93,* 3908–3913.

Singer, A., Wonnermann, M. & Müller, W. (1999). Hyperforin, a major antidepressant constituent of St John's wort, inhibits serotonin uptake by elevating free intracellular Na^+. *Journal of Pharmacology and Experimental Therapeutics, 290,* 1363–1368.

Smith, D., Dempster, C., Glanville, J., Freemantle, N. & Anderson, I. (2002). Efficacy and tolerability of venlafaxine compared with selective serotonin reuptake inhibitors and other antidepressants: A meta-analysis. *British Journal of Psychiatry, 180,* 396–404.

Stimpson, N., Agrawal, N. & Lewis, G. (2002). Randomised controlled trials investigating pharmacological and psychological interventions for treatment-refractory depression. Systematic review. *British Journal of Psychiatry, 181,* 284–294.

Stokes, P.E., Shamoian, C.A., Stoll, P.M. & Patton, M.J. (1971). Efficacy of lithium as acute treatment of manic-depressive illness. *Lancet, i,* 1319–1325.

Stuart, G.W. (1985). The Northwick Park ECT trial. *British Journal of Psychiatry, 147*, 727–729.

Swann, A.C., Bowden, C.L., Morris, J., Calabrese, J.R., Petty, F. & Small, J. (1997). Depression during mania: Treatment response to lithium or divalproex. *Archives of General Psychiatry, 32*, 1310–1318.

Tondo, L., Baldessarini, R.J. & Floris, G. (2001). Long-term clinical effectiveness of lithium maintenance treatment in types I and II bipolar disorders. *British Journal of Psychiatry, 41*, (Suppl.), S184–S190.

Tondo, L., Jamison, K.R. & Baldessarini, R.J. (1997). Effect of lithium maintenance on suicidal behaviour in major mood disorders. *Annals of the New York Academy of Sciences, 836*, 339–351.

Trollor, J.N. & Sachdev, P.S. (1999). Electroconvulsive treatment of neuroleptic malignant syndrome: A review and report of cases. *Australian and New Zealand Journal of Psychiatry, 33*, 650–659.

Vogel, G. (2000). New brain cells prompt new theories of depression. *Science, 290*, 258–259.

Weiner, R.D. (2000). Retrograde amnesia with electroconvulsive therapy—characteristics and implications. *Archives of General Psychiatry, 57*, 591–592.

Wheatley, D. (1997). LI 160, an extract of St. John's wort, versus amitriptyline in mildly to moderately depressed outpatients—a controlled 6-week clinical trial. *Pharmacopsychiatry, 30*, (Suppl 2), 77–80.

Woelk, H. (2000). Comparison of St John's wort and imipramine for treating depression: Randomised controlled trial. *British Medical Journal, 321*, 7260, 536–539.

Wolkowitz, O.M. & Reus, V.I. (1999). Treatment of depression with antiglucocorticoid drugs. *Psychosomatic Medicine, 61*, 698–711.

Yatham, L.N. (2002). The role of novel antipsychotics in bipolar disorders. *Journal of Clinical Psychiatry, 63* (Suppl. 3), 10–14.

Young, L.T., Joffe, R.T., Robb, J.C., MacQueen, G.M., Marriott, M. & Patelis-Siotis, I. (2000). Double-blind comparison of addition of a second mood stabilizer versus an antidepressant to an initial mood stabilizer for treatment of patients with bipolar depression. *American Journal of Psychiatry, 157*, 124–126.

Young, M.A., Meaden, P.M., Fogg, L.F., Cherin, E.A. & Eastman, C.I. (1997). Which environmental variables are related to the onset of seasonal affective disorder? *Journal of Abnormal Psychology, 106*, 554–562.

8

COGNITIVE BEHAVIOURAL THERAPY FOR DEPRESSION

Mick Power

INTRODUCTION

Depression has been known as a disorder for thousands of years. One of the most vivid descriptions is presented in the Bible when Job loses his possessions and his family, and laments:

> My days are past, my purposes are broken off, even the thoughts of my heart. They change the night into day: the light is short because of darkness. If I wait, the grave is mine house: I have made my bed in the darkness. I have said to corruption, Thou art my father: to the worm, Thou art my mother, and my sister. And where is now my hope?

Hippocrates in the fifth century BC coined the term "melancholia" (the Latinised form of the original Greek term) to cover this disorder, though he considered it to result from an excess of one of the four humours, black bile. The term "depression" (from the Latin "deprimere" meaning "to press down") was not introduced into English until the 17th century, though it was only in the late 19th century, and early 20th century, in the writings of Griesinger and Kraepelin, that the term began to replace "melancholia" as a diagnostic label (see Jackson, 1986, for a detailed history).

The term "depression" now refers to a wide range of disorders and a number of different classification systems. Nevertheless, the majority of these systems consider depression to be a combination of depressed mood and at least some of the following symptoms:

(1) loss of interest in normal activities (anhedonia)
(2) slowness in thinking and, in severe cases, slowness in movement (retardation)
(3) feelings of self-condemnation
(4) appetite disturbance
(5) excessive tiredness
(6) sleep disturbance
(7) loss of libido
(8) suicidal thoughts and attempts.

Mood Disorders: A Handbook of Science and Practice. Edited by M. Power.
© 2004 John Wiley & Sons, Ltd. ISBN 0-470-84390-X.

There have been various attempts at classification which have made distinctions such as *reactive-endogenous* and *neurotic-psychotic*. However, it has now been shown that the majority of depressions of all types are preceded by negative life events, so the attempt to distinguish reactive from non-reactive types has largely been abandoned (see Champion, 2000). One distinction that does appear to be useful, though, is that between unipolar and bipolar depression. Bipolar disorders typically show periods of mania or hypomania in addition to periods of severe depression; in contrast to unipolar depression, bipolar disorders have a high genetic loading; and the primary form of treatment is with lithium (Goodwin & Jamison, 1990). Nevertheless, there are interesting signs that even such an apparently biologically determined form of depression may also demonstrate considerable sensitivity to psychosocial factors, in relation both to first onset and to the course of the disorder, and that approaches such as cognitive behavioural therapy (CBT) and interpersonal psychotherapy (IPT) are useful adjunctive therapies (see Chapters 14 and 15).

COGNITIVE-BEHAVIOURAL MODELS

There are a number of theoretical and clinical models of depression in both the behavioural and the cognitive literatures. Early behavioural models (e.g., Lewinsohn, 1974) tended to focus on the symptoms of anhedonia (see above) with the general assumption that reduced rates of positive reinforcement, or lower rates of self-reinforcement that would follow from a withdrawal from everyday activities, would lead to a state of depression. Seligman's (1975) learned helplessness model initially argued that it was the lack of control over reinforcement that was more important than whether or not the patient received reinforcement. However, as we have pointed out elsewhere (Power & Wykes, 1996), the learned helplessness model would predict that people should become depressed if an anonymous well-wisher dropped £100 through their letter box every week, an idea that we definitely find counter-intuitive. Although it has become clear, as we will discuss in detail below, that the straightforward behavioural models are too simplistic in their accounts of depression, because they focus primarily on anhedonia, in the treatment of depression the early assessment and, if needed, intervention in activity levels has become a standard part of cognitive-behavioural approaches.

We will concentrate in this chapter on the main CBT approach to depression, that of Beck (1976). However, it should first be pointed out that Beck's theory was in fact presaged by the work of the ego analyst Bibring (1953), who revised Freud's original psychoanalytic formulation (presented in his classic work, *Mourning and Melancholia* [1917]). Bibring proposed that it was the failure of certain aspirations, such as to be loved or to be admired, that was the primary cause of depression in vulnerable individuals. Although it is unclear to what extent Beck was influenced by Bibring's work (Weishaar, 1993), this idea lies at the core of Beck's cognitive therapy.

The general cognitive therapy model of depression is outlined in Figure 8.1. The figure shows that dysfunctional schemas are typically formed in childhood as a consequence of socialisation processes developed in interaction with parents and other significant individuals within the child's social network. These early socialisation processes lead the child to believe that his or her worth is especially dependent on the views of others, or that self-worth can be achieved only through the successful pursuit of certain goals and through gaining the admiration of others. Beck (1983) characterised dependent individuals as "sociotropic", and achievement-oriented individuals who often avoid dependency on others as "autonomous".

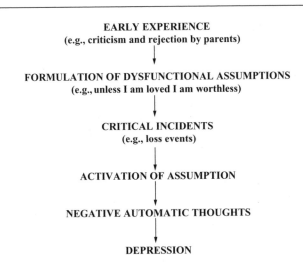

EARLY EXPERIENCE
(e.g., criticism and rejection by parents)

FORMULATION OF DYSFUNCTIONAL ASSUMPTIONS
(e.g., unless I am loved I am worthless)

CRITICAL INCIDENTS
(e.g., loss events)

ACTIVATION OF ASSUMPTION

NEGATIVE AUTOMATIC THOUGHTS

DEPRESSION

Figure 8.1   A summary of Beck's model of depression

Within the model, both types of individual are considered to have dysfunctional schemas which are normally latent, but which become activated when a negative event occurs that matches that particular schema. For example, the adolescent who has an excessive need to be loved by others may find that the first rejection in a love relationship leads to a state of depression in which the self is believed to be unlovable and worthless. Of course, not everyone who has the dysfunctional schemas need become depressed; the successful pursuit of a role or goal may prevent some individuals from becoming depressed despite their vulnerability. This model may also explain why some individuals might become depressed for the first time only later in life (e.g., Champion & Power, 1995).

Figure 8.1 also shows that activation of dysfunctional schemas leads to a range of cognitive phenomena that form the focus of the main part of therapy. One of the innovations of Beck's approach was the focus on so-called negative automatic thoughts (NATs), the experience of which typically leads the individual to believe that he or she is a failure. For example, a thought such as "I'm worthless" or "No one will ever love me" can lead to a sudden downturn in mood; one of the aims of therapy therefore is to help the individual identify what these NATs are and, subsequently, to learn how to challenge them rather than simply believe them to be absolute truths.

A second feature of cognitive processes that are consequent on the activation of the dysfunctional schemas is that they lead to so-called logical errors of thinking. These logical errors have been variously grouped into the following sorts of categories (Beck et al., 1979):

(1) All-or-nothing thinking: "If I can't do it perfectly, there's no point in doing it at all."
(2) Overgeneralisation: "I always get things wrong."
(3) Discounting the positive (selective abstraction): "I've finished my work today, but I should have done more."
(4) Jumping to conclusions (mind-reading): "Everyone is fed up with me because I'm depressed again."
(5) Catastrophising (magnification and minimisation): "It's all going to go wrong, and I can't change it."
(6) Emotional reasoning: "I feel bad therefore I must have done something wrong."

(7) Shoulds: "I should pull my socks up and get on with it."
(8) Personalisation: "It always rains when I arrange to go out."

In the early writings on cognitive therapy, these logical errors were presented in a way that implied that depressed individuals are irrational and illogical in their thinking, with the implication that normal individuals are rational and logical. However, more recent analyses have accepted the demonstrations from studies of reasoning in normal individuals that such individuals may also demonstrate characteristic biases (e.g., Garnham & Oakhill, 1996), and even that under certain conditions depressed individuals may be *more* accurate rather than less accurate than normal controls (e.g., Alloy & Abramson, 1979). Cognitive therapists now assume, therefore, that depression causes self-related information processing to be biased in a negative way (e.g., Haaga et al., 1991; Weishaar, 1993). A negative bias does not, however, invariably imply a distortion of information processing (see Power & Dalgleish, 1997). In fact, normal non-depressed individuals typically are mildly positively biased for self-related information processing and are also prone to the same types of logical errors as are depressed individuals, but in the opposite direction, as the following examples illustrate (Power & Wykes, 1996):

(1) All-or-nothing thinking: "This place would fall apart without me."
(2) Overgeneralisation: "You know I'm always right."
(3) Discounting the negative (selective abstraction): "I was just doing my duty and following orders."
(4) Jumping to conclusions (mind-reading): "I feel happy and everyone thinks I'm wonderful."
(5) Magnification and minimisation: "If I were running the country, I'd soon sort this mess out."
(6) Emotional reasoning: "I feel so good I know I'm going to win the National Lottery today."
(7) Shoulds: "Other people should pay me more respect and recognise my talents."
(8) Personalisation: "The sun always shines when I arrange to go out."

The moral of this story is that both normal and depressed individuals can be biased in how they process information, though the biases are typically positive for normal individuals and negative for depressed individuals. Therefore, the task of the therapist is made even more difficult than the original cognitive therapy approach implied, in that some of the depressed client's negative statements may be incisively accurate. The therapist should not be misled into thinking, however, that the accuracy of some negative statements means that all negative statements are true, for therein lies the therapist's skill in distinguishing one from the other (Power, 2002).

THE PRACTICE OF THERAPY

General comments

As in work with any client group, there are a number of issues that are common to work in therapy and a number of issues that are specific to the client group in particular. The most general issue for any therapy is, of course, the development of a collaborative therapeutic relationship; without such a relationship, effective therapeutic work is well-nigh impossible (e.g., Frank, 1982). In fact, the establishment of a good relationship is typically easier than with some other client groups, especially with those clients with strong dependency needs. As for the "autonomous" depressed individuals mentioned above, who normally aim to be self-sufficient, when they enter therapy, it is often because their attempts at self-sufficiency have broken down under the pressure of a significant life crisis. They may experience their need for help from the therapist as shameful or humiliating; nevertheless, one of the functions of depression may be to force individuals to question interpersonal and other goal-related issues which they have attempted to deny. It is more likely to be on recovery from depression that the autonomous individual becomes difficult to work with in therapy. Of course, the issue of the therapeutic relationship remains throughout therapy and is particularly relevant in short-term work for depression where termination issues are always just around the corner, a problem that we will return to later.

Assessment

The functions of the initial assessment sessions with any client are twofold, involving both the collection of basic information about the individual's background and history, and testing likely problems in the establishment of the collaborative therapeutic relationship (see Power, 2002). The cognitive model of depression (Beck et al., 1979) highlights issues about the individual's early background and relationships with significant others (see Figure 8.1); therefore, careful attention needs to be paid both to early losses that have been followed by experience of neglect (cf. Rutter, 1972), and to subtler issues about the acceptability of the individual or characteristics of the individual to those significant others. Of course, it is not uncommon for clients initially to report that they had happy childhoods with loving parents. However, as Bowlby (e.g., 1980) and a number of subsequent commentators have observed, clients may often report what they have been instructed to say by parents—"I'm doing this because I love you, dear". Thus, the client may have conflicting schematic models (Power & Dalgleish, 1997), and it may only be in the reporting of specific incidents from childhood that the nature of the different and inconsistent parental models comes to light.

Turning to more specific aspects of the assessment, it is necessary for the therapist to assess the severity and chronicity of depression. Severity is commonly measured with the Beck Depression Inventory (BDI) (Beck et al., 1961), though, as Kendall et al. (1987) noted, the BDI is not a diagnostic instrument, and it is only in conjunction with a clinical diagnosis of depression that the scale can be assumed to measure depression. In conjunction with assessment of the severity of depression, particular care needs to be taken with the assessment of suicide risk in depressed individuals; thus, an estimated 15% of depressed individuals succeed in killing themselves, and upwards of 40% of depressed clients may attempt suicide (e.g., Champion, 2000). It is incumbent on the therapist, therefore, to help a client feel safe about the discussion of current suicide ideation and any past attempts, in order both to gauge the severity of the attempts and to identify the high-risk situations in which such attempts are likely to occur in the future. Where such a risk is identified, clear action plans must be in place and agreed with the client and other key individuals, where appropriate.

Other features of depression that should be addressed during the assessment include the experience of recent negative life events, which are known to be significantly increased prior to the onset of depression (e.g., Brown & Harris, 1978). One of the risks of depression, however, is that not only may there have been an increase in so-called independent events prior to the episode of depression, but also, subsequent to the episode, there may have been an increase in the number of dependent events (that is, events dependent on the individual's own actions). These dependent events may be especially destructive of the person's relationships and career, but may be preventable with an appropriate intervention in therapy (Champion, 2000).

Information should also be collected about the individual's current sources of social support; in particular, whether or not the person is able to mobilise support during a crisis, or, indeed, whether, for example, the lack of support from the person's partner may be one of the reasons for the depressive episode.

In our own recent attempt to put the emotion back into cognition (Power & Dalgleish, 1997), an additional feature that we emphasised for assessment for therapy is people's beliefs about their own emotional states. In the case of depression, we have suggested that the maintenance of the depressed state may, in part, be due to the coupling of emotion states, especially sadness and shame (that is, self-disgust in our analysis). The experience of self-disgust may arise in a number of ways, not only in the ways emphasised traditionally in cognitive therapy; that is, because of a belief of being worthless, unlovable, or a failure. In addition, people may be depressed because they have, in their own view, allowed themselves to experience an unacceptable emotional state. For example, in many cultures, men are not supposed to experience or express sadness because it is a weak, effeminate emotion, and women are not supposed to express anger because it is not "ladylike" (Power, 1999). Although we know better, clients often enter therapy ashamed of the emotions that they are experiencing, perhaps because, for familial and societal reasons, they have been brought up to reject these emotions. The task of the therapist is to enable the person to accept the experience and expression of these rejected emotional states and to integrate the states into the normal experience of the self (cf. Greenberg et al., 1993).

The educational component

One of the strengths of the cognitive behavioural approach (e.g., Beck et al., 1979) is that the therapist presents the client with a rationale for therapy and also presents relevant educational information, or bibliotherapy, about the problems being experienced. The booklet, *Coping with Depression*, was designed by Beck and his colleagues to provide information to depressed clients about the experiences they may be having, in addition to introducing the main characteristics of the cognitive approach. The booklet is handed out during the first or second session to be read for homework. The client's response to the booklet has been shown to be a good predictor of whether or not the cognitive approach is likely to be effective with that particular client (Fennell & Teasdale, 1987), such that a client who clearly disagrees or does not relate to the description of the model in any way is unlikely to do well in cognitive therapy. In such a case, the therapist might be advised to discuss alternative forms of treatment with the client to see whether one of these might be more suitable.

One of the frequent experiences that therapists share is that clients may have little or no information about the problems that they are experiencing and, indeed, may even have mistaken beliefs. For example, the person may believe that he or she is the only person to have had this experience, that depression will never go away, or that depression is cured by pulling one's socks up. A crucial aspect of the early stages of cognitive therapy is therefore to explore the person's own model of depression and to provide facts and information with, when appropriate, additional reading material relevant to the person's problems. This additional information can range from specific handouts to workbooks such as that of Greenberger and Padesky (1995), which presents useful information and includes relevant exercises. A meta-analysis of the use of CBT bibliotherapy showed a clear benefit for this approach even in the absence of other intervention (Cuijpers, 1997).

Daily activities

In addition to handing out the *Coping with Depression* manual early in therapy, the therapist should also ask the client to complete an activities schedule for at least the first few weeks of therapy. A reduction in usual activities can be quickly identified from the completed schedule. Exploration should then be made of what normal activities have been dropped and why this has occurred. For example, some depressed people believe that they would be a burden on other people and that they would spoil other people's fun; others think that there is no point in trying because they would not enjoy any of their former activities. Using this information, the therapist can identify a range of graded tasks that starts with the easiest one that the person is both most likely to succeed at and perhaps even enjoy. In cases where the person has become extremely inactive, one of the early aims of therapy should be to help the individual increase his or her activity levels. In very extreme cases, the depressed individual may perceive almost any activity or even physical movement as "too much effort". In such cases, it may first be necessary to focus on beliefs about effort, while encouraging the individual to practise small tasks that no longer seem to be carried out under automatic control, but have to be consciously controlled throughout; this situation may parallel a similar problem that is experienced in chronic fatigue syndrome, in which everyday physical and mental activities are perceived to be excessively effortful and are therefore no longer carried out (Lawrie et al., 1997).

In the case of some depressed clients, it is not the reduction in activity that is the problem, but rather the excessive focus on one type of activity. The classic case is that of the workaholic whose waking hours are all spent in the pursuit of ambition and success, often of an unrealistic nature. In such cases, the activities schedule is full of so-called mastery items, but there is an absence of pleasurable activities. The focus on one dominant role or goal and the undervaluing of other roles and goals is, of course, a classic presentation in depression (e.g., Champion & Power, 1995), so the therapist may have to identify and explore long-held quasi-religious beliefs about the importance of such an approach. Indeed, the focus of therapy may become those schematic models that lead the person to exclude happiness or pleasure from day-to-day life.

Monitoring thoughts and feelings

After the client has been recording daily activities for a week or two, it is useful to introduce the idea of structured diaries (e.g., Greenberger & Padesky, 1995). The technique provides individuals with a new way of approaching and thinking about distressing situations because of the way that they are taught to structure their experiences. With the collection of a number of such situations, the therapist and client may become aware of certain themes emerging from the material. The first column typically asks for a brief description of the situation that led to the experience of distress. The second column asks the individual to list the emotion experienced in the situation; it can usefully include a percentage rating of the strength of the emotion so that the therapist can readily gauge exactly how distressing the situation was. The third column is designed for the recording of negative automatic thoughts (NATs) that occurred in the situation. The identification of NATs is straightforward for some people with depression (and other emotional disorders), and within a week or two such individuals readily make the distinction between feelings and automatic thoughts. However, some individuals need more practice before they can make the distinction, but it is important to continue the monitoring exercise until the distinction becomes clearer. Some individuals, even with practice, report that they have no thoughts to record and that the emotional reactions simply occur "out of the blue". We will return to this problem shortly.

Once clients have mastered the simpler three-column technique, the next step is to introduce a more complex monitoring form which expands the structured monitoring to five columns. The additional two columns require clients to find one or more alternative interpretations to the interpretation that is reflected in their automatic thoughts. Having found an alternative interpretation, the clients are then asked to rerate their degree of belief in the original interpretation.

The crucial part of the five-column technique obviously depends on clients' willingness to search for alternative interpretations of situations that they may have interpreted in a particular way for many years. It is well known from studies of reasoning that individuals (in whatever mood state) find it difficult to draw alternative conclusions when they have already reached a conclusion that is congenial with a current mental model; indeed, many biases reflect the early termination of a search for conclusions when such an interpretation has been found (e.g., Power & Wykes, 1996). For example, if someone's currently dominant schematic model represents the self as a failure, then the interpretation of a situation as another instance of failing is congenial with this model, and no alternatives will normally be sought. The converse occurs for someone whose dominant schematic model of the self is that of a success, when situations will be readily interpreted to reflect instances of further success, even though such interpretations may not necessarily be accurate. Depressed clients may need considerable encouragement to search for alternative explanations to their favoured conclusions in many situations. The therapist should carefully avoid being drawn to dispute and argue with these cherished interpretations, but, instead, as Padesky (1994) has cogently argued, should try to use the process of guided discovery, which enables clients themselves to identify alternatives, rather than having the alternatives thrust upon them.

One of the key problems that we noted above with the three- and the five-column techniques is that clients sometimes report that emotions "come out of the blue" without any prior automatic thoughts. The early cognitive therapy view of this problem was that it was merely a matter of time and of practice before such clients would be able to identify their NATs. Of course, such a strategy does run the risk that has sometimes been attributed to psychoanalytic therapies, namely, of bringing about the phenomenon rather than the phenomenon having genuine causal validity; that is, cognitive therapy clients might come to experience NATs, just as Freudian patients come to have Freudian dreams and Jungian patients come to have Jungian dreams. An alternative theory that we have spelled out in our SPAARS model is that some emotions really do come "out of the blue" (Power & Dalgleish, 1997; 1999). Although some emotional reactions follow the occurrence of

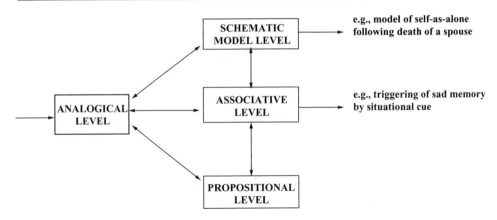

Figure 8.2   The SPAARS model of emotion, showing sadness-related outcomes

conscious appraisals, there appear to be a number of phenomena that do not require such conscious processes (see Figure 8.2). In addition, we propose that emotions can also result from automatic processes that occur outside awareness; these automatic processes may be the consequence of the frequent repetition of particular appraisal-emotion sequences, as in the child who is shouted at repeatedly coming to be afraid of anyone shouting, and this reaction continuing into adulthood as an automatic reaction. With such cases, the best way forward is to explore where the reactions have originated rather than insist that the NATs are there, while, nevertheless, continuing to encourage the client to record as much information as possible about these automatic responses.

Schematic models of self and others

One of the key aims of cognitive therapy is to explore the underlying assumptions that people have of themselves and of significant others in their lives. The continued monitoring of critical situations week to week in therapy will soon provide the therapist with clear indications of the themes underlying a particular client's difficulties, information that can be supplemented with assessments of attitudes by tools such as the Dysfunctional Attitudes Scale (Weissman & Beck, 1978) and the Schema Questionnaire (Young, 1999). Let us imagine that we have a client, part of whose formulation is that he has a fear of success in competitive situations because of other people's envy that would ensue from his winning. Exploration of the origins of this schematic model might indicate that the client's father behaved in a very overbearing manner whenever there was a competitive situation in which the client was involved. The client may also back down or appear to withdraw statements in therapy in order to avoid imagined conflict with the therapist. The therapist therefore accrues information from a variety of past and present situations, including the therapeutic relationship, which supports the existence of this key self-defeating schematic model. This model had a particular value in a previous significant relationship, but, unfortunately, has been generalised now to cover all relationships that are perceived to be competitive. Having reached such clarity, the therapist has a variety of options, all of which probably should be explored in parallel.

[handwritten note in top margin: "Must be to write with work therapist"]

First, there may be a number of experiments that can be set as homework in which the client puts to the test his belief that any competitive situation will lead to destructive attacks from other individuals; thus, there are many situations in which, in theory, there is no limit on the number of winners or losers because the outcome is primarily dependent on the individual's own performance (as in taking a driving test).

Second, the therapist may also explore the client's thoughts and feelings where schematic models become obvious in therapy—for example, in an apparent conflict over who is right in therapy. The therapist can also use these situations in therapy as indications of other past and present relationships and how significant others might react in relation to the client's actions; in addition, the client's perceptions of how the other person really feels about his winning can also be explored (cf. Safran & Segal, 1990).

Third, the therapist can help the client restrict the range of applicability of the self–other schematic model, or, alternatively, may help the client to develop a more sophisticated and appropriate mental model of why his father related to him in the way he did (cf. Padesky, 1994). In fact, his father reacted badly towards *anyone's* success, not just the client's; his father covered up his own feelings of being a failure by attacks on other people's success, not only his son's. Although the client had believed that he was the only one that his father had related to in this manner, he realised, when for the first time he began to talk to other relatives about his father's reactions, that they all shared his feelings, but were not prepared to fail in order to avoid his father's envy and destructive attacks.

This example illustrates that schematic models are complex, have their origins in the past, and typically relate self and one or more significant others in a rigid, repeating pattern. The themes involved in depression normally relate to issues of loss, failure, and shame. The self is viewed positively when an overinvested role or goal is being pursued successfully—for example, the perfect wife or mother, the high-flying student or executive who can deal with everything, or the would-be pop star who will finally get the recognition that she deserves. Unfortunately, the experience of events and difficulties that are a threat to such goals or roles leaves the person feeling worthless, unlovable, and shameful, because the self-concept is so bound up with them, and little or nothing else is seen to be of value.

Termination issues, including relapse prevention

Issues related to termination may be more critical for individuals suffering from depression than for most other disorders, because of the role that loss and abandonment plays in the onset of depression (Power, 2002). In addition, in short-term treatments such as CBT, the therapist may have had little or no opportunity to observe a client's reactions to natural breaks in therapy, such as those caused by holidays, which normally occur in longer-term treatments and provide invaluable clues about how the client deals with issues related to loss. In working with short-term therapies for depression, it is essential, therefore, that termination issues are considered early in therapy and that the therapist remains vigilant throughout. Of course, many short-term therapies have a pre-specified number of sessions, so that the client knows from the start the number of sessions involved. In other cases, however, the therapist may need to make some judgement about when the client is likely to be ready for the end of therapy. Such judgements must obviously take account of the client's own views, they may include some formal assessment of symptomatology and relevant cognitive variables, and they should also include a judgement of the extent to which the client has understood and been able to put into practice the CBT model. Casement's (1985) notion of the internalisation of a positive model of the therapist also seems like a useful proposal that can be applied to any form of therapy. For example, clues that the client has internalised a model of the therapist can be gleaned when the client reports something along the lines: "I was just about to jump over the till in the supermarket on Friday and escape in a panic, when I suddenly thought to myself, 'Oh, I wonder what my therapist would say to me now.' I then managed to calm down and continue with my shopping."

Of course, such statements are powerful indicators that the client has an internal model of both the therapist and the skills of therapy, in that the model is being applied in critical situations.

However, the real risk in short-term CBT for depression is that the therapy will merely have been palliative, and not have dealt with the high risk of relapse which runs at approximately 50% over 2 years after recovery from depression (e.g., Hammen, 1997). Therefore, one of the tasks towards the end of CBT is to develop potential relapse-prevention measures with clients, which include the identification of and working through potential high-risk situations (e.g., Segal et al., 2002). An additional focus of relapse prevention is the client's reactions to such situations. For example, if a client begins to feel miserable because of an upset at work, but then begins to worry that feeling moderately miserable means that serious long-term depression will inevitably follow, a vicious cycle downward will have begun that pulls the client further into depression (cf. Teasdale, 1988). The focus of relapse prevention should therefore be both on the likely events or situations that will lead to the client's feeling miserable, and on how the client reacts to such feelings when they occur (e.g., Segal et al., 2002). As we noted above, many individuals with emotional disorders have unrealistic beliefs about their emotional states, in that they often want to rid themselves of feelings of anxiety, depression, or sadness, and live a future filled only with the experience of happiness. Relapse prevention must therefore emphasise to clients that living happily ever after happens only in fairy tales, not in real life, and that our emotional reactions are as inherent and essential a part of us as the experience of physical pain.

Finally, on a more practical level, it is useful to include one or two "booster" sessions approximately 3–6 months after the end of therapy. These sessions allow a review of the successes and the problems that the client has faced since the end of therapy. They allow the therapist to assess how well the client has worked with the model without the support of therapy. Booster sessions also provide a tangible lifeline for the client at times when things feel difficult, and they may help the client to pull through without the need for additional professional intervention.

EVALUATION OF CBT FOR DEPRESSION

There have now been a number of meta-analytic reviews of the comparative effectiveness of CBT for depression that have clearly demonstrated its effectiveness (e.g., Dobson, 1989; Reinecke et al., 1998; Robinson et al., 1990). These studies show a reduction in symptom severity across treatment by about two-thirds in comparison to pre-treatment depression levels. The meta-analysis of Reinecke et al. (1998) is of interest in that they demonstrated the effectiveness of CBT for the treatment of adolescent depression with effect sizes compared to controls of 1.02 at immediate post-treatment, and continuing at 0.61 at short to medium length follow-up (see Chapter 5). Laidlaw (2001) (see Chapter 19) has summarised the work to date with CBT for depression in older adults, concluding that CBT is probably efficacious, but that more large-scale studies are needed. The American Psychological Association Task Force (see Crits-Cristoph, 1998, for a revised summary) concluded that both CBT and IPT are well-established treatments for adult depression.

However, the results from these studies have been overshadowed by the large-scale National Institute of Mental Health multisite study of CBT, IPT, imipramine, and placebo (Elkin et al., 1989). In this study, 250 patients with major depressive disorder were randomly assigned to one of four treatment types at one of three treatment centres. The immediate post-treatment results showed that, overall, there were no significant differences between any of the treatment types, the surprising comparison being that imipramine was no more effective than placebo. Only on a post hoc division of cases into moderate versus severe levels of depression did some effects emerge for the more severe group, with imipramine being clearly more effective than placebo, and there being some possible benefits for IPT in comparison to placebo. More recent analyses of follow-up over 18 months have again shown surprisingly few significant comparisons, though there was some evidence that CBT was slightly more effective than imipramine or placebo in relation to a range of measures of relapse, need for further treatment, and length of time symptom free (Shea et al., 1992). Perhaps one of the more interesting revelations from this large-scale study has been comment about *site* differences for the various therapies (e.g., Elkin, 1994); however, a more revealing analysis might be of *therapist* differences rather than leaving the differences attributed to sites, though, understandably, individual therapists may wish to avoid such direct scrutiny. Perhaps one of the most intriguing of the subsequent analyses of this large dataset has been the recent study by Ablon and Jones (2002). In their analyses of therapy process in transcripts of CBT and IPT sessions, they developed a rating system of the "ideal CBT prototype" and the "ideal IPT prototype". They found, however, that *both* CBT and IPT corresponded more closely to the CBT prototype rather than the IPT prototype. Moreover, the better the correspondence to the CBT prototype, the better the outcome for both types of therapy. Of course, this finding highlights many issues that have been long discussed about theory versus actual practice in therapy, with findings, such as those going back to Sloane et al. (1975), that expert therapists of different therapy types are more similar to each other than predicted when the content of their therapy sessions is analysed (see Holmes & Bateman, 2002, for a recent summary).

CONCLUSIONS

The evidence to date for the effectiveness of CBT shows that it is clearly an effective treatment for depression and that it may be particularly beneficial for the prevention of relapse, especially with training in relapse-prevention strategies. The approach is now well established and may be the treatment of choice for many groups. Notwithstanding these strengths, however, there are a number of aspects of both the theory and the practice of CBT that can still be improved. One important such area is that of the role of emotion in the therapy and the theoretical models of understanding cognition and emotion. Modern multilevel theories of emotion (e.g., Power & Dalgleish, 1997; Teasdale & Barnard, 1993) provide more sophisticated models on which to base CBT and, in the process, offer different implications for practice (e.g., Power & Dalgleish, 1999). In addition, there is the continuing accumulation of evidence that good therapists of all persuasions may be more similar in their practice than bad therapists who simply follow textbook accounts of therapy. Future large-scale studies, such as those funded in the USA by NIMH, will provide unique opportunities to disentangle mechanisms of change common across therapies; these analyses will take us to the next level of evidence and beyond the mere percentage game that the current level of evidence provides.

REFERENCES

Ablon, J.S. & Jones, E.E. (2002). Validity of controlled clinical trials of psychotherapy: Findings from the NIMH Treatment of Depression Collaborative Research Program. *American Journal of Psychiatry, 159*, 775–783.

Alloy, L.B. & Abramson, L.Y. (1979). Judgment of contingency in depressed and nondepressed students: Sadder but wiser? *Journal of Experimental Psychology: General, 108*, 441–485.

Beck, A.T. (1976). *Cognitive Therapy and the Emotional Disorders*. New York: Meridian.

Beck, A.T. (1983). Cognitive therapy of depression: New perspectives. In P.J. Clayton & J.E. Barrett (Eds), *Treatment of Depression: Old Controversies and New Approaches* (pp. 265–290). New York: Raven Press.

Beck, A.T., Rush, A.J., Shaw, B.F. & Emery, G. (1979). *Cognitive Therapy of Depression: A Treatment Manual*. New York: Guilford.

Beck, A.T., Ward, C.H., Mendelsohn, M., Mock, J. & Erbaugh, J. (1961). An inventory for measuring depression. *Archives of General Psychiatry, 4*, 561–571.

Bibring, E. (1953). The mechanism of depression. In P. Greenacre (Ed.), *Affective Disorders* (pp. 14–47). New York: International Universities Press.

Bowlby, J. (1980). *Attachment and Loss*. Vol. III. *Loss: Sadness and Depression*. Harmondsworth: Penguin.

Brown, G.W. & Harris, T.O. (1978). *Social Origins of Depression: A Study of Psychiatric Disorder in Women*. London: Tavistock.

Casement, P. (1985). *On Learning from the Patient*. London: Tavistock.

Champion, L.A. (2000). Depression. In L.A. Champion & M.J. Power (Eds), *Adult Psychological Problems: An Introduction* (2nd edn) (pp. 29–53). Hove: Psychology Press.

Champion, L.A. & Power, M.J. (1995). Social and cognitive approaches to depression: Towards a new synthesis. *British Journal of Clinical Psychology, 34*, 485–503.

Crits-Cristoph, P. (1998). Training in empirically validated treatments: The Division 12 APA Task Force recommendations. In K.S. Dobson & K.D. Craig (Eds), *Empirically Supported Therapies: Best Practice in Professional Psychology* (pp. 5–14). Thousand Oaks, CA: Sage.

Cuijpers, P. (1997). Bibliotherapy in unipolar depression: A meta-analysis. *Journal of Behavior Therapy and Experimental Psychiatry, 28*, 139–147.

Dobson, K. (1989). A meta-analysis of the efficacy of cognitive therapy for depression. *Journal of Consulting and Clinical Psychology, 57*, 414–419.

Elkin, I. (1994). The NIMH Treatment of Depression Collaborative Research Program: Where we began and where we are now. In A.E. Bergin & S.L. Garfield (Eds), *Handbook of Psychotherapy and Behavior Change* (4th edn) (pp. 114–139), New York: Wiley.

Elkin, I., Shea, T., Watkins, J.T., et al. (1989). National Institute of Mental Health Treatment of Depression Collaborative Research Program. *Archives of General Psychiatry, 46*, 971–982.

Fennell, M.J.V. & Teasdale, J.D. (1987). Cognitive therapy for depression: Individual differences and the process of change. *Cognitive Therapy and Research, 11*, 253–272.

Frank, J.D. (1982). Therapeutic components shared by all psychotherapies. In J.H. Harvey & M.M. Parks (Eds), *Psychotherapy Research and Behavior Change* (pp. 9–37). Washington, DC: American Psychological Association.

Freud, S. (1917/1984). *Mourning and Melancholia*. Pelican Freud Library, Vol. 11. Harmondsworth: Penguin.

Garnham, A. & Oakhill, J. (1996). *Thinking and Reasoning*. Oxford: Blackwell.

Goodwin, F.K. & Jamison, K.R. (1990). *Manic Depressive Illness*. Oxford: Oxford University Press.

Greenberg, L.S., Rice, L.N. & Elliott, R. (1993). *Facilitating Emotional Change: The Moment by Moment Process*. New York: Guilford.

Greenberger, D. & Padesky, C. (1995). *Mind Over Mood: A Cognitive Therapy Treatment Manual for Clients*. New York: Guilford.

Haaga, D.A.F., Dyck, M.J. & Ernst, D. (1991). Empirical status of cognitive therapy of depression. *Psychological Bulletin, 110*, 215–236.

Hammen, C. (1997). *Depression*. Hove: Psychology Press.

Holmes, J. & Bateman, A. (2002). *Integration in Psychotherapy: Models and Methods*. Oxford: Oxford University Press.

Jackson, S.W. (1986). *Melancholia and Depression: From Hippocratic Times to Modern Times*. New Haven, CT: Yale University Press.

Kendall, P.C., Hollon, S.D., Beck, A.T., Hammen, C.L. & Ingram, R.E. (1987). Issues and recommendations regarding use of the Beck Depression Inventory. *Cognitive Therapy and Research, 11*, 289–300.

Laidlaw, K. (2001). An empirical review of cognitive therapy for late life depression: Does research evidence suggest adaptations are necessary for cognitive therapy with older adults? *Clinical Psychology and Psychotherapy, 8*, 1–14.

Lawrie, S.M., MacHale, S.M., Power, M.J. & Goodwin, G.M. (1997). Is the chronic fatigue syndrome best understood as a primary disturbance of the sense of effort? *Psychological Medicine, 27*, 995–999.

Lewinsohn, P. (1974). A behavioural approach to depression. In R. Friedman & M. Katz (Eds), *The Psychology of Depression: Contemporary Theory and Research* (pp. 157–185). New York: Winston-Wiley.

Padesky, C.A. (1994). Schema changes processes in cognitive therapy. *Clinical Psychology and Psychotherapy, 1*, 267–278.

Power, M.J. (1999). Sadness. In T. Dalgleish, & M.J. Power (Eds), *Handbook of Cognition and Emotion* (pp. 497–519). Chichester: Wiley.

Power, M.J. (2002). Integrative therapy from a cognitive-behavioural perspective. In J. Holmes & A. Bateman (Eds), *Integration in Psychotherapy: Models and Methods* (pp. 27–47). Oxford: Oxford University Press.

Power, M.J. & Dalgleish, T. (1997). *Cognition and Emotion: From Order to Disorder*. Hove: Psychology Press.

Power, M.J. & Dalgleish, T. (1999). Two routes to emotion: Some implications of multi-level theories of emotion for therapeutic practice. *Behavioural and Cognitive Psychotherapy, 27*, 129–141.

Power, M.J. & Wykes, T. (1996). The mental health of mental models and the mental models of mental health. In J. Oakhill & A. Garnham (Eds), *Mental Models in Cognitive Science: Essays in Honour of Phil Johnson-Laird* (pp. 197–222). Hove: Psychology Press.

Reinecke, M.A., Ryan, N.E. & DuBois, D.L. (1998). Cognitive-behavioral therapy of depression and depressive symptoms during adolescence: A review and meta-analysis. *Journal of the American Academy of Child and Adolescent Psychiatry, 37*, 26–34.

Robinson, L.A., Berman, J.S. & Neimeyer, R.A. (1990). Psychotherapy for the treatment of depression: A comprehensive review of controlled outcome research. *Psychological Bulletin, 108*, 30–49.

Rutter, M. (1972). *Maternal Deprivation Reassessed*. Harmondsworth: Penguin.

Safran, J.D. & Segal, Z.V. (1990). *Interpersonal Process in Cognitive Therapy*. New York: Basic Books.

Segal, Z.V., Williams, J.M.G. & Teasdale, J.D. (2002). Mindfulness-Based Cognitive Therapy for Depression. New York: Guilford.

Seligman, M.E.P. (1975). *Helplessness: On Depression, Development and Death*. San Francisco, CA: Freeman.

Shea, T.M., Elkin, I., Imber, S.D., et al. (1992). Course of depressive symptoms over follow-up: Findings from the National Institute of Mental Health Treatment of Depression Collaborative Research Program. *Archives of General Psychiatry, 49*, 782–787.

Sloane, R.B., Staples, F.R., Cristol, A.H., Yorkston, N.J. & Whipple, K. (1975). *Psychotherapy Versus Behavior Therapy*. Cambridge, MA: Harvard University Press.

Teasdale, J.D. (1988). Cognitive vulnerability to persistent depression. *Cognition and Emotion, 2,* 247–274.

Teasdale, J. & Barnard, P. (1993). *Affect, Cognition and Change.* Hove: Erlbaum.

Weishaar, M. (1993). *Aaron T. Beck.* London: Sage.

Weissman, A.N. & Beck, A.T. (1978). Development and validation of the Dysfunctional Attitude Scale: A preliminary investigation. Paper presented at the meeting of the American Educational Research Association, Toronto.

Young, J.E. (1999). *Cognitive Therapy for Personality Disorders: A Schema-Focussed Approach* (3rd edn). Sarasota, FL: Professional Resource Press.

9

INTERPERSONAL PSYCHOTHERAPY OF DEPRESSION*

John C. Markowitz

Interpersonal psychotherapy (IPT) is a time-limited, diagnosis-targeted, empirically tested treatment. Relative to most psychotherapies, it has been carefully studied and relatively little practiced: until recently, most of its practitioners were researchers. Yet, the success of IPT in the treatment of outpatients with major depression has led to its testing for an expanded range of diagnostic indications, and to its increasing clinical dissemination.

In our era, the empirical grounding of treatments and economic pressures on treatment have both gained increasing importance, according greater stature to treatments such as IPT. This has been reflected not only in a growing interest in clinical training in IPT, but in treatment guidelines from several countries and professional organizations. A local example is *What Works for Whom?*, based on a report commissioned for the National Health Service of the UK Department of Health (Roth & Fonagy, 1996). This chapter is intended for clinicians in the UK who are interested in exploring IPT as one of the available interventions for mood and other disorders. Readers should also know that there is a British Interpersonal Psychotherapy Society as well as an international one (www.interpersonalpsychotherapy.org/). A recent meeting of the latter group indicated that IPT training for clinicians has advanced farther in the UK than elsewhere in the world.

This chapter provides a brief overview of IPT for clinicians. For greater depth of discussion, the reader is referred to the IPT manual (Weissman et al., 2000).

BACKGROUND

Klerman, Weissman, and colleagues developed IPT as a treatment arm for a pharmacotherapy study of depression. They recognized that many outpatients in clinical practice received talking therapy as well as medication, and felt that their study would gain face validity by

* This chapter is based in part on a chapter previously published as Markowitz, J.C. (2003). Interpersonal Psychotherapy. In R.E. Hales and S.C. Yudofsky (Eds) *The American Psychiatric Publishing Textbook of Clinical Psychiatry* (4th edn) (pp. 1207–1223). Washington, DC: American Psychiatric Publishing. www.appi.org. Reproduced with permission.

Mood Disorders: A Handbook of Science and Practice. Edited by M. Power.
© 2004 John Wiley & Sons, Ltd. ISBN 0-470-84390-X.

including both modalities. Yet, they had no idea what was actually practiced in the surround-ing offices in New England—as, indeed, we have little grasp of what is presumably eclectic community practice today. Being researchers, they developed a psychotherapy based on research data, as well as to some degree on existing interpersonal theory.

IPT is based on principles derived from psychosocial and life events research on de-pression, which has demonstrated relationships between depression and complicated be-reavement, role disputes (as in bad marriages), role transitions (and meaningful life changes), and interpersonal deficits. Life stressors can trigger depressive episodes in vulnerable indi-viduals, and, conversely, depressive episodes compromise psychosocial functioning, lead-ing to further negative life events. In contrast, social supports protect against depression. IPT theory borrows from the post-World War II work of Adolph Meyer and Harry Stack Sullivan (1953), as well as the attachment theory of John Bowlby and others. Sullivan, who popularized the term "interpersonal", emphasized that life events occurring after the early childhood years influence psychopathology. This idea, which seems commonplace enough today, was radical in an era dominated by psychoanalysis, when the focus was almost exclu-sively on early childhood experiences. IPT uses this principle for practical, not etiological purposes. Without presuming to know the *cause* of a depressive episode, whose etiology is presumably multifactorial, IPT therapists pragmatically use the connection between current life events and onset of depressive symptoms to help patients understand and combat their episode of illness.

TREATMENT WITH IPT

IPT therapists use a few simple principles to explain the patient's situation and illness. These are simple enough that dysphoric patients with poor concentration can grasp them. First, they define depression as a *medical illness*, a treatable condition that is not the patient's fault. This definition displaces the burdensome guilt from the depressed patients to their illness, making the symptoms ego-dystonic and discrete. It also provides hope for a response to treatment. The therapist uses ICD-10 or DSM-IV (American Psychiatric Association, 1994) criteria to make the mood diagnosis, and rating scales, such as the Hamilton Depression Rating Scale (HDRS) (Hamilton, 1960) or Beck Depression Inventory (BDI) (Beck, 1978), to assess symptoms.

Indeed, the therapist temporarily gives the patient the "sick role" (Parsons, 1951), which helps patients to recognize that they suffer from a common mood disorder with a predictable set of symptoms—not the personal failure, weakness, or character flaw that depressed pa-tients often believe is the problem. The sick role excuses patients from what the illness prevents them from doing, but also obliges patients to work *as* patients in order ultimately to recover the lost healthy role. I am told that in the UK (unlike the USA), clinicians hear the term "sick role" as a tainted term associated with long-term psychiatric disability. This is not at all its IPT connotation. On the contrary, the sick role is intended as a temporary role, coincident with the term of a time-limited treatment, to relieve self-blame while fo-cusing the patient on a medical diagnosis. The time limit and brief duration of IPT, and the IPT therapist's frequent encouragement of patients to take social risks and improve their situation, guard against regression and passivity.

A second principle of IPT is to focus the treatment on an interpersonal crisis in the patient's life, a problem area connected to the patient's episode of illness. By solving an interpersonal problem—complicated bereavement, or a role dispute or transition—IPT patients can both improve their life situation and simultaneously relieve the symptoms of the depressive episode. Since randomized, controlled outcome studies have repeatedly validated this coupled formula, IPT can be offered with confidence and optimism similar to that accompanying an antidepressant prescription. This therapeutic optimism, while hardly specific to IPT, very likely provides part of its power in remoralizing the patient.

IPT is an eclectic therapy, using techniques seen in other treatment approaches. It makes use of the so-called common factors of psychotherapy (Frank, 1971). These include building a therapeutic alliance, helping the patient feel understood (through use of a medical disease model and relating mood to event), facilitation of affect, a rationale for improvement (if you fix your situation, your mood should improve), support and encouragement, a treatment ritual, and success experiences (that is, actual life changes). Beyond this, its medical model of depressive illness is consistent with pharmacotherapy (and makes IPT highly compatible with medication in combination treatment). IPT shares role-playing and a "here and now" focus with cognitive behavior therapy (CBT), and addresses interpersonal issues in a manner marital therapists would find familiar. It is not its particular techniques but its overall strategies that make IPT a unique and coherent approach. Although IPT overlaps to some degree with psychodynamic psychotherapies, and many of its early research therapists came from psychodynamic backgrounds, IPT meaningfully differs from them. It focuses on the present, not the past; it focuses on real life change rather than self-understanding; it employs a medical model; and it avoids exploration of the transference and genetic and dream interpretations (Markowitz et al., 1998). Like CBT, IPT is a time-limited treatment targeting a syndromal constellation (such as major depression); however, it is much less structured, assigns no explicit homework, and focuses on affect and interpersonal problem areas rather than automatic thoughts. Each of the four IPT interpersonal problem areas has discrete, if somewhat overlapping, goals for therapist and patient to pursue.

IPT techniques help the patient to pursue these interpersonal goals. The therapist repeatedly helps the patient relate life events to mood and other symptoms. These techniques include an *opening question,* which elicits an interval history of mood and events; *communication analysis,* the reconstruction and evaluation of recent, affectively charged life circumstances; *exploration of patient wishes and options,* in order to pursue these goals in particular interpersonal situations; *decision analysis,* to help the patient choose which options to employ; and *role-playing,* to help patients prepare interpersonal tactics for real life. The reformulation of cases using an IPT focal problem area often makes difficult cases more manageable both for patient and clinician.

IPT deals with current interpersonal relationships, focusing on the patient's immediate social context rather than on the past. The IPT therapist attempts to intervene in depressive symptom formation and social dysfunction rather than enduring aspects of personality. In any case, it is difficult to assess accurately personality traits when confounded by the state changes of an Axis I disorder such as a depressive episode (Hirschfeld et al., 1983). IPT builds new social skills (Weissman et al., 1981), which may be as valuable as changing personality traits.

Phases of treatment

Acute IPT treatment has three phases. The *first phase,* usually 1–3 sessions, involves diagnostic evaluation, psychiatric anamnesis, and setting the treatment framework. The therapist reviews symptoms, gives the patient a diagnosis as depressed by standard criteria (such as ICD-10), and gives the patient the sick role. The psychiatric history includes the *interpersonal inventory*, which is not a structured instrument but a careful review of the patient's past and current social functioning and close relationships, and their patterns and mutual expectations. The therapist should gain a sense of who the patient is with other people, how he or she interacts with them, and how relationships may have contributed to or have been altered by the depressive episode. Depressed patients frequently have difficulty in asserting their needs, confronting others or getting angry effectively, and taking social risks. Changes in relationships proximal to the onset of symptoms are elucidated: for example, the death of a loved one (potential complicated bereavement), children leaving home (a role transition), or worsening marital strife (a role dispute). The interpersonal inventory supplies a framework for understanding the social and interpersonal context in which the depressive symptoms occur and should lead to a treatment focus.

The therapist assesses the need for medication, based on symptom severity, past illness history, treatment response, and patient preference, and then provides psychoeducation by discussing the constellation of symptoms that define major depression, their psychosocial concomitants, and what the patient may expect from treatment. The therapist next links the depressive syndrome to the patient's interpersonal situation in a formulation (Markowitz & Swartz, 1997) centered on one of four interpersonal problem areas: (1) *grief*; (2) interpersonal *role disputes*; (3) *role transitions*; or (4) *interpersonal deficits*. With the patient's explicit acceptance of this formulation as a focus for further treatment, therapy enters the middle phase.

Any formulation necessarily simplifies a patient's complex situation. It is important, however, to keep antidepressant treatment focused on a simple theme that even a highly distractible depressed patient can grasp. When patients present with multiple interpersonal problems, the goal of formulation is to isolate one or at most two salient problems that are related (either as precipitant or consequence) to the patient's depressive episode. Having more than two foci means an unfocused treatment. Choosing the focal problem area requires clinical acumen, although research has shown that IPT therapists agree in choosing such areas (Markowitz et al., 2000), and patients seem to find the foci credible.

In the *middle phase*, the IPT therapist follows strategies specific to the chosen interpersonal problem area. For grief—complicated bereavement following the death of a loved one—the therapist encourages the catharsis of mourning and, as that affect is released, helps the patient find new activities and relationships to compensate for the loss. For role disputes, which are overt or covert conflicts with a spouse, other family member, coworker, or close friend, the therapist helps the patient explore the relationship, the nature of the dispute, whether it has reached an impasse, and available options to resolve it. Should these options fail, therapist and patient may conclude that the relationship has reached an impasse and consider ways to change or live with the impasse, or to end the relationship.

A role transition is a change in life status defined by a life event: beginning or ending a relationship or career, a geographic move, job promotion or demotion, retirement, graduation, or diagnosis of a medical illness. The patient learns to manage the change by mourning the loss of the old role while recognizing the positive and negative aspects of the new role he or she is assuming, and taking steps to gain mastery over the new role. Frequently, the new role, while undesired, is discovered to have previously unseen benefits. Interpersonal deficits, the residual fourth IPT problem area, is reserved for patients who lack one of the first three problem areas: that is, patient who report no recent life events. The category is poorly named, and really means that the patient is presenting without the kind of defining recent life event on which IPT usually focuses. Interpersonal deficits recognizes that the patient is usually quite socially isolated, and defines the patient as lacking social skills, including having problems in initiating or sustaining relationships, and helps the patient to develop new relationships and skills. Some, or indeed most, patients who might fall into this category in fact suffer from dysthymic disorder, for which separate strategies have been developed (Markowitz, 1998).

IPT sessions address current, "here and now" problems rather than childhood or developmental issues. Each session after the first begins with the question, "How have things been since we last met?" This focuses the patient on recent mood and events, which the therapist helps the patient to connect. The therapist provides empathic support for the patient's suffering, but takes an active, nonneutral, supportive, and hopeful stance to counter depressive pessimism. The therapist elicits the options that the patient has to make positive changes in his or her life in order to resolve the focal interpersonal problem, options that the depressive episode may have kept the patient from seeing or exploring fully. Simply understanding the situation is insufficient: therapists stress the need for patients to test these options in order to improve their lives and simultaneously treat their depressive episodes. It can be seen why this focus on interpersonal functioning might build social skills and lead the patient to make meaningful life changes in a relatively brief treatment interval.

The *final phase* of IPT occupies the last few sessions of acute treatment (or the last months of a maintenance phase). Here the therapist's goal is to build the patient's newly regained sense of independence and competence by having him or her recognize and consolidate therapeutic gains. The therapist anchors self-esteem by elucidating how the patient's depressive episode has improved because of the changes the patient has made in his or her life situation and in resolving the interpersonal problem area ("Why do you think you're feeling so much better? It's impressive what you've accomplished!")—at a time when the patient had felt weak and impotent. The therapist also helps the patient to anticipate depressive symptoms that might arise in the future, and their potential triggers and remedies. Compared to psychodynamic psychotherapy, IPT de-emphasizes termination, which is simply a graduation from successful treatment. The therapist helps the patient see the sadness of parting as a normal interpersonal response to separation, distinct from depressive feelings. If the patient has not improved, the therapist emphasizes that it is the treatment that has failed, not the patient, and that alternative effective treatment options exist. This is analogous to a failed pharmacotherapy trial; if one treatment fails, it is the illness rather than the patient who is resistant, and, thankfully, other treatment options remain. Patients who have a successful acute response, but whose multiple prior depressive episodes leave them at high risk of recurrence, may contract for maintenance therapy as acute treatment draws to a close. Another strength of IPT is that its maintenance form, like its acute format, has also demonstrated efficacy in rigorous trials.

IPT FOR UNIPOLAR MOOD DISORDERS: EFFICACY AND ADAPTATIONS

The history of IPT has been a sequence of manual-based clinical trials, often adapting IPT to the particular psychosocial problems and needs of the target treatment population.

Acute treatment of major depression

The first acute study of IPT was a four-cell, 16-week randomized trial comparing IPT, amitriptyline (AMI), combined IPT and AMI, and a nonscheduled control treatment for 81 outpatients with major depression (DiMascio et al., 1979; Weissman et al., 1979). Amitriptyline more rapidly alleviated symptoms, but, at treatment completion, there was no significant difference between IPT and AMI in symptom reduction. Each reduced symptoms more efficaciously than the control condition, and combined AMI-IPT was more efficacious than either active monotherapy. Patients with psychotic depression did poorly on IPT alone. One-year follow-up found that many patients remained improved after the brief IPT intervention. Moreover, IPT patients had developed significantly better psychosocial functioning at 1 year, whether or not they received medication. This effect on social function was not found for AMI alone, nor was it evident for IPT immediately after the 16-week trial (Weissman et al., 1981).

The ambitious, multisite National Institute of Mental Health Treatment of Depression Collaborative Research Program (NIMH TDCRP) (Elkin et al., 1989), randomly assigned 250 outpatients with major depression to 16 weeks of IPT, CBT, or either imipramine (IMI) or placebo plus clinical management. Most subjects completed at least 15 weeks or 12 sessions. Mildly depressed patients (17-item HDRS score of <20) showed equal improvement in all treatments. For more severely depressed patients (HDRS of ≥20), IMI worked fastest and most consistently outperformed placebo. IPT fared comparably to IMI on several outcome measures, including HDRS, and was superior to placebo for more severely depressed patients. The great surprise of this study was that CBT was not superior to placebo (albeit not significantly worse than IPT or IMI) among more depressed patients. Reanalyzing the NIMH TDCRP data by the Johnson-Neyman technique, Klein and Ross (1993) found "medication superior to psychotherapy, [and] the psychotherapies somewhat superior to placebo . . . particularly among the symptomatic and impaired patients" (Klein & Ross, 1993, p. 241), and "CBT relatively inferior to IPT for patients with BDI scores greater than approximately 30, generally considered the boundary between moderate and severe depression" (p. 247).

Shea et al. (1992) conducted an 18-month, naturalistic, follow-up study of TDCRP subjects and found no significant differences in recovery among remitters (who had responded with minimal or no symptoms by the end of treatment, sustained during follow-up) across the four treatments. Twenty-six percent of IPT, 30% of CBT, 19% of imipramine, and 20% of placebo subjects who had acutely remitted remained in remission 18 months later. Among acute remitters, relapse over the year and a half was 33% for IPT, 36% for CBT, 50% for imipramine (medication having been stopped at 16 weeks), and 33% for placebo. The authors concluded that 16 weeks of specific treatments was insufficient to achieve full and lasting recovery for many patients.

An IPT research group in the Hague has completed a study of IPT versus nefazodone, alone and in combination, for acute treatment of major depression (Blom et al., 1996; Blom, personal communication, 2003).

Maintenance treatment

IPT was first developed and tested in an 8-month, six-cell study (Klerman et al., 1974; Paykel et al., 1975). In today's parlance, this study would be considered a "continuation" treatment, as the concept of maintenance antidepressant treatment has lengthened. One hundred and fifty acutely depressed women outpatients who responded (with at least 50% symptom reduction as rated by a clinical interviewer) to 4–6 weeks of AMI were randomly assigned to receive 8 months of weekly IPT alone, AMI alone, placebo alone, combined IPT-AMI, IPT-placebo, or no pill. Randomization to IPT or a low-contact psychotherapy condition at entry into the continuation phase, followed by randomization to medication, placebo, or no pill at the end of the second month of continuation. Maintenance pharmacotherapy prevented relapse and symptom exacerbation, whereas IPT improved social functioning (Weissman et al., 1974). The effects of IPT on social functioning were not apparent for 6–8 months, and combined psychotherapy-pharmacotherapy had the best outcome.

Two studies in Pittsburgh, Pennsylvania, have assessed longer antidepressant maintenance trials of IPT. Frank et al. (1990, 1991; Frank 1991a), studied 128 outpatients with multiply, rapidly recurrent depression. Patients, who had had, on average, seven episodes of major depression, were initially treated with combined high-dose imipramine (>200 mg/day) and weekly IPT. Responders remained on high-dosage medication while IPT was tapered to a monthly frequency during a 4-month continuation phase. Patients remaining remitted were then randomly assigned to 3 years of one of the following:

(1) ongoing high-dose imipramine plus clinical management
(2) high-dose imipramine plus monthly IPT
(3) monthly IPT alone
(4) monthly IPT plus placebo
(5) placebo plus clinical management.

High-dose imipramine, with or without maintenance IPT, was the most efficacious treatment, protecting more than 80% of patients over 3 years. In contrast, most patients on placebo relapsed within the first few months. Once-monthly IPT, while less efficacious than medication, was statistically and clinically superior to placebo in this high-risk patient population. Reynolds and colleagues (1999) essentially replicated these maintenance findings in a study of geriatric patients with major depression that compared IPT and nortriptyline. It is notable that both of these studies used unusually high doses (that is, maintenance of acute levels, rather than a dosage taper) of antidepressant medications, while employing the lowest ever (albeit only ever) monthly maintenance dosage of a psychotherapy.

The modal depressed patient is a woman of childbearing age, but many depressed pregnant or nursing women prefer to avoid pharmacotherapy. Frank and colleagues' finding of an 82-week survival time without recurrence with monthly maintenance IPT alone would suffice to protect many women with recurrent depression through pregnancy and nursing without medication. Further research is needed to determine the relative efficacy of IPT to newer medications, such as selective serotonin reuptake inhibitors, as well as the efficacy of more-frequent-than-monthly doses of maintenance IPT. A study underway in Pittsburgh compares differing doses of maintenance IPT for depressed patients.

Geriatric depressed patients

IPT was initially used as an addition to a pharmacotherapy trial of geriatric patients with major depression to enhance compliance and to provide some treatment for the placebo control group (Rothblum et al., 1982; Sholomskas et al., 1983). Investigators noted that grief and role transition specific to life changes were the prime interpersonal treatment foci. These researchers suggested modifying IPT to include more flexible duration of sessions, more use of practical advice and support (for example, arranging transportation, calling physicians), and the recognition that major role changes (for example, divorce at age 75) may be impractical and detrimental. The 6-week trial compared standard IPT to nortriptyline in 30 geriatric, depressed patients. The results showed some advantages for IPT, largely due to higher attrition from side effects in the medication group (Sloane et al., 1985).

Reynolds et al. (1999) conducted a 3-year maintenance study for geriatric patients with recurrent depression in Pittsburgh, using IPT and nortriptyline in a design similar to the Frank et al. (1990) study. The IPT manual was modified to allow greater flexibility in session length under the assumption that some elderly patients might not tolerate 50-minute sessions. The authors found that older patients needed to address early life relationships in psychotherapy in addition to the usual "here and now" IPT focus. The study treated 187 patients, 60 years or older, with recurrent major depression, using a combination of IPT and nortriptyline. The 107 who acutely remitted and then achieved recovery after continuation therapy were randomly assigned to one of four 3-year maintenance conditions:

(1) medication clinic with nortriptyline alone, with steady-state nortriptyline plasma levels maintained in a therapeutic window of 80–120 ng/ml
(2) medication clinic with placebo
(3) monthly maintenance IPT with placebo
(4) monthly IPT (IPT-M) plus nortriptyline.

Recurrence rates were 20% for combined treatment, 43% for nortriptyline alone, 64% for IPT with placebo, and 90% for placebo alone. Each monotherapy was statistically superior to placebo, whereas combined therapy was superior to IPT alone and had a trend for superiority over medication alone. Patients 70 years or older were more likely to have a depressive recurrence and to do so more quickly than patients in their sixties. This study corroborated the maintenance results of Frank and colleagues, except that in this geriatric trial combined treatment had advantages over pharmacotherapy alone as well as psychotherapy alone.

It is easy to misinterpret the comparison of high-dose tricyclic antidepressants to low-dose IPT-M in both these studies. First, it should be noted that no patients in this study received only medication or IPT: even patients in the "medication-only" maintenance phase had received a longer course of acute and continuation IPT than most patients ever get. Second, had the tricyclics been lowered comparably to the reduced psychotherapy dosage, as had been the case in earlier antidepressant medication maintenance trials, recurrence in the medication groups might well have been greater. Meanwhile, there were no precedents for dosing maintenance psychotherapy, for which the choice of a monthly interval for IPT-M was reasonable, and indeed somewhat clinically beneficial. For less severely recurrent major depression, or at somewhat higher IPT doses, how might maintenance IPT fare?

Depressed adolescents (IPT-A)

Mufson et al. (1993) modified IPT to address developmental issues of adolescence. In adapting IPT to this population, they added a fifth problem area and potential focus: the single-parent family. This interpersonal situation appeared frequently in their adolescent treatment population, and actually reflected multiple wider social problems in an economically deprived, high-crime, and drug-filled neighborhood. Other adaptations included family and school contacts. The researchers conducted an open feasibility trial before completing a controlled 12-week clinical trial comparing IPT-A to clinical monitoring in 48 clinic-referred, 12–18-year-old patients who met DSM-III-R criteria for major depressive disorder. Thirty-two patients completed the protocol (21 IPT-A, 11 controls). Patients who received IPT-A reported significantly greater improvement in depressive symptoms and social functioning, including interpersonal functioning and problem-solving skills. In the intent-to-treat sample, 75% of IPT-A patients met the criterion for recovery (HDRS score of ≤6) compared to 46% of controls (Mufson et al., 1999). Mufson is completing a follow-up trial of IPT-A in a large-scale effectiveness study in school-based clinics and is also piloting it in a group format for depressed adolescents.

Rossello and Bernal (1999) compared 12 weeks of randomly assigned IPT ($n = 22$), CBT ($n = 25$), and a waiting-list control condition ($n = 24$) for adolescents ages 13–18 in Puerto Rico who met DSM-III-R criteria for major depression, dysthymia, or both. The investigators did not use Mufson's IPT-A modification. Both IPT and CBT were more efficacious than the waiting list in improving adolescents' self-rated depressive symptoms. IPT was more efficacious than CBT in increasing self-esteem and social adaptation (effect size for IPT = 0.73; for CBT = 0.43) (Rossello & Bernal, 1999).

Depressed HIV-positive patients (IPT-HIV)

Recognizing that medical illness is the kind of serious life event that might lend itself to IPT treatment, Markowitz et al. (1992) modified IPT for depressed HIV patients (IPT-HIV), emphasizing common issues among this population, including concerns about illness and death, grief, and role transitions. A pilot open trial found that 21 of the 24 depressed patients responded. In a 16-week controlled study, 101 subjects were randomized to IPT-HIV, CBT, supportive psychotherapy (SP), or IMI plus SP (Markowitz et al., 1998). All treatments were associated with symptom reduction, but IPT and IMI-SP produced symptomatic and functional improvement significantly greater than CBT or SP. These results recall those of more severely depressed subjects in the NIMH TDCRP study (Elkin et al., 1989). Many HIV-positive patients responding to treatment reported improvement of neurovegetative physical symptoms that they had mistakenly attributed to HIV infection.

Depressed primary care patients

Many depressed individuals are willing to accept medical but not mental health treatment. Schulberg and colleagues compared IPT to nortriptyline pharmacotherapy for depressed ambulatory medical patients in a primary-care setting (Schulberg & Scott, 1991; Schulberg et al., 1993). IPT was integrated into the routine of the primary-care center: for example, nurses took vital signs before each session, and if patients were medically hospitalized, IPT was continued in the hospital when possible.

Patients with current major depression ($n = 276$) were randomly assigned to IPT, nortriptyline, or primary-care physicians' usual care. They received 16 weekly sessions followed by four monthly sessions of IPT (Schulberg et al., 1996). Depressive symptoms improved more rapidly with IPT or nortriptyline than in usual care. About 70% of treatment completers receiving nortriptyline or IPT recovered after 8 months, compared to 20% in usual care. This study had an odd design for treatment in the USA in bringing mental health treatment into medical clinics, but might inform treatment in the UK, where a greater proportion of antidepressant treatments are delivered in primary-care settings.

In the Schulberg et al. study, subjects with a lifetime history of comorbid panic disorder had a poor response across treatments compared to those with major depression alone (Brown et al., 1996). These predictive findings on comorbid panic disorder were corroborated by Frank et al. (2000a).

Conjoint IPT for depressed patients with marital disputes (IPT-CM)

It is well established that marital conflict, separation, and divorce can precipitate or complicate depressive episodes (Rounsaville et al., 1979). Some clinicians have feared that individual psychotherapy for depressed patients in marital disputes can lead to premature rupture of marriages (Gurman & Kniskern, 1978). To test and address these concerns, Klerman and Weissman developed an IPT manual for conjoint therapy of depressed patients with marital disputes (Klerman & Weissman, 1993). Both spouses participate in all sessions, and treatment focuses on the current marital dispute. Eighteen patients with major depression linked to the onset or exacerbation of marital disputes were randomly assigned to 16 weeks of either individual IPT or IPT-CM. Patients in both treatments showed similar improvement in depressive symptoms, but patients receiving IPT-CM reported significantly better marital adjustment, marital affection, and sexual relations than did individual IPT patients (Foley et al., 1989). These pilot findings require replication in a larger sample and with other control groups.

Antepartum/postpartum depression

Pregnancy and the postpartum period are times of heightened depressive risk for patients who may wish to avoid pharmacotherapy. Spinelli at Columbia University is using IPT to treat women with antepartum depression. Pregnancy is deemed a role transition that involves the depressed pregnant woman's self-evaluation as a parent, physiological changes of pregnancy, and altered relationships with the spouse or significant other and with other children. "Complicated pregnancy" has been added as a fifth potential interpersonal problem area. Session timing and duration are adjusted for bed rest, delivery, obstetrical complications, and child care, and postpartum mothers may bring children to sessions. As with depressed HIV-positive patients, therapists use telephone sessions and hospital visits as necessary (Spinelli, 1997). A controlled clinical trial is comparing 16 weeks of acute IPT and 6-month follow-up sessions to a didactic parent education group in depressed pregnant women.

O'Hara et al. (2000) compared 12 weeks of IPT to a waiting list for 120 women with postpartum depression. The investigators assessed both the mothers' symptom states and their interactions with their infants (Stuart & O'Hara, 1995). In the IPT group, 38% met HDRS and 44% met BDI remission criteria, whereas comparable responses on each measure in the waiting-list control group were 14%. Sixty percent of IPT patients and 16%

of controls reported more than a 50% BDI improvement. Postpartum women receiving IPT also improved significantly on social-adjustment measures relative to the control group.

Klier et al. (2001) adapted IPT to a 9-week, 90-minute group format and treated 17 women with postpartum depression. Scores on the 21-item Ham-D fell from 19.7 to 8.0, suggesting efficacy. In a still more intriguing study, Zlotnick et al. (2001) treated 37 women at risk for postpartum depression with either four 60-minute sessions of an IPT-based group approach or usual treatment. This preventive application resembles a group form of interpersonal counseling (Klerman et al., 1987), a simplified version of IPT. Six of 18 women in the control condition, but none of 17 in the interpersonal group, developed depression at 3 months postpartum.

Dysthymic disorder (IPT-D)

IPT was modified for dysthymic disorder, a disorder whose chronicity does not fit the standard IPT model. This adaptation also may provide a better fit for dysthymic patients without acute life events who previously would have been put in the interpersonal deficits category of acute IPT. IPT-D encourages patients to reconceptualize what they have considered lifelong character flaws as ego-dystonic, chronic mood-dependent symptoms: as chronic but treatable "state" rather than immutable "trait". Therapy itself was defined as an "iatrogenic role transition" from believing oneself flawed in personality to recognizing and treating the mood disorder. Markowitz (1994, 1998) openly treated 17 pilot subjects with 16 sessions of IPT-D, of whom none worsened and 11 remitted. Medication benefits many dysthymic patients (Kocsis et al., 1988; Thase et al., 1996), but nonresponders may need psychotherapy, and even medication responders may benefit from combined treatment (Markowitz, 1994). Based on these pilot results, a comparative study of 16 weeks of IPT-D alone, SP, and sertraline plus clinical management, as well as a combined IPT/sertraline cell, has been completed at Weill Medical College of Cornell University.

Browne, Steiner, and others at McMaster University in Hamilton, Canada, treated more than 700 dysthymic patients in the community with either 12 sessions of standard IPT over 4 months, sertraline for 2 years, or their combination. Patients were followed for 2 years (Browne et al., 2002). Based on an improvement criterion of at least a 40% reduction in score of the Montgomery–Asberg Depression Rating Scale (MADRS) at 1-year follow-up, 51% of IPT-alone subjects improved, fewer than the 63% taking sertraline and 62% in combined treatment. On follow-up, however, IPT was associated with significant economic savings in use of health care and social services. Combined treatment was thus most cost-effective, and was as efficacious as, but less expensive than, sertraline alone.

In a comparison of medication to combined treatment, Feijò de Mello and colleagues (2001) randomly assigned 35 dysthymic outpatients to moclobemide with or without 16 veekly sessions of IPT. Both groups improved, but with a nonsignificant trend for greater improvement on the Ham-D and MADRS in the combined treatment group.

Subsyndromally depressed hospitalized elderly patients

Recognizing that subthreshold symptoms for major depression impeded recovery of hospitalized elderly patients, Mossey et al. (1996) conducted a trial using a modification of

IPT called interpersonal counseling (IPC) (Klerman et al., 1987). Nonpsychiatric nurses treated geriatric, medically hospitalized patients with minor depressive symptoms for 10 1-hour sessions flexibly scheduled to accommodate the patient's medical status. Seventy-six hospitalized patients over age 60 who had subsyndromal depressive symptoms on two consecutive assessments were randomly assigned to either IPC or usual care (UC). A euthymic, untreated control group was also followed. Patients found IPC feasible and tolerable. Three-month assessment showed nonsignificantly greater improvement in depressive symptoms and on all outcome variables for IPC relative to UC, whereas controls showed mild symptomatic worsening. In the IPC and euthymic control groups, rates of rehospitalization were similar (11–15%), and significantly less than the subsyndromally depressed group receiving UC (50%). Differences between IPC and UC became statistically significant after 6 months on depressive symptoms and self-rated health, but not physical or social functioning. The investigators felt 10 sessions were not enough for some patients, and that maintenance IPC might have been useful.

OTHER APPLICATIONS

The success of IPT in treating unipolar mood disorders has led to its expansion to treat other psychiatric disorders. Frank and colleagues in Pittsburgh have been assessing a behaviorally modified version of IPT as a treatment adjunctive to pharmacotherapy for bipolar disorder. They report on this adaptation elsewhere in this volume (Chapter 15) (Frank, 1991b; Frank et al., 1999; 2000a;b).

Furthermore, IPT is increasingly being applied to a range of nonmood disorders. There are intriguing applications of IPT as treatment for bulimia (Agras et al., 2000; Fairburn et al., 1993; Wilfley et al.,1993; 2000) and anorexia nervosa, social phobia (Lipsitz et al., 1999), post-traumatic stress disorder, and other conditions. Life events, the substrate of IPT, are ubiquitous, but how useful it is to focus on them may vary from disorder to disorder. There have been two negative trials of IPT for substance disorders (Carroll et al., 1991; Rounsaville et al., 1983), and it seems unlikely that an outwardly focused treatment such as IPT would be useful for such an internally focused diagnosis as obsessive compulsive disorder. In the continuing IPT tradition, clinical outcome research should clarify the question of its utility. IPT is also being modified for use in other formats—for example, as group therapy (Klier et al., 2001; Wilfley et al. 1993, 2000; Zlotnick et al., 2001) and as a telephone intervention. Weissman (1995) developed an IPT patient guide with worksheets for depressed readers that may be used in conjunction with IPT.

In summary, IPT is one of the best tested psychotherapies, particularly for mood disorders, where it has demonstrated efficacy as both an acute and maintenance monotherapy and as a component of combined treatment for major depressive disorder. It appears to have utility for other mood and nonmood syndromes, although evidence for most of these is sparser. Monotherapy with either IPT or pharmacotherapy is likely to treat successfully most patients with major depression, so combined treatment should probably be reserved for more severely or chronically ill patients (Rush & Thase, 1999). How best to combine time-limited psychotherapy with pharmacotherapy is an exciting area for future research: when is it indicated, in what sequence, and for which patients?

Comparative trials have begun to reveal moderating factors that predict treatment outcome. The NIMH TIDCRP, which compared IPT and CBT, suggested factors that might predict better outcome with either IPT or CBT. Sotsky and colleagues (1991) found that depressed patients with low baseline social dysfunction responded well to IPT, whereas those with severe social deficits (probably equivalent to the "interpersonal deficits" problem area) responded less well. Greater symptom severity and difficulty in concentrating responded poorly to CBT. Initial severity of major depression and of impaired functioning responded best in that study to IPT and to imipramine. Imipramine worked most efficaciously for patients with difficulty in functioning at work, reflecting its faster onset of action. Patients with atypical depression responded better to IPT or CBT than to imipramine or placebo (Shea et al., 1999).

Barber and Muenz (1996), in a study of the TDCRP completers, found IPT more efficacious than CBT for patients with obsessive personality disorder, whereas CBT fared better for avoidant personality disorder. This finding did not hold for the intent-to-treat sample. Biological factors, such as abnormal sleep profiles on EEG, predicted significantly poorer response to IPT than for patients with normal sleep parameters (Thase et al., 1997). Frank and colleagues (1991) found that psychotherapist adherence to a focused IPT approach may enhance outcome. Moreover, sleep EEG and adherence, the first a biological and the latter a psychotherapy factor, had additive effects in that study. Replication and further elaboration of these predictive factors deserve ongoing study.

Another exciting development is the use of neuroimaging studies to compare IPT and pharmacotherapy outcomes. In Sunderland, Martin et al. (2001), using SPECT, found that IPT and venlafaxine had overlapping but also differing effects on right posterior cingulate (IPT), right posterior temporal (venlafaxine), and right basal ganglia activation (both treatments). Brody et al. (2001) in Los Angeles reported slightly different but roughly analogous findings with positron-emission tomography (PET) scanning of patients treated with IPT and paroxetine.

TRAINING

Until very recently, IPT therapy was delivered almost entirely by research study therapists. As the research base of IPT has grown and it has become included in treatment guidelines, there has been a growing clinical demand for this empirically supported treatment. IPT training is now increasingly included in professional workshops and conferences, with training courses conducted at university centers in the UK, Canada, Continental Europe, Asia, New Zealand, and Australia, in addition to the USA. IPT is taught in a still small but growing number of psychiatric residency training programs in the USA (Markowitz, 1995) and has been included in family-practice and primary-care training. It was not, however, included in a recent mandate for psychotherapy proficiency of US psychiatric residency programs.

The principles and practice of IPT are straightforward. Yet, any psychotherapy requires innate therapeutic ability, and IPT training requires more than reading the manual (Rounsaville et al., 1988; Weissman et al., 1982). Therapists learn psychotherapy by practicing it. IPT training programs generally are designed to help already experienced therapists refocus their treatment by learning new techniques, not to teach novices psychotherapy. This makes sense, given its development as a focal research therapy: IPT has never been intended as a universal treatment for all patients, a conceptualization of psychotherapy that in any case seems naively grandiose in the modern era.

IPT candidates should have a graduate clinical degree (M.D., Ph.D., M.S.W., or R.N.), several years of experience conducting psychotherapy, and clinical familiarity with the diagnosis of patients they plan to treat. The training developed for the TDCRP (Elkin et al., 1989) became the model for subsequent research studies. It included a brief didactic program, review of the manual, and a longer practicum in which the therapist treated two to three patients under close supervision and monitored by videotapes of the sessions (Chevron & Rounsaville, 1983). Rounsaville et al. (1986) found that psychotherapists who successfully conducted an initial supervised IPT case often did not require further intensive supervision, and that experienced therapists committed to the approach required less supervision than others (Rounsaville et al., 1988). Some clinicians have taught themselves IPT with the IPT manual (Klerman et al., 1984) and peer supervision to guide them. For research certification, we recommend at least two or three successfully treated cases with hour for hour supervision of taped sessions (Markowitz, 2001).

There has been no formal certificate for IPT proficiency and no accrediting board. When the practice of IPT was restricted to a few research settings, this was not a problem, as one research group taught another in the manner described above. As IPT spreads into clinical practice, issues arise about standards for clinical training, and questions of competence and accreditation gain greater urgency. Training programs in IPT are still not widely available, as a recent US Surgeon General's report noted (Satcher, 1999). Many psychiatry residency and psychology training programs still focus exclusively on long-term psychodynamic psychotherapy or on CBT. In these programs, too, the lack of exposure to time-limited treatment has been noted (Sanderson & Woody, 1995).

The educational process for IPT in clinical practice requires further study. We do not know, for example, what levels of education and experience are required to learn IPT, or how much supervision an already experienced psychotherapist is likely to require. The International Society for Interpersonal Psychotherapy is currently debating how best to set standards for clinical practice of IPT, which doubtless varies from country to country. The UK is in better shape than most: IPT therapists in Britain have agreed on standards for clinical training and practice that are essentially equivalent to those for researchers. These rigorous standards should ensure high-quality IPT in the UK.

REFERENCES

Agras, W.S., Walsh, B.T., Fairburn, C.G., Wilson, G.T. & Kraemer, H.C. (2000). A multicenter comparison of cognitive-behavioral therapy and interpersonal psychotherapy for bulimia nervosa. *Arch Gen Psychiatry, 57*, 459–466.

American Psychiatric Association (APA). (1994). *Diagnostic and Statistical Manual of Mental Disorders* (DSM-IV), 4th edn. Washington, DC: American Psychiatric Association.

Barber, J.P. & Muenz, L.R. (1996). The role of avoidance and obsessiveness in matching patients to cognitive and interpersonal psychotherapy: Empirical findings from the Treatment for Depression Collaborative Research Program. *J Consult Clin Psychol, 64*, 951–958.

Beck, A.T. (1978). *Depression Inventory*. Philadelphia: Center for Cognitive Therapy.

Blom, M.B.J., Hoencamp, E. & Zwaan , T. (1996). Interpersoonlijke psychotherapie voor depressie: Een pilot-onderzoek. *Tijdschr voor Psychiatr, 38*, 398–402.

Brody, A.L., Saxena, S., Stoessel, P., et al. (2001). Regional brain metabolic changes in patients with major depression treated with either paroxetine or interpersonal therapy: Preliminary findings. *Arch Gen Psychiatry, 58*, 631–640.

Brown, C., Schulberg, H.C., Madonia, M.J., Shear, M.K. & Houck, P.R. (1996). Treatment outcomes for primary care patients with major depression and lifetime anxiety disorders. *Am J Psychiatry, 153*, 1293–1300.

Browne, G., Steiner, M., Roberts, J., et al. (2002). Sertraline and/or interpersonal psychotherapy for patients with dysthymic disorder in primary care: 6-month comparison with longitudinal 2-year follow-up of effectiveness and costs. *J. Affect Disord, 68*, 317–330.

Carroll, K.M., Rounsaville, B.J. & Gawin, F.H. (1991). A comparative trial of psychotherapies for ambulatory cocaine abusers: Relapse prevention and interpersonal psychotherapy. *Am J Drug Alcohol Abuse, 17*, 229–247.

Chevron, E.S. & Rounsavillle, B.J. (1983). Evaluating the clinical skills of psychotherapists: A comparison of techniques. *Arch Gen Psychiatry, 40*, 1129–1132.

DiMascio, A., Weissman, M.M., Prusoff, B.A., Neu, C., Zwilling, M. & Klerman, G.L. (1979). Differential symptom reduction by drugs and psychotherapy in acute depression. *Arch Gen Psychiatry, 36*, 1450–1456.

Elkin, I., Shea, M.T., Watkins, J.T., et al. (1989). National Institute of Mental Health Treatment of Depression Collaborative Research Program: General effectiveness of treatments. *Arch Gen Psychiatry, 46*, 971–982.

Fairburn, C.G., Jones, R., Peveler, R.C., Hope, R.A. & O'Connor, M. (1993). Psychotherapy and bulimia nervosa: Longer-term effects of interpersonal psychotherapy, behavior therapy, and cognitive behavior therapy. *Arch Gen Psychiatry, 50*, 419–428.

Feijò de Mello, M., Myczowisk, L.M. & Menezes, P.R. (2001). A randomized controlled trial comparing moclobemide and moclobemide plus interpersonal psychotherapy in the treatment of dysthymic disorder. *J Psychother Prac Res, 10*, 117–123.

Foley, S.H., Rounsaville, B.J., Weissman, M.M., Sholomskas, D. & Chevron, E. (1989). Individual versus conjoint interpersonal psychotherapy for depressed patients with marital disputes. *Int J Fam Psychiatry, 10*, 29–42.

Frank, E. (1991a). Interpersonal psychotherapy as a maintenance treatment for patients with recurrent depression. *Psychotherapy, 28*, 259–266.

Frank, E. (1991b). Biological order and bipolar disorder. Presented at the meeting of the American Psychosomatic Society, Santa Fe, NM, March.

Frank, E., Kupfer, D.J., Perel, J.M., et al. (1990). Three-year outcomes for maintenance therapies in recurrent depression. *Arch Gen Psychiatry, 47*, 1093–1099.

Frank, E. Kupfer, D.J., Wagner, E.F., McEachran, A.B. & Cornes, C. (1991). Efficacy of interpersonal psychotherapy as a maintenance treatment of recurrent depression. *Arch Gen Psychiatry, 48*, 1053–1059.

Frank, E., Shear, M.K., Rucci, P., et al. (2000a). Influence of panic-agoraphobic spectrum symptoms on treatment response in patients with recurrent major depression. *Am J Psychiatry, 157*, 1101–1107.

Frank, E., Swartz, H.A., Mallinger, A.G., Thase, M.E., Weaver, E.V. & Kupfer, D.J. (1999). Adjunctive psychotherapy for bipolar disorder: Effects of changing treatment modality. *J Abnorm Psychol, 108*, 579–587.

Frank, E., Swartz, H.A. & Kupfer, D.J. (2000b). Interpersonal and social rhythm therapy: Managing the chaos of bipolar disorder. *Biol Psychiatry, 48*, 593–604.

Frank, J. (1971). Therapeutic factors in psychotherapy. *Am J Psychotherapy, 25*, 350–361.

Gurman, A.S. & Kniskern, D.P. (1978). Research on marital and family therapy: Progress, perspective, and prospect. In S.B. Garfield & A.B. Bergen (Eds), *Handbook of Psychotherapy and Behavior Change* (pp. 817–902). New York: Wiley.

Hamilton, M. (1960). A rating scale for depression. *J Neurol Neurosurg Psychiatry, 25*, 56–62.

Hirschfeld, R.M.A., Klerman, G.L., Clayton, P.J., et al. (1983). Assessing personality: Effects of the depressive state on trait measurement. *Am J Psychiatry, 140*, 695–699.

Klein, D.F. & Ross, D.C. (1993). Reanalysis of the National Institute of Mental Health Treatment of Depression Collaborative Research Program general effectiveness report. *Neuropsychopharmacology, 8*, 241–251.

Klerman, G.L., Budman, S., Berwick, D., et al. (1987). Efficacy of a brief psychosocial intervention for symptoms of stress and distress among patients in primary care. *Med Care, 25*, 1078–1088.

Klerman, G.L., DiMascio, A., Weissman, M.M., Prusoff, B.A. & Paykel, E.S. (1974). Treatment of depression by drugs and psychotherapy. *Am J Psychiatry, 131*, 186–191.

Klerman, G.L. & Weissman, M.M. (1993). *New Applications of Interpersonal Psychotherapy.* Washington, DC: American Psychiatric Press.

Klerman, G.L., Weissman, M.M. Rounsaville, B.J. & Chevron, E.S. (1984). *Interpersonal Psychotherapy of Depression.* New York: Basic Books.

Klier, C.M., Muzik, M., Rosenblum, K.L. & Lenz, G. (2001). Interpersonal psychotherapy adapted for the group setting in the treatment of postpartum depression. *J Psychother Prac Res, 10,* 124–131.

Kocsis, J.H., Frances, A.J., Voss, C., Mann, J.J., Mason, B.J. & Sweeney, J. (1988). Imipramine treatment for chronic depression. *Arch Gen Psychiatry, 45,* 253–257.

Lipsitz, J.D., Fyer, A.J., Markowitz, J.C. & Cherry, S. (1999). An open trial of interpersonal psychotherapy for social phobia. *Am J Psychiatry, 156,* 1814–1816.

Markowitz, J.C. (1994). Psychotherapy of dysthymia. *Am J Psychiatry, 151,* 1114–1121.

Markowitz, J.C. (1995). Teaching interpersonal psychotherapy to psychiatric residents. *Acad Psychiatry, 19,* 167–173.

Markowitz, J.C. (1998). *Interpersonal Psychotherapy for Dysthymic Disorder.* Washington, DC: American Psychiatric Press.

Markowitz, J.C. (2001). Learning the new psychotherapies. In M.M. Weissman (Ed.), *Treatment of Depression: Bridging the 21st Century* (pp. 281–300). Washington, DC: American Psychiatric Press.

Markowitz, J.C. & Swartz, H.A. (1997). Case formulation in interpersonal psychotherapy of depression. In T.D. Eels (Ed.), *Handbook of Psychotherapy Case Formulation* (pp. 192–222). New York: Guilford.

Markowitz, J.C., Klerman, G.L., Perry, S.W., Clougherty, K.F. & Mayers, A. (1992). Interpersonal therapy of depressed HIV-seropositive patients. *Hosp Comm Psychiatry, 43,* 885–890.

Markowitz, J.C., Kocsis, J.H., Fishman, B., et al. (1998). Treatment of HIV-positive patients with depressive symptoms. *Arch Gen Psychiatry, 55,* 452–457.

Markowitz, J.C., Leon, A.C., Miller, N.L., Cherry, S., Clougherty, K.F. & Villalobos, L. (2000). Rater agreement on interpersonal psychotherapy problem areas. *J Psychother Pract Res, 9,* 131–135.

Markowitz, J.C., Svartberg, M. & Swartz, H.A. (1998). Is IPT time-limited psychodynamic psychotherapy? *J Psychother Prac Res, 7,* 185–195.

Martin, S.D., Martin, E., Rai, S.S., Richardson, M.A. & Royall, R. (2001). Brain blood flow changes in depressed patients treated with interpersonal psychotherapy or venlafaxine hydrochloride. *Arch Gen Psychiatry, 58,* 641–648.

Mossey, J.M., Knott, K.A., Higgins, M. & Talerico, K. (1996). Effectiveness of a psychosocial intervention, interpersonal counseling, for subdysthymic depression in medically ill elderly. *J Gerontol, 51A,* M172–M178.

Mufson, L., Moreau, D. & Weissman, M.M. (1993). *Interpersonal Therapy for Depressed Adolescents.* New York: Guilford.

Mufson, L., Weissman, M.M., Moreau, D. & Garfinkel, R. (1999). Efficacy of interpersonal psychotherapy for depressed adolescents. *Arch Gen Psychiatry, 56,* 573–579.

O'Hara, M.W., Stuart, S., Gorman, L.L. & Wenzel, A. (2000). Efficacy of interpersonal psychotherapy for postpartum depression. *Arch Gen Psychiatry, 57,* 1039–1045.

Parsons, T. (1951). Illness and the role of the physician: A sociological perspective. *Am J Orthopsychiatry, 21,* 452–460.

Paykel, E.S., DiMascio, A., Haskell, D. & Prusoff, B.A. (1975). Effects of maintenance amitriptyline and psychotherapy on symptoms of depression. *Psychol Med, 5,* 67–77.

Reynolds, C.F. III, Frank, E., Perel, J.M., et al., (1999). Nortriptyline and interpersonal psychotherapy as maintenance therapies for recurrent major depression: A randomized controlled trial in patients older than fifty-nine years. *JAMA, 281,* 39–45.

Rossello, J. & Bernal, G. (1999). The efficacy of cognitive-behavioral and interpersonal treatments for depression in Puerto Rican adolescents. *J Consult Clin Psychol, 67,* 734–745.

Roth, A. & Fonagy, P. (1996). *What Works for Whom?: A Critical Review of Psychotherapy Research* (p. iv). New York: Guilford.

Rothblum, E.D., Sholomskas, A.J., Berry, C. & Prusoff, B.A. (1982). Issues in clinical trials with the depressed elderly. *J Am Geriatr Soc, 30,* 694–699.

Rounsaville, B.J., Chevron, E.S., Weissman, M.M., Prusoff, B.A. & Frank, E. (1986). Training therapists to perform interpersonal psychotherapy in clinical trials. *Compr Psychiatry, 27,* 364–437.

Rounsaville, B.J., Glazer, W., Wilber, C.H., Weissman, M.M. & Kleber, H.D. (1983). Short-term interpersonal psychotherapy in methadone-maintained opiate addicts. *Arch Gen Psychiatry, 40,* 629–636.

Rounsaville, B.J., O'Malley, S.S., Foley, S.H. & Weissman, M.M. (1988). The role of manual-guided training in the conduct and efficacy of interpersonal psychotherapy for depression. *J Consult Clin Psychol, 56,* 681–688.

Rounsaville, B.J., Weissman, M.M., Prusoff, B.A. & Herceg-Baron, R.L. (1979). Marital disputes and treatment outcome in depressed women. *Compr Psychiatry, 20,* 483–490.

Rush, A.J. & Thase, M.E. (1999). Psychotherapies for depressive disorders: A review. In M. Maj & N. Sartorius (Eds), *Depressive Disorders: WPA Series Evidence and Experience in Psychiatry* (pp. 161–206). Chichester: Wiley.

Sanderson, W.C. & Woody S. (1995). Manuals for empirically validated treatments: A project of the Task Force on Psychological Interventions. Vol. 48. Washington, DC: Division of Clinical Psychology, American Psychological Association. *Clin Psychol, 48,* 7–11.

Satcher, D. (1999). *Surgeon General's Reference: Mental Health: A Report of the Surgeon General.* Rockville, MD: US Department of Health and Human Services.

Schulberg, H.C. & Scott, C.P. (1991). Depression in primary care: Treating depression with interpersonal psychotherapy. In C.S. Austad & W.H. Berman (Eds), *Psychotherapy in Managed Health Care: The Optimal Use of Time and Resources* (pp. 153–170). Washington, DC: American Psychological Association.

Schulberg, H.C., Block, M.R., Madonia, M.J., et al. (1996). Treating major depression in primary care practice. *Arch Gen Psychiatry, 53,* 913–919.

Schulberg, H.C., Scott, C.P., Madonia, M.J. & Imber, S.D. (1993). Applications of interpersonal psychotherapy to depression in primary care practice. In G.L. Klerman & M.M. Weissman (Eds), *New Applications of Interpersonal Psychotherapy* (pp. 265–291). Washington, DC: American Psychiatric Press.

Shea, M.T., Elkin, I., Imber, S.D., et al. (1992). Course of depressive symptoms over follow-up: Findings from the National Institute of Mental Health Treatment for Depression Collaborative Research Program. *Arch Gen Psychiatry, 49,* 782–794.

Shea, M.T., Elkin, I. & Sotsky, S.M. (1999). Patient characteristics associated with successful treatment: Outcome findings from the NIMH Treatment of Depression Collaborative Research Program. In D.S. Janowsky (Ed.), *Psychotherapy Indications and Outcomes* (pp. 71–90). Washington, DC: American Psychiatric Press.

Sholomskas, A.J., Chevron, E.S., Prusoff, B.A. & Berry, C. (1983). Short-term interpersonal therapy (IPT) with the depressed elderly: Case reports and discussion. *Am J Psychother, 36,* 552–566.

Sloane, R.B., Stapes, F.R. & Schneider, L.S. (1985). Interpersonal therapy versus nortriptyline for depression in the elderly. In G.D. Burrows, T.R. Norman & L. Dennerstein (Eds), *Clinical and Pharmacological Studies in Psychiatric Disorders* (pp. 344–346). London: John Libbey.

Sotsky, S.M., Glass, D.R., Shea, M.T., et al. (1991). Patient predictors of response to psychotherapy and pharmacotherapy: Findings in the NIMH Treatment of Depression Collaborative Research Program. *Am J Psychiatry, 148,* 997–1008.

Spinelli, M. (1997). Manual of interpersonal psychotherapy for antepartum depressed women (IPT-P). Available through Dr Spinelli, Columbia University College of Physicians and Surgeons, New York.

Stuart, S. & O'Hara, M.W. (1995). IPT for postpartum depression. *J Psychother Prac Res, 4,* 18–29.

Sullivan, H.S. (Ed.) (1953). *The Interpersonal Theory of Psychiatry.* New York: W.W. Norton.

Thase, M.E., Buysse, D.J, Frank, E., et al. (1997). Which depressed patients will respond to interpersonal psychotherapy? The role of abnormal EEG profiles. *Am J Psychiatry, 154,* 502–509.

Thase, M.E., Fava, M., Halbreich, U., et al. (1996). A placebo-controlled, randomized clinical trial comparing sertraline and imipramine for the treatment of dysthymia. *Arch Gen Psychiatry, 53,* 777–784.

Weissman, M.M. (1995). *Mastering Depression: A Patient Guide to Interpersonal Psychotherapy.* Albany, NY: Graywind Publications. Currently available through the Psychological Corporation, Order Service Center, P. O. Box 839954, San Antonio, TX 78283–3954, USA; Tel. 1-800-228-0752, Fax 1-800-232-1223.

Weissman, M.M., Klerman, G.L., Paykel, E.S., Prusoff, B.A. & Hanson B. (1974). Treatment effects on the social adjustment of depressed patients. *Arch Gen Psychiatry, 30,* 771–778.

Weissman, M.M., Klerman, G.L., Prusoff, B.A., Sholomskas, D. & Padian, N. (1981). Depressed outpatients: Results one year after treatment with drugs and/or interpersonal psychotherapy. *Arch Gen Psychiatry, 38,* 52–55.

Weissman, M.M., Markowitz, J.C. & Klerman, G.L. (2000). *Comprehensive Guide to Interpersonal Psychotherapy.* New York: Basic Books.

Weissman, M.M., Prusoff, B.A., DiMascio, A., Neu, C., Goklaney, M. & Klerman, G.L. (1979). The efficacy of drugs and psychotherapy in the treatment of acute depressive episodes. *Am J Psychiatry, 136,* 555–558.

Weissman, M.M., Rounsaville, B.J. & Chevron, E.S. (1982). Training psychotherapists to participate in psychotherapy outcome studies: Identifying and dealing with the research requirement. *Am J Psychiatry, 139,* 1442–1446.

Wilfley, D.E., Agras, W.S., Telch, C.F., et al. (1993). Group cognitive-behavioral therapy and group interpersonal psychotherapy for the nonpurging bulimic individual: A controlled comparison. *J Consult Clin Psychol, 61,* 296–305.

Wilfley, D.E., MacKenzie, R.K., Welch, R.R., Ayres, V.E. & Weissman, M.M. (2000). *Interpersonal Psychotherapy for Groups.* New York: Basic Books.

Zlotnick, C., Johnson, S.L., Miller, I.W., Pearlstein, T. & Howard, M. (2001). Postpartum depression in women receiving public assistance: Pilot study of an interpersonal-therapy-oriented group intervention. *Am J Psychiatry, 158,* 638–640.

Part II

BIPOLAR DEPRESSION

10

EPIDEMIOLOGY AND CLASSIFICATION
OF BIPOLAR DISORDER

Jonathan Cavanagh

CLASSIFICATION

Categories or continuua?

We have in front of us a fruit called psychosis, and we don't know whether it's a citrus that
will divide itself into separable sections or an apple that we must divide along arbitrary lines.
Belmaker and Van Praag (1980)

Bipolar affective disorder and schizophrenia constitute the twin pillars of classically defined
psychosis. As Goodwin and Jamison (1990) point out, Kraepelin's (somewhat unintentional)
legacy has divided psychotic illness into two entities, schizophrenia and manic depression.
This can leave many patients in a diagnostic no man's land. Kendler (1986) has stated that
"no area in psychiatric nosology has been as controversial". This controversy has formed
the scaffolding for contemporary classification. However, excessive reliance on presenting
symptoms and narrative and too little on the history of patients and their families can
lead to undue reliance on one set of diagnostic rules at the expense of the true picture.
Argument about the validity of the dichotomous classification of the major psychoses has
been in progress for the last century, beginning soon after Kraepelin (1896) described his
classification of dementia praecox and manic-depressive insanity in the fifth edition of his
textbook.

The basic concept behind the classification of psychosis is that of the nosological entity
(Jablensky, 1999), which has remained unchanged since formulated by Kahlbaum (1874);
that is, a close correspondence between clinical symptoms, course and outcome, cerebral
pathology and aetiology as the criteria for correlated clinical states constituting a "natural
disease entity".

The resulting construction of the clinical entities of dementia praecox and manic-
depressive illness from previously chaotic or arbitrarily subdivided clinical material represented an immense step forward (Jablensky, 1999). However, no neuropathological

Mood Disorders: A Handbook of Science and Practice. Edited by M. Power.
© 2004 John Wiley & Sons, Ltd. ISBN 0-470-84390-X.

validation of these entities has been forthcoming, and the validating criteria have been restricted to:

(1) internal cohesion of the clinical picture
(2) course and outcome.

Kraepelin's manic-depressive insanity was a broader group than the modern concept of bipolar disorder, and the dementia praecox was narrower than ICD-10 or DSM-IV schizophrenia. This was reflected in the relative frequencies of the two diagnoses in Kraepelin's Munich University Clinic; manic-depressive illness accounted for 18.6% but dementia praecox for only 7.3% of all admissions in 1908 (Jablensky et al., 1993). These figures are substantially different from the typical annual admission rates expected in the contemporary setting, which would not record twice the number of manic-depressive as schizophrenic admissions.

Using the Present State Examination and CATEGO (Wing et al., 1973), Jablensky (1999) recoded Kraepelin's original case summaries of 53 cases of dementia praecox and 134 cases of manic-depression recognized in 1908. The overall concordance between Kraepelin's original diagnoses and the CATEGO was 80.2%. The coded raw data were applied to an independent taxonomic method, grade of membership analysis (Woodbury & Manton, 1982), to obtain a statistical grouping of clinical disorders and patients that could be compared with Kraepelin's original classification (Jablensky & Woodbury, 1995). The methods resulted in three groups of disorder clearly corresponding to bipolar affective disorder, unipolar depression, and dementia praecox. There was significant overlap between dementia praecox and bipolar disorder, with 19% of dementia praecox cases having secondary membership in the bipolar group and 17% vice versa. These results suggest a respectable level of concurrence between Kraepelin's typology of the psychoses and the clinical data on which it was based.

"Splitters" and "lumpers"

These terms summarize the different conceptualizations of the major psychoses throughout the early twentieth century. "Splitters" favour separation in terms of aetiology by way of categories. "Lumpers" postulate clustering of characteristics at the root of a predisposition to any of the major psychoses.

Wernicke (1906) proceeded conceptually from neurology, describing three functional brain systems involving the association cortex; namely, the *psychomotor* (awareness of own body), the *psychosensory* (awareness of external world), and the *intrapsychic* (awareness of one's personality). According to Wernicke, disturbances of these systems resulting from different aetiologies led to psychotic syndromes which could be classified as *somatopsychoses, allopsychoses, and autopsychoses*.

These ideas influenced Kleist (1947) and Leonhard (1979), who developed complex classifications incorporating Wernicke's ideas. Leonhard split schizophrenia into two disease groups—systematic and unsystematic, with contrasting aetiologies. The disorder was genetic in the case of the unsystematic form and developmental/environmental in the systematic form. Leonhard was the first to separate bipolar and unipolar disorders—a dichotomy which has now been adopted by the classificatory systems. There is now some evidence to support the prognostic validity of this classification (Astrup, 1979; Perris, 1974).

Kretschmer (1927) provided a prototype multidimensional classification of the major psychoses, using character trait clusters, that is, schizothyhmic, cyclothymic, and viscous, which, respectively, reflected an underlying predisposition to schizophrenia, affective psychoses, and epilepsy.

Kretschmer did not concur with the view that the psychoses were circumscribed disease phenomena, but instead held that they were episodes "rooted in the biological constitution of the individual with all possible phenomena from subclinical to florid". The genome was responsible for the "underlying all-embracing genotype"; hence, the correlation between body build and the diathesis to a particular type of psychosis—complex or mixed psychopathological pictures were the result of additive or interaction effects of inherited predispositions.

Kraepelin challenged his own dichotomous orthodoxy. He was careful to emphasize that the disease entities of dementia praecox and manic-depressive insanity were *provisional*. In "Patterns of mental disorder", Kraepelin (1920) described a different approach from previous views: "It is natural to turn away from arranging illnesses in orderly well-defined groups and to set ourselves instead the undoubtedly higher and more satisfying goal of understanding their structure."

Jablensky (1999) summarized Kraepelin's view as follows: "The affective and schizophrenic forms of mental disorder do not represent the expression of particular pathological processes but rather areas of our personality in which these processes unfold." Thus, schizophrenia and manic depression were not seen as due to particular pathological processes but rather as pre-existing response templates of the human brain to a variety of aetiological factors rooted in genetics and evolution.

In his concept of strata or "registers" of response patterns to pathogenic stimuli, Kraepelin suggested three registers or strata of response:

(1) affective, hysterical and paranoid forms
(2) schizophrenic form
(3) encephalopathic form.

While the affective and schizophrenic forms could easily combine, they would not normally involve demonstrable organic tissue damage. But if a pathological lesion is deep enough to cause an encephalopathic response, it could be expected to activate both the schizophrenic and affective levels of reaction.

Kraepelin's ultimate view of the affective–schizophrenic dichotomy was that "we cannot distinguish satisfactorily between these two illnesses and this brings home the suspicion that our formulation of the problem may be incorrect" (Kraepelin, 1920).

After Kraepelin, the major change in classification of the psychoses came in 1911 with Bleuler, who renamed "dementia praecox" as "schizophrenia". In this new system, certain symptoms were seen as schizophrenic and pathognomonically so—these symptoms defined the splitting of thought from feeling and behaviour; that is, formal thought disorder, blunted affect, autism, and ambivalence. These fundamental symptoms demanded a diagnosis of schizophrenia. Affective symptoms were regarded as non-specific, and manic depression was diagnosed only when schizophrenia was excluded. One of the main effects of the introduction of Schneiderian concepts in the UK in the 1960s was a split in "Anglophone" psychiatry (UK–USA), American psychiatry using a very broad definition of schizophrenia and diagnosing affective patients as schizophrenic.

The convergence of ICD-10 and DSM-IV has bridged the gap. However, as Andreasen (1987) puts it, "The boundary between schizophrenia and affective disorders must remain flexible, depending on whether the goal is research or patient care."

In terms of the conceptualization of bipolar disorders, there has been a discernible split over the boundaries applied to these disorders. Akiskal and others have been calling for a radical extension of the boundaries of bipolar disorder to include various subcategories, such as bipolar II and bipolar III. Klerman (1981) has extended this subdivision by reminding us that mania is not a condition which is the sole preserve of bipolar, but can arise in neurological and toxic states. The following seven subcategories of bipolar disorder are proposed:

type I—mania and depression
type II—depression and hypomania
type III—mania in response to antidepressants
type IV—cyclothymic personality
type V—depression with a family history of bipolar disorder
type VI—mania without depression
type VII—secondary mania.

In contrast, calls have been made to preserve the integrity of the bipolar disorder concept. For example, Baldessarini (2000) criticizes the distinction of the type II bipolar syndrome as lacking any test of its relationship to bipolar I by standard biomedical criteria. Similarly, little has been done in terms of evaluating differential therapeutics.

Furthermore, Baldessarini describes the dilution of the bipolar concept as premature and potentially misleading. He urges restraint, owing to the impression that classical bipolar disorder is "as close to a disease as we have in modern psychiatry.... It offers hope of a coherent and tractable phenotypic target for genetic, biological and experimental therapeutic studies."

One of the great debates in nosology has been that of the reality of the difference between bipolar disorder and schizophrenia (Jablensky, 1999). Whether they are two distinct and discrete entities, two partially overlapping clusters of clinical and biological characteristics, or a single continuum is the subject of continuing contemporary debate. The availability of increasingly sophisticated technologies with which to investigate disorders (molecular biology, genetics, and neuroimaging) raises the question of how useful the categorical classification systems, such as ICD-10 and DSM-IV, are in understanding the aetiologies of these disorders.

For example, genome scans of large samples of families with schizophrenic and affective psychoses have identified candidate regions for further study; moreover, several of these regions of interest have loaded for both schizophrenia and bipolar disorder (DeLisi 1999). Similarly, overlaps between the two disorders have been recorded in neuroimaging studies (Elliot, 1997). Lastly, epidemiological studies of possible risk factors, such as obstetric/perinatal complications, suggest that these may operate in similar ways across diagnostic/categorical boundaries (Kinney et al., 1993).

These studies represent a clinical-epidemiological approach to the issue of classification. Another approach has been from a neurobiological angle, asking whether, in fact, bipolar disorder and schizophrenia are variations on a theme and represent differing degrees of abnormality within the cognitive-emotional-behavioural circuits that are being mapped currently in neuroscience. Evidence from neuroimaging and from neuropsychology can offer insights into what factors separate these conditions and whether these factors are artefacts of categorization systems, or whether they do represent biological differences both in terms of pathophysiology and in terms of the long-term effects on the brain and thus on prognostication.

EPIDEMIOLOGY

In the best circumstances, epidemiological data can be a measure of the distribution of an illness in the population, its extent, and the associated risk factors. Epidemiological data can also link genetic, psychological, environmental, biological, and sociological factors.

There are problems with the epidemiology of bipolar affective disorder, including inconsistencies in diagnosis, treatment, and research design. For example, bipolar disorder is not always included as a separate diagnostic class in epidemiological studies; consequently, the true epidemiological picture remains unclear. However, Goodwin and Jamison (1990) argue that most of the biases in the literature are in the direction of underestimating, rather than overestimating, the incidence and prevalence of bipolar disorder.

Despite methodological variation and consequent interpretative difficulties, a level of agreement is evident. Bipolar disorder is a relatively common condition affecting men and women equally. Cultural, marital, social, and ethnic variation is less clearly defined.

Classification and epidemiology are intimately linked. The accuracy of the latter is essentially dependent on the former. In psychiatry, a branch of medicine which, so far, is devoid of objective physical signs and testing, classification and clinical assessment is all. The epidemiology of bipolar disorder is therefore governed by what classification system is in place and in what way the diagnosis is reached. Modern epidemiology must also take account of the elasticity of diagnostic boundaries, in terms of both broadening and narrowing the definition of bipolar disorder.

A summary of factors which influence rates of psychiatric disorders follows:

- breadth of criteria
- instruments used
- lay versus clinical interviewers
- population studied
- sample size
- single versus repeated observations
- interview of patients versus relatives
- timing of interviews.

While we accept these limitations, establishing the epidemiology of a disorder is an essential part of researching the condition. A crucial factor in this is the completeness of case ascertainment. To achieve complete ascertainment, the options include total population surveys, which are expensive and difficult, especially if the condition under study is rare. An alternative is random sampling, which can have problems surrounding the yield obtained.

Problems more specifically associated with bipolar affective disorder include the problem of "polarity" itself. There is an intrinsic problem in establishing the prevalence of a disorder that can be recognized only at an unpredictable point in its course—namely, when polarity changes.

In their seminal work on bipolar disorder, Goodwin and Jamison (1990) conducted a systematic assessment of the incidence and prevalence of bipolar disorder, using the best studies available to them at that time. The summary statistics from this review showed that the lifetime risk of bipolar disorder was generally less than 1% in industrialized nations (range 0.6–0.9%, 1.2% being a combination of bipolar I and II patients). The annual incidence rate of bipolar was estimated for men at 0.009–0.015%; that is, 9–15 new cases per 100 000 per year. For women, the figures were estimated at 0.007–0.03; that is, 7–30 new cases per 100 000 per year.

Perhaps the most influential epidemiological surveys remain the Epidemiologic Catchment Area (ECA) and the National Comorbidity Survey (NCS) (Kessler et al., 1994; Regier et al., 1988). However, future challenges for psychiatric epidemiology include the limitations in currently available surveys as tools for mental health service planning, which include these two large community surveys, the National Institute of Mental Health (NIMH) ECA and the NCS. Both have been the main sources of estimates of treatment need in the USA.

These surveys showed the following prevalence rates of psychiatric and addictive disorders: 1-year prevalence of 30% and a lifetime prevalence of 50%. These very high figures have led to the questioning of their usefulness as proxies for treatment need (Bebbington, 2000; Regier et al., 1998). The high disorder rates were accompanied by low service-use rates, with less than a third of people with active mental disorder using mental health services in a 1-year period (Kessler et al., 1999; Regier et al., 1993). The extent to which untreated cases represent unmet need for treatment, as opposed to absence of the need for treatment because of mild or transient symptoms, is unclear.

Methodological differences

The NIMH ECA study was conducted between 1980 and 1985 in five sites. The survey provided 18 571 household and 2290 institution residents aged 18 and over. Two face-to-face interviews were conducted 12 months apart, described as wave 1 and wave 2. A telephone interview was conducted of household respondents and was carried out 6 months after wave 1. Questions on the use of health services were asked at each interview. Diagnostic data were obtained at waves 1 and 2 only. DSM-III diagnoses were assessed with the Diagnostic Interview Schedule (DIS).

The NCS was a cross-sectional survey of a nationally representative household sample of 8098 adolescents and adults aged 15–54. It was conducted from 1990 to 1992. The University of Michigan version of the Composite International Diagnostic Interview (UM-CIDI) was used to obtain DSM-III-R diagnoses.

Generalized anxiety disorder and post-traumatic stress disorder were assessed only in the NCS, whereas obsessive compulsive disorder, anorexia nervosa, somatization disorder, and cognitive impairment were assessed only in the ECA.

Narrow et al. (2002) used the concept of clinical significance of mental disorders to re-examine these data. As an idea, clinical significance is increasingly important, especially from the perspective of service provision. Interestingly, clinical significance has been part of the DSM definition of mental disorder. DSM-IV defines a mental disorder as "a clinically significant behavioural or psychological syndrome or pattern that occurs in an individual and that is associated with present distress (eg a painful symptom) or disability (ie impairment in one or more important areas of functioning) or with a significantly increased risk of suffering death, pain, disability or an important loss of freedom".

Clinical significance has also been incorporated in the diagnostic criteria for many disorders in DSM-IV in the context of distress or impairment in social, occupational, or other

Table 10.1   The use of the clinical significance criterion in estimates of affective disorder

Comparison of 1-year prevalence rates from the NCS study

Before clinical significance criteria		With clinical significance criteria
Any mood disorder	11.1 (9.7–12.5)	7.5 (6.3–8.7)
Major depressive episode	10.1 (8.7–11.5)	6.4 (5.4–7.4)
Unipolar major depression	8.9 (7.7–10.1)	5.4 (4.4–6.4)
Dysthymia	2.5 (2.1–2.9)	1.8 (1.4–2.2)
Bipolar I	1.3 (0.9–1.7)	1.3 (0.9–1.7)
Bipolar II	0.2 (0.0–0.4)	0.2 (0.0–0.4)

Comparison of 1-year prevalence rates from the ECA study (all ages)

Before clinical significance		With clinical significance
Any mood disorder	9.5 (8.9–10.1)	5.1 (4.7–5.5)
Major depressive episode	5.8 (5.4–6.2)	4.5 (4.1–4.9)
Unipolar major depression	4.9 (4.5–5.3)	4.0 (3.6–4.4)
Dysthymia	5.5 (5.1–5.9)	1.7 (1.5–1.9)
Bipolar I	0.9 (0.7–1.1)	0.5 (0.3–0.7)
Bipolar II	0.4 (0.2–0.6)	0.2 (0.0–0.4)

important areas of functioning. However, despite this prominence of clinical significance as a concept, there is no consensus as to its definition, nor are there any operationalized criteria.

In the study by Narrow et al. (2002), the use of data on clinical significance *lowered* the past year prevalence rates of "any (psychiatric) disorder" among those aged 18–54 by 17% in the ECA and 32% in the NCS. For adults older than 18 years, the revised estimate for any disorder was 18.5%. The use of the clinical significance criterion reduced disparities between estimates in the two surveys. The validity of the criterion was supported by the positive associations between clinical significance with disabilities and suicidal behaviour. The discrepancies between the ECA and NCS, a source of considerable controversy, were largely attributed to methodological differences (Table 10.1).

Comorbidity

The issue of comorbid conditions has been more readily recognized in contemporary studies. For example, McElroy et al. (2001) evaluated 288 outpatients with bipolar I or bipolar II, using structured diagnostic interviews to determine the diagnosis of bipolar, comorbid Axis I diagnoses and demographics. They found that 187 (65%) with bipolar disorder also met DSM-IV criteria for at least one comorbid lifetime Axis I disorder. More had anxiety (42%) and substance misuse (42%) than eating disorder (5%). There were no differences in comorbidity between bipolar I and bipolar II. Both lifetime and current Axis I comorbidity were associated with an earlier age of onset. Current Axis I comorbidity was associated with history of both cycle acceleration and more severe episodes over time.

One overarching problem in the epidemiology of bipolar disorder is the debate surrounding broad or narrow criteria. The above discussion illustrates the case for more specific criteria. However, there has been a move by some toward considerable expansion of the concept. Akiskal et al. (2000) have challenged the narrow definition of what constitutes bipolar disorder. Kraepelin's own broad-brush, inclusive definitions included hypomania; temperamental dispositions of a cyclothymic, irritable, manic type; and a family history of manic depression.

The current classifications are narrower and adopt the unipolar/bipolar approach. Conservative criteria have estimated bipolar disorder to account for 1% of the population and only 10–15% of all mood disorders (Regier et al., 1988; Weissman et al., 1996). These figures have been challenged by Akiskal et al. (2000) on the basis of the broader concept of bipolarity that has evolved over the last 20 years to include manic hypomanic, rapid-cycling, and mixed mania.

The unipolar–bipolar distinction (proposed, among others, by Angst, 1966/1973, and Winokur et al., 1969) has become the accepted nomenclature of most clinicians and researchers. As Akiskal et al. (2000) put it, the dichotomy may have a degree of heuristic value but fails to help in placing and understanding those affective disorders which lie between.

The rise in genetic studies of bipolar pedigrees has uncovered many affected individuals with principally depressive features (Akiskal et al., 1985; Gershon et al., 1982; Tsuang et al., 1985). Akiskal and Mallya (1987) estimated that 4–5% of the general population belongs to a broad bipolar spectrum with chiefly depressive phenomenology coupled with less-than-manic excitements.

The clinical reality of these "less-than-manic" patients has led to various reclassifications. For example, Dunner et al. (1976) described less-than-manic patients as bipolar II on the basis of hospitalization for depression and excited periods that did not require hospitalization. Fieve and Dunner (1975) had reserved bipolar I for those who were admitted for mania. It should be remembered that "less-than-manic" excitements are very controversial concepts, and the debate remains active. The "soft bipolar spectrum" (Akiskal & Mallya, 1987), a more inclusive term for bipolar conditions beyond classical mania, revises previous definitions of bipolar II by incorporating depressions with hypomanic episodes, and cyclothymic and hyperthymic traits, as well as familial bipolarity. The spectrum also includes hypomanic episodes which occur during pharmacotherapy or other somatic treatments.

Other terms used for "less-than-manic" bipolar conditions with depressive presentations include "Dm" (Angst et al., 1980), "unipolar–L" (Kupfer et al., 1975), and "pseudo-unipolar" depression (Mendels, 1976).

In a series of more formal bipolar spectrum proposals (Akiskal, 1983, 1996; Akiskal & Akiskal, 1988), bipolarity is categorized into the following types:

type I: mania with or without depression
type II: depression with hypomania and/or cyclothymia
type III: hypomania associated with antidepressants, as well as depression with hyperthymic temperament and/or bipolar family history.

Table 10.2 illustrates the results of a consecutive series of cases examined by Akiskal and Mallya (1987) in response to an American Psychiatric Association request for an assessment of whether the (then) new DSM-III provided sufficient coverage for all affective diagnoses. It demonstrates that the bipolar spectrum conditions were as prevalent as their unipolar counterparts.

Angst (1998) demonstrated a high prevalence of brief hypomanic episodes below the 4-day requirement of DSM-IV. His work argues in favour of a broadening of the bipolar

Table 10.2   Primarily affective
diagnoses in a community
setting (adapted from Akiskal
et al., 2000)

Diagnosis	%
BP I	18
BP II	18
BP III	9
Cyclothymia	5
Unipolar	44
Dysthymia	6

concept to include both the severe—psychotic mania—end of the spectrum and the sub-threshold end—brief hypomania.

Subthreshold does not equate with subclinical or clinically insignificant. Indeed, sub-threshold episodes have been shown to have significant psychosocial consequences. However, the question of whether this constitutes inclusion criteria in a categorical classification remains unanswered. The real question might be whether categories are appropriate for these criteria or whether they are better placed in the context of continua.

Genetic research in the form of twin studies has provided evidence for, rather than against, the broader concept of bipolarity. Monozygotic twins that were discordant for strictly defined mood disorders were broadly concordant for mood-labile temperaments at the milder, untreated end of the spectrum and mood-incongruent psychoses beyond the boundaries of the classical affective psychoses at the severe end of the spectrum (Bertelsen et al., 1977).

Most epidemiological surveys have excluded less-than-manic forms of bipolar disorder. Rates of bipolar disorder, based mainly on ascertaining a history of mania, have been found to be 1%.

The two US national studies which affected the received wisdom with respect to rates of bipolar are the ECA (Regier et al., 1988) and the NCS (Kessler et al., 1994). Respectively, the rates of bipolar disorder recorded from these surveys are 1.2% and 1.6%. Weissman et al. (1996) conducted a cross-national study of rates and reported a range of 0.3–1.5%.

Newer data demonstrate higher rates owing to the broadening of the concept of bipolar disorder to include mania of less than 4 days, hypomania, brief hypomania, and cyclothymia.

Epidemiological literature from community studies in the USA and several European countries has included soft bipolar within the spectrum of bipolar (Table 10.3). This newer

Table 10.3   Lifetime prevalence rates of bipolar
disorder

Study/country	Rate (%)
Regier et al. (1988)/USA	1.2
Kessler et al. (1994)/USA	1.6
Lewinsohn et al. (1995)/USA	5.7
Weissman et al. (1996)/cross-national	0.3–1.5
Szadoczky et al. (1998)/Hungary	5.0
Angst (1998)/Switzerland	8.3

literature broadens the bipolar spectrum from 1% to at least 5%. This is hardly a surprising change. Broader criteria are bound to increase the rates recorded. By contrast, the data from Narrrow et al. (2002) showed that using clinical significance criteria, rather than simply broadening the concept of bipolar, reduced prevalence rates.

Cyclothymia, hypomania, hyperthymia, and personality disorder (Axis II)

Despite the vagaries of epidemiology and the interpretation of various rates, it is useful to spend a moment reflecting on what constitute the "outer edges" of bipolar disorder. Kraepelin (1921) and Kretschmer (1936) both described affective states which ranged from the severest to the mildest and which existed on a continuum that included personal predisposition or temperament. Both described cyclothymic people in whom low-grade subdepressive and hypomanic presentations occurred.

DESCRIPTIONS OF CYCLOTHYMIA

Some people with cyclothymia exhibit depressive or irritable moodiness, while, in others, trait hypomanic features (hyperthymic temperament) predominate. These characteristics can be present throughout life but never progress to major episodes of affective illness. Or they can herald predisposing or prodromal of more severe episodes. Upon recovery, patients customarily return to baseline temperament.

Some large-scale studies have investigated cyclothymia. These studies differ from more typical epidemiology in that they concentrate on student or clinical populations.

Akiskal et al. (1977) at the University of Tennessee (USA) reported that just less than 10% of the mental health clinic conformed to subsyndromal mood changes over extended periods of time. Placidi et al. (1998) in Italy found subthreshold variation between hypomanic and subdepressive periods occurring in 6.3% of the population. It should be remembered, however, that these two studies employed operationalized criteria developed at the University of Tennessee by Akiskal et al., a group which favour the broadening of bipolar criteria. Nevertheless, all of these studies tend to show very similar levels of "bipolar diathesis".

PERSONALITY DISORDER

One of the difficulties of this area of research is the separation on the continuum between personality disorder features and the point at which symptoms become disorder in terms of bipolar disorder rather than abnormalities of personality or temperament. An awareness of boundaries is important, as personality tests in common use have been known to misattribute subthreshold mood changes to borderline personality disorder (O'Connell et al., 1991).

DESCRIPTIONS OF HYPOMANIA

There is also a very real clinical problem in separating hypomania from mania by the criteria laid down in DSM-IV (1994). One point of contention focuses on the length of time during which the symptoms must be present. Those studies validating a shorter than 4-day duration for hypomania were all conducted before the availability of DSM-IV. For example, a study by Wicki and Angst (1991) found a modal duration of 1–3 days.

Cassano et al. (1992), who used a definition of 2 days in a study of bipolar II disorder, found that these patients had rates of bipolar family history statistically indistinguishable from that of bipolar I disorder—both of which were significantly higher than that of major depressive disorders.

The most common manifestations of hypomania in a community study (Angst, 1998) were the following:

- less sleep
- more energy and strength
- more self-confidence
- increased activities (including working more)
- enjoying work more than usual
- more social activities
- spending too much money
- more plans and ideas
- less shy and inhibited
- more talkative than usual
- increased sex drive
- increased consumption of coffee, cigarettes, and alcohol
- overly optimistic
- increased laughter
- thinking fast/sudden ideas.

THE BOUNDARY BETWEEN MANIA AND HYPOMANIA

In a recent editorial commentary, Goodwin (2002) clearly described the difficulties surrounding the contemporary use of the two descriptors, mania and hypomania. The outstanding issue remains of where the boundary falls between hypomania and mania, and between hypomania and normality. DSM-IV defines both hypomania and cyclothymia as milder conditions than does ICD-10.

The boundary between hypomania and mania pivots on a definition of functional disturbance that is different between DSM-IV and ICD-10 but is dependent upon qualifications such as "severe" and "marked" whose meaning is open to interpretation. Goodwin (2002) argues that DSM-IV splits mania from hypomania in a clinically significant way. The community cohort study carried out by Angst (1998) exerts a major influence in terms of lifetime prevalence estimates. This study found DSM-IV diagnoses of mania and hypomania in 5.5% of the population. But extending the boundaries resulted in the inclusion of a further 14.1% of the population. The Angst study also revealed a population rate of bipolar I of 0.5% and of bipolar II of 3%.

Although the inclusion or exclusion of bipolar spectrum disorders is the subject of contemporary controversy (Baldessarini, 2000), findings from US studies support those of Angst (Carlson & Kashani, 1988; Lewisohn et al., 1995). Despite the epidemiological and nosological caveats, Goodwin emphasizes that something is being detected that requires explanation and clarification. Moreover, the diagnosis of hypomania is not merely one of abundant good health, and while it may be benign, it often is less so.

The question remains as to whether treatment paradigms specific for bipolar I disorder might be indicated in clinically significant spectrum conditions. As Goodwin concludes, accurate diagnosis has become clinically important for elated states. Moreover, the challenge remains of defining where hypomania ends and individual differences begin. Goodwin states that to make the distinction between hypomania and mania as it is drawn in DSM-IV appears to have important advantages (Goodwin, 2002).

DESCRIPTIONS OF HYPERTHYMIA

Clinically, hyperthymia is regarded as subthreshold, lifelong hypomanic symptoms. Psychometrically established traits in hyperthymia are as follows:

- warm, people-seeking, or extroverted
- cheerful, over-optimistic, or exuberant
- uninhibited, stimulus-seeking, or promiscuous
- over-involved and meddlesome
- vigorous, full of plans, improvident, or carried away by restless impulses
- overconfident, self-assured, boastful, bombastic, or grandiose
- articulate and eloquent.

Current data cast an uncertain light on the boundary between hyperthymic temperament and normality (Akiskal et al., 1998), and this temperament may be considered abnormal only in the presence of clinical depression.

DESCRIPTIONS OF BIPOLAR II

A common clinical situation is a patient presenting with a major depressive episode and further examination revealing a history of hypomania. The accuracy of the diagnosis is dependent on the sharpness of the patient's memory, and recall bias can be a significant problem. It can be seen as a problem with state-dependent memory in particular. When high, all previous highs are remembered; when low, only previous depressions are remembered (Kelsoe, personal communication to Akiskal, 31 March 2000).

Bipolar II is a complex diagnosis owing to the reportedly high levels of comorbidity, such as anxiety, bulimia, substance misuse, and personality disorder (Benazi, 1999; Perugi et al., 1998). There is also some evidence that so-called atypical depressions frequently progress to bipolar spectrum disorders (Ebert et al., 1993).

An analysis of the NIMH Collaborative Depression Study on unipolar patients who switched to bipolar II examined 559 patients with unipolar depression at entry during a prospective observation period of 11 years. Of these, 48 converted to bipolar II (Akiskal et al., 1995)—that is, just over 8.5%. It has been suggested that mood lability is a key variable in the cyclothymic temperament and the hallmark of those unipolar patients who switch to bipolar II. However, more systematic evidence is required before this claim can be substantiated. According to Coryell et al. (1995), in those with at least a 5-year history of affective illness, a diagnosis of bipolar II represents a stable condition which rarely progresses to bipolar I.

PHARMACOLOGICAL HYPOMANIA

This is a form of hypomania that manifests itself on treatment with antidepressants. Neither of the major classification systems (ICD-10 and DSM-IV) have accorded bipolar status to these patients. Some authors disagree and regard this as a separate bipolar state, which they call "bipolar III" (Akiskal et al., 2000).

RAPID-CYCLING BIPOLAR DISORDER

According to standard classification systems (ICD-10 and DMS-IV), those with rapid cycling suffer a minimum of four episodes of illness per year (Maj et al., 1994). The term "alternating" has been advocated as preferable, as many patients have no remission from episodes during a rapid-cycling phase.

There are degrees of cycling severity: rapid (four per year), ultrarapid (four per month), and ultradian (within a day). Coryell et al. (1992) regard rapid cycling as a phase in the illness rather than a distinct subtype. There is no clear indication from current literature on what risk factors exist for rapid cycling. Those highlighted include female gender, cyclothymic temperament, borderline hypothyroidism, and excessive use of antidepressants (Bauer et al., 1994; Koukopoulos et al., 1980; Wehr et al., 1988). By no means are all these agreed upon. Indeed, in one meta-analysis, Tondo and Baldessarini (1998) found an inconsistent association with female gender. One important factor in this literature is the difficulty associated with what is essentially a post hoc diagnosis.

One retrospective analysis of a large sample showed that bipolar illness with depression as the primary onset illness was significantly more likely than manic/mixed onsets to develop rapid cycling, suicidal behaviour, and psychotic symptoms (Perugi et al., 2000).

MIXED STATES

Mixed states of bipolar affective disorder have been recognized since the earliest days of modern classification (Kraepelin, 1921; Weygandt, 1901). Kraepelin described depressive admixtures occurring during mania as well as hypomanic intrusions into depression. His categorization included six subtypes. Mixed states are not fully reflected in ICD-10, and the DSM-IV definition requires manic and depressive symptoms in their full manifestations.

In their review of the phenomenology of mania, Goodwin and Jamison (1990) found that symptoms of depression and irritability, rather than elation, occur in 70–80% of patients with mania. Recent research has attempted to define mixed states with greater precision (e.g., Cassidy et al., 1998; McElroy et al., 1992). Various conceptualizations have included transitional states between mania and depression, an intermediate state, and a distinct affective state. However, little consensus has emerged on how best to diagnose mixed states. DSM-IV remains the most widely accepted convention, but there is growing criticism of its rigidity (e.g., Perugi et al., 1997). This has prompted alternative definitions; for example, the criteria derived from existing depression-rating scales (Post et al., 1989, Prien et al., 1988, Secunda et al., 1985, Swann et al., 1993), the use of depression items or subscales from general rating instruments (Cohen et al., 1988; Himmelhoch & Garfinkel, 1986), and a reduction in the number of DSM-IV major depression criteria required to make the diagnosis (Tohen et al., 1990; McElroy et al., 1992). Another approach has involved revisiting the essential constituents of mania. Cassidy et al. (1998) have produced the most comprehensive factor analysis of manic symptoms on a large sample to date. Five independent factors were found. Importantly, the most significant factor, dysphoric mood, was found to have a bimodal distribution. This finding raises the possibility that mixed bipolar disorder is a distinct entity.

Although it has been little studied, estimates have been made of the clinical epidemiology of mixed states. Cassidy and Carroll (2001) concluded that an earlier age of first hospitalization and increased duration of illness were compatible with the view that mixed manic episodes occur more frequently later in the course of bipolar disorder. Differences in ethnicity, gender, and clinical history also add to the evidence supporting the separation of mixed mania as a diagnostic subtype.

SYNTHESIS

In the 2002 edition of the *British Medical Journal*, its editor Richard Smith attempted to define the concept of "non-disease". His conclusions are summarized as follows: the concept of "disease" is a slippery one—so is "medicine". Health is also impossible to define. To have a condition labelled as a disease may bring considerable benefit—both material and emotional. But the diagnosis of a disease may also create problems in the denial of insurance, mortgage, and employment. A diagnosis may also lead to patients regarding themselves as forever flawed and unable to "rise above" their problem.

There is increasing evidence of a neurobiological, genetic, psychological, and social nature which indicates that bipolar disorder is at the very least a disorder. If disease is defined as the presence of clear and reproducible pathology, such evidence is not yet available in the case of bipolar disorder. However, modern biotechnology is providing methods which can provide information in vivo concerning the nature of the functional abnormalities in conditions such as schizophrenia and the affective disorders.

The issues for the future include the questions of whether schizophrenia and bipolar affective disorder are on a continuum of psychosis and whether a broad or narrow definition of bipolar is the most useful from both a clinical and a research viewpoint.

As new research techniques develop, it will be possible to answer part or all of these questions. The central diagnostic importance placed on alterations in mood distracts from the more subtle but nevertheless meaningful symptoms, such as changes in psychomotor function and cognition. Advances in neuroimaging paradigms which incorporate neuropsychological tests have revealed some of the neurofunctional similarities and differences between diagnostic subgroups. Importantly, more information than ever is available concerning the correlation between structural and functional brain changes and symptoms expressed by patients suffering from bipolar disorder and schizophrenia. One of the great challenges ahead is the separation of state from trait phenomena and to increase our understanding of common fundamentals in mental disorder. In other words, what are the first principles which underlie mental functions and the abnormalities therein? Cognition, emotion, and behaviour offer templates with which to examine the symptoms in disorders such as the bipolar. Clinical observation, while useful, is no longer sufficient for exploring the baseline abnormalities in these disabling disorders. Debates surrounding definitions, broad versus narrow, inclusive versus exclusive, may be answered by greater understanding of the common pathways that underlie the symptoms expressed.

REFERENCES

Akiskal, H.S. (1983). The bipolar spectrum: New concepts in classification and diagnosis. In L. Grinspoon (Ed.), *Psychiatry Update: The American Psychiatric Association Annual Review*, vol II (pp. 271–292). Washington, DC: American Psychiatry Press.

Akiskal, H.S. (1996). The prevalent clinical spectrum of bipolar disorders: Beyond DSM IV. *Journal of Clinical Psychopharmacology, 17* (Suppl. 3), 117–122.

Akiskal, H.S. & Akiskal, K. (1988). Re-assessing the prevalence of bipolar disorders: Clinical significance and artistic creativity. *Psychiatrie et Psychobiologie, 3*, 29s–36s.

Akiskal, H.S. & Mallya, G. (1987). Criteria for the 'soft' bipolar spectrum: Treatment implications. *Psychopharmacology Bulletin, 23*, 68–73.

Akiskal, H.S., Bourgeois, M.L., Angst, J., Post, R., Moller, H-J. & Hirschfeld, R. (2000). Re-evaluating the prevalence of and diagnostic composition within the broad clinical spectrum of bipolar disorders. *Journal of Affective Disorders, 59*, S5–S30.

Akiskal, H.S., Djenderedjian, A.H., Rosenthal, R.H. & Khani, M.K. (1977). Cyclothymic disorder: Validating criteria for inclusion in the bipolar affective group. *American Journal of Psychiatry, 134*, 1227–1233.

Akiskal, H.S., Downs, I., Jordan, P., Watson, S., Daugherty, D. & Pruitt, D.B. (1985). Affective disorders in referred children and younger siblings of manic depressives: Mode of onset and prospective course. *Archives of General Psychiatry, 42*, 996–1003.

Akiskal, H.S., Maser, J.D., Zeller, P., Endicott, J., Coryell, W. & Keller, M. (1995). Switching from 'unipolar' to 'bipolar II': An 11-year prospective study of clinical and temperamental predictor in 559 patients. *Archives of General Psychiatry, 52*, 114–123.

Akiskal, H.S., Placidi, G.F., Signoretta, S., et al. (1998). TEMPS–I: Delineating the most discriminant traits of cyclothymic, depressive, irritable and hyperthymic temperaments in a non-patient population. *Journal of Affective Disorders, 51*, 7–19.

American Psychiatric Association (1994). *Diagnostic and Statistical Manual of Mental Disorders*, 4th edn. Washington, DC: APA.

Andreasen, N.C. (1987). The diagnosis of schizophrenia. *Schizophrenia Bulletin, 13*, 9–22.

Angst, J. (1966/1973). The etiology and nosology of endogenous depressive psychoses. *Foreign Psychiatry, 2*,

Angst, J. (1998). The emerging epidemiology of hypomania and bipolar II disorder. *Journal of Affective Disorders, 50*, 143–151.

Angst, J., Frey, R,. Lohmeyer, B. & Zerbin-Rudin, E. (1980). Bipolar manic-depressive psychoses: Results of a genetic investigation. *Human Genetics, 55*, 237–254.

Astrup, C. (1979). *The Chronic Schizophrenias*. Oslo: Universitetsforlaget.

Baldessarini, R.J. (2000). A plea for intergrity of the bipolar concept. *Bipolar Disorders, 2*, 3–7.

Bauer, M.S., Calabrese, J., Dunner, D.L., et al. (1994). Multisite data re-analysis of the validity of rapid cycling as a course modifier for bipolar disorder in DSM-IV. *American Journal of Psychiatry, 151*, 506–515.

Bebbington, P. (2000). The need for psychiatric treatment in the general population. In G. Andrews & S. Henderson (Eds), *Unmet Need in Psychiatry* (pp. 85–96). Cambridge: Cambridge University Press.

Belmaker, R.H. & Van Praag (Eds) (1980). *Mania: An Evolving Concept*. New York: Spectrum Publications.

Bertelsen, A., Llaovald, B. & Hauge, M. (1977). A Danish twin study of manic-depressive disorders. *British Journal of Psychiatry, 130*, 330–351.

Benazi, F. (1999). Prevalence of bipolar II disorder in atypical depression. *European Archives of Psychiatry and Clinical Neurosciences, 249*, 62–65.

Carlson, G.A. & Kashani, J.H. (1988). Manic symptoms in a non-referred adolescent population. *Journal of Affective Disorders, 15*, 219–226.

Cassano, G.B., Akiskal, H.S., Savino, M., Musetti, L., Perugi, G. & Soriani, A. (1992). Proposed subtypes of bipolar II and related disorders: With hypomanic episodes (or cyclothymia) and with hyperthymic temperament. *Journal of Affective Disorders, 26*, 127–140.

Cassidy, F. & Carroll, B.J. (2001). The clinical epidemiology of pure and mixed manic episodes. *Bipolar Disorders, 3*, 35–40.

Cassidy, F., Forest, K., Murry, E. & Carroll, B.J. (1998). A factor analysis of the signs and symptoms of mania. *Archives of General Psychiatry, 55,* 27–32.

Cohen, S., Khan, A. & Robison, J. (1988). Significance of mixed features in acute mania. *Comprehensive Psychiatry, 29,* 421–426.

Coryell, W., Endicott, J. & Keller, M. (1992). Rapidly cycling affective Disorder: Demographics, diagnosis, family history and course. *Archives of General Psychiatry, 49,* 126–131.

Coryell, W., Endicott, J., Maser, J.D., Keller, M.B., Leon, A.C. & Akiskal, H.S. (1995). Long-term stability of polarity distinctions in the affective disorders. *American Journal of Psychiatry, 152,* 385–390.

DeLisi, L. (1999). A critical overview of recent investigations into the genetics of schizophrenia. *Current Opinion in Psychiatry, 12,* 29–39.

Dunner, D.L., Gershon, E.S. & Goodwin, F.K. (1976). Heritable factors in the severity of affective illness. *Biological Psychiatry, 11,* 31–42.

Ebert, D., Barocka, A., Kalb, R. & Ott, G. (1993). Atypical depression as a bipolar spectrum disease: Evidence from a longitudinal study; the early course of atypical depression. *Psychiatria Danubia, 5,* 133–136.

Elliot, R. (1997). Prefrontal dysfunction in depressed patients performing a complex planning task: A study using positron emission tomography. *Psychological Medicine, 27,* 931–942.

Fieve, R.R. & Dunner, D.L. (1975). Unipolar and bipolar affective states. In F.F. Flach & S.S. Draghi (Eds), *The Nature and Treatment of Depression* (pp.145–160). New York: Wiley.

Gershon, E.S., Hamovit, J., Guroff, J.J., et al. (1982). A family study of schizoaffective, bipolar I, bipolar II, unipolar and control probands. *Archives of General Psychiatry, 39,* 1157–1167.

Goodwin, F.K. & Jamison, K.R., (1990). *Manic-Depressive Illness.* New York: Oxford University Press.

Goodwin, G. (2002). Hypomania: What's in a name? *British Journal of Psychiatry, 181,* 94–95.

Himmelhoch, J.M. & Garfinkel, M.E. (1986). Sources of lithium resistance in mixed mania. *Psychopharmacology Bulletin, 22,* 613–620.

Jablensky, A. (1999). The conflict of the nosologists: Views on schizophrenia and manic-depressive illness in the early part of the 20th century. *Schizophrenia Research, 39,* 95–100.

Jablensky, A. & Woodbury, M.A. (1995). Dementia praecox and manic-depressive insanity in 1908: A grade of membership analysis of the Kraepelinian dichotomy. *European Archives of Psychiatry and Clinical Neuroscience, 245,* 202–209.

Jablensky, A., Hugler, H., von Cranach, M. & Kalinov, K. (1993). Kraepelin revisited: A reassessment and statistical analysis of dementia praecox and manic depressive insanity in 1908. *Psychological Medicine, 23,* 843–858.

Kahlbaum, K. (1874). *Die Katatonie oder das Spannnungsirresein.* Berlin: Hirschwald.

Kelsoe, (personal communication to Akiskal, 31 March 2000).

Kendler, K.S. (1986). Kraepelin and differential diagnosis of dementia praecox and manic depressive insanity. *Comprehensive Psychiatry, 27,* 549–558.

Kessler, R.C., McGonagle, K.A., Zhao, S., et al. (1994). Lifetime and 12-month prevalence of DSM-III-R psychiatric disorders in the United States. Results from the National Comorbidity Survey. *Archives of General Psychiatry, 51,* 8–19.

Kessler, R.C., Zhao, S., Katz, S.J., et al. (1999). Past-year use of outpatient services for psychiatric problems in the National Comorbidity Survey. *American Journal of Psychiatry, 156,* 115–123.

Kinney, D.K., Yurgelun-Todd, D.A., Levy, D.L., Medoff, D., Lajonchere, C.M. & Radford-Paregol, M. (1993). Obstetrical complications in patients with bipolar disorder and their siblings. *Psychiatry Research, 48,* 47–56.

Kleist, K. (1947). *Fortschritte der Psychiatrie.* Frankfurt: Kramer.

Klerman, G. (1981). The spectrum of mania. *Comprehensive Psychiatry, 22,* 11–20.

Koukopoulos, A., Reginaldi, D., Laddomada, P., Floris, G., Serra, G. & Tondo, L. (1980). Course of the manic-depressive cycle and changes caused by treatment. *Pharmakopsychiatr, 13,* 156–167.

Kraepelin, E. (1896). *Psychiatrie. Ein Lehrbuch für Studirende und Aerzte.* Leipzig: Funfte, vollstandig umgearbeiete Auflage Barth.

Kraepelin, E. (1921). *Manic Depressive Insanity and Paranoia* (Ed. G.M. Robertson; trans. R.M. Barclay). Edinburgh: Livingstone.

Kraepelin, E. (1974) [1920]. Die Erscheinungsformen des Irreseins. [English trans.] In S.R. Hirsch & M. Shepherd (Eds), *Themes and Variations in European Psychiatry* (pp. 7–44). Bristol: John Wright.

Kretschmer, E. (1927). *Der sensitive Beziehungswahn*. Berlin: Springer.

Kretschmer, E. (1936). *Physique and Character*. London: Kegan, Paul, Trench, Trubner.

Kupfer, D.J., Pickar, D., Himmelhoch, J.M. & Detre, T.P. (1975). Are there two types of unipolar depression? *Archives of General Psychiatry, 32*, 866–871.

Leonhard, K. (1979). The Classification of Endogenous Psychoses. New York: Halsted Press.

Lewisohn, P.M., Klein, D.N. & Seeley, J.R. (1995). Bipolar disorders in a community sample of older adolescents: Prevalence, phenomenology, comorbidity and course. *Journal of the American Academy of Child and Adolescent Psychiatry, 34*, 454–463.

Maj, M., Magliano, L., Pirozzi, R., Marasco, C. & Guarneri, M. (1994). Validity of rapid cycling as a course specifier for bipolar disorder. *American Journal of Psychiatry, 151*, 1015–1019.

McElroy, S.L., Altshuler, L.L., Suppes, T., et al. (2001). Axis I psychiatric comorbidity and its relationship to historical illness variables in 288 patients with bipolar disorder. *American Journal of Psychiatry, 158*, 420–426.

McElroy, S.L., Keck, P.E., Pope, H.G., Hudson, J.I., Faedda, G.L. & Swann A.C. (1992). Clinical and research implications of the diagnosis of dysphoric or mixed mania or hypomania. *American Journal of Psychiatry, 149*, 1433–1444.

Mendels, J. (1976). Lithium in the treatment of depression. *American Journal of Psychiatry, 133*, 373–378.

Narrow, W.E., Rae, D.S., Robins, L.N. & Regier, D.A. (2002). Revised prevalence estimates of mental disorders in the United States. *Archives of General Psychiatry, 59*, 115–123.

O'Connell, C.A., Mayo, J.A. & Sciutto, M.S. (1991). PDQ-R personality disorders in bipolar patients. *Journal of Affective Disorders, 23*, 217–221.

Perris, C. (1974). A study of cycloid psychoses. *Acta Psychiatrica Scandinavica, 253* (Suppl.), 1–77.

Perugi, G., Akiskal, H.S., Lattanzi, L., et al. (1998). The high prevalence of soft bipolar II features in atypical depression. *Comprehensive Psychiatry, 39*, 63–71.

Perugi, G., Akiskal, H.S., Micheli, C., et al. (1997). Clinical subtypes of bipolar mixed states: Validating a broader European definition in 143 cases. *Journal of Affective Disorder, 43*, 169–180.

Perugi, G., Micheli, C., Akiskal, H.S., et al. (2000). Polarity of the first episode, clinical characteristics and course of manic depressive illness; a systematic retrospective investigation of 320 bipolar I patients. *Comprehensive Psychiatry, 41*, 13–18.

Placidi, G.F., Signoretta, S., Liguori, A., Gervasi, R., Maremanni, I. & Akiskal, H.S. (1998). The Semi-Structured Affective Temperament Interview (TEMPS-I): Reliability and psychometric properties in 1010 14–26-old year students. *Journal of Affective Disorders, 47*, 1–10.

Post, R.M., Rubinow, D.R., Uhde, T.W., et al. (1989). Dysphoric mania, clinical and biological correlation. *Archives of General Psychiatry, 46*, 353–358.

Prien, F.R., Himmelhoch, J.M. & Kupfer, D.J. (1988). Treatment of mixed mania. *Journal of Affective Disorders, 15*, 9–15.

Regier, D.A., Boyd, J.H., Burke, J.D. Jr, et al. (1988). One month prevalence of mental disorders in the United States. Based on five epidemiologic catchment area sites. *Archives of General Psychiatry, 45*, 977–986.

Regier, D.A., Kaelber, C.T., Rae, D.S., et al. (1998). Limitations of diagnostic criteria and assessment instruments for mental disorders: Implications for research and policy. *Archives of General Psychiatry, 55*, 109–115.

Regier, D.A., Narrow, W.E., Rae, D.A., Manderscheid, R.W., Locke, B.Z. & Goodwin, F.K. (1993). The de facto US mental and addictive disorders service system: Epidemiologic catchment area prospective 1-year prevalence rates of disorders and services. *Archives of General Psychiatry, 50*, 85–94.

Secunda, S.K., Katz, M.M., Swann. A., et al. (1985). Mania. Diagnosis, state measurement and prediction of treatment response. *Journal of Affective Disorders, 8*, 113–121.

Smith, R. (2002). In search of "non-disease". *British Medical Journal*, 7342; 883.

Swann, A.C., Secunda, S.K., Katz, M.M., et al. (1993). Specificity of mixed affective states: clinical comparison of dysphoric mania and agitated depression. *Journal of Affective Disorders, 28*, 81–89.

Szadoczky, E., Papp, Z., Vitrai, I., Rihmer, Z. & Furedi, J. (1998). The prevalance of major depressive and bipolar disorder in Hungary. *Journal of Affective Disorders, 50*, 155–162.

Tohen, M., Waternaux, C.X. & Tsuang, M.Y. (1990). Outcome in mania: A 4 year prospective follow-up study of 75 patients utilizing survival analysis. *Archives of General Psychiatry, 47*, 1106–1111.

Tondo, L. & Baldessarini, L.U. (1998). Rapid cycling in women and men with bipolar manic-depressive disorders. *American Journal of Psychiatry, 155*, 1434–1436.

Tsuang, M.T., Faraone, S.V. & Fleming, J.A. (1985). Familial transmission of major affective disorders; is there evidence supporting the distinction between unipolar and bipolar disorders? *British Journal of Psychiatry, 146*, 268–271.

Wehr, T.A., Sack, D.A., Rosenthal, N.E. & Cowdry, R.W. (1988). Rapid cycling affective disorder: Contributing factors and treatment responses in 51 patients. *American Journal of Psychiatry, 145*, 179–184.

Weissman, M.M., Bland, R.C., Canino, G.J., et al. (1996). Cross-national epidemiology of major depression and bipolar disorder. *Journal of the American Medical Association, 276*, 293–299.

Wernicke, C. (1906). *Grunriß der Psychiatrie in klinischen Vorlesungen*. Leipzig: Thieme.

Weygandt, W. (1901). Ueber das manisch-depressive Irresein. *Berliner Klinischer Wochenschrift, 4*, 105–106.

Wicki, W. & Angst, J. (1991). The Zurich study X Hypomania in a 28- to 30-year-old cohort. *European Archives of Psychiatry and Clinical Neurosciences, 40*, 339–348.

Wing, J.K. Cooper, J.E. & Sartorius, N. (1973). Measurement and classification of psychiatric symptoms. London: Cambridge University Press.

Winokur, G., Clayton P.J. & Reich, T. (1969). *Manic Depressive Illness*. St Louis, MO: Mosby.

Woodbury, M.A. & Manton, K.G. (1982). A new procedure for the analysis of medical classifications. *Methods of Information in Medicine, 21*, 210–220.

11

BIOLOGICAL THEORIES OF BIPOLAR DISORDER

Douglas Blackwood and Walter Muir

The neurobiological basis of bipolar disorders and the complex interactions of environmental and inherited factors that create vulnerability to abnormal moods remain essentially unknown. However, several lines of research are providing important clues about the type of biological processes underlying moods and their disorders. The established approaches of neurochemistry and pharmacology that gave rise to the present generation of antidepressant and mood-stabilising drugs have highlighted the importance of neurotransmitters and cell signalling pathways. Advances in neuroimaging techniques have identified several brain regions showing structural or functional changes in subjects with mood disorders, and cognitive deficits found in patients are in keeping with these imaging findings. It is also now firmly established that genetic factors have a major role in determining the risk of bipolar disorder, and recent developments in genomics and proteomics since the sequencing of the human and mouse genomes are now providing powerful new approaches to the study of these brain disorders. Genetic strategies can identify previously unknown genes as candidates for a role in mood disorders, and it is hoped that elucidating the novel neurochemical pathways and cellular processes in which these genes operate will give a fresh understanding of the biology of complex behaviours and moods.

NEUROIMAGING AND NEUROPSYCHOLOGY OF BIPOLAR DISORDER

Bipolar disorder was traditionally considered an episodic illness showing complete remission of symptoms between bouts of elevated or depressed moods. However, many patients experience significant social impairment between episodes, and different lines of investigation, including brain imaging and neurocognitive assessment, provide evidence of structural or functional brain alterations that are independent of the illness episode. Neuroimaging studies have reported increased size and reduced glucose utilisation in the amygdala and basal ganglia, and parts of the prefrontal cortex appear to be smaller in

Mood Disorders: A Handbook of Science and Practice. Edited by M. Power.
© 2004 John Wiley & Sons, Ltd. ISBN 0-470-84390-X.

bipolar patients than in controls. Phosphorous magnetic resonance spectroscopy (MRS) has revealed abnormalities of membrane phospholipid metabolism in frontal and striatal regions (Strakowski et al., 2000). The subgenual prefrontal cortex, which is part of the cingulate cortex, is of particular interest (Drevets et al., 1997). Abnormalities in this region were first identified in depression; subsequently positron-emission tomography (PET), magnetic resonance imaging (MRI) and post-mortem data have confirmed a significant reduction in grey matter volume in the subgenual prefrontal cortex in bipolar disorder (Ongur et al., 1998). These changes may be a feature of all types of depression; imaging studies have not identified consistent changes specific to bipolar disorder. Overall, there is converging evidence from imaging studies that dysfunctions in the prefrontal cortex, amygdala and striatum play a part in bipolar mood swings.

Investigations of cognitive function in bipolar disorder suggest that patients experience impairment of memory and concentration during periods of illness, and some deficits persist after recovery. During an episode of acute mania, patients show deficits in sustained attention and verbal learning rather than in tests of executive function (Clark, et al., 2001). In some bipolar patients, cognitive deficits persist after the remission of acute symptoms, especially those with a chronic form of illness (Bearden et al., 2001). These studies are difficult to interpret because the states of depression and mania strongly influence the administration of tests and the subjects' motivation to take part. However, there is converging evidence from several studies that bipolar subjects, compared with controls, show impairments in verbal and visuospatial memory, and tasks requiring serial processing and higher-order cognitive functioning, such as abstraction. Results from some, but not all, studies distinguish bipolar from unipolar subjects. In one comparison of neuropsychological performance during an acute depressive episode, patients with bipolar disorder showed a higher degree of cognitive dysfunction connected with frontal lobe activity than patients with unipolar depression (Borkowska & Rybakowski, 2001). The difference between bipolar and unipolar patients could not be accounted for by differences in symptom severity or duration of the illness, and the level of cognitive dysfunction led the authors to suggest that there may be similarities between cognitive deficits observed in bipolar disorder and schizophrenia. Alterations in memory and executive function are not specific to bipolar disorder, and their neural correlates remain extremely speculative, but it has been suggested that these are consistent with impairment in the prefrontal cortex and striatal systems, as identified in imaging studies. A major question is whether the cognitive deficits found in patients during episodes of depression or of mania persist after full recovery when the patient is euthymic. Several studies on this have provided evidence for lasting deficits that are trait- rather than state-related variables. Both good- and poor-outcome bipolar patients performed worse than controls on a number of neuropsychological tests, and after controlling for age, premorbid IQ and depressive symptoms, it was found that executive function was consistently impaired (Ferrier et al., 1999). Another study testing verbal learning, memory and executive function in euthymic patients and in controls found persisting impairment of verbal learning in bipolar subjects when fully recovered from a previous manic or depressive episode (Cavanagh et al., 2002).

PHARMACOLOGY AND NEUROCHEMISTRY OF BIPOLAR DISORDER

Pharmacological treatments are central to the management of bipolar disorder in the acute phase and for the prevention of further episodes. Theories of the neurochemical basis of bipolar disorder have traditionally been based on knowledge of the targets of drugs known to be effective in the treatment of depression and mania, drugs known to cause mood changes and mood stabilisers effective in prophylaxis.

One of the earliest biological theories of mood disorder, the monoamine hypothesis, proposed that depression was due to a deficiency of the monoamine neurotransmitters noradrenalin (norepinephrenine), 5-hydroxytryptamine or serotonin (5-HT), and dopamine. This was based on the pharmacology of the first effective antidepressant drugs, the tricyclic antidepressants and monoamineoxidase inhibitors, which are known to increase the availability of monoamines at the synapse, in contrast to drugs, such as reserpine, that deplete monoamines and caused depression. Support came from biochemical and pharmacological studies of neurotransmitters, and their precursors and metabolites in serum, platelets and cerebrospinal fluid (CSF), and in post-mortem brain tissue, where receptor function has been directly and extensively studied (Stahl, 2000). Overall, evidence from these studies has been inconclusive. Direct measurement of brain monoamine receptors in post-mortem tissue has failed to reveal consistent changes linked to mood disorder, apart from the striking and consistent finding of increased $5-HT_2$ receptors in the frontal cortex of suicide victims. Noradrenalin metabolites are reduced in some depressed patients, and the main metabolite of 5-HT, 5-hydroxy indole acetic acid (5HIAA), is reduced in the CSF of depressed subjects.

However, the simple hypothesis that reduced monoamine availability at certain synapses is a cause of depression does not explain the delayed response to antidepressants, for, although antidepressants cause an immediate increase in monoamines, their therapeutic response is felt by the patient sometimes after a delay of several weeks. The focus of research has moved from neurotransmitters and their metabolites to their receptors, the control of gene expression regulating their synthesis and the post-synaptic signalling events of the downstream transmission of synaptic signals.

Long-term prophylaxis with mood stabilisers is an essential element of treatment for most patients. Lithium carbonate, first discovered as a treatment over 50 years ago, remains the first choice of mood stabiliser, firmly backed by clinical trials that prove its efficacy in the treatment and prophylaxis of mania and recurrent depression. The anticonvulsants sodium valproate (or valproate semisodium) and carbamazepine are alternatives to lithium and lamotrigine; moreover, an anticonvulsant is being increasingly used as a second-line treatment.

Post-synaptic signal transduction, the cascade of post-synaptic events set in train by the depolarisation of a monoamine receptor, involves a complex second-messenger system, part of which is the family of proteins called guanine nucleotide-binding proteins (G proteins). These bind to the post-synaptic receptor and are responsible for the further transmission of the signal initiated when the neurotransmitter binds to its receptor at the synapse. A number of enzymes, including inositol, modify the second-messenger system by binding to G proteins, and it is thought that lithium exerts its effects by depleting the level of inositol (Berridge et al., 1989).

The potential importance of the inositol system is enhanced by the recent discovery that three major mood stabilisers, lithium, carbamazepine and sodium valproate, have a common mode of action, causing inositol depletion via the cytoplasmic inositol-regulating protein prolyl oligopeptidase in a model system. Inositol depletion is likely to have an important effect in the regulation of signal transduction and indeed in neuronal growth (Williams et al., 2002). Much attention has been directed to these intracellular signalling pathways. G protein levels and function measured in peripheral blood mononuclear leucocytes are reported to be increased in mania, decreased in depression and altered in post-mortem tissue from bipolar patients. However, no DNA sequence variants associated with bipolar disorder have yet been detected in genes coding for proteins involved in these signal-transduction pathways (Avissar & Schreiber, 2002).

GENETICS OF BIPOLAR DISORDER

It has long been suspected and is now firmly established that bipolar disorder is familial, and there is a 10-fold increase in the risk of illness in a first-degree relative of someone with the disorder compared to the population risk. That this is partly due to genetic rather than purely environmental factors is confirmed by adoption studies and the well-replicated observation that concordance rates are significantly higher in identical than fraternal twins. However, the type of inheritance observed in families with bipolar disorder is not well understood. It is clear that the disorder is not usually caused by the dysfunction of any single gene or even two or three genes, and analysis of the segregation of the illness in families has not provided a clear explanation of how the illness is inherited. Diagnosis is essentially descriptive and is based on symptoms described by patients and observation of their behaviour, and there are no reliable biological markers to validate the descriptive definition. The disorder is most probably heterogeneous, encompassing several distinct disorders each with a different genetic basis. For example, an early age of onset or a maternal inheritance pattern may identify two subtypes. Some studies of the segregation of the disorder in families support a model in which single genes of large effect cause illness in families, and different genes are responsible for illness in different families (major genes with locus heterogeneity). This model is supported by some segregation analyses and linkage studies in large families (Blackwood et al., 2001; Blangero & Elston, 1989; Rice et al., 1987; Spence et al., 1995). However, there is evidence that subtypes of the disorder may be the result of the presence of several additive or interacting genes, each one alone being neither sufficient nor necessary for illness to develop (polygenic model). Further complexity arises when we consider other genetic effects that may be important in some forms of the illness. So-called epigenetic phenomena include anticipation, defined as an increase in illness severity and progressively earlier age at onset with each generation. The importance of anticipation, for which there is some evidence in familial bipolar disorder, is that, if present, it suggests a possible molecular mechanism to explain the clinical phenomenon. Other disorders showing anticipation, such as Huntington's disease, are caused by the expansion of unstable repeat DNA sequences in genes. Two other epigenetic phenomena of possible relevance to bipolar disorder are imprinting, describing a different expression of a disease when transmitted maternally as opposed to paternally, and mitochondrial inheritance, caused by a mutation in the mitochondrial genome, in which the disease is always transmitted from the maternal side. Each of these genetic hypotheses suggests candidate genes that have been investigated by linkage and association studies, as decribed below.

LINKAGE STUDIES

The success of linkage studies as the first step in mapping genes in other complex disorders, including Alzheimer's disease, diabetes and breast cancer, has given a strong stimulus to the search for genes in bipolar disorder (Baron, 2002; Craddock et al., 2001; Potash & DePaulo,

2000). Genetic linkage studies involve families where two or more members are affected by illness. The statistical analyses aim to detect the cosegregation of a genetic marker with the disease phenotype in a family. Studies can be based on extended, multiply affected families or collections of sibling pairs where both siblings are affected. Before the era of molecular genetics, one of the first linkages to be reported in bipolar disorder was with colour blindness and the glucose-6-phosphate dehydrogenase locus, highlighting the possibility of an X chromosome locus in bipolar disorder, since both of these markers were known to be on the X chromosome. Initial reports were not replicated, but subsequent linkage studies have maintained interest in a possible locus of bipolar disorder on the X chromosome (Baron, 2002). As a product of the Human Genome Project, many thousands of polymorphic markers are now available. These include microsatellites and single nucleotide polymorphisms (SNPs), each precisely mapped to a known location on a chromosome. Today, sequencing techniques can be used to detect SNPs directly, and a huge number have been generated by the SNP-mapping consortium and other sources, allowing the detailed mapping of large stretches of the genome (Taylor et al., 2001). In a typical linkage study, a series of polymorphic DNA markers, evenly spaced across the region of interest (that may include the whole genome), are typed with DNA obtained from family members. Typically, about 400 evenly spaced microsatellite markers may be used in a genome-wide scan for linkage. During the past decade, family linkage studies have identified several chromosome regions likely to harbour genes implicated in bipolar disorder. Recent results have been encouraging, and several chromosome regions have been identified in more than one linkage study. Chromosome regions where linkage has been confirmed or is suggestive include 1q, 4p, 6p, 10p, 10q, 12q, 13q, 18p, 18q, 21q, 22q and Xp. Further linkage studies may show that some of these are false-positive findings, but it is likely that some are true linkages. The task of finding genes in these regions by methods of association (linkage disequilibrium mapping) and direct sequencing of candidate genes is not trivial, because linkage typically has low resolution for locating genes and defines a broad chromosome region. For example, the candidate region identified by linkage on chromosome 4 may contain around 50 genes, several of which are good candidates for a role in mental disorders.

ASSOCIATION STUDIES

Linkage and association studies assume the existence of a DNA variant that, by altering the expression of a gene, changes a person's risk of developing illness. However, association studies test this assumption by comparing the distribution of different types of a DNA variant (alleles) in populations of "affecteds" and "unaffecteds" (Cardon & Bell, 2001). When a candidate gene has been identified, direct DNA sequencing may reveal mutations that cause the expression of the gene to change.

In the absence of a clearly biological hypothesis, the choice of candidate genes is large because almost any gene expressed in the brain can be construed as a possible candidate for bipolar disorder. In practice, candidates have been selected for several reasons. Positive linkage studies or consistent chromosome abnormalities in patients with bipolar disorder can provide pointers to a particular chromosomal region (candidate loci). Candidates may also arise from assumptions made about proteins or systems of proteins connected with the assumed underlying pathology of the illness, or from our knowledge of the targets of drugs that are useful in treating the disorder (candidate genes).

A major limitation of the candidate-gene approach is our incomplete knowledge of the neurochemistry and pathophysiology of bipolar disorders, so that a reasonable case can be argued to include almost any of the 10 000 genes known to be expressed in the human brain in a list of candidate genes worth investigating. A second difficulty of candidate gene association is that bipolar disorder is a heterogeneous group of conditions, and very large sample sizes are required to detect small population effects. To date, the results of association studies have been inconclusive.

Candidate gene association studies

POSITIONAL CANDIDATES

Genes mapped within narrow regions of chromosomes 4, 12, 18 and 22, where strong evidence for linkage in families has been reported, are being systematically studied.

NEUROTRANSMITTER SYSTEMS

A large proportion of candidate-gene studies have focused on key enzymes and proteins involved in dopamine-norepinephrine- and serotonin-based neurotransmitter systems. Among the first candidates to be studied by association analysis was the gene for tyrosine hydroxylase, a rate-limiting enzyme in the metabolism of catecholamines. The apparent success of linkage to chromosome 11p15 in the large Old Order Amish kindreds with multiple cases of bipolar disorder (Egeland et al., 1987) led to further studies of genes in the area. Initial promising results (Leboyer et al., 1990) were followed by a series of conflicting, but overall negative studies (Furlong et al., 1999; Turecki et al., 1997). This story has been repeated for many of the other candidates subsequently investigated, and, at present, even partly replicated findings have to be approached with some caution.

The enzyme catechol-*o*-methyl transferase (COMT) is also involved in the degradation of monoamines. The gene coding for this enzyme is associated with a common and functional polymorphism that alters the activity of the protein. Alleles associated with low enzyme activity may increase the likelihood of developing bipolar illness and increase the likelihood that the illness will take a rapid cycling form (Kirov et al., 1998). Monoamine oxidase (MAO) is another key enzyme in amine metabolism. There are several forms of the enzyme, and the gene for type A has been quite extensively studied. A modest association has been found between forms of the microsatellite polymorphism and the likelihood of bipolar disorder, especially in females; the gene is on the X chromosome (Furlong et al., 1999; Preisig et al., 2000).

Specific serotonin reuptake inhibitors (SSRIs) are a mainstay of pharmacotherapy in the treatment of depressive phases of bipolar disorder. It is logical that their substrate, the human serotonin reuptake transporter (hSERT), and its gene on the long arm of chromosome 17 have been the focus of intensive study. A polymorphism (a variable number tandem repeat [VNTR]) affects the function of the gene, and there is evidence that the 12-repeat allele modestly increases the susceptibility to bipolar disorder in Caucasian populations (Craddock et al., 2001). The effect is relatively small, but studies have been consistent, and the concept of a secondary "push" on top of another more substantial genetic weighting factor (or factors) could explain some of the variability in the penetrance of the condition. The primary function of aminergic neurotransmitters is to interact with a post-synaptic receptor to achieve their signalling actions. These membrane-bound receptor proteins are key candidates for dysfunction in bipolar illness. The serotonergic receptor system has been examined both at the sequence level (Shimron-Abarbanell et al., 1996) and by association analysis for seven of the 5-HT receptor types, with very mixed results and with both positive and negative findings in abundance (Potash & DePaulo, 2000).

Dopaminergic receptors have perhaps been more extensively studied in patients with schizophrenia than bipolar disorder, and here again the results have been mixed (Potash & DePaulo, 2000). An interesting example is *DRD5*, the gene encoding the type 5 dopamine receptor, which is found especially in the limbic and frontal cortex in human brain. This is strongly associated with schizophrenia, but not bipolar disorder (Muir et al., 2001), and yet it lies within the region of highest linkage (at 4p16.3) in a large Scottish family with bipolar disorder (Blackwood et al., 1996). The gene for wolframin, the protein involved in Wolfram's syndrome, which is commonly associated with psychiatric disorders, is also in the region, although it is not mutated in the Scottish bipolar pedigree. The *DRD3* gene codes for the type 3 dopamine receptor, and its localisation is largely confined to limbic brain regions. Although it is postulated to have a role in the precipitation of mania by dopamine agonists, studies of relevant polymorphisms have not shown convincing evidence for association in bipolar disorder.

The confusing results that emerge from association studies of neurotransmitter systems may arise because the studies are too small to detect genes that are relatively rare in the population as a whole or have a small individual effect in causing disease that has polygenic causation.

GENES INVOLVED IN INTRACELLULAR SIGNAL TRANSDUCTION

There has been a great deal of recent interest in the part played by intracellular signalling cascades in both the genesis of mood disorders and the actions of pharmacotherapeutic agents. Common to these has been the realisation that the adult brain is a much more functionally and anatomically plastic organ than previously thought, and that changes in neuronal intracellular messenger cascades are vitally important in controlling such changes (Manji & Lenox, 2000). Long-term stress has been shown to induce neuronal apoptosis and prevent neurogenesis in the hippocampus, and several studies have suggested that severe mood disorders can induce significant damage (perhaps by glucocorticoid overactivity) in key brain regions thought to be affected in bipolar disorder, such as the hippocampus (Manji et al., 2001).

Antidepressants and mood stabilisers, such as lithium, are known to have important effects on intracellular signalling mechanisms that influence cellular plasticity and apoptosis, in a time-dependent fashion that more closely mimics their clinical activity than direct effects on the extracellular neurotransmitter systems. Of the intracellular mechanisms, the protein cascades that involve cyclic (c) AMP are especially interesting. Long-term antidepressant medication (various classes) increases intracellular levels of cAMP and activates the intranuclear response elements, including cAMP response element-binding protein (CREB) and brain-derived neurotrophic factor (BDNF), via the protein kinase A system (Vaidya & Duman, 2001). BDNF is thought to play a crucial role in neuronal plasticity and survival, perhaps via the antiapoptotic activities of bcl-2 proteins. The phosphodiesterase PDE4 is involved in the cytoplasmic breakdown of cAMP, and inhibitors such as rolipram have an antidepressant effect, again potentially by the chronic upregulation of the CREB–BDNF system via cAMP.

The intracellular signalling cascades provide many candidates for association studies with bipolar disorder, but few studies have been conducted. The G protein-coupled receptor kinase-3 gene (*GRK-3*) is located at 22q11 near the velocardiofacial region (see below), and its expression was decreased in a family with bipolar disorder. The gene for inositol monophosphatase type 2 is located at 18p11.2, where there is evidence of linkage in bipolar disorder (Kato, 2001).

TRIPLET REPEATS AND ANTICIPATION

Trinucleotide repeats consist of three nucleotides consecutively repeated within a region of DNA. The commonest of these comprise of strings of the nucleotide sequence (CGG), (CAG) or (CTG). Their presence may confer instability on a gene because they are prone to undergo a novel type of mutation known as triplet repeat, expansion, a dynamic mutation that results in an expansion of the length of the repeat, sometimes to hundreds of bases, that ultimately disrupts gene function. Diseases caused by trinucleotide repeat expansion include Huntington's disease and fragile X syndrome, and the mechanism, though not yet fully understood, explains some of the unusual nonmendelian patterns of inheritance found in these disorders. Unstable repeats have the property of extending in length during meiosis, and this leads to the clinical phenomenon of "anticipation", which describes the increase in severity of symptoms of illness and a progressively earlier age at onset in successive generations. Longer expansions cause greater disruption of gene function, leading to greater severity of illness. Analysis of bipolar pedigrees has been consistent with anticipation, showing, on average, a 6–10-year advance in age at onset from one generation to the next (Margolis et al., 1999), although the interpretation of the apparent anticipation is confounded by other population trends in age of onset (Visscher et al., 2001). Several studies have reported association between bipolar disorder and CAG and CTG repeats in the genome, but a role for repeats has not been confirmed by the analysis of any single candidate gene. Repeat expansion remains an interesting but unconfirmed possibility in a subgroup of bipolar disorder.

THE MITOCHONDRIAL HYPOTHESIS OF BIPOLAR DISORDER

Genomic imprinting mediated by DNA methylation was proposed as the explanation of an apparent bias towards paternal inheritance in linkage to chromosome 18p in bipolar disorder following the observation that around 20% of families collected for a linkage study appeared to be maternally inherited (McMahon et al., 1995; Stine et al., 1995). Mitochondrial inheritance is another possible explanation of maternal inheritance in a subgroup of families (Kato & Kato, 2000). There are single case reports of patients comorbid with depression and known mitochondrial diseases. In human postmortem brain tissue, an increase in a deletion in mitochondrial (mt)DNA was found, but the frequency of this deletion was not sufficient to have clinical effect. Two mtDNA polymorphisms that caused amino-acid substitutions were significantly associated with bipolar disorder. However, the mitochondrial hypothesis was not supported when the whole mitochondrial genome was sequenced in nine bipolar probands from families showing exclusively maternal transmission (McMahon et al., 2000). There were no differences in the frequency of mtDNA haplotypes between bipolar patients and controls, although a small effect was found with one polymorphism that had previously been associated in a Japanese study.

PHARMACOGENOMICS

Association studies are a useful way to study the response of individuals to drug treatments. A goal of pharmacogenomic research is to detect genetic variation that predicts a person's response to a particular type of treatment and to measure the likelihood of unwanted side effects to drugs, information that could save unnecessary prescribing and reduce the incidence of adverse reactions. Determining the rates of drug metabolism mediated by the cytochrome system and the detection of good and poor responders to lithium by measuring variants of the gene are two examples of this approach.

GENE-EXPRESSION ANALYSIS

New tools for measuring the expression of genes on a large scale are now available with oligonucleotide or cDNA microarrays and by proteomic technologies (Avissar & Schreiber, 2002). Advances in genomics and proteomics make it possible to screen very large numbers of candidate genes and proteins. One example of this approach was a study in which methamphetamine-treated rats were used as a model for mania (Niculescu et al., 2000). Gene expression in specific brain regions was compared in treated and untreated animals by oligonucleotide microarrays. Amphetamine administration led to changes in the expression of several genes in rat cortex, and the human homologues of these genes were considered candidates for a role in the pathogenesis of bipolar disorder, including a G-protein coupled receptor kinase (*GRK3*). This was selected for further examination, as it was mapped to a region of chromosome 22 where linkage to bipolar disorder had previously been reported and weak evidence for association to illness was reported. A parallel approach is to use proteomic technology to survey post-mortem brain material to detect subtle alterations of protein linked to bipolar disorder. In one study, the levels of proteins in the frontal cortex were compared in post-mortem tissue from individuals with bipolar disorder, schizophrenia and depression, and eight protein species displayed disease-specific alterations in the frontal cortex. Positional cloning strategies, microarray methods for genome analysis and proteomic technologies are powerful new methods to identify completely novel pathogenic mechanisms of bipolar disorder.

CYTOGENETIC STUDIES MAY HELP TO LOCALISE GENES CONTRIBUTING TO BIPOLAR DISORDER

Cloning genes disrupted by chromosome rearrangements has been a very fruitful approach for a wide variety of inherited neurological conditions. In contrast to linkage and association studies, where the results, even if positive, define broad areas at the molecular level, abnormalities of chromosomes can precisely pinpoint the position of disrupted genes (Evans et al., 2001).

One of the earliest areas of interest was chromosome 21, stemming from the long-held idea that Down's syndrome (trisomy 21) as a condition is mutually exclusive with bipolar disorder. This is not the case, and there are good descriptions of both mania and depression in Down's syndrome, although the risk of bipolar disorder may be decreased, and unipolar disorder is held by some to be increased in frequency. Trisomies involving the sex chromosomes have also been implicated, but the initial studies were not well controlled, and more recent work has not provided good evidence that they are a substantial risk factor for bipolar disorder (Mors et al., 2001).

Carriers of a reciprocal translocation t(1;11)(q42.2;q21), which was stably inherited in a large Scottish pedigree, were shown to have very high rates of major psychiatric illness when compared to non-carriers. The strongest evidence for linkage (Lod score of 7.1) was found with a phenotype that included both schizophrenia and affective psychosis—with cases of bipolar and recurrent unipolar disorder in translocation carriers (Blackwood et al., 2001; St Clair et al., 1990).

Candidate genes for schizophrenia and bipolar disorder isolated by a direct molecular genetic analysis of the breakpoint, *DISC1* and *DISC2*, were detected by cloning of a translocation breakpoint that disrupted their exonic structure (Millar et al., 2000).

A small pedigree has been described with a t(9;11)(p24;q23.1) translocation where five carriers had bipolar disorder and one had early-onset recurrent major depression that co-segregated with affective disorder. There are four unaffected carriers, but the pedigree is probably too small to yield to linkage analysis (Baysal et al., 1998). However, recently, a mannosyltransferase gene has been shown to be disrupted by the chromosome 11q23 breakpoint (Baysal et al., 2002). This has been labelled *DIBD1* (disrupted in bipolar disorder 1), a 15-exon brain-expressed gene that is possibly involved in protein *n*-glycosylation. Linkage analyses in two separate sets of NIMH bipolar pedigrees did not yield conclusive results, but one polymorphic marker pair did show evidence of increased allele sharing in the first series of multiplex pedigrees. Further studies on this gene will be interesting, and, as the region is also a "hot spot" for schizophrenia, it may also be one that transcends the usual diagnostic boundaries.

A recent and striking observation has been made of a high rate of affective psychosis in patients with Prader-Willi syndrome, especially where this has originated through uniparental disomy of chromosome 15 (Boer et al., 2002). This region contains several imprinted genes that could be candidates. A similar situation where a contiguous gene syndrome may be associated with bipolar disorder is the Velocardiofacial syndrome, involving an interstitial deletion on chromosome 22 (Papolos et al., 1996; Pulver et al., 1994). This deletion includes several genes, and the completion of the full sequence of chromosome 22 should rapidly yield candidate genes for further testing in the general population.

A cross-referencing search of two large cytogenetic registers, one in Scotland and the other in Denmark, revealed two unrelated individuals with the rare pericentric inversion inv(18) (p11.3q21.1), in which one subject had schizophrenia and the other bipolar disorder (Mors et al., 1997). Linkage has been reported at both breakpoint regions for schizophrenia and bipolar disorder. A breakpoint at 18q22.1 was also reported in a patient with schizoaffective disorder by Overhauser et al. (1998), and two related individuals with a translocation at 18q22.3 were diagnosed as having schizoaffective disorder and bipolar disorder (Calzolari et al., 1996).

FUTURE DIRECTIONS

Despite promising positive linkage findings, no genes have been identified as being un-equivocally involved in bipolar disorder. However, powerful new approaches are becoming available to elucidate the neurobiological basis of the disorder. These include microarrays in genomics and proteomics, permitting the rapid, simultaneous screening of many genes and proteins in large patient samples. Another development is the combination of struc-tural brain imaging with a candidate-gene approach that has shown, in a recent study, an association between a variant of the serotonin transporter gene and increased neuronal ac-tivity in the amygdala, as assessed by functional magnetic resonance imaging (Hariri et al., 2002).

REFERENCES

Avissar, S. & Schreiber, G. (2002). Toward molecular diagnostics of mood disorders in psychiatry. *Trends Mol Med, 8*, 294–300.

Baron, M. (2002). Manic-depression genes and the new millennium: poised for discovery. *Mol Psychiatry, 7*, 342–358.

Baysal, B.E., Potkin, S.G., Farr, J.E., et al. (1998). Bipolar affective disorder partially cosegregates with a balanced t(9;11)(p24;q23.1) chromosomal translocation in a small pedigree. *Am J Med Genet, 81*, 81–91.

Baysal, B.E., Willett-Brozick, J.E., Badner, J.A., et al. (2002). A mannosyltransrerase gene at 11q23 is disrupted by a translocation breakpoint that co-segregates with bipolar affective disorder in a small family. *Neurogenetics, 4*, 43–53.

Bearden, C.E., Hoffman, K.M. & Cannon, T.D. (2001). The neuropsychology and neuroanatomy of bipolar affective disorder: a critical review. *Bipolar Disord, 3*, 106–150; discussion 151–153.

Berridge, M.J., Downes, C.P. & Hanley M.R. (1989). Neural and developmental actions of lithium: a unifying hypothesis. *Cell, 59*, 411–419.

Blackwood, D.H., He, L., Morris, S.W., et al. (1996). A locus for bipolar affective disorder on chromosome 4p. *Nat Genet, 12*, 427–430.

Blackwood, D.H., Fordyce, A., Walker, M.T., St Clair, D.M., Porteous, D.J. & Muir, W.J. (2001). Schizophrenia and affective disorders—cosegregation with a translocation at chromosome 1q42 that directly disrupts brain-expressed genes: clinical and P300 findings in a family. *Am J Hum Genet, 69*, 428–433.

Blackwood, D.H., Visscher, P.M. & Muir, W.J. (2001). Genetic studies of bipolar affective disorder in large families. *Br J Psychiatry Suppl, 41*, s134–136.

Blangero, J. & Elston, R.C. (1989). Familial analysis of bipolar affective disorder using logistic models. *Genet Epidemiol, 6*, 221–227.

Boer, H., Holland, A., Whittington, J., Butler, J., Webb, T. & Clarke, D. (2002). Psychotic illness in people with Prader Willi syndrome due to chromosome 15 maternal uniparental disomy. *Lancet, 359*(9301), 135–136.

Borkowska, A. & Rybakowski, J.K. (2001). Neuropsychological frontal lobe tests indicate that bipolar depressed patients are more impaired than unipolar. *Bipolar Disord, 3*, 88–94.

Calzolari, E., Aiello, V., Palazzi, P., et al. (1996). Psychiatric disorder in a familial 15;18 translocation and sublocalization of myelin basic protein of 18q22.3. *Am J Med Genet, 67*, 154–161.

Cardon, L.R. & Bell, J.I. (2001). Association study designs for complex diseases. *Nat Rev Genet, 2*, 91–99.

Cavanagh, J.T., Van Beck, M., Muir, W. & Blackwood, D.H. (2002). Case-control study of neuro-cognitive function in euthymic patients with bipolar disorder: an association with mania. *Br J Psychiatry, 180*, 320–326.

Clark, L., Iversen, S.D. & Goodwin G.M. (2001). A neuropsychological investigation of prefrontal cortex involvement in acute mania. *Am J Psychiatry, 158*, 1605–1611.

Craddock, N., Dave, S. & Greening, J. (2001). Association studies of bipolar disorder. *Bipolar Disorders, 3*, 284–298.

Drevets, W.C., Price, J.L. & Simpson, J.R., Jr., et al. (1997). Subgenual prefrontal cortex abnormalities in mood disorders. *Nature, 386*(6627), 824–827.

Egeland, J.A., Gerhard, D.S., Pauls, D.L., et al. (1987). Bipolar affective disorders linked to DNA markers on chromosome 11. *Nature, 325*(6107), 783–787.

Evans, K.L., Muir, W.J., Blackwood, D.H. & Porteous, D.J. (2001). Nuts and bolts of psychiatric genetics: building on the Human Genome Project. *Trends Genet, 17*, 35–40.

Ferrier, I.N., Stanton, B.R., Kelly, T.P. & Scott, J. (1999). Neuropsychological function in euthymic patients with bipolar disorder. *Br J Psychiatry, 175*, 246–251.

Furlong, R.A., Rubinsztein, J.S., Ho, L., et al. (1999). Analysis and metaanalysis of two polymorphisms within the tyrosine hydroxylase gene in bipolar and unipolar affective disorders. *Am J Med Genet, 88*, 88–94.

Furlong, R.A., Ho, L., Rubinsztein, J.S., Walsh, C., Paykel, E.S. & Rubinsztein, D.C. (1999). Analysis of the monoamine oxidase A (MAOA) gene in bipolar affective disorder by association studies, meta-analyses, and sequencing of the promoter. *Am J Med Genet, 88*, 398–406.

Hariri, A.R., Mattay, V.S., Tessitore, A., et al. (2002). Serotonin transporter genetic variation and the response of the human amygdala. *Science, 297*(5580), 400–403.

Kato, T. (2001). Molecular genetics of bipolar disorder. *Neurosci Res, 40*, 105–113.

Kato, T. & Kato N. (2000). Mitochondrial dysfunction in bipolar disorder. *Bipolar Disord, 2*(3 Pt 1), 180–190.

Kirov, G., Murphy, K.C., Arranz, M.J., et al. (1998). Low activity allele of catechol-*O*-methyltransferase gene associated with rapid cycling bipolar disorder. *Mol Psychiatry, 3*, 342–345.

Leboyer, M., Malafosse, A., Boularand, S., et al. (1990). Tyrosine hydroxylase polymorphisms associated with manic-depressive illness. *Lancet, 335*(8699), 1219.

Manji, H.K. & Lenox, R.H. (2000). Signaling: cellular insights into the pathophysiology of bipolar disorder. *Biol Psychiatry, 48*, 518–530.

Manji, H.K., Drevets, W.C. & Charney, D.S. (2001). The cellular neurobiology of depression. *Nat Med, 7*, 541–547.

Margolis, R.L., McInnis, M.G., Rosenblatt, A. & Ross, C.A. (1999). Trinucleotide repeat expansion and neuropsychiatric disease. *Arch Gen Psychiatry, 56*, 1019–1031.

McMahon, F.J., Stine, O.C., Meyers, D.A., Simpson, S.G. & DePaulo, J.R. (1995). Patterns of maternal transmission in bipolar affective disorder. *Am J Hum Genet, 56*, 1277–1286.

McMahon, F.J., Chen, Y.S., Patel, S., et al. (2000). Mitochondrial DNA sequence diversity in bipolar affective disorder. *Am J Psychiatry, 157*, 1058–1064.

Millar, J.K., Wilson-Annan, J.C., Anderson, S. et al. (2000). Disruption of two novel genes by a translocation co-segregating with schizophrenia. *Hum Mol Genet, 9*, 1415–1423.

Mors, O., Ewald, H., Blackwood, D. & Muir, W. (1997). Cytogenetic abnormalities on chromosome 18 associated with bipolar affective disorder or schizophrenia. *Br J Psychiatry, 170*, 278–280.

Mors, O., Mortensen, P.B. & Ewald, H. (2001). No evidence of increased risk for schizophrenia or bipolar affective disorder in persons with aneuploidies of the sex chromosomes. *Psychol Med, 31*, 425–430.

Muir, W.J., Thomson, M.L., McKeon, P., et al. (2001). Markers close to the dopamine D5 receptor gene (DRD5) show significant association with schizophrenia but not bipolar disorder. *Am J Med Genet, 105*, 152–158.

Niculescu, A.B., III, Segal, D.S., Kuczenski, R., Barrett, T., Hauger, R.L. & Kelsoe, J.R. (2000). Identifying a series of candidate genes for mania and psychosis: a convergent functional genomics approach. *Physiol Genomics, 4*, 83–91.

Ongur, D., Drevets, W.C. & Price, J.L. (1998). Glial reduction in the subgenual prefrontal cortex in mood disorders. *Proc Natl Acad Sci USA, 95*, 13290–13295.

Overhauser, J., Berrettini, W.H. & Rojas, K. (1998). Affective disorder associated with a balanced translocation involving chromosome 14 and 18. *Psychiatr Genet, 8*, 53–56.

Papolos, D.F., Faedda, G.L., Veit, S., et al. (1996). Bipolar spectrum disorders in patients diagnosed with velo-cardio- facial syndrome: does a hemizygous deletion of chromosome 22q11 result in bipolar affective disorder? *Am J Psychiatry, 153*, 1541–1547.

Potash, J.B. & DePaulo, J.R., Jr. (2000). Searching high and low: a review of the genetics of bipolar disorder. *Bipolar Disord, 2,* 8–26.

Preisig, M., Bellivier, F., Fenton, B.T., et al. (2000). Association between bipolar disorder and monoamine oxidase A gene polymorphisms: results of a multicenter study. *Am J Psychiatry, 157,* 948–955.

Pulver, A.E., Nestadt, G., Goldberg, R., et al. (1994). Psychotic illness in patients diagnosed with velo-cardio-facial syndrome and their relatives. *J Nerv Ment Dis, 182,* 476–478.

Rice, J., Reich, T., Andreasen, N.C., et al. (1987). The familial transmission of bipolar illness. *Arch Gen Psychiatry, 44,* 441–447.

Shimron-Abarbanell, D., Harms, H., Erdmann, J., et al. (1996). Systematic screening for mutations in the human serotonin 1F receptor gene in patients with bipolar affective disorder and schizophrenia. *Am J Med Genet, 67,* 225–228.

Spence, M.A., Flodman, P.L., Sadovnick, A.D., Bailey-Wilson, J.E., Ameli, H. & Remick, R.A. (1995). Bipolar disorder: evidence for a major locus. *Am J Med Genet, 60,* 370–376.

St Clair, D., Blackwood, D., Muir, W., et al. (1990). Association within a family of a balanced autosomal translocation with major mental illness. *Lancet, 336,* 13–16.

Stahl, S. (2000). *Essential Psychopharmacology of Depression and Bipolar Disorder,* Cambridge University Press.

Stine, O.C., Xu, J., Koskela, R., et al. (1995). Evidence for linkage of bipolar disorder to chromosome 18 with a parent-of-origin effect. *Am J Hum Genet, 57,* 1384–1394.

Strakowski, S.M., DelBello, M.P., Adler, C., Cecll, D.M. & Sax K.W. (2000). Neuroimaging in bipolar disorder. *Bipolar Disord, 2*(3 Pt 1), 148–164.

Taylor, J.G., Choi, E.H., Foster, C.B. & Chanock, S.J. (2001). Using genetic variation to study human disease. *Trends Mol Med, 7,* 507–512.

Turecki, G., Rouleau, G.A., Mari, J., Joober, R. & Morgan, K. (1997). Lack of association between bipolar disorder and tyrosine hydroxylase: a meta-analysis. *Am J Med Genet, 74,* 348–352.

Vaidya, V.A. & Duman, R.S. (2001). Depresssion—emerging insights from neurobiology. *BMJ, 57,* 61–79.

Visscher, P.M., Yazdi, M.H., Jackson, A.D., et al. (2001). Genetic survival analysis of age-at-onset of bipolar disorder: evidence for anticipation or cohort effect in families. *Psychiatr Genet, 11,* 129–137.

Williams, R.S., Cheng, L., Mudge, A.W. & Harwood, A.J. (2002). A common mechanism of action for three mood-stabilizing drugs. *Nature, 417*(6886), 292–295.

12

BIPOLAR AFFECTIVE DISORDER: CURRENT PERSPECTIVES ON PSYCHOLOGICAL THEORY AND TREATMENT

Kim Wright and Dominic Lam

While extensive research into unipolar depressive disorder has resulted in the formulation of various cognitive and behavioural models (e.g., Abramson et al., 1978; Beck, 1967; Lewinsohn, 1974), comprehensive psychological theories of bipolar disorder remain limited in terms of both quantity and empirical support. Some studies comparing the somatic and cognitive symptoms of unipolar and bipolar depression have concluded that the two states are very similar, while others have found differences in the prevalence of symptoms such as psychomotor agitation, anxiety and irritability (Depue & Monroe, 1978; Mitchell et al., 1992). Thus, at present, difficulties exist in applying the findings of unipolar research to the study of bipolar disorder. Moreover, despite depressive symptoms often being present during a manic episode, any comprehensive model of bipolar disorder must account for the development of manic symptoms as well as for those of depression: "The salient fact to bear in mind when contemplating these switches of hedonic capacity is that it is the same person, with the same developmental history and a constant environment, who cycles between, for example, incompetent versus omnipotent self-perceptions" (Carroll, 1994).

In this chapter, we will consider two theories of bipolar affective disorder that have the potential to account for both ends of the bipolar spectrum: a cognitive behavioural approach, and a model that proposes dysregulation of the behavioural activation system (BAS). Both are psychobiological in nature, acknowledging the strong evidence for a genetic contribution to the condition (e.g., Allen et al., 1974; Bertelsen et al., 1977; Cardno et al., 1999; Kringlen, 1967; Mendlewicz & Rainer, 1977), while proposing a mediating role for cognitive factors in the expression of biological vulnerability. The two approaches converge, and it will be suggested that, taken together, they provide direction for the further development of psychological interventions as well as support for current clinical practice.

Mood Disorders: A Handbook of Science and Practice. Edited by M. Power.
© 2004 John Wiley & Sons, Ltd. ISBN 0-470-84390-X.

COGNITIVE BEHAVIOURAL MODEL

Cognitive therapy is guided by the principle that thinking, behaviour, mood and physical state can affect each other. The cognitive model for bipolar affective disorder that we propose is largely based on the generic cognitive model for affective disorder (Beck, 1967). According to Beck's cognitive theory of affective disorder, individuals with extreme dysfunctional assumptions are prone to developing affective disorders such as depression. These assumptions are latent when the individuals are outside a mood episode. However, in the face of a congruent life event, these assumptions are activated and may lead to a mood episode such as depression. Once in a depressive state, the individual is prone to make thinking errors and to experience negative automatic thoughts.

The following model is largely pragmatic and takes into account the complex picture of biological, psychological and social elements surrounding manic depression. Figure 12.1 summarises the cognitive model of bipolar affective disorder, which is discussed below in terms of the interaction between dysfunctional cognitions, behaviour, biological vulnerability and mood.

Dysfunctional attitudes

Beck (1983) proposed that individuals in a manic phase can exhibit an autonomous tendency and individuals in a depressive state can exhibit a tendency towards over-dependence upon others. Within the cognitive model framework, it is also postulated by Lam et al. (1999) that extreme achievement-orientated attitudes in bipolar affective disorder might lead to extreme striving behaviour and irregular daily routine. Lam et al. (in press) carried out a principal component analysis of the Dysfunctional Attitude Scale for 143 bipolar 1 patients. Four factors were derived: (1) "goal-attainment", (2) "dependency", (3) "achievement" and (4) "antidependency". No significant differences were found when the validation sample was compared with 109 patients suffering from unipolar depression in any of the four factors. However, the DAS scores correlated significantly with the depression scores. When subjects who were likely to be in a major depressive episode were excluded and any residual depression symptoms controlled for, the scores of bipolar patients were significantly higher than euthymic unipolar patients in factor 1 ("goal-attainment") and factor 4 ("antidependency").

The goal-attainment subscale appears to capture the risky attitudes described earlier. Examples of the goal-attainment subscale are as follows: "I should be happy all the time", "A person should do well at everything he undertakes", "I ought to be able to solve problems quickly and without a great deal of effort" and "If I try hard enough, I should be able to excel at anything I attempt". The antidependency subscale consists of two items (see Figure 12.1), which are congruent with the tendency towards autonomy proposed previously.

Lam et al. also found that, as postulated by Beck (1983), depressed bipolar patients exhibit similar dependency needs to those expressed by patients suffering from unipolar depression. However, in this study, the euthymic bipolar subjects also endorsed beliefs centring on antidependency, and to a significantly greater extent than did the euthymic unipolar subjects. This difference remained despite the inclusion of those subjects with depressive symptoms. Hence, the evidence suggests that bipolar individuals may have ambivalent attitudes of wanting to depend on and validate their personal worth via others and yet at the same time want to be independent from others.

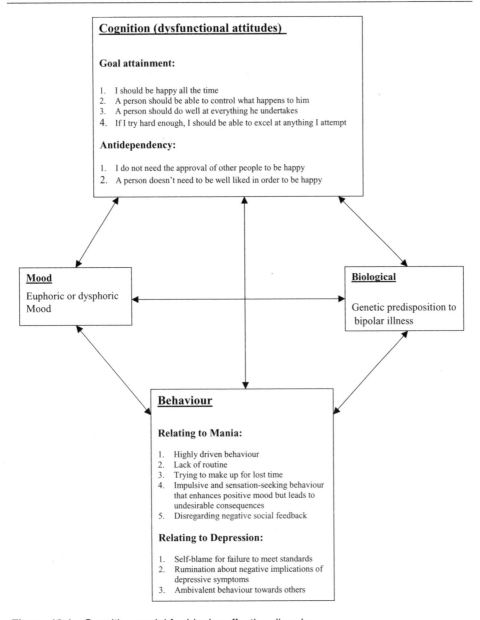

Figure 12.1 Cognitive model for bipolar affective disorder

Goal-attainment, autonomy and the development of mania

Two previous studies have suggested a link between goal achievement and the development of mania: Lozano and Johnson (2001) found achievement-striving scores predictive of increases in manic symptoms, while an earlier study found goal-attainment life events to be predictive of increases in manic symptoms, whereas more general positive life events were not (Johnson et al., 1999).

The extremely high goal-attainment beliefs described above may lead to working excessively long hours, and seeking activities that may lead to positive mood but are impulsive and may have long-term undesirable consequences. Furthermore, as a way of coping with frequent relapses and hospitalisation, patients with these high goal-attainment goals may engage in extreme and driven behaviour, such as overworking to "make up for lost time", due to their illness episodes. This behaviour may disrupt the individual's important social routines, such as regular meal times and regular exercise. Disruption of routine and sleep can lead to a bipolar episode: empirically, there is evidence that life events, which disrupt sleep-wake routines, play an important role prior to the onset of a bipolar episode. In the 8 weeks prior to manic episodes, a significantly greater proportion of patients had social rhythm disruption events in the 8-week episode-free control period (Malkoff-Schwartz et al., 1998). Bipolar patients are also known to relapse after long-distance travel or jet lag (American Psychiatric Association, 1994; Healy & Williams, 1989). Clinically, it has been observed that chaos can lead to more episodes; hence, having a regular routine seems very important for bipolar patients. Therefore, extreme attitudes may—through effects upon behaviour—interact with biological vulnerability to precipitate a manic episode.

Extreme beliefs of an autonomous nature may exacerbate the onset of hypomania by motivating the bipolar individual to disregard negative social feedback. As social feedback can aid in identifying the prodromal symptoms of hypomania, this may precipitate increases in hypomanic symptoms.

Goal-striving, dependency and depression

When personal effort is perceived as being successful, the goal-attainment beliefs described may lead to feelings of potency. However, this belief set could lead to feelings of failure and self-blame if the ideal outcome is not achieved. Thus, an individual with these extreme beliefs is particularly vulnerable to marked changes in affect. These changes may exacerbate a biological predisposition to mood fluctuation, and, in turn, depressive symptoms, such as physical retardation, slowed thinking and low mood, might be viewed as further evidence of failure to "do well at everything" or "be happy all the time".

A tendency towards over-dependence upon others appears to be characteristic of both bipolar and unipolar depression (Hollon et at., 1986) and to be mood-state dependent (Miranda & Persons, 1988; Miranda et al., 1998). The findings described previously indicate that in bipolar individuals belief in the importance of autonomy may exist concurrently with feelings of dependency. As the need to depend upon others during depression is at odds with the ideal of autonomous functioning, such a conflicting set of beliefs may generate further perceptions of failure and frustration in bipolar individuals during the depressive phase, and in this way strong autonomous beliefs may act as a maintenance factor in bipolar depression.

BEHAVIOURAL ACTIVATION SYSTEM DYSREGULATION MODEL

Another system that has been considered as a possible site of pathology in bipolar disorder is the behavioural activation system (BAS). The concept of the BAS was derived from investigations of the motivational effects of appetitive and aversive stimuli upon the behaviour of animals (Gray, 1982). The BAS governs approach behaviour, such that it is activated by, and seeks to bring the animal into contact with, conditioned and unconditioned positive incentive stimuli (Gray, 1990). Exposure to reward elicits behavioural patterns associated with BAS activity, such as approach, exploration and engagement, as well as activating underlying processes governed by the BAS. The latter includes incentive-reward motivation and the emotional states of desire and curiosity. Cognitive activity will also be affected, as increased interaction with the environment will produce the need for increased evaluation.

Depue and colleagues (Depue et al., 1987; Goplerud & Depue, 1985) have suggested that in bipolar-spectrum disorders the BAS is poorly regulated, such that the limits that define the extent of BAS variation are weak in these individuals. They note the correspondence between the features that characterise high levels of BAS activity (for example, high non-specific arousal, positive emotion, and engagement in goal-directed activity), and the symptoms of a hypomanic state, as well as observing that disengagement from reward-seeking activities, anhedonia and psychomotor retardation often characterise bipolar depression. In a study of the effects of naturally occurring stress on BAS level, Goplerud and Depue (1985) found that, after a stressful event, cyclothymic individuals took longer than did normal controls to return to baseline levels of BAS functioning. This suggests that in bipolar spectrum disorders, BAS dysregulation may exist not in terms of the initial appearance of a mood state, but in the inability of the system to return the mood state to its set point.

However, the development of a bipolar episode from a prolonged period of abnormal BAS level would seem to rely upon more than delayed achievement of homeostasis. One possibility is that associated changes in cognition may act to excite or depress the system further. Meyer et al. (2001) have investigated the link between BAS functioning and symptom onset: using a scale designed to measure the extent to which the BAS becomes activated after exposure to reward or potential reward (the Reward Responsiveness Scale of the BIS/BAS sensitivity scale) (Carver & White, 1994), they found that responsivity to reward not only correlates with levels of manic symptoms, but is also predictive of increases in manic symptoms, even when baseline levels of manic symptoms are controlled for.

Thus, while elevated BAS levels are a normal part of reaction to reward, it is possible that bipolar individuals show oversensitivity to rewarding events once in this state. There is some evidence of increased expectation of reward in bipolar-spectrum individuals following initial success: Stern and Berrenberg (1979) found that, after success feedback, individuals with a history of hypomanic symptoms were more likely to expect success on future laboratory tasks than were control participants, a difference that was not apparent when feedback was less positive. Such a tendency to focus upon—and overestimate—potential for reward in the environment constitutes a cognitive bias that may promote further-reward seeking behaviour, thus exciting the system further. Figure 12.2 illustrates the BAS model in the case of mood and BAS elevation.

With regard to the relationship between BAS dysregulation and bipolar depression, Depue and colleagues have proposed that bipolar depression represents extreme underactivity of the BAS, and there is some biological evidence to support this view. Several studies have found a relative decrease in left-frontal cortical activity in currently depressed individuals as compared with a non-depressed sample, and in previously depressed as compared with never depressed individuals (Allen et al., 1993; Henriques & Davidson, 1990; 1991), and relative level of activity in this area has been found to correlate positively with BAS sensitivity to reward as measured by Carver and White's (1994) scale (Harmon-Jones & Allen, 1997).

In keeping with the above approach, it could be postulated that at low levels of BAS activity, the BAS is abnormally sensitive to frustrative non-reward in bipolar individuals, such that it is easily subdued by failure to attain reward. A similar suggestion has been made

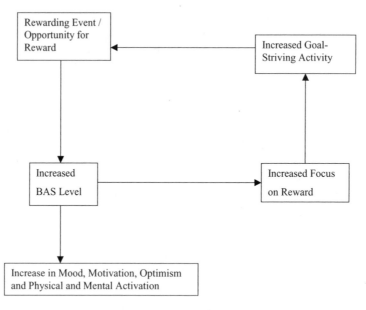

Figure 12.2   BAS model for the development of hypomania

by Strauman (1999), and Carver and Scheier (1998), who postulate that depression results from a failure to attain approach goals. A need for further work investigating the relationship between frustrative non-reward, BAS level and symptoms of depression is indicated. Figure 12.3 illustrates the BAS model in the case of a decrease in mood and BAS activity.

In summary, the BAS model proposes that weak regulatory mechanisms within a biological system constitute the biological vulnerability in bipolar disorder, and that associated

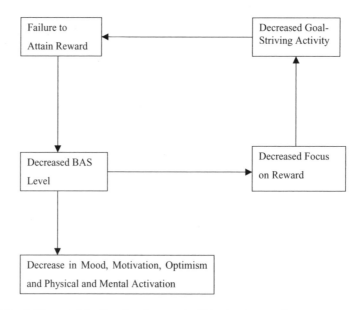

Figure 12.3   BAS model for the development of bipolar depression

changes in cognition—specifically, changes in the processing of signals of reward—act to maintain this dysregulation by channelling behaviour towards or away from further reward. Figure 12.2 illustrates this model in the case of mood and BAS elevation, while Figure 12.3 depicts this cycle in the case of a decrease in mood and in BAS activity.

It should be noted that increased BAS level in this model may be triggered not only by the occurrence of a rewarding event but also by the opportunity for reward or success. Such an opportunity may arise from apparently negative circumstances depending upon the particular values and goals of the individual: for example, the end of a romantic relationship may be perceived as an opportunity to pursue relationship or career prospects that were previously not possible. Stressful events may also affect daily rhythms such as sleep-wake patterns: as mentioned previously, disruption of this kind has been linked to the onset of mood disturbance. This disruption may provide a separate path by which stressful negative events could trigger mania or depression, augmenting the direct effect of the event on the BAS system.

INTERACTION BETWEEN THE TWO APPROACHES

Abnormality in the processing of goal-attainment and reward is a common feature of the two models; indeed, the two approaches complement each other. In the case of BAS elevation and hypomania, extreme goal-attainment attitudes may promote goal-striving activity that would lead to further elevations in BAS level. High BAS activation results in greater attentional focus upon reward as well as increased optimism, which may confirm goal-attainment attitudes such as, "If I try hard enough, I should be able to excel at anything I attempt".

With regard to lowered BAS activity, attitudes such as "I should be able to control what happens to me" and "I should be happy all the time" will intensify the feelings of failure that might result from the low mood and the subnormal energy and motivation levels that accompany a decrease in BAS level. These feelings of failure are proposed to decrease BAS level further, perpetuating the cycle.

We propose that vulnerability to BAS dysregulation serves as a biological diathesis in bipolar affective disorder, and that this vulnerability may even distinguish those individuals prone to developing bipolar affective disorder from those who are not. Extreme goal-attainment beliefs are proposed to interact with the course of the illness, because people with these beliefs will be likely to engage in behaviour that could precipitate the development of an episode. Correspondingly, the very experience of mania or depression may well serve to generate and reinforce particular beliefs, even at an early stage in the course of the illness.

TREATMENT IMPLICATIONS

Psychoeducation and monitoring

The BAS theory claims that bipolar individuals are particularly susceptible to biobehavioural dysregulation, and therefore deliberate regulation of behaviour patterns may limit periods of vulnerability. Current therapy packages for bipolar affective disorder often adopt a diathesis-stress model (e.g., Lam et al., 1999; Scott, 2001) and teach clients the importance of having a balanced lifestyle and ensuring regularity of social routines in order to minimise sleep disruption, as keeping regular sleeping patterns and daily routines appears to be very important for bipolar patients (Wehr et al., 1987). Having knowledge of what may trigger an illness episode can lead to establishing a routine in daily living that avoids excessive stress and limits mood swings. Prediction, anticipation and prevention of any disruption in routine and sleep by stressors such as life events can be an important aspect in the psychosocial management of bipolar affective disorders.

Periods of BAS over- or underactivity would appear to constitute risky periods, despite the fact that clear symptoms of hypomania or depression may be absent at this stage. Therefore, a first step would be to monitor mood level in order to identify such periods. While mood and activity diary-keeping already form a part of existing therapy packages, the BAS theory suggests that monitoring should also take into account the status of BAS outputs such as level of motivation, optimism, physical restlessness and speed of thought. In fact, these are common prodromes of bipolar disorder, as measured by spontaneous self-report (Lam & Wong, 1997).

Coping with prodromes

Monitoring will facilitate the identification of early warning signs—or prodromes—of illness. Although prodromes are idiosyncratic, there is research evidence that bipolar patients report a fairly consistent pattern of prodromes over time (Lam et al., 2001; Molnar et al., 1988). An effective coping strategy for dealing with prodromes is associated with higher social functioning (Lam & Wong, 1997), which, in turn, predicted longer intervals between episodes (Gitlin et al., 1995) or fewer bipolar episodes (Lam et al., 2001). In Lam et al.'s study, avoiding the temptation to seek further stimulation and engaging in calming activities in the prodromal phase of mania were associated with fewer manic episodes during the following 18 months. Likewise, engaging systematically in pleasure or mastery activities, seeking support and reality-testing one's negative cognitions during the prodromal stage of a depression were associated with fewer depressive episodes.

The BAS model suggests specifically that activities should be considered in terms of their potential to reward or frustrate as a means of understanding how they might interact with current mood state. When the BAS level appears elevated, potential sources of reward should be regulated, with a view to avoiding further elevation that may result in hypomania. For example, stimulating social events and work-related challenges could be avoided or reduced. Encouraging realistic appraisal of circumstances or planned actions to incorporate a balanced view of the risks and downsides involved would be one way of dealing with overoptimistic thinking that might lead to unwise actions and further mood elevation. Similarly, when the BAS level appears low, potential sources of reward should be encouraged, while challenges with a high risk of failure should be avoided—for example, through use of graded task assignments. Potential sources of social support could be investigated and, if necessary, instigated, and regular social contact encouraged.

Challenging dysfunctional attitudes

The presence of extreme goal-striving attitudes represents another point with potential for intervention. The task of challenging these beliefs may be approached by illustrating to the individual how these assumptions have served them ill in the past. This may be achieved through examining carefully the period immediately preceding a previous manic episode: by definition, mania involves significant functional impairment, admission to hospital or the experience of psychotic symptoms (American Psychiatric Association, 1994); therefore, it often results in unpleasant consequences for the individual. Investigating the link between these consequences and the antecedent behaviour—and more importantly, perhaps, the assumptions guiding this behaviour—is one method of opening a discussion of the value of extreme goal-striving beliefs.

The high value placed upon autonomy is another aspect of this model that could be explored in therapy. The therapeutic approaches described previously encourage clients to identify prodromal signs of mania and depression, in order that action may be taken to prevent deterioration. In clinical practice, many clients report difficulty in recognising their warning signs once in the prodromal stages of an episode, particularly in the early phase of hypomania. Feedback from trusted others may aid early recognition of warning signs, but this feedback may well be ignored if the individual believes that the opinions of others are of little importance. High levels of social support have been found to predict a more favourable course in bipolar depression (Johnson et al., 1999). Thus, encouraging clients to put into place—and make use of—social support networks may provide some protection against the development of depression. The desire to operate autonomously may thwart attempts to encourage social interdependency. Again, these incidents may be used as examples of the way in which these beliefs might be unhelpful and impede recovery from hypomania and depression.

These beliefs also have implications within the treatment sphere. Reluctance to become dependent upon medication and the health services may result in lowered compliance with medication. Discussion within a treatment setting of the pros and cons of taking medication has been shown to improve outcome in this group (Cochran, 1984), and this component is present in the treatment packages described earlier. Issues of dependency and autonomy may also be raised within the process of therapy itself, and, if this is the case, an emphasis upon collaboration between therapist and client is particularly important.

In more general terms, a collaborative and empathic approach is of importance, given the focus upon regulation and moderation that the techniques outlined require. The experience of hypomania and the early stages of mania may be a positive one in many respects: some bipolar individuals report enjoying increased speed of thought, confidence and energy, as well as feeling more productive and creative (Lam et al., 1999). The appeal of this state should not be underestimated: recent findings suggest that euthymic bipolar individuals who view themselves as possessing these hypomanic-like traits and believe this to be positive are less likely to respond well to cognitive behavioural therapy (Lam et al., submitted), which requires clients to be willing to engage in monitoring and regulating mood and behaviour.

In addition, whereas some of the unhelpful cognitions that might be tackled in the treatment of depression could be considered undesirable by Western society—for example, over-dependency upon others, and ideas of passivity and helplessness—it could be argued that the notion of autonomous goal-striving is idealised by contemporary Western culture (e.g., Resnick, 1999). Therefore, in terms of challenging these beliefs in therapy, recourse to standards of desirable behaviour may be problematic. Acknowledging the attractions of hypomania, and of goal-driven behaviour, may be important if a balanced discussion of the advantages and disadvantages of mood and activity regulation is to be undertaken.

CONCLUSION

The two theoretical approaches described recognise the importance of biological vulnerability in bipolar affective disorder, which may take the form of a genetic predisposition to the illness manifested as instability in biological systems such as the BAS and those governing circadian rhythms. However, both approaches propose a key role for cognitive biases in the maintenance of the condition. Attitudes towards—and processing of—reward and goal attainment have been indicated by a number of studies as possible sites of cognitive dysfunction in bipolar disorder, and these theories suggest several ways in which this dysfunction may operate. At present, the evidence for a causal link between reward sensitivity and the development of manic symptoms is largely correlational: more detailed experimental work investigating abnormal behavioural and emotional response to reward in euthymic bipolar individuals would aid in testing the model proposed.

In clinical practice, not all clients are observed to hold clear extreme goal-striving beliefs. It is possible that these beliefs characterise a subset of bipolar individuals, for whom the course of their illness is greatly affected by the unhelpful nature of such attitudes. Another possibility is that such attitudes are mood-state dependent: several studies report the level of dysfunctional attitudes to change significantly in affectively disordered individuals after both negative and positive mood induction (Miranda & Persons, 1988; Miranda et al., 1998). Thus, highly goal-striving attitudes may be active only when mood is raised. Again, experimental work could test this possibility in bipolar individuals. Finally, studies examining dysfunctional assumptions in bipolar disorder have employed a limited range of measures. Excessive goal-striving may be manifested in many different ways, and in many different spheres of life. While theoretical research can work to uncover the essential common elements of these beliefs within the bipolar population, therapists must expect great variation between individuals in the extent to which these cognitive biases dominate the course of the illness, and when and where they might be most harmful.

REFERENCES

Abramson, L.Y., Seligman, M.E.P. & Teasdale, J. (1978). Learned helplessness in humans: Critique and reformulation. *Journal of Abnormal Psychology, 87*, 49–74.

Allen, J.J., Iacono, W.G., Depue, R.A. & Arbisi, P. (1993). Regional electroencephalographic asymmetries in bipolar seasonal affective disorder before and after exposure to bright light. *Biological Psychiatry, 33*, 642–646.

Allen, M.G., Cohen, S., Pollin, W., et al. (1974). Affective illness in veteran twins: A diagnostic review. *American Journal of Psychiatry, 131*, 1234–1239.

American Psychiatric Association (1994). Practice guidelines for the treatment of patients with bipolar disorder. *American Journal of Psychiatry*, December Supplement, *151*, 1–36.

American Psychiatric Association (1994). *Diagnostic and Statistical Manual for the DSM-V.* Washington, DC: American Psychiatric Association.

Beck, A.T. (1967). *Depression: Clinical, Experimental and Theoretical Aspects.* New York: Hoeber.

Beck, A.T. (1983). Cognitive therapy of depression: New perspectives. In P.J. Clayton & J.E. Barrett (Eds), *Treatment of Depression: Old Controversies and New Approaches* (pp. 5–37). New York: Raven Press.

Beck, A.T., Rush, A. J., Shaw, B. & Emery, G. (1979). *Cognitive Therapy of Depression.* New York: Guilford.

Bertelsen, A., Harvald, B. & Hauge, M. (1977). A Danish twin study of manic-depressive disorder. *British Journal of Psychiatry, 130*, 330–351.

Cardno, A.G., Marshall, E.J., Coid, B., et al. (1999). Heritability estimates for psychotic disorders. *Archives of General Psychiatry, 56*, 162–168.

Carroll, B.J. (1994). Brain mechanisms in manic depression. *Clinical Chemistry, 40*, 303–308.

Carver, C.S. & Scheier, M.F. (1998). *On the Self-Regulation of Behavior* (pp. 166–170). Cambridge: Cambridge University Press.

Carver, C.S. & White, T.L. (1994). Behavioral inhibition, behavioral activation, and affective responses to impending reward and punishment: The BIS/BAS scales. *Journal of Personality and Social Psychology, 67*, 319–333.

Cochran, S.D. (1984). Preventing medical noncompliance in the outpatient treatment of bipolar affective disorders. *Journal of Consulting and Clinical Psychology, 52*, 873–878.

Depue, R.A. & Monroe, S.M. (1978). The unipolar-bipolar distinction in the depressive disorders. *Psychological Bulletin, 85*, 1001–1029.

Depue, R.A., Krauss, S.P. & Spoont, M.R. (1987). A two-dimensional threshold model of seasonal bipolar affective disorder. In D. Magnusson & A. Ohman (Eds), *Psychopathology: An interactionist Perspective* (pp. 95–123). New York: Academic Press.

Gitlin, M.J., Swendsen, J., Heller, T.L. & Hammen, C. (1995). Relapse and impairment in bipolar disorder. *American Journal of Psychiatry, 152*, 1635–1640.

Goplerud, E. & Depue, R.A. (1985). Behavioral response to naturally occurring stress in cyclothymia and dysthymia. *Journal of Abnormal Psychology, 94*, 128–139.

Gray, J.A. (1982). *The Neuropsychology of Anxiety*. New York: Oxford University Press.

Gray, J.A. (1990). Brain systems that mediate both emotion and cognition. *Cognition and Emotion, 4*, 269–288.

Harmon-Jones, E. & Allen, J.J. (1997). Behavioral activation sensitivity and resting frontal EEG asymmetry: Covariation of putative indicators related to risk for mood disorders. *Journal of Abnormal Psychology, 106*, 159–163.

Healy, D. & Williams, J.M.G. (1989). Moods, misattributions and mania: An interaction of biological and psychological factors in the pathogenesis of mania. *Psychiatric Developments, 1*, 49–70.

Henriques, J.B. & Davidson, R.J. (1990). Regional brain electrical asymmetries discriminate between previously depressed and healthy control subjects. *Journal of Abnormal Psychology, 99*, 22–31.

Henriques, J.B. & Davidson, R.J. (1991). Left frontal hypoactivation in depression. *Journal of Abnormal Psychology, 100*, 535–545.

Hollon, S.D., Kendall, P.C. & Lumry, A. (1986). Specificity of depressotypic cognitions in clinical depression. *Journal of Abnormal Psychology, 95*, 52–59.

Johnson, S.L., Sandrow, D., Meyer, B., et al. (1999). Increases in manic symptoms after life events involving goal attainment. *Journal of Abnormal Psychology, 109*, 721–727.

Kringlen, E. (1967). *Heredity and Environment in the Functional Psychoses*. London: Heinemann.

Lam, D.H. & Wong, G. (1997). Prodromes, coping strategies, insight and social functioning in bipolar affective disorders. *Psychological Medicine, 27*, 1091–1100.

Lam, D.H., Jones, S.H., Haywood, P. & Bright, J.A. (1999). *Cognitive Therapy for Manic Depression*. Chichester: Wiley.

Lam, D., Wong, G. & Sham, P. (2001). Prodromes, coping strategies and course of illness in bipolar affective disorders—a naturalistic study. *Psychological Medicine, 31*, 1397–1402.

Lam, D., Wright, K. & Sham, P. (paper submitted). Sense of self and response to cognitive therapy for bipolar disorder.

Lam, D., Wright, K. & Smith, N. (in press). Dysfunctional assumptions in bipolar disorder. *Journal of Affective Disorders*.

Lewinsohn, P.M. (1974). A behavioral approach to depression. In R.J. Friedman & M.M. Katz (Eds), *The Psychology of Depression: Contemporary Theory and Research* (pp. 157–185). New York: Wiley.

Lozano, B.E. & Johnson, S.L. (2001). Can personality predict increases in manic and depressive symptoms? *Journal of Affective Disorders, 63*, 103–111.

Malkoff-Schwartz, S., Frank, E. & Andersen, B. (1998). Stressful life events and social rhythm disruption in the onset of manic and depressive bipolar episodes. *Archives of General Psychiatry, 55*, 702–707.

Mendlewicz, J. & Rainer, J.D. (1977). Adoption study supporting genetic transmission in manic-depressive illness. *Nature, 268*, 327–329.

Meyer, B., Johnson, S.L. & Winters, R. (2001). Responsiveness to threat and incentive in bipolar disorder: Relations of the BIS/BAS scales with symptoms. *Journal of Psychopathology and Behavioral Assessment, 23*, 133–143.

Miranda, J. & Persons, J.B. (1988). Dysfunctional attitudes are mood-state dependent. *Journal of Abnormal Psychology, 97*, 76–79.

Miranda, J., Gross, J.J., Persons, J.B. & Hahn, J. (1998). Mood matters: Negative mood induction activates dysfunctional attitudes in women vulnerable to depression. *Cognitive Therapy and Research, 22*, 363–376.

Mitchell, P., Parker, G., Jamieson, K., et al. (1992). Are there any differences between bipolar and unipolar melancholia? *Journal of Affective Disorders, 25*, 97–106.

Molnar, G., Feeney, M.G. & Fava, G.A. (1988). Duration and symptoms of bipolar prodromes. *American Journal of Psychiatry, 145*, 1576–1578.

Resnick, C.A. (1999). How interdependence in cultures promotes well-being. *Dissertation Abstracts International: Section B: The Sciences and Engineering, 59*.

Scott, J. (2001). Cognitive therapy as an adjunct to medication in bipolar disorder. *British Journal of Psychiatry, 178* (Suppl. 41), s164–s168.

Stern, G.S. & Berrenberg, J.L. (1979). Skill-set, success outcome, and mania as determinants of the illusion of control. *Journal of Research in Personality, 13*, 206–220.

Strauman, T.J. (1999). Reply to Depue and Collins. *Behavioral and Brain Sciences, 22*, 536.

Wehr, T.A., Sack, D.A. & Rosenthal, N.E. (1987). Sleep reduction as a final common pathway in the genesis of mania. *American Journal of Psychiatry, 144*, 201–204.

13

INTEGRATION OF PATIENT, PROVIDER, AND SYSTEMS TREATMENT APPROACHES IN BIPOLAR DISORDER

WHERE EVIDENCE MEETS PRACTICE REALITY

Sagar V. Parikh and Sidney H. Kennedy

Bipolar disorder is often characterized by grandiosity as a cardinal symptom of mania, but grandiosity may also characterize the illness from another perspective: virtually no other psychiatric disorder is as grand in its plethora of clinical presentations (Goldberg & Harrow, 1999; Goodwin & Jamison, 1990). Depression, mania, and mixed states each require substantially different biological, psychological, and social interventions, and even the same episode can be approached very differently by two biological psychiatrists or two psychotherapists (Prien & Potter, 1990; Prien & Rush, 1996). How is a practitioner to choose among the many pathways to treatment? The science of medicine identifies the efficacy of each particular path, but only the art of medicine—the weighing of individual circumstances with clinical judgement and the capacity to integrate approaches—allows for truly effective treatment. This chapter explores several dominant approaches to treatment, each of which has been discussed in detail in this book—but it then attempts to provide a model for weaving a therapeutic tapestry.

The challenges of treatment are perhaps best shown by examining a common clinical scenario illustrating how different experts might approach the problem and then offering a sequence of recommendations based on the integration of approaches at the end of the chapter.

Vignette: Bipolar depression. Mr Y is a 22-year-old college student with a previous history of a psychotic manic episode requiring 3 weeks of inpatient treatment at age 19. He had discontinued lithium and antipsychotics after 6 months of treatment originally, because he "didn't need pills to be well". He was successful in his studies, was in a serious relationship, and had become an impassioned animal rights activist. He was particularly skeptical of medical research for its reliance on animals, and fond of movies that depicted

---

Mood Disorders: A Handbook of Science and Practice. Edited by M. Power.
© 2004 John Wiley & Sons, Ltd. ISBN 0-470-84390-X.

psychiatric problems as a result of individuals struggling to assert individuality in the face of oppressive societal norms. Two months prior to the current assessment, he developed low energy and difficulty in concentrating; this had evolved to more explicit major depression with excessive sleepiness, overeating, severe depressive ruminations, social withdrawal, hopelessness, and suicidal ideation. Nevertheless, he felt that it was not right to kill—either animals or himself—and so he sought help to "get over the suicidal urges and get my energy back".

How should he be treated?

Most psychiatrists would agree that medication—most likely a mood stabilizer such as lithium—would be a critical first step. Major treatment guidelines on bipolar disorder stress the importance of this step, and cite the substantial evidence on the use of lithium mono-therapy for bipolar depression (Bauer et al., 1999; Kusumakar & Yatham, 1997). Common clinical practice, however, often includes starting both a mood stabilizer and an antidepres-sant concurrently, to treat fully the depression, despite limited research evidence for this. Further complicating the biological approach is the lack of agreement on which antidepres-sant should be used, although most, if not all, biological psychiatrists would probably agree on the mood stabilizer/antidepressant combination in conjunction with "medication visits".

Psychotherapists might take a more complex approach (Roth et al., 1996). Most would grudgingly accept the need for a mood stabilizer, but the target and technique for psycho-therapy would differ markedly. Cognitive-behavioral therapy (CBT) practitioners would target the depressive ruminations, social withdrawal, hopelessness, and suicidality. Inter-personal psychotherapy (IPT) practitioners might attend to the sleep changes while search-ing for evidence of interpersonal deficits or conflicts underlying this particular episode. Still other therapists would also look to family/couple or even psychodynamic issues for intervention. Members of the public and self-help advocates might counsel the wisdom of avoiding the formal health-care system and looking to time, social support, and environmen-tal change as key steps to be pursued. In particular, stigma as a barrier to recovery would be targeted by some (Perlick, 2001). Idealists would look at integrating a variety of interven-tions in the most "person-centered" way. For each intervention—biological, psychological, and social—advice would be available in the literature, and, indeed, in this volume—yet how to decide what is right for this person? Furthermore, how would one design a bipolar treatment service that would best suit situations such as this?

A THEORETICAL FRAMEWORK: MEDICAL MODELS AND CHRONIC DISEASE MANAGEMENT

Evidence-based medicine is a dominant mantra currently, and correctly stresses the im-portance of using a systematic search for efficacious treatments (Sackett et al., 2000). An afterthought of this approach is the larger factors that may also influence outcomes, such as patient treatment preference (Bedi et al., 2000; Lin & Parikh, 1999), local health system re-sources, and practitioner characteristics and training (Donohoe, 1998; Parikh et al., 1997a). Several theoretical models provide guidance on how to understand these other relevant factors—models looking at "population health" (Ibrahim et al., 2001) or the "determinants of health" and models explicitly designed for chronic disease management. In fact, in the leading model of chronic disease management (Wagner et al., 1996), four categories of intervention have been identified: (1) practice design (reorganization), (2) patient education, (3) expert systems (provider education, guidelines, and decision support), and (4) computer-based support (reminder programs, feedback of automated clinical measures, or alerts to the clinician on matters such as nonrenewal of prescribed medications). By blending these models into a hybrid, which reflects the perspective of the clinician, it is possible to look at treatment success as a product of successful negotiation of barriers at three key levels: patient, provider, and system.

PATIENT INTERVENTIONS

Medication remains the cornerstone of treatment for bipolar disorder, so prescription of at least a mood stabilizer would be routine. Furthermore, while there may be cost factors in seeing a physician and filling a prescription, for all practical purposes such interventions are feasible in virtually all health-care environments in the developed world. Specific medication recommendations are outlined elsewhere in this volume, and would be combined with basic clinical management (supportive therapy including specifying treatment and monitoring outcome, offering practical advice for immediate problems such as work or school stressors, and instilling hope for relief of symptoms). However, abundant data demonstrate poor medication adherence in bipolar disorder (Cohen et al., 2000); thus, the next level of intervention would be compliance-enhancing strategies. Such strategies would generally fall into the category of psychoeducation, which multiple studies have demonstrated to improve medication compliance and overall treatment adherence (Sperry, 1995). Key studies have also shown that psychoeducation improves clinical outcomes; a median of nine sessions designed to educate the patient on the signs and symptoms of early relapse and the development of an early-warning strategy dramatically reduced time to relapse into mania and improved quality of life in a randomized controlled trial (Perry et al., 1999). A manual on group psychotherapy for bipolar disorder, which includes detailed instructions for a six-session "phase I of the Life Goals Program", could be a template for either individual or group psychoeducation (Bauer & McBride, 1996). This psychoeducational intervention has been validated in a pilot study (Bauer et al., 1998); we are now comparing this to a 20-session CBT intervention in a randomized controlled trial of 210 bipolar patients across multiple sites in Canada, which will also provide further delineation of the benefits of psychoeducation.

Beyond psychoeducation, specific psychotherapeutic interventions are now emerging. At the time of our earlier reviews (Huxley et al., 2000; Parikh et al., 1997b), we found 32 peer-reviewed reports involving just 1052 bipolar patients (average number per study was just 33), with only 13 studies having some form of control group. Since 1999, various reports of psychosocial interventions have been published, including many randomized, controlled trials, some of which involved close to 100 subjects each.

Findings from these latest studies have been summarized elsewhere in this volume, but bear brief summary to allow consideration of treatment choice. A randomized, controlled comparison of intensive clinical management (CM) versus interpersonal and social rhythm therapy (IPSRT) involving 82 subjects revealed few differences in impact, with significant increases in relapses when subjects were crossed over from one modality to the other as part of the research design (Frank et al., 1997; 1999). The authors suggested that disruption to the psychosocial treatment routine itself was a sufficient stressor to provoke relapse—an important demonstration of the value of "continuity of care" (Hammen et al., 1992; Hammen & Gitlin, 1997). Several studies—some pilot, others full trials (Hirschfeld et al., 1998; Lam et al., 2000; 2003; Scott et al., 2001)—have demonstrated marked efficacy of CBT versus "treatment as usual" in overall illness course, incorporating both prevention of relapse and reduction in overall affective and functional morbidity. However, each of these interventions was lengthy (16–20 sessions), and all were delivered as individual psychotherapy. Access to CBT therapists, particularly those who are comfortable with and knowledgeable about bipolar disorder, is universally difficult, and offering 20 sessions of individual CBT to every new bipolar patient is impractical and costly. Moreover, a significant portion of CBT interventions for bipolar disorder incorporates basic psychoeducation, including illness recognition and development of relapse-prevention strategies. Such difficulties have led us to conduct a series of studies on psychoeducation alone (five sessions) versus treatment as usual (Parikh et al., 2001), individual psychoeducation (seven sessions) versus individual CBT (20 sessions) (Zaretsky et al., 2001), and a recent comparison of six sessions of group psychoeducation versus 20 sessions of individual CBT (Parikh et al., unpublished). Preliminary findings from a recently completed 'randomized, controlled trial (Zaretsky et al., 2001) involving seven individual sessions of psychoeducation compared to the same seven sessions plus 13 sessions of CBT, all drawn from another manual (Basco & Rush, 1996), suggest that a brief psychoeducational intervention was indeed very similar in impact to the longer psychoeducation (PE) plus CBT. One key difference in our study was that CBT was clearly more successful than PE in reducing dysfunctional attitudes in those who entered CBT (during the maintenance phase of bipolar disorder) with very high dysfunctional attitudes scores. If we keep in mind earlier findings about persistent negative cognitions in many patients with bipolar depression (Zaretsky et al., 1999), as well as abnormal cognitive styles (Reilly-Harrington et al., 1999), and the additional costs of CBT, a picture may be emerging that suggests brief group psychoeducation for all nonpsychotic bipolar patients as an initial step, with CBT being relegated to a secondary role for individuals with persistent problems and, in particular, persistent dysfunctional attitudes.

A similar analysis may be done regarding the role of family and marital interventions for bipolar disorder. As we previously reviewed (Huxley et al., 2000), 13 earlier studies of marital or family therapy, though severely limited methodologically, did suggest benefit from these interventions. Of the six controlled studies, the two with the fewest subjects and shortest interventions (Van Gent & Zwart, 1991, who used a five-session intervention for partners of bipolar patients and Honig et al., 1997, who used a six-session intervention with couples) showed the fewest benefits. Among the two controlled studies showing the most clinical benefit, Clarkin et al. (1998) used a 25-session marital intervention for couples; Miklowitz and Goldstein (1990) used a 21-session family therapy treatment to achieve results (in a pilot study). A larger (involving 101 bipolar patients with their families) randomized, controlled study by Miklowitz et al. (2000) used the 21-session family intervention compared to two family sessions and follow-up crisis management, and did show improvements in terms of fewer depressive relapses for the family-intervention group, but primarily in those families prospectively identified as having the highest negative expressed emotion. Furthermore, outcome was not related to therapist fidelity to the model (Weisman et al., 2002). Such findings are sobering; high-intensity treatments of typically more than 20 sessions, involving considerable patient effort to involve family, offer some benefit. The direct and indirect costs of such an intervention surely must be high. The ability of the health-care system to support such an intervention or the likelihood of many patients and families being able to attend such an intervention must surely be low. Balancing resources with need, and wisdom with evidence, perhaps such intensive family interventions are best reserved for those with early evidence of high need, such as high negative expressed emotion and obvious conflict—a recommendation that would mirror common clinical practice.

PROVIDER INTERVENTIONS

Specific provider interventions in bipolar disorder have not been reported. In a pilot study we have just completed (Parikh et al., unpublished), we created a "bipolar treatment optimization program" that incorporated a patient intervention and a simultaneous provider education and support intervention for the patient's primary care physician. Patients benefited, but it is too early to determine to what extent the provider intervention was effective.

However, the larger context of medical care, and depression in particular, has been studied exhaustively with respect to provider interventions, such as providing education in the form of treatment guidelines, continuing medical education events, and providing feedback of screening tools such as depression self-report scales routinely administered to all patients in a practice setting. From medicine as a whole, traditional education in the form of conventional continuing medical education events, distribution and teaching of guidelines, grand rounds, and conferences have shown little impact on clinical practice (Davis et al., 1995; 1999). As summarized by Von Korff and Goldberg (2001), randomized, controlled trials of interventions to improve depression treatment in primary care have been negative when the intervention focused only on provider or provider plus patient interventions. In the same spirit, single-session training events in depression did not change practice patterns, but there is evidence that longitudinal programs alter practice (Hodges et al., 2001; Parikh et al., 1999). However, simple mass screening with rating scales and provision of results to the relevant primary-care physician have not been found particularly effective in altering disease outcomes (Gilbody et al., 2001). Taken together and extrapolated, these findings suggest that provider interventions may be a necessary, but are clearly not a sufficient, intervention to make an improvement in the treatment of bipolar disorder.

SYSTEM INTERVENTIONS

System interventions incorporate multiple elements, and inevitably overlap with the domains of patient and provider maneuvers. Furthermore, studies of system reorganization strategies do not easily allow "unbundling" of the different components to identify the most potent elements. Nonetheless, such system interventions are clear to specify and clear to study. Historically, the establishment of "lithium" clinics for bipolar disorder was an early example of a relatively pure system intervention, as reviewed by Gitlin and Jamison (1984). The staff of these clinics fostered a clear understanding of the medical model for bipolar disorder, built care along multidisciplinary lines, and established routines for the evaluation and monitoring of patients, as well as the provision of basic psychoeducation. Virtually no advances in systems interventions in bipolar disorder had been reported until the launching of two randomized, controlled studies (comparison condition is treatment-as-usual), both of which are still ongoing. In the first program, Bauer (2001) is comparing a "comprehensive patient education package", with specific treatment guidelines for providers, and a special nurse provider care facilitation/treatment with "usual care".

In the second similar study, Simon et al. (2002) are using a collaborative treatment model involving the same structured psychoeducation for patients, feedback of "automatic" monitoring results and algorithm-based medication recommendations to providers, and a nurse care manager to provide monthly telephone monitoring, outreach, psychoeducation, and care coordination. While results for bipolar disorder are not yet available, the findings from the depression literature are very clear: nine randomized, controlled treatment trials involving depressed patients in primary care show strong positive results from the adoption of a model where therapeutic maneuvers include some degree of care management, reorganization of typical care pathways, and incorporation of patient and provider education and support (Von Korff & Goldberg, 2001). Similarly, in a US multicenter clinical trial involving practice nurses in care management over 24 months, remission rates improved by 33 percentage points compared to the "treatment-as-usual group" (a remarkable 74% remission rate versus 41% at 24 months; Rost et al., 2002). Such results, paralleling the success in employing chronic disease-management strategies for diabetes (Renders et al., 2001), suggest that bipolar disorder will be best served by a chronic disease model involving an emphasis on system reorganization to include nurse care facilitation, telephone interventions, and full use of a multidisciplinary "patient care team" (Wagner, 2000)—but in conjunction with the patient and provider programs described earlier.

INTEGRATION OF PATIENT, PROVIDER, AND SYSTEMS APPROACHES

This chapter began by citing the example of a young man with bipolar disorder, and posed a question about the best treatment approach. Surely, the start of the answer is rooted in evidence, and some of the evidence has been reviewed briefly earlier. But clinical reality is influenced by a number of variables that extend beyond research evidence or "best practices". Patient attitudes, stigma on the part of both the patient and the provider, costs, availability of suitable providers, convenience, transportation access, the enthusiasm of providers, the nature of the treatment alliance, and the specific treatment preferences of a local environment are among the determinants of treatment initiation and continuation (Parikh, 1998). Large epidemiological surveys, such as the US National Comorbidity Survey (Kessler et al., 1994) and the Mental Health Supplement to the Ontario Health Survey (Parikh et al., 1996; 1997a; 1999), document that most individuals who fulfill diagnostic criteria for various mood disorders are not receiving treatment; among those in treatment, the median annual treatment frequency is less than 10 visits to any type of provider. Faced with this evidence and cognizant of the cost of high-intensity services, we must make recommendations for treatment that reflect what is readily achievable as well as what might constitute "best practice".

Integration of all of these perspectives would suggest that treatment be conceptualized in a pyramid form, much like Maslow's hierarchy of needs (Maslow, 1987), as noted in Figure 13.1. At the base of the pyramid in this figure is the need for pharmacotherapy and clinical management (supportive therapy including specifying treatment and monitoring outcome, offering practical advice for immediate problems such as work or school stressors, and instilling hope for relief of symptoms), essential for all patients. The second layer,

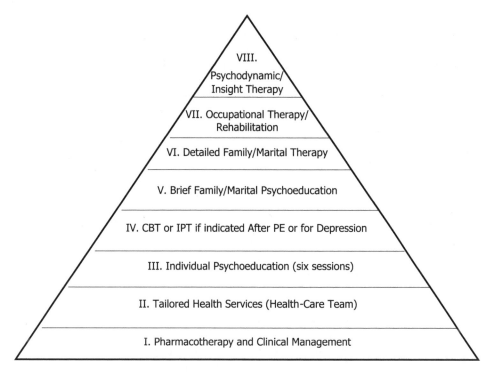

Figure 13.1   Hierarchy of treatment interventions for bipolar disorder (Parikh, 2002)

involving appropriate health-system design (tailored health services), would benefit most patients, and would involve specific suggestions on the use of the chronic disease model for bipolar disorder, with the creation of a health-care team for bipolar disorder. The treatment team would probably include nurse care coordinators/practitioners as key components, together with the ready availability of educational and other supports for both patients and health-care providers. The third layer, necessary for almost all patients, would be individual psychoeducation; based on the evidence and cost, brief group psychoeducation would be the ideal model. Various studies are employing Bauer and McBride's manual (1996) for group psychotherapy, from which a six-session psychoeducational component (phase I of the Life Goals Program) may be extracted. The highly readable and scripted format of the manual, its use in many studies, and even its translation into French and adoption in various clinical sites in Quebec and Europe suggest that this manual may be a prime model for cost-effective group psychoeducation.

The fourth layer of the pyramid, now necessary for fewer patients, would be specific individual psychotherapy—most likely, CBT or IPSRT. However, in reality, the benefits of both of these treatments include the fact that a key component of CBT includes illness education, relapse-prevention drills, and attention to sleep and other behavioral routines—in other words, topics already covered through the basic psychoeducation. Similarly, IPSRT includes many psychoeducational components as well. The unique features of CBT revolve around challenges to distorted cognitions and more detailed modulation of behavioral routines than would be done in basic psychoeducation. Similarly, the unique features of IPSRT would include the extremely meticulous attention to social and biological rhythms, and, to some extent, interpersonal conflict/deficit resolution (Malkoff–Schwartz et al., 1998). In view of this, CBT could perhaps be reserved for those with poor illness management despite receipt of psychoeducation, and particularly those with very high dysfunctional attitudes at outset (easily quantified by the Dysfunctional Attitudes Scale [Weissman, 1979]). Recommendations of IPSRT would also be limited to those individuals both with poor illness management despite psychoeducation and with prominent interpersonal issues. In addition, pending additional research, both CBT and IPT may be appropriate to target specific types of episodes, such as bipolar depression (Swartz & Frank, 2001; Zaretsky et al., 1999).

Above the CBT and IPT layers of the pyramid, family and marital interventions would include basic psychoeducation as the fifth layer, possibly integrated with the original psychoeducation of the patient (Reinares et al., 2002). A separate sixth layer would be the more extensive and costly "gold standard" treatments, as described by Miklowitz and Goldstein (1990; 1997) or Clarkin et al. (1998), restricted to those with severe family and/or marital discord (Miklowitz et al., 1998). At the seventh level of the pyramid would be a rehabilitation layer; for purposes of this model, simple management of basic return to work and school would be incorporated into the first layers of pharmacotherapy and clinical management as well as in individual psychoeducation. In layer seven, "rehabilitation" refers to much more complex and detailed efforts to restore functioning, suitable for a small group of patients. Finally, the last layer of the pyramid would utilize psychotherapy models, such as psychodynamic therapy, to deal with more complex issues, personality problems, etc.

To return to the example, cited at the beginning of the chapter, of the young man with bipolar depression and a background of medication noncompliance and skepticism about the medical model, we can now develop some recommendations.

(1) Start a mood stabilizer, consider an antidepressant, offer practical advice (such as consider time off work or school, spend time with friends, etc.) and instill hope.
(2) In addition to the treating physician, consider enlisting a nurse who will more closely monitor the patient and may be able to form a more detailed treatment alliance that permits other interventions as below.
(3) Add basic psychoeducation (six sessions from Bauer and McBride's (1996) manual).
(4) Consider phase-specific psychotherapy: CBT for bipolar depression, particularly if a simple administration of the Dysfunctional Attitudes Scale shows an extremely high score.
(5) Consider adding IPSRT if the above measures are insufficient, particularly after medication and CBT interventions.
(6) Evaluate for family discord; provide one to two sessions of family psychoeducation.
(7) Consider an occupational therapy consultation if difficulty in returning to work or school is anticipated.
(8) Initiate family interventions as acute episode stabilizes, if indicated.
(9) Consider detailed psychotherapy if indicated after episode stabilizes; issues such as shame, stigma, and diminished self-esteem and future potential are common.

This sequence of steps assumes that treatment expertise is available in each modality; in reality, many jurisdictions will not be able to provide all treatments. But based on the treatment pyramid model, and in view of the fact that the most basic layers of the pyramid are those with both evidence and feasibility with respect to cost and practicality, it is advisable for any clinic undertaking to treat bipolar disorder to attempt to organize resources to provide as many of the basic layers of treatment as possible. To invest clinic resources heavily in IPSRT or family interventions, for example, without adequate efforts at more basic interventions would result in a mismatch between treatment needs and treatment available. The challenges of bipolar disorder are many; so, too, are the methods of treatment. Construction of a treatment model incorporating chronic disease-management principles allows for rational clinic planning, and for wise delivery of care to patients.

REFERENCES

Basco, M.R. & Rush, A.J. (1996). *Cognitive-Behavioral Therapy for Bipolar Disorder*. New York: Guilford.

Bauer, M. (2001). The collaborative practice model for bipolar disorder: Design and implementation in a multi-site randomized controlled trial. *Bipolar Disord, 3*, 233–244.

Bauer, M. & McBride, L. (1996). *Structured Group Psychotherapy for Bipolar Disorder*. New York: Springer.

Bauer, M.S., Callahan, A.M., Jampala, C., et al. (1999). Clinical practice guidelines for bipolar disorder from the Department of Veterans Affairs. *J Clin Psychiatry, 60*, 9–21.

Bauer, M., McBride, L., Chase, C., Sachs, G. & Shea, N. (1998). Manual based group psychotherapy for bipolar disorder: A feasibility study. *J Clin Psychiatry, 59*, 449–455.

Bedi, N., Chilvers, C., Churchill, R., et al. (2000). Assessing effectiveness of treatment of depression in primary care. Partially randomised preference trial. *Br J Psychiatry, 177*, 312–318.

Clarkin, J.F., Carpenter, D., Hull, J., Wilner, P. & Glick, I. (1998). Effect of psychoeducational intervention for married patients with bipolar disorder and their spouses. *Psychiatr Serv, 29*, 531–533.

Cohen, N.L., Parikh, S.V. & Kennedy, S.H. (2000). Medication compliance in unipolar depression and bipolar disorder: Determinants and methods of assessment. *Primary Care Psychiatry, 6*, 101–110.

Davis, D., Thomson, M.A., Freemantle, N., Wolf, F.M., Mazmanian, P. & Taylor-Vaisey, A. (1999). Impact of formal continuing medical education: Do conferences, workshops, rounds, and other traditional continuing education activities change physician behavior or health care outcomes? *JAMA, 282*, 867–874.

Davis. D.A., Thomson, M., Oxman, A., et al. (1995). Changing physician performance: A systematic review of the effect of continuing medical education strategies. *JAMA, 274*, 700–705.

Donohoe, M.T. (1998). Comparing generalist and specialty care. *Arch Intern Med, 158*, 1596–1608.

Frank, E., Hlastala, S., Ritenour, A., et al. (1997). Inducing lifestyle regularity in recovering bipolar disorder patients: Results from the maintenance therapies in bipolar disorder protocol. *Biol Psychiatry, 41*, 1165–1173.

Frank, E., Swartz, H.A., Mallinger, A.G., Thase, M.E., Weaver, E. & Kupfer, D.J. (1999). Adjunctive psychotherapy for bipolar disorder: Effects of changing treatment modality. *J Abnorm Psychol, 108*, 579–587.

Gilbody, S.M., House, A.O. & Sheldon T.A. (2001). Routinely administered questionnaires for depression and anxiety: Sytematic review. *BMJ, 322*, 406–409.

Gitlin, M.J. & Jamison, K.R. (1984). Lithium clinics: Theory and practice. *Hosp Community Psychiatry, 35*, 363–368.

Goldberg, J.F. & Harrow, M (1999). *Bipolar Disorders: Clinical Course and Outcome*. Washington, DC: American Psychiatric Association Press.

Goodwin, F. & Jamison, K. (1990). *Manic-Depressive Illness*. Oxford: Oxford University Press.

Hammen, C. & Gitlin, M.J. (1997). Stress reactivity in bipolar patients and its relation to prior history of disorder. *Am J Psychiatry, 154*, 856–857.

Hammen, C., Ellicott, A. & Gitlin, M. (1992). Stressors and sociotropy/autonomy: A longitudinal study of their relationship to the course of bipolar disorder. *Cogn Ther, 16*, 409–418.

Hirschfeld, D.R., Gould, R.A., Reilly-Harrington, N.A., et al. (1998). Short-term adjunctive cognitive-behavioural group therapy for bipolar disorder: Preliminary results from a controlled trial. Paper presented at the annual meeting of the Association of the Advancement of Behaviour Therapy Conference, Washington, DC.

Hodges, B., Inch, C. & Silver, I. (2001). Improving the psychiatric knowledge, skills, and attitudes of primary care physicians, 1950–2000: A review. *Am J Psychiatry, 158,* 1579–1586.

Honig, A., Hofman, A., Rozenndaal, N. & Dingemans, P. (1997). Psychoeducation in bipolar disorder: Effect on expressed emotion. *Psychiatry Res, 72,* 17–22.

Huxley, N.A., Parikh, S.V. & Baldessarini, R.J. (2000). Effectiveness of psychosocial treatments in bipolar disorder: State of the evidence. *Harvard Rev Psychiatry, 8,* 126–140.

Ibrahim, M.A., Savitz, L.A., Carey, T.S. & Wagner, E.H. (2001). Population based health principles in medical and public health practice. *J Public Health Manag Pract, 7,* 75–81.

Kessler, R.C., McGonagle, K.A., Zhao, S., et al. (1994). Lifetime and 12 month prevalence of DSM-IIIR psychiatric disorders in the United States. *Arch Gen Psychiatry, 51,* 8–19.

Kusumakar, V. & Yatham, L.N. (Eds) (1997). The treatment of bipolar disorders: Review of the literature, guidelines, and options. *Can J Psychiatry, 42* (Suppl. 2), 67S–100S.

Lam, D.H., Watkins, E.R., Hayward, P., et al. (2003). A randomized controlled study of congnitive therapy for relapse prevention for bipolar affective disorder: Outcome of the first year. *Arch Gen Psychiatry, 60,* 145–152.

Lam, D.H., Bright, J., Jones S., et al. (2000). Cognitive therapy for bipolar disorder—A pilot study of relapse prevention. *Cogn Ther Res, 24,* 503–520.

Lin, E. & Parikh, S.V. (1999). Clinical, demographic, and attitudinal characteristics of the untreated depressed in Ontario. *J Affective Disord, 53,* 153–162.

Malkoff-Schwartz, S.F., Frank, E., Anderson, B., et al. (1998). Stressful life events and social rhythm disruption in the onset of manic and depressive bipolar episodes. A preliminary investigation. *Arch Gen Psychiatry, 55,* 702–707.

Maslow, A.H. (1987). *Motivation and Personality,* 3rd edn. New York: Harper & Row.

Miklowitz, D. & Goldstein M. (1990). Behavioral family treatment for patients with bipolar affective disorder. *Behav Modif, 14,* 457–489.

Miklowitz, D.J. & Goldstein, M.J. (1997). *Bipolar Disorder: A Family Focussed Treatment Approach.* New York: Guilford.

Miklowitz, D.J., Simoneau, T.L., George, E.L., et al. (2000). Family-focussed treatment of bipolar disorder; 1-year effects of a psychoeducational program in conjunction with pharmacotherapy. *Biol Psychiatry, 48,* 582–592.

Miklowitz, D.J., Wendel, J.S. & Simoneau, T.L. (1998). Targeting dysfunctional family interactions and high expressed emotion in the psychosocial treatment of bipolar disorder. *In-Session: Psychother Pract, 4,* 25–38.

Parikh, S.V. (1998). Improving Bipolar Disorder Treatment: Integrating Epidemiologic and Clinical Data to Design Better Mental Health Services. Annual meeting, Canadian Psychiatric Association, Halifax.

Parikh, S.V. (2002). New Treatments for Bipolar Disorder. 7th Annual International Continuing Professional Development Conference of the Canadian Psychiatric Association, Varadero, Cuba, February.

Parikh, S.V. & Parker, K (1999). Improving Detection and Management of Psychiatric Illnesses: Linking Family Medicine and Psychiatry with an Innovative Longitudinal Course. Alliance for Continuing Medical Education Annual Meeting, Atlanta, January 1999.

Parikh, S.V., Kusumakar, V., Haslam, D.R.S., Matte, R., Sharma, V. & Yatham, L.N. (1997b). Psychosocial interventions as an adjunct to pharmacotherapy in bipolar disorder. *Can J Psychiatry, 42,* (Suppl. 2) 74S–78S.

Parikh, S.V., Kusznir, A., Cooke, R.G., et al. (2001). Bipolar education treatment trial: Preliminary results. *Bipolar Disord, 3* (Suppl. 1) 50.

Parikh, S.V., Lesage, A.D., Kennedy, S.H. & Goering, P.N. (1999). Depression in Ontario: Undertreatment and factors associated with antidepressant use. *J Affective Disord, 52* (1–3), 67–76.

Parikh, S.V., Lin, E. & Lesage, A.D. (1997a). Mental health treatment in Ontario: Selected comparisons between the primary care and specialty sectors. *Can J Psychiatry, 42,* 929–934.

Parikh, S.V., Wasylenki, D., Goering, P. & Wong, J. (1996). Mood disorders: Rural/urban differences in prevalence, health care utilization, and disability in Ontario. *J Affective Disord, 38,* 57–65.

Perlick, D.A. (2001). Special section on stigma as a barrier to recovery: Introduction. *Psychiatr Serv, 52,* 1613–1614.

Perry, A., Tarrier, N., Morriss, R., McCarthy, E. & Limb, K. (1999). Randomized controlled trial of efficacy of teaching patients with bipolar disorder to identify early symptoms of relapse and obtain treatment. *BMJ, 318*, 149–153.

Prien, R.F. & Potter, W.Z. (1990). NIMH Workshop report on treatment of bipolar disorders. *Psychopharmacol Bull, 28*, 409–427.

Prien, R.F. & Rush, A.J. (1996). National Institute of Mental Health Workshop report on the treatment of bipolar disorder. *Biol Psychiatry, 40*, 215–220.

Reilly-Harrington, N.A., Alloy, L.B., Fresco, D.M. & Whitehouse, WG. (1999). Cognitive styles and life events interact to predict bipolar and unipolar symptomatology. *J Abnorm Psychol, 108*, 567–578.

Reinares, M., Colom, F., Martinez-Aran, A., Benabarre, A. & Vieta, E. (2002). Therapeutic interventions focused on the family of bipolar patients. *Psychother Psychosom, 71*, 2–10.

Renders, C.M., Valk, G.D., Griffin, S.J., Wagner, E.H., Van Eijk, J.T.M. & Assendelft, W.J.J. (2001). Interventions to improve the management of diabetes in primary care, outpatient, and community settings. *Diabetes Care, 24*, 1821–1833.

Rost, K., Nutting, P., Smith, J.L., Elliott, C.E. & Dickinson, M. (2002). Managing depression as a chronic disease: A randomized trial of ongoing treatment in primary care. *BMJ, 325*, 934–940.

Roth, A., Fonagy, P., Parry, G., et al. (1996). *What Works for Whom? A Critical Review of Psychotherapy Research.* New York: Guilford.

Sackett, D.L., Straus, S.E., Richardson, W.S., Rosenberg, W. & Haynes, R.B. (2000). *Evidence Based Medicine.* Edinburgh: Churchill Livingstone.

Scott, J., Garland, A. & Moorhead, S. (2001). A pilot study of cognitive therapy in bipolar disorders. *Psychol Med, 31*, 459–467.

Simon, G.E., Lundman, E.J., Unutzer, J. & Bauer, M.S. (2002). Design and implementation of a randomized trial evaluating systematic care for bipolar disorder. *Bipolar Disord, 4*, 226–236.

Sperry, L. (1995). *Psychopharmacology and Psychotherapy: Strategies for Maximizing Outcomes.* New York: Brunner/Mazel.

Swartz, H.A. & Frank, E. (2001). Psychotherapy for bipolar depression: A phase-specific treatment strategy? *Bipolar Disord, 3*, 11–22.

Van Gent, E.M. & Zwart, F.M. (1991). Psychoeducation of partners of bipolar manic patients. *J Affective Disord, 21*, 15–18.

Von Korff, M. & Goldberg, D. (2001). Improving outcomes in depression. *BMJ, 323*, 948–949.

Wagner, E.H. (2000). The role of patient care teams in chronic disease management. *BMJ, 320*, 569–572.

Wagner, E.H., Austin, B.T. & Von Korff, M. (1996). Organizing care for patients with chronic illness. *Millbank Q, 74*, 511–543.

Weisman, A., Tompson, M.C., Okazaki, S., et al. (2002). Clinicians' fidelity to a manual-based family treatment as a predictor of the one-year course of bipolar disorder. *Fam Process, 41*, 123–131.

Weissman, A. (1979). The Dysfunctional Attitudes Scale: A validation study. *Disserations Abstracts International, 40*, 1389–1390B (University Microfilm N.) 79–19, 533.

Zaretsky, A.E., Parikh, S.V. & Lancee, W.E. (2001). A randomized controlled trial of CBT in the maintenance treatment of bipolar disorder. *Bipolar Disord, 3* (Suppl. 1), 63.

Zaretsky, A.E., Segal, Z.V. & Gemar, M. (1999). Cognitive therapy for bipolar depression: A pilot study. *Can J Psychiatry, 44*, 491–494.

14

COGNITIVE BEHAVIOURAL THERAPY FOR BIPOLAR AFFECTIVE DISORDER

Matthias Schwannauer

The following chapter on the cognitive behavioural therapy (CBT) of bipolar affective disorder is divided into three main parts. The first section gives an overview of the specific issues facing the clinician when considering a psychological intervention for patients suffering from bipolar affective disorder. The second part outlines specific cognitive behavioural techniques found particularly relevant in the application of the cognitive behavioural model to this disorder group. Finally, the last section provides a summary of the empirical evidence to date for CTB in bipolar populations.

INTRODUCTION

Bipolar disorder affects 0.8–1.6% of the population (e.g., Kessler et al., 1994, 1997), and is equally distributed between men and women. The mean onset is in late adolescence and early adulthood, causing lasting psychosocial difficulties, partly due to the impact of the age of onset and the crucial impact on individual development (Ramana & Bebbington, 1995), but also as a result of the high likelihood of repeated episodes within a few years in 80–90% of the bipolar population (Goodwin & Jamieson, 1990). One of the tragic manifestations of the complexity and the lasting impairments often caused by the traumatic impact of early and multiple episodes is the high suicide rate in bipolar disorder; the mean rate is 15–20% (e.g., Iometsa, 1993; Simpson & Jamieson, 1999). This places the issue of suicidal risk at the centre of the therapeutic intervention.

One of the first challenges facing the CBT therapist in bipolar disorder is the strong heterogeneity of this disorder group and its various phenomenological manifestations. In comparison with other mood disorders, the emotional, cognitive, and behavioural problems associated with bipolar disorder range from long periods of depression to varying degrees of euphoria, irritability, agitation, and psychotic symptomatology. Most individuals suffering from bipolar disorder experience cyclical symptoms and multiple episodes of both depression and mania over their lifetime, causing significant disruptions in their lives as well as lasting psychological and psychosocial difficulties.

Mood Disorders: A Handbook of Science and Practice. Edited by M. Power.
© 2004 John Wiley & Sons, Ltd. ISBN 0-470-84390-X.

A second challenge for the treatment of bipolar disorder is the high proportion of comorbidity. Clinically significant are the high prevalence rates of substance abuse, up to 61% (Brady & Lydiard, 1992); a large proportion of the 21% of individuals suffering from a bipolar disorder also suffer from an anxiety disorder (Himmelhoch, 1999), and 50% display difficulties associated with personality disorders (Peselow et al., 1995). These high rates of comorbidity create clinical complexity not only in the assessment of current difficulties and realistic treatment goals, but also in terms of the CBT of core symptoms and psychosocial impairments, as these difficulties are often masked by heightened depressive or manic symptoms.

CBT has been shown to be a highly effective short-term psychotherapeutic intervention for a wide range of disorder groups, especially recent developments in CBT for treatment-resistant schizophrenia and severe and enduring depressive disorder, and the increasing positive evidence base has opened the prospect of the development of psychological interventions for bipolar disorders. To date, there have been several efficacy studies and some experimental trials reporting on the effectiveness of adapted CBT in bipolar disorder (see Chapter 12). Overall, these preliminary findings are promising and support the feasibility and clinical effectiveness of CBT for individuals suffering from bipolar disorder.

The relatively late development of psychological therapies for bipolar disorder might be due to the historical predominance of a biological paradigm in this disorder group; research investigating genetic and biological factors has been dominant, and there seemed to be a common misconception that most patients with bipolar disorder make a full interepisode recovery. Secondly, earlier psychotherapeutic approaches to bipolar disorder came with the warning that patients suffering from bipolar disorder were poor candidates for psychotherapy, as they lacked sufficient introspection, showed a high degree of dependency, and formed poor therapeutic relationships.

THE COGNITIVE BEHAVIOURAL MODEL OF BIPOLAR DISORDER

Many authors have argued that there is a marked lack of a coherent psychological model of bipolar disorder (e.g., Jones, 2001; Scott, 2001a). Recent research, however, highlights the role of cognitive and psychosocial factors in the development and course of bipolar disorder, and the first treatment manuals were published in recent years, delineating the application of CBT principles to bipolar disorders (Basco & Rush, 1996; Lam et al., 1999; Newman et al., 2002; Scott, 2001b). A body of research focused on cognitive factors such as attributional styles (Alloy et al., 1999); perfectionism, deficits in problem-solving skills, and elevated scores of sociotropy and autonomy (Lam et al., 2000); and maladaptive schemata (Young, 1999). These factors appear to play a significant role in the interaction of severe changes in behaviour, reactions to and the creation of significant psychosocial stressors, disruptions in chronobiological functioning and varied responsiveness to psychotropic medications. One of the reasons for the complex pattern of factors influencing each individual's phenomenology and course of the disorder is the huge variability in the spectrum of bipolar disorders, ranging from chronic cyclothymic presentations to episodic manifestations of severe depression and mania with psychotic features.

Overall, the cognitive behavioural model aids our clinical understanding of the psychopathology of bipolar disorder and the ways in which specific problems and interactions can be targeted, rather than offering aetiological clarification of this disorder. Researchers have suggested that similar cognitive structures and biases underlie both unipolar and bipolar depression (Alloy et al., 1999; Lam et al., 2000; Reilly-Harrington et al., 1999), particularly in terms of systematic attributional errors and sensitivity to failure or interpersonal rejection. Specific to individuals suffering from bipolar disorder, however, is the extreme valence shift in the content of their thinking. A cognitive model of bipolar disorder needs to integrate the variability in the stress responses of individuals. In other words, some individuals with bipolar disorder respond to stress by developing depressive symptoms, and others with the development of manic responses. The model also needs to take into account that bipolar individuals display trait-like thought processes in the form of long-standing predispositions and state-like responses to environmental triggers and physiological activation. Furthermore, it needs to take into account the specific effects of significant life events and environmental stressors on individuals' affect regulation, in line with a diathesis-stress model of mood disorders (Lam et al., 1999); in particular, the fact that only certain life events appear to be able to predict mania, while others do not (Johnson et al., 1999). Therefore, a clinical working model of bipolar disorder needs to encompass biology, individual beliefs and behavioural reactions, interpersonal functioning, environmental triggers and life events, and the individual's idiosyncratic conceptualisation of these events.

Beck's (1979) cognitive behavioural model suggests that depressed mood is mediated by particular patterns of thinking that accentuate mood shifts. Individuals who are depressed become more negative in how they perceive themselves, others, and the world in general; as a result, they are prone to systematic cognitive distortions in that they tend to overgeneralise, self-blame, jump to negative conclusions, and view things in black- and-white terms. The avoidance of social contacts and other safety behaviours often result as an interaction of mood shifts and negative thinking patterns. These cognitive styles of depression are thought to arise out of early learning experiences. Beck suggested in his cognitive model that mania is a mirror image of depression, as determined by a hyperpositive triad of self, others, and the future. Scott and colleagues (2000) found that individuals with bipolar disorder demonstrated lower levels of self-esteem, over-general memory, poorer problem-solving skills, and higher levels of dysfunctional attitudes, particularly those related to need for social approval and perfectionism. They further found that these vulnerabilities persisted between episodes in patients who were adherent to prophylactic treatment. Beck and colleagues worked on a reformulation of the original linear cognitive model for bipolar disorders (Beck, 1996; Newman et al., 2002). This recent reconceptualisation includes the notion of "modes". Modes are understood as integrated "cognitive affective behavioural networks" of powerful combinations of schemata, overlearned behaviour patterns, and intense, difficult-to-modulate emotions. When schemata and modes are activated by specific life events, chronobiological disruption, or other such triggers, the bipolar individuals' predispositional reactions become expressed by extremities in emotional and behavioural functioning. The authors argue that individuals' belief systems interact with their inherent perception of current stressors and events. This activation of long-standing beliefs and schemata determines their affect and behaviour, and influences their information processing by directing the individual towards information consistent with the schema. In this way, a negatively valenced schema is activated during a depressed phase, directing memory retrieval towards events of loss and rejection, and focusing current attention on the possibility of failure. In a manic phase, a positively valenced schema is activated, and is likely to lead to problematic decision making by selectively ignoring the need for adaptive caution and inhibition.

Clinically, a reliable understanding of the individual's cognitive assumptions and core beliefs, encompassing self-perception and perception of the world and the future, helps the therapist to demonstrate an accurate understanding of the individual's experiences and to focus on the assumptions and beliefs that cause most distress and dysfunction. It is therefore important to assess individuals' core beliefs independently of their presenting symptom pattern. A grandiose and manic individual might have the same core schema of "unlovability" and "incompetence" as a depressed patient. Bipolar individuals appear to maintain consistent, maladaptive core beliefs and schemata that shift polarity in their manifestations. The successful modification of these beliefs through cognitive therapy should result in the reduced amplification of the dysfunctional mood swings of the bipolar client.

Apart from the reformulation of the cognitive model for bipolar disorder by Beck and his colleagues, other alternatives have been formulated to capture the complex interactions between thoughts and emotions. Teasdale and Barnard (1993) differentiate between propositional and implicational "schematic" levels of information processing. They argue that propositional-level cognitions, or direct appraisals of any given information, do not directly activate emotional reactions, but are mediated on a level of implicational meaning by a process of schematic appraisal, in the context of present and past propositional information. Power and Dalgleish (1997, 1999) support this model and add an additional direct or associative route to emotions. This model has several clinical implications in disentangling the rational or schematic processes of change that appear to be primarily focused on by classical cognitive therapy approaches from the associative or direct associations of certain cues and emotional reactions. Jones (2001) utilised this multilevel approach to emotion and cognition to investigate the vulnerability of bipolar individuals to mood changes following disruptions in their circadian rhythms. Applying this model in individuals with bipolar disorder schema change is achieved by associative links through behaviour modification and corrective experiences, rather than rational cognitive techniques such as the challenging of automatic thoughts and restructuring. Patients should therefore be encouraged to experience subsyndromal mood changes and stimulation through adaptive coping strategies with the subsequent absence of prodromal symptoms.

THE APPLICATION OF CBT IN THE TREATMENT OF BIPOLAR DISORDER

Overall, the cognitive behavioural approach to the treatment of bipolar disorder aims to enhance non-pharmacological coping skills, to enhance elements of self-efficacy and responsibility in the treatment of the condition, to support individuals in recognising and managing psychosocial stressors and the impact of past episodes, to introduce specific strategies to deal with cognitive and behavioural difficulties, and to modify underlying schemata and core assumptions.

CBT for bipolar disorder relies on the basic characteristics of a CBT model. In that the cognitive behavioural model is most effective when the individuals are full collaborative partners in the treatment process. The therapist educates individuals about the diathesis-stress model of bipolar disorder, socialises them into the cognitive model of mood changes, and appraises them of the rationale for particular interventions. An assessment of the individual's core beliefs and underlying schemata is essential in the case formulation of individual vulnerabilities that form an integral part of the treatment plan.

CBT for bipolar disorder is naturally phase specific. The specific focus of the intervention varies depending on the individual formulation of treatment goals and the phase of the disorder in which the patient presents. For example, if a patient presents in an acute phase of a bipolar episode, the cognitive behavioural strategies will be aimed at crisis intervention, the treatment of acute symptoms, an assessment of risk and the factors that are maintaining the episode, and the establishment of a good therapeutic alliance. If a patient presents in the recovery phase following a recent episode or in a phase of stabilisation between episodes, CBT would aim to be insight oriented; to explore the meaning and context of symptoms, interpersonal functioning, preventative cognitive strategies, and self-management skills; to reduce the psychosocial impact of the disorder; and to build resilience regarding ongoing stressors.

The following section will outline the four main components of cognitive behavioural psychotherapy for bipolar disorder: psychoeducation; early warning signs and coping with prodromal symptoms; cognitive behavioural strategies for dealing with manic, hypomanic, or depressive symptoms; and finally the targeting of associated difficulties in psychosocial functioning, especially interpersonal difficulties.

Crucial for the adaptation of a cognitive behavioural intervention to any psychiatric disorder is the individual case formulation. This should be developed in collaboration with the patient, and it should be based on a developmental and cognitive model of the specific phenomenology of the bipolar disorder. The cognitive formulation is the starting point for the therapeutic intervention; it can be used as an alternative explanation of the patient's difficulties and will help to engage the patient into a cognitive way of understanding and working with the presenting problems.

SELF-MONITORING AND PRODROMAL CHANGES

Dealing with manic and hypomanic phases has been described as being the biggest clinical challenge in the treatment of bipolar individuals. Most individuals suffering from bipolar disorder would describe a manic phase as being inescapable. Once their mood starts to rise, the initial positive reinforcement of experiencing new sources of energy and creativity develops. Especially when this happens after long periods of depressed mood, it easily develops into a self-reinforcing pattern that seems impossible to stop.

The psychoeducational component of the cognitive behavioural intervention is an important starting point in this stage of problematic mood changes. The individual's awareness of possible consequences and that manic episodes are developing in a way that requires increased external control and medication seems crucial in preventing the negative impact of full-blown manic episodes. Past episodes provide the best source for information.

The early warning signs paradigm, originally developed for relapse prevention in early-onset psychotic disorders, especially schizophrenia, has been adapted for use with people suffering from bipolar disorders (Lam & Wong, 1997). Patients learn to identify prodromal and early symptoms of relapse and develop a range of behavioural techniques to improve their coping skills in order to counteract early symptoms effectively and to avoid their development into a full-blown episode.

In most cases, the change in mood, cognition, and behaviour is a gradual process. This allows time for the clinician and the individual to utilise psychological interventions while he or she is still responsive to cognitive and behavioural techniques. Teaching patients to recognise early symptoms of psychotic relapse and to seek early treatment is associated with important clinical improvements (Perry et al., 1999). Recent advances in the identification and formulation of individualised early warning signs (Lam & Wong, 1997) and the prodromal "relapse signature" (Smith & Tarrier, 1992) allow clinicians to reformulate the process of cycling into mania as an interaction of the individual's life situation, cognitive processing, and general level of coping skills. We can help patients to develop an individualised profile of prodromal changes and to be sensitised to significant mood changes early enough to curtail vicious cycles. This therapeutic step is influenced by the idiosyncratic beliefs that patients associate with changes in mood and that might compromise their coping abilities in the face of prodromal changes. For example, patients who believe that their manic episodes follow a predetermined course no matter what they do, might well be less cautious and responsible in the face of early hypomanic mood changes, and therefore might exacerbate the development of manic symptoms. These maladaptive beliefs underlying the individual's coping strategies and reactions are crucial, especially in the prevention of manic episodes. In utilising cognitive therapy strategies such as cognitive reframing and guided discovery, patients can learn to view new behaviours as an active process in which they execute a choice and that, despite the undeniable attraction of hypomanic impulses, some degree of control may be established.

One of the difficulties described by many patients is that of developing hypervigilance against minor changes in mood and their misinterpretation as onset of a manic episode rather than an accurate reflection of ordinary happiness, a mistake which can lead to inappropriate safety behaviours and avoidance. Within a cognitive behavioural framework, this can be avoided by teaching patients to monitor their mood on an ongoing basis, using individualised mood-monitoring tools that allow patients to look out for several specific prodromal signs in connection with actual environmental stressors and events, in order to avoid the generalisation of mood changes. Patients may also learn to employ coping strategies in response to prodromal changes that are appropriate to the mood changes observed. These coping strategies include activity schedules, the observation of sleep and dietary routines, the practice of relaxation exercises and graded task assignments, time-delay rules and problem-solving techniques in the face of impulsive decision making, and stimulus-control techniques, such as the regulation of alcohol and caffeine consumption, and the reduction of risk-seeking behaviours and stimulating activities. In a review discussing the benefits of cognitive behavioural interventions for individuals suffering bipolar disorder, Jones argues that the indicated mechanisms of change, over and above the known benefits of cognitive therapy, indicate behavioural techniques, such as extended activity scheduling and stabilisation of daily routines and sleep cycles, that predominantly influence circadian rhythm (Jones, 2001).

Disruption and irregularity in circadian rhythms, social events, and activities have been found to impact significantly on mood and can trigger affective episodes in people suffering from bipolar disorders. In support of this effect, the regulation of social interactions and balanced sleep–wake cycles have been found to be effective in preventing relapse and subsyndromal mood swings in bipolar disorders. Bipolar patients are highly sensitive to disruptions in their biological rhythms (Malkoff-Schwartz et al., 1998). The regularity of daily routines and activities, as well as the regularity of sleep–wake cycles, has been identified as a major protective factor (Frank et al., 1999). The psychological factors that influence individuals' ability to maintain stability, such as advance planning, attention to detail, and self-restraint, are the very difficulties that are associated with bipolarity. The therapist must therefore be very cautious in introducing these ideas that might easily be perceived as being overly controlling and meet significant resistance from the patient. One way to evaluate whether positive mood changes are indicative of a hypomanic or manic episode is to engage in calming activities and "time out" as a way of self-assessment of whether it is possible for the patient to remain still and to concentrate for significant periods of time.

The most effective intervention for successful coping with prodromal symptoms and counteracting mood changes is to re-evaluate the experience of past episodes and their consequences, and to engage in a cost-benefit analysis of letting things take their natural course, or to engage in constructive self-monitoring and self-regulating strategies. A useful therapeutic step within this is the acknowledgement of the difficulties in resisting especially hypomanic mood changes and the initial gratification that goes along with it. In this, we need to bear in mind that both appraisals of current symptoms and the memory of past episodes are influenced by mood-congruent biases. It is therefore valuable to use life-charting techniques and diary keeping to encourage patients to process recent changes in the context of past experience and in interaction with other life changes (Basco & Rush, 1996).

COGNITIVE STRATEGIES

The cognitive therapy techniques used for bipolar disorders include strategies aimed at the processing of symptoms and cognitive distortions relating to hypomanic and manic episodes. Furthermore, they aim to address beliefs and attributional biases linked to the psychological effects of long-term impairment through chronic mood-related difficulties and/or residual symptoms.

Most patients suffering from bipolar disorders describe mood-related difficulties and their social and interpersonal consequences as dating back to early adolescence. The long-standing nature of many of the associated difficulties and variation in intensity and severity over time make it difficult for many patients to identify areas of normal functioning or the clear demarcations of the "healthy self". Some schema work can therefore prove to be extremely useful in re-examining the value and evidence of old belief systems and the generation of new sets of beliefs adaptive to the current actuality.

Cognitive therapy follows a constructionist view of reality as being created by the individual's idiosyncratic preconceptions, perceptions, and memories. Cognitive therapy strategies, in the face of significant emotional difficulties, take into account the systematic distortions and maladaptation that can significantly influence the individual patient's world-view. This approach aims at the correction or re-evaluation of these systematic mood-congruent biases by re-examination of actual experiences and current interpersonal interactions, including the therapeutic relationship (e.g., Newman et al., 2002). In the presence of signs of mania and hypomania, cognitive therapists would aim to help patients to reality-test and re-examine their extremely positive world-view and self-perception, taking into consideration their current interactions and environmental stressors. Similar microtechniques and strategies come into play, for example, in the observance of daily thought records. Systematic thinking errors are driven by hyperpositive automatic thought patterns and beliefs not unlike the ones observed in depression, but with the opposite valence, such as overgeneralisation, mind-reading, and personalisation. In the re-evaluation of these thought patterns, it is important for the therapist to support patients in the process of rationalising by emphasising the maladaptive nature of such styles and consideration of the likely consequences of hyperpositive thinking.

Especially for manic or hypomanic patients, these attempts might be perceived as extremely counter-intuitive and controlling in the light of their self-perception of enjoying life and their new-found energy. It is therefore important for cognitive therapists working with bipolar patients to aim at preserving their sense of autonomy, self-efficacy, and control over their own lives. Techniques that support the self-efficacy and the re-evaluation of maladaptive beliefs include behavioural experiments, the feedback of close others, and anticipatory problem solving.

Patients can be encouraged to test their assumptions by creating real-life experiments. In hypomanic patients, this technique could lead to some reckless behaviour when hyperpositive thoughts are put to the test. In hypomania, therefore, behavioural experiments can be constructed to test the assumed consequences of not following impulses, acting with caution, and time-delays. To make constructive use of their social support system, bipolar patients often have to meet previous agreements with significant others regarding their intervention and advice, as hypomanic individuals often do not appreciate the influence of others.

One of the main features of manic or hypomanic phases is excessive risk taking. This is accompanied by a set of cognitive biases that leads many bipolar patients to underestimate the potential harm or overestimate the potential benefits of their behaviours (Leahy, 1999). Newman and colleagues (2002) introduce a version of the cost-benefit sheets often employed in CBT problem-solving techniques to get bipolar patients to balance the risk and benefit of actions prospectively—the "productive potential versus destructive risk rating technique". In this technique, patients use a two-column table balancing the "productive potential" and the "destructive potential" with the support of the therapist, a procedure which should allow individuals in a hypomanic or manic phase to consider the potentially negative consequences of their actions for others.

Related to these techniques which attempt to help bipolar patients to re-evaluate their hyperpositive thoughts are the following CBT applications to moderate their impulsivity. One example of this is the "time-delay" rule, encompassing contracted agreements to delay the execution of "spontaneous" ideas that might include adventurous activities or large purchases. The CBT technique of scheduling daily activities is commonly used to help depressed patients to master day-to-day activities and to reactivate the enjoyment of favourite pastimes; for bipolar patients, this technique can be employed to slow down the vicious cycle of mania driven by excessive activities, poor decision making, and more poorly deliberated and ineffective activities. Anticipatory problem solving regarding early warning signs of imminent mood swings and in relation to life stressors that might exacerbate symptoms (Johnson & Miller, 1997) appears to be crucial in these two areas where the coping abilities of bipolar patients can be particularly challenged. Therapeutically, the process of anticipatory problem solving includes the retrospective evaluation of past crises to identify potential problem areas in major life domains, and using problem-solving techniques to deal with these problem areas and obstacles in advance. Another technique to moderate hypomanic and manic mood is stimulus control. This includes the ability to moderate drug and alcohol use, and not to engage in extreme sports and other risk-taking and "exciting" activities. Medium to long-term choices in this connection include the regulation of working patterns that do not include extreme hours and frequent disruptions of sleep cycles. These strategies, especially when viewed medium to long term, might seem very challenging to individuals who are prone to act impulsively and like to engage in activities without much prior consideration and planning. To avoid conflict with the high autonomy of bipolar patients, the therapist needs to take as collaborative a position as possible.

Many bipolar patients argue that, in particular, their high moods, euphoria, and heightened irritability are autonomous from their volition. Therapeutically, it can be extremely challenging to moderate these mood states and to increase patients' willingness to participate in interventions that are incongruent with their current mood. Cognitive behavioural techniques that can be applied in that context are relaxation and breathing exercises, cognitive strategies to compare the lasting effects of pleasant affective states with their intensity, and the appraisal of positive beliefs that are linked to the high feelings themselves.

Individuals with bipolar disorder experience frequent and prolonged periods of depression which gradually foster feelings of hopelessness strongly associated with suicidal thinking and suicide. This is seen as being directly related to the problems created by frequent mood swings and associated behaviours. Bipolar patients frequently have to reassemble their lives after episodes of manic acting out and depressive withdrawal; they find it difficult to trust their euthymic mood and not to worry about the impending relapse. The diagnosis itself, its cyclical episodes, and their treatments are further associated with stigma and shame, making it harder for individuals to utilise and maintain their social support network, and prolonging their depressogenic beliefs and hence their vulnerability to relapse (Lundin, 1998). In sum, bipolar disorder contains painful and unstable affect, extremes of cognitions and behaviours, interpersonal deficits, and a lasting sense of Sisyphus' despairing exhaustion. As a result, the lifetime suicide rates have been found to be 15–25% (Goodwin & Jamieson, 1990; Simpson & Jamieson, 1999; see Chapter 18). An assessment of risk therefore needs to be an ongoing feature in the treatment of individuals suffering from bipolar disorder.

The CBT of depression is discussed in detail elsewhere in this volume (see Chapter 8) and generally applies well to the depressed mood states within bipolar disorder. Here I would only like to point to a few specific aspects that might be more specifically relevant to individuals suffering from bipolar disorder.

Many people suffering from bipolar disorders report a long history of several significant illness episodes, the traumatic impact of multiple hospital admissions, and partially successful treatment regimens involving several different psychotropic medications. Individuals in this disorder group often suffer from significant residual symptoms and have experienced short periods of remission followed by frequent relapses. This poses a particular challenge to the clinician, and patients and their significant others might express increased hopelessness regarding remission and scepticism regarding the model offered by the clinician. Key characteristics of chronic or partially remitted disorders, such as suicidal ideation, hopelessness, low self-esteem and self-efficacy, avoidant coping strategies, and poor problem solving are amenable to change through cognitive behavioural strategies.

In a high-risk population, such as patients with bipolar disorder, it is advisable to negotiate an antisuicide agreement, and although such contracts do not prevent suicides, they highlight and validate the importance of a safe environment for patients and therapists alike (Kleepsies & Dettmer, 2000; Stanford et al., 1994). In the face of intense suicidal ideation, the therapist aims to reveal the beliefs underlying suicidal thoughts and to engage the patient in the exploration of alternative and life-affirming beliefs. These interventions include the open investigation of the pros and cons of suicide, the gentle challenging of assumptions behind suicidal thoughts (for example, suicide as solution to all problems), and consideration of the social context and the consequences of such thoughts and actions. As utilised in the CBT of unipolar depression, the increase of mastery and pleasure in productive and enjoyable activities can instil hope and encourage self-efficacy. Cognitive factors associated with increased risk of suicidality are "cognitive rigidity", perfectionism, and poor autobiographical recall (Blatt, 1995; Ellis & Ratcliff, 1986; Evans et al., 1992; Scott et al., 2000). Cognitive rigidity refers to depressogenic, all-or-nothing thinking and has a strong link with the hopelessness and despair associated with suicidality. This particular thinking style is therefore at the core of cognitive interventions. Likewise, perfectionism describes a set of beliefs that makes individuals vulnerable to depression and hopelessness, and it compromises constructive problem solving. Zuroff and colleagues (2000) suggest that perfectionist beliefs are related to self-criticism, perceived stress, and increased interpersonal problems, and they can further impede the therapeutic alliance. Poor autobiographical recall has been linked to problem-solving deficits in unipolar and bipolar depressed individuals (Evans et al., 1992; Scott et al., 2000); it compromises their ability to learn from past experience, and it can thus confirm old dysfunctional beliefs.

Central to the effective treatment of chronic or acute depressive difficulties in bipolar patients is the optimal utilisation of their social support network. The consequences and interactional styles of both manic and depressed episodes can easily compromise the individuals' relationships. A careful assessment of the individuals' social network and the relationships that survived following many mania-induced conflicts and depression-induced estrangements will provide a fruitful starting point for the rebuilding of a stable and supportive social environment. Detailed analysis of specific interactions or situations as well as role-playing and other social skills-training techniques might provide crucial assets in the cognitive behavioural intervention.

INTERPERSONAL FUNCTIONING

The third phase of the treatment is targeted on the interpersonal difficulties that precipitate or resulted from the disorder. This is where cognitive strategies address core beliefs and schemata. The goals for this phase of the treatment include the experience of increased self-efficacy and the rebuilding of a more solid and autonomous sense of self. This takes account of the impact of the illness, which often occurs in a developmentally critical time when self-esteem and identity are formed. It further appears that the impact of mania and depression at an early age are significant, as they dramatically affect important developmental milestones such as educational achievements, early work experience, and important interpersonal relationships. Essential cognitive structures such as dysfunctional core beliefs will probably become self-perpetuating. Examples of these beliefs include a distorted sense of autonomy or personal capability, vulnerability to harm or illness, and a sense of defectiveness and unlovableness. Maladaptive core beliefs that may have been established by the early onset of the disorder or traumatic events are important to address, as it will help those individuals to understand and cope with the specific psychosocial impairments experienced later in the life course.

These interpersonal vulnerabilities and risk factors can play a major part in the recovery and prevention of relapse of the individual. Therapeutically, some of this process will consist of the facilitation of successful transitions following major episodes, significant psychosocial changes, and the adjustment to necessary lifestyle changes. As in the above mentioned model of the importance of corrective experiences and behaviour change in individuals with bipolar disorder, these changes in the cognitive emotional schemata of the bipolar patient are achieved through consistent behavioural adaptations to the vulnerabilities intrinsic to the disorder. In their reformulation of the interpersonal psychotherapy (IPT) framework for bipolar disorder (IP/SRT), Frank and colleagues (1997) combine the key interpersonal difficulties associated with bipolar disorder with an introduction to the strict monitoring of social routines and circadian rhythms (see Chapter 15). By addressing interpersonal problems and the regularity of daily routines, this method deals with both concurrent symptoms and the impact of interpersonally based stressors on patients' life, and increases their resistance to potential vulnerabilities.

The application of these techniques within a CBT framework allows the patient to develop an understanding of how adverse interpersonal experiences create maladaptive schemata about the self, foster dysfunctional attachment beliefs, and impair the acquisition of effective interpersonal problem-solving strategies. Patients also advance their understanding of how these might alter the threshold of stress needed to trigger a depressive or manic reaction, and how the generation of these events might be maintained by dysfunctional ways of solving emerging interpersonal difficulties and by conflicts arising from maladaptive expectations about others (Lovejoy & Steuerwald, 1997). The direct therapeutic targeting of these interpersonal vulnerabilities can lead to schema change and the development of stable supportive interactions in the presence of negative life events that aid the prevention of relapse.

OUTCOMES

Early investigations of CBT techniques in bipolar disorder focused almost solely on the adherence to medical treatments. The main studies of this particular CBT application are by Benson (1975) and Cochran (1984). Benson (1975) reports a retrospective analysis of 31 bipolar disorder patients who were all in a manic phase at the start of treatment, receiving a combination treatment of lithium and psychotherapy. Comparisons were made between relapse in this group of people with a diagnosis of bipolar disorder and previous reports of relapse rates with lithium alone. He reports that 14% of his patients relapsed compared with the reported mean relapse rate of 34% with lithium alone. He suggests that psychotherapy is important to keep the patient motivated to continue lithium, to provide basic therapeutic support, and to monitor the patient's mood as a way of early detection of falling serum lithium levels.

Cochran's (1984) study is probably the most cited paper in the context of cognitive therapy for bipolar disorders. He evaluated the effectiveness of a preventative treatment-adherence intervention with 28 outpatients with a diagnosis of bipolar disorder who had recently started lithium treatment. The intervention consisted of six sessions of modified CBT aimed at cognitions and behaviour that seemed to be interfering with treatment adherence. Comparison was made with a control group who received standard outpatient follow-up, at the end of treatment and after 6-month follow-up. Neither the patient self-report nor the lithium levels showed an effect of the intervention; only the psychiatrists' observation showed better perceived adherence in the treatment group after therapy. At 6-month follow-up, patients in the treatment group showed significantly less hospitalisations and affective episodes. The intervention as described does not seem to take into account symptoms and other manifestations of the disorder, but pays attention only to compliance with pharmacological treatment.

A number of studies have since focused predominantly on relapse prevention and the identification of prodromal symptoms and early signs of relapse. Perry and colleagues (1999) investigated 69 patients with a diagnosis of bipolar disorder who had had a relapse in the previous 12 months. Subjects were randomised into two conditions, 7–12 sessions with a research psychologist plus routine care or routine care alone. The CBT intervention consisted of teaching patients to recognise early symptoms of manic and depressive relapse and producing and rehearsing an action plan. By comparison, the treatment group experienced significantly longer intervals until manic relapse than the control group. Furthermore, the authors found significant improvements on measures of social functioning and employment in the treatment group compared with the control group 18 months after the baseline assessment.

Several more comprehensive studies utilising a CBT framework focused not only on treatment adherence, relapse prevention, and reduction of symptomatic distress but also on psychosocial functioning. Palmer and colleagues (1995) describe a psychoeducational and CBT programme in a group format for people with a diagnosis of bipolar disorder, currently in remission. Four participants attended 17 weekly group sessions. At the end of treatment, three of the four participants showed significant improvements in depressive and manic symptoms. Three of the four of the participants showed significant improvement in their social adjustment at the end of treatment and two at follow-up. Zaretsky and colleagues (1999) designed a cognitive behavioural intervention focusing on the treatment of acute symptoms rather than relapse prevention. In a matched case controlled design, they demonstrated the effectiveness of a 20-session CBT intervention for acute depression in the context of a bipolar disorder compared to the effectiveness in recurrent unipolar depression by comparing both groups in parallel. They found that depressive symptoms in eight bipolar and eight unipolar patients were significantly reduced after CBT intervention. Lam and colleagues (2000) describe a cognitive therapy approach for a total of 12 bipolar patients. The treatment consisted of 12–20 sessions over 6 months. On a global symptom level (over 12 months), the treatment group had significantly fewer episodes and fewer hospitalisations than to the control group. The monthly self-report and observer ratings of manic and depressive symptoms confirmed that there was significantly lower level of manic and depressive symptoms in the treatment group over the course of the 12 months. The therapy group performed significantly better on medication compliance, social functioning, self-controlled behaviour, and coping with mania and depression prodromes. Patelis-Siotis (2001) reported outcomes of a 14-session adjunctive group CBT for patients suffering from a bipolar disorder. Forty-nine outpatients with a diagnosis of bipolar disorder currently maintained on a stable mood level on medication participated in a CBT group programme focusing on psychoeducation and cognitive behavioural intervention strategies. The results indicate no significant changes in mood-related symptoms between baseline and end of treatment. However, a significant increase in psychosocial functioning was found. Scott and colleagues (2001a) report the outcome of a randomised controlled study testing the feasibility and potential benefits of cognitive therapy for people with a diagnosis of bipolar disorder. Following assessment, patients were randomly assigned to immediate cognitive therapy or a 6-month waiting-list control condition. Both groups contained 21 subjects. Patients were followed up at 6-month intervals for a maximum of 18 months. In comparison with the waiting-list control groups, the CBT group showed significant reductions in symptoms and improvement in global functioning. They also found that significantly fewer subjects met criteria for relapse after CBT than before, and hospitalisation rates were significantly lower in the year after CBT intervention.

CONCLUSIONS

In conclusion, it seems that there is mounting evidence of the clinical efficacy and effectiveness of CBT, which can be a most useful mode of psychological intervention for individuals suffering from bipolar disorder. It appears that CBT is acceptable and appeals to patients with bipolar disorder for its structured application, the high level of autonomy, and its potential to integrate past and current experiences in a comprehensive and applicable framework. Furthermore, reformulations and adaptations of the cognitive behavioural model of affective and psychotic disorders allow the integration of developmental and interpersonal facets of bipolar disorder in a beneficial way. Discussion of the most optimal form of delivery of this psychotherapeutic intervention remains inconclusive. The significant deficits and losses experienced by patients with bipolar disorder in all aspects of their lives support longer and more integrated treatment modalities and call for the investigation of a comprehensive developmental model of bipolar psychopathology.

REFERENCES

Alloy, L., Reilly-Harrington, N.A., Fresco, D.M., Whitehouse, W.G. & Zechmeister, J.S. (1999). Cognitive styles and life-events in subsyndromal unipolar and bipolar disorders: Stability and prospective prediction of depressive and hypomanic mood swings. *Journal of Cognitive Psychotherapy, 13*, 21–40.

Basco, M.R. & Rush, A.J. (1996). *Cognitive Behavioural Therapy for Bipolar Disorder*. New York: Guilford.

Beck, A.T. (1979). *Cognitive Therapy and the Emotional Disorders*. New York: Guilford.

Beck, A.T. (1996). Beyond belief: A theory of modes, personality and psychopathology. In P.M. Salkovskis (Ed.), *Frontiers of Cognitive Therapy* (pp. 1–25). New York: Guilford.

Benson, R. (1975). The forgotten treatment modality in bipolar illness: Psychotherapy. *Diseases of the Nervous System, 36*, 634–638.

Blatt, S.J. (1995). The destructiveness of perfectionism: Implications for the treatment of depression. *American Psychologist, 50*, 1003–1020.

Brady, K.T. & Lydiard, B. (1992). Bipolar affective disorder and substance abuse. *Journal of Clinical Psychopharmacology, 12*,17s–22s.

Cochran, S.D. (1984). Preventing medical non-compliance in the outpatient treatment of bipolar affective disorder. *Journal of Consulting and Clinical Psychology, 52*, 873–878.

Ellis, T.E. & Ratcliff, K.G. (1986). Cognitive characteristics of suicidal and non-suicidal psychiatric inpatients. *Cognitive Therapy and Research, 10*, 625–634.

Evans, J., Williams, J., O'Loughlin, S. & Howells, K. (1992). Autobiographical memory and problem-solving strategies of parasuicidal patients. *Psychological Medicine, 22*, 399–405.

Frank, E., Hlastala, S., Ritenour, A., et al. (1997). Inducing lifestyle regularity in recovering bipolar disorder patients: Results from the maintenance therapies in bipolar disorder protocol. *Biological Psychiatry, 41*, 1165–1173.

Frank, E., Swartz, A.H., Mallinger, A.G., Thase, M.E., Waever, E.V. & Kupfer D.J. (1999). Adjunctive psychotherapy for bipolar disorder: Effects of changing treatment modality. *Journal of Abnormal Psychology, 108*, 579–587.

Goodwin, F. & Jamieson, K. (1990). *Manic Depressive Illness*. Oxford: Oxford University Press.

Himmelhoch, J.M. (1999). The paradox of anxiety syndromes in comorbid with the bipolar illnesses. In J.F. Goldberg & M. Harrow (Eds), *Bipolar Disorders: Clinical Course and Outcome* (pp. 237–258). Washington, DC: American Psychiatric Press.

Isometsa, E.T. (1993). Course, outcome and suicide risk in bipolar disorder: A review. *Psychiatrica Fennica, 24*, 113–124.

Johnson, S.L. & Miller, I. (1997). Negative life events and time to recovery from episodes of bipolar disorder. *Journal of Abnormal Psychology, 106*, 449–457.

Johnson, S.L., Winett, C., Meyer, B., Greenhouse, W. & Miller, I. (1999). Social support and the course of bipolar disorder. *Journal of Abnormal psychology, 108*, 558–566.

Jones, S.H. (2001). Circadian rhythms, multilevel models of emotion and bipolar disorder—an initial step towards integration? *Clinical Psychology Review, 21*, 1193–1209.

Kessler, R.C., McGonagle, K.A., Zhao, S., et al. (1994). Lifetime and 12 month prevalence of DMS-III-R psychiatric disorders in the United States: Results from the national Comorbidity Survey. *Archives of General Psychiatry, 51*, 8–19.

Kessler, R.C., Rubinow, D.R., Holmes, C., Abelson, J.M. & Zhao, S. (1997). The epidemiology of DSM-III-R bipolar I disorder in a general population survey. *Psychological Medicine, 27*, 1079–1089.

Kleepsies, P.M. & Dettmer, E.L. (2000). An evidence-based approach to evaluating and managing suicidal emergencies. *Journal of Clinical Psychology, 56*, 1109–1130.

Lam, D.H. & Wong, G. (1997). Prodromes, coping strategies, insight and social functioning in bipolar affective disorder. *Psychological Medicine, 27*, 1091–1100.

Lam, D.H., Bright, J., Jones, S., et al. (2000). Cognitive therapy for bipolar illness. A pilot study of relapse prevention. *Cognitive Therapy and Research, 24*, 503–520.

Lam, D.H., Jones, S.H., Hayward, P. & Bright, J.A. (1999). *Cognitive Therapy for Bipolar Disorder*. Chichester: Wiley.

Leahy, R.L. (1999). An investment model of depressive resistance. *Journal of Cognitive Psychotherapy, 11*, 3–19.

Lovejoy, M.C. & Steuerwald, B.L. (1997). Subsyndromal unipolar and bipolar disorders. II. Comparisons on daily stress levels. *Cognitive Therapy and Research, 21*, 607–618.

Lundin, R.K. (1998). Living with mental illness: A personal experience. *Cognitive and Behavioural Practice, 5*, 223–230.

Malkoff-Schwartz, S., Frank, E., Anderson, B., et al. (1998). Stressful life events and social rhythm disruption in the onset of manic and depressive bipolar episodes: A preliminary investigation. *Archives of General Psychiatry, 55*, 702–707.

Newman, C.F., Leahy, R.L., Beck, A.T., Reilly-Harrington, N.A. & Gyulai, L. (2002). *Bipolar Disorder—a Cognitive Therapy Approach*. Washington, DC: American Psychological Association.

Palmer, A.G., Williams, H. & Adams, M. (1995). CBT in a group format for bipolar affective disorder. *Behavioural and Cognitive Psychotherapy, 23*, 153–168.

Patelis-Siotis, I. (2001). Cognitive-behavioural therapy: Application for the management of bipolar disorder. *Bipolar Disorder, 3*, 1–10.

Perry, A., Tarrier, N., Morriss, R., McCarthy, E. & Limb, K. (1999). Randomised controlled trial of efficacy of teaching patients with bipolar disorder to identify early symptoms of relapse and obtain treatment. *British Medical Journal, 318*, 149–153.

Peselow, E., Sanfilipo, M. & Fieve, R. (1995). Relationship between hypomania and personality disorders before and after successful treatment. *American Journal of Psychiatry, 152*, 232–238.

Power, M.J. & Dalgleish, T. (1997). *Cognition and Emotion: From Order to Disorder*. Hove: Psychology Press.

Power, M.J. & Dalgleish, T. (1999). Two routes to emotion: Some implications of multi-level theories of emotion for therapeutic practice. *Behaviour and Cognitive Psychotherapy, 27*, 129–141.

Ramana, R. & Bebbington, P. (1995). Social influences on bipolar affective disorders. *Social Psychiatry and Psychiatric Epidemiology, 30*, 152–160.

Reilly-Harrington, N.A., Alloy, L.B., Fresco, W. & Whitehouse, W.G. (1999). Cognitive styles and life events interact to predict bipolar and unipolar symptomatology. *Journal of Abnormal Psychology, 108*, 567–578.

Scott, J. (2001a). Cognitive therapy as an adjunct to medication in bipolar disorder. *British Journal of Psychiatry, 178*, 164–168.

Scott, J. (2001b). *Overcoming Mood Swings: A Self-Help Guide Using Cognitive and Behavioural Techniques*. London: Constable Robinson.

Scott, J., Stanton, B., Garland, A. & Ferrier, N. (2000). Cognitive vulnerability to bipolar disorder. *Psychological Medicine, 30*, 467–472.

Simpson, S.G. & Jamieson, K.R. (1999). The risk of suicide in patients with bipolar disorder. *Journal of Clinical Psychiatry, 60* (Suppl. 2), 53–56.

Smith, J.A. & Tarrier, N. (1992). Prodromal symptoms in manic depressive psychosis. *Social Psychiatry and Psychiatric Epidemiology, 27*, 245–248.

Stanford, E., Goetz, R. & Bloom, J. (1994). The no harm contract in the emergency assessment of suicidal risk. *Journal of Clinical Psychiatry, 55*, 344–348.

Teasdale, J.D. & Barnard, P.J.B. (1993). *Affect, Cognition and Change: Remodelling Depressive Thought*. Hove: Erlbaum.

Young, J.E. (1999). *Cognitive Therapy for Personality Disorder: A Schema-Focused Approach* (3rd edn). Sarasota, FL: Professional Resource Exchange.

Zaretsky, A.E., Zindel, V.S. & Gemar, M. (1999). Cognitive therapy for bipolar depression: A pilot study. *Canadian Journal of Psychiatry, 44*, 491–494.

Zuroff, D.C., Blatt, S.J., Sotsky, S.M., et al. (2000). Relation of therapeutic alliance and perfectionism to outcome in brief outpatient treatment of depression. *Journal of Consulting and Clinical Psychology, 68*, 114–124.

15

INTERPERSONAL AND SOCIAL RHYTHM THERAPY

*Holly A. Swartz, Ellen Frank, Heather N. Spielvogle,
and David J. Kupfer*

INTRODUCTION

Pharmacotherapy constitutes the mainstay of treatment for bipolar disorder. Nevertheless, for individuals suffering from bipolar disorder, treatment with pharmacotherapy alone is associated with incomplete remission (Goodwin & Jamison, 1990), substantial risk for recurrence (Gitlin et al., 1995), and persistent impairments in functioning (Coryell et al., 1993). Psychotherapies that address psychosocial difficulties and enhance illness management (that is, medication adherence, and detection of warning signs of relapse) may play an important role in bridging the gap between symptom improvement brought about by medications and a full recovery from illness. Indeed, a growing body of research suggests that, when compared to treatment with pharmacotherapy alone, treatment with the combination of medication and a bipolar-specific psychotherapy results in better outcomes for patients (Craighead et al., 1998; Kusumakar et al., 1997; Swartz & Frank, 2001). Current expert treatment guidelines recommend the combination of psychotherapy and medication for the acute management of bipolar depression and during the maintenance phase of the disorder (American Psychiatric Association, 2002). Thus, psychotherapy is considered an integral component of treatment for individuals suffering from bipolar disorder. In this chapter, we will describe interpersonal and social rhythm therapy (IPSRT), a bipolar-specific psychotherapy currently being tested in a large clinical trial at the University of Pittsburgh.

OVERVIEW OF INTERPERSONAL AND SOCIAL RHYTHM THERAPY (IPSRT)

IPSRT was developed as a response to the observation that pharmacotherapy, although essential to the treatment of bipolar disorder, is often not enough for patients suffering from

Mood Disorders: A Handbook of Science and Practice. Edited by M. Power.
© 2004 John Wiley & Sons, Ltd. ISBN 0-470-84390-X.

the disorder. Studies of maintenance treatment with mood stabilizers alone demonstrate unacceptably high rates of recurrence over a 2–3 year period (Gelenberg et al., 1989; Markar & Mander, 1989), and persistence of residual psychosocial difficulties despite syndromal recovery (Goldberg et al., 1995). In order to address these clinical dilemmas, Dr Ellen Frank at the University of Pittsburgh developed a psychotherapy designed both to facilitate full recovery from illness and promote long-term wellness. IPSRT, built on the principles of interpersonal psychotherapy (IPT) for unipolar depression (Klerman et al., 1984) and theories of circadian rhythm biology (Ehlers et al., 1988), has the tripartite goals of supporting medication adherence, minimizing the impact of disruptive life events on social rhythms, and addressing interpersonal difficulties as they arise in the context of a mood disorder. In a broader sense, IPSRT strives to dampen the most extreme oscillations of mood and energy by helping patients to manage provocative social and environmental factors more effectively. IPSRT integrates psychoeducational, interpersonal, and behavioral strategies in order to reduce symptoms, improve functioning, and prevent recurrence of episodes.

Theoretical background

The framework of IPSRT rests on three related theoretical constructs:

(1) the "instability model" of bipolar disorder proposed by Goodwin and Jamison (1990)
(2) theories regarding the function of social and environmental cues in promoting/disrupting circadian rhythm integrity (Ehlers et al., 1988; 1993)
(3) the principles of IPT conceptualized by Klerman and Weissman, (Klerman et al., 1984).

We discuss the theoretical underpinnings of each component below.

INSTABILITY MODEL

In their instability model, Goodwin and Jamison (1990) define three interconnected pathways to episode recurrence: taxing life events, medication noncompliance, and social rhythm disruption. Each pathway potentially leads a stable patient towards an episode of depression or mania. Their model suggests that individuals with bipolar disorder are fundamentally (biologically) vulnerable to disruptions in circadian rhythms. Psychosocial stressors, in turn, interact with this biological vulnerability to cause symptoms. For instance, stressful life events (such as the birth of a child) disrupt social rhythms, causing disturbances in circadian integrity, which, in turn, may lead to recurrence. Alternately, problematic interpersonal relationships or irregular work schedules contribute to nonadherence to a medication regimen, which, again, may lead to recurrence. Conversely, a patient's ambivalent feelings about medications or intolerable side effects may lead the patient to skip doses or discontinue medication. As medication is decreased, symptoms and rhythm irregularities emerge. As a direct consequence of this model, one would assume that helping patients learn to take their medication regularly, lead more orderly lives, and resolve interpersonal problems more effectively would promote circadian integrity and minimize risk of recurrence. IPSRT focuses on all three of these pathways in an effort to stabilize mood.

ZEITGEBERS AND ZEITSTÖRERS

Related to the model elaborated by Goodwin and Jamison (above), circadian rhythm researchers have identified reciprocal relationships among circadian rhythms, sleep-wake cycles, and mood. It is well documented, for instance, that sleep reduction can lead to mania in bipolar subjects (Leibenluft et al., 1996; Wehr et al., 1987). Furthermore, sleep deprivation has significant (if transient) antidepressant effects in both unipolar and bipolar depressed subjects (Barbini et al., 1998; Leibenluft et al., 1993; Leibenluft & Suppes, 1999). Ehlers and colleagues (1988), attempting to bridge the biological and psychosocial models of depression, hypothesized that there are specific social cues that entrain biological cycles (*Zeitgebers*) and others that disrupt them (*Zeitstörers*). Social Zeitgebers are defined as personal relationships, social demands, or tasks that entrain biological rhythms (for example, meeting school-age children at the bus stop at 3 p.m. each day). They further hypothesized that losing a social Zeitgeber (for example, summer vacation with the attendant loss of the school bus pickup) could trigger an episode by causing the dysregulation of biological rhythms (Ehlers et al., 1993). Another example of a social Zeitgeber is a regular job. Losing a job that may have previously determined sleep/wake times, rest periods, and meal times represents a lost Zeitgeber. In an individual with the genetic predisposition to depression, the physiological and chronobiological disturbances produced by losing the social cues for sleep and meal times could be as important in the genesis of an episode as the psychological distress generated by the event.

In contrast to Zeitgebers, Zeitstörers are defined as physical, chemical, or psychosocial events that *disturb* the biological clock. For instance, travel across time zones represents a prototypical Zeitstörer. The abrupt change in the timing of light exposure, rest times, and sleep schedule can produce a range of symptoms from mild jet lag to a full-blown affective episode in predisposed individuals. Other examples of potential Zeitstörers include newborn babies, marital separations, work deadlines (especially those that require an individual to stay at work into the night, missing meals and sleep), and rotating shift work. Each of these disruptions has the potential to alter significantly an individual's circadian and sleep-wake rhythms and, in turn, provoke an affective episode. IPSRT was built on the idea that helping patients to regulate social rhythms (modulate Zeitgebers and Zeitstörers) may help vulnerable individuals reduce the risk of developing mood symptoms.

INTERPERSONAL PSYCHOTHERAPY (IPT)

IPT was developed by Klerman and colleagues as a treatment for unipolar depression (Klerman et al., 1984). This treatment is described in detail elsewhere in this textbook (See Chapter 9). Built on the tenets of social psychology and the observations of interpersonal theorists such as Harry Stack Sullivan, IPT focuses on the link between mood and interpersonal life events. IPT postulates that psychosocial and interpersonal factors are associated with the onset and maintenance of mood episodes in individuals biologically predisposed to affective disorders, and that symptoms of mood disorders interfere with the interpersonal coping skills of the afflicted individuals. In IPSRT, therapists use IPT strategies both to resolve interpersonal difficulties and to lessen the impact of stressful interpersonal events on daily routines.

TREATMENT STRATEGIES

A hybrid model

Built on these overlapping paradigms, IPSRT fuses three distinct interventions—psychoeducation, social rhythm therapy, and IPT—into a single psychosocial treatment. IPSRT helps patients optimize daily schedules, resolve interpersonal difficulties, and understand their illness in order to achieve symptom remission and improve interpersonal functioning. By intervening in these potential pathways to recurrence, IPSRT ultimately strives to prevent new episodes of illness in a highly vulnerable population. Each treatment intervention (psychoeducation, social rhythm therapy, and IPT) will be described separately. In practice, however, these strategies are administered flexibly and fluidly, without distinct boundaries between modalities. During the course of a single session, the therapist moves seamlessly among the techniques, according to the particular needs of the patient. Thus, the IPSRT represents a true integration of these disparate approaches. Table 15.1 summarizes these three strategies and the treatment techniques associated with them.

Table 15.1 IPSRT treatment strategies

Strategy	Techniques
Psychoeducation	Provide education regarding: ❑ medications and their side effects ❑ course and symptoms of bipolar disorder Teach patients to recognize: ❑ early warning signs of recurrence ❑ prodromal symptoms Encourage patient to: ❑ become "expert" on their illness ❑ collaboratively manage illness with therapist and psychiatrist
Social rhythm therapy	Balance stimulation and stability Complete Social Rhythm Metric ❑ monitor frequency/intensity of social interactions ❑ monitor daily mood Search for specific triggers of rhythm disruption Gradually regularize social rhythms
Interpersonal psychotherapy	Conduct in-depth psychiatric evaluation Link mood to life events Establish interpersonal case formulation (focus on one or two problem areas): ❑ grief ❑ role transition ❑ role dispute ❑ interpersonal deficits Grieve for the lost "healthy self"

PSYCHOEDUCATION

Psychoeducation subsumes a heterogeneous group of interventions that are deployed in the service of treating a wide variety of disorders. Virtually all bipolar-specific psychotherapies incorporate psychoeducation—albeit to varying degrees. Psychoeducation is also an integral part of standard IPT (see discussion below). In IPSRT, psychoeducation focuses on (a) the illness and its consequences, (b) medications and their side effects, and (c) prodromal symptoms/detection of early warning symptoms. Patients receive information from the therapist about the symptoms and course of bipolar disorder, the impact of the illness on vocational and social functioning, and the medications used to treat bipolar disorder. In the course of IPSRT, patients are encouraged to become "experts" in bipolar disorder so that they can collaborate more effectively in the management of their illness. In the instance of a physician-clinician treatment team, the nonphysician therapist must also develop familiarity with the major classes of medications used to treat the disorder and their side effects in order to help the patient recognize medication-related problems and collaborate with the physician to manage them. Therapists are encouraged to work collaboratively with the patient to understand and remedy sources of nonadherence—including management of side effects—that interfere with optimal quality of life.

In order to encourage early identification of prodromal symptoms, the therapist reviews with the patient prior episodes of depression and mania. Jointly, the therapist and patient identify characteristic behaviors or symptoms that may herald the onset of an episode, and agree to assess the patient routinely for these harbingers of exacerbation. In addition, family members of IPSRT patients are encouraged to attend a 1-day psychoeducation workshop in order to facilitate medication compliance and help detect early warning signs of recurrence.

Clinical vignette 1

Amy is a 31-year-old single woman with a 10-year history of bipolar disorder. Recent plasma levels of her current primary mood stabilizer, sodium divalproex, were perplexingly low. In IPSRT, the therapist reviewed with Amy the parameters of therapeutic blood levels and then pointed out that the two most recent blood tests fell below the therapeutic range. The therapist reminded Amy about the risk of nonadherence to pharmacotherapy, and gently asked her whether she had any insight into her uncharacteristically low blood levels. Amy burst into tears, revealing that her boyfriend had threatened to leave her because of her 30-pound weight gain over the past year, which he attributed to sodium divalproex. The therapist acknowledged that weight gain can be a troubling side effect of many of the medications used to treat bipolar disorder. Together, they reviewed Amy's currently prescribed medications, which, in addition to the divalproex, included olanzapine and citalopram. Given the complex medication regimen currently prescribed for Amy, the therapist suggested that the weight gain might not be attributable solely to the divalproex. They discussed other options besides abruptly discontinuing her medication, such as consulting with her psychiatrist to discuss alternatives and pursuing an exercise regimen. In addition to helping Amy understand the importance of raising this issue specifically with her psychiatrist, the therapist discussed with Amy how her weight gain had affected her relationship. They reviewed the importance of educating her boyfriend about her medications, explored other areas of conflict in the relationship, and discussed the negative impact of the weight gain on Amy's sex life with her boyfriend (related to her shame about her changing body).

SOCIAL RHYTHM THERAPY

Social rhythm therapy is based on the theory that stable daily rhythms lead to enhanced stability of mood. This component of treatment focuses on developing strategies to promote regular, rhythm-entraining, social Zeitgebers and manage the negative impact of disrupting Zeistörers. Each week, patients are asked to complete an instrument, the Social Rhythm Metric (SRM), that helps them optimize their daily rhythms. This 17-item self-report form asks patients to record daily activities (that is, time out of bed, first contact with another person, meal times, and bedtime), whether each occurred alone or with others present, and whether or not they involved significant amounts of social stimulation (that is, quiet versus interactive). Patients are also asked to rate their moods each day. A shorter version of the SRM (five items) has also been validated and may be more easily implemented than the longer form in most clinical settings (Monk et al., 2002).

In the beginning stages of treatment, the patient is asked to complete the SRM weekly. The first 3–4 weeks of SRMs are used to establish the patient's baseline social rhythms. The therapist and patient jointly review the SRMs, identifying both stable and unstable daily rhythms. For instance, is the patient going to bed at a reasonable hour during the week but then staying out late on the weekends? Does the patient's mood dip on days when she or he skips meals? By examining the SRMs, the therapist and patient can begin to identify behaviors that negatively influence the patient's rhythm stability.

Once baseline SRMs are collected and patterns of regularity/irregularity identified, the therapist and patient begin working towards rhythm stability through graded, sequential lifestyle changes. The therapist and patient identify short-term, intermediate, and long-term goals to bring social rhythms gradually into a tighter, less variable range. For example, a short-term goal may be going to bed at a fixed time for a period of 1 week. In order to achieve that goal, the patient may need to make changes in his or her social behaviors (for example, curtailing late-night social activities) and health-related behaviors (for example, working with the psychiatrist to move all sedating medications to bedtime). Intermediate goals may include sleeping 8 hours a night with no naps during the day or decrease the number of hours spent at work. In order to accomplish these goals, the patient will build on short-terms gains but also institute some new social cues (such as signing up for afternoon classes to decrease napping). The therapist emphasizes the importance of establishing a *regular* schedule, even if the schedule most comfortable to the patient is phase shifted. For instance, many patients with bipolar disorder prefer to establish regular routines that include a late bedtime (such as 2 a.m.) and a later awakening time (such as 10 a.m.). The therapist helps patients understand that virtually any regular schedule is acceptable as long as they are able to meet their social obligations and to sleep for an adequate duration in a single time block (for most individuals, 7–9 hours). Long-term goals may consist of encouraging patients to find a job which allows them to keep a more regular schedule (for example, a job in a movie theater that does not begin until noon). In an effort to regulate rhythms, the therapist will also monitor the frequency and intensity of social interactions and identify connections between mood and activity level. If a patient is depressed, the therapist may encourage the patient to participate in more stimulating activities; if hypomanic, the patient will be encouraged to minimize overstimulation.

During the course of treatment, the therapist continues to review SRMs. The weekly SRM provides the therapist with the opportunity to review progress toward identified social rhythm goals and address impediments to change. In addition, the SRM is used to help the patient self-monitor for evidence of an exacerbation of the mood disorder. When a patient begins to slip into an episode of mania or depression, changes in sleep and activity levels may be detected on the SRM before the patient is aware of a shift in mood. Thus, the SRM is used as both a measure of therapeutic change and an ancillary mechanism for monitoring symptoms.

Clinical vignette 2

Bob is a 52-year-old married man with bipolar disorder who began treatment with IP-SRT because of a 6-month history of depression that was unresponsive to sequential trials of mood stabilizers plus antidepressants. He had been a successful businessman, but several devastating manic episodes had left him bankrupt and estranged from his family. After he completed 3 weeks of SRMs, it became apparent that Bob consistently reversed his days and nights, spent hours on the Internet from midnight to 5 a.m., and slept routinely during the daytime. He was also very isolated, with few social contacts. Bob acknowledged that he felt lonely and disconnected from "the rest of the world". The therapist helped the patient see that his sleep schedule was contributing to his isolation and perhaps his depression. Together, they worked out a plan to shift his bedtime gradually from 6 a.m. to 2 a.m. over a period of several weeks. Bob agreed to participate in some regular activities during daytime hours, such as a daily walk to buy the newspaper at a neighborhood store, and at least one phone call to a friend or relative around the conventional dinner hour. Although progress was slow, the patient noted some improvement in his mood as he began the process of reconnecting with his social network. The social rhythm therapy component of IPSRT helped provide opportunities for social interactions; IPT strategies were then used to help Bob develop new skills to manage these interactions.

INTERPERSONAL PSYCHOTHERAPY (IPT)

IPT is thoroughly described elsewhere in this text (Chapter 9) and will be described very briefly in this chapter. The initial phase of IPT begins with an in-depth psychiatric evaluation. The therapist conceptualizes the patient's "problem" as a medical illness characterized by specific symptoms linked to biological processes, equating bipolar disorder with medical illnesses such as diabetes or heart disease. The therapist educates the patient, making direct statements about diagnosis, the heritability of the disorder, and treatment options. This approach, in addition to ensuring an accurate diagnosis, relieves the patient of the guilt associated with this syndrome. During the initial phase of treatment, the therapist also gives patients the *sick role* (Parsons, 1951), a role that encourages patients to participate actively in treatment, helps them accept that symptoms are manifestations of a medical condition, and relieves them of unmanageable social obligations. The therapist conceptualizes the sick role as a temporary status for the patient, who is expected to work in treatment toward resuming the healthy role.

During the initial phase, the therapist conducts the *interpersonal inventory*, a systematic exploration of the important individuals in the patient's past and present life. When inquiring about these significant relationships, the therapist explores the quality of the relationships including the fulfilling and unsatisfying aspects of the relationships. In addition, the therapist investigates seemingly important relationships the patient does not mention. A good understanding of the patient's interpersonal difficulties will then allow the therapist to see connections between interpersonal events and symptom exacerbation.

The centerpiece of IPT is the *interpersonal case formulation* (Markowitz & Swartz, 1997), a summary statement that reiterates the patient's diagnosis and links it to one (or at most two) interpersonal problem areas. In the formulation, the therapist explicitly links the onset and maintenance of the mood episode to a specific interpersonal problem area. A salient problem area is chosen, based on information collected during the psychiatric interview and interpersonal inventory. In IPT, there are four possible interpersonal problem areas: grief, role transition, interpersonal role dispute, and interpersonal deficits. These four problem areas are discussed below, with a specific focus on their relevance in the treatment of bipolar disorder.

Grief

The patient and therapist will choose grief or complicated bereavement as the focal problem area when the current affective episode is linked to the death of an important person in the patient's life. Treatment focuses on facilitation of the mourning process. The therapist reviews in detail the relationship with the deceased person, encourages the expression of previously suppressed affect in order to facilitate catharsis, and helps the patient recognize distorted (either overly positive or overly negative) memories of the relationship with the deceased. In standard IPT, the problem area of grief is selected only when an important person in the patient's life has died. Individuals with bipolar disorder, however, often experience the symbolic loss of *the person they would have become* were they not afflicted with bipolar disorder. In IPSRT, this is referred to as *grieving for the lost healthy self.* Subsumed under the broader category of grief, grieving for the lost healthy self involves encouraging patients to talk about the limits placed on their life by the illness, lost hopes, and missed opportunities. After mourning these losses, the patient is helped to recognize his or her strengths (rather than focusing on the losses), and gently encouraged to set new, realistic goals.

Role transition

A role transition is defined as a major life change. Examples of a role change include moving to a new city, starting a new job, becoming a parent, graduating from college, etc. Although role transitions are a normal part of the human experience, for individuals who are vulnerable to mood disorders, these changes may provoke an episode. Patients with bipolar disorder are especially vulnerable to change, even of the face of relatively minor perturbations of their environment (Frank et al., 1999). IPT strategies for addressing a role transition include helping the patient develop more realistic views of both the old and new roles (patients tend to idealize the old role and devalue the new one) and acquiring new interpersonal skills to master the new role.

It is important to keep in mind that bipolar illness itself may bring about role transitions. For instance, mania-driven, inappropriate behavior may lead to job loss; depression-associated social isolation may lead to failed relationships. Paradoxically, the process of achieving mood stability may represent a role transition for many patients. In particular, many patients miss the pleasurable hypomanic episodes associated with more variable mood states. It is important that the therapist help the patient mourn the loss of these episodes, identify their negative consequences, and help the patient find pleasures associated with new-found mood stability.

Interpersonal role dispute

An interpersonal role dispute occurs when nonreciprocal expectations are present in intimate relationships. The goals of treatment include identification of the dispute, alteration of role expectations and communication patterns, and development of a change plan. Therapeutic strategies include role-play, investigation of realistic options, and communication analysis. Role disputes are common sequelae of bipolar disorder. Irritability associated with both depression and mania can contribute to the erosion of close interpersonal relationships. Similarly, protracted social withdrawal associated with bipolar depression can destroy close relationships. Friends and family members may be perplexed and ultimately vexed by the patient's wild swings in mood and energy states, leading to misunderstandings and ultimately entrenched role disputes.

Interpersonal deficits

Patients with interpersonal deficits have long histories of unsuccessful relationships. Typically, the therapist is not able to identify a clear interpersonal event associated with episode onset. Thus, this problem area is used as a "default" category, applied only when the three other categories do not capture the patient's circumstances. Patients with long-standing bipolar disorder who have destroyed virtually all close relationships may be best characterized as experiencing interpersonal deficits. This problem area is the least well conceptualized of the four and is associated with poorer outcomes (Weissman et al., 2000).

Clinical vignette 3

Clara is a 27-year-old single white woman, a physician who graduated from medical school but experienced psychotic mania during her first year of surgical training. After recovering from the manic episode, she transferred to a less stressful residency in pathology. She was able to complete her pathology residency but became severely depressed as she attempted to find a job afterwards. In therapy, Clara focused initially on the IPSRT-specific strategy of mourning for the lost healthy self. She discussed her early career aspirations, including plans to become a trauma surgeon. She felt defeated by her illness, choosing pathology because "I had no other options". Clara and the therapist also explored the toll that the illness had taken on relationships, leaving Clara feeling incapable of sustaining a relationship or confiding in others about her illness. Through the mourning process, Clara came to accept the limitations of her illness, while recognizing that there were still many options open to her. The next part of treatment helped Clara make the transition from pathology resident to working physician. The therapist helped Clara explore the importance of finding a career that was intellectually challenging but not too pressured. They also discussed the importance of selecting a job that enabled her to maintain a regular schedule. After exploring several options, Clara decided that she did not wish to pursue an academic career in pathology, but should consider a less time-intensive job in the pharmaceutical industry. Clara's mood improved as she began to pursue new career options that were compatible with both her illness and her modified career aspirations.

Although built on the principles of IPT, IPSRT differs from IPT in several respects (Swartz et al., 2002). Firstly, IPT focuses on the links between life events and mood. In IPSRT, life events are viewed not only as sources of mood dysregulation but also as potential triggers of rhythm disruption. Thus, IPSRT addresses interpersonal problems using both IPT strategies and behavioral strategies designed to regulate the social rhythm disruptions associated with the interpersonal problem. In addition, IPT for unipolar depression is a therapy of interpersonal change. The therapist actively encourages depressed patients to take interpersonal risks and make relatively large changes in their interpersonal circumstances in a brief period of time. By contrast, patients who suffer from bipolar disorder may destabilize in the face of relatively minor change (Frank et al., 1999), and are likely to deteriorate in the setting of very stimulating shifts in their interpersonal lives. Therefore, in IPSRT, the therapist helps the patient *adapt to change* and *find a healthy balance between spontaneity and stability*. Changes are made gradually, and both therapist and patient remain alert to signs of clinical deterioration in the face of change.

Integrating the components

IPSRT is organized into three discrete treatment phases (the initial, intermediate, and maintenance phases). Within each phase, the components of IPSRT are administered variably, in order to accommodate the specific needs of each patient. The relative emphasis of psychoeducation, social rhythm therapy, and IPT strategies will vary according to the phase of treatment and the acuity of the patient's symptoms.

INITIAL PHASE

The initial phase of IPSRT consists of gathering a psychiatric history, providing psychoeducation about bipolar disorder, carrying out the interpersonal inventory, and introducing the patient to the SRM. During this phase, all patients are evaluated by a psychiatrist (if the therapist is not a physician) to optimize pharmacotherapy. Patients may enter IPSRT when they are euthymic, subsyndromal, or fully symptomatic. Thus, the duration of the initial phase varies considerably, ranging from 2 weeks to 2 months. During this time, the patient is seen weekly by the therapist and as often as needed by the psychiatrist in order to stabilize medications.

The first step of the initial phase involves gathering a thorough medical and psychiatric history. In the course of conducting the history, the therapist listens carefully for descriptions of disrupted daily routines or interpersonal relationships that may have preceded current or previous mood episodes. By carefully reviewing these events, the therapist develops an understanding of specific episode triggers and begins to conceptualize possible vulnerabilities in the patient's interpersonal life. The therapist uses this information to introduce the IPSRT paradigm to the patient, illustrating the connections among interpersonal events, social rhythms, and episode onset with examples from the patient's own life.

In the initial phase, the therapist also initiates the SRM. As discussed previously, most of the items on the SRM are prespecified on the instrument itself (that is, wake times, sleep times, meal times, and time of morning beverage). However, two items must be individually tailored to each patient. Therefore, in the initial phase, the therapist helps the patient identify two daily activities, such as exercise, watching a specific television program, walking the dog, etc., that will be used throughout treatment as anchors for the patient's daily routines. SRMs are collected weekly to define trends in the patient's daily rhythms; however, no effort is made to modify these rhythms unless there are clinically pressing concerns such as wildly erratic sleep times. For patients with limited interest in this area (many patients are actually very interested in making changes in this arena once they see the connection between routines and their moods and episodes), or more limited literacy or intelligence, or whom the therapist suspects will have difficulty complying with this aspect of the treatment for other reasons, there is the option of using a five-item version that captures most of the essential features of the monitoring process (Monk et al., 2002).

The final component of the initial phase is the interpersonal case formulation. The case formulation links the current mood episode to one of the four IPT problem areas and sets the interpersonal agenda for the next phase of treatment (Markowitz & Swartz, 1997). If the patient is manic or hypomanic during the initial phase, it may be difficult to complete the interpersonal inventory and establish a case formulation until medications have been initiated and some degree of symptom control has been established. In some instances, therefore, the initial phase of treatment may focus on psychoeducation and containment until the patient is able to engage fully in the therapy enterprise.

INTERMEDIATE PHASE

The intermediate phase follows from the interpersonal case formulation and SRM goals. Therapy focuses on resolving the chosen interpersonal problem, identifying and meeting intermediate and long-term SRM goals, and optimizing pharmacotherapy (in consultation with a psychiatrist). In addition, therapist and patient continue to monitor symptoms and side effects closely, using standardized rating scales such as the 25-item, modified version of the Hamilton Rating Scale for Depression (HRSD) (Thase et al., 1991) and the Bech–Rafaelsen Mania Scale (Bech et al., 1979) to track shifts in mood states. The intermediate phase typically lasts for several months, and sessions are conducted weekly.

During the intermediate phase, SRMs are reviewed weekly, searching for evidence of rhythm dysregularity. The therapist and patient jointly attempt to understand sources of rhythm instability, which may include emergent bipolar symptoms (for example, later sleep times driven by an evolving hypomania), interpersonal events (for example, very irregular meal and sleep times stemming from the chaos of caring for three children under the age of 6), or their combination. The therapist helps patients find ways to regulate their rhythms by setting clear, graduated SRM goals, and then using the SRMs to track progress over time.

An important issue that typically arises during the middle phase of treatment is the balance between stability and spontaneity. Many patients suffering from bipolar disorder are accustomed to hectic variations in mood and energy states. The prodigious efforts of the therapist to curb the variability in their mood and activities are not always welcomed by the patient. In fact, many patients believe they will find regularity boring and unappealing. If sensitive to this issue, the therapist can help the patient determine how much stability is required to lessen the risk of recurrence while encouraging patients to seek some degree of "safe" spontaneity in other areas of their life. For instance, if a patient's work schedule has variable demands (for example, big projects followed by lulls in activity), the therapist may encourage the patient to avoid rhythm-disrupting projects during the spring and summer when the patient is historically at risk of manic episodes, instead shifting them to the autumn and winter months when the patient is more likely to tolerate less structured social rhythms. Alternately, by using IPT strategies, such as grieving for the lost healthy self or managing the role transition from variable mood states to euthymia, the therapist can help the patient understand and mourn the lost highs while learning to value greater stability in mood and, ultimately, functioning.

During the intermediate phase of therapy, as in life, patients invariably experience changes in life circumstances that lead to changes in routine. For instance, patients may begin new jobs, start new relationships, move to a new apartment, or resume classes. The therapist helps the patient work through these changes in a manner that minimizes disruptions of daily rhythms. For instance, the therapist may encourage patients in a new relationship to speak with their new partner about the importance of routines, helping patients establish new patterns that do not deviate substantially from old ones. Patients starting new jobs are encouraged to shift their schedules gradually in order to minimize abrupt changes in daily habits and degree of activity. IPSRT uses social rhythm therapy techniques to protect rhythm integrity, and IPT techniques to explore and manage the interpersonal consequences of these events.

During the intermediate phase of IPSRT, the therapist uses the IPT strategies discussed in Chapter 9 to resolve the interpersonal problem identified in the case formulation. In addition to helping the patient see connections between the problem area and mood, the therapist explores the impact of the interpersonal problem area on social rhythm stability and medication adherence. For instance, if the selected problem area is a role dispute with a spouse, the therapist will ask the patient about the marital conflict over the past week. If the patient reveals that his wife now insists that he drop the children off at school early in the morning (this had previously been the wife's responsibility), the therapist will explore both the impact of the new schedule on the patient's daily rhythms (Will he have to get up earlier? Should he go to bed earlier? Will this interfere with his morning dose of lithium?), as well as the interpersonal meaning of the event (How does the patient feel about the new arrangements? How did the couple make this decision?). The relative emphasis and sequencing of the techniques are determined by the clinical judgement of the therapist.

MAINTENANCE PHASE

The maintenance phase is designed to consolidate treatment gains, optimize interpersonal functioning in the absence of syndromal illness, and prevent recurrence. Treatment frequency is tapered to biweekly for 2 months and then monthly. This phase of treatment lasts 2 years in our research protocol, although, in clinical practice, some patients may stay in maintenance psychotherapy indefinitely. Crisis intervention is provided on an as-needed basis in this phase of treatment.

Because bipolar disorder is a chronic illness, some might argue that combination treatment (that is, medication plus psychotherapy) is indicated indefinitely. In other cases, a patient may demonstrate appreciable improvement in multiple domains and may feel comfortable in changing to maintenance medication without psychotherapy. In the absence of data to guide this choice, the decision to end maintenance treatment is necessarily an individual decision. When maintenance treatment ends, we recommend a very gradual process of termination, over four to six monthly sessions.

The termination stage should be a period of reflection and encouragement. The therapist reviews the patient's progress and identifies areas in which additional improvement is needed. The therapist underscores the fact that the patient has acquired both new interpersonal skills and a new understanding of the importance of maintaining regular social rhythms, reinforcing the importance of practicing these skills in order to perpetuate therapeutic gains. In this final phase, it is also important to identify additional resources for the patient in the event that symptoms worsen. Virtually all patients with bipolar I disorder will continue maintenance medication indefinitely and should be referred to a psychiatrist for follow-up.

Clinical vignette 4

Doreen is a 34-year-old, single mother of four, with a history of two prior hospitalizations for suicide attempts during mixed states. Doreen entered IPSRT during a mixed-state episode following the birth of her fourth child. She had stopped her mood stabilizers during the pregnancy and had not yet resumed them, despite instructions from her psychiatrist to restart them immediately after delivery (Doreen did not plan to breast-feed). The initial phase of treatment emphasized psychoeducation, including the importance of following the psychiatrist's recommendations in order to prevent another hospitalization (the patient was not currently suicidal). It was immediately apparent that Doreen's erratic sleep schedule, driven by the needs of her newborn infant, contributed substantially to her symptoms. Thus, the therapist moved rapidly to help Doreen enlist assistance from her extended family. Doreen's mother and several sisters each agreed to stay with Doreen one night per week in order to provide her with some relief from nighttime feedings as well as assistance with other household responsibilities. Doreen restarted lithium and olanzapine, and immediately began to feel better.

As Doreen's mood began to stabilize, it became clear that the interpersonal problem area most salient to Doreen's current mood episode was a role dispute with Roger, her boyfriend of 2 years. Roger, the father of Doreen's two youngest children, was unemployed and had a history of drug use. He denied current drug use, but Doreen said, "I'm not so sure." Roger was very suspicious of doctors and medication, routinely disparaging Doreen's efforts to enter treatment and actively discouraging her from taking medication. In fact, he routinely took her medications from the cabinet, perhaps selling them on the street, claiming, "You don't need these." He did not contribute financially to the household, and instead often demanded money from Doreen. The intermediate phase of treatment focused on helping Doreen set some limits with Roger. She had no wish to end the relationship; however, she admitted that she had trouble getting her needs met in it. Therefore, her therapist began to help Doreen's identify and articulate what she wanted from Roger.

The therapist suggested that they first work on the conflict over Doreen's seeking treatment for bipolar disorder. Doreen asked for some educational materials to give Roger in the hope that he would eventually "come around", but also decided to hide her medications in a new, secure location so that he would be unable to take them from her.

Because Roger often showed up unannounced in the middle of the night, contributing to Doreen's erratic SRM, they also worked toward helping Roger understand that he was only welcome to "show up" before 10 p.m. Initially, Roger was enraged by these limits and disappeared for 2 weeks. When he returned, however, he was conciliatory, and Doreen felt empowered by her capacity to "stand firm" with him. She then decided that she would refuse to give any more money to Roger unless he did some things around the house to help her (fix a broken door, etc.), a decision which helped her feel more competent in the management of both her household and her relationship.

Doreen's mood stabilized after 4 months of treatment, and she graduated to the maintenance phase, which focused on helping her tolerate medication side effects, develop more effective ways to manage her hectic schedule at home, and manage disputes with Roger. Given her multiple psychosocial problems and history of stopping medications precipitously, the therapist felt it important that Doreen continue psychotherapy indefinitely.

PRELIMINARY FINDINGS

Study design

A single large trial of IPSRT as a treatment for bipolar disorder (in combination with medication) is currently nearing completion at the University of Pittsburgh. This study, Maintenance Therapies in Bipolar Disorder (MTBD), is funded by a grant from the National Institute of Mental Health (R37 MH29618). In MTBD, acutely ill patients meeting criteria for bipolar I disorder are treated with medication and randomly assigned to either IPSRT or intensive clinical management (ICM). In order to enter the protocol, subjects must meet the Schedule for Affective Disorders and Schizophrenia criteria (Spitzer & Endicott, 1978) or the Research Diagnostic Criteria (Endicott et al., 1977) for bipolar I disorder with a score of 15 or greater on the 24-item HRSD (Hamilton, 1960; Thase et al., 1991) or the Bech–Rafaelson Mania Scale (Bech et al., 1979). Exclusion criteria include pregnancy, chronic alcohol and drug abuse, rapid cycling (defined as four or more affective episodes in 1 year), or an unstable comorbid medical condition. In addition, individuals meeting criteria for antisocial and borderline personality disorder or schizophrenia are excluded from this study.

Once stabilized (defined as 4 weeks of symptom scores averaging ≤ 7 on the 24-item version of the HRSD and ≤ 7 on the Bech–Rafaelsen Mania Scale while on a stable medication regimen), patients are reassigned to either IPSRT or ICM (in conjunction with the medication regimen that led to stabilization) for 2 years of monthly maintenance treatment. The maintenance phase of treatment consists of 3 months of bimonthly sessions followed by 21 months of monthly session. Thus, four treatment sequences are possible in this study: IPSRT followed by IPSRT; IPSRT followed by ICM; ICM followed by ICM; and ICM followed by IPSRT. See Figure 15.1 for a schematic depiction of the MTBD study design.

Although used as a comparison condition in MTBD, ICM is an important psychotherapeutic intervention in its own right. It should not be mistaken for an inactive control. Influenced by the medical model of clinical management, ICM focuses on fostering support, promoting treatment adherence, assessing symptoms, and providing psychoeducation.

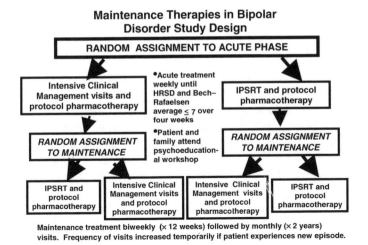

Figure 15.1 Maintenance therapies in bipolar disorder: study design

Thus, ICM incorporates many general psychotherapeutic strategies that contribute to the successful management of bipolar illness. See Table 15.2 for a summary of ICM techniques. In contrast to IPSRT, therapists providing ICM are proscribed from discussing interpersonal stressors and social rhythm stability. In MTBD, all therapists are trained to administer reliably both IPSRT and ICM.

In MTBD, all patients receive pharmacotherapy according to a specified algorithm (available from the authors). Unless contraindicated, pharmacotherapy begins with lithium. Neuroleptics, additional mood stabilizers, benzodiazepines, and antidepressants are added in stepwise fashion, guided by weekly symptom scores. Once stable, attempts are made to withdraw all medication except for the primary mood stabilizer (or combination of mood stabilizers, in some cases). If patients cannot tolerate a reduction of medications (that is, of an antidepressant or antipsychotic), they are permitted to remain on the combination that keeps them well. Once reassigned to the maintenance phase of the study, medication cannot be changed unless a recurrence is declared (except for 5 days of "rescue" medications, such as lorazepam, administered under specified conditions for subsyndromal hypomanic symptoms).

Table 15.2 Intensive clinical management

Elements of intensive clinical management (ICM)

1. Education about bipolar disorder
2. Education about medications used to treat bipolar disorder
3. Education about basic sleep hygiene
4. Careful review of side effects
5. Medical and behavioral management of side effects
6. Nonspecific support
7. Education regarding early warning signs of impending episodes and use of rescue medication
8. 24-hour on-call service

Results

The first published report from the MTBD protocol examined the relative impact of ICM and IPSRT on stability of daily routines (Frank et al., 1997). This analysis included 38 subjects (18 receiving IPSRT and 20 receiving ICM) followed in the acute phase of treatment for up to 52 weeks. As measured by the SRM (Monk et al., 1991), a random regression analysis illustrated that individuals who received IPSRT achieved greater stability in their social rhythms when compared to ICM treatment over a similar time period (chi square $= 3.96$; $P = 0.047$). The two groups did not differ on levels of symptomatology over 52 weeks (measured by the HRSD and the Bech–Rafaelson; chi square $= 0.12$; $P = 0.73$). These analyses demonstrate that IPSRT effectively enhances stability of daily routines.

We have also reported on the effects of episode polarity on time to stabilization in the acute phase of the study (Hlastala et al., 1997; Kupfer et al., 2000). We first reported on differential time to stabilization among subjects treated for depression ($n = 22$), mania ($n = 8$), or a mixed state ($n = 12$) during the acute phase of the study (Hlastala et al., 1997), finding significant differences among groups (chi square $= 14.80$, $P = 0.0006$). Subsequent analyses of a larger sample ($n = 151$) demonstrated longer median times to stabilization in depressed and mixed/cycling subjects: 11.0 weeks for subjects treated for mania, 24.0 weeks for subjects treated for depression, and 40.3 weeks for subjects treated for mixed/cycling episodes. Between-group comparisons of survival analyses (time to stabilization) were significantly different (for all, $P < 0.05$). In the earlier report, although no specific treatment effects were found, among depressed subjects, those who received IPSRT had a median time to remission of 22 weeks, versus 40 weeks in subjects assigned to ICM. Although not statistically significant, this finding suggests that IPSRT may selectively hasten recovery from a depressive episode.

We have only recently begun to analyze data from the maintenance phase of the study. As shown in Figure 15.1, subjects can receive one of four possible treatment assignments in MTBD: IPSRT followed by IPSRT; IPSRT followed by ICM; ICM followed by ICM; or ICM followed by IPSRT. In one report, we looked at the effects of changing psychotherapy assignment between acute and maintenance treatment (Frank et al., 1999). Among the first 82 subjects to enter the maintenance phase of the study, we found that subjects who received the same treatment for both acute and maintenance phases (IPSRT/IPSRT or ICM/ICM) trended toward lower levels of manic and depressive symptomatology ($P = 0.06$) and had a significantly lower risk of recurrence ($P = 0.03$) over 52 weeks than those assigned to altered treatments (IPSRT/ICM or ICM/IPSRT). We also showed that subjects assigned to IPSRT in the acute phase who then "lost" it (IPSRT/ICM) had significantly higher symptom scores than the other three groups during the 52 weeks of maintenance treatment. These finding were particularly remarkable in light of the fact that, according to our protocol, patients change neither the timing of their appointments nor their therapists when treatment content is altered. Because only subjects who achieved stability in the acute phase were permitted to enter the maintenance phase, these data also suggest that treatments that get patients well keep them well (subjects who fail to achieve remission with their assigned treatment condition are withdrawn from the study). In keeping with our theory that stabilizing routines encourage wellness in patients suffering from bipolar disorder, we concluded that a constant treatment regimen contributes to enhanced stability in this population.

We also observed that subjects assigned to either IPSRT or ICM during the maintenance phase of MTBD remain relatively well (recurrence-free) compared to historical reports of subjects assigned to medication alone. It seems likely that both "high-dose" (IPSRT) and "low-dose" (ICM) adjunctive psychotherapy contribute to enhanced wellness in this population (Frank et al., 1999), resulting in improved stability for many of the patients in our protocol. In a subsequent analysis of the first 90 subjects to enter the preventative phase of the study, we found that, over time, patients assigned to IPSRT were increasingly likely to experience euthymia and decreasingly likely to experience periods characterized by depressive symptoms, compared to patients assigned to ICM (Frank, 1999).

Some subjects express a preference for assignment to IPSRT, stating that they want to receive psychotherapy (although these preferences do not affect the random assignment process). We believe that the desire for psychotherapy may play into observed dropout rates among groups. Thus far, dropout rates are highest among those assigned to ICM in both the acute and maintenance phases (25%; 8/32) and lowest among those assigned to ICM in the acute phase followed by IPSRT in the maintenance phase (6%; 2/31). Dropout rates in the IPSRT/ICM and IPSRT/IPSRT groups are intermediate to the other groups (19% or 6/32 and 15% or 4/27, respectively) (Swartz et al., 2001). Patients assigned to ICM in the acute phase who discover that they are again assigned to ICM for maintenance may drop out of the study and seek more intensive psychotherapy elsewhere. Alternately, some patients who are assigned to ICM initially and then assigned to IPSRT for maintenance may be relieved to "finally get psychotherapy", leading to lower attrition in this group.

CONCLUSION

Because the study is not complete, we cannot yet draw final conclusions from MTBD. Our experience so far suggests that IPSRT successfully promotes rhythm stability and may lead to improved outcomes in subsets of patients with bipolar disorder, such as those with acute depression. However, the less intensive ICM intervention also promotes wellness in some of our patients. Given the complexities of this illness, it seems likely that IPSRT will prove to be an effective intervention for some patients during some phases of the illness. For bipolar disorder, the adage, "one size doesn't fit all" seems particularly apt. We may learn that IPSRT contributes significantly to improvements in symptoms and functioning for some individuals, but that for others, adjunctive ICM suffices.

Our quest to find better treatments for patients suffering from bipolar disorder led to the development and testing of IPSRT. We hope that, in the final analysis, IPSRT will provide yet another option for the treatment of bipolar disorder, helping some patients to achieve a fuller and more stable recovery than would have been possible with medications alone.

ACKNOWLEDGEMENT

This study was supported by the National Institute of Mental Health, Grants MH-29618, MH-30915, and MH-64518.

REFERENCES

American Psychiatric Association (2002). *Practice Guideline for the Treatment of Patients with Bipolar Disorder (Revision). American Journal of Psychiatry, 159 (April Suppl.).*

Barbini, B., Colombo, C., Benedetti, F., Campori, E., Bellodi, L. & Smeraldi, E. (1998). The unipolar-bipolar dichotomy and the response to sleep deprivation. *Psychiatry Research, 79*, 43–50.

Bech, P., Bolwig, T.G., Kramp, P. & Rafaelsen, O.J. (1979). The Bech-Rafaelsen Mania Scale and the Hamilton Depression Scale: Evaluation of homogeneity and inter-observer reliability. *Acta Psychiatrica Scandinavica, 59*, 420–430.

Coryell, W., Scheftner, W., Keller, M., et al. (1993). The enduring psychosocial consequences of mania and depression. *American Journal of Psychiatry, 150*, 720–727.

Craighead, W.E., Miklowitz, D.J., Vajk, F.C. & Frank, E. (1998). Psychosocial treatments for bipolar disorder. In P.E. Nathan & J.M. Gorman (Eds), *A Guide to Treatments That Work* (pp. 240–248). New York: Oxford University Press.

Ehlers, C.L., Frank, E. & Kupfer, D.J. (1988). Social zeitgebers and biological rhythms. *Archives of General Psychiatry, 45*, 948–952.

Ehlers, C.L., Kupfer, D.J., Frank, E. & Monk, T.H. (1993). Biological rhythms and depression: The role of zeitgebers and zeitstorers. *Depression, 1*, 285–293.

Endicott, J., Spitzer, R.L. & Winokur, G. (1977). Research diagnostic criteria: Rationale and reliability. *Archives of General Psychiatry, 34*, 1229–1235.

Frank, E. (1999). Interpersonal and social rhythm therapy prevents depressive symptomatology in bipolar 1 patients [Abstract]. *Bipolar Disorders, 1*[Suppl. 1], 13.

Frank, E., Hlastala, S., Ritenour, A., et al. (1997). Inducing lifestyle regularity in recovering bipolar disorder patients: Results from the maintenance therapies in bipolar disorder protocol. *Biological Psychiatry, 41*, 1165–1173.

Frank, E., Swartz, H.A., Mallinger, A.G., Thase, M.E., Weaver, E.V. & Kupfer, D.J. (1999). Adjunctive psychotherapy for bipolar disorder: Effects of changing treatment modality. *Journal of Abnormal Psychology, 108*, 579–587.

Gelenberg, A.J., Kane, J.M., Keller, M.B., et al. (1989). Comparison of standard and low serum levels of lithium for maintenance treatment of bipolar disorder. *New England Journal of Medicine, 321*, 1489–1493.

Gitlin, M.J., Swendsen, J., Heller, T.L. & Hammen, C. (1995). Relapse and impairment in bipolar disorder. *American Journal of Psychiatry, 152*, 1635–1640.

Goldberg, J.F., Harrow, M. & Grossman, L.S. (1995). Course and outcome in bipolar affective disorder: A longitudinal follow-up study. *American Journal of Psychiatry, 152*, 379–384.

Goodwin, F. & Jamison, K. (1990). *Manic-Depressive Illness*. New York: Oxford University Press.

Hamilton, M. (1960). A rating scale for depression. *Journal of Neurology, Neurosurgery, and Psychiatry, 25*, 56–62.

Hlastala, S.A., Frank, E., Mallinger, A.G., Thase, M.E., Ritenour, A.M. & Kupfer, D.J. (1997). Bipolar depression: An underestimated treatment challenge. *Depression and Anxiety, 5*, 73–83.

Klerman, G.L., Weissman, M.M., Rounsaville, B.J. & Chevron, E.S. (1984). *Interpersonal Psychotherapy of Depression*. New York: Basic Books.

Kupfer, D.J., Frank, E., Grochocinski, V.J., et al. (2000). Stabilization in the treatment of mania, depression, and mixed states. *Acta Neuropsychiatrica, 12*, 110–114.

Kusumakar, V., Yatham, L.N., Haslam, D.R.S., et al. (1997). The foundations of effective management of bipolar disorder. *Canadian Journal of Psychiatry, 42*(Suppl. 2), 69S–73S.

Leibenluft, E. & Suppes, T. (1999). Treating bipolar illness: Focus on treatment algorithms and management of the sleep-wake cycle. *American Journal of Psychiatry, 156*, 1976–1979.

Leibenluft, E., Albert, P.S., Rosenthal, N.E. & Wehr, T.A. (1996). Relationship between sleep and mood in patients with rapid-cycling bipolar disorder. *Psychiatry Research, 63*(2–3), 161–168.

Leibenluft, E., Moul, D.E., Schwartz, P.J., Madden, P.A. & Wehr, T.A. (1993). A clinical trial of sleep deprivation in combination with antidepressant medication. *Psychiatry Research, 46*, 213–227.

Markar, H. & Mander, A. (1989). Efficacy of lithium prophylaxis in clinical practice. *British Journal of Psychiatry, 155*, 496–500.

Markowitz, J.C. & Swartz, H.A. (1997). Case formulation in interpersonal psychotherapy of depression. In T.D. Eells (Ed.), *Handbook of Psychotherapy Case Formulation* (pp. 192–222). New York: Guilford.

Monk, T.H., Frank, E., Potts, J.M. & Kupfer, D.J. (2002). A simple way to measure daily lifestyle regularity. *Journal of Sleep Research, 11*, 183–190.

Monk, T.H., Kupfer, D.J., Frank, E. & Ritenour, A.M. (1991). The Social Rhythm Metric (SRM): Measuring daily social rhythms over 12 weeks. *Psychiatry Research, 36*, 195–207.

Parsons, T. (1951). Illness and the role of the physician: A sociological perspective. *American Journal of Orthopsychiatry, 21*, 452–460.

Spitzer, R.L. & Endicott, J. (1978). Use of the Research Diagnostic Criteria and the Schedule for Affective Disorders and Schizophrenia to study affective disorders. *Archives of General Psychiatry, 35*, 837–844.

Swartz, H.A. & Frank, E. (2001). Psychotherapy for bipolar depression: A phase-specific strategy? *Bipolar Disorders, 3*, 11–22.

Swartz, H.A., Frank, E., Mallinger, A.G., Houck, P.R. & Kupfer, D.J. (2001). *Improving quality of life for patients with bipolar disorder.* Paper presented at the 154th Annual Meeting of the American Psychiatric Association, New Orleans, LA.

Swartz, H.A., Markowitz, J.C. & Frank, E. (2002). Interpersonal psychotherapy for unipolar and bipolar disorders. In S.G. Hofmann & M. Tompson (Eds), *Treating Chronic and Severe Mental Disorders: A Handbook of Empirically Supported Interventions* (pp. 131–158). New York: Guilford.

Thase, M.E., Carpenter, L., Kupfer, D.J. & Frank, E.F. (1991). Clinical significance of reversed vegetative subtypes of recurrent major depression. *Psychopharmacology Bulletin, 27*, 17–22.

Wehr, T.A., Sack, D.A. & Rosenthal, N.E. (1987). Sleep reduction as a final common pathway in the genesis of mania. *American Journal of Psychiatry, 144*, 201–204.

Weissman, M.M., Markowitz, J.C. & Klerman, G.L. (2000). *Comprehensive Guide to Interpersonal Psychotherapy*. New York: Basic Books.

16

SELF-MANAGEMENT AND THE EXPERT PATIENT

Anne Palmer and Jan Scott

INTRODUCTION

This chapter focuses on the philosophy and role of self-management programmes for bipolar disorder (BD). The term "self-management" came to prominence in the 1960s and 1970s, reflecting the rise of the "self-help" movement. The latter evolved partly as a consequence of dissatisfaction with traditional models of medical care that assumed patients would comply without question with the advice and instructions proffered by health professionals. Many people with long-term physical or mental disorders found more acceptable approaches to their health problems and took greater control of their lives through sharing experiences and seeking support from their peers instead of relying on organised health-care systems. In some instances, this idea was taken to the extreme, and individuals sought to cope without any professional input. In other settings, the user-led self-help groups and the professionally led mental health services worked side by side. Although their interactions spanned the spectrum from the truly harmonious to the overtly antagonistic, the ensuing dialogue and negotiation between service users and service providers created an environment in which self-management programmes became a reality for many individuals with persistent health problems.

Self-management has now come to mean any programme that gives people with a long-term health problem the information and skills to help them actively manage some or all of the key aspects of their disorder. The underpinning philosophy of self-management programmes is to enable individuals to make informed choices about the treatments and approaches they wish to pursue to manage their health and well-being. The added benefit is that they gain confidence about their capacity to take control of their lives. The expertise and experience of both professionals and service users have been pivotal in the recent development of self-management programmes for BD. Before we review these programmes, an outline of the contemporary literature about individual responsibility for health risks and the associated political context will be discussed. There are obvious advantages in an approach that promotes the idea that individuals with a serious health problem can and should be

Mood Disorders: A Handbook of Science and Practice. Edited by M. Power.
© 2004 John Wiley & Sons, Ltd. ISBN 0-470-84390-X.

actively involved in the process of managing their disorder. However, this chapter will also highlight that there are potential dangers in giving individuals too much responsibility for their state of health or in promoting unrealistic expectations of what they can control or achieve through their own efforts.

CHANGES IN THE CONCEPT OF THE INDIVIDUAL AND THE LOCATION OF RISKS TO HEALTH

From her review of contemporary psychological literature, Ogden (1995) argues that, in the twentieth century, there have been fundamental shifts in our view of the individual and his or her relationship to the environment.

In the 1960s, there was a move away from the notion that individuals were passive, without agency, their behaviours being a response to external circumstances, towards a view of the individual as an interactive being. The revised model proposed that individuals processed and appraised information from the external world and that their behaviours were then shaped by the interactions between them and their environment. Thus, the nexus of "illness risk" moved, from being identified with factors that were outside the individual (biomedical models), to being the product of interpersonal interactions with external factors (the biopsychosocial model).

In the last decades of the twentieth century, there was a further shift to the view of the individual as being "intra-active". The intra-active individual is still conceptualised as an interactive being, but is also viewed as having a sense of authorship over actions, thoughts and emotional experiences, as having volition and control over behaviours, and as being the architect of intentions and plans (see also Harter, 1999).

Changing views about individual identity are reflected in contemporary cultural views about the nexus of health risks. Ogden writes that, following the paradigm shifts discussed above, current models emphasise that health risks and health-related behaviours are inherent within the individual, who has personal control and responsibility over his or her own (healthy or unhealthy) lifestyle. If this model were applied to a person with BD, it would suggest that individuals have the ability to control their own behaviour and to manage and master health treatments. In this context, risks to health are viewed as a breakdown in self-control and self-efficacy. Ogden terms this the creation of the "risky self", which is implicit in both the concept of the "expert patient" (Donaldson, 2001) and the definition of "recovery", which are discussed in the next sections.

THE POLITICAL CONTEXT AND SELF-MANAGEMENT

The expert patient's programme holds out the promise of thousands of confident and more informed patients and large numbers of lay people involved in evidence based self-management programmes of one kind or another. However, in order to achieve this there will need to be a major shift in cultural attitudes, and this in turn will depend in part on convincing patients and professionals of the value of this approach (Donaldson 2001).

Because he is the Chief Medical Officer for England and Wales, Liam Donaldson's paper has significantly influenced the dialogue between service users and service providers. The document clearly states that the main challenges to the provision of a quality health service are not from acute, but from long-term disorders, because the latter are the predominant disease pattern in the UK and across most of the developed and developing world.

The paper found that comprehensive health programmes have not yet been provided, and Donaldson suggests that one reason for this is the failure to use as a resource the knowledge and experience of the individuals with long-term disorders. He recommends a fundamental shift in the way in which such disorders are managed, and central to this proposal is the active recruitment and involvement of "expert patients".

The expert patient may be defined as someone who has "confidence, skills, input and knowledge to play a central role in the management of life with chronic disease, and to minimise its impact on their day to day living". Essentially, this means that people with a long-term disorder take a central role in decisions about their problems. They must be regarded as experienced partners in the process of health care, instead of as inexperienced recipients of treatment (Lorig et al., 1993). It follows that policies to modernise the design and delivery of services within the National Health Service (NHS) must emphasise the role of patients as partners who share their expertise with other health-care providers.

THE PHILOSOPHY OF RECOVERY

Yanos et al. (2001) write that the focus of recovery in BD should be on good community adjustment rather than just the alleviation of psychiatric symptoms. Copeland (1994) also challenged the definition of recovery as a mere reduction in symptoms, and strongly argued, from her own and other peoples' experiences of BD, that fuller recovery from a severe and enduring health problem is possible.

Since the publication of Anthony's (1993) synthesis of the writings of people with experience of recovery, this perspective (or "the recovery model", as it has come to be known) has become more widely recognised, and adopted, within service-user and professional circles. Evidence for this recognition comes from the growing number of recovery-orientated programmes established, and from individuals writing about their recovery.

A recent review of the literature identified involvement in self-managed care and other types of consumer-delivered mental health services as one of the main factors in recovery (Yanos et al., 2001). Beliefs about the disorder and the ability to manage it are also important in recovery, and these will now be considered.

BELIEFS AND SELF-MANAGEMENT

We have talked about contemporary literature, and the political and recovery models which inform current thinking about self-management, but in a clinical setting we need to know where the individual client sits with regard to these models. As will be demonstrated, the beliefs people have will dictate the strategies they are prepared to endorse, and this includes any treatment proposals.

Leventhal et al.'s (1980) self-regulatory model is a model about "illness beliefs" and provides a framework for understanding the self-regulation processes that determine health-related behaviours, such as self-management. It is made up of interrelated components.

The first component is the interpretation of the health problem. People confronted with a health problem, in this case, BD, must first get to grips with the health problem itself and what it seems to them to involve. The ways in which people think about (interpret) their health problem creates a representation of that problem. This representation gives personal meaning to the health problem and is organised around five themes:

(1) *What is it?* (identity): the label given to the health problem such as a medical, or self-diagnosis.
(2) *Why has it happened?* (cause): the perceived cause of the health problem, which can, for example, be based on cultural ideas, myths or medical knowledge.
(3) *How long will it last?* (time line): an estimation of how long the health problem or the phase of the health problem will last, and whether it will recur.
(4) *What effects will it have?* (consequences): a prediction about possible effects on the person's life, which can be about finance, relationships, the person's own health, etc., and can be seen as positive or negative, and serious or minor.
(5) *What can I do to make it go away?* (cure/control): the possibility that the health problem can be cured or ameliorated and perceptions of control over the health problem by the client and/or others.

The second component concerns how an individual copes with or manages his or her own health problem. According to Leventhal et al., beliefs or cognitive representations about the health problems described above provide a framework which functions to guide a return to, or maintenance of, a state of good health. Two broad forms of coping have been described. These are "approach coping (for example, "take the pills" or "joining self-management groups") and "avoidance coping" (for example, disengagement or venting).

The third component is the individuals' appraisal of their coping strategy. The individual evaluates the effectiveness of the coping strategy and decides whether to continue it or use a new one. Not everyone will move to this stage, especially where avoidance is a form of coping, and is not recognised as such.

Leventhal et al. postulate that the association between health problem representations and emotional responses, such as fear, can lead to avoidance coping as a protective measure. For example, if self-management is seen as symbolic of having a feared health problem, then non-adherence, or changing the identity of the health problem to something more trivial, may be a strategy to avoid exposure to threat.

Avoidance coping is also linked to Weinstein's (1984) concept of unrealistic optimism. Individuals vary in their optimism, and those whose optimism is unrealistically high may, for example, interpret their health problems as follows: "It isn't serious"; "they've got it wrong" and "it's normal—other people have highs and lows". They may then not monitor for early warning signs and fail to develop appropriate strategies to avoid or prevent escalation of episodes. In addition, they may feel so safe that they are very likely to engage in dangerous behaviours, such as sleep-disrupting activities. For these reasons, if the individual's optimism is unrealistic, it is likely to lead to avoidance of self-management.

Just as individuals with BD have beliefs about their health problems, they also have beliefs about their ability to carry out health-related behaviours. These seem to be crucial in the stages of self-regulation of health behaviours.

Bandura (1977) used the term self-efficacy not as a trait, but to describe people's beliefs about the extent to which they can control a particular behaviour in a particular situation. Self-efficacy beliefs are associated with feelings of helplessness (Seligman, 1975). In learned helplessness, individuals perceive their responses as futile, leading to failure to initiate coping responses.

Self-efficacy is a widely applied construct in models of health behaviour and is considered one of the best predictors of health behaviour (Conner & Norman, 1996). One of the advantages of learning self-management may be that practising new coping skills increases self-confidence, and a new self model ("self as able to manage health problem") is formed.

The building up of self-efficacy beliefs or self-confidence is aided by having an expert tutor. Bray et al. (2001) found that when people first take responsibility for their own health, an expert tutor is vital. They investigated the role of what they term "proxy efficacy", which they define as the belief that another person has the skills and ability to deal with issues on our behalf, a belief that, in turn, increases people's confidence to carry out health-enhancing behaviours. It is speculated that having a credible fellow sufferer as tutor may further enhance the individual's perception of capability and efficiency. A final and important point about Bray's work is that it gives a rationale for why self-management might be effective besides being acceptable to people with BD.

STUDIES WHICH ILLUSTRATE THE IMPORTANCE OF SELF-MANAGEMENT

There has been little written about self-management for BD and, at the present time, there are few adequate trials that attest to its success or otherwise. Before we talk about a user-led self-management programme, other group approaches will be discussed.

The idea of people with BD self-managing their own problems is implicit in cognitive behavioural therapy (CBT) groups for BD (Palmer et al., 1995, Palmer & Gilbert, 1997). These authors write that participants were helped to recognise and then to challenge their own attitudes and beliefs, and to acquire active problem-solving and coping strategies through repeated experiences within therapy and homework practice. The emphasis placed on repeated homework in CBT is important, not just for the people to practise managing their disorder, but to build up modified or new schematic models such as "self as able to manage BD". Thus, use of the strategies learnt in group sessions may be the key to promoting changes in the people's confidence and belief that they can be an active agent in their own actions and can reinstate control over their life should the early symptoms of a BD episode recur. This further encourages the use of self-management strategies, and a virtuous circle is formed.

Bauer (2002) takes up this theme of the person with BD as a comanager when he writes that, in contrast to a paternalistic order-following approach to treatment, a collaborative model expects clients to be partners in managing their own health problems. He argues that the organisation of clinical resources to deliver care to clients who present for treatment can also build on the collaborative approach of CBT (Bauer, 2002; Bauer et al., 1998). Bauer et al. (1998) provided an "easy access service", whereby individuals with BD learnt self-management in groups led by two nurses. The participants in the group had access both to information about the disorder and to opportunities to learn problem-solving skills, compared with those receiving treatment as usual. Results showed that participants in the group did better than those participants receiving "treatment as usual" in terms of reduced symptoms, improved social functioning, and reduced health-care costs. Although Bauer et al.'s service was initially a "stand-alone" one, it has now been extended so that it is part of an integrated service, and the effectiveness of this model is currently being evaluated in a very large multicentre, randomised, controlled trial (Bauer, 2002).

The above studies are important because the resolution of the acute symptoms of BD is too often regarded as the treatment end point in health services. However, current research indicates that individuals with BD experience profound and ongoing functional disabilities even when the acute episode is resolved (Bauer, 2002). It is therefore noteworthy that interventions that help individuals with BD to enhance or acquire problem-solving skills, provide encouraging evidence not only of reductions in symptoms but also of restoring social functioning (Scott et al., 2001). The emphasis on functional outcomes is consistent with the philosophy of the recovery model. Furthermore, Yanos et al.'s (2001) review of the literature identifies self-managed care as one of the main factors in promoting the perception of recovery in an individual.

"User-led" self-management programmes, previously known as expert patient programmes, have developed over the last 20 years for people with chronic physical health problems in disorders such as arthritis and asthma. One example is the Chronic Disease Self-Management Programme developed at Stanford, in which professionally trained instructors with chronic disease train volunteer course tutors with various long-term health problems (Lorig et al., 1993). In this country, patient groups and organisations for long-term physical health problems have developed a number of similar programmes (Donaldson, 2001), but only one has been developed for long-term mental disorders.

The Manic Depression Fellowship (MDF) have played an important role in developing self-management programmes. The MDF argue that most individuals with BD have the potential, with optimal treatment, to return to normal social and occupational functioning, so avoiding poor long-term outcomes and becoming a burden on carers and families. However, such an outcome is often not achieved. One reason for people with BD not reaching optimal functioning is that the NHS is poorly resourced for their care. In our experience, comprehensive treatment programmes are far from being routinely provided. This is despite the fact that epidemiological data show that there are an estimated 500 000 people with BD in the UK (Weissman et al., 1998) and when burden of disease is measured by "disability-adjusted life years", mood disorders are at the top of the list in America and third in Europe (WHO, 1999). Another reason may be that we have not regarded those people with BD as potential deliverers of health-care services.

In the development stage of the MDF programme, the organisation consulted both within their own membership and with professionals working in the field. This meant that right from the beginning, the skills and expertise of both professional and user were incorporated into the programme. However, the programme is now organised and delivered entirely by people with BD and the MDF, their representative organisation, rather than professionals.

The programme has been designed to give information about BD, and also to enable the participants to take an active role in their own care, improving self-efficacy in dealing with problems when the disorder affects their daily living or undermines their self-image. It is comprehensive, and it teaches the participants how to identify triggers and warning signs and how to implement strategies to reduce the severity of an episode. Unlike many readily available self-help manuals and books that claim to provide an absolute solution to keeping well, the MDF programme is currently the subject of a research evaluation where, in addition to standard outcome measures, the quality of life of the participants will also be assessed.

A NOTE OF CAUTION

As discussed at the beginning of this chapter, reconfiguring individual identity as "intra-active" and relocating the risks to health to within the individual gives a rationale for the philosophy of self-management. However, in his presidential address at Yale University,

Brownell (1991) sounded a note of caution about over-emphasising individual personal responsibility and individual control over health.

Brownell described American culture as one that places immense emphasis on the power and responsibility of the individual. This description is mirrored in Ogden's views about the concept of personal responsibility for health being deeply ingrained in the individualism and self-reliance of the new Right in the USA. Brownlow postulated that whereas good health was seen as a means of attaining personal goals, it now also symbolises self-control, hard work, ambition and success in life. People expect and are expected to control their health, and this has moral implications. Those who have good health or remain well are judged as having positive qualities (strong and hard-working), in contrast to those who fall ill or have less than perfect health, who are judged as having negative qualities (passive and weak).

Those who fail to maintain or gain good health are likely to feel frightened, overwhelmed and vulnerable, and they may add to their own distress by making harsh judgements about themselves. The ensuing feelings of guilt and shame are likely to escalate their distress further. Moreover, they may be harshly judged and blamed by others, especially by what Brownlow termed the "self-righteous healthy". Exposure to people with health problems also makes healthy individuals feel more vulnerable and uncertain. This often leads to rationalisations or coping strategies that focus on the belief that the world is a just and fair place. As such "people get what they deserve and deserve what they get" (Lerner et al., 1976; Wortman & Lehman, 1985).

Other writers have also questioned whether, in contemporary Western culture, the point has been reached where it is not possible for an individual to become unwell without being at fault (Marantz, 1990). Marantz highlights the dangers of characterising episodes of illness as preventable, because this implies that the individual with that health problem becomes responsible for any recurrence. He argues that responsibility is attributed in this deterministic way because we all like to be able to explain why something has happened. However, calculating risk is meaningful only with respect to whole populations, and not to individuals, and were a risk factor to be correctly identified, it would not be an absolute cause of disorder. Marantz goes on to state that there is no known lifestyle (or self-management programme) which can ensure absence of health problems. For these reasons, he concludes that we should encourage people to modify known risk factors while, at the same time, "allowing them the luxury of getting sick without feeling guilty".

Brownlow argues that one of the reasons that people are so ready to attribute personal blame to others for disease is to be found in the paradoxical but coexisting beliefs about control. That is, we have control over our health yet at the same time are vulnerable to unpredictable factors. One resolution of this seeming paradox is overstating personal control and responsibility because it enables individuals to cope with the fear of having no or little control. Given the phenomenology of BD, in which an individual experiences marked and often unpredictable mood swings, it is vital to accept the limitations of personal responsibility and try to work within the realms of what can or cannot realistically be controlled or managed by any one individual.

The models described also have implications for health professionals. A collaborative working relationship between client and clinician requires the clinician to acknowledge and work with the clients' perceptions of their problems and an exploration of the clients' representation of the illness model. At the same time, clinicians should neither collude with inappropriate models nor be so rigid in their own theoretical stance that they cannot find common territory to form a working alliance. This is a challenge that many clinicians find frustrating. But, in reality, for the collaboration to be effective, the clinician and client must first develop a shared and accepted model of what is happening for that individual. Only when that negotiation is complete can they use this agreed (individualised) formulation to identify and prioritise the treatment or management interventions to be used. For many clinicians, this requires three things: a change in their style of interviewing and interaction, an acceptance of stress–vulnerability models of the disorder being treated, and an acceptance that health or well-being is not simply the absence of symptoms but is also the presence of a positive sense of self, and restoration or development of an appropriate quality of life for that individual.

CONCLUSIONS

This chapter highlights the development of the self-management approach to BD. As conceptualisations about the individual have changed, so have ideas about the location of health risks (Ogden, 1995). The contemporary view is that health risks reside within the individual, who has personal control and responsibility for his or her health. The rise of self-efficacy and personal responsibility models have had an impact at the national (expert patients), service (collaborative clinician-client approaches to treatment) and community (user-led self-management programmes) levels. The philosophy is well accepted, and the future of such approaches appears to be ensured. Furthermore, the idea of user-led programmes fits well into the general 'stepped-care' model of multidimensional approaches to the clinical treatment of BD. However, self-management is not for the faint-hearted. The difficulties of understanding and coping with a disorder such as BD should not be underestimated. However, as strongly expressed by one of the participants in Pollack's (1996) study, "It is a lot easier for me to take control of my life than to have someone run it for me."

The notion of self-management and empowerment is also implicit in professionally led therapies such as CBT. What was a chasm between those who treat mental disorders and those who have a disorder is reduced, and the therapist and the person with BD work together to understand and manage the problems that arise. This divide has been further reduced as people with BD are beginning to make a special contribution through the development of user-led self-management programmes.

Efforts to self-manage a disorder such as BD, where the expected health change is valued, are certainly worthwhile. However, there are risks inherent in the tendency to overstate personal control over health. Biology, like random events and factors, limits the degree to which health is under the control of the individual. It is vitally important that the limits on self-control and personal responsibility are recognised. One obvious consequence of setting unattainable standards is that many people will be blamed by themselves or others for their assumed failings, further undermining self-esteem. Nothing will more undermine individuals' confidence (self-efficacy) than to receive messages from care professionals and the wider society that they have failed as people when, or if, they become unwell.

The theme that runs through the shifting ideas about individual identity, the recovery model, and government policy is that an individual with a long-term disorder is someone with knowledge and expertise to contribute to the management of that disorder and the services provided. People with BD are no longer passive recipients of care but have personal control over their own health care and are a central component of health-care delivery for other people with BD. However, with control goes responsibility, and it is also important to set realistic limits—individuals need to be aware of what they can control and what is beyond their sphere of influence, so that we do not promise more than any of us is capable of delivering.

REFERENCES

Anthony, W.A. (1993). Recovery from mental illness: The guiding vision of the mental health service system in the 1990s. *Psychosocial Rehabilitation Journal, 16*, 11–23.

Bandura, A. (1977). Self efficacy: Toward a unifying theory of behaviour change. *Psychological Review, 84*, 191–215.

Bauer, M. (2002). Psychosocial Interventions for bipolar disorder: A Review. In M. Maj, J.J. Lopez-Ibor & N. Sartorius (Eds), *Evidence and Experience in Psychiatry*, vol. 5, WPA Series. Chichester: Wiley.

Bauer, M.S., McBride, L., Chase, C.V., Sachs, G. & Shea, N. (1998). Manual-based group psychotherapy for bipolar disorder: A feasibility study. *Journal of Clinical Psychiatry, 59*, 449–455.

Bray, S.R., Gyurcsik, N.C., Culos-Reed, S.N., Dawson, K.A. & Martin, K.A. (2001). An exploratory investigation of the relationship between proxy efficacy, self efficacy and exercise attendance. *Journal of Health Psychology, 6*, 425–434.

Brownell, K.D. (1991). Personal responsibility and control over our bodies: When expectation exceeds reality. *Health Psychology, 10*, 303–310.

Conner, M. & Norman, P. (1996). *The Role of Social Cognitions in Health Behaviours: Research and Practice with Social Cognitive Models*. Buckingham: Open University Press.

Copeland, M.E. (1994). *Living Without Depression and Manic Depression*. Oakland, CA: New Harbinger Publications.

Donaldson, L. (2001). *The Expert Patient: A New Approach to Chronic Disease Management for the 21st Century*. Department of Health.

Harter, S. (1999). *The Construction of Self: A Developmental Perspective*. New York: Guilford.

Lerner, M.J., Miller, D.T. & Holmes, J. (1976). Deserving and the emergence of justice. In L. Berkowitz & E. Walster (Eds), *Advances in Experimental Social Psychology* (pp. 47–69). New York: Academic.

Leventhal, H., Meyer, D. & Nerenz, D. (1980). The common sense representations of illness danger. In S. Rachman (Ed.), *Medical Psychology*, vol. 2 New York: Pergamon.

Lorig, K.R., Mazonson, P.D. & Holman, H.R. (1993). Evidence suggesting that health education for self management in patients with chronic arthritis has sustained health benefits while reducing health care costs. *Arthritis and Rheumatism, 36*, 439–446.

Marantz, P.R. (1990). Blaming the victim: The negative consequence of preventative medicine. *American Journal of Public Health, 80*, 1186–1187.

Ogden, J. (1995). Psychosocial theory and the creation of the risky self. *Social Science and Medicine, 40*, 409–415.

Palmer, A.G. & Gilbert, P. (1997). Manic depression: What psychologists can do to help. In V. P. Varma (Ed.), *Managing Manic Depressive Disorder* (pp. 42–60). Bristol: Jessica Kingsley Publications.

Palmer, A.G., Williams, H. & Adams, M. (1995). Cognitive behavioural therapy for bipolar affective disorder in a group format. *Behavioural and Cognitive Psychotherapy, 23*, 153–168.

Pollack, L.E. (1996). Inpatients with BD: Their quest to understand. *Journal of Psychosocial Nursing and Mental Health, 34*, 19–24.

Scott, J., Garland, A. & Moorehead, S. (2001). A pilot study of cognitive therapy in bipolar disorders. *Psychological Medicine, 31*, 459–467.

Seligman, M.E.P. (1975). *Helplessness*. San Francisco, CA: WH Freeman.

Weinstein, N. (1984). Why it won't happen to me: Perceptions of risk factors and susceptibility. *Health Psychology, 3*, 431–457.

Weissman, M.M., Leaf, P.J., Tischler, G.L., et al. (1998). Affective disorders in five United States communities. *Psychological Medicine, 18*, 141–153.

World Health Organization (1999). *Annual Report.*

Wortman, C.B. & Lehman, D.R. (1985). Reactions to victims of life crises: Support attempts that fail. In I.G. Sarson & B.R. Sarson (Eds), *Social Support: Theory, research and applications* (pp. 463–490). Boston, MA: Martinus Nijhoff.

Yanos, P.T., Primavera, L.H. & Knight, L.E. (2001). Consumer-run service participation, recovery of social functioning, and the mediating role of psychological factors. *Psychiatric Services, 52,* 493–500.

Part III

GENERAL ISSUES

17

CURRENT APPROACHES TO THE ASSESSMENT OF DEPRESSION

Dave Peck

Bebbington (Chapter 1) has outlined current thinking about the classification of depression. Although some debate exists, it is generally recognised that depression is best construed as a unitary disorder along a continuum of severity. The main exception to this simple classification is bipolar depression, in which periods of depression are interspersed with periods of excitement and mania.

Snaith (1993) examined the content of a range of depression rating scales and noted great divergence, some apparently focusing on items more associated with anxiety than with mood. He concluded with a plea for a more sophisticated approach to the construction and validation of rating scales; in particular, that they should be more closely related to accepted clinical definitions of depression. Despite such pleas, the most commonly used measures of depression, in clinical practice and in research studies, are still standard rating scales and questionnaires.

There are several alternatives to the traditional questionnaires and rating scales in the measurement of depression, using quite different methodologies. These alternatives can and perhaps should be used in conjunction with more traditional methods; the methods tap aspects of depression that are often neglected by scales and questionnaires, such as slowness. Many of them have levels of validity that suggest that they could be used to monitor changes in the level of depression. In this chapter, these alternatives will be termed 'behavioural' methods. They will receive more attention than might seem to be justified on the basis of the frequency of their reported use, in the hope that readers will consider using them in their own clinical and research endeavours. All measurements are subject to measurement error; however, the sources of error in behavioural methods are different from those of the traditional scales. A more rounded and comprehensive assessment of depression should result if behavioural measures are included in assessment batteries, despite their being more time-consuming than questionnaires.

Bebbington has already noted that many instruments have been devised to detect or diagnose mental illness, including depression, such as Schedules for Clinical Assessment in Neuropsychiatry (SCAN), Structured Clinical Interview for DSM IV (SCID) and the

Mood Disorders: A Handbook of Science and Practice. Edited by M. Power.
© 2004 John Wiley & Sons, Ltd. ISBN 0-470-84390-X.

Present State Examination (PSE). Although some of these diagnostic instruments are used to assess levels of depression, this is not their main function; they will not be covered in this chapter.

The focus of this chapter is therefore on psychometric instruments and other methods that are used to assess, and monitor change in, levels of depression. Most of the rating scales are copyrighted and are only available commercially. However, some are available free on the Internet, courtesy of pharmaceutical firms; for example, the Hamilton and the Zung scales can be downloaded from www.wellbutrin-sr.com/hcp/depression/hamilton.html.

PSYCHOMETRIC MEASURES

It is possible to classify psychometric measures of depression in several ways. One useful way is according to whether the measure is nomothetic or idiographic; that is, whether the measure is a standard instrument with set questions and a set of norms against which an individual score can be compared (nomothetic); or whether the instrument has a standard format, but with the content entirely determined by the specifics of the individual's problems (idiographic). A second way is according to whether the instrument is completed by the client (self-completed) or by the clinician (observer-completed); the latter can be subdivided into instruments based on standard rating scales and those based on structured interviews. A third classification is according to whether the instrument is designed to assess depression alone, or whether it includes assessments of other mental states (multistate instruments).

These differences are important because the different kinds of instrument often tap different aspects of depression, and may be differentially sensitive to the occurrence and rate of clinical change.

A comprehensive guide to psychometric measures of depression, including sample copies of some instruments, has been published (Nezu et al., 2000).

Nomothetic observer-completed instruments

These instruments should be administered by a trained interviewer, but, in practice, it is unlikely that all clinicians will have received the relevant training. The advantages of observer-completed instruments are several: they are more suitable if clients are very depressed, uncooperative or distracted; clients can be given the opportunity to elaborate on their responses; and clinicians often have a different but equally valuable and valid perspective on client problems. A disadvantage is that clients may be unwilling to respond openly to certain items if they are face-to-face with a clinician.

There are many instruments in this category, but, in practice, the instrument overwhelmingly used in research publications is the Hamilton Depression Rating Scale (HDRS). For example, Snaith (1996) reported that the HDRS was used in 66% of publications that employed a depression rating scale. Similarly, a survey (carried out in the preparation of this chapter) of the *British Journal of Psychiatry* and the *American Journal of Psychiatry* from 1990 to 2002 showed that the HDRS was employed in 152 papers, with the next most common instrument in this category being the Montgomery-Asberg Depression Rating Scale (three papers). Although it is more difficult to estimate its use in clinical practice, it is likely that the HDRS predominates here as well. This predominance is puzzling because much dissatisfaction has been expressed with the HDRS (Snaith, 1996).

THE HAMILTON DEPRESSION RATING SCALE (HDRS)

The HDRS comprises 17 items, rated 0–2 or 0–4, and emphasises somatic symptoms. There are several alternative versions of the HDRS, with extra items to cover more psychological symptoms, but mostly the 17-item version is employed. It focuses on symptoms over the last week or so. Little guidance is provided on how to administer the scale; the lack of published guidance suggests that the observer should be an experienced clinician. Specific training is required for its use, and it should be used only as part of a comprehensive assessment, along with information from a variety of other sources; unfortunately, such recommendations in the use of the HDRS are widely ignored (Snaith, 1996). Hamilton (1967) is the key reference. The psychometric properties of HDRS have been extensively investigated. Interrater reliability is generally good (O'Hara & Rehm, 1983).

Questions have been raised about the sensitivity of the HDRS to detect differences between drug treatments, and this lack of sensitivity may reduce the statistical power of studies using this scale (Faries et al., 2000). A six-item version of the HDRS has been developed; O'Sullivan et al. (1997) reported that this short version was as useful as the longer versions in terms of sensitivity to change after drug treatments.

MONTGOMERY-ASBERG DEPRESSION RATING SCALE (MADRS)

The MADRS contains 10 items, rated on a four-point scale; useful descriptions of all the items are provided, as well as cues at each rating point. The administration should be preceded by a flexible clinical interview. The MADRS focuses entirely on psychological aspects of depression; this lack of somatic items is said to make it particularly suitable for use in general medical populations because it omits aspects of depression such as poor appetite that could also occur in a physical illness with no depressive component.

Nomothetic self-completed instruments

The same survey of the two journals referred to above indicated that the Beck Depression Inventory (BDI) is similarly predominant, especially in research studies. The BDI was employed in 54 papers in the journals examined; the next most frequent (the Zung Self-Rating Depression Scale) was employed in six papers. Similarly, Richter et al. (1998) claimed that the BDI has been used in more than 2000 research studies. It is likely that the BDI has a similar predominant position in clinical practice. Again this predominance is puzzling because the BDI has been the subject of much criticism (see below). However, the extensive knowledge that has accumulated about this inventory, and practitioner inertia, may explain its continued popularity.

BECK DEPRESSION INVENTORY (BDI)

The BDI has 21 items, rated on a four-point scale of severity (0–3), focusing mainly on psychological aspects of depression. Items were derived from the authors' clinical experience. The original reference is Beck et al. (1961). According to Richter et al. (1998), scores on the BDI tend to be markedly skewed, most scores being in the lower ranges. These authors also note that even in a sample of psychiatric patients, the mean item score on the three-point scale rarely exceeds 2, suggesting that the BDI scales do not discriminate well between levels of severity; internal consistency is acceptable but test-retest reliability is poor. Some factor-analytic studies report that the BDI is multifactorial; others, that it measures just one factor. A more recent version of the BDI (BDI II) has been developed (Beck et al., 1996). Some of the original items have been replaced (such as symptoms of weight loss), and the BDI II is now explicitly linked to DSM-IV criteria, with a common time frame of 2 weeks. The psychometric properties of BDI II are promising (Dozois et al., 1998; Steer et al., 2001), and many of the deficiencies of the original version appear to have been rectified.

Although the BDI was not designed to detect cases, several studies have indicated that it can be usefully employed in this way; for example, after myocardial infarction (Strik et al., 2001) and in low back pain (Love, 1987).

MADRS-S

This is a self-completed version of the observer-completed MADRS. Svanborg and Asberg (2001) compared it with the BDI. The instruments correlated at +0.87 and were equally effective in discriminating between different diagnoses and in assessing sensitivity to change. The authors criticised the content of the BDI, claiming that the items are unduly influenced by 'maladaptive personality traits'.

ZUNG SELF-RATING DEPRESSION SCALE (SDS) (ZUNG, 1965)

This scale comprises 20 items rated on a four-point scale covering symptoms over the last week. Psychological and somatic items have similar weight. It correlates moderately with other scales, but there is inconsistent evidence on its sensitivity to change. Becker (1988) has provided a useful short review.

Multistate instruments

The Minnesota Multiphasic Personality Inventory (MMPI) is a long questionnaire comprising 567 items in a 'true/false' format. There are 10 clinical scales including one for depression, as well as several other groups of subscales, some of which may also be used for assessing aspects of depression. It has recently been extensively revised (Butcher & Williams, 2000).

The Kellner Symptom Questionnaire is a 92-item adjective checklist measuring depression, anxiety, hostility, and somatic concern. Reliability, validity and sensitivity to change are good. British norms are available (Zeffert et al., 1996).

The Symptom Check List (SCL-90) is a 90-item self-report instrument designed to measure nine different dimensions of mental health problems on a five-point scale, including depression, as well as such dimensions as phobic anxiety, hostility and interpersonal sensitivity. Depression items include loss of interest in sex, no interest in things, and feeling hopeless. Global scores (such as overall severity) can also be derived. Normative data are extensive, and reliability and validity are good. A key reference is Derogatis et al. (1970). A revised version (SCL-90-R) is now available.

The Brief Symptom Inventory (BSI) is a short form of the SCL-90-R. It comprises 53 items rated on a five-point scale, and takes about 10 minutes to complete. There are nine symptom scales and three global indices.

The General Health Questionnaire (GHQ) has four different versions, with, respectively, 12, 28, 30 or 60 items. It is very widely used in studies to detect mental health problems 'over the last few weeks' in non-psychiatric settings. It should not be used to arrive at a clinical diagnosis, or to assess long-standing problems. Subjects are asked to rate a series of statements on a four-point scale assessing change from the 'usual'; responses can be scored in four different ways. There are four sets of items, measuring, respectively, depression, anxiety, social dysfunction and somatic symptoms. A key reference is Goldberg (1972).

The Brief Psychiatric Rating Scale (BPRS) comprises 24 items rated on a seven-point scale from 'not present' to 'extremely severe'. There is one specific item for depression, but other relevant items include 'suicidality', 'guilt' and 'motor retardation'. The original reference is Overall and Gorham (1962). Crippa et al. (2001) have produced a structured interview guide to accompany the BPRS, which is said to increase interrater agreement.

The Hospital Anxiety and Depression Scale (HADS) is a widely used scale, developed by Zigmond and Snaith (1983); items concerned with biological aspects of depression are excluded, permitting its use to assess depression in physically ill populations. There are seven items in each of the two subscales, rated on a 0–3 scale. It is quick to complete and to score. The psychometric properties have been extensively investigated, most impressively by Mykletun et al. (2001), who used the HADS with a population of over 50 000 subjects; with such a large sample, they were able to rerun their principal components analysis and other analyses with numerous subgroups. Their findings strongly supported the clinical and research value of the HADS, in that the factor structure corresponded closely (but not perfectly) to the two subscales of anxiety and depression, the subscales correlated with each other at about +0.55, the items had an acceptable level of homogeneity, and internal consistency was high (about 0.80). The psychometric properties were even better when a more psychologically disturbed subsample was selected. It appears that HADS is a useful instrument for clinical and research purposes, but its value in detecting psychological morbidity in early breast cancer has been questioned (Hall et al., 1999).

In intercorrelations of the various scales within a multistate instrument, strong relationships are often reported, particularly between depression and anxiety. This has led some researchers (e.g., Tyrer, 1990) to suggest that anxiety and depression may not be distinct states, but form a single dimension.

Recently developed scales

A number of scales have been developed recently that appear promising for use in particular circumstances, but need further investigation before they can be recommended for routine clinical or research use. Teasdale and Cox (2001) developed a checklist of affective and self-devaluing cognitions (such as 'downhearted' and 'worthless') that may be activated when people are entering a depressive phase, particularly those who have a history of depression. It could be useful as an assessment of cognitive vulnerability to depression, and for use in clinical work or in epidemiological studies. McKenzie and Marks (1999) used a single-item rating scale to assess depression in patients with anxiety disorders; it was completed by clinicians and by patients. The scale correlated at over +0.70 with the BDI.

A self-report device was developed by Bech et al. (2001) to measure severity in moderate to severe depression. It is consistent with DSM-IV and ICD-10. Sensitivity and specificity were reported as high (0.82–0.92). An observer-completed scale for assessing depression in elderly medical patients, particularly those who can not communicate, has been described by Hammond et al. (2000). It comprises six items, selected using psychometric criteria from an original set of nine items. The six items refer to looking sad, crying, agitation, lethargy, needing encouragement and withdrawal from surroundings. Sensitivity, specificity and predictive values were acceptable.

Idiographic instruments

As noted earlier, idiographic instruments have a standard structure, but a content that is tailored to the requirements of a particular study or individual. They are not used to assess depression exclusively, but they have been used sufficiently often in depression to warrant their inclusion in this chapter.

GOAL-ATTAINMENT SCALE (GAS)

The GAS was designed to assess how far goals have been achieved, on a five-point scale. Typically, the scores range from +2 to −2, with 0 as the expected level of attainment. At least two points, preferably more, should be behaviourally 'anchored' by descriptors. For example, the expected goal may be 'spends at least 6 hours out of bed'; +2 could be 'gets up regularly before 8 a.m. and remains up'; +1 could be 'spends most of the day out of bed'; −1 could be 'gets up for occasional meals'; −2 could be 'spends nearly all the time in bed'. The method was originally devised to monitor broad treatment strategies and intervention programmes (Kiresuk & Sherman, 1968), but is now often used to assess individual progress.

VISUAL ANALOGUE SCALE (VAS)

This consists of a 10-cm line with bipolar adjectives at each end. Subjects are asked to put a cross anywhere on the line that best describes how they are feeling in terms of the adjectives. Scoring is simply the distance from the end of the line to the point of endorsement. It has long been used to measure aspects of mood (Zealley & Aitken, 1969). It is particularly useful when there are no standard scales available to measure a particular construct, or to rate a concept on many different dimensions but with the same format. It is quick to complete and to score. When administered longitudinally, VAS ratings are moderately correlated with questionnaire scores of mental state, but only in about 60% of subjects (Morrison & Peck, 1990).

SEMANTIC DIFFERENTIAL (SD)

As its name implies, the SD was originally devised to measure the meanings of particular concepts across different individuals (Osgood et al., 1957). It consists of a concept to be rated above a line divided into seven boxes. Subjects are asked to put a cross in the box that most accurately reflects their view or interpretation of the concept. The concepts can be rated on any number of bipolar scales. It could be regarded as a special form of the VAS.

PERSONAL QUESTIONNAIRE RAPID SCORING TECHNIQUE (PQRST)

This ingenious method requires subjects to state their problems (up to 10) in their own words, and to rate them from 'maximum possible' to 'absolutely none' in a series of paired comparisons. It is particularly useful for detailed analyses of an individual's problems, and for tracking them over time. Versions of different lengths are available. A key reference is Mulhall (1976); it has been used in a number of clinical areas—for example, to analyse change in different forms of psychotherapy (Barkham et al., 1989).

CORRELATIONS BETWEEN RATING SCALES

Correlations between observer- and self-completed scales were investigated by Sayer et al. (1993); the correlations between the HDRS and the BDI varied between +0.16 and +0.73 (that is, low to high). The reported low correlations may reflect the use of a restricted range of severity in the participating subjects; thus, Fitzgibbon et al. (1988) found moderate correlations in samples with restricted scores (for example, r = +0.43 in medical patients), but higher correlations when samples were wider and included depressed patients, medical patients and healthy volunteers (r = +0.89). The finding of a high correlation may give a misleading impression of the degree of agreement between instruments; patients categorised as mild on one measure may be judged as severe on other measures (Enns et al., 2000).

BEHAVIOURAL ASSESSMENT OF DEPRESSION

The value of direct behavioural observations of motor activity in depressed people was outlined over 20 years ago by Lewinsohn and Lee (1981); they noted that simple ratings of ward behaviour correlated well with the HDRS and with the BDI (about +0.70). Tryon (1991) published a review of the measurement of activity in psychology and in medicine ('actigraphy'). He reported that actigraphy was useful in examining sleep-wake periods, and in assessing psychomotor agitation and retardation in depression. Activity levels (as measured from the wrist) changed markedly from admission to discharge, and immobility was a particularly sensitive indicator of the intensity of depression. Actigraphy has also been successfully used with outpatients. More recently, Caligiuri and Ellwanger (2000) found that 60% of depressed patients displayed abnormal psychomotor activity on a variety of tests, many of the patients showing signs similar to those found in parkinsonian disease. Changes in actigraphy have been shown to be sufficiently sensitive to detect differential responses to various antidepressant drugs, especially via early morning recordings (Stanley et al., 1999).

Alessi (2001) claims that the motor aspects of depression, in contrast to the affective aspects, have been neglected by researchers, partly because of difficulties in recording and analysing changes in motor behaviour. He suggested that recent advances in motion-capture technology will facilitate a greater focus on these aspects and broaden our understanding of a wider range of depressive phenomena.

Sobin and Hackheim (1997) provided a useful literature review of psychomotor abnormalities in depression. They reported that activity increases in bipolar patients during manic phases and decreases during depressive phases, and that 24-hour gross motor activity is higher in unipolar patients than in schizophrenic patients and bipolar patients, these differences being particularly marked during the night. Depressed patients also manifest more self-touching, less eye contact, less smiling and fewer eyebrow movements. Overall reaction times, decision times and motor-response times are all slower in depression. Sobin and Hackheim (1997) conclude that such measures are sufficiently sensitive to warrant consideration as viable objective measures of depressive states. Finally, they stress that retardation and agitation are not mutually exclusive, and that both should be measured in any comprehensive assessment of psychomotor symptoms in depression.

In the performance of psychomotor tests, significant levels of cognitive effort are also involved (such as memory). In an attempt to obtain an uncontaminated measure of motor activity, Sabbe et al. (1999) used a simple task in which cognitive demands were minimal. Depressed patients were asked to carry out 10 simple line-drawing tasks, and a range of measures were taken, such as movement time per line, pen lifts and time intervals between starting lines. Compared with healthy controls, depressed patients showed marked slowing on all tasks. Similarly, van Hoof et al. (1998) demonstrated that, whereas schizophrenic patients were characterised mainly by cognitive retardation, depressed patients were characterised by both cognitive and motor retardation.

In addition to such direct physical measures, questionnaire measures of psychomotor activity have also been developed. The CORE system (a sign-based method of rating psychomotor disturbances) has been shown to be helpful in distinguishing melancholia from other types of depression (Parker et al., 2000), and in the prediction of response to electroconvulsive therapy (ECT) (Hickie et al., 1996). However, its content validity has been questioned (Sobin et al., 1998). The Motor Agitation and Retardation Scale (Sobin et al., 1998) has been shown to distinguish clearly between normals and depressed inpatients; and scores on the Depressive Retardation Rating Scale (Lemelin & Baruch, 1998) are associated with global attentional deficits in major depression. Finally, the Saltpetre Retardation Rating Scale correlates with depression severity and with prognosis, and is sensitive to change (Dantchev & Widloecher, 1998).

Speech Patterns and Depression

Lewinsohn and Lee (1981) described a method of coding and monitoring the verbal interactions of depressed people in their own homes and during group therapy, using time-sampling methodology. More recently, Hale et al. (1997) recorded verbal interactions between depressed people and others, including their partners. During speech, patients displayed more movements (such as self-touching), and fewer head nods and shakes. However, the value of such measures of verbal interaction in monitoring changes in level of depression remains to be demonstrated.

Measurement of formal speech characteristics appears to be more promising. Early work by Szabadi et al. (1976) demonstrated that speech pause time was lengthened in depression. More recently, Vanger et al. (1992) found that overall speech activity decreased and silences increased, in line with the level of depression, and with the emotional salience of the discussion topic. Kuny and Stassen (1993) observed speech patterns and measured voice sound characteristics in 30 recovering depressives, on seven occasions throughout their hospital stay. Several of their measures were closely related to the time course of recovery, such as voice timbre, loudness and variability of loudness. These associations were clear in about two-thirds of their sample, but not in the remaining third (mainly those with poor or variable recovery). These results were replicated in a later study, using the HDRS to assess severity; in addition, they reported a marked relationship between early signs of recovery and later outcome (Stassen et al., 1998). Sobin and Hackheim (1997) listed a number of speech and voice characteristics related to depression, including low voice amplitude, decreased monitoring and correction of speech, and reduced speaking time.

SUMMARY AND CONCLUSIONS

Depression is a multifaceted phenomenon, with a variety of psychological and motor components. However, in the measurement of depression, clinicians and researchers tend to use a narrow range of scales and questionnaires that relate only to psychological aspects, especially mood. The HDRS and the BDI are by far the most popular psychometric instruments for measuring depression, and there are no signs that they are about to be supplanted, despite their being subject to much criticism. An unfortunate consequence of the narrow focus on affective aspects is that other aspects, such as speech patterns and motor abnormalities, have been largely neglected as measures of depression in research studies. A more comprehensive assessment of the full range of depressive phenomena by a wide range of measurement techniques would be helpful in casting further light on this complex clinical condition.

REFERENCES

Alessi, N. (2001). Is there a future for depression digital motion constructs in psychiatry? *CyberPsychology and Behaviour, 4*, 457–463.

Barkham, M., Shapiro, D.A. & Firth-Cozens, L. (1989). Personal questionnaire changes in prescriptive versus exploratory psychotherapy. *British Journal of Clinical Psychology, 28*, 97–107.

Bech, P., Rasmussen, N., Olsen, L.R., Noerholm, V. & Abildgaard, W. (2001). The sensitivity and specificity of the Major Depression Inventory, using the Present State Examination as the index of diagnostic validity. *Journal of Affective Disorders, 66*, 159–164.

Beck, A., Steer, R.A. & Brown, G.K. (1996). *Beck Depression Inventory Manual*. San Antonio, TX: Psychological Corporation.

Beck, A., Ward, C.H., Mendelson, M., Mock, J. & Erbaugh, J. (1961). An inventory for measuring depression. *Archives of General Psychiatry, 4*, 561–571.

Becker, R.E. (1988). Zung Self-Rating Depression Scale. In M. Hersen & A.S. Bellack (Eds), *Dictionary of Behavioral Assessment Techniques*. New York: Pergamon.

Butcher, J.N. & Williams, C.L. (2000). *Essentials of MMPI-2 and MMPI-A Interpretation*. Minneapolis, MN: University of Minnesota Press.

Caligiuri, M.P. & Ellwanger, J. (2000). Motor and cognitive aspects of motor retardation in depression. *Journal of Affective Disorders, 57*, 83–93.

Crippa, J.A., Sanches, R.F., Hallak, J.E., Loureiro, S.R. & Zuardi, A.W. (2001). A structured interview guide increases Brief Psychiatric Rating Scale reliability in raters with low clinical experience. *Acta Psychiatrica Scandinavica, 103*, 465–470.

Dantchev, N. & Widloecher, D.J. (1998). The measurement of retardation in depression. *Journal of Clinical Psychiatry, 59*, (Suppl. 14), 19–25.

Derogatis, L.R., Limpman, R. & Covi, L. (1970). SCL-90: An outpatient psychiatric rating scale—preliminary report. *Psychopharmacology Bulletin, 9*, 13–28.

Dozois, D., Dobson, K.S. & Ahnberg, J.L. (1998). A psychometric evaluation of the Beck Depression Inventory. II. *Psychological Assessment, 10*, 83–89.

Enns, M.W., Larsen, D.K. & Cox, B.J. (2000). Discrepancies between self and observer ratings of depression. The relationship to demographic, clinical and personality variables. *Journal of Affective Disorders, 60*, 33–41.

Faries, D., Herrera, J., Rayamajhi, J., DeBrota, D., Demitrack, M. & Potter, W.Z. (2000). The responsiveness of the Hamilton Depression Rating Scale. *Journal of Psychiatric Research, 34*, 3–10.

Fitzgibbon, M.L., Cella, D.F. & Sweeney, J.A. (1988). Redundancy in measures of depression. *Journal of Clinical Psychology, 44*, 372–374.

Goldberg, D. (1972). *The Detection of Psychiatric Illness by Questionnaire*. Maudsley Monograph 21. London: Oxford University Press.

Hall, A., A'Hern R. & Fallowfield, L. (1999). Are we using appropriate self-report questionnaires for detecting anxiety and depression in women with early breast cancer? *European Journal of Cancer, 35*, 79–85.

Hale, W.W., Jansen, J.H., Bouhuys, A.L., Jenner, J.A. & van den Hoofdakker, R.H. (1997). Non-verbal behavioral interactions of depressed patients with partners and strangers: The role of behavioral social support and involvement in depression persistence. *Journal of Affective Disorders, 44*, 111–122.

Hamilton, M. (1967). Development of a rating scale for primary depressive illness. *British Journal of Social and Clinical Psychology, 6*, 278–296.

Hammond, M.F., O'Keeffe, S.T. & Barer, D.H. (2000). Development and validation of a brief observer-rated screening scale for depression in elderly medical patients. *Age and Ageing, 29*, 511–515.

Hickie, I., Mason, C., Parker, G. & Brodaty, H. (1996). Prediction of ECT response: Validation of a refined sign-based (CORE) system for defining melancholia. *British Journal of Psychiatry, 169*, 68–74.

Kiresuk, T.J. & Sherman, R.E. (1968). Goal attainment scaling: A general method for evaluating comprehensive community mental health programmes. *Community Mental Health Journal, 4*, 443–453.

Kuny, S. & Stassen, H.H. (1993). Speaking behavior and voice sound characteristics in depressive patients during recovery. *Journal of Psychiatric Research, 27*, 289–307.

Lemelin, S. & Baruch, P. (1998). Clinical psychomotor retardation and attention in depression. *Journal of Psychiatric Research, 32*, 81–88.

Lewinsohn, P.M. & Lee, W. (1981). Assessment of affective disorders. In D.H. Barlow (Ed.), *Behavioral Assessment of Adult Disorders* (pp. 129–179). New York: Guilford.

Love, A.W. (1987). Depression in chronic low back pain patients: Diagnostic efficiency of three self report questionnaires. *Journal of Clinical Psychology, 43*, 84–89.

McKenzie, N. & Marks, I. (1999). Quick rating of depressed mood in patients with anxiety disorders. *British Journal of Psychiatry, 174*, 266–269.

Morrison, D.P. & Peck, D.F. (1990). Do self-report measures of affect agree? A longitudinal study. *British Journal of Clinical Psychology, 29*, 395–400.

Mulhall, D. (1976). Systematic self assessment by PQRST (Personal Questionnaire Rapid Scaling Technique). *Psychological Medicine, 6*, 591–597.

Mykeltun, A., Stordal, E. & Dahl, A.A. (2001). Hospital Anxiety and Depression (HAD) scale: Factor structure, item analyses and internal consistency in a large population. *British Journal of Psychiatry, 179*, 540–544.

Nezu, A.M., Ronan, G.F., Meadows, E.A. & McClure, K.S. (2000). *Practitioner's Guide to Empirically-Based Measures of Depression*. New York: Plenum.

O'Hara, M.W. & Rehm, L.P. (1983). Hamilton Rating Scale for Depression: Reliability and validity of judgements of novice raters. *Journal of Consulting and Clinical Psychology, 51*, 318–319.

Osgood, C.E., Suci, G.J. & Tannenbaum, P.H. (1957). *The Measurement of Meaning*. Urbana, IL: University of Illinois Press.

O'Sullivan, R.L., Fava, M., Agustin, C., Baer, L. & Rosenbaum, J.F. (1997). Sensitivity of the six-item Hamilton Depression Rating Scale. *Acta Psychiatrica Scandinavica, 95*, 379–384.

Overall, J.E. & Gorham, D.R. (1962). The Brief Psychiatric Rating Scale. *Psychological Reports, 10*, 799–812.

Parker, G., Roy, K., Hadzi-Pavlovic, D., et al. (2000). Subtyping depression by clinical features: The Australian database. *Acta Psychiatrica Scandinavica, 101*, 21–28.

Richter, P., Werner, J., Heerlein, A., Kraus, A. & Sauer, H. (1998). On the validity of the Beck Depression Inventory. A review. *Psychopathology, 31*, 160–168.

Sabbe, B., Hulstijn, W., van Hoof, J., Tuynman-Qua, H.G. & Zitman, F. (1999). Retardation in depression: assessment by means of simple motor tasks. *Journal of Affective Disorders, 55*, 39–44.

Sayer, N.A., Sackheim, H.A., Moeller, J.R., et al. (1993). The relations between observer-rating and self-report of depressive symptomatology. *Psychological Assessment, 5*, 350–360.

Snaith, R.P. (1993). What do depression rating scales measure? *British Journal of Psychiatry, 163*, 293–298.

Snaith, R.P. (1996). Present use of the Hamilton Depression Rating Scale: Observation on method of assessment in research on depressive disorders. *British Journal of Psychiatry, 168*, 594–597.

Sobin, C. & Hackheim, H.A. (1997). Psychomotor symptoms of depression. *American Journal of Psychiatry, 154*, 4–17.

Sobin, C., Mayer, L. & Endicott, J. (1998). The Motor Agitation Retardation Scale: A scale for the assessment of motor abnormalities in depressed patients. *Journal of Neuropsychiatry and Clinical Neurosciences, 10*, 85–92.

Stanley, N., Fairweather, D.B. & Hindmarch, I. (1999). Effects of fluoxetine and dothiepin on 24-hour activity in depressed patients. *Neuropsychobiology, 39*, 44–48.

Stassen, H.H., Kuny, S. & Hell D. (1998). The speech analysis approach to determining onset of improvement under antidepressants. *European Neuropsychopharmacology, 8*, 303–310.

Steer, R.A., Brown, G.K., Beck, A.T. & Sanderson, W.C. (2001). Mean Beck Depression Inventory II scores by severity of major depressive episode. *Psychological Reports, 88*, 1075–1076.

Strik, J.J., Honig, A., Lousberg, R. & Denollet, J. (2001). Sensitivity and specificity of observer and self report questionnaires in major and minor depression following myocardial infarction. *Psychosomatics, 42*, 423–428.

Svanborg, P. & Asberg, M. (2001). A comparison between the Beck Depression Inventory (BDI) and the self rating version of the Montgomery-Asberg Depression Rating Scale (MADRS). *Journal of Affective Disorders, 64*, 203–216.

Szabadi, E., Bradshaw, C.M. & Besson, J.A. (1976). Elongation of pause-time in speech: A simple, objective measure of motor retardation in depression. *British Journal of Psychiatry, 129*, 592–597.

Teasdale, J.D. & Cox, S.G. (2001). Dysphoria: Self-devaluative and affective components in recovered depressed patients and never depressed controls. *Psychological Medicine, 31*, 1311–1316.

Tryon, W.W. (1991). *Activity Measurement in Psychology and Medicine*. New York: Plenum.

Tyrer, P. (1990). The division of neurosis: A failed classification. *Journal of the Royal Society of Medicine, 83*, 614–616.

Vanger, P., Summerfield, A.B., Rosen, B.K. & Watson, J.P. (1992). Effects of communication content on speech behaviour of depressives. *Comprehensive Psychiatry, 33*, 39–41.

van Hoof, J., Jogems-Kostermen, B., Sabbe, B., Zitman, F. & Hulstijn, W. (1998). Differentiation of cognitive and motor slowing in the Digit Symbol Test (DST): Differences between depression and schizophrenia. *Journal of Psychiatric Research, 32*, 99–103.

Zealley, A.K. & Aitken, R.C.B. (1969). Measurement of mood. *Proceedings of the Royal Society of Medicine, 62*, 993–996.

Zeffert, S., Clark, A., Dobson, C.J., Jones, A. & Peck, D.F. (1996). The Symptom Questionnaire: British standardisation data. *British Journal of Clinical Psychology, 35*, 85–90.

Zigmond, A.S. & Snaith, R.P. (1983). The Hospital Anxiety and Depression Scale. *Acta Psychiatrica Scandinavica, 67*, 361–370.

Zung, W.W.K. (1965). A self-rating depression scale. *Archives of General Psychiatry, 12*, 63–70.

18

SUICIDE AND ATTEMPTED SUICIDE

Andrew K. MacLeod

Suicidal behaviour is often assumed to be linked to depression. This chapter addresses some key questions about the relationship between depression and suicidal behaviour. First, evidence will be reviewed concerning the prevalence of suicidal behaviour in those who are depressed and the rates of depression in those who are suicidal. It will become clear that there is a strong link but that the non-overlap is much greater than the overlap: many people who commit suicide or attempt suicide are not depressed, and the overwhelming majority of depressed people will not attempt or commit suicide. The chapter will then move on to discuss *how* depression might be related to suicidality. Several factors will be discussed that might account for both the overlap and the lack of overlap. The final two sections of the chapter will cover evidence on risk assessment and treatment of suicidal behaviour. The evidence reviewed is not always specific to depression, as often studies on suicidality do not differentiate between depressed and non-depressed suicidal behaviour. However, given the overlap between depression and suicidality, the evidence is very relevant to depressed, suicidal behaviour. Before proceeding, it is important to clarify what is meant by suicidal behaviour.

TYPES OF SUICIDAL BEHAVIOUR

The concept of suicide is relatively straightforward, as it is defined by a legal judgement where there is clear evidence that the person intended to take his or her own life. Cases where clear evidence is lacking but the suspicion is of suicide are usually recorded as undetermined deaths and are often included in the suicide statistics. Non-fatal suicidal behaviour is more complicated because of the range of behaviours encompassed and the variety of terms used. The terms usually imply something about the level of intent to die; for example, 'attempted suicide' implies a strong intention to die, whereas 'deliberate self-harm' does not. It is tempting to make judgements about the level of intent, but this is difficult to do in practice. People are often unaware of the medical lethality of the overdose they have taken (by far the most common type of self-harm), thus rendering this a poor criterion. Moreover, when asked, most commonly, people simply say they wanted to escape; they may not be clear

Mood Disorders: A Handbook of Science and Practice. Edited by M. Power.
© 2004 John Wiley & Sons, Ltd. ISBN 0-470-84390-X.

about whether they wanted to die or not (Bancroft et al., 1979). Finally, individuals with more than one episode of self-harm are quite likely to have a mixture of levels of intent across different episodes (Brown et al., 2002; Sakinofsky, 2000). One solution suggested by Kreitman (1977) was to use the term 'parasuicide' as a descriptive term to cover all deliberate but non-fatal acts of self-harm, thus, remaining neutral about level of intent to die. As Kerkhof (2000) has pointed out, this term has not really caught on with clinicians, who tend to use attempted suicide or deliberate self-harm. In this chapter, the terms 'parasuicide', 'deliberate self-harm', and 'attempted suicide' will be used interchangeably to describe a deliberate but non-fatal act of self-harm whatever the medical lethality or motivation behind the behaviour. A final reason for not distinguishing types of parasuicide is that, although some studies have specifically addressed the issue of measuring intent, most have not; therefore, the literature typically groups together all non-lethal suicidal behaviour.

HOW MANY PEOPLE ENGAGE IN SUICIDAL BEHAVIOUR?

In England and Wales in a typical year, about 1% of deaths are from suicide (Office for National Statistics, 1999). This translates into a rate of about 10 per 100 000 of the population, the rate also found in the UK confidential inquiry into suicide and homicide, which looked at suicides occurring over a 5-year period (Department of Health, 2001). Rates do vary in different countries (World Health Organisation [WHO], 2001). For example, the rates in northern European countries and most, but not all, former Soviet republics are high (for example, Ukraine 30/100 000), and the rates in Mediterranean countries tend to be low (for example, Greece 4/100 000). Suicide is predominantly a male behaviour: the aggregate male/female ratio across countries is 3.5:1 (WHO, 2001); in the UK, it is 3:1 (Department of Health, 2001).

Parasuicide is much more common than suicide, although the data tend to be less reliable due to the varying ways they are collected as well as the different definitions of parasuicide being used in different places. A WHO multicentre study using standardised recording of parasuicides presenting to hospital in centres in 16 European countries found a mean, age-standardised rate per annum of 186/100 000 (Kerkhof, 2000). The rates varied across countries from 69/100 000 in the Spanish centre to 462/100 000 in the French centre. The UK rates, where Oxford was the centre, were the second highest, with 384/100 000. Unlike suicide, parasuicide is more common in females—the female to male ratio in the WHO European study was 1.5:1. Kerkhof (2000) estimated that, in that WHO study, the lifetime prevalence of medically treated suicide attempts was about 2% for males and 3% for females. Estimates have also been made from population surveys rather than hospital presentations. This has the benefit of potentially detecting non-presenting cases, but the reliability of the data is unknown. The finding of prevalence will depend on the exact question asked. Most surveys estimate that 1–4% of the population have engaged in parasuicide, though some figures are higher (Kerkhof, 2000). From a recent large population survey in the USA, 4.6% reported having made a suicide attempt (Kessler et al., 1999). About half said it was a serious attempt with at least some intent to die, even if ambivalent, and half said it was a cry for help where they did not want to die. Suicidal thoughts or ideation is probably more common again, but is very difficult to estimate. Kessler et al. (1999) found that 13.5% reported having suicide ideation at some point in their lives. Again, the exact question asked will have a bearing on the rate found.

Repetition of parasuicide is common and represents a serious clinical problem. In the WHO European study, 54% of attempters had a previous attempt, and 30% made another attempt during the 1-year follow-up (Kerkhof, 2000). Approximately 1% of attempters go on to complete suicide within 1 year, and studies with a follow-up period of at least 5 years show rates of 3–13% (Sakinofsky, 2000). Between one-third and two-thirds of those who die by suicide will have made a previous attempt (Sakinofsky, 2000).

SUICIDAL BEHAVIOUR IN DEPRESSION

Completed suicide

How many depressed people commit suicide? An influential study by Guze and Robins (1970) estimated that the lifetime risk of a depressed person committing suicide was about 15%. This figure has been widely quoted since, but recently has been questioned. Bostwick and Pankratz (2000) argued that this figure is an overestimate because the studies analysed by Guze and Robins used only the most severe (that is, hospitalised) depressed patients and had fairly short follow-up periods. As the risk of suicide is greatest after discharge from hospital (Harris & Barraclough, 1997), projecting rates within a short, post-discharge follow-up to lifetime rates is likely to lead to overestimation, particularly when the figure is based on proportionate mortality prevalence—the number of deaths by suicide relative to the number of deaths in the sample. Bostwick and Pankratz (2000) reanalysed the data from the Guze and Robins review, as well as newer data, using case fatality prevalence (proportion of total sample that died by suicide) rather than proportionate mortality prevalence (proportion of deaths that were suicides). They also divided the new data by severity into patients that were hospitalised because of suicide concerns, inpatients who were not specifically hospitalised because of suicide risk, and outpatients. Their estimates of lifetime prevalence of suicide in affective disorder patients for the newer data were 8.6% for those hospitalised because of suicidal risk, 4.0% for those hospitalised without risk specified, and 2.2% for outpatients. For the non-affectively ill population, the risk was less than 0.5%. The data used by Guze and Robins reanalysed in this way yielded a lifetime risk of 4.8%.

Some studies have actually followed up patients and reported suicide rates over a longer period. In a very substantial study, Ostby et al. (2001) followed up over 39 000 unipolar, major depression patients and 15 000 bipolar patients who had been inpatients in Sweden between 1973 and 1975. The average follow-up period was 10 years. During the follow-up period, 5.2% of the unipolar group and 4.4% of the bipolar group committed suicide. Both groups had elevated general mortality rates, as indicated by standardised mortality ratios (SMRs). The SMR is the number of deaths from a particular cause divided by what would be expected in the population from that cause. Thus, an SMR of 2 means that the group had twice the number of deaths from that particular cause than would have been expected. Interestingly, most causes of death, including natural causes, were overrepresented in both patient groups. However, death by suicide was by far the most overrepresented. The SMRs for death by suicide were 20 in the unipolar group and 10 in the bipolar group. These SMRs are actually very similar to those reported by Harris and Barraclough (1997) in a meta-analysis of studies that had at least a 2-year follow-up and had lost fewer than 10% of patients at follow-up. These authors found a mean SMR of 20 for major depression, 15 for bipolar disorder, and 12 for dysthymia.

Attempted suicide and ideation

Rates of attempted suicide are, as would be expected, higher than rates of suicide. Fombonne et al. (2001) reported a 20-year follow-up of a sample of individuals who had been depressed as youths. The suicide risk in the sample was 2.5%, but 44% had attempted suicide at least once. This sample of early-onset depression may represent an unusually high risk of attempts. Most other studies have found lower rates of a history of attempted suicide in depressed patients. For example, Bottlender et al. (2000) reported a history of self-harm in 27% of bipolar patients and 18% of unipolar patients. As in the case for suicide in bipolar patients, depression seems to be key. Lopez et al. (2001) found that 33% of their sample of 169 bipolar I disorder patients in northern Spain reported one or more previous suicide attempts. Severity of depressive episodes was one factor that distinguished those with and without a history of attempts.

How many of those who are depressed have suicidal ideation? Of course, it depends on what is meant by suicidal ideation, but it is probably accurate to say that more than half of depressed people have suicidal thoughts (Lonnqvist, 2000). For example, Schaffer et al. (2000) retrospectively reviewed 533 patients with major depression and found that 58% had suicidal ideation. There are also high rates of suicidal thoughts in bipolar patients, though it seems to be mainly accounted for by levels of depression rather than mania. Dilsaver et al. (1994) studied a sample of bipolar I patients, some of whom also met criteria for concurrent major depression, which they termed 'depressive mania'. Of the 49 pure mania patients, only one exhibited suicidal ideation. In contrast, 24 out of 44 depressive mania patients showed suicidal thoughts. Strakowski et al. (1996) also found higher rates of suicidal ideation in patients with mixed bipolar disorder than those with manic bipolar disorder. Further analysis showed that depression levels rather than group status (mixed versus manic) predicted suicide ideation. Oquendo et al. (2000) found that bipolar patients who had a history of suicide attempts had more episodes of depression than did those without a suicidal history.

There is no doubt that the relative risk of suicide, attempted suicide, and suicide ideation is very substantially increased in depression, both unipolar and bipolar. However, estimates do vary, influenced mainly by the particular samples studied and the methods used. A reasonable estimate would be that just over half of depressed patients have suicidal ideation and somewhere between 20% and 33% have a non-fatal attempt. Lifetime suicide risk in unipolar depression is almost certainly lower than the 15% commonly cited. The evidence is that bipolar disorder carries a lower risk than unipolar disorder, and depressive episodes would seem to be the key factor for suicide risk in bipolar disorder.

DEPRESSION IN SUICIDAL BEHAVIOUR

Estimates vary considerably of how many people who commit suicide were depressed (Lonnqvist, 2000). This is perhaps not surprising, as accurate data are difficult to arrive at and usually rely on a retrospective method of trying to build a picture of the person, called psychological autopsy. For example, Foster et al. (1997) conducted interviews with general practitioners, family, friends, and work colleagues to study the characteristics of 118 people out of 154 who committed suicide in Northern Ireland in 1 year. They estimated that an Axis

I disorder was present in 86% of cases, but that this was major unipolar depression in only 32% and bipolar depression in 4% of cases. One very large-scale study looked at reported suicides over a 5-year period in the UK (Department of Health, 2001). The study found that about one-quarter of almost 21 000 suicides over the period were in contact with mental health services, and so consultants were able to provide diagnostic information about these individuals. Of those in contact with services, 42% met criteria for major affective disorder and 10% for bipolar disorder. It is reasonable to assume that the rates of depression might be lower in those not in contact with the services, so the overall rate may have been lower than 42%.

It does appear that depression is more common in non-fatal self-harm than it is in suicide. This is true even when comparable methods of assessment are used. In a sample of 202 suicides in New Zealand, Beautrais (2001) found that 56% met diagnostic criteria for a mood disorder, according to information supplied by a significant other. She compared this to patients who had made a medically serious but non-fatal suicide attempt, also using a significant other as a source of information for direct comparability. She found that 78% of the attempters met criteria for a mood disorder. Even where data are not restricted to medically serious attempters, there is a high rate of depression in parasuicide. For example, Haw et al. (2001) found that 71% of their unselected sample of 150 self-harm patients presenting at accident and emergency departments met diagnostic criteria for major depressive episode (only one patient met criteria for bipolar disorder).

To summarise, depression is common in those who commit suicide, and especially in those who attempt suicide. Estimates vary considerably, and there is no definitive figure in either case. However, it appears likely that somewhere between one-third and one-half of those who commit suicide are depressed, whereas between one-half and three-quarters of attempters are depressed.

REASONS FOR DISCORDANCE

Obviously, there will be pathways to suicide other than depression, and many other risk factors have been identified (e.g., Maris et al., 1992). But, why is depression without suicidal behaviour so common? Why is there not a higher incidence of suicidal behaviour in depression? One possibility is that it is necessary to have additional risk factors that add to the risk that depression carries. Or, it may be that those who are depressed but not at suicidal risk have certain protective factors which offset any depressive risk. A second possibility lies within the nature of the depressive experience itself: are there certain facets or features of depression that are particularly related to suicidality?

Additional risk factors

High comorbidity is generally associated with greater risk of suicidal behaviour. One particular type of comorbidity that has received attention is comorbid Axis I and Axis II disorders. For example, Foster et al. (1999) found in the Northern Ireland study a much higher risk of suicide in those with Axis I–Axis II morbidity than those with Axis I morbidity only. Personality disorder has also been found to be an additional risk factor in the case of suicide attempts. Soloff et al. (2000) compared the characteristics of suicide attempts in patients who had both borderline personality disorder and major depression with those who had only major depression or only borderline personality disorder. Depressed and borderline patients did not differ from each other in characteristics of suicide attempts (number of attempts, level of lethal intent, medical damage, objective planning, or degree of violence of method), but those with both disorders had higher levels of objective planning and a greater number of attempts. Comorbid depression and alcoholism are also associated with higher rates of suicidality than is depression alone (Cornelius et al., 1995).

A number of studies have examined psychological variables that differentiate depressed suicidal from depressed non-suicidal individuals. Roy (1998) found that depressed patients who had attempted suicide were more introverted than depressed patients who had never attempted suicide. Seidlitz et al. (2001) measured a range of emotion traits in older (over 50) depressed inpatients who either had or had not attempted suicide. Attempters were lower in warmth and positive emotions, but the groups did not differ on other emotions, such as anger, sadness, and guilt. Importantly, the groups did not differ on severity of depression as measured by the Hamilton depression score (excluding the suicide item), ruling out severity of depression as an overriding explanation for both emotions and suicidality. The strategy of comparing suicidal and non-suicidal depressed patients has also been used to look at problem-solving skills. Schotte and Clum (1987) measured problem-solving skills in depressed inpatients with suicidal ideation and inpatients who were equally depressed but did not have any suicidal ideation. The suicidal group performed more poorly than the depressed, non-suicidal group in a number of ways: they thought of fewer relevant steps to solve problems, gave more irrelevant solutions, thought of more drawbacks to their solutions, and said they were less likely to implement their solutions. Williams and colleagues have linked this difficulty with problem solving to the difficulties that suicidal individuals have in recalling specific autobiographical memories (e.g., Williams, 2001).

As well as additional risk factors, lack of factors that protect against suicidality in the face of depression might play an important role. Linehan and colleagues (Linehan et al., 1983) developed the Reasons for Living Inventory (RFL) to assess beliefs that inhibit suicidal behaviour. The scale has six subscales covering survival and coping beliefs (for example, I still have many things left to do—I am curious about what will happen in the future), responsibility to family, child-related concerns, fear of suicide, fear of social disapproval, and moral objections to suicide. Those who have attempted suicide endorse fewer reasons for living than psychiatric controls or the general population (Linehan et al., 1993). In the context of depression and suicidality, Malone et al. (2000) measured reasons for living in patients with major depression who either had or had not attempted suicide. The attempters and non-attempters had comparable Hamilton depression scores, though the attempters were significantly higher on depression as measured by the Beck Depression Inventory. The attempters had lower scores on the RFL generally and particularly on the subscales of responsibility to family, survival and coping beliefs, fear of social disapproval, and moral objections.

The nature of the depressive experience— hopelessness

Are certain features or aspects of the experience of depression linked to suicidality? Perhaps the most obvious question is whether severity of depression is related to suicidal behaviour. Not surprisingly, the evidence suggests that it is. In a large follow-up study, Simon and von Korff (1998) found that the risk of suicide greatly increased with the type of treatment received. The rates in those treated as inpatients were much higher than those treated as outpatients. Assuming that treatment reflects severity, it is reasonable to conclude that rates are related to severity of depression. Alexopoulos et al. (1999) found that suicide ideation and suicide attempts in an elderly depressed sample were predicted by severity of depression, along with low social support and having previous attempts with high intent.

A more interesting question is whether there are particular aspects of depression that link to suicidality. The evidence is very clear that hopelessness about the future is the component of depressive experience that relates to suicidal behaviour (see Nimeus et al., 1997). Studies report that hopelessness mediates the relationship between depression and suicidal intent within parasuicide populations (Salter & Platt, 1990; Wetzel et al., 1980). Furthermore, hopelessness has also been found to be related to repetition of parasuicide 6 months later (Petrie et al., 1988) and completed suicides up to 10 years later (Beck et al., 1989; Fawcett et al., 1990).

Lack of positive future thinking

Studies of suicidal future thinking have generally relied on the Beck Hopelessness Scale (Beck et al., 1974) as a measure of hopelessness about the future. This is a 20-item true/false self-report measure that assesses global outlook for the future (for example, 'the future seems dark to me'). More recently, MacLeod and colleagues (MacLeod et al., 1993; 1997; 1998) examined future-directed thinking in parasuicidal patients more directly by adapting the standard verbal fluency paradigm. In the standard verbal fluency task, participants are given a time limit and asked to generate as many exemplars of a category as they can, for example words beginning with a particular letter. In the 'future-thinking task' developed by these authors, individuals were asked to think of future positive events (things they were looking forward to) and negative events (things they were not looking forward to), for a range of time periods, ranging from the next 24 hours to the next 10 years. Participants were given a time limit, and a fluency measure of the number of different events that they generated for each category was recorded. This method has the advantage of being a direct measure rather than a self-report measure; that is, it provides an objective measure (count) of responses rather than relying on participants saying how many items of each type they could generate if they were asked. The second major advantage is that it provides separate scores for positive and negative future thinking, in line with a range of theoretical approaches which distinguish between positively valenced and negatively valenced psychological systems (e.g., Ito & Cacciopo, 1998). The results have consistently shown that parasuicide patients are less able than controls to provide events they are looking forward to, but do not differ from controls in the number of events they are not looking forward to (MacLeod et al., 1993; 1997; 1998). It therefore appears that the future thinking of parasuicidal individuals is characterised by a lack of positive anticipation in the absence of any increase in negative anticipation.

The lack of positive anticipation that characterises suicidal individuals fits well with the research on reasons for living. One of the main ways that reasons for living might inhibit suicidality is by protecting people from hopelessness about the future. In fact, a number of the items on the RFL specifically measure a view of the future that anticipates positive and meaningful experiences. A study by Greene (1989) also indirectly supports this view. She found that depressed women high in hopelessness differed from equally depressed women who were low in hopelessness by having young children. One interpretation is that having young children provides a trajectory into the future that protects the person from hopelessness in the face of depression.

It has been suggested that suicidal behaviour is fundamentally about wanting to escape (Shneidman, 1999; Williams, 2001). The person might be trying to escape from depression or from other, different painful states of awareness. Hopelessness about the future is the key element of depression that leads to suicidal behaviour. In the case of hopelessness, the escape is not necessarily about escaping stress or negative experiences, but it can be about trying to get away from the painful state of mind that arises when someone has no positive future to look forward to.

RISK ASSESSMENT

There are two main clinical issues in relation to suicidal behaviour: can it be predicted and can it be prevented? More specifically in relation to depression, how useful is depression in predicting suicidal behaviour and is treating depression an adequate treatment for suicidal behaviour? As will be seen, suicidal behaviour cannot be predicted accurately with the whole range of known risk factors, let alone depression. Treating suicidal behaviour has proved to be equally difficult. As would be expected from the discordance between suicidality and depression, treating depression is not an adequate treatment for suicidality.

Predicting suicidal behaviour

Hopelessness is often cited as a good predictor of suicidality, as touched upon earlier. For example, Beck and colleagues have found that hopelessness predicts suicide in patients who had been hospitalised because of suicide ideation (Beck et al., 1985) and in general psychiatric outpatients (Beck et al., 1990). For suicidal inpatients, a score of 10 or more (out of 20) on the Beck Hopelessness Scale successfully identified 10 of 11 patients who completed suicide in a 5–10-year follow-up (Beck et al., 1985). In a sample of almost 2000 outpatients, a score of 9 or above correctly identified 16 out of the 17 suicides that occurred in a 3–4-year follow-up. As would be expected, hopelessness outperformed depression in prediction. However, the cost of such high sensitivity (not missing those who are at risk) was poor specificity. Specificity refers to the ability to avoid labelling people as being at risk when they are not; that is, the ability to avoid false positives. In both of these studies, the rate of false positives was very high. In the inpatient study, 88% of those identified as being at risk did not commit suicide, and the rate was 98% in the outpatient study.

Other studies have used a much wider range of factors to try to predict suicidal behaviour, with similar results. There are many ways in which those who commit suicide or attempt suicide differ, on average, from those who do not. These risk factors include socio-demographic factors, such as gender, class, and employment status; psychological factors, such as poor problem solving and hopelessness; and psychiatric factors, notably depression. Sometimes completers and attempters differ from the general population in the same way, and sometimes they diverge. These factors are discussed in more detail by Maris et al. (1992) and Williams (2001). Pokorny (1983) followed almost 4800 psychiatric inpatients over a 5-year period. Sixty-seven of the group committed suicide, a rate of 1.4%. A predictive model based on a range of known risk factors correctly identified 35 of the 67 as being at high risk. This moderate success of 'hits' was offset by over 1000 false positives. Trying to improve specificity has the effect of reducing sensitivity. For example, in a similar type of study, Goldstein et al. (1991) managed to reduce the false-positive rate but at the cost of 'missing' all 46 suicides in their sample! The problem is translating group differences into prediction at the individual level. Powell et al. (2000) compared 112 people who committed suicide while in hospital with a group of randomly selected control patients from the same hospitals. There were many differences between the two groups, and a number of the variables were statistically significant risk factors (that is, clearly differentiated between the groups). However, using these factors to predict at an *individual* level whether someone would commit suicide was of little use: only two of the 112 patients who committed suicide had a predicted risk of suicide above 5% based on these risk factors.

Predicting parasuicide has also been shown to be difficult, though one of the problems that besets suicide prediction—low base rates—is less marked. Kreitman and Foster (1991) identified 11 factors that predicted repetition of parasuicide, including previous parasuicide, having a personality disorder, and having high alcohol consumption. Depression was not one of the identified risk factors in their study. Repetition was linked with the number of risk factors present: those who had three or fewer risk factors showed a 5% repetition rate, whereas those with eight or more had a 42% repetition rate. However, as Kreitman and Foster (1991) point out, a large majority of their repeaters were in the mid-range of risk scores, a finding which simply reflected the fact that the vast majority of the sample scored in the mid-range. If a cutoff of 8 or above was adopted for prediction, 76% of those who repeat would be missed. Adopting a lower cutoff would improve the hit rate, but it rapidly increases the number of false positives.

Predictive models fail for a number of reasons. Suicidal behaviour, especially suicide, is relatively rare, and rare behaviours are inherently difficult to predict. Many of the factors used in these predictive studies do not reflect the psychological state of individuals but instead appear to be quite distant from the actual behaviour (MacLeod et al., 1992). This can be seen most clearly in socio-demographic variables such as ethnicity, gender, and age, where, although there may be a statistical connection between these variables and suicidality, there are clearly many mediating factors that translate these variables into suicidal behaviour. More generally, predictive models, or summative checklist approaches to risk, cannot take into account the individuality of the person. Someone may have many risk factors, but these can be 'trumped' by an overriding protective factor, such as a feeling of duty or responsibility to family, or religious beliefs prohibiting suicide. Conversely, someone may have very few risk factors, but the few that they do have are very important, such as a recent major loss, and so they may be at high risk. As Shea (1999) notes,

> people don't kill themselves because statistics suggest that they should. The call to suicide comes from psychological pain. Each person is unique. Statistical power is at its best when applied to large populations, and at its weakest when applied to individuals. But it is the individual who clinicians must assess. (Shea, 1999, p. 11)

Clinical risk assessment

The arguments outlined above and the failure of prediction to work at the individual level have led to a more or less consensual view that the emphasis should not be on *prediction* but on assessing *risk* (Maris et al., 1992). In other words, the task for the clinician is to gauge whether risk is elevated, not to forecast whether people will kill or harm themselves or not. The window of increased possibility of suicidal behaviour is what Litman (1990) has called the 'suicide zone'. People are in the suicide zone when they are in a state where killing themselves is a possibility, but, at the same time, perhaps only about one or two in every 100 who are in that zone of acutely high risk will kill themselves (Litman, 1990).

Clinical assessment differs from the predictive research in that it is concerned with immediate or short-term risk. It also differs from the predictive research in focusing more on individual factors than 'objective' factors. In fact, many of the factors that dominate the predictive models seem to be largely ignored by clinicians. Jobes et al. (1995) surveyed practising clinicians on their methods of assessing suicide risk. They found that their respondents rarely used any formal risk-assessment measures, relying much more on a clinical interview covering a broad range of questions. Interestingly, though not suprisingly, the three areas of questioning given the highest utility rating for arriving at an assessment were whether the person had a suicidal plan, suicidal thoughts, and a method of suicide available. Observations that were considered by clinicians to be most useful in making their assessments were difficulty in establishing an alliance with the patient, evidence of alcohol or drug use, and evidence of depressed affect.

In summary, hopelessness or, indeed, any known combination of variables is not a good predictor of suicidal behaviour. The cost of identifying those who will commit or attempt suicide is that many of those who will not are incorrectly labelled as being at risk. Reducing this high number of false positives results in missing those who are at risk. Predictive models perform poorly because suicidal behaviour is rare and because they cannot take account of individual variability. The focus has shifted from prediction to risk assessment, where the emphasis is on relative risk (is it possible?) rather than absolute risk (will it happen?). Clinical assessment of individuals can take account of individual factors, but the accuracy of such assessment is not known, and perhaps is not generally knowable, as it will depend on who is doing the assessing. The challenge is to integrate the empirical research base with an individually sensitive approach to clinical assessment.

INTERVENTION

There are two broad strategies of intervening in suicide. One approach is to treat suicidal behaviour indirectly by treating any accompanying psychiatric disorder, of which the main candidate would be depression. The second approach is to develop treatments that focus specifically on tackling suicidal ideation and behaviour. Due to the clear discordance between depression and suicidal behaviour, even a highly effective treatment for depression is unlikely to be an effective treatment for suicidal behaviour. A recent review by Khan et al. (2000) illustrates the point. These authors reviewed suicide rates in documented trials of new antidepressants over a 10-year period in the USA. Data from almost 20 000 patients were included. The overall rate of suicidal behaviour was low—just less than 1% committed suicide and almost 3% attempted suicide. Importantly for the argument here, the active treatments produced depressive symptom reduction of 41% compared to 31% for placebo, but the groups did not differ in rates of suicide. There are some limitations to generalising from these findings. The trials were very brief—4–8 weeks—and the patients in the trials were not typical in that they were not actively suicidal and not comorbid (Hirschfeld, 2000). However, the data demonstrate that reductions in depression can take place without accompanying reductions in suicidality. Studies of recovery also show that improvements in depression, hopelessness, and psychosocial function can all occur without any reduction in repetition of suicidal behaviour (Townsend et al., 2001). One possible exception to this is the use of lithium to treat bipolar disorder in particular. There is evidence from epidemiological studies that patients taking lithium have reduced suicide risk. However, this is mainly based on naturalistic studies of those attending lithium clinics (Verkes & Cowen, 2000). Clearly, there may be selection factors operating in that those motivated and able to adhere to a lithium regimen might be at lower risk to start with.

There is a wide range of psychological treatments aimed specifically at reducing suicidal behaviour. Treatments tend to focus on preventing repetition of parasuicide, partly because of the near impossibility of demonstrating treatment effectiveness in such a rare behaviour as completed suicide. On the whole, treatments show limited effectiveness, many studies finding no difference in parasuicide rates in those given a specific treatment and those given standard treatment (Hawton et al., 1998; Heard, 2000). The difficulty in demonstrating effectiveness of treatment is undoubtedly influenced by the relative rarity of suicidal behaviour. An additional major factor, increasingly recognised, is the heterogeneity of those who engage in suicidal behaviour. The only thing that these individuals necessarily have in common is a single behavioural act.

Some studies have shown positive results. There is no really clear pattern to those studies: they include brief treatments as well as longer-term treatments, and treatments based on psychodynamic principles as well as those based on broadly cognitive-behavioural principles. Linehan reported significantly lower rates of self-harm in borderline personality disorder patients given dialectical behaviour therapy (DBT) (Linehan et al., 1991). DBT is an intensive intervention, with weekly individual and group session for about 1 year. The group sessions aim to teach skills, such as interpersonal problem-solving skills, strategies for regulating emotions, and ways of tolerating distress, and the individual sessions focus on understanding suicidal episodes and dealing with issues of adherence to treatment. Bateman and Fonagy (1999) also reported a statistically significant reduction in self-harm rates along with other outcome measures in borderline personality disorder patients, this time those receiving psychoanalytically oriented partial hospitalisation (maximum 18 months), compared to those receiving standard psychiatric treatment. In both of these cases, benefits were maintained at follow-up (Bateman & Fonagy, 2001; Linehan et al., 1993).

Brief treatments with unselected samples have also shown evidence of effectiveness. Salkovskis et al. (1990) employed a brief (five sessions) home-based, problem-solving approach with patients who had a history of self-harm. The sessions covered standard problem-solving training, such as help with identifying problems, generating solutions, and implementing solutions, all applied flexibly to the individual's situation. Compared to a treatment-as-usual group, those receiving the intervention showed reduced depression, hopelessness, and suicide ideation and also significantly lower repetition rates at 6 months, although at 18-month follow-up the groups were no longer significantly different on repetition. Guthrie et al. (2001) found that recent suicide attempters given four sessions of home-based brief psychodynamic interpersonal therapy aimed at resolving interpersonal problems showed lower parasuicide rates at 6-month follow-up than those receiving treatment as usual.

It is difficult to say why some studies have found a positive effect against a background of most showing no difference between a targeted intervention and treatment as usual. The Linehan et al. (1991) and Bateman and Fonagy (1999) studies focus on a particular subset of attempters—those meeting criteria for borderline personality disorder—thus reducing the heterogeneity of the sample and also targeting a group with higher rates of self-harm. The Salkovskis study may have accommodated heterogeneity, as the authors emphasised the flexible application of the treatment to individual cases. In contrast, a group intervention that included problem solving reported by Rudd et al. (1996) found no significant benefit over and above treatment as usual. The problem-solving intervention in the Rudd et al. study was implemented in groups of 12–14, thus necessarily limiting the extent to which treatment could be tailored to the individual. These explanations are post hoc, but it is clear that the heterogeneity of patients, as well as low base rates, represent major obstacles to successful intervention.

Individualising treatment

Heterogeneous conditions call for multifaceted treatments that can be delivered flexibly, depending on the individual. In a climate of evidence-based, often manualised treatments, this represents a challenge. Davison (1998) points out that empirically supported manualised treatments do not take account of patient variability. Can an evidence base be reconciled with individualised treatment? Over 20 years ago, Liberman (1981) outlined a framework for doing just that. Liberman described a *modular* approach to the treatment of depression where, because of the complexity of the condition, a broad spectrum, multicomponent approach to treatment is needed. Crucially, although many factors are involved in causing and maintaining depression, not all factors contribute equally to all patients. As not everyone has all factors equally, a broad-spectrum approach is "intrusive and encumbers the patient with many interventions, some of which may not be necessary or applicable" (Liberman, 1981, p. 241). A modular approach consists of an array of treatment strategies that are selected after a careful assessment of the individual patient's needs. The modules for each condition would be specified and determined in advance on the basis of empirical evidence. Some modules may be more primary. For example, Liberman suggests that all depressed patients start with a problem-solving module and move beyond that to modules that match their particular problems if needed. Interestingly, the same idea of starting with problem solving has recently been advocated for suicidal behaviour (Hawton & van Heeringen, 2000). Treatment for suicidal behaviour would have modules for tackling poor problem-solving skills, hopelessness or lack of future positivity, and so on. A similar approach has been described by Evans et al. (1999), but without the explicit feature of selective targeting of different modules for different individuals. The modular approach provides a framework for containing the diversity of interventions needed to approach a heterogeneous population such as suicide attempters.

In fact, although not fully specified by Liberman (1981), a modular approach provides a framework for a full scientist-practitioner programme. The initial, research-based steps would consist of establishing the characteristics of those with the particular condition. In the case of suicidal behaviour, much progress has been made in respect to this. Therapeutic strategies to target those particular deficits would then be developed and evaluated for effectiveness. At the level of clinical application, each patient would be assessed on each characteristic, and the module would be selected according to assessment outcome. Evaluation would include the target behaviour (suicidal behaviour) but also the specific focus of the treatment module that is delivered (such as hopelessness or lack of positive future thinking). In the case of suicidal behaviour, some of this work has already been done (e.g., Linehan, 1993), but there is a need to develop intervention strategies that specifically target hopelessness or lack of positive future thinking. This may focus on formulating positive goals but is particularly likely to need strategies to help individuals to form plans to achieve positive goals. Vincent et al. (in press) found that parasuicide patients had less difficulty in thinking of goals than they had in thinking of plans to achieve those goals.

SUMMARY AND CONCLUSIONS

There is a strong link between depression and suicidal behaviour, but there is also high divergence, as shown especially by the fact that the vast majority of depressed people do not commit or attempt suicide. The presence or absence of other factors might help explain this divergence. Factors such as other psychiatric diagnoses, especially personality disorder; protective factors; and other psychological factors, such as personality and affective traits, and problem-solving skills, have all been shown to distinguish suicidal from non-suicidal depressed individuals. The relationship between depression and suicidality is mainly dependent on one particular facet of depression—hopelessness about the future. Hopelessness appears to consist mainly of a lack of positive thoughts about the future rather than preoccupation with a negative future. Risk assessment and intervention in suicidal behaviour are difficult because of the relatively low base rate of suicidal behaviour and the heterogeneity of those who engage in it. Predictive models, whether using depressive hopelessness or a range of factors, are able to identify those at risk only through incorrectly classifying unacceptably high numbers of people as at risk. Because of predictive inaccuracy, the emphasis has shifted to assessment of relative risk rather than absolute risk. Treatments of depression are themselves never likely to be effective treatments for suicidal behaviour per se. The majority of studies testing specific interventions for suicidal behaviour have shown no benefit over treatment as usual, though a number of studies have shown positive results. There is no obvious pattern to the successful interventions in terms of their content, though they do seem either to target a specific subgroup of parasuicides or to involve a brief, flexible treatment delivered at home. Both these strategies potentially limit the problem of heterogeneity. A modular approach provides a framework for incorporating a range of treatment strategies derived from the interface between basic and applied research. Developing strategies to tackle depressive hopelessness, particularly lack of positivity about the future, is one of the most needed and promising lines for future research.

REFERENCES

Alexopoulos, G.S., Bruce, M.L., Hull, J., Sirey, J.A. & Kakuma, T. (1999). Clinical determinants of suicidal ideation and behaviour in geriatric depression. *Archives of General Psychiatry, 56*, 1048–1053.

Bancroft, J., Hawton, K., Simkin, S., Kingston, B., Cumming, C. & Whitwell, D. (1979). The reasons people give for taking overdoses. *British Journal of Medical Psychology, 52*, 353–365.

Bateman, A. & Fonagy, P. (1999). Effectiveness of partial hospitalization in the treatment of borderline personality disorder: A randomized controlled trial. *American Journal of Psychiatry, 156*, 1563–1569.

Bateman, A. & Fonagy, P. (2001). Treatment of borderline personality disorder with psychoanalytically oriented partial hospitalization: An 18-month follow-up. *American Journal of Psychiatry, 158*, 36–42.

Beautrais, A.L. (2001). Suicides and serious suicide attempts: Two populations or one? *Psychological Medicine, 31*, 837–845.

Beck, A.T., Brown, G., Berchick, R.J., Stewart, B.L. & Steer, R.A. (1990). Relationship between hopelessness and ultimate suicide: A replication with psychiatric outpatients. *American Journal of Psychiatry, 147*, 190–195.

Beck, A.T., Brown, G. & Steer, R.A. (1989). Prediction of eventual suicide in psychiatric inpatients by clinical ratings of hopelessness. *Journal of Consulting and Clinical Psychology, 57*, 309–310.

Beck, A.T., Steer, R.A., Kovacs, M. & Garrison, B. (1985). Hopelessness and eventual suicide: A 10-year prospective study of patients hospitalized with suicidal ideation. *American Journal of Psychiatry, 145*, 559–563.

Beck, A.T., Weissman, A., Lester, D. & Trexler, L. (1974). The measurement of pessimism: The hopelessness scale. *Journal of Consulting and Clinical Psychology, 42*, 861–865.

Bostwick, J.M. & Pankratz, V.S. (2000). Affective disorders and suicide risk: a re-examination. *American Journal of Psychiatry, 157*, 1925–1932.

Bottlender, R., Jager, M., Strauss, A. & Moller, H.J. (2000). Suicidality in bipolar compared to unipolar depressed inpatients. *European Archives of Psychiatry and Clinical Neuroscience, 250*, 257–261.

Brown, M., Comtois, K.A. & Linehan, M.M. (2002). Reasons for suicide attempts and nonsuicidal self-injury in women with borderline personality disorder. *Journal of Abnormal Psychology, 111*, 198–202.

Cornelius, J.R., Salloum, I.M., Mezzich, J., et al. (1995). Disproportionate suicidality in patients with comorbid major depression and alcoholism. *American Journal of Psychiatry, 152*, 358–364.

Davison, G.C. (1998). Being bolder with the Boulder model: The challenge of education and training in empirically supported treatments. *Journal of Consulting and Clinical Psychology, 66*, 163–167.

Department of Health (2001). *Safety first: Five-year report of the national confidential inquiry into suicide and homicide by people with mental illness.* London: Department of Health Publications.

Dilsaver, S.C., Chen, Y., Swann, A.C., Shoaib, A.M. & Krajewski, K.J. (1994). Suicidality in patients with pure and depressive mania. *American Journal of Psychiatry, 151*, 1312–1315.

Evans, K., Tyrer, P., Catalan, J., et al. (1999). Manual-assisted cognitive-behaviour therapy (MACT): A randomized controlled trial of a brief intervention with bibliotherapy in the treatment of recurrent deliberate self-harm. *Psychological Medicine, 29*, 19–25.

Fawcett, J., Scheftner, W.A., Fogg, L., et al. (1990). Time-related predictors of suicide in major affective disorder. *American Journal of Psychiatry, 147*, 1189–1194.

Fombonne, E., Wostear, G., Cooper, V., Harrington, R. & Rutter, M. (2001). The Maudsley long-term follow-up of child and adolescent depression. II. Suicidality, criminality and social dysfunction in adulthood. *British Journal of Psychiatry, 179*, 218–223.

Foster, T., Gillespie, K. & McClelland, R. (1997). Mental disorders and suicide in Northern Ireland. *British Journal of Psychiatry, 170*, 447–452.

Foster, T., Gillespie, K., McClelland, R. & Patterson, C. (1999). Risk factors for suicide independent of DSM-III-R Axis I disorder—case-control psychological autopsy study in Northern Ireland. *British Journal of Psychiatry, 175*, 175–179.

Goldstein, R.B., Black, D.W., Nasrallah, A. & Winokur, G. (1991). The prediction of suicide—sensitivity, specificity and predictive value of a multivariate model applied to suicide among 1906 patients with affective disorders. *Archives of General Psychiatry, 48*, 418–422.

Greene, S.M. (1989). The relationship between depression and hopelessness. *British Journal of Psychiatry, 154*, 650–659.

Guthrie, E., Kapur, N., Mackway-Jones, K., et al. (2001). Randomised controlled trial of brief psychological intervention after deliberate self-poisoning. *British Medical Journal, 323*, 1–5.

Guze, S.B. & Robins, E. (1970). Suicide and primary affective disorders. *British Journal of Psychiatry, 117*, 437–438.

Harris, C.E. & Barraclough, B.M. (1997). Suicide as an outcome for mental disorders. *British Journal of Psychiatry, 170*, 205–228.

Haw, C., Hawton, K., Houston, K. & Townsend, E. (2001). Psychiatric and personality disorders in deliberate self-harm patients. *British Journal of Psychiatry, 178*, 48–54.

Hawton, K. & van Heeringen, K. (2000). Future perspectives. In K. Hawton & K. van Heeringen (Eds), *The International Handbook of Suicide and Attempted Suicide* (pp. 713–723). Chichester: Wiley.

Hawton, K., Arensman, E., Townsend, E., et al. (1998). Deliberate self-harm: Systematic review of efficacy of psychosocial and pharmacological treatments in preventing repetition. *British Medical Journal, 317*, 441–447.

Heard, H.L. (2000). Psychotherapeutic approaches to suicidal ideation and behaviour. In K. Hawton & K. van Heeringen (Eds), *The International Handbook of Suicide and Attempted Suicide* (pp. 503–518). Chichester: Wiley.

Hirschfeld, R.M.A. (2000). Suicide and antidepressant treatment. *Archives of General Psychiatry, 57*, 325–326.

Ito, T.A. & Cacciopo, J.T. (1998). Representations of the contours of positive human health. *Psychological Inquiry, 9*, 43–48.

Jobes, D.A., Eyman, J.R. & Yufit, R.I. (1995). How clinicians assess suicide risk in adolescents and adults. *Crisis Intervention and Time Limited Treatment, 2*, 1–12.

Kerkhof, A.J.F.M. (2000). Attempted suicide: Patterns and trends. In K. Hawton & K. van Heeringen (Eds), *The International Handbook of Suicide and Attempted Suicide* (pp. 49–64). Chichester: Wiley.

Kessler, R.C., Borges, G. & Walters, E.E. (1999). Prevalence of and risk factors for lifetime suicide attempts in the national comorbidity survey. *Archives of General Psychiatry, 56*, 617–626.

Khan, A., Warner, A. & Brown, W.A. (2000). Symptom reduction and suicide risk in patients treated with placebo in antidepressant clinical trials. *Archives of General Psychiatry, 57*, 311–326.

Kreitman, N. (1977). *Parasuicide*. London: Wiley.

Kreitman, N. & Foster, J. (1991). The construction and selection of predictive scales, with special reference to parasuicide. *British Journal of Psychiatry, 159*, 185–192.

Liberman, R.P. (1981). A model for individualizing treatment. In L.P. Rehm (Ed.), *Behaviour Therapy for Depression: Present Status and Future Directions* (pp. 231–253). New York: Academic Press.

Linehan, M.M. (1993). *Skills Training Manual for Treating Borderline Personality Disorder*. New York: Guilford.

Linehan, M.M., Armstrong, H.E., Suarez, A., Allmon, D. & Heard, H.L. (1991). Cognitive behavioural treatment of chronically parasuicidal borderline patients. *Archives of General Psychiatry, 48*, 1060–1064.

Linehan, M.M., Goodstein, J.L., Neilsen, S.L. & Chiles, J.A. (1983). Reasons for staying alive when you are thinking of killing yourself: The Reasons for Living Inventory. *Journal of Consulting and Clinical Psychology, 51*, 276–286.

Linehan, M.M., Heard, H.L. & Armstrong, H.E. (1993). Naturalistic follow-up of a behavioural treatment for chronically parasuicidal borderline patients. *Archives of General Psychiatry, 50*, 971–974.

Litman, R.E. (1990). Suicides: What do they have in mind? In D. Jacobs & H.N. Brown (Eds), *Suicide: Understanding and Responding* (pp. 143–156). Madison, CT: International Universities Press.

Lonnqvist, J.K. (2000). Psychiatric aspects of suicidal behaviour: Depression. In K. Hawton & K. van Heeringen (Eds), *The International Handbook of Suicide and Attempted Suicide* (pp. 107–120). Chichester: Wiley.

Lopez, P., Mosquera, F., de Leon, J., et al. (2001). Suicide attempts in bipolar patients. *Journal of Clinical Psychiatry, 62*, 963–966.

MacLeod, A.K., Pankhania, B., Lee, M. & Mitchell, D. (1997). Depression, hopelessness and future-directed thinking in parasuicide. *Psychological Medicine, 27*, 973–977.

MacLeod, A.K., Rose, G.S. & Williams, J.M.G. (1993). Components of hopelessness about the future in parasuicide. *Cognitive Therapy and Research, 17*, 441–455.

MacLeod, A.K., Tata, P., Evans, K., et al. (1998). Recovery of positive future thinking within a high risk parasuicide group: Results from a pilot randomized controlled trial. *British Journal of Clinical Psychology, 37*, 371–379.

MacLeod, A.K., Williams, J.M.G. & Linehan, M.M. (1992). New developments in the understanding and treatment of suicidal behaviour. *Behavioural Psychotherapy, 20*, 193–218.

Malone, K.M., Oquendo, M.A., Haas, G.L., Ellis, S.P., Li S. & Mann, J.J. (2000). Protective factors against suicidal acts in major depression: Reasons for living. *American Journal of Psychiatry, 157*, 1084–1088.

Maris, R.W., Berman, A.L., Maltsberger, J.T. & Yufit, R.I. (Eds) (1992). *Assessment and Prediction of Suicide*. New York: Guilford.

Nimeus, A., Traskman-Bendz, L. & Alsen, M. (1997). Hopelessness and suicidal behaviour. *Journal of Affective Disorders, 42*, 137–144.

Office for National Statistics (1999). *Health Statistics Quarterly, Autumn, 1999*. London: ONS.

Oquendo, M.A., Waternauz, C., Brodsky, B., et al. (2000). Suicidal behaviour in bipolar mood disorder: Clinical characteristics of attempters and non-attempters. *Journal of Affective Disorders, 59*, 107–117.

Ostby, U., Brandt, L., Correia, N., Ekbom, A. & Sparen, P. (2001). Excess mortality in bipolar and unipolar disorder in Sweden. *Archives of General Psychiatry, 58*, 844–850.

Petrie, K., Chamberlain, K. & Clarke, D. (1988). Psychological predictors of future suicidal behaviour in hospitalized suicide attempters. *British Journal of Clinical Psychology, 27*, 247–258.

Pokorny, A.D. (1983). Prediction of suicide in psychiatric in-patients—report of a prospective study. *Archives of General Psychiatry, 40*, 249–257.

Powell, J., Geddes, J., Deeks, J., Goldacre, M. & Hawton, K. (2000). Suicide in psychiatric hospital in-patients: Risk factors and their predictive power. *British Journal of Psychiatry, 176*, 266–272.

Roy, A. (1998). Is introversion a risk factor for suicidal behaviour in depression? *Psychological Medicine, 28*, 1457–1461.

Rudd, M.D., Rajab, M.H., Orman, D.T., Stulman, D.A., Joiner, T. & Dixon, W. (1996). Effectiveness of an outpatient intervention targeting suicidal young adults: Preliminary results. *Journal of Consulting and Clinical Psychology, 64*, 179–190.

Sakinofsky, I. (2000). Repetition of suicidal behaviour. In K. Hawton & K. van Heeringen (Eds), *The International Handbook of Suicide and Attempted Suicide* (pp. 385–404). Chichester: Wiley.

Salkovskis, P.M., Atha, C. & Storer, D. (1990). Cognitive-behavioural problem solving in the treatment of patients who repeatedly attempt suicide. *British Journal of Psychiatry, 157*, 871–876.

Salter, D. & Platt, S. (1990). Suicidal intent, hopelessness and depression in a parasuicide population: The influence of social desirability and elapsed time. *British Journal of Clinical Psychology, 29*, 361–371.

Schaffer, A., Levitt, A.J., Bagby, R.M., Kennedy, S.H., Levitan, R.D. & Joffe, R.T. (2000). Suicidal ideation in major depression: Sex differences and impact of comorbid anxiety. *Canadian Journal of Psychiatry, 45*, 822–826.

Schotte, D.E. & Clum, G.A. (1987). Problem-solving skills in suicidal psychiatric patients. *Journal of Consulting and Clinical Psychology, 55*, 49–54.

Seidlitz, L., Conwell, Y., Duberstein, P., Cox, C. & Denning, D. (2001). Emotion traits in older suicide attempters and non-attempters. *Journal of Affective Disorders, 66*, 123–131.

Shea, S.C. (1999). *The practical art of suicide assessment: A guide for mental health professionals and substance abuse counsellors*. New York: Wiley.

Shneidman, E.S. (1999). Conceptual contribution—The Psychological Pain Assessment Scale. *Suicide and Life-Threatening Behavior, 29*, 287–294.

Simon, G.E. & von Korff, M. (1998). Suicide mortality among patients treated for depression in an insured population. *American Journal of Epidemiology, 147*, 155–160.

Soloff, P.H., Lynch, K.G., Kelly, T.M., Malone, K.M. & Mann, J.J. (2000). Characteristics of suicide attempts of patients with major depressive episode and borderline personality disorder: A comparative study. *American Journal of Psychiatry, 157*, 601–608.

Strakowski, S.M., McElroy, S.L., Keck, P.E. & West, S.A. (1996). Suicidality among patients with mixed and manic bipolar disorder. *American Journal of Psychiatry, 153*, 674–676.

Townsend, E., Hawton, K., Altman, D.G., et al. (2001). The efficacy of problem-solving treatments after deliberate self-harm: Meta-analysis of randomized controlled trials with respect to depression, hopelessness, and improvements in problems. *Psychological Medicine, 31*, 979–988.

Verkes, R.J. & Cowen, P.J. (2000). Pharmacotherapy of suicidal ideation and behaviour. In K. Hawton & K. van Heeringen (Eds), *The International Handbook of Suicide and Attempted Suicide* (pp. 487–502). Chichester: Wiley.

Vincent, P.J., Boddana, P. & MacLeod, A.K. (in press). Positive life goals and plans in parasuicide. *Clinical Psychology and Psychotherapy*.

Wetzel, R.D., Margulies, T., Davis, R. & Karam, E. (1980). Hopelessness, depression, and suicidal intent. *Journal of Clinical Psychiatry, 41*, 159–160.

Williams, J.M.G. (2001). *Suicide and Attempted Suicide*. London: Penguin.

World Health Organization (2001). *The World Health Report*. Geneva: WHO.

19

DEPRESSION IN OLDER ADULTS

Ken Laidlaw

INTRODUCTION

This chapter reviews the science and practice of psychological treatment for depression in older adults. In work with older people with depression, knowledge of normal age-related changes is necessary. While it may be a mistake to adopt too positive a perspective on ageing, a negative perspective is much more harmful and unhelpful when working with older people, closing, as it does, one's mind to the possibility of change and learning at all ages. In this chapter, depression in older people is considered within the context of societal attitudes and the demographic changes taking place globally. The increase in longevity suggests that more psychotherapists will come into contact with older people and will need to become much more aware of treatment issues and efficacy data for this population. The chapter also briefly reviews information on the prevalence of depression in older people, and the risk of suicide in older people is also reviewed. To understand the importance of late-life depression, as distinct from depression in younger adult age groups, a number of important concepts are introduced. The chapter also focuses upon the efficacy data on the use of psychological treatments for depression in late life. The chapter concludes with a brief discussion of treatment issues when working psychologically with older people.

DEMOGRAPHIC CHANGES AND THE GLOBALISATION OF AGEING

The need for mental health-care professionals to receive specialist training in working with older people in order to provide effective psychological treatments for late-life depression will become increasingly important in the light of demographic changes currently taking place globally. From recent statistics (UN, 2001), it is estimated that the world's older adult population will show a threefold increase over the next 50 years, from 606 million people today to 2 billion in 2050. As people live longer, it is the oldest old section of society (people aged over 80 years) that will show the most dramatic increase, with an almost fivefold increase from 69 million in 2000 to 379 million older people in 2050.

Mood Disorders: A Handbook of Science and Practice. Edited by M. Power.
© 2004 John Wiley & Sons, Ltd. ISBN 0-470-84390-X.

The ageing index and dependency ratios are important indicators of how developed and developing societies are ageing. The ageing index is calculated by comparing the number of people aged 65 years and over per 100 young people aged 15 years and younger. In the year 2000 in the UK, the ageing index was 82, meaning that, for every 100 youths, there were 82 people aged 65 years and above living in the UK. This index is set to rise to 152 by the year 2030. In the USA, the ageing index is currently 59, and by the year 2030 it is set to rise to 102. By the year 2030, Italy, Bulgaria, the Czech Republic, Greece and Japan will all have age indices above 200, meaning that there will be two older people for every one young person in these societies (Kinsella & Velkoff, 2001). The dependency ratio is calculated by dividing the total population over the age of 60, of retirement age, by the total population aged 15–60, of working age. In 2002 in North America, the dependency ratio was 0.26, and for the countries of the European Union, the ratio was 0.36. In 2025, it is estimated that the ratio will rise to 0.44 in the US and to 0.56 in Europe (World Health Organisation [WHO], 2002).

UK DEMOGRAPHIC DATA

In the UK in 1931, life expectancy at birth for men was 58 years and for women 62 years. Currently, a man aged 60 years can expect to live for another 18.9 years and a woman aged 60 years for another 22.7 years. In 2000 in the UK, life expectancy at birth increased to 75 years for men and 80 years for women, with older people accounting for one-sixth of the total population (Kinsella & Velkoff, 2001). There is a gender gap in life expectancy, resulting in larger numbers of older women than older men. The 'feminization of ageing' (WHO, 1999) is reflected in the fact that, in the UK in 1997, there were 5523 centenarians, and only 580 of these were men. The gender gap is important for therapists to take note of, as women tend to report higher levels of depression than men and are more likely to come to the attention of the psychiatric services (Crawford et al., 1998).

THE PREVALENCE OF DEPRESSION IN OLDER PEOPLE

Depression is generally considered to be the most common psychiatric disorder among older adults (Ames & Allen, 1991; Blazer, 1994), although recent evidence suggests that anxiety disorders may actually be more common (Blazer, 1997). Data from the Epidemiological Catchment Area Study (Regier et al., 1988) suggest that rates of major depressive disorder among older adults are lower than rates for younger adults (for review, see Futterman et al., 1995). A recent systematic review of community-based studies assessing the prevalence of late-life depression carried out by Beekman et al. (1999) calculated an average prevalence rate of 13.5% for clinically relevant depression symptoms. Data from the UK suggest that major depressive disorder affects only a minority of older people, Livingston et al. (1990) identifying an overall prevalence rate of 16% for depression symptoms in their inner-London sample. Consistent with other prevalence studies of depression in older adults, Livingston et al. (1990) found that depressed older adults were more likely to be living alone and to have been in recent contact with GPs and hospital services. Lindesay et al. (1989) report similar rates of depression in older adults living in the community, with 13.5% of their sample identified with mild to moderate depressive symptoms and 4.3% identified with severe depressive symptoms.

Katona et al. (1997) note that, in younger people, the comorbidity of depression with other psychiatric conditions has received much attention, yet depression comorbidity in older adults has received relatively little attention. This would appear to be surprising, as Katona et al. (1997) found very high rates of comorbid generalised anxiety in older adults diagnosed with depression. The association between depression and heightened levels of generalised anxiety was so great in their sample that they suggest depression should be looked for whenever anxiety is present in older people. These findings correspond to reports by Flint (1999) that late-life generalised anxiety disorder is usually associated with depression. Lenze et al. (2001) comment that older adults with depression and comorbid anxiety are more likely to present with greater severity levels and are more likely to experience poorer treatment response.

Rates of depression in older people vary depending upon the sample considered. For example, Katz et al. (1989) identified a prevalence rate of major depressive disorder among nursing home residents of 18–20%, and up to 27–44% overall for other dysphoric mood states. Likewise, Abrams et al. (1992) describe depression as being widespread in nursing-home residents. Unfortunately, although nurses are good at detecting depression in nursing-home residents, levels of treatment are low (Katz et al., 1989).

Levels of depression in community samples are much higher when disability is present; for example, in Parkinson's disease, prevalence rates of depression have been reported in up to 40–50% of people diagnosed with Parkinson's disease (Zesiewicz et al., 1999).

However, although there is an association between physical illness and depression, it is important to remember that the majority of older people with physical illness do not meet criteria for major depression (Zeiss et al., 1996), and it is the extent and personal importance of limitations imposed on an individual that is more important for determining disability (Zeiss et al., 1996). Koenig et al. (1992) demonstrate that the presence of a medical condition reduces the rate of detection and treatment of depression in older adults.

PREVALENCE OF SUICIDE IN LATER LIFE

Suicide rates for persons aged 65 years and older are higher than for any other age group, and the suicide rate for persons over 85 is the highest of all (Beautrais, 2002; Gallagher-Thompson & Osgood, 1997; Kinsella & Velkoff, 2001; Pearson & Brown, 2000). While depression does not necessarily result in suicide, among older people who make suicide attempts, depression is the most frequent diagnosis (Blank et al., 2001; Pearson & Brown, 2000; WHO, 2001). Suicide rates for men and women tend to rise with age, but are highest for men aged 75 years and above (Kinsella & Velkoff, 2001; WHO, 2001). The high suicide rate among older people, especially older men living on their own, may be partly explained by the fact that older people are more likely to use high-lethality methods of suicide and are much less likely to communicate their intent beforehand (Blank et al., 2001; WHO, 2001). In the UK, drug overdose was the most frequent method of suicide among older people (Draper, 1996). Sadly, although many older people who committed suicide visited their family doctor within 1 month of their act, this did not always result in recognition and treatment (Blank et al., 2001). For example, Caine et al. (1996) carried out a review of the cases of 97 older people who had committed suicide and discovered that while 51 had visited their GP within 1 month prior to their suicide and 47 had been diagnosed with a psychiatric problem, only 19 had received treatment. Caine et al. (1996) reviewed the treatment received by these individuals and concluded that only two had received adequate treatment. The reality is that suicide rates for older people are probably underestimates, as the true cause of death may not always be recorded on the death certificate, either from the reticence of the family doctor reluctant to cause a family distress or because the means of death is uncertain (Pearson & Brown, 2000).

There are two paradoxes about suicide in later life; first, older people are living longer, and yet those surviving longer (especially older men) are more likely than ever to die by their own hand. The second paradox is that it is older women, especially those aged 85 years and above, that are faced with the greatest challenges of ageing, and yet they have much lower rates of suicide than men of the same ages. For anyone working with depressed older adults, a thorough evaluation of suicide risk needs to be made during treatment.

DIAGNOSIS AND MANAGEMENT OF DEPRESSION IN OLDER PEOPLE

Depression in older people cannot be dismissed as unimportant, not least because suicide in older people is much higher than in younger people (Kinsella & Velkoff, 2001; Pearson & Brown, 2000; WHO, 2001), but also because depression in later life appears to have a negative impact on life expectancy, with an increased risk of death that may not be completely accounted for by physical ill health (Ames & Allen, 1991) or by suicide (Burvill & Hall, 1994). Unfortunately, depression in older people is often overlooked, as it is commonly assumed that depression is a natural consequence of the losses experienced by older people in terms of emotional attachments, physical independence and socio-economic hardship (Laidlaw, 2001). The 'understandability phenomenon' (Blanchard, 1996) or the 'fallacy of good reasons' (Unutzer et al., 1999) is the notion that depression in older people is in some way to be expected and is a normal part of ageing. Assumptions such as these can influence the expectations of client, therapist and physician alike, resulting in a sense of the hopelessness of treatment (Unutzer et al., 1999). Seeing depression as understandable produces shared therapeutic nihilism and lowers expectations for treatment in both the providers and recipients of care (Montano, 1999).

Treatment for depression in older people is commonly managed by GPs in primary care (Rothera et al., 2002). McDonald (1986) demonstrated that GPs were able to identify depressive symptoms in primary-care settings; however, in very few cases was diagnosis translated into treatment or referral to other agencies. Crawford et al. (1998) report that GPs were aware of depression in a little over one-half of their patients aged 65 years and above, but that men living alone, those with the least education and those with visual impairment were much less likely to be identified by GPs as depressed. Levels of active treatment were very low, the majority of older people receiving little or no treatment for their depression. For those patients receiving treatment, this consisted mainly of antidepressants.

When GPs use antidepressants to treat depression in older people, they usually prescribe subtherapeutic dosages (Heeren et al., 1997; Isometsa et al., 1998; Orrell et al., 1995). Nelson (2001) comments that, although there is good evidence for the efficacy of pharmacotherapy, due to changes in metabolism in older people, there is an increased risk of toxicity from antidepressants, especially tricyclic antidepressants (TCAs), and that makes this class of drugs less tolerable. However, even newer types of antidepressants, such as the selective serotonin reuptake inhibitors (SSRIs), can cause water retention (the consequences include headaches, lethargy and, in more severe cases, confusion), weight loss and balance problems (Nelson, 2001). Balance problems are potentially very difficult to tolerate in older people, especially for older women, who, due to osteoporosis, are at increased risk of hip fractures after falls. Mittmann et al. (1997) noted that, although it is commonly stated that older adults tolerate SSRIs better than TCAs, their meta-analysis of the safety and tolerability of antidepressants suggested there were no differences in the rates of adverse events with the different classes of antidepressants. Interestingly, Mittmann et al. (1997) also note that while older adults generally do not tolerate TCAs very well, those who can tolerate these medications generally have a good treatment outcome.

Despite a fear of side effects from antidepressant medications, such as cardiac arrhythmias (Ryynanen, 1993) and problems to do with tolerability of medications, treatments with recognised efficacy for the alleviation of depression, such as cognitive behavioural therapy (CBT), are often not recognised by GPs as viable options for older adults with depression. The provision of psychological treatment for depression in older people is hampered by factors such as a lack of knowledge among GPs regarding the effectiveness of psychotherapy with older people (Collins et al., 1997; Laidlaw et al., 1998), the low numbers of trained geriatricians and psychogeriatricians and the continuing legacy of Freud's assertion that older people lack the mental plasticity to change or to benefit from psychotherapy (Lovestone, 1983). Service providers have also tended to neglect the psychological needs of older people, so that older adults expect to receive physical treatment for a range of psychological difficulties (Woods, 1995).

Another reason that older people have traditionally been underserved in terms of psychological treatment is the pervasive idea that older people do not want to take part in psychotherapy sessions (Lebowitz et al., 1997). Landreville et al. (2001) investigated the acceptability of psychological and pharmacological treatments for depression in older people. Using a series of case vignettes, older people reported cognitive, cognitive-behavioural and antidepressant medications as being acceptable treatments for late-life depression. Interestingly, the acceptability of treatment types varies according to the level of severity of depression symptoms; for more severe depression symptoms, older people rated cognitive therapy as more acceptable than antidepressants.

META-ANALYSIS OF THE EFFICACY OF PSYCHOLOGICAL TREATMENTS FOR DEPRESSION IN OLDER ADULTS

Scogin & McElreath (1994) produced the first meta-analysis of the efficacy of psychosocial treatments for late-life depression mainly in response to the National Institutes of Health (NIH) consensus statement (NIH, 1991) that suggested limited supporting evidence for psychotherapy for late-life depression. In 1997, the consensus statement was updated to take account of important new information in a range of areas pertinent to psychotherapy for depression in older adults. Lebowitz et al. (1997) concluded that cognitive-behavioural and interpersonal approaches had established evidence for treatment efficacy, and that psychological treatments deserved greater emphasis as a treatment alternative to anti-depressant medications and ECT. Scogin & McElreath (1994) produced effect sizes for treatment versus no treatment or placebo that were substantial and very similar to the effect sizes calculated by Robinson et al. (1990) in their review of psychotherapy for depression across all age ranges. Despite the clear superiority of psychological treatments to no treatment or waiting list control, there was no evidence to support the superiority of any single treatment modality. Cross-comparisons investigating differences in efficacy between brief forms of psychotherapy suggested that many treatments were equally successful in treating late-life depression (Scogin & McElreath, 1994).

Scogin and McElreath (1994) included personal construct therapy, self-administered bibliotherapy, and behaviour therapy within their broad definition of psychosocial treatments. In consequence, their overall meta-analyses were too broad and over-inclusive. There would appear to be questions over the merits of combining apparently markedly different treatments (psychodynamic psychotherapy and behaviour therapy) to derive a single composite measure of effect. More information would appear to be lost than is gained by such an approach. Overall, the review by Scogin and McElreath (1994) was a timely and thorough evaluation of the effectiveness of psychological treatments for depression, but the analyses by Scogin and McElreath ought to be supplemented by more focused meta-analytic reviews.

A useful supplementary meta-analytic review to that performed by Scogin and McElreath (1994) was published by Koder et al. (1996), who evaluated cognitive therapy for the treatment of depression in older adults. Koder et al. (1996) identified seven treatment comparison studies between 1981 and 1994. Three of these seven studies favoured CBT over other treatment modalities, three failed to find significant treatment differences between modalities, and one study was positive for some aspects of cognitive treatment.

A minor point to note is that this meta-analysis contains an unfortunate error in that Koder et al. (1996) counted the studies by Jarvik et al. (1982) and Steuer et al. (1984) as separate studies, whereas Jarvik et al. (1982) reported interim results and Steuer et al. (1984) reported the final analysis (Jarvik et al., 1997). Koder et al. (1996) concluded that while there were too few studies of sufficient scientific and methodological merit upon which a definitive conclusion could be reached over the relative efficacy of cognitive therapy and other treatment modalities, cognitive therapy is undoubtedly an effective treatment procedure for late-life depression.

Engels and Verney (1997) reviewed 17 psychological outcome studies for late-life depression published between 1974 and 1992. The mean effect size calculated in this meta-analysis was moderate at 0.63, although lower than other reported effect sizes; on average, older adults receiving treatment for depression are better off than 74% of older people not receiving treatment. Cognitive therapy and behavioural therapy were the most effective treatments. A surprising result showing that CBT was less effective than either cognitive treatment or behavioural therapy alone may be explained in part by narrow inclusion criteria for CBT. Engels and Verney (1997) characterised studies as purely cognitive that are probably more accurately described as cognitive-behavioural. For example, studies published by Gallagher-Thompson, Thompson and colleagues are much more accurately characterised as CBT, as these researchers generally stress the behavioural components of treatment within a framework of cognitive strategies.

An important finding from the analysis by Engels and Verney (1997) is that individual therapy is more efficacious than group therapy in older adults. This would appear to be particularly so for cognitive and behavioural treatments. Overall, in this meta-analysis, psychotherapy with older adults appears to be most efficacious when the diagnosis is major depression or depression rather than multiple complaints. A possible difficulty in this conclusion is that information about achievement of diagnoses was often unclear in a number of studies.

In a departure from meta-analyses that looked at only pharmacological or only psychosocial treatments for late-life depression, Gerson et al. (1999) investigated the effectiveness of pharmacological and psychological treatments for depression in older people. Gerson et al. (1999) reviewed 45 studies carried out between 1974 and 1998. Four of the 45 studies used non-drug (psychological) methods of treatment for depression in later life. All patients were diagnosed with major depressive disorder. Gerson et al. (1999) also utilised stricter inclusion criteria for their analyses, such as a minimum of 15 patients in each treatment group, description of dose regimen in both treatment and control groups, documentation of side effects by self-report or questionnaire, specification of attrition rates and, lastly, statistical evaluation. The stricter criteria reduced the number of studies entered into the meta-analysis to 28, two of which used psychological methods of treatment.

The results of Gerson et al.'s meta-analyses were identical with either criteria (inclusive versus strict) in that pharmacological and psychological treatments for major depressive disorder in late life were equally efficacious. There were no significant differences in the relative reduction of quantitative measures of mood between treatments. Analyses also revealed no significant difference in attrition rates between pharmacological and psychological treatments. Gerson et al. (1999: 20) conclude: 'Effective psychological interventions constitute a much-needed addition to antidepressant medication for depressed older patients.'

COGNITIVE BEHAVIOUR THERAPY (CBT) FOR DEPRESSION IN OLDER ADULTS

Description of CBT

CBT is an active, directive, time-limited and structured treatment approach. The most common form of CBT used in the UK is based upon the cognitive model of dysfunctional information processing in emotional disorders developed by Beck and colleagues (Beck et al., 1979). In the Beck model, cognitions (which can be thoughts or images) are determined by underlying beliefs (termed 'schemas'), attitudes and assumptions. The most basic premise of CBT is that how a person feels and behaves determines the way that person thinks and makes sense of experiences. CBT can be distinguished from other forms of psychotherapy by its emphasis on the empirical investigation of the patient's thoughts, appraisals, inferences and assumptions. This aim is achieved through the explicit use of cognitive and behavioural techniques such as activity scheduling, graded task assignments, problem-solving techniques, thought identification and monitoring, and examining and challenging core beliefs about the self, world and future. Morris and Morris (1991) state the following reasons why CBT can be particularly effective with older people:

(1) The focus is on the 'here and now'; the individual's current needs are identified and interventions are developed to target-specific stressors.

(2) CBT is *skills-enhancing* and practical; people are taught specific ways to manage their individual stressors.

(3) Sessions are *structured*; the organised nature of therapy keeps the person oriented to tasks within and across sessions, and homework is used to keep the focus on managing problems.

(4) *Self-monitoring* is used; the individual is taught to recognise mood fluctuations and emotional vulnerabilities, and to develop strategies that enhance coping ability.

(5) CBT adopts a *psychoeducative approach*; the connection between thoughts, mood and behaviour is explained.

(6) CBT is *goal-oriented*; interventions are developed to target and challenge stereotyped beliefs, such as, 'You can't teach an old dog new tricks'.

Summary of efficacy data

Cognitive therapy has proven efficacy as a treatment for depression in older people (Dick et al., 1996; Gatz et al., 1998; Karel & Hinrichsen, 2000; Knight & Satre, 1999; Koder et al., 1996; Laidlaw, 2001). In a broad review of the empirical evidence for the psychological treatment of depression in older adults, Gatz et al. (1998) concluded that CBT meets strict American Psychological Association criteria as a *probably efficacious* treatment. According to Gatz et al. (1998: 13), CBT did not meet criteria as a 'well-established' treatment because 'superiority to psychological placebo has not been demonstrated with sufficiently large samples, and superiority to another treatment has not been found with sufficient consistency'. The conservative conclusion drawn by Gatz et al. (1998) may well be warranted at this stage, as too few studies have been conducted to evaluate properly cognitive therapy's efficacy. For an in-depth evaluation of the efficacy of CBT, see Laidlaw (2001).

CBT has been the most systematically studied psychological treatment for depression in older adults (Karel & Hinrichsen, 2000). The methodological differences across studies investigating the outcome of psychological treatments for late-life depression make cross-comparison difficult. Some studies do not include control conditions (Fry, 1984; Leung & Orrell, 1993; Steuer et al., 1984). It is rare for any study to report data on long-term follow-up of up to 2 years (Gallagher-Thompson et al., 1990). Some studies have evaluated group cognitive therapy (Arean et al., 1993; Beutler et al., 1987; Kemp et al., 1991/2; Leung & Orrell, 1993; Rokke et al., 2000; Steuer et al., 1984), whereas others have evaluated individual cognitive therapy (Dick & Gallagher-Thompson, 1995; Gallagher & Thompson, 1982; 1983; Gallagher-Thompson et al., 1990; Gallagher-Thompson & Steffen, 1994; Kaplan & Gallagher-Thompson, 1995; Thompson et al., 1987, 2001). In terms of attrition rates, there are wide variations across studies (see Laidlaw, 2001, for a more thorough discussion). Surprisingly few studies report upon comorbidity of physical illness, with the studies that do comment upon this reporting very high rates of physical illnesses (Rokke et al., 2000; Steuer et al., 1984). A major criticism of the research conducted so far is that the majority of studies have very small sample sizes.

Overall, the evidence supports the applicability of CBT as an effective treatment alternative to antidepressant medication for late-life depression (see especially Thompson et al., 2001). Although one cannot specify whether any particular type of therapy is most effective for late-life depression, cognitive therapy is an effective treatment for depression in older people.

INTERPERSONAL PSYCHOTHERAPY (IPT) AND DEPRESSION IN OLDER ADULTS

Description of IPT

IPT was originally developed by Gerald Klerman, Myrna Weissman and associates (see Klerman et al., 1984). IPT, a short-term, focused treatment programme for depression, recognises that many of the stressors that may predispose an individual to develop depression are interpersonal in nature. IPT was included as an active treatment comparator in the Treatment of Depression Collaborative Research Programme (Elkin et al., 1989), and appeared to outperform CBT (Thompson et al., 2001).

IPT focuses on four main problem areas in its treatment approach to depression: (1) grief; (2) interpersonal disputes (conflict with significant others); (3) role transitions (changes in a significant life situation); (4) interpersonal deficits (problems with an individual's initiating, maintaining or sustaining relationships). A number of authors have argued that the approach IPT takes and its focus upon the four problem areas identified above make this form of psychotherapy particularly well suited for use with older adults (Hinrichsen, 1999; Karel & Hinrichsen, 2000; Miller et al., 1998; Miller & Silberman, 1996). As Hinrichsen (1999) states, late life is a time of change and adjustment; many older people will be dealing with the loss of a spouse, many will be negotiating changes in the nature of their relationships with friends, spouses and adult children, and many will be dealing with role transitions due to retirement or adjustments to functional health status. Miller and Silberman (1996) state that IPT is easily relevant to depression in older adults as it is short-term, practical and goal-oriented with a focus on the 'here and now', especially as many older adults may be dealing with adjustments due to the changing nature of later life. As described by Miller and Silberman (1996), IPT and CBT share many features in terms of their relevance as treatments for older adults.

Summary of efficacy data of IPT for depression in older adults

Charles Reynolds, Ellen Frank and colleagues have carried out much of the research investigating IPT's efficacy as a treatment for depression in older adults in Pittsburgh (Reynolds et al., 1996, 1999a, 1999b). In reviewing the evidence for the treatment efficacy of IPT for late-life depression, Gatz et al. (1998) state that, while IPT is a treatment of 'well-established' efficacy for depression in adults, there is insufficient evidence to come to this conclusion for older adults.

A number of individual studies have evaluated IPT for depression in older adults. Miller et al. (1998) report that 80% of patients receiving a combination of IPT and the antidepressant nortriptyline (NT) show a full response to treatment (defined as a score of less than 10 on the Hamilton Rating Scale for Depression for at least 3 consecutive weeks). Reynolds et al. (1999b) evaluated the effectiveness of maintenance NT and IPT for the prevention of recurrence of depression in older adults. Maintenance IPT and NT in combination were superior to either treatment alone, and all active treatments were superior to placebo and medication clinic visits. Thus, overall, there are some good grounds for optimism that IPT represents another treatment option for depression in older adults. As much of the research in this form of psychological treatment comes from one specialist psychiatric research laboratory, there is a need for more research before definitive conclusions can be reached about the efficacy of IPT for depression in older adults.

PSYCHODYNAMIC APPROACHES AND DEPRESSION IN OLDER ADULTS

Description of psychodynamic approaches

There is no one single form of psychodynamic psychotherapy with older people (Gatz et al., 1998; Karel & Hinrichsen, 2000; Knight, 1996). While the view of Freud that people over the age of 50 are uneducable has in many ways prevented psychodynamic approaches from being applied to the treatment of depression in older adults, as Steuer (1982) points out, not all the early pioneers of psychodynamic theory held such ageist attitudes. Eriksson and Jung considered analysis a very worthwhile exercise for older people. Jung saw the purpose of later life as individuation or integrating previously unacknowledged or unconscious aspects of the psyche (Steuer, 1982). There are a number of commonalities among the various forms of psychodynamic psychotherapy, such as an emphasis on the role of unresolved developmental issues for the later development of psychopathology or difficulties in coping, and an emphasis on the curative aspects of a corrective emotional relationship between patient and therapist (Nordhus & Nielson, 1999). In many descriptions of psychodynamic psychotherapy with older people, transference and countertransference are considered especially important (Karel & Hinrichsen, 2000; Nordhus & Neilson, 1999; Steuer, 1982).

Summary of the efficacy data of psychodynamic psychotherapy for depression in older adults

Much of the empirical support for psychodynamic psychotherapy with older people comes, surprisingly, from research carried out in CBT trials (Gallagher & Thompson, 1983; Thompson et al., 1987). In the research trials carried out by the Thompson group, the form of psychodynamic psychotherapy used in their treatment trials (insight-oriented psychotherapy) was broadly as effective as cognitive or behavioural treatments. Steuer et al. (1984) also concluded that psychodynamic and cognitive treatments were equally efficacious in the treatment of depression in older adults. In addition, the meta-analysis literature provides empirical support for the use of psychodynamic approaches in the treatment of depression in older adults, as results suggest equivalence in outcome between different forms of psychological treatments.

WORKING PSYCHOTHERAPEUTICALLY WITH OLDER PEOPLE

The following discussion outlines some basics in working with older adults. For a fuller discussion of the psychological approach to treating depression in older adults, the reader should consult Laidlaw et al. (2003). As Knight (1999) comments, there are two key questions for psychotherapists when working with older adults; can psychological interventions developed in adult settings be expected to work for older adults, and does one need to adapt these psychological interventions for use with older adults? From the foregoing, the first key question may be answered with a resounding yes. In this section, the second key question is explored and answered. It is important to understand that older adults are *the least* homogeneous of all age groups. Older adults often have many more dissimilarities than similarities (Steuer & Hammen, 1983). As Zeiss and Steffen (1996) point out, there are at least two generations contained within this age grouping. With the increase in longevity, there can be four decades separating the youngest old from the oldest old. In working psychologically with older people, it can often be useful to bear in mind the importance of cohort beliefs (Knight, 1999), which refer to the set of cultural norms, historical events, and personal events that obtained or occurred during a specific generation. Cohort beliefs may influence how easily older adults, particularly older men, will find discussing their feelings, and they may also influence stigmatising beliefs about mental illness. Cohort beliefs can act as a barrier to older adults receiving treatment for depression. Understanding older people in terms of their generational cohort allows therapists to gain insight into the societal norms and rules that may influence an individual's behaviour. Understanding cohort experiences and taking these into account when working psychotherapeutically with older people is no more difficult, and no less important, than when working with cohorts such as ethnic minority groups.

Koder et al. (1996: 105) state: 'The debate is not whether CT is applicable to elderly depressed patients, but how to modify existing CT programmes so that they incorporate differences in thinking styles in elderly people and age related psychological adjustment.' However, chronological age is the worst marker for determining whether therapeutic adaptations are necessary in cognitive therapy (Zeiss & Steffen, 1996).

WHAT ADAPTATIONS AND UNDER WHAT CIRCUMSTANCES?

Adaptations are not always essential for older people to benefit from treatment with cognitive therapy for depression (Steuer & Hammen, 1983; Zeiss & Steffen, 1996). Modification of therapy may be indicated and may be required to take account of issues to do with normal age-related changes, such as the presence of chronic physical illness and slowed cognitive processing (Grant & Casey, 1995). Modifications are intended to enhance treatment outcome within the model of therapy (that is, CT), whereas adaptations are intended to alert clinicians to the possibility that the treatment model they have chosen may be inadequate for the circumstances (Laidlaw, 2001). Cognitive therapy is particularly appropriate as an intervention for older adults, as it takes into account normal age-related changes in the formulation of an individual's problems (Thompson, 1996). In more ways than not, cognitive therapy with older people is similar to therapy with younger people. Interestingly, Miller and Silberman (1996: 93) come to a very similar conclusion when discussing the issue of adapting IPT for use with older adults, concluding that 'IPT with elders shares far more similarities than differences to IPT with younger patients'.

When it is argued that adaptations are unnecessary, the assertion is that structural elements of cognitive therapy such as agenda setting, collaborative empiricism, cognitive conceptualisation, cognitive restructuring and homework setting are all essential elements. Cognitive therapy is a relevant and accessible therapy precisely because it deals with older people's current concerns, whether grief, physical limitations following a stroke or general emotional distress.

Two pieces of evidence from the empirical literature caution the clinician against drawing the conclusion that in order for cognitive therapy to be effective with older people it must be adapted. The first piece of evidence against the adaptation of CBT comes from the meta-analysis literature. Results of meta-analyses carried out in older adult populations report near identical effect sizes (Robinson et al., 1990; Scogin & McElreath, 1994) to those reported by meta-analyses studies looking at CBT across all age groups. In their review of empirical evidence of psychological treatments for late-life depression, Gatz et al. (1988) note that in studies little fundamental adjustment of techniques appears to be necessary. The idea that CBT has to be adapted for use with older people (see Wilkinson, 1997) has another very unfortunate consequence. The accumulated knowledge and empirical evidence demonstrating the effectiveness of CBT as an effective alternative to antidepressant medication is disregarded because of questions about the relevance and effectiveness of non-adapted psychological therapy.

CONCLUSIONS

Depression in older people is very often under-diagnosed and under-treated. There are ageist beliefs among professionals and among older people themselves that may prevent older people from receiving adequate access to effective psychological treatment for depression. This is very unfortunate, as there is a growing evidence base demonstrating the effectiveness of psychological treatments for older people. As many older adults are unable to tolerate antidepressants or there may be contraindications to their use with older people with cardiac problems (Orrell et al., 1995), psychological treatments are a much-needed, effective treatment alternative (Gerson et al., 1999). In many cases, psychological treatments can be considered an effective treatment of first choice for depression in older people (Thompson et al., 2001). It is argued that there is no empirical evidence or therapeutic necessity to adapt psychological therapies such as CBT in order to make them suitable and accessible for older adults without cognitive impairment or in the absence of frailty. Older people themselves appear to want the opportunity to participate in psychotherapy. Given the increase in the numbers of older people with the increase in life expectancy, the psychological needs of this important section of society are likely to increase rather than decrease.

Future research into the effectiveness of psychological treatment for depression in older people needs to examine their effectiveness in physical conditions with high levels of psychological distress, such as dementia, post-stroke depression and Parkinson's disease. Many of these conditions are currently at early stages of evaluation of efficacy in terms of psychological and physical treatments for depression. At present, there is a large unmet need. Likewise in other populations with high levels of emotional distress, such as in nursing homes, it is important to assess the potential impact of psychological treatments to alleviate suffering. Finally, suicide among older people is on the increase, and the future research extension of psychological treatments for older people cannot afford to ignore the potential for alleviating distress and reducing tragedy at the end of life. Suicide in older people left untargeted is a terrible, damning judgement on the priorities of the society we live in.

REFERENCES

Abrams, R.C., Teresi, J.A. & Butin, D.N. (1992) Depression in nursing home residents. *Clinics in Geriatric Medicine, 8*, 309–312.

Ames, D. & Allen, N. (1991). The prognosis of depression in old age: Good, bad or indifferent? *International Journal of Geriatric Psychiatry, 6*, 477–481.

Arean, P.A., Perri, M.G., Nezu, A.M., Schein, R.L., Frima, C. & Joseph, T.X. (1993). Comparative effectiveness of social problem-solving therapy and reminiscence therapy as treatments for depression in older adults. *Journal of Consulting and Clinical Psychology, 61*, 1003–1010.

Beautrais, A. (2002). A case control study of suicide and attempted suicide in older adults. *Suicide and Life-Threatening Behavior, 32*, 1–9.

Beck, A.T., Rush, A.J., Shaw, B.F. & Emery, G. (1979). *Cognitive Therapy of Depression.* New York: Guilford.

Beekman, A.T., Copeland, J.R.M. & Prince, M.J. (1999). Review of community prevalence of depression in later life. *British Journal of Psychiatry, 174*, 307–311.

Beutler, L.E., Scogin, F., Kirkish, P., et al. (1987). Group cognitive therapy and alprazolam in the treatment of depression in older adults. *Journal of Consulting and Clinical Psychology, 55*, 550–556.

Blanchard, M. (1996). Old age depression—a biological inevitability? *International Review of Psychiatry, 8*, 379–385.

Blank, K., Cohen, C., Cohen, G., et al. (2001). Failure to adequately detect suicidal intent in elderly patients in the primary care setting. *Psychiatry, 9*, 26–36.

Blazer, D.G. (1994). Epidemiology of depression: Prevalence and incidence. In J.R.M. Copeland, M.T. Abou-Saleh & D.G. Blazer (Eds), *Principles and Practice of Geriatric Psychiatry* (pp. 519–524). Chichester: Wiley.

Blazer, D. (1997). Generalized anxiety disorder and panic disorder in the elderly: A review. *Harvard Review of Psychiatry, 5*, 18–27.

Burvill, P.W. & Hall, W.D. (1994). Predictors of increased mortality in elderly depressed patients. *International Journal of Geriatric Psychiatry, 9*, 219–227.

Caine, E., Lyness, J. & Conwell, Y. (1996). Diagnosis of late life depression: Preliminary studies in primary care settings. *American Journal of Geriatric Psychiatry, 4*, s45–s50.

Collins, E., Katona, C. & Orrell, M.W. (1997). Management of depression in the elderly by general practitioners: Referral for psychological treatments. British *Journal of Clinical Psychology, 36*, 445–448.

Crawford, M., Prince, M., Menezs, P. & Mann, A. (1998). The recognition and treatment of depression in older people in primary care. *International Journal of Geriatric Psychiatry, 13*, 172–176.

Dick, L.P. & Gallagher-Thompson, D. (1995). Cognitive therapy with the core beliefs of a distressed lonely caregiver. *Journal of Cognitive Psychotherapy: An International Quarterly, 9*, 215–227.

Dick, L.P., Gallagher-Thompson, D. & Thompson, L.W. (1996). Cognitive-behavioural therapy. In R.T. Woods (Ed.), *Handbook of the Clinical Psychology of Ageing.* Chichester: Wiley.

Draper, B. (1996). Attempted suicide in old age. *International Journal of Geriatric Psychiatry, 11*, 577–587.

Elkin, I., Shea, T., Watkins, J.J., et al. (1989). National Institute of Mental Health treatment of depression collaborative research program. *Archives of General Psychiatry, 46*, 971–982.

Engels, G.I. & Verney, M. (1997). Efficacy of nonmedical treatments of depression in elders: A quantative analysis. *Journal of Clinical Geropsychology, 3*, 17–35.

Flint, A.J. (1999). Anxiety disorders in late life. *Canadian Family Physician, 11*, 2672–2679.

Fry, P.S. (1984). Cognitive training and cognitive-behavioral variables in the treatment of depression in the elderly. *Clinical Gerontologist, 3*, 25–45.

Futterman, A., Thompson, L.W., Gallagher-Thompson, D. & Ferris, R. (1995). Depression in later life: Epidemiology, assessment, etiology, and treatment. In E.E. Beckham & W.R. Leber (Eds), *Handbook of Depression,* 2nd edn, (pp. 494–525). New York: Guilford.

Gallagher, D. & Thompson, L.W. (1982). Treatment of major depressive disorder in older adult outpatients with brief psychotherapies. *Psychotherapy: Theory, Research and Practice, 19*, 482–490.

Gallagher, D.E. & Thompson, L.W. (1983). Effectiveness of psychotherapy for both endogenous and nonendogenous depression in older adult outpatients. *Journal of Gerontology, 38*, 707–712.

Gallagher-Thompson, D., Hanley-Peterson, P. & Thompson, L.W. (1990). Maintenance of gains versus relapse following brief psychotherapy for depression. *Journal of Consulting and Clinical Psychology, 58*, 371–374.

Gallagher-Thompson, D. & Osgood, N. (1997). Suicide in later life. *Behavior Therapy, 28*, 23–41.

Gallagher-Thompson, D. & Steffen, A. (1994). Comparative effects of cognitive-behavioral and brief psychodynamic psychotherapies for depressed family caregivers. *Journal of Consulting and Clinical Psychology, 62*, 543–549.

Gatz, M., Fiske, A., Fox, L.S., et al. (1998). Empirically validated psychological treatments for older adults, *Journal of Mental Health and Aging, 4*, 9–46.

Gerson, S., Belin, T.R., Kaufman, M.S., Mintz, J. & Jarvik, L. (1999). Pharmacological and psychological treatments for depressed older patients: A meta-analysis and overview of recent findings. *Harvard Review of Psychiatry, 7*, 1–28.

Grant, R.W. & Casey, D.A. (1995). Adapting cognitive behavioral therapy for the frail elderly. *International Psychogeriatrics, 7*, 561–571.

Heeren, T.J., Derksen, B.F., Heycop, T.H. & Van Gent, P. (1997). Treatment, outcome and predictors of response in elderly depressed in-patients. *British Journal of Psychiatry, 170*, 436–440.

Hinrichsen, G.A. (1999). Treating older adults with interpersonal psychotherapy for depression. *Journal of Clinical Psychology, 55*, 949–960.

Isometsa, E., Seppala, I., Henriksson, M., Kekki, P. & Lonnqvist, J. (1998). Inadequate dosaging in general practice of tricyclic vs other antidepressants for depression. *Acta Psychiatrica Scandinavica, 98*, 429–431.

Jarvik, L.F., Mintz, J., Gerner, R. & Steuer, J. (1997). Cognitive therapy for depression in the elderly. *International Journal of Geriatric Psychiatry, 12*, 131–132.

Jarvik, L.F., Mintz, J., Steuer, J. & Gerner, R. (1982). Treating geriatric depression: A 26-week interim analysis. *Journal of the American Geriatrics Society, 30*, 713–717.

Kaplan, C.P. & Gallagher-Thompson, D. (1995). Treatment of clinical depression in caregivers of spouses with dementia. *Journal of Cognitive Psychotherapy: An International Quarterly, 9*, 35–44.

Karel, M.J. & Hinrichsen, G. (2000). Treatment of depression in late life: Psychotherapeutic interventions. *Clinical Psychology Review, 20*, 707–729.

Katona, C., Manela, M.V. & Livingston, G. (1997). Comorbidity with depression in older people: The Islington study. *Ageing & Mental Health, 1*, 57–61.

Katz, I.R., Lesher, E., Kleban, M., Jethanandani, V. & Parmalee, P. (1989). Clinical features of depression in the nursing home. *International Psychogeriatrics, 1*, 5–15.

Kemp, B.J., Corgiat, M. & Gill, C. (1991/2). Effects of brief cognitive-behavioral group psychotherapy on older persons with and without disabling illness. *Behavior, Health and Aging, 2*, 21–28.

Kinsella, K. & Velkoff, V.A. (2001). US Census Bureau, Series P95/01–1. An Aging World. Washington, DC: US Government Printing Office.

Klerman, G.L., Weissman, M.M., Rounsaville, B.J. & Chevron, E. (1984). *Interpersonal Psychotherapy of Depression*. New York: Basic Books.

Knight, B. (1996). Overview of psychotherapy with the elderly: The contextual, cohort-based, maturity-specific-challenge model. In S.H. Zarit & B.G. Knight (Eds), *A Guide to Psychotherapy and Aging: Effective Clinical Interventions in a Life-Stage Context* (pp. 17–34). Washington, DC: American Psychological Association.

Knight, B. (1999). The scientific basis for psychotherapeutic interventions with older adults: An overview. *Journal of Clinical Psychology, 55*, 927–934.

Knight, B.G. & Satre, D.D. (1999). Cognitive behavioral psychotherapy with older adults. *Clinical Psychology, 6*, 188–203.

Koder, D.A., Brodaty, H. & Anstey, K.J. (1996). Cognitive therapy for depression in the elderly. *International Journal of Geriatric Psychiatry, 11*, 97–107.

Koenig, H.G., Meador, K.G., Cohen, H.J. & Blazer, D.G. (1992). Screening for depression in hospitalized elderly medical patients: Taking a closer look. *Journal of the American Geriatrics Society, 40*, 1013–1017.

Laidlaw, K. (2001). An empirical review of cognitive therapy for late life depression: Does research evidence suggest adaptations are necessary for cognitive therapy with older adults? *Clinical Psychology and Psychotherapy, 8*, 1–14.

Laidlaw, K., Davidson, K.M. & Arbuthnot, C. (1998). GP referrals to clinical psychology and treatment for depression: A pilot study. *Newsletter of the Psychologist Special Interest Group in Elderly People (PSIGE), 67*, 6–8.

Laidlaw, K., Thompson, L.W., Gallagher-Thompson, D.G. & Siskin, L. (2003). *Cognitive Behaviour Therapy with Older People*. Chichester: Wiley.

Landreville, P., Landry, J., Baillargeon, L., Guerette, A. & Matteau, E. (2001). Older adults' acceptance of psychological and pharmacological treatments for depression. *Journals of Gerontology; Psychological Sciences, 50B*, P285–P291.

Lebowitz, B.D., Pearson, J.L., Schneider, L.S., et al. (1997). Diagnosis and treatment of depression in late life: Consensus statement update. *Journal of the American Medical Association, 278,* 1186–1190.

Lenze, E.J., Mulsant, B.H., Shear, M.K., Alexopoulos, G.S., Frank, E. & Reynolds, C.F. (2001). Comorbidity of depression and anxiety disorders in later life. *Depression and Anxiety, 14,* 86–93.

Leung, S.N.M. & Orrell, M.W. (1993). A brief cognitive behavioural therapy group for the elderly: Who benefits? *International Journal of Geriatric Psychiatry, 8,* 593–598.

Lindesay, J., Brigs, K. & Murphy, E. (1989). The Guys/Age Concern Survey: Prevalence rates of cognitive impairment, depression and anxiety in an urban elderly community. *British Journal of Psychiatry, 155,* 317–329.

Livingston, G., Hawkins, A., Graham, N., Blizard, B. & Mann, A. (1990). The Gospel Oak study: Prevalence rates of dementia, depression and activity limitation among elderly residents in inner London. *Psychological Medicine, 20,* 137–146.

Lovestone, S. (1983). Cognitive therapy with the elderly depressed: A rational and efficacious approach? In R. Levy & A. Burns (Eds), *Treatment and Care in Old Age Psychiatry* (pp. 183–189). New York: Biomedical Publishing.

McDonald, A. (1986). Do general practitioners 'miss' depression in elderly patients? *British Medical Journal, 292,* 1365–1367.

Miller, M.D. & Silberman, R.L. (1996). Using interpersonal psychotherapy with elders. In S.H. Zarit & B.G. Knight (Eds), *A Guide to Psychotherapy and Aging: Effective Clinical Interventions in a Life-Stage Context* (pp. 83–93). Washington, DC: American Psychological Association.

Miller, M.D., Wolfson, L., Frank, E., et al. (1998). Using interpersonal psychotherapy (IPT) in a combined psychotherapy/medication research protocol with depressed elders. *Journal of Psychotherapy Practice and Research, 7,* 47–55.

Mittmann, N., Herrmann, N., Einarson, T.R., et al. (1997). The efficacy, safety and tolerability of antidepressants in late life depression: A meta-analysis. *Journal of Affective Disorders, 46,* 191–217.

Montano, C.B. (1999). Primary care issues related to the treatment of depression in elderly patients. *Journal of Clinical Psychiatry, 60* (Suppl. 20), 45–51.

Morris, R.G. & Morris, L.W. (1991). Cognitive and behavioural approaches with the depressed elderly. *International Journal of Geriatric Psychiatry, 6,* 407–413.

Nelson, J.C. (2001). Diagnosing and treating depression in the elderly. *Journal of Clinical Psychiatry, 62* (Suppl. 24), 18–22.

NIH (1991). Diagnosis and treatment of depression in later life. *NIH Consensus Statement.*

Nordhus, I.H. & Nielson, G.H. (1999). Brief dynamic psychotherapy with older adults. *Journal of Clinical Psychology, 55,* 935–947.

Orrell, M., Collins, E., Shergill, S. & Katona, C. (1995). Management of depression in the elderly by general practitioners. I. Use of antidepressants. *Family Practice, 12,* 5–11.

Pearson, J.L. & Brown, G.K. (2000). Suicide prevention in late life: Directions for science and practice. *Clinical Psychology Review, 20,* 685–705.

Regier, D.A., Boyd, J.H., Burke, J.D., et al. (1988). One month prevalence of mental disorders in the United States. *Archives of General Psychiatry, 45,* 977–986.

Reynolds, C.F., Frank, E., Dew, M.A., et al. (1999a). Treatment of 70+ year olds with recurrent major depression: Excellent short-term but brittle long term response. *American Journal of Geriatric Psychiatry, 7,* 64–69.

Reynolds, C.F., Frank, E., Kupfer, D.J., et al. (1996). Treatment outcome in recurrent major depression: A post hoc comparison of elderly ('young old') and midlife patients. *American Journal of Psychiatry, 153,* 1288–1292.

Reynolds, C.F., Frank, E., Perel, J.M., et al. (1999b). Nortriptyline and interpersonal psychotherapy as maintenance therapies for recurrent major depression: A randomized controlled trial in patients older than 59 years. *Journal of the American Medical Association, 281,* 39–45.

Robinson, L.A., Berman, J.S. & Neimeyer, R.A. (1990). Psychotherapy for the treatment of depression: A comprehensive review of controlled outcome research. *Psychological Bulletin, 108,* 30–49.

Rokke, P.D., Tomhave, J.A. & Jocic, Z. (2000). Self-management therapy and educational group therapy for depressed elders. *Cognitive Therapy and Research, 24*, 99–119.

Rothera, I., Jones, R. & Gordon, C. (2002). An examination of the attitudes and practice of general practitioners in the diagnosis and treatment of depression in older people. *International Journal of Geriatric Psychiatry, 17*, 354–358.

Ryynanen, O.P. (1993). Psychotropic medication and quality of life in the elderly. *Nordic Journal of Psychiatry, 47* (Suppl. 28), 67–72.

Scogin, F. & McElreath, L. (1994). Efficacy of psychosocial treatments for geriatric depression: A quantitative review. *Journal of Consulting and Clinical Psychology, 62*, 69–74.

Steuer, J.L. (1982). Psychotherapy with the elderly. *Psychiatric Clinics of North America, 5*, 199–213.

Steuer, J.L. & Hammen, C.L. (1983). Cognitive-behavioral group therapy for the depressed elderly: Issues and adaptations. *Cognitive Therapy and Research, 7*, 285–296.

Steuer, J.L., Mintz, J., Hammen, C.L., et al. (1984). Cognitive-behavioral and psychodynamic group psychotherapy in the treatment of geriatric depression. *Journal of Consulting and Clinical Psychology, 52*, 180–189.

Thompson, L.W. (1996). Cognitive-behavioral therapy and treatment for late life depression. *Journal of Clinical Psychiatry, 57* (Suppl. 5), 29–37.

Thompson, L.W., Coon, D.W., Gallagher-Thompson, D.G., Sommer, B.R. & Koin, D. (2001). Comparison of desipramine and cognitive behavioral therapy in the treatment of elderly outpatients with mild-to-moderate depression. *American Journal of Geriatric Psychiatry, 9*, 225–240.

Thompson, L.W., Gallagher, D. & Breckenridge, J.S. (1987). Comparative effectiveness of psychotherapies for depressed elders. *Journal of Consulting and Clinical Psychology, 55*, 385–390.

UN (2001). *World Population Prospects: The 2000 Revision (Highlights)*. New York: United Nations Population Division, Department of Economic and Social Affairs.

Unutzer, J., Katon, W., Sullivan, M. & Miranda, J. (1999). Treating depressed older adults in primary care: Narrowing the gap between efficacy and effectiveness. *Milbank Quarterly, 77*, 225–256.

Wilkinson, P. (1997). Cognitive therapy with elderly people. *Age and Ageing, 26*, 53–59.

WHO (1999). *Ageing: Exploding the Myths*. Geneva: World Health Organization.

WHO (2001). *Men, Ageing and Health: Achieving Health Across the Lifespan*. Geneva: World Health Organization.

WHO (2002). *Active Ageing: A Policy Framework*. Geneva: World Health Organization.

Woods, R.T. (1985). Psychological treatments I: Behavioural and cognitive approaches. In J. Lindesay (Ed.), *Neurotic Disorders in the Elderly* (pp. 97–113). Oxford: Oxford University Press.

Zeiss, A.M. & Steffen, A. (1996). Treatment issues with elderly clients. *Cognitive and Behavioral Practice, 3*, 371–389.

Zeiss, A.M., Lewinsohn, P.M., Rohde, P. & Seeley, J.R. (1996). Relationship of physical disease and functional impairment to depression in older people. *Psychology and Aging, 11*, 572–581.

Zesiewicz, T.A., Gold, M., Chari, G. & Hauser, R.A. (1999). Current issues in depression in Parkinson's disease. *American Journal of Geriatric Psychiatry, 7*, 110–118.

20

SUMMARY AND NEW DIRECTIONS

Mick Power

INTRODUCTION

The previous chapters in this book are a testament to the healthy state of developments in research and in clinical practice in the mood disorders. The juxtaposition of the unipolar and bipolar disorders has, it is hoped, provided the opportunity to consider these disorders in a more unified and cross-fertilising fashion than is often the case. The view that psychotic phenomena, whether in depression or in other disorders such as schizophrenia, are something qualitatively different from "everyday experience" can reasonably be questioned in the case of the mood disorders, however controversial this questioning may appear for schizophrenia (e.g., Lavender, 2000). Medicine has advanced through the recognition that the "devils" and "miasmas" of earlier times are in fact a number of disease entities and acute illnesses; this same approach has also benefited psychiatry through, for example, the identification of the organic process in tertiary syphilis, or the identification of the brain's role in the "noble" disease of epilepsy. In parallel, developments in cell and molecular biology have begun to offer up the actual mechanisms by which our genes provide a starting point for the process of development. Fractional differences in starting points can manifest themselves in major differences in outcome, as chaos theory tells us (see Chapter 6); thus, even in twins with the same genotype and with one twin affected by bipolar disorder, there are significant differences in whether or not the second twin will go on to develop bipolar disorder. The issue of the high genetic contribution to bipolar disorders has for too long led to the adoption of simplistic approaches to the bipolar disorders, when it may be more useful to view the unipolar–bipolar distinction as an heuristic one, but in which there is no clear demarcation between different subtypes of depression. As Cavanagh (Chapter 10) quotes memorably, should we consider depression more like a citrus fruit that divides naturally along certain segments, or like an apple that can be divided along any point or direction? One of the major starting points for mood disorders must be still the question of classification and diagnosis; therefore, pointers in this direction will be considered first. We will then briefly review some of the other key developments including epidemiology, theoretical models, and treatment issues, together with one or two additional points, before drawing to a conclusion.

Mood Disorders: A Handbook of Science and Practice. Edited by M. Power.
© 2004 John Wiley & Sons, Ltd. ISBN 0-470-84390-X.

DIAGNOSIS

Of course, it is very easy and very tempting to take pot-shots at classification and diagnosis in psychiatry. From a sceptical viewpoint, it appears to the outside that every few years a bunch of experts sit around and "horse-trade" their favourite, often self-promoting diagnoses. The history of the classification and diagnosis of depression has witnessed, for example, a varying set of categories such as neurotic-endogenous, reactive-endogenous, and neurotic-psychotic. As Bebbington (Chapter 1) summarises, these and other distinctions appear to reflect a dimension of severity of depression, in which rarer symptoms (for example, delusions of guilt) appear in only the most extreme variants.

The problem for classification and diagnosis in depression—indeed, for all psychological disorders—is that there is no *theoretical* basis for the systems in use. Indeed, the systems such as DSM are explicitly atheoretical. Imagine that Mendeleev had approached the periodic table of the chemical elements in the same way; there are clearly substances that are "shiny, silver ones" (such as aluminium, silver, and iron), while there is another group that are "shiny, golden ones" (such as copper and gold). Another distinction could be made between "soft, malleable" substances that explode (such as potassium, sodium, and phosphorus) and "hard, non-explosive" substances (such as zinc, tin, and silicon). These distinctions would have some value, at least for a while, but because they are not theoretically based, they will be inconsistent, contradictory, and change with fashion.

So what is the answer for classification and diagnosis in depression? The first step, and one that many chapters in this book argue explicitly for, is that there needs to be a dimensional approach, in which the severity of the disorder ranges from minimal to maximal. But how should this dimension be conceptualised? Indeed, should there be only one dimension considered? These two questions are significant, first, because we need to know whether the opposite to "very depressed" on the severity dimension is "not depressed", or whether it is the bipolar opposite of depression, "very happy". The traditional approach to the manic state in bipolar disorders might suggest this latter option; namely, that the "opposite" state to depression is a state of elation. However, this traditional account fails to explain why recent empirical studies of the manic and hypomanic states show that elation may not be the most highly characteristic aspect, but that "mixed states" and mood lability may be more accurate conceptualisations (Cassidy et al., 1998; Cavanagh et al., submitted). This issue certainly demands a broader approach to the assessment of depression than the current reliance on self-report and on clinical interviews, as Peck has cogently argued (Chapter 17).

The second question is, if there is more than one dimension, what should these other dimensions be? A starting point may be that there are two possible dimensions, both capturing severity, but one relating to genetic/biological factors and one relating to psychological/social factors. Of course, such factors are aetiological rather than merely symptom-based, and are generally avoided in DSM-type classification systems, with the one exception of post-traumatic stress disorder, in which the stressor is both aetiological and nosological. The dimensions have the advantage that they provide a dimensional classification system within which both the unipolar and bipolar disorders can be placed according to their putative aetiology, while acknowledging that the majority of depressions have a contribution from both. Such an approach would also allow the incorporation of some of the recent problems highlighted with bipolar disorders, in which the initial diagnosis is almost always wrong if the first episode is a depressed one, given that the diagnostician can really be certain only after further episodes whether or not these are manic/hypomanic ones. Recently, there have been suggestions that very short periods of "highs" might be predictive of later manic episodes, and that short "highs" in reaction to antidepressant treatment might be similarly indicative (e.g., Perugi et al., 1997).

A two-dimensional approach might provide a starting point for the nosology of depression, but it still may not go far enough in overcoming the consensus-driven versus theory-driven approaches. Even the proposal mentioned above that all depressions should be treated as bipolar until proven otherwise, and that there may be further bipolar 1, 2, 3, 4, etc., subtypes may simply amount to further atheoretical, descriptive game-playing, however useful the distinctions might be. A more radical approach to depression and its classification might be to get a theory! To return to the periodic table, by analogy, the best theory cannot simply be a theory of just the alkaline metals but has to place depression in the context of other psychological disorders, especially given the high rates of comorbidity with other disorders such as anxiety (see Chapter 1). There can be no accusations of modesty for the following speculations, but they are provided as an illustration of how one might go about developing a theoretically based classification; they are not being presented as *the* correct one.

The basic-emotions approach has a long and distinguished history that includes Descartes and Darwin, and recent exponents such as Ekman, Plutchik, Izzard, and Tomkins. The approach was extended by Oatley and Johnson-Laird (1987) in their functional account of emotion, which assumed that a set of five basic emotions could be used to derive all the other more complex emotions. Power and Dalgleish (1997) further extended this proposal and argued that emotional disorders might also be explicable in such a system with certain additional theoretical assumptions, such as the idea of "coupling" or "blending" of emotions (cf. Plutchik, 1980). The preliminary conceptual analysis suggested that, from a basic-emotions point of view, many emotional disorders could be viewed as the coupling of two or more basic emotions, and that many supposedly "unitary" disorders, such as obsessional compulsive disorders and phobias, might be more appropriately derived from different basic emotions. In relation to depression, there are a number of possible combinations of coupled emotions. If sadness is taken as the commonest emotion in depression, when it is combined with disgust, especially in the form of self-disgust (that is, as self-loathing, shame, and guilt, which are complex emotions derived from the basic emotion of disgust; see Power, 1999; Power & Dalgleish, 1997), the coupling provides for one subtype of depression together with some inhibition of happiness. However, other combinations are also possible; for example, anxious depression could occur from the coupling of sadness and anxiety, perhaps with some disgust plus some happiness inhibition. Agitated or irritable depression is likely to be a coupling of sadness and anger, and again some increased disgust and inhibited happiness. When happiness is increased rather than inhibited, the mixed states occur, especially in the dysphoric mania category, where both increased happiness and increased anxiety occur. Combinations such as sadness and anger, but without increased disgust, are more likely to be seen in examples of extreme or "pathological grief"; for example, after the sudden and unexpected loss of a loved one (see Power & Dalgleish, 1997).

Although we are yet to obtain solid and replicated data for the full range of this basic-emotions analysis of the emotional disorders, in a recent study (Power & Tarsia, submitted) we compared basic-emotion profiles across groups of normal controls, depressed, anxious, and mixed anxiety depression (not, however, the subclinical category appendixed in DSM-IV, but rather a group of patients who met DSM criteria for both major depression and one of the anxiety disorders, such as Generalised Anxiety Disorder (GAD) or phobia). The basic-emotion profiles, obtained with the Basic Emotions Scale (Power, submitted) showed no elevation of anger, but the sadness and the disgust levels were significantly higher in the depressed and the mixed groups than in the anxiety and control groups. The anxiety levels were elevated in all of the clinical groups in comparison to the controls, but the clinical groups did not differ significantly from each other. Whether this reflects the fact that the patients were primarily an outpatient group, or that the findings will be replicated in larger, more extensive studies remains to be seen. Finally, the happiness levels were highest in the control, intermediate in the anxious, and lowest in the mixed and depressed groups. In sum, the Basic Emotions Scale showed that different profiles of basic emotions are found across different emotional disorders, though whether or not such profiles could ever provide a theoretical basis for the classification and diagnosis of the emotional disorders remains to be seen.

EPIDEMIOLOGY

Of course, the epidemiology of depression still remains a mystery, but how could it be otherwise without a good theoretically based diagnostic and classification system? The situation is akin to trying to study astronomy with nothing but a dirty milk bottle. Nevertheless, despite the considerable inadequacies in the measuring tools, there are still some surprises in the epidemiology that no theory of depression has yet been able to cope with. That is, the lifespan and gender data on depression (see Chapter 1 and Chapter 5) seem to show that the approximate 2:1 ratio of women to men for depression appears sometime around puberty and then disappears sometime in later life; children show an approximately equal rate, and this is also true in older adults. In addition, these are clearly both cultural effects in that cultures in which women have been traditionally devalued show higher rates of depression in women, but there are also generational cohort effects in that some Western cultures seem to be showing an increase in depression and suicide rates in young men (Chapter 18). The good news for depression research is that no simplistic model can account for the epidemiological data. The bad news is that there is as yet no complex model that can account for it either.

The present and immediate future for epidemiology is showing increased use of genetic epidemiology methods to study both unipolar and bipolar depressions through the use of large-scale twin studies (e.g., Kendler & Prescott, 1999) and large-scale family studies that can look at, for example, obligate carriers (see Chapter 11). A recent such study by Sullivan et al. (2002) found that for unipolar depression there was 37% heritability and no significant shared environment effects, but only individual-specific environmental factors (such as specific individual life events or traumas) in their analysis of the presence and absence of depression in a large family study. These genetic epidemiology studies show great promise and can begin to disentangle genetic, gender, age, and cultural effects in their contributions to both unipolar and bipolar disorders in the next decade. However, large-scale, prospective, high-risk studies, in which adolescents and young adults who are at increased risk because of affected family members and other factors, must also be carried out to examine exactly how genetic and psychosocial factors interact to produce or protect the individual from depression.

THEORETICAL MODELS

Theories of depression are like other theories that span the biopsychological domain in that either they are of the "mindless brain" variety and focus solely on putative biochemical or brain-circuit mechanisms, or they are of the "brainless mind" variety and focus solely on fashionable psychological models that might be impossible to implement in the brain. Western culture does, of course, have a long philosophical tradition that has encouraged this mind–brain dualism, so one should not be harder on theories of depression than on theories in other areas. Many of the chapters in this book have fallen, not surprisingly, into one or other of these categories, but it is hoped that at least some of the chapters have begun to hint at what these integrative mind–brain theories might look at in the area of depression and that they have begun to "mind the gap".

However, before a consideration of these theories, perhaps we should first point to the means by which advances can be made in these integrated mind–brain theories. That is, what methods in themselves span this false divide, in order to provide progress in our knowledge base about depression? One of these methods was discussed in the last section through the use of genetic epidemiology, by means of which some approximations to the genetic and non-genetic contributions can begin to be sketched. Such methods can help to identify candidate genes, and from there an exploration of their biological mechanisms can begin. However, there are also many other methods that span this divide and by means of which empirical progress can be made. One such is that of neuroimaging, which is very much in its early days in relation to depression (see Chapters 2 and 11). I have to confess to having been one of the sceptics initially about imaging approaches such as functional magnetic resonance imaging (f-MRI), because they seemed to be simply the "new phrenology" (though maybe, in fact, we have been too harsh in our long dismissal of phrenology!). Anyway, methods such as f-MRI offer the possibility of a method that immediately integrates the biological and the psychological; carefully designed "subtraction methodologies" can lead to important advances in understanding the underlying substrate and the brain circuits involved in those particular psychological processes. However, although the "subtraction methodology" can provide a very elegant approach, it does have its own pitfalls that are not yet understood. One of the key concerns is the subtraction methodology itself; it amounts to the fundamental question, "does $3 - 2 = 2 - 1$?" In fact, the original exponent of the subtraction methodology approach in the nineteenth century, the Danish physiologist F.C. Donders, used the subtraction approach to study reaction times to simple and complex stimuli, the argument being that additional processes were involved, for example, if there were greater numbers of choices between stimuli. Although the method was both elegant and influential, later approaches in cognitive psychology demonstrated that Donders' principles broke down under certain important conditions (e.g., Neisser, 1967). To give a concrete example for f-MRI, let us say that a subtraction study is set up that shows neutral faces and faces showing a specific emotion such as disgust to groups of depressed and control subjects. The argument then is that any remaining differences reflect the unique status of the processing of disgust in depression. But the question, "does $3 - 2 = 2 - 1$?", then applies; for example, if the control group were anxious patients rather than controls, would the same findings occur? Or if only female faces were used? Or if the faces were all familiar to the individual? Or if the stimuli were short video clips rather than photographs? So even an example as apparently straightforward as the processing of facial stimuli proves to be extremely complex once it is argued that the "equivalent" subtraction has to be achieved in several different ways before some confidence can be gained in the conclusions.

A further point that can be made briefly concerns the types of neuropsychological tests that can be used in studies such as f-MRI, psychological priming, genetic epidemiology, and so on. The tradition in cognitive psychology, and therefore in the development of neuropsychological and related tests, has been to use *emotionally neutral* stimuli; thus, the question, "What is the capital of Albania?", is an emotionally neutral knowledge question for most people, in contrast to "When did your father stop beating you?", which is emotionally valenced for everyone. Between these two extremes, we need to develop emotionally valenced tasks that are the equivalent of the emotionally neutral tasks currently in use, especially when these can be linked to f-MRI type studies. For example, in relation to depression (and other emotional disorders), there are key questions of the role of the frontal cortex in the executive control of emotion and emotion processing that have only begun to be asked. However, in order to study emotional disorders, executive function tasks need to be modified so that they have emotionally valenced versions (cf. Power et al., 2000).

Further developments will also be made in our understanding of the evolutionary role of depression (see Chapter 6), and in our understanding of the animal models that may offer the possibility of testing human models, such as in the work of LeDoux. The area of anxiety research has clearly benefited from the animal work by LeDoux (e.g., 1996), which has offered considerable support for multilevel approaches and should provide an impetus for such developments in the area of depression. Classic experimental psychology methods, such as those based on priming and subliminal activation methods of non-conscious processes, should also continue to provide further data for richer theorising about depression (see Chapters 3 and 4), but they may now be of greatest use when they are tied into f-MRI and other electrophysiological methods, so that bridges continue to be made across the mind–brain gap. They will also be of most value when they explore emotionally valenced stimuli rather than the emotionally neutral stimuli that have been used traditionally in experimental psychology. Fast-acting and other non-conscious brain mechanisms have evolved to process "emotional meaning" or the "emotional significance" of events, as noted above in the comments on developing emotionally significant neuropsychological tests.

Before we finish this section, some comments must also be made specifically about theoretical developments in the bipolar disorders. The study of bipolar disorders has suddenly opened up to psychological and social approaches, having long been ignored and left to the medicobiological approach. Even here, there have been few significant advances in theory, and the approach has focused primarily on pharmacotherapy (see Chapters 11 and 7). The promise of the psychological and the social approaches has been raised both by Wright and Lam (Chapter 12) and by Swartz et al. (Chapter 15). Although the primary focus of the last two chapters was on treatment (see also next section), the fact that the cognitive behavioural therapy (CBT) and interpersonal psychotherapy (IPT) models have an impact on the course of bipolar disorders is in itself of theoretical importance. Wright and Lam have highlighted both the role of specific types of dysfunctional beliefs that may be specific to bipolar disorders and have considered an integration of these CBT-based concepts into a conditioning-based model of approach-avoidance. In contrast, Swartz et al. (Chapter 15) have extended proposals made earlier by Goodwin and Jamison (1990) that individuals with bipolar disorders may be especially sensitive to disruption of psychosocial rhythms, a problem that many significant life events (such as job loss, the birth of a child, or retirement) and even more minor events (such as vacations, weekends, and jet-lag) possess.

TREATMENT

The development and adaptation of treatment approaches for both unipolar and bipolar disorders continues to gather pace. In the area of unipolar disorders, there are now well-established pharmacotherapeutic treatments that continue to be added to with new generations of antidepressants (see Chapter 7). Psychological treatments such as CBT and IPT have been shown to be efficacious in randomised, controlled trials in adults (see Chapters 8 and 9). The main challenge now for psychosocial approaches, and one that Markowitz (Chapter 9) details most clearly, is how these effective psychosocial treatments can be adapted for use with different populations such as adolescents (see also Chapter 5), older adults (see also Chapter 19), and specific disorder groups such as suicidal patients (see also Chapter 18).

In some ways, perhaps the most exciting area for the development of psychosocial treatments is now the neglected area of the bipolar disorders. Kay Redfield Jamison's writings, both her autobiography (1995) and her accounts of other famous sufferers (1993), have been at the forefront of drawing both lay and scientific attention to the bipolar disorders. In large part, the development of psychological treatments is a consequence of her major contributions. In Chapter 14, Schwannauer outlined the recent development of CBT approaches to bipolar disorders; in particular, the work of Newman et al. (2001) and Lam et al. (1999). Swartz and colleagues (Chapter 15) have shown one way in which IPT can be adapted to bipolar work. Both the CBT and the IPT adaptations have highlighted specific aspects of the disorder to focus on. For the CBT adaptation, the work on early warning signs that has proven fruitful in CBT work with schizophrenia (e.g., Birchwood, 2000) provides an important new clinical tool. When such early warning signs are identifiable, we have the possibility for sufferers and carers of alternative management strategies (see Chapter 16). A problem arises when early warning signs do not occur, as when there is a rapid transition into the disordered state. In these cases, perhaps the adapted IPT approach, IPSRT, with its focus on disrupted circadian rhythms, may provide an additional clinical strategy. However, because these CBT and IPT approaches are at an early stage of development, they are currently being compared with each other, and with pharmacotherapy, in a substantial NIMH-funded randomised controlled trial. Ultimately, though, one suspects that the best psychosocial approaches to the management of these difficult and tragic disorders will require combined pharmacotherapy, CBT, IPT, and family approaches (e.g., Miklowitz & Goldstein, 1997) as appropriate (see Chapter 13).

CONCLUSIONS

This crystal-ball gazing into the future of depression has occurred with the help of a cast of leading experts in all of the relevant areas. There is no aspect of depression where any sitting back and resting on laurels can yet be done, but both the science and the practice in this area should see considerable developments in the next decade. It is hoped that the juxtaposition of the unipolar and bipolar disorders will offer the possibility of cross-fertilisation in the areas of classification and diagnosis, theory, research, and clinical practice. Too often, these disorders are considered separately, or the focus on bipolar disorders takes an overly psychosis-based viewpoint. Both unipolar and bipolar disorders can, at the extremes, include psychotic aspects, such as loss of contact with reality, and delusions and hallucinations.

The view taken here is that these phenomena can occur at the extremes of dysregulated emotion systems (Power & Dalgleish, 1997); similar examples from other areas include the extremes of love seen in De Clerambault syndrome, the delusional beliefs about contamination or danger to self and others seen in extreme obsessive-compulsive disorder cases, the delusional beliefs about body shape and size seen in anorexia, and so on. In all areas of psychopathology, there are cases at the extremes in which delusion and reality become confused. Emotions have evolved to produce heuristic short cuts under circumstances of great significance to the individual and to the group, but evolutionary systems that provide advantage can also produce disadvantage. The emotional disorders, of which the unipolar and bipolar disorders are one set of examples, show how both the advantages and disadvantages can be apparent even in the same individual. Throughout history, these disorders have made remarkable contributions through remarkable individuals. To quote one such individual, Winston Churchill, "We are all worms. But I do believe that I am a glow-worm." Churchill's life was a testament to both the tragedy and the greatness that depression can bring. For the great majority of sufferers and carers, however, the experience of these disorders seems to be an experience only of tragedy; the work presented in this volume will, it is hoped, provide some pointers as to how such tragedy can be turned into everyday misery, and even offer the occasional experience of genuine success.

REFERENCES

Birchwood, M. (2000). The critical period for early intervention. In M. Birchwood, D. Fowler & C. Jackson (Eds), *Early Intervention in Psychosis: A Guide to Concepts, Evidence and Interventions* (pp. 28–63). Chichester: Wiley.

Cassidy, F., Forest, K., Murry, E. & Carroll, B.J. (1998). A factor analysis of the signs and symptoms of mania. *Archives of General Psychiatry, 55*, 27–32.

Cavanagh, J., Power, M.J. & Goodwin, G. (submitted). The Bipolar Longitudinal Investigation of Problems (BLIP) scale

Goodwin, F.K. & Jamison, K.R. (1990). *Manic-Depressive Illness.* New York: Oxford University Press.

Jamison, K.R. (1993). *Touched with Fire: Manic-Depressive Illness and the Artistic Temperament.* New York: Free Press.

Jamison, K.R. (1995). *An Unquiet Mind: A Memoir of Moods and Madness.* New York: Knopf.

Kendler, K.S. & Prescott, C.A. (1999). A population-based twin study of lifetime major depression in men and women. *Archives of General Psychiatry, 56*, 39–44.

Lam, D.H., Jones, S.H., Hayward, P. & Bright, J.A. (1999). *Cognitive Therapy for Bipolar Disorder: A Therapist's Guide to Concepts, Methods and Practice.* Chichester: Wiley.

Lavender, T. (2000). Schizophrenia. In L.A. Champion & M.J. Power (Eds), *Adult Psychological Problems: An Introduction* (2nd edn) (pp. 201–230). Hove: Psychology Press.

LeDoux, J.E. (1996). *The Emotional Brain: The Mysterious Underpinnings of Emotional Life.* New York: Simon & Schuster.

Miklowitz, D. & Goldstein, M.J. (1997). *Bipolar Disorder: A Family-Focused Treatment Approach.* New York: Guilford.

Neisser, U. (1967). *Cognitive Psychology.* New York: Appleton-Century-Crofts.

Newman, C.F., Leahy, R.L., Beck, A.T., Reilly-Harrington, N.A. & Gyulai, L. (2001). *Bipolar Disorder: A Cognitive Therapy Approach.* Washington, DC: American Psychological Association.

Oatley, K. & Johnson-Laird, P.N. (1987). Towards a cognitive theory of emotions. *Cognition and Emotion, 1*, 29–50.

Perugi, G., Akiskal, H.S., Micheli, C., et al. (1997). Clinical subtypes of bipolar mixed states: Validating a broader European definition in 143 cases. *Journal of Affective Disorders, 43*, 169–180.

Plutchik, R. (1980). *Emotion: A Psychoevolutionary Synthesis.* New York: Harper & Row.

Power, M.J. (1999). Sadness and its Disorders. In T. Dalgleish and M.J. Power (Eds), *Handbook of Cognition and Emotion* (pp. 497–519). Chichester: Wiley.

Power, M.J. (submitted). The structure of emotion: An empirical comparison of six models.

Power, M.J. & Dalgleish, T. (1997). *Cognition and Emotion: From Order to Disorder*. Hove: Psychology Press.

Power, M.J., Dalgleish, T., Claudio, V., Tata, P. & Kentish, J. (2000). The directed forgetting task: Application to emotionally valent material. *Journal of Affective Disorders, 57*, 147–157.

Power, M.J. & Tarsia, M. (submitted). Basic emotions in depression and anxiety.

Sullivan, P.F., Neale, M.C. & Kendler, K.S. (2002). Genetic epidemiology of major depression: Review and meta-analysis. *American Journal of Psychiatry, 157*, 1552–1562.

AUTHOR INDEX

SUBJECT INDEX

Acetylcholine, 36
Adolescence, 7, 80, 82, 83, 84, 85, 86, 87, 89,
    177, 190–191
Aetiology, 4, 17, 204
Age effects, 14
Amphetamine, 147, 229
Anhedonia, 70, 168
Anticonvulsants, 150
Antidepressants, 34, 35, 36, 38, 47, 143, 144,
    146, 147, 189, 215, 223, 227, 340–341
Antipsychotics, 151
Anxiety, 33, 41, 50, 62, 101, 110, 125
Appetitive system, 67, 70, 72
Assessment, 171
Attachment, 104, 108, 124
Attachment theory, 62–63
Atypical depression, 41, 42
Augmentation, 143, 151
Automatic Thoughts Questionnaire (ATQ), 49
Autonomy, 168

Bech–Rafaelsen Mania Scale, 285
Beck Depression Inventory (BDI), 171, 184,
    309–310, 315
Beck Hopelessness Scale (BHS), 325
Beck's cognitive therapy, 48, 49, 100, 130,
    168–169, 170–171, 236, 261–262
Behavioural activation system (BAS), 63, 235,
    238–242, 244
Behavioural assessment, 313–314
Behavioural inhibition system (BIS), 63
Behavioural models, 168
Behaviourism, 48
Benzodiazepines, 151
Biological markers, 145
Biological model, 43, 88, 100
Biological vulnerability, 16, 84–85
Biopsychosocial model, 106
Bipolar disorders, 3, 101, 117, 149, 152, 168,
    194, 203, 204, 206, 207–208, 209, 211,
    213, 214, 221, 236, 247, 259, 322
Bipolar spectrum, 117, 150, 210, 213, 214
Booster sessions, 177

Brief Psychiatric Rating Scale (BPRS), 311
Brief Symptom Inventory (BSI), 311
Buddhism, 130, 132
Bulimia, 194
Bupropion, 36

Carbamazepine, 150, 152
Case identification, 9
Case management, 252
Chaos theory, 353
Child abuse, 18, 121, 126
Childhood experience, 18, 55, 56, 87, 103, 107,
    119
Cholinergics, 36
Circadian rhythms, 264, 276
Classification, 3, 7, 89, 100, 167, 168, 203, 204,
    205, 206, 207, 307, 353, 354–355
Clinical Interview Schedule-Revised (CIS-R),
    11
Clinical management, 249, 289
Clonidine, 39
Cognitive Behaviour Therapy, 178, 188, 236,
    248, 253, 254, 259, 260, 261, 262–263,
    265, 266, 269, 299, 343–344, 347–348,
    358, 359
Cognitive bias, 38, 49, 51, 68, 127, 169–170,
    265, 266
Cognitive deficits, 222
Cognitive models, 47, 48, 49, 50, 51, 56, 171,
    177
Cognitive vulnerability, 84
Comorbidity, 7, 8, 101, 192, 209, 214, 260, 323,
    339, 355
Compliance, 249, 254
Composite International Diagnostic Interview
    (CIDI), 10, 11, 12, 13, 208
Continuity, 87, 88
Coping With Depression booklet, 172, 173
CORE rating system, 314
Cortisol, 32, 34, 41, 43, 85, 105, 146
Cross-cultural effects, 16
Cyclothymia, 212
Cystic fibrosis, 117